HOWARD RUFF
FROM A to Z

Other books by the author

**HOW TO PROSPER DURING
THE COMING BAD YEARS**

FAMINE AND SURVIVAL IN AMERICA

HOWARD RUFF FROM A to Z

A TIMELESS MONEY MAKING
ODYSSEY THROUGH THE
FIRST FOUR YEARS
OF AMERICA'S
LEADING FINANCIAL
ADVISORY SERVICE

Howard J. Ruff

TARGET
PUBLISHERS

Published by Target Publishers
P.O. Box 2000
San Ramon, California 94583
Second printing, June 1980

Library of Congress Catalog Card Number: 80-50360

Manufactured in the United States of America

This publication is designed to provide the Author's opinion in regard to the subject matter covered. It is sold with the understanding that the Publisher or Author is not engaged in rendering legal, accounting or other professional service. If legal advice or other expert assistance is required, the services of a competent professional should be sought.

The Author specifically disclaims any personal liability, loss or risk incurred as a consequence of the use and application, either directly or indirectly, of any advice or information presented herein.

CONTENTS

CONTENTS

CONTENTS

CONTENTS

CONTENTS

CONTENTS

CONTENTS

CONTENTS

CONTENTS

CONTENTS

CONTENTS

CONTENTS

CONTENTS

CONTENTS

CONTENTS

CONTENTS

CONTENTS

HOWARD RUFF
FROM A to Z

INTRODUCTION

Some years ago a friend of mine was browsing through the racks at a used book store and saw a book entitled *HOW TO HUG*. He was in a bit of a hurry, it was only $1.00 so he grabbed it, paid for it and ran. When he got home he found he had just bought Volume 9 of the *ENCYCLOPAEDIA BRITANNICA*. It wasn't exactly what he thought when he picked it up.

Well, this book also is a bit different from what you might have thought. It's not primarily designed to be read from beginning to end, although I certainly wouldn't object to that. *HOWARD RUFF FROM A TO Z* is a collection of almost everything I've ever written in *THE RUFF TIMES*. Some of the material has been published in *HOW TO PROSPER DURING THE COMING BAD YEARS*, but we have reshuffled it and added new material. You can find out my opinion at any given time on almost any subject. We've done some judicious editing, which, for the most part, has been limited to straightening out some of the syntax and clarity problems that developed, especially during my early period as a writer. I guess I couldn't keep my editorial hands off it, but I didn't want you to misunderstand anything I had written. We've also knocked out some duplication of concepts, where I have come back to the same theme several times for the benefit of new subscribers. In addition to that, we have deleted topical articles, those which have no relevance or value past the date of the issue in which they appeared.

I've left "all the warts on," so to speak, with no attempt to make myself look better than I am. My track record as a forecaster and prognosticator is not perfect, but it's pretty darn good. If you had zeroed in on any one piece of my advice relative to the deployment of your money and followed it, the odds are roughly seven to three that it would have worked out well for you, and that isn't bad. If you had taken all of my advice clear across the board, you would be way ahead of the game, as your gains would have substantially out-paced your losses. Heck, nobody's perfect—not even me.

The reason we embarked on this whole project is because our Member Services Department needed this compilation to help new subscribers to *THE RUFF TIMES* understand material which had been covered prior to their coming aboard. With this encyclopedia, they now have that information at their finger tips. In fact, we are putting the information on our consultants' desk computers so that, with the punching of a few buttons, it will appear on a display screen. We also wanted to have something as a useful premium to offer as an incentive for those who would subscribe to *THE RUFF TIMES* so they could catch up on things, and above all, I wanted something to protect me from being misquoted or misrepresented. My views have been considered controversial and are often taken out of context inadvertently. In a few instances, my statements have been deliberately misrepresented in the media, although, for the most part, I think they have tried to be fair.

The Table of Contents is pretty thorough, listing all major topics and most sub-topics, but the World Index at the back is even more thorough. You should be able to chase down almost any subject by the use of either one of these tools. Because many of the original articles covered several subjects, we have tried to pick the central theme and include larger segments, even though they might cover several peripheral ideas. There were difficult decisions to make as to how far to break down an article. If we subdivided too far, by sentences, for example, we would have had a fragmented, impossible to read, dull reference work. We made a calculated decision to use larger segments of material and paint with rather broad brush strokes in setting up our categories for the Table of Contents, while giving you a detailed track to run on through the Word Index.

Throughout the text there are numerous references to books, newsletters and other resource material. For your convenience in obtaining more information about these materials, we have compiled a list (a bibliography), complete with addresses, and entered them in one section called Reference Materials. I hope you'll find this useful and convenient.

THE RUFF TIMES has been a very personal sort of newsletter. Whenever anyone else has written for it, their work has been clearly labeled as their own. I use no ghost writers and do most of my own research, although lately I have added some very competent research and editorial help, particularly Kent Tipton, who was in charge of organizing the material in this volume. I wish to thank him for his efforts in tackling this monster. Also, Bob Bishop, from *THE RUFF TIMES* Member Services Department, has given editorial and proofreading help. Of course, Cathy Brabec, our Word Processing Department Manager, Linda Parker, her assistant, and Judy Kimball, my personal assistant and secretary, have been invaluable. Without these capable people, the project never would have made it to first base, or E, to be more accurate.

You may agree or disagree with any principle espoused in this book, but that's OK. If I ever met anyone who totally agreed with everything I said, I'd probably sever the relationship out of sheer boredom. In any event, I hope that what you read here will be stimulating, thought-provoking, and above all, helpful.

A Coherent Philosophy

One major difficulty in preparing such a volume is that readers may not be able to grasp the overall philosophy of government, economics, investment, and society that is well understood by most of *THE RUFF TIMES* subscribers. This philosophy is covered thoroughly in *HOW TO PROSPER DURING THE COMING BAD YEARS*, and this encyclopedia will make a lot more sense if it is used as a research source in the context of that total philosophy.

Just to make things a bit easier though, I will sum up the fundamentals of the Howard Ruff Philosophy and the premises on which *THE RUFF TIMES* is based.

I won't attempt to argue for each of these points, as I feel that is done adequately in the body of the material.

1. The United States is caught up in an irreversible inflationary spiral that moves in a series of advances and retreats, each advance being to higher levels of inflation. It will eventually run out of control.

2. This process is politically impossible to reverse because doing so would involve cancellation of government programs which have large constituencies and on which large numbers of people have become dependent. The ensuing political pain is unacceptable, so government must inflate or die.

3. In a period of inflation, certain types of investments do well and others do badly.

4. Inflation's principal evil is that it confiscates the capital of savers and "prudent" investors. Those who engage in the usual conservative kind of investing will be the losers during inflation; namely those who buy certificates of deposits, bonds, cash value insurance, annuities and all forms of fixed-value, interest-bearing loans to institutions.

5. Those who invest in hard assets such as gold, silver, diamonds, real estate, collectible items, etc., will prosper, as their capital will

increase in value faster than inflation is chewing up their purchasing power.

6. Inflation is not rising prices. Inflation is caused by an increase in the money supply and means "falling money." Another workable definition is: "The money is going broke."

7. Government can be a profitable servant but a fearful master. We are living in an era where it is more and more our master and we have a responsibility to work to ensure that government continues to be chained by the Constitution, as intended by the Founding Fathers.

8. The basic economic unit of society is the family and when it comes under assault, as it is today, it creates social and economic problems. The breakdown of the family is one of the principal factors in the inflationary problems our society faces.

9. Self-education is the key to making wise decisions about your life, your money, and your future, and it is to this end that *THE RUFF TIMES* is dedicated.

So read on and enjoy, whether you read for information, or whether you read just to argue with me. I hope that I have presented you with a stimulating and enjoyable experience. God bless you all.

A

ABORTION

(5/15/76)   I am sick to death of hearing an expectant woman say, "It's my body and I can do what I want with it." It's just not that simple. There is a second life within her body and she can't take it upon herself to destroy it. I must admit to bias. I believe that abortion is murder, and leaves physical and psychological scars. It fosters a disregard for human life and turns sex solely into a plaything, without responsibility. Sex cannot and should not be engaged in without a great reverence for the responsibility that it produces within us to nurture any life it may create.

Spiritual values and intangibles have built nations, and their loss has destroyed empires. This nation was not built upon the material wealth of its founders, but upon their principles. The great principle of reverence for life, and the clear acceptance of the responsibility to provide the best life possible for any life created is one of man's highest values. Abortion is not the answer to the world's problems of preventing starvation, because overpopulation is not the problem. (see: Population Control)

(9/1/76)   Perhaps another reason why I feel that abortion is wrong is my own personal experience. I have one older brother. A few years after his birth, my mother lost a baby during pregnancy. When she became pregnant with me, she was told that an abortion was necessary to save her life. She resolved that she was going to have this baby. She stayed 7 ½ months in bed, with her life in danger every bit of the way. In today's social and political environment, my mother probably would have been induced to have an abortion, and I would never have seen the light of day. Now you might argue that the world could have one less Howard Ruff and not be any worse off, but I believe that I'm performing a constructive purpose in this world. History is full of great composers, artists, scientists, and innovators

7

who have improved the world, who were the last of several children, or who were even unwanted or who were handicapped, or who, by today's standards, would never have been allowed to be born.

Perhaps an argument could be made that there should be one standard for this nation and another standard for the rest of the world. I have not made a judgment on that matter. Perhaps it is wrong for desperately poor nations like India and Pakistan to continue to produce babies into squalor. Perhaps they should encourage limitation of births. I truly don't know. I haven't worked this out to my own satisfaction.

But I do know that in this country, where we have the resources to see that every child has a proper life, education, and a chance to contribute to the world; people should be allowed to have the children they are prepared to accept and be responsible for, without feeling that they are somehow traitors to the human race. So, let's get this problem back into perspective. The economic facts say that if you're not growing, you're shrinking, and if the United States' economy ever shrinks, we will weep for the entire world.

AFFIRMATIVE ACTION

(4/15/78)   By Patrick J. Buchanan

In his classic *ANIMAL FARM*, George Orwell suggests that what revolutionaries often seek is not the equal justice of their slogans, but the power and privilege of those they dispossess.

The indictment made may be handed up against the leaders of the civil rights revoution. The smoking pistol is there. It can be found resting between the lines of the civil service regulations demanding that once again race, sex, and national origin be listed upon a job seeker's application.

When these designations were removed years ago it was judged a victory for human rights, another step toward the ideals of American democracy, where merit and ability, not race or sex, would determine which men and women would rise and which would not.

Well, "equality of opportunity" is no longer sufficient for the black caucus or its white auxiliaries. What is demanded now is preferential treatment.

The new discrimination is defended upon various grounds. We are told, it is only a temporary expedient. It is progressive and noble, since it rectifies the results of past discrimination. It is essential to bring more blacks, Spanish-speaking, and women into economic parity with all Americans.

The noble end, we are told, justifies the distasteful means.

"We can and we do approve . . .," declared *The New York Times*, all six of whose celebrated syndicated columnists are white and male.

Others argue that the nameless, faceless, jobless men who fail to win the position to which they are entitled by education, experience and ability are actually martyrs in a great cause. Where the old discrimination which favored white men was odious and deplorable, the new is praiseworthy.

But all the rhetoric does not erase the simple injustice of punishing a job-seeker for an act of racism he did not commit, and for an ethnic heritage over which he had no control. Nor does it diminish the rank hypocrisy of those enthusiasts of affirmative action so anxious to impose upon others sacrifices they are unwilling to make themselves.

When was the last time you saw a liberal Congressman, Senator, Assistant Secretary, columnist or commentator voluntarily surrender his position and salary to a black man—to help move this racial minority into the mainstream of American life.

If American liberalism is in such disrepute, is it not because it does so much sermonizing and makes so few sacrifices?

The loudest champions of forced busing almost always have their children in private schools. The leading advocates of public housing in working class suburbs will take you to court if you dare disturb the "ecological balance" of their own estates.

Is it not time the leading proponents of affirmative action become its leading practitioners?

If only 10 liberal Senators would step forward and resign their office on the condition that the incumbent governor name a black or a woman to this all-male club, imagine the impact Kennedy, Bayh, Muskie and McGovern could have as they returned to private life.

And surely there is no more articulate champion of affirmative action than Walter Mondale. Imagine the applause in the Democratic Party if tomorrow he resigned his position on condition that Jimmy Carter send to Congress for confirmation as his successor Barbara Jordan of Texas.

But if these guiding lights of national liberalism are unwilling to sacrifice their salaries, positions or status to advance the cause they espouse so eloquently, how then do they demand such sacrifices of men less secure, less privileged than themselves?

AMERICA—ITS DESTINY

(5/1/79) I have a confession to make. It's so earth-shaking and far-reaching that it might totally alter your opinion of me, but honesty has finally prompted repentance, and the nasty truth had to come out. I hope you are ready for this.

I AM AN OPTIMIST!

I know this will come as a shock to all of you who have accepted me as your resident pessimist and "Prophet Of Doom." I am not a pessimist, and never was one, and I'm tired of reading about it.

It's my own darned fault that people say that. I spend so much time dealing with the ostriches of the world who don't think that anything can ever go wrong, trying to prepare them for a few bad years, that I have not done a good job on the real pessimists and "prophets of doom" who have no faith in the ultimate destiny of this country. So here is my POLLYANNA POLEMIC; or, if you wish, my MODERATION MANIFESTO.

There are some hard money writers who believe that the end of America is at hand, maybe even the end of Western Civilization. They believe you should have armed retreats in the mountains, and lots of guns to defend your dehydrated food, gold, and silver. Another manifestation of this fatalism is the philosophy of getting all of their money out of America and stashing it in Swiss banks, the Cayman Islands or Costa Rica, and, if possible, following that with your body, so you can be away from America when it descends into total savagery.

I respect the sincerity of these people. The problems they describe are real, and there's no denying that there is at least some possibility that the end is near, but I believe they are making one fundamental mistake. They are underestimating the inherent strength and resilience of America and understating the severity of the crises through which it has suffered triumphantly in its turbulent past.

Some people are optimistic by nature, no matter how dire the circumstances. They are very attractive and fun to be around, but they make lousy counselors. Life consists of ups and downs, and the optimists will never foresee and avoid the downs.

Then there are the pessimists who always expect the worst. They are unpleasant fellows, but they have the virtue of helping you avoid all the pitfalls, if you believe them, but they will also miss all the booms and opportunities. Sooner or later, they'll both be right. Even a stopped clock is right twice a day.

A wise advisor is inherently neither an optimist nor a pessimist. He sees the world as it is. He is emotionally prepared to be either bullish or bearish, and he has no emotional stake on either side of the issue.

Am I such a perfect advisor? Probably not, but I try like heck. I have a vested interest only in being right. I have no vested interest in being optimistic or pessimistic. I am not a tenured economics professor who will always have a job, even if he's wrong 90% of the time. I have to meet the test of the marketplace with a respectable track record.

Now, after all of that rather hard-to-argue-with rationale, let me tell you what I really believe about the future of this country and make my case for coming "out of the closet" as a pragmatic optimist, based on the evidence, not temperament.

It is true that in the short-term, we face runaway inflation, possible collapse of the monetary system, and civil disorders in the big cities, we also face a form of federal, state and municipal bankruptcy, achieved by paying everybody off, to the penny, in depreciated dollars, through inflation. But don't underestimate the Rasputin-like recuperative powers of this nation.

The smartest money in the world is pouring into America. The ARABS, the GERMANS, the JAPANESE, and the SWISS are all buying our real estate, and our basic industries. Just as I'm suggesting, they are buying a lot of gold and silver and diamonds as inflation hedges, too. Those people know that this nation is the most likely to have its institutions survive intact.

Gadflies like me spend most of their time telling you what's wrong, because, if nobody points out what's wrong, nothing gets corrected. As the classic cliche goes, "Eternal vigilance is the price of liberty." But let's make sure we understand what is right, or we will make dumb mistakes with our money.

America is the hope of the world! Half of the world's population would migrate here if it could. Even while they blast us in the United Nations and play footsie with our enemies, they still know about our immense productive strength.

Runaway inflation and the collapse of the currency will force us to return to sound fiscal policies, and we will produce ourselves out of our troubles.

I'm convinced we will still have churches and schools and the Bill of Rights and a judicial system and the right to "throw the rascals out" by the ballot box. The system is being attacked from within, but ultimately, we will repel every assault.

11

I believe that the civil disorders that can come through breakdowns in an inflationary economy will be basically limited to the core of our large cities. I have no fears for my safety in small-town America.

There is not a currency in the world that will be immune from the world-wide disease of inflation as long as ours is afflicted by it. However, this nation will be the first to recover and will continue to be "a light unto the world." I don't want my money in Switzerland or Costa Rica or Mexico, except perhaps for some small portion of it in case our current government temporarily does something stupid with the banking system. I'd rather have the bulk of my wealth in hard money assets or in real estate right here in the United States. That's where it's safest. That's where my freedom to enjoy it is most likely to survive. And the Arabs, Germans, Japanese and Iranians think so too!

In playing the gadfly, I may have conveyed the false impression that I think this nation is wrong every time it turns around. Our problems are real, but most people can identify with my position that "I love my country but I fear my government." Thomas Jefferson, among others, told us that a healthy state of skepticism toward government would prevent it from evolving into our master rather than our servant, which is the nature of all governments. There's nothing new about that. It's an ongoing battle which I, my children, and their children, will fight for all our lives. But America has such inherent strengths that it is virtually unthinkable that it will not survive.

It is because of my basic optimism that I have not abandoned the system and joined the tax revolt, or advised bailing out of the country. I reject the conclusion that "all is lost" and that the system can be saved only by directly rejecting and confronting it. That attitude is much like the tactics of burning a Vietnamese village in order to save it. I happen to believe that the inflationary excesses of the system and the abuses of government power will be squeezed out of the system by the inevitable currency collapse, which will result from the inflation I'm predicting. When a pendulum swings, it usually swings back.

So there it is folks. I am a pragmatic optimist because I think the facts warrant it.

I'm also optimistic for one last reason. There is no conceivable set of circumstances in which there are not opportunities. Those who seize these opportunities and act will benefit. I believe we can survive; I believe we can prosper. I believe the first duty of a responsible citizen is to survive financially so that he will have the financial security and the leisure to be influential in the years to come. (see: Economy of U.S.)

ARABS

ARAB MONEY

(3/15/76) The Federal Reserve reported on March 9, 1976, that the oil-producing countries of the Middle East and North Africa have $18 billion on deposit in 21 of the largest United States banks. (Somewhere between $60 billion and $100 billion by January, 1979. No one really knows exactly how much. HJR) About half of this money held by the six largest banks in the Federal Reserve survey represents deposits which can be withdrawn by the oil-producing nations within 30 days.

In previous articles on banking, I have warned you that this was "hot" money and that at the first sign of real serious trouble, the Arabs could withdraw their money rapidly. They have shown no hesitancy in pulling money out of troubled banks and troubled economies, as they have demonstrated in Great Britain, and in Lebanon. This is only one of the serious threats to the American banking system, which at the present time is being held together with spit and bailing wire.

(5/15/77) They had extended an olive branch when SAUDI ARABIA and THE UNITED ARAB EMIRATES held their price increase to only five percent. They made it clear that they expected a response from us in our Israeli policy. We not only did not respond, but we offered them some calculated insults. ANDREW YOUNG at the United Nations referred to the Arabs' "Ku Klux Klan mentality" towards Israel. Then Congress passed the anti-boycott legislation, penalizing American companies who comply with Arab terms for doing business with them.

Then came the final insult. About three weeks ago, the Arabs responded to the request of the INTERNATIONAL MONETARY FUND to provide $7 billion for the help of the poor nations, by demanding that they have a vote in the IMF equal to that of the United States, since they were putting up as much money as the U.S. This request was summarily shot down by Mr. Blumenthal, the Secretary of the Treasury. Finally, the Arabs had had enough, so they walked into the offices of the BANK FOR INTERNATIONAL SETTLEMENTS (BIS) in Switzerland and said, "Gentlemen, we wish to join." The BIS consists of the central banks of the COMMON MARKET Countries; Japan, South Africa—and now the Arabs. They are the pro-gold forces of the world. They have opposed the IMF. The Arabs have now aligned themselves with the pro-gold forces. The are alarmed at our policies in several ways: They don't like our support of Russian revolutionary aims in Africa. They feel threatened by Russian control of the sea lanes along the whole coast line of Africa. They are worried about safely shipping oil, and they don't trust the Russians.

They are worried about being able to get uranium from South Africa for their nuclear plants, as also is Germany, another member of the BIS, which has $35 billion dollars in nuclear reactor contracts all over the world.

I have reason to believe that when Mr. Carter visited Europe last weekend, he was quietly presented with an ultimatum from the Arabs: the U.S. must cease its war on gold and its support of Communist movements in Africa. I believe the Arabs are preparing to bluff, either with their black gold in the ground or with their incredible monetary holdings in the United States. They're not quite ready yet. They would stand to lose too much at this point by dumping the United States economy. However, they were heavy buyers at the last IMF gold auction, and if they gradually begin to withdraw their short-term deposits in banks, and sell their Treasury Bills, they are preparing for an economic confrontation.

If you don't believe they are prepared to use their power, then you don't remember 1973 when they had far fewer chips than they do now, and they didn't hesitate to throw our economy into a tailspin by embargoing oil.

(11/15/77)   Just imagine that you are the Finance Minister of an Arab monarchy. You have to please your King, who has the power to have your hand (or your head) cut off in the public square, if he wishes. Your job is to see that he gets the maximum return from his oil revenues. You have put his money into short-term deposits in New York banks, which in turn, have loaned it to insolvent countries. You thought this was a great idea at the time, because that would leave the banks on the hook—responsible for both the loans they made and the money you deposited. But now, those things which your King has been importing (heavy construction equipment, building materials, high technology) are inflating in price at between 15% and 25% a year, so his dollars are getting chewed up by inflation. In addition, the dollar has been sinking against virtually every other currency in the

14

world, and you are in the uncomfortable position of informing your monarch that he needs a 20% to 25% increase in oil prices just to break even.

If you think you feel sick now, look at your alternatives:

1.   You can hedge your dollar losses by buying gold, which you have done covertly for almost a year. As the dollar sinks, currencies get into trouble; gold will rise and compensate for your losses, but there. isn't enough of it around.

2.   You can stay with the dollar, tough it out and hope that your ruler doesn't lose patience during the several years it will take for the U.S. Government to correct its balance-of-payments deficit, balance its budgets and bring its dollar back to some semblance of strength.

3.   You can carefully pull your money out of the New York banks and throw it into some other currency, but you had better do it just right or you will throw the dollar and the U.S. banking system into a disastrous tailspin before you can get most of your money out safely.

4.   You can invest in hard, tangible assets including factories, electrical power systems, farms and basic industries. However, if you do this just at the beginning of a world depression, you could have cash-flow losses for the next ten years.

5.   You can raise the price of oil and trigger a world-wide depression.

6.   Or, you can just slit your throat now. You have just discovered a 600 lb. gorilla can't sit anywhere he wants when most of the chairs are small.

Bad Choices

Now, after you have chosen your best course of action, you have to persuade a fiercely independent, somewhat anarchistic group of oil producers, with totally different problems, they should go along. The Iranians are spending their money as fast as they make it, so they don't have your problem. They need higher prices. The Venezuelans can absorb any of their revenues in internal development. So you (probably being a Saudi Arabian, or from one of the Persian Gulf sheikdoms) have a tough row to hoe.

I think I know what the Finance Minister has decided and that's why I advised you to get out of banks, savings and loans, credit unions, and long-term bonds. There were several reasons why I took that drastic step.

The Arabs are, for the first time, showing signs of great interest in currencies and government securities other than the United States.

They are also the major factor in the recent upsurge of gold prices. They are buying Japanese securities. They really didn't have much choice because the Yen is the only world-wide currency large enough to accommodate them. They have been buying Swiss francs and British pounds, and all of these currencies have been exploding upward against the dollar. The continued inflow of Arab money into New York, which kept our balance of payments deficit from being worse than it would have been, may now be ended. The monstrous transfer of wealth to the oil nations has not totally destroyed the dollar, only because the Arabs were recycling their profits back into this country through the aforementioned short-term deposits. They don't even have to pull their money out in order to destabilize us. All they have to do is stop pouring money in, and THAT HAS NOW HAPPENED. Their task is to get out as much money as possible before things come entirely unglued.

If we react by freezing Arab money, it would open up the possibility of an Arab oil boycott, and the insane price control policies that have made us dependent upon foreign oil will then rise up to bite us. These actions could force a rupture in OPEC, particularly between Saudi Arabia and Iran. As I've written before in *THE RUFF TIMES*, these people don't like each other. They do not have the same ethnic heritage. The Iranians are not Arabs. They have religion in common, much in the same divisive way that Catholics and Protestants do. The Shah of Iran is building a monstrous military force. It is offensive in nature and designed to move large amounts of troops across the Tigris-Euphrates Delta and down the Persian Gulf. The Near-East is a terrible tinder-box, and it's not just Israel and its neighbors who might be fighting.

Examine the history. All during the Arab boycott in the last Israeli war, Iran continued to supply Israel with their oil needs. The Shah needed more cash; the Saudis needed safety for their cash. I do not see how they can continue to be unified.

Now, what does this mean to you? If we get a crisis in the New York banks, I don't think they will fail, although they could close for awhile and tie up your money for years under Executive Order #11490 (see: Executive Order #11490). Uncle Sam will be forced to provide them between $50 and $100 billion dollars of printing press money which could thrust inflation over that invisible line where it becomes self-feeding and irreversible. The Federal Reserve Board will counter by attempting to tighten the money supply as they are doing now, and you will get interest rates through the ceiling, AND inflation, AND depression, all at the same time.

FROM A TO Z

There is a great secret struggle going on right now over Arab money, with some very frightened bankers. That money ain't there. It's loaned out to Blue Chip borrowers, like Zaire and Peru. When you borrow money from somebody for 120 days, and loan it out for 5 years, you are in trouble if your creditor wants his money. The consequences for western civilization are awesome.

ARAB BOYCOTT

(5/1/77) While all the world was listening to Mr. Carter, an event of earth-shaking proportions managed to sneak by. Congress passed legislation invoking various penalties upon American firms which comply with the Arab oil-producers' boycott against Israel, as a condition of doing business with them. This news came to the Arabs as the finance ministers were meeting in Abu Dhabi to establish an Arab monetary fund. Shortly after Congress acted, the following dispatch came across the Dow Jones tape, and I was notified of it by Douglas Johnston:

ARAB LEADERS ASTONISHED BY CONGRESSIONAL MOVES TO PASS PRO-ISRAEL ANTI-BOYCOTT LAW
ABU DHABI UNITED ARAB EMIRATES -AP- ARAB LEADERS MEETING HERE EXPRESSED ASTONISHMENT AT CONGRESSIONAL MOVES TO PASS A TOUGH ANTI-BOYCOTT LAW FAVORING ISRAEL.
'THIS IS CERTAINLY A STRANGE TIME FOR THE UNITED STATES TO BE CARRYING ON LIKE THIS,' SAID MOHAMMED NABULSI, JORDAN'S CENTRAL BANK GOVERNOR, HERE WITH 20 OTHER MINISTERS AND CENTRAL BANKERS FOR THE INAUGURAL MEETING OF THE ARAB MONETARY FUND.
A CLOSE ADVISOR TO THE HEAD OF STATE OF ONE OF THE LARGEST ARAB OIL PRODUCERS SAID HIS CONSERVATIVE PRO-AMERICAN LEADER IS DUMB-FOUNDED AT WHAT APPEARS TO BE U.S. DISREGARD FOR ITS OWN INTERESTS.
'NOW WITH TWO OIL PRODUCERS—SAUDI ARABIA AND THE UNITED ARAB EMIRATES—ARTIFICIALLY HOLDING DOWN OIL PRICES AND WAITING FOR THE AMERICANS TO ABANDON THEIR ONE-SIDED SUPPORT OF ISRAEL NOW YOUR CONGRESS THROWS THE BOY-COTT ISSUE AT US. IT IS INCREDIBLE,' THIS OFFICIAL SAID.
KUWAIT FINANCE MINISTER, ABDUL RAHMAN

ATIQI SAID HIS COUNTRY'S OIL EXPORTS ARE DOWN BY 25% THIS YEAR BECAUSE OF THE TWO-TIER PRICE DISPUTE WITHIN THE ORGANIZATION OF PETROLEUM EXPORTING COUNTRIES.

'THIS SUITS US FINE,' HE SAID, EXPLAINING THAT SURPLUS OIL PRODUCERS ARE NERVOUS ABOUT THE LARGE CASH RESERVES THEY ARE BUILDING UP MOSTLY IN WESTERN CURRENCIES AND INVESTMENTS.

'IF ALL ARAB COUNTRIES REDUCED PRODUCTION LIKE THIS, THE UNITED STATES WOULD HAVE A REAL ENERGY CRISIS BECAUSE THEY CANNOT INCREASE IMPORTS FROM ANY OTHER AREA,' SAID A UAE OFFICIAL.

'BUT WE CAN GET OUR IMPORTS FROM EUROPE AND JAPAN IF THE AMERICANS COMMIT COMMERCIAL SUICIDE WITH THE BOYCOTT BILLS.'

What this means is that the Arabs just may decide to teach us about our total vulnerability to them. It will take us three to ten years to offset our vulnerability. If, as the Saudis said, their "moderate" price policy was a signal to us to reciprocate in our Israeli policy, then this action would be interpreted as a repudiation of this "olive branch." I can see the Arabs unsheathing their threat to our monetary system with their vast short-term deposits in our banks and their holdings of U.S. Treasury Bills. Remember, they hold close to 20% of all U.S. government short-term securities and can destroy the market for those securities overnight by dumping a fraction of them. They could cut oil production 25%, as the dispatch indicates, and immediately throw our economy into a tailspin, from which it might never recover.

Mr. Carter is right. The energy threat may be the greatest threat we will face in our lifetimes, but if we are swallowed up by this problem, it will be a case of national suicide. We have caused the problem, and it is the government's fault. The proposed solutions are totally inappropriate. And even if they took the right actions today, we would have a period of vulnerability for three to ten years where our throat would be laid bare to the political pressures of this group of primitive desert sheiks.

B

BALANCE OF PAYMENTS

(12/15/76)   Our balance of payments is a most critical matter. We export many, many billions of dollars worth of agricultural goods. If we didn't, the dollar would sink sharply in the international currency marketplace. If the dollar sinks, you would find large foreign financial interests beginning to divest themselves of American government debt securities, such as Treasury bills, Treasury notes, municipal bonds, etc.

Approximately 20% of our short-term debt securities are in the hands of FRENCH, GERMAN, SWISS, JAPANESE and ARAB money interests. This group is the second largest U.S. creditor, behind only the U.S. Banking System.

When the Arabs increased the price of oil by three to four times, they, in effect, exacted a tax on oil. Billions of new dollars flowed into the Arab coffers. It did not immediately destabilize the world's monetary system, as many, including me, thought it might. It was because the Arabs turned right around and put much of that money into American short-term securities, in effect, recycling it. Now the Arabs own so much of our debt, that if they ever decided to unload their dollar holdings, they could literally destroy the dollar. The value of Treasury bills and notes would be driven into the floor by a wave of selling. American banks would be in terrible danger, as they are holding approximately 20% of the outstanding T-bills and notes. The system could be upset, bringing a chain-reaction of failures in the American banking system.

All it would take for this event to occur, would be one super bad crop year or two moderately bad crop years, causing a few billion dollars more balance-of-payment deficits.

If you don't think your friendly Swiss banker or your friendly Arab oil sheik would ever do anything to hurt America, you're crazy. As the British pound weakened, these foreign interests, who held tremendous amounts of pound sterling in deposits in British banks, simply began bailing out. The pound has dropped through the floor.

These people would do the same here in a moment's notice, if they felt their money would be safer somewhere else—such as in gold. They are now heavy buyers of gold.

It is my opinion that the American dollar has been weakening for a long time. Its weakness is disguised by the fact that other currencies are weakening faster. We have had the recent devaluations of the Mexican peso and the Australian and New Zealand dollars relative to the American dollar. The Canadian dollar is sinking. Some experts feel it may drop to as low as 85 cents in American currency.

The American dollar's fundamental weakness could become apparent to everyone if we should have crop troubles. It isn't just a question of feeding our people. The question is: Will the glue holding the American monetary system and world civilization together continue to spring up from American soil? (see: Currency)

BALANCE THE BUDGET AMENDMENT

(2/15/79)   Who Shall Bell The Cat?

On October 26, 1642, in a basement room in Buckingham Palace, a historic meeting occurred which would affect the fate of generations unborn. The palace mice held a convention to decide what to do about the cat who had been decimating their ranks. Finally, a brilliant proposal was made to put a bell on the cat so the palace mice could hear him coming. With a squeak of acclamation, the assembled delegates passed the motion unanimously, and the minor details were entrusted to a committee. One such detail—who shall bell the cat?

The National Taxpayers Union, headed by JAMES DAVIDSON, whom I interviewed recently on my show, has persuaded twenty-two state legislatures to pass resolutions calling for a new U.S. Constitutional Convention—the first since 1787—to pass an amendment requiring a balanced Federal budget. This proposal has met with screams of outrage and fear from all across the political spectrum.

That noted skin-diver and protector of the public purse, TEDDY KENNEDY, has called it, "a dark, ominous development for the nation and a serious threat to the integrity of the Constitution." A group of liberal Republicans headed by Senator HEINZ presented its own watered-down version of tax limitation to head off the landslide movement toward a Constitutional Convention. House Speaker, TIP O'NEILL, says the best way to "drive them to their senses," referring to the states that are considering such an amendment, "would be to take a hard look at Federal aid to those states"—a rather nasty piece of Congressional bullying.

What does that have to do with mice and cats?

If we ever succeed in getting a hard-nosed limitation on government spending, requiring major budget slashing, then we will have to turn over to some committee the resolution of such minor details as "whose ox gets gored."

The likelihood of some form of limitation on spending is less than 50-50, but improving. No less a political figure than JERRY BROWN has pressed for a Constitutional Convention. He almost got left behind on the Proposition 13 issue. He realizes that his chameleon-like reversal of his pre-election position was a political tight-rope act without a net, too dangerous to repeat. So he has grabbed the reins of the front bandwagon and he is now a Born-Again enemy of big spending.

A Constitutional spending straitjacket is anathema to all but the most hide-bound conservative politicians. Political success is based on (1) spending enough to get elected while (2) not taxing enough to cross the voter rebellion threshhold, and there is no relationship between the two. Tying them together by law doesn't just change the rules. It's a whole different game, a prospect that strikes terror in the heart of any savvy politician.

There is a developing head-on confrontation between the convention proposal and the weaker measure proposed by 103 members of the House, which would limit spending to some percentage of the Gross National Product, including a bail-out clause allowing more spending if approved by two-thirds of both houses. Such a law, it is assumed, would take some of the steam out of the Constitutional Amendment drive for a stronger law, just as in California a weaker tax relief law was passed, hoping to head off Proposition 13. It should work this time.

If, despite this, we get a spending limitation, there will be a vicious political blood-letting over "whose ox gets gored" and "who shall bell the cat." The liberals will want to cut defense and the conservatives have the votes to block it. The conservatives want to cut HEW, and the liberals have the votes to block it. But when the finally get down to goring the oxen, every political career in Washington will be on the line.

Actually, it is a better-than-even bet that Congress will raise business taxes, rather than cut spending. Massachusetts' voters overwhelmingly approved a November referendum shifting the tax burden from home owners to businesses, which was pushed through with liberal doses of propaganda and money from Massachusetts' city mayors, trade unions and consumers. Of course, higher business taxes mean higher consumer prices, but that can be blamed on the businessmen.

It is not clear that a Constitutional Convention, once convened, can be limited to this issue only. I realize that this spectre has been raised by the spenders in order to derail the Constitutional juggernaut, but they just might be right. The world is full of single-issue groups from each end of the political spectrum, ranging from abortion to redistribution of the income, all of which will be elbowing to get their cause before the Convention. As of now, no one knows what really would come out of the Convention. In the final analysis, the threat of such a Convention might force some real limitations in spending through Congressional action.

Now, let's assume we have voted to bell the cat and the oxen are about to be gored. I am convinced that there is a great potential for revolution in the streets. The anger of those who will have their promised benefits withdrawn could be considerable, and the cuts would be restored to buy peace. This nation is less restrained and less law-abiding every year. The propensity to challenge legal authority no longer is limited to the radical, anti-Vietnam War left. Conservative farmers have indulged in illegal confrontation tactics and several have said they now understand what motivated the Vietnam protestors. The confrontation tax rebels on the right are willing to violate regulations and statutes in order to support a higher Constitutional principle. The potential for revolt, urban guerrilla warfare, violent labor problems, etc., from the left, right and center, is considerable, if spending cuts are more than superficial. For example, VERNON JORDAN, the head of the Urban League, testified on MR. CARTER'S proposed budget for fiscal year 1980. He said that if the proposed budget were passed there was great potential for "racial riots in the streets," as we had in the 1960s.

I believe that a slashing and balancing of the budget would thrust us into a deflationary depression of the same proportions as the 1930s. But don't worry. It isn't likely to happen.

Does that mean I'm against it? Absolutely not! I'm for it. The depression of the 1930s may have saved the American system from the excesses of the 1920s. T' ⌣ value of the dollar rose and a loaf of bread only required a nickel (if you had one). Deflation produces great economic dislocation: lots of people out of work and a lot of suffering, but the purchasing power of money increases. Deflation would save the currency, but would be so unpleasant that no politician would want to be identified as having voted for whatever would cause it.

The only way you can make most addicts kick their habits is to somehow confine them against their will. The only way we are going to make our nation go through it is to enchain it with a Constitutional Amendment.

Tax limitation is a most treacherous enterprise, but I think we ought to take the chance. The odds are against real limitation. Too many people have a vested interest in deficit spending and inflation. But let's keep trying.

BANKS

HOW TO SELECT ONE

(2/15/76)   Most of our readers use banks for disbursing funds for business and personal needs, payment collections, etc. . . . so your choice of banks is critical.

Rule number 1. Avoid banks with high "loan-to-deposit" ratios. Get the figures from the financial statement of the banks, or perhaps from your stockbroker. Information regarding publicly held companies is routinely published in *Standard & Poors Stock Guide. Forbes* magazine's January 1 issue has detailed reports on major banks.

Rule number 2. Avoid banks with the highest ratio of international deposits to total deposits on the liability side of the ledger. (To get the ratio, divide the international deposits by the total deposits.) Pick the banks with the lowest ratio. This could be "hot" Eurodollar or Arab money that could be withdrawn quick as a flash at the first sign of bank insolvency.

Rule number 3. Avoid the banks with the highest "Asset-to-Capital ratios." Assets include loans. If the ratio is high, then the bank's capital, which is the ultimate protection against losses, is supporting too many loans. It could be quickly drawn on, to the point of insolvency, if loan defaults rise.

Here are some other check points.

1.   Is the Bank's capital heavily invested in Municipal bonds or notes? If so, forget it.

2. Does it have a large, active Foreign Exchange trading department? Watch out, as it was foreign exchange trading losses that started Franklin Bank's demise.

3. Has it recently changed from a Federally Chartered to a State Chartered bank, or is it contemplating doing so? Check the last annual report, or ask your Branch Manager. Many banks are now doing this because State bank examiners are reputed to be easier to deal with in interpreting regulations than are the Federal examiners. There are no short cuts.

I don't see anyway to avoid this homework. I can't do it for every bank in America. You must do it for your region. In my area, the Bank of America meets most of the tests reasonably well. It seems to be the best of the bad lot.

ENDANGERED BANKS

(3/1/76)   Let's look at the scorecard:

BANK FAILURES THIS YEAR (1976)
Hamilton National Bank of Chattanooga (the third
largest failure in American banking history)
Franklin Bank of Houston
The Astro Bank of Houston
NEAR FAILURE
Farmer's Bank of the State of Delaware

(2/1/76)   Here is the Federal Reserve list of problem banks:

MORE SERIOUS PROBLEMS:

CENTRAL BANKING SYSTEM, Oakland, CA
(Central Bank National Association)
DATA LEASE FINANCIAL CORP., North Palm Beach, FL
(Miami Nat'l Bank)
FIRST PENNSYLVANIA CORP., Bala Cynwyd, PA,
21st largest (1st Penn Bank/Trust Co)
FIRST WISCONSIN CORP., Milwaukee, WI 35th largest
(First Wisconsin Nat'l Bank of Milwaukee)
HAMILTON BANCSHARES INC., Chattanooga, TN
(Hamilton Nat'l Bank)
IMPERIAL BANCORP, Los Angeles, CA
(Imperial Bank)
INDUSTRIAL NAT'L CORP., Providence, RI
(Industrial Nat'l Bank)

FROM A TO Z

MARINE MIDLAND BANKS, Buffalo, NY
13th largest (Marine Midland Bank-NY)
NCNB CORP., Charlotte, NC 30th largest
(North Carolina Nat'l Bank)
UNION BANCORP INC., Los Angeles, CA
28th largest (Union Bank)
UNION PLANTERS CORP., Memphis, TN
(Union Planters Nat'l Bank)

OTHER "PROBLEM" BANKS:

AMERICAN BANKSHARES CORP., Milwaukee, WI
(American City Bank & Trust Co.)
AMERICAN BANK & TRUST CORP., New York, NY
(American Bank & Trust Co.)
AMERICAN FLETCHER CORP., Indianapolis, IN
(American Fletcher Nat'l Bank & Trust Co)
BANCAL TRI-STATE CORP., San Francisco, CA 38th largest
(Bank of California)
BANCSHARES OF NORTH CAROLINA, Jacksonville, NC
(Bank of N.C.)
CAMERON FINANCIAL CORP., Charlotte, NC
(First Union Nat'l Bank)
CENTRAL NATIONAL CHICAGO CORP., Chicago, IL
(Central Nat'l Bank in Chicago)
CHASE MANHATTAN CORP., New York, NY 3rd largest
(Chase Manhattan Bank)
CITIZENS & SOUTHERN NAT'L BANK, Atlanta, GA
44th largest (Citizens & Southern Nat'l Bank)
CITIZENS BANCSHARES INC., Atlanta, GA
(Citizens Trust Bank)
CITY NATIONAL CORP., Beverly Hills, CA
(City Nat'l Bank)
FIRST MERCHANTS CORP., Richmond, VA
(First & Merchants Nat'l Bank)
FIRST COOLIDGE CORP., Watertown, MA
(Coolidge Bank & Trust Co.)
FIRST GEORGIA BANCSHARES INC., Atlanta, GA
(First Georgia Bank)
FIRST NAT'L BOSTON CORP., Boston, MA 17th largest
(First Nat'l Bank of Boston)
ICB CORP., New Orleans, LA
(Int'l. City Bank & Trust Co.)

LIBERTY NATIONAL CORP., Oklahoma City, OK
(Liberty Nat'l Bank & Trust Co. of Oklahoma)
PACIFIC BANCORPORATION, Bakersfield, CA
(Community Nat'l Bank)
PATAGONIA CORP., Tucson, AZ
(Great Western Bank & Trust Co.)
REPUBLIC OF TEXAS CORP., Dallas, TX 24th largest
(Republic Nat'l Bank of Dallas)
SECURITY NEW YORK STATE CORP., Rochester, NY
(Security Trust Co. of Rochester)
SECURITY PACIFIC CORP., Los Angeles, CA 11th largest
(Security Pacific Nat'l Bank)
UNITED JERSEY BANKS, Princeton, NJ
(People Trust of New Jersey)
WELLS FARGO & CO., San Francisco, CA 12th largest
(Wells Fargo Bank)

MONEY EXPANSION

(10/1/76) Sam Paige gives a remarkably simple explanation of how the money supply expands through the banking system. He says there are three possible sources of money from which the bank can make you a loan:
1. Bank capital.
2. Bank deposits.
3. Out of thin air!

Which do they use? Number 3, of course! When the bank approves your loan, they simply create a deposit to your account on the books. This loan is a bank asset. It is also a liability, because it is a deposit against which you can draw. SO THE BANK'S BOOKS BALANCE!

Simple, isn't it? As an asset, it also adds to reserves against which they can make other loans. The only restriction on expansion is that the Federal Reserve requirement that they deposit 15 percent of the deposit at the district Federal Reserve Bank.

And that's how banks grow.

(12/15/78) Do All My Business With One Bank?

Q. Wouldn't it be a good idea to put my money in the same bank or savings and loan that holds my mortgage? Then I can merely claim an off-set against my indebtedness if the institution should go broke.

FROM A TO Z

A. When a bank fails nowadays, sometimes the assets (loans) are bought by another bank and the liabilities (deposits) are assumed by the FDIC, so you could have your loan in one place, and your deposit in another, and it might not off-set.

NOTICE OF WITHDRAWALS

(4/15/78)   Here is a copy of a fascinating document published by the FIRST NATIONAL BANK OF McMINNVILLE in Tennessee. This, unfortunately, is typical of similar statements published by most banks. It's a real confidence builder.

> Depositor(s) may at any time be required by Bank to give notice of an intended withdrawal, not less than 60 days before a withdrawal is made. The intent of this provision is to protect the best interests of the Bank and depositors alike, and it will be enforced only in cases of financial excitement or when it may be deemed expedient, by the Bank's Board of Directors.

That's why I suggest that any substantial amounts of money be somewhere other than your bank. The chances of a period of "financial excitement" are very high, and that's precisely what I'm trying to guard against. Keep in the bank only what is necessary for current transactions and to maintain an orderly account.

SAFETY OF BANKS

(5/15/76)   San Francisco Seminar
Let me pass on a few interesting concepts from James Benham, President of the Capital Preservation Fund of Palo Alto, California.
He told us the banks aren't safe. He knew that wasn't new to us, but perhaps it would be interesting to hear it from the founder of a $50 million mutual fund: "In 1974, if banks had been required to mark their investment holdings down to their true market value, there would have been no capital left in the banks of America. The FDIC was not designed for crises, but for normal times."
He gave us an interesting analysis of the Bank of America's financial statement. Of the $6.6 billion of the United States Treasury Securities held by the bank, less than 10%, or approximately 600 million, are available to secure private depositors. The rest is committed to secure public depositors, such as cities, counties, states, etc.
Because of overnight "repurchase agreement" sales of their Treas-

ury bills, on occasion, big banks will find themselves for a day, with no municipal or Treasury bonds in their portfolios. Our banks hold $90 billion in foreign loans held, much of this from insolvent, underdeveloped countries. If the Federal Reserve ever had to bail out our banks, they would be bailing out the whole world. Banks have the strongest lobbies in the world. There are ten companies of over a billion dollar sales that paid no taxes last year, and four of them were banks. They make the rules.

(Special Report #4, 10/76)

Q: Is it safe to have my money in banks?

A: Yes—NOW! We came very close to losing the banking system during the recession of 1974-75, but the banks have pulled back from the brink temporarily, as of this date. The time will come, however, when they will be in serious trouble. In my opinion, the banking system is still substantially weakened and will be much more vulnerable to the next downturn than they were to the last one. They could be in serious trouble with a world-wide depression. For now, however, I wouldn't worry about your bank.

Q: How can I tell whether my bank is safer than the others?

A: I wouldn't worry about it too much. If you should select one of the first banks to go broke, you're probably lucky. The FED-ERAL DEPOSIT INSURANCE CORPORATION is well-equipped to see that you suffer no loss, or even inconvenience. With great fanfare and public acclaim, they will announce the bank was taken over by someone else overnight and opened under a new name, and your deposits are secure and you have nothing to worry about. The FDIC attempts to protect you, not only with the money, but with a smooth transition.

However, the FDIC was not designed to deal with a general collapse of the banking system, but only the occasional bank failure. Don't worry about whether your individual bank is safe. Worry about whether the banking system is in danger. The time will come when you will want to take your money from the banks and put it into tangible assets, such as precious metals, food and land.

BANKING INDUSTRY PROBLEMS

(2/1/76) Well, it's out now. The banks aren't as sound as they told us they were. Senator Proxmire, Chairman of the Senate Banking

Committee, says: "A relatively limited economic set-back could result, conceivably, in the failure of some of the nation's largest banks."

If that statement came from me, it would be called inflammatory, extreme and dangerous.

Senator Proxmire recommended a subpoena for representatives of Chase Manhattan and First National City Bank to appear before the committee. They refused!

I told you in Special Report No. 1, last October, that the greatest threat to the banking system was "disclosure." Well, I was right.

Arthur Burns says the banks are "generally sound." Sure! So sound, that looking too deeply into the condition of individual banks carries the enormous risk of triggering a bank panic?

Burns told the House Banking Committee, "When you cast doubt on the solvency of individual banks, you are taking grave risks, not only of causing a run on the individual banks, but also causing broad tremors in a very large part of our financial system. The risk is enormous, even nationwide, and it may extend beyond the boundary of the nation."

Here are their problems.

1. Huge investments in municipal bonds, including New York City, New York State, Big M.A.C. and many defaulting Housing Authorities.

2. Billions in oil tanker loans in default because of gross over-building.

3. Huge loans to insolvent nations. Zaire has already defaulted on several billion dollars.

4. Billions in Real Estate Investment Trust loans (R.E.I.T.) in default.

5. A wave of personal and corporate bankruptcies and defaulting loans.

6. An inability to raise equity capital because of depressed bank stocks.

7. DISCLOSURE of these problems triggering enough runs to tip them into insolvency. (It wouldn't take much.)

(2/15/76) When things start really going sour, here's what the banks do:

1. They shore up public confidence by showing high earnings. Thanks to the miracle of modern accounting, losses can be shown on the balance sheet by the reduction of loan loss reserves, and not debits against earnings. So we are seeing some glorious earnings reports from

some very sick banks.

Also a loss this year need not be all charged off against this year's income—only 20% a year for five years.

Then you make some "bridge loans" to buy time and hope for the best.

2.   They launch a massive PR campaign. Tell the world how sound the banking system is! Runs must be avoided at all costs. Money running around from one bank to another looking for safety is like water sloshing around in a boat. If there's enough of it, the shifting weight can capsize the boat, and they know this.

3.   They demand secrecy! Disclosure could be fatal, triggering withdrawals. The power of the banks to avoid disclosure is incredible. (see also: Banks, Robert Hartline Letter)

The White House, "executive privilege" notwithstanding, couldn't maintain its secrecy. The C.I.A. and the F.B.I. couldn't avoid the cold light of public exposure.

I think, however, the banks have a good chance to keep the lid on their present troubles, for a while anyway.

4.   They tell everyone how the government protects deposits.

The Federal Deposit Insurance Corporation (FDIC) insures your deposit up to $40,000. Wonderful! These insurance funds add up to 1.3 percent of the deposits in America. That's one dollar of insurance for every $76 on deposit.

If Banks Go Broke

If banks go broke, any one of three scenarios could effect you.

1.   Your bank could go under and you would be paid by the FDIC with no loss.

2.   Several banks could go under, including yours, and it could overwhelm the FDIC fund and you would lose all or part of your money.

3.   Your bank could survive, but the combination of major banks failing and the infusion of billions in printing press money by the Fed, in an effort to meet the panic runs, could cause a gigantic depression characterized by severe monetary inflation. Your dollars would decline in value at a rapid pace. You cannot escape completely, even if you choose a sound bank.

(1/1/77) The United States' banking system is dominated by no more than fifteen banking groups, most of them controlled by giant holding companies. They are: The First National City Bank, Chase-Manhattan, Chemical, Manufacturer's Hanover, Marine Midland,

Morgan Guarantee, Bank of America, Wachovia, Continental Bank of Chicago, The Mellon Bank, Security Pacific, and Western Bancorporation. These are the banks where nearly all of the thousands of smaller banks in the country do their banking. This is where all of the money and credit in the United States comes together. They are the key log in the jam. If you pull it out, the entire system crumbles. What is their status?

On November 4, 1976, the Federal Deposit Insurance Corporation reported that their "problem bank" list has lengthened this year. The number of big problem banks has expanded faster in the West as a whole. Nevertheless, all three Federal Bank Regulatory Agencies assure us the banking system is in better shape now than it was in January, despite a record number of failures and forced mergers.

What do you expect them to say? It's their job to see that the system doesn't crumble. They know the biggest single factor in the safety of banks is public confidence. The public interest requires them to lie, if necessary. Remember that the FDIC has roughly $1 of insurance on hand for every $76 of deposits. This is ordinarily sufficient when there are no serious problems in the economic system.

What would happen if a few big banks went broke?

The failure of any two of the top twenty could wipe out the FDIC funds.

The banks are vulnerable in two ways. Remember, bank loans are ASSETS and the banks are in trouble on the asset side of their balance sheet, and vulnerable on the liability side, too. Their liabilities are primarily the obligation to pay depositors on demand. The classic 1933 run on the banks consisted of liabilities coming due unexpectedly when long lines of depositors wanted their money, forcing the banks to shut down. On any given day, if 10 percent of the depositors demanded their funds, even the strongest banks could fail, but it is the assets that worry me the most.

It is my opinion that 25 percent of the assets of the top fifteen banks in the United States are worthless. They are carried on the books at full value, but are simply not there. They have gone down the drain.

By 1979, it is reasonable to expect that the total assets of all the commercial banks in the United States will be over $800 billion. Now remember, the big banks hold about 25 percent of that in government and municipal bonds, real estate, loans to the largest corporations, tankers, and foreign governments.

What about their real estate loans? Immense amounts of money are tied up in the Real Estate Investment Trusts (REIT). The REIT loans are listed on the asset side of the balance sheet. At least half of it is irrevocably lost. There's somewhere between $10 and $20 billion down the tubes. This is depositors' money. Sooner or later, it will have to be written off.

Now, according to the bank regulatory agencies and under current accounting rules, these losses do not have to be deducted at the time it is evident the loans are no longer paying interest and aren't any good. They can be written off over five years. So the banks still continue to show most of these loans as assets.

The banks have poured about $15 billion into loans against tankers. Between $5 and $10 billion of these loans will never be repaid.

Back in 1974, the U.S. Controller of the Currency suggested it would be unwise for any American bank to loan any more money to Italy, but they kept on doing it anyway. Italy is not an example of a credit-worthy borrower. She is in desperate shape and we're going to have to continue to throw good money after bad, simply to prevent her total collapse and default on the money she's borrowed.

But if you think Italy is bad, take a look at the so-called Lesser Developed Countries (LDC). American banks have loaned them over $50 billion of your money. This is done primarily so they can pay the OPEC nations their exorbitant prices for oil. The loans are primarily backed by U.S. Governmental guarantees. If those countries default, Uncle Sugar is going to have to bail out the banks.

This is why Jim Benham, in our recent interview, referred to the Federal Reserve as "the lender of last resort to the entire world." Loans to the Lesser Developed Countries have the potential for explosive printing press inflation.

The recent price increase of the OPEC nations, even though it was held to only 5%, is no source of satisfaction. It makes the LDC loans shakier, at the same time forcing the banks to throw more good money on the table to avoid defaults. When a man owes you money you desperately need, he is now your general partner. He controls you.

Banks are still loaning to the Lesser Developed Countries, under the assumption that a world-wide economic recovery will improve things well enough to bail them out. The world-wide economic recovery is not yet developing. It is chancy at best.

It takes approximately 30 percent of the total earnings of these countries just to service their outstanding debt to the American banks. There is no way these loans are going to be paid off. All the banks can do is postpone the day of reckoning with more loans.

After that come the billions of dollars the banks have invested in suspect municipal bonds, such as the State of Massachusetts, which, we have been informed, is going to be broke sometime this spring, to say nothing of New York, Detroit, Cleveland, San Francisco, and a lot of other pretty shaky borrowers.

Bear in mind, all these loans can be called "good" if they simply continue to loan sufficient money to these lousy borrowers so they can make regular interest payments. So they send good money after bad and really dig a deeper hole for themselves. For the same reason, they loaned $600 million to W. T. Grant just weeks before it filed bankruptcy.

It is a formula for disaster to borrow short and lend long. Loans are being financed by selling 90-day Certificates of Deposits, so a modern run on the banks consists not only of investors and deposits lining up to get their money back; it includes the non-renewal of Certificates of Deposit.

The bank balance sheets are shot full of troubles, but it boils down to this on the bottom line. There are approximately $200 billion in assets held by the top fifteen banks in the U.S. Approximately $40 billion of this is worthless.

THEIR COMBINED NET WORTH, PART OF WHICH IS STOCKHOLDER MONEY THAT CANNOT BE WITHDRAWN BY DEPOSITORS, IS ONLY ABOUT $20 BILLION. THEIR PHONY ASSETS ARE ROUGHLY TWICE THEIR NET WORTH. This is a recipe for disaster.

If the system eventually goes, it doesn't matter whether your money is in a sound bank, or a weak bank. You will lose it. If the system DOESN'T go, it doesn't matter whether your money is in a sound bank or a weak bank, because if you choose the wrong bank, the FDIC will pay you off, as long as the system is intact.

What it adds up to is this: the potential to bring down the American banking system is already in the system. There is a potential for bank troubles to trigger a desperate flood of paper money to save the banking system, triggering hyper-inflation. It is my opinion that the government will not politely stand by and watch the system go, but will attempt to flood the system with cash reserves in order to meet the depositor demand when the ultimate calamity occurs; which is, of course, the depositor run on the banks. That's why I'm betting on an explosive inflation. You will eventually have to switch your money into "counter-cyclical" investments. Gold and silver are counter-cyclical to the economy, generally. As troubles get bad, those investments leap forward. It is not time yet to bail out of the banks and put all your money into hard money assets. The time will come, and we will let you know, probably too early. But it is better to be early than late. In the meantime, don't renew your CDs. Don't tie up your money more than 120 days, except in suburban or small town residential and agricultural real estate. Liquidity is the key right now. Begin to shift some of your funds into gold or silver-related investments, and tangible assets such as food, and keep the rest liquid.

Remember, the failure of the banking system means depression, municipal bankruptcy and urban chaos, no automated paychecks, welfare, or Social Security checks. You must be prepared to live independently of this interdependent economic system, until normal commerce resumes.

(3/15/76)   Let's review their troubles. They are loaded down with Real Estate Investment Trust Loans in default, New York City and State securities, loans to such marvelous credit risks as Penn Central and W.T. Grant, with a rising incidence of corporate bankruptcies and companies in trouble due to the past recession, and billions in loans to insolvent third world countries. Their ratio of ready cash-to-deposits are at an historic all-time low, and a withdrawal of $18 billion in oil money from the U.S. banking system could well be a fatal blow.

These data were finally released by the banks as a result of demands from the Senate Foreign Relations Subcommittee on Multi-National Corporations. This group is launching a new investigation into the extent, impact and effectiveness of U.S. banks overseas.

The only two banks whose names have leaked out were Wells Fargo and Bank of America. Interestingly enough, Wells Fargo and Bank of America were alleged to be among the 25 American banks which cooperate with the Arab nations' boycott against Israel, in a list released by the Anti-Defamation League of B'nai Brith. If true, it is interesting to note how successful "hot money" can be in influencing bank policy. It is a measure of the banks' fear and concern.

This is just another reason for avoiding banks except for the most limited use of checking account services.

(5/15/77)   The Bank "Wolf"

Our banks are threatened by technical insolvency. They are O.K. as long as the economic winds are calm, but their weaknesses would be exposed by economic downturn.

Much of the paper they hold is worthless and will have to eventually be written off. They are tremendously exposed to Lesser

Developed Counties with loans which will never be repaid. They are holding the paper of near-to-bankrupt communities, which will be forced over the brink during the next downturn when the costs of supporting the unemployed become too great.

As the Nation goes, so go the banks, and vice-versa. The Government will do everything it can to save the banks—but this will result in printing press inflation.

(8/1/78)   On Friday, July 14, two interesting articles appeared in *THE WALL STREET JOURNAL*. They will sound just like vintage Ruff to you old-timers.

> BANKS' TROUBLES WORRY FEDERAL OVERSEERS, THOUGH THEIR DANGER LIST IS DOWN NOW.
>
> Some officials see the industry facing an economic slow-down now in poorer shape than before the 1974-75 recession. Big banks still struggle with a huge post-recession hangover from real-estate loans gone sour. Their real-estate holdings, swollen by foreclosures, approach $1.2 billion; experts say part must ultimately be written off as losses.
>
> The big institutions suffer from capital shortages. Senate Banking Chairman Proxmire calls the capital of the largest banks 'grossly inadequate.' The main reason: Their retained earnings have fallen short of the inflation rate. Washington bank watchers agree big banks may have trouble in an economic slow-down; no one is sure what to do about it.

I've said over and over in print, from the lecture platform, and on radio and television, that the banks will go into the next recession weaker than they went into the last one. It's about time that some of the "mainstream" publications recognized that.

In the same *WSJ* there was an interesting report about savings banks in New York.

> Savings banks in New York State sustained significant outflows of deposits in June despite paying higher interest rates on two newly authorized types of certificate accounts. (The banks had a net out-flow of $162 million in the month, the worst experience for a June since the 1974 credit crunch, when a net of $205 million flowed out, according to the Savings Bank Association of New York State.) Banks and Savings and Loan Associations recently were authorized to offer 6-month certificates whose rate is pegged to the interest rate on 6-month Treasury bills. They were also authorized to offer a high-yielding 8-year account. 'It appears so far that the net effect of the new certificates had been to increase the

cost of money with little more impact on cash flow,' lamented Ira Scott, Executive Vice-President of the Association.

We face the same kinds of banking dangers that we faced in 1974 except the system is now weaker. One of the major distorting effects of inflation is high interest rates. High interest rates tend to motivate savers to pull their money out of bank deposits and look for higher yields in Treasury bills and other short-term instruments. This can also accelerate from a stream into a torrent if people get worried about the status of the banks. Runs on the banks still are possible and if anybody tells you the FDIC can prevent a run on all the banks, you can tell them they are crazy. It is argued that the FDIC insurance would have prevented the 1930's runs on the banks. No way! Events would have totally overwhelmed the FDIC.

Mark my words, you are now watching the unfolding of the next recession, and possibly the beginning of the Big Inflationary Depression. It's happening right now all around you. The danger signals? Higher interest rates, a falling dollar, bank deposit outflows, an erratic but continually climbing inflation rate, soaring gold prices, and deteriorating public confidence.

NEW YORK CITY LOANS

(Special Report #3, 9/76)   One of the world's largest industries is the financial group which funds federal, local and state deficits. It consists of banks, insurance companies, and investment houses. Without deficits, billions in income to these firms would be eliminated. They may have overreached themselves in New York's case, but they did it under the assumption the Federal Reserve Board would bail them out. So, perhaps they knew exactly what they were doing. If I could find some way to make them pay the penalty for their greed, without the rest of the nation suffering, I would do so. But unfortunately, they can't be punished without adversely affecting the lives of every American. We have to look no farther than Manhattan to find the villains. And perhaps, we must all share in the blame that comes from these self-inflicted wounds—those who so complacently sat back and said:

"Nothing can go wrong. The nation is in good hands. Our resources are unlimited. We must be compassionate. Don't count the costs. Who says America can fail?"

Let us all pray to God that Howard Ruff is wrong.

FROM A TO Z

ROBERT HARTLINE LETTER

(2/1/79)   You remember the story of the Watchbird (see: Regulatory Agencies)? Well, it's finally happened. A Watchbird is circling me. I just received a fascinating letter from Mr. Robert H. Hartline, Supervisory Agent of the Eleventh District of the FEDERAL HOME LOAN BANK BOARD, as follows:

> Dear Mr. Ruff:
>
> We understand that during a December 24, 1978 telecast of the program, RUFF HOUSE, you made a statement to the effect that people should not put their savings into savings and loan associations.
>
> We request that you provide us with a copy of the text of that statement and any explanation of the reason for such a statement, so that we may determine the propriety of the statement and whether it complies with applicable laws.
>
> Your early response will be appreciated.

I'm not personally afraid of Mr. Hartline, but it is frightening that a government agency would consider it had the right to "determine the propriety" of something I said.

In the show under question, I had an inquiry from a viewer wanting to know whether he should put his money in a Federally insured bank or savings and loan. My answer was:

> No. I wouldn't put it in a bank or savings and loan right now. Your rate of return on those investments will be less than the rate of inflation. That, plus the fact that the "profit" is taxed, makes you a loser. Second, we're moving into a recession, and possibly into a depression, and our banking system and our savings and loan system are moving into this in considerably weaker condition than when we went into the recession in 1974-75. I happen to believe that we will see headlines in the not too distant future telling us that there are some very serious things wrong with our banking system (as we did in 1975). If you want to sleep well, no, I would not put money there.
>
> We're going to see some headlines that will shake our confidence. The Federal Deposit Insurance Corporation only has enough money to insure about 1.3 percent of all bank deposits. That is also true of the Federal Savings and Loan Insurance Corporation. I don't think that is adequate to deal with serious runs on the banks, which I think are possible in the next year or two. So in the interest of sleeping well, I'd rather be out of the banking system."

A little research by my attorney produced the fact that Mr. Hartline's objection is based on a law passed February 3, 1938, which says:

> Whoever willfully and knowingly makes, circulates, or transmits to another or others any statement or rumor, written, printed or by word of mouth, which is untrue in fact or is directly, or by inference, derogatory to the financial condition, or affects the solvency or financial standing of the Federal Savings and Loan Insurance Corporation, shall be fined not more than $1,000 or imprisoned not more than one year, or both.

This allows an official policy of concealment of the true condition of a bank or the banking system, and allows people to blithely make commercial deposits, buy bank stocks, and purchase CDs in troubled or even insolvent banks, while the government works secretly behind the scenes to bail them out. That's fine as long as the whole system is basically stable, and only an occasional mismanaged bank gets in trouble. In this case you go to your bank one day and see that it has another name over the door, having been secretly acquired by another bank. But if the whole system should come under great strain, then the FDIC could have a monstrous liability, as it would have been partners to a conspiracy to conceal material facts important to prospective investors and depositors. This law would prevent anyone from warning depositors and investors. As I indicated in *HOW TO PROSPER DURING THE COMING BAD YEARS*, it is the government's policy to pay all claims on all deposits, even over and above the insured amounts, to avoid lawsuits over losses resulting from your naive investment in a secretly insolvent bank.

The issue raised by Mr. Hartline's letter is the government's power to intimidate my free speech. There are two basic principles in conflict. One is my First Amendment right and need to warn people of financial dangers for their own individual decision making. The other is the government's desire to have privacy while it maneuvers behind the scenes. This assumes that statements such as mine could cause a banking panic, which, if true, puts me in an interesting dilemma. Do I speak the truth in time to allow some people to get their money out of the system? Or do I swallow my tongue, hoping somehow the system will survive and everyone will be all right? You may not agree with my choice, but I hope you agree I have a genuine moral dilemma.

Free speech might have its hazards, and in some cases, might prove embarrassing in the short run, but in the long haul, free speech is indispensable to our system. This fundamental human right was intended to prevail over momentary governmental expediency. Without it, the system is vulnerable to bureaucratic tyranny. And that's precisely what I may have walked into.

I don't know if Mr. Hartline will pursue this further. I know that I do not intend to send him a transcript. Neither the law nor principles requires me to do so. I deny his right to determine "the propriety" of my statements. If he chooses to bring charges against me, I propose to fight. I may lose, but on appeal, we will raise the Constitutional issue. If we don't win, I fear for the fate of the great American experiment.

If the banking system is sound, my statements won't hurt it. If it is so precarious it fears statements from an obscure newsletter writer and fringe-time talk-show host, then it is in sorry shape indeed, and the sooner we know, the better. In that case, collapse would be inevitable anyway.

As a practical matter, the government is not going to let the banking system "fail" in the classic meaning of the word. If we have runs on the banks due to a collapsing dollar, a liquidity squeeze with lots of bankruptcies, the Arabs withdrawing their short-term deposits, etc., the government will be loading up C-141's with mountains of paper money and flying off to cover the banks until it has run out of steam. This explosion of paper money could convert us quickly from a credit economy into a printing press economy, but that's another subject. In the final analysis, if the banking system gets in trouble publicly the banks might be shut down for a few days and then you might not be able to withdraw as much money as you want when you want it. Your money could be tied up for days, weeks or even months, limiting your financial freedom while prices and precious metals are blowing through the roof. Such problems would probably trigger the President to invoke Executive Order #11490 (*HOW TO PROSPER DURING THE COMING BAD YEARS*, Chapter 9). Ultimately, you will be repaid in inflationary funny-money, too late to get rid of it.

This is a different world with a lot of ingenious governmental weapons to prevent the classic bank problems of the 1930s, but this new scenario would be just as unpleasant as the old style banking collapse. The dangers are very real. Not right now, of course, but later.

Even if there is no upheaval of the system in the next recession or depression, I still think a savings deposit or CD is a lousy investment, just from a dollars-and-cents-return point of view. I think banks are lousy places to keep money other than money necessary to maintain orderly personal and business affairs. Your money is better off in Treasury bills and money market funds, or in gold, silver, diamonds, and all the other things I have consistently recommended over the past three years.

TREASURY SECURITIES

(5/15/76)   James Benham makes the point that for now, Treasury Securities are the safest of all the investments because the United States Government will be the last to go broke and we will certainly see signs of other problems, giving us time to bail out. Individuals hold less than 2 percent of the $162 billion in Treasury notes and bills in circulation. Banks own most of the rest, and the Federal Reserve gives the banks the money to buy them.

BARTER

(6/1/79)   Governors On Thermometers Now?

I saw an interesting poll the other day indicating that 57 percent of the people of this country were in favor of wage and price controls—one of the signs I was looking for to signal the possible advent of such controls. We are getting local rent controls in several major cities, including Los Angeles and San Francisco; the all-inclusive national wage, price and rent controls are inevitable. I think the time is very close when we will have to cope with shortages in the economy, and it will be illegal for many merchants to sell items at profitable prices. They'll refuse to sell, go out of business, find loopholes, deal in the Black Markets—or barter. One important tool for functioning in this distorted, crippled marketplace is to learn how to barter, and hook up with a dependable barter network.

How would you like to learn how to use silver coins to sell things at the face value of the coin, and save capital gains taxes? (Page 143, hard-bound, *HOW TO PROSPER DURING THE COMING BAD YEARS.*) How would you like to be able to exchange vacation homes with other barter exchange members? How would you like to be able to trade goods and services directly with others? How would you like to get a thorough education on how to barter? Well, you have your chance with the COMSTOCK TRADING COMPANY. I will be an active "barterer," and COMSTOCK TRADING COMPANY will become a Ruff Recommended vendor. That's how highly I value the concept. It's my job to anticipate trends and prepare you for them; and learning to barter will be critical.

A lot of interesting things end up in our files that don't merit some of the precious space in our 8 pages every two weeks, but in a catalog, published and updated on a monthly basis, there's room for all kinds of barter or purchase opportunities in land, wood stoves, wholesale deals, etc. You name it, it will probably be in the catalog. We anticipate several thousand members right off the bat. The price is more than reasonable and we have negotiated an outstanding arrangement for *RUFF TIMES'* subscribers.

As is the case with all vendors, we have no financial interest in your dealings with COMSTOCK TRADING. I have divested myself of my interest, and neither I, nor Target, will benefit from your membership. (see: Price and Wage Controls)

BETER, DR. PETER

(1/15/77) PETER BETER rose to fame some years back by claiming all of the gold in Fort Knox had been removed by ROCKEFELLER interests.

He recently made the rather startling announcement that the Soviets have placed dozens of nuclear missiles in American coastal waters, and can demolish the United States at any time. He said the United States government knows it and has been removing these missiles, but they are being replaced by the Soviets as rapidly as they are removed. He has even given specific coordinates as to the location of each missile. He has been campaigning to put public pressure on the Pentagon to publicly announce it. The question is, is it true?

I had a call from Dr. Beter. Let me tell you what I think about this whole situation.

Dr. Beter is an enigma. His past credentials are certainly impressive, but he seems to specialize in great sweeping allegations, which can be neither proven nor disproven.

I know for a fact that one of his statements, regarding missiles in San Pablo Bay (the northern part of San Francisco) simply is not correct. I have fished those waters for many years. They have an average depth of eight feet. There is no way a Soviet submarine could sneak in and plant missiles. There is a heavily traveled deep channel south of the bay, which is narrow and barely deep enough to accommodate deep-water vessels, but it simply isn't deep enough, and the currents are too fast and treacherous to permit a Soviet submarine to negotiate these waters. When I presented this to him, he said he had simply missed on his coordinates by two miles. Well, I have looked at my map and there is no place within a two-mile radius of San Pablo Bay where this could be done. Insofar as San Pablo Bay is concerned, he's dead wrong. This, to me, casts doubt on the rest of his allegations.

In our conversation, he told me he knew of the location of 89 other missiles, which he has refused to reveal to the government until they "go public" with his statements and vindicate him. And, at that time, he will reveal those locations to the government.

He claims his sources are primarily former or present disgruntled Intelligence Agents, but he cannot reveal his sources. He told me he will gradually reveal his sources as he receives permission from the individuals involved.

I have given you as accurate an account of his claims as possible. Now for my opinion.

At the present time, I don't believe it. I don't know whether Dr. Beter is an outright fraud or whether he is being led by the nose by some people who are crying wolf, hoping we won't listen when it really happens, or those who would like to discredit the political conservative movement by making claims, which on the face, seem ridiculous.

I must emphasize that I don't know for sure whether that's wrong. I happen to believe that the Soviets are morally capable of taking such an action; I don't know whether it is physically possible. I remain inherently skeptical of someone who makes a sweeping allegation that cannot be proven or disproven.

I challenge Dr. Beter to bring that information to me, reveal his sources and his documentation, and I will evaluate it. I will keep everything he says to me in the strictest confidence and will only release information to the public as he gives me his permission. I am even prepared to give him a legal agreement with severe penalties attached if I should violate that trust. If the information is convincing, I will prepare my next meal from humble pie and crow, and will tell the world through my publication, that Dr. Beter is right.

If true, it makes the Cuban Missile Crisis seem like kids playing cops and robbers with cap guns. It means the Soviet Union can now simply say, "Lay down your arms or we will destroy you on a moment's notice." If our government knows of this and is removing these missiles and not informing us, it is wrong and they should tell us. If Dr. Beter knows of additional missiles and he is not informing our government, he should make this known. Until I receive some documentation, it is my personal opinion that his claims are unfounded.

I have no animosity towards Dr. Beter. I find him to be a most interesting man. I'm inclined to think that if he is wrong, he is not intentionally defrauding us. He may have been given some incorrect information and he perhaps has made some leaping assumptions. I also am prepared to say, if he turns out to be right, that he is one of America's bravest citizens and deserves to be honored as such.

How about it, Dr. Beter? (No response was ever received—5/79. HJR)

BONDS & BOND MARKET

(2/15/76)   Some fundamentals:

1. As interest rates go up, bond prices go down, and vice versa. That seems to defy logic, but bond interest, unlike stock dividends, never changes in dollar terms, except in case of total default or bankruptcy.

For example, most bonds have a face value at redemption time of $1,000. If it carries a stated interest rate of 6%, the owner would receive $60 a year in cash payments, because $60 is 6% of $1,000. That $60 amount never changes.

2. Bonds can be bought and sold in the secondary market after they are issued, just as stocks can be. However, the market value of bonds will go up or down, depending upon prevailing interest rates in the general marketplace. For example, if interest generally were to rise to 12 percent, a prospective buyer of your 6% bond wouldn't be willing to pay the face value of the bond ($1000) because the interest payments are only $60, a 6 percent return, and he can probably get 12 percent interest somewhere else for his money, perhaps in bank certificates of deposit. He would probably be willing to pay $500 for the bonds, however, because $60 interest on $500 is 12%.

Conversely, if interest rates dropped to 3%, the price of the bonds could theoretically rise to $2,000, because $60 is 3% of $2000, and that might be what an investor would be willing to pay.

Now, this is all an over-simplification, because other factors can modify these price movements, such as the general market's opinion of future interest rate trends; the closeness to the maturity date of the particular bond issue when the bond holder would receive the face value in full; changes in the credit rating of the bond issuer; or the rate of inflation, with investors demanding a return high enough to compensate for a loss of purchasing power. But the principle is correct, interest rates and bond prices move in opposite directions.

Banks rely on their economists and computer forecasts, and economic forecasting has been dismally wrong for over four years.

The consenus has been consistently wrong as to the direction the economy has been going. Economists have overstated the up side and underestimated the down side.

Relying on this advice, the banks have made some hellacious blunders. While treating the small businessman like a potential thief when he applies for a loan, until he can prove he doesn't really need the money, they shovelled it out to such credit-worthy petitioners as New York City, Penn Central, Lockheed, and W. T. Grant, when all the data indicated the chance of repayment was small.

Why?

Arrogance probably. After the "go-go banking" years, when everybody could do no wrong, bankers couldn't conceive of their peers of the corporate or political aristocracy defaulting on a loan.

Later it was "good money after bad" to try to give the borrower time to work it out so there would be no loss at all. But they underestimated the length and severity of the recession and they were covering up the severity of their problems. A loan isn't a bad loan until they call it a bad loan, and if you loan a troubled borrower some more money so he can pay interest on his old loans, it's still a "good" loan.

CORPORATE BONDS

(11/76) When corporate bonds are purchased at or near par, even an 8% return isn't enough. Inflation and taxes, remember?

There are two ways to beat that game.

1. Guess correctly on interest rates. If you guess right and buy bonds when rates are high, and sell them when rates go down, you can make some interesting capital gains. If you guess wrong, you lose money.

2. Buy "junk bonds." These are distressed merchandise. These bonds are issued by companies in trouble and are selling as low as 50% of par. If you spread your money around between 10 or 15 issues and borrow 50% against them, the risks are low and the potential return is high. The odds are that only one will actually default. The odds heavily favor all the rest paying interest as agreed, with no default, and at an average yield of 20% to 24% on your money.

XYZ BOND:

$1,000	par value
70	interest (7 percent on the par value)
500	Purchase price to you
250	Your money invested (50 percent loan)
70	gross interest received
25	less interest paid on 50 percent loan
45	Net yield (18 percent return on $250 investment)

When the company's fortunes improve, or the bonds mature, or interest rates fall, the odds are that they will pay off at par, or close to it.

If you hold those bonds for one year, and they rise to par ($1,000), your $250 investment shows a $500 capital gain. Now deduct the capital gains tax (25 percent—$125). Interest costs on your margin loan have already been deducted from your annual yield. Don't forget an inflation loss (perhaps $35). You now have a real profit of $340, PLUS the $45 net interest ($385 total) or a true 154 percent after inflation return. This could offset the total loss of one of your issues due to default, and leave you with a $135 profit, plus the interest earned on your other holdings.

Only one junk bond issue in 25 actually defaults. Even if the company is liquidated, bond holders come first, and usually make out O.K. Remember, even if it only pays 50 cents on the dollar, you're still doing well.

The odds are that at least one out of 10 issues will show a spectacular rise to near par.

This kind of investment is only for those who have risk money available after taking the basic survival steps you've heard from me time and time again—an emergency food supply, reduced debt, high liquidity, some gold and silver coins, and a secure home.

It also takes a certain kind of temperament. You had better be prepared to worry a lot.

Any good broker should be able to find some appropriate issues for you to consider, but he will probably think you're crazy. Just be sure they are currently paying interest. Avoid rails, airlines, and financial institutions, as government meddling (regulations) can hurt you.

MUNICIPAL BONDS

(1/1/78)   Tax-Free Municipals

Q. Don't you think that tax-free municipal bonds are a good buy
right now?

A. Tax advantages can sometimes lead you into bad investments, and
tax considerations can force businesses to do things that would be
dumb from any other point of view. Right now, there is no
question that if you are in a high tax bracket, you get a better true
yield on municipals. They have been greatly in demand, and the
marketplace has generally recovered temporarily from the fears of
the New York debacle. If you insist on staying with municipal
bonds, watch the market very carefully, and when you become
convinced, as I have, that the interest rate trend is up, bail out.
(That happened shortly after this article was published, and I
turned bearish on bonds—HJR.) The tax advantage could be
more than offset by the loss of principal through a falling market
price. Also, because of the currently favorable climate for
municipals, cities will flood the market with new issues. This will
tend to drive down prices.

BONDS AND ECONOMIC COLLAPSE

(9/15/78)   One early sign is the collapse of the bond markets as a
result of rising interest rates. The bond markets have been very weak
with occasional corrections over the last several months. The bond
markets collapsed in 1920 and 1921 in Germany, and one of the
reasons the printing presses had to run all night was because the
German government was not able to go into the capital markets and
borrow money. The bond markets had collapsed, so they went
directly to the printing press and monetized the debt.

Two of the reasons I have contended we are headed for inflation
instead of deflation are rising prices and rising interest rates which
lead to a collapse of the bond market. In each instance the collapse of
the bond market has turned out to be highly inflationary. During our
deflationary depression of the 1930s, bond prices were at all time
highs and interest rates were under 1 percent for a good part of this
period. By the same token, in an inflationary spiral with rising interest
rates, bond prices go through the floor. This makes it very difficult for
public and private borrowers to find money at any price, and the only
solution is the printing of additional money.

That's what I think we are headed for. The only question is, when do we pass some "point of no return" when the process becomes irreversible? Nobody knows that and I don't either, but I see some similarities between today's circumstances and the period of about six months into the German four-year inflation. I think we have passed it politically already.

BUREAUCRATS

A GOOD ONE

(9/15/77) I've spent enough time tearing into bureaucrats and when I run across a good one, I ought to say so.

In trying to close an escrow on the sale of my home, I found the IRS had a very large lien filed against me relating to an obligation over eight years old. It had not been cleared on the county records, although it had been satisfied. I was told by functionaries at the IRS it would take over a month to get the necessary information to file a "release of lien" against my property so I could close escrow, and there was no way to short-cut the process. I simply didn't believe it, so I phoned the special Procedures Branch of the IRS in San Francisco. After being kicked around to four different people, I finally found a human being, a marvelous Mr. O'Connor, who said, "You have been kicked around enough, let me hear the story." He listened patiently, interrupted twice for clarification and then said, "I'll be back to you within an hour." Ten minutes later the phone rang, he had obtained the necessary information by telephone, indicated that the records would be in his hand the following Monday, and I would be able to pick up the appropriate releases.

Now, I have mixed emotions about Mr. O'Connor. What's a man like him doing in government? He must feel dreadfully out of place. And my second reaction? Why aren't more men like Mr. O'Connor in government? We might have a chance for some sanity in our national affairs if there were more Mr. O'Connors in the world. Thank you, Mr. O'Connors.

ALL THE REST

(6/1/76)   Death by Drowning

On June 5, 1976, the bureaucracies of the United States of America and the State of Idaho were directly responsible for the death by drowning of at least nine people. A new dam burst, wiping out some communities, killing stock, tearing up highways, destroying irrigation systems and killing people. The property damage couldn't be helped, but most of the loss of life was tragically unnecessary.

Here are the facts:

ENGINEERS AT THE DAM KNEW IT WAS GOING TO BURST THREE AND ONE-HALF HOURS BEFORE THE WARNING WENT OUT. THE WARNING WENT OUT FIVE MINUTES BEFORE THE ACTUAL BREAK.

How could such incredible fumbling occur?

At 8:10 a.m., the engineers on the spot concluded the dam was going to go. Water had been seeping under the dam, and whirlpools had appeared in the lake next to the dam. Also there were visible cracks.

As the dam is U.S. Government owned and operated, government procedures for emergencies were followed. No warning could be sent without clearance from Denver and from Washington, D.C. This being Saturday morning, it took almost three hours. At 11:00, a local sheriff was called. He didn't believe it, and insisted on driving up to see. That took about 45 minutes. He radioed a warning at 11:43 a.m. Five minutes later the dam burst, sweeping away campers on the river below the dam.

Governor Andrus had been notified, with sufficient time to fly from Boise some 300 miles away to the dam. Flying over the dam, he commented that there had to be a great loss of life, as he had watched the campers get swept away.

What lesson is there in this for all of us?

First, I have always contended that many of the ills that attend our nation are the result of well-intended fumbling efforts on the part of Big Government to help us. The dam should never have been built. It was unneeded by anyone but the Bureau of Reclamation, to justify its existence.

Second, once Big Government has decided to "help you," the help gets bogged down in a swamp of regulations, each one seeming to be useful. Then the cost of helping you goes out of sight and the benefits are lost in the costs of administration. The bureaucrats substitute regulations for judgment. Usually this costs money, time, or both. Often it bankrupts people and distorts the economy. In this case, it killed people.

The intent of procedures, in this case, was to avoid false alarms which could cause chaos. It was probably assumed an emergency would happen during office hours. It also assumed Washington, D.C.

was smarter than Idaho.

Why didn't the dam personnel warn the campers?

When one sheriff didn't believe them, why didn't they call another?

Why didn't the Governor send someone from close by to check it out, and then put out the warning himself? Why was he up there sight-seeing, instead of taking administrative action to prepare?

The greatest lesson in this tragedy was the value of individual preparedness and initiative. The food stores were destroyed in Rexburg and Sugar City, but many people had food storage programs because about 75 percent of them are Mormons. If the food had been properly canned or containerized, and if the home had not been washed away entirely (which usually wasn't the case), when the flood waters receded, it was still there. No one went hungry. Those living on higher ground shared their stored food and their homes with the unfortunate. Churches in Idaho Falls each sponsored a church or neighborhood in Rexburg or Sugar City and sent carloads of workers and food.

The parents of Terry Jeffers, Target's President, living in Idaho Falls, dug into their food storage supplies and sent food and punch to feed the homeless and the workers pouring in to help.

What was the government doing all this time? They sent troops. To work? No! The troops were there to prevent looting, which is stupid if you know anything about those small eastern Idaho towns. They tried to block entry of the hundreds of organized volunteers trying to get in to help clean up and bring supplies. Then the troops just stood around and watched, while men and women started shoveling mud out of homes and shops.

So what have we learned?

1. Government built a dam that wasn't needed or wanted.

2. Government is responsible for a number of needless deaths through bureaucratic red tape.

3. Government impeded volunteer help efforts.

4. Self-reliant people who had routinely stored food, were able to eat, or provide help to others, reducing the need for government relief efforts.

5. Whole communities responded with commodities and muscle to share in the face of a calamity.

6. Food supplies which weren't properly containerized were damaged or destroyed, arguing that if food is stored it should be done right.

(7/15/76)   Tunnel Vision

The recent widely publicized action of HEW in banning father-son and mother-daughter events in schools is a great example of "tunnel vision" at work, and President Ford's response, although encouraging, missed the point.

To bring you up to date, here's what happened.

Scottsdale, Arizona school officials wrote to the Equal Opportunities section of HEW last February asking clarification of Title IX, the anti-sex discrimination provision of the Education Amendments of 1972. "Were father-son banquets forbidden?" the officials asked.

The request landed on the desk of Helen Walsh, Title IX coordinator for the region.

Ms. Walsh remembered how, when she was a child, her school in Massachusetts sponsored a father-son banquet featuring Bob Cousy and Tom Heinsohn, the Boston Celtics' superstars. Because she was a girl, she couldn't go, but she sneaked out and watched through a crack in the door.

Now, it was her chance to get even. "No, Scottsdale, Arizona, you can't have father-son events because it discriminates between the sexes," was her stance.

Recently she was asked to rule on whether or not a school could select an outstanding boy student, and an outstanding girl student.

Here is what Ms. Walsh said about that:

"The answer, of course, is 'no'. You can pick out two outstanding students, but they might be two boys or two girls.

"You couldn't say the valedictorian has to be a boy and the salutatorian a girl—they're just the two top scholars."

President Ford, seeing the perfect chance to act "Presidential" denounced the "dingle-brained bureaucrat" who produced the ruling. But everyone has missed the real points involved.

This is not just a "dingle-brained bureaucrat" acting irrationally. This decision was approved by her boss and cleared through HEW's office of General Counsel. It's a "dingle-brained" system that chooses to regulate every aspect of our lives. Ms. Walsh's actions were rational, according to the rules, and consistent with the highest traditions of bureaucratic thinking. That's scary!

In the last issue, I said, "There's always a good reason." Every new rule, every new law has a reason. There are real problems out there. But solving all of life's problems—leveling all of life's inequities by law—is like walking through a minefield. Remember Ruff's First Law of Government:

"When government solves a problem, it then creates two or more problems of equal or much greater dimension."

Alexis de Tocqueville's Warning To Modern America

Alexis de Tocqueville should perhaps be enshrined as a modern prophet. His immense insight into the nature, character, and personality of America could have been written today rather than in the nineteenth century. Perhaps none of his observations of the future of this country is more pertinent than his vision of our over-regulated present, and our omnipresent government, which "...every day renders the exercise of the free agency of man less useful and less frequent; it circumscribes the will within a narrower range and gradually robs a man of all the uses of himself. The principle of equality has prepared man for these things; it has predisposed men to endure them and often to look on them as benefits."

"After having thus successfully taken each member of the community in its powerful grasp and fashioned him at will, the supreme power then extends its arm over the whole community. It covers the surface of society with a network of small complicated rules, minute and uniform, through which the most original mind and the most energetic characters cannot penetrate, to rise above the crowd. The will of man is not shattered, but softened, bent, and guided; men are seldom forced by it to act, but they are constantly restrained from acting. Such a power does not destroy, but it prevents existence; it does not tyrannize, but it compresses, enervates, extinguishes, and stupifies a people, until each nation is reduced to nothing better than a flock of timid and industrious animals of which the government is the shepherd."

(9/1/76)   Sex On The Brain

A Los Angeles County Probation Officer, assigned to counsel young girls at a detention school, was arrested on charges that he had lured a delinquent fifteen-year-old girl inmate to his home, got her drunk, and then had sexual intercourse with her, while being photographed by a sixteen-year-old girl. Ordinarily, this might just be considered one of the strange things that happens even in the best of probation departments. However, the case prompted Department District Attorney, Ralph Mayer, who is acting head of the District Attorney's Special Investigations Division, to question some of the practices at Las Palmas School, where the probation officer worked. Mayer said:

> Both men and women probation officers are assigned to oversee

these girls in cottages, and it is my understanding that male probation officers are often designated to make sure that girls get showered and in bed by 9:30 at night. Probation officers are assigned to this duty regardless of sex. No one seems aghast at this sort of involvement when teenage girls are involved."

WHEN HE WAS INFORMED OF MAYER'S CRITICISM, A PROBATION DEPARTMENT SPOKESMAN SAID THAT FEDERAL LAWS THAT PROHIBIT SEX DISCRIMINATION WERE THE REASON MALE OFFICERS WERE ASSIGNED TO GIRL WARDS AND FEMALE OFFICERS TO BOY WARDS.

This piece of tragic foolishness regarding sex discrimination, and the attempt to blur the natural distinctions between the sexes can only result in societal distortion, but again, we're back to a fundamental issue: Is the United States Government wise enough to foresee the implications of every attempt they make at solving society's problems through rules, regulations and legislation?

The Letter Of The Law

Another bizarre example of bureaucracy-run-wild occurred recently when a school district requested a clarification on the legality of having an all-boy chorus in an elementary school. They were informed that it would be illegal sex discrimination and they could lose their various grants and Federal subsidies.

The school had been totally unsuccessful at getting the boys to join the chorus and sing with the girls, but they decided that if they could first get the boys singing in an all boy's chorus, sooner or later they could bring the choruses together for special events and it would result in a strong mixed chorus.

Despite the fact that their intentions were well within the spirit of the regulations, unfortunately, some letter-of-the-law Pharisee concluded it was not legal.

The strength of America rests in its freedom (see: Freedom). The economic strength of this country lies in the ability of citizens to freely make decisions in their best interests, based on their own good judgment. For example, there are dislocations in residential patterns when forced busing takes place. People who might have bought a home in one area because of the good schools close by, might make another decision based on their knowledge of busing; their children might not be attending the school which they have so carefully checked out. This affects home-buying patterns in the real estate market.

When the government legislates a morality that differs from that which we would like to teach our children, then we have a battle at home over what's right and what's wrong. This means great stress in American families and the American family is the basic building block of this country (see: Family). Freedom to make our own decision in our own lives is the mortar holding the building together.

(12/15/76)   Dear Sir, You're Dead

The National Taxpayers Union recently reported one of the most incredible examples of government mindlessness I've seen in a long time.

> Illinois bureaucrats sent out form letters to deceased welfare recipients, informing them their benefits have been cut off because they are dead. Thousands of copies of the letters have been mailed out, reading: 'Your assistance benefits will be discontinued. Reason: It has been reported to our offices that you have expired.'

Helen Schumacher of the Illinois Welfare Division says she is merely following HEW regulations which required notification of recipients who lose their benefits. The regulations, she says, make no exception for the dead:

> We're required to notify deceased persons of the cessation of their benefits. Recipients who want to dispute the decision are allowed an appeal.

This would be funny if it were not merely the logical extension of the bureaucratic state of mind and the mindless juggernaut that government seems to spawn on every level.

(7/15/78)   The Controllocrats

Well, Uncle Sam has finally found a problem worthy of his attention. It seems that Iowa girls need to have their basketball rules regulated by the Department of HEALTH, EDUCATION AND WELFARE, or at least they thought so until Governor Ray telephoned HEW Secretary Joseph Califano to complain. HEW had scheduled a press conference in Washington to make an announcement about whether six-girl basketball discriminates against the players. It seems that girls' rules are different from boys' in that three girls play on offense and three stay back on defense and there are six players on the floor at all times. Critics have said the six-girl system fails to prepare the players for the full-court five "person" game played by colleges, professional and international teams, which, of course, consist entirely of men. That seems logical enough. How can girls expect to play with Rick Barry and Doctor "J" if they don't get practice in the full-court game?

HEW feels they have every right to come up with such reasonable, logical rules as these, because the Iowa schools get $25 million from Title IX (federal school programs).

Governor Ray came up with a very constructive comment, "I suggested that . . . maybe they should require boys to play six-man basketball so they could be equal to girls."

What won't they think of next? Aren't you glad you have those people in Washington looking out for you?

BUSINESS

"PROFITS"

(10/1/76)   In a recent Gallup Poll, Americans were asked what percentage of the sales dollar in American industry ends up as profit. The average response was 35 percent. And the strong feeling was that immoral price rigging was responsible for these "huge" profits.

The true figure is five percent. Some industries, such as food retailing, average 1½ percent. This is before taxes. Taxes cut that figure in half. Out of what's left, companies must set aside operating capital, reserves for plant modernization and expansion, and pay dividends to those who risked their invested funds. No profits? No reward for risked capital! No reward? No capital! No capital? That's the end of the American Dream. It's just that serious.

This horrible misconception on the part of the public, along with unscrupulous and ignorant politicians pandering to this misconception by screaming at "obscene profits," is causing an anti-business mood, reflected in punitive tax changes and a hostile regulatory climate, that could stall the great productive American Machine.

This attitude and these actions can only hurt the investors who own shares of American industries, by reducing dividends and depressing the stock market.

While no one was looking, an incredible phenomenon has developed.

Over half of the shares of the securities listed on the New York Stock Exchange are held by middle-income Americans: mutual funds (owned by millions of small investors), union pension funds, insurance companies, churches, trust funds, and college endowments.

If punitive tax and anti-trust actions reduce corporate profits, middle Americans and conservative small investors who put their savings into blue chips, mutual funds, pension funds, and insurance cash values will find their future jeopardized by a falling stock market and disappearing dividends.

Let's look at the claim of "obscene profits." For instance, the oil companies were lynched in the press when their 1974 net profits showed gains of 50 percent, 100 percent and, in some instances, 200 percent over the previous year. It was claimed that this was the result of greedy gouging to take advantage of the energy shortage. Sounds incriminating, doesn't it?

I don't love the oil companies. I'm sure they took some advantage of the situation. But the high-percentage profit increases were increases over the worst profit year in decades and, in most instances, merely returned profits to more normal levels. For example, if profits were $5 million in 1972, dropped to $1 million in 1973, and went to $3 million in 1974, you could argue that 1974 profits increased three times over 1973, even though they were still 40 percent below 1972. On $100 million in sales, that would mean profits were 5 percent, 1 percent and 3 percent.

The Reward-Risk Ratio

Politically popular price controls on natural gas and petroleum, plus inflating cost, and a changing tax structure, have reduced the reward for new exploration to the point where investing in high risk exploration for new oil has slowed drastically. The potential profit reward is too low for the financial risk involved. As a result, domestic oil and gas production has declined sharply, and demand is rising. That makes us more vulnerable to the Arabs. Dependence on foreign oil is 44 percent, up from only 20 percent in 1973 when the oil boycott almost put America out of business. And yet, we cut the depletion allowance, increasing risk and reducing profit. We are trying to break up big oil companies to "increase competition," despite the fact that this is the most cutthroat, competitive business in the world. Environmentalists delay the Alaska pipeline and block new drilling, not just to force safer methods of drilling, but to stop it completely.

In Congress, we threaten to impose extra taxes on the oil companies, if they meet the Arab conditions on boycotting Israel. No conditions, no oil!

Now, I believe Israel's existence is justified by its courage, its hard work, and scriptural prophecy.

But, even Israel agrees the business boycotts don't hurt them much.

Punitive action will only result in higher gas and oil costs here if the companies face higher U.S. taxes.

Then we institute school busing on a grand scale, using millions of gallons of gasoline daily for a dubious social experiment that isn't improving education for anyone. We know another Israeli war is inevitable, the Arabs can permanently damage us by cutting off our oil and remove their billions in deposits in our banks. Yet, we obligingly put our necks on the block, sharpen the sword, hand it to the executioner (who hates us) and proceed on the assumption he will not strike.

Healthy profits, when reinvested, create jobs and prosperity. Blue chip stocks with stable growing earnings can turn into sound inflation hedges again through moderately rising stock prices. They assure healthy pension plans, colleges, and insurance dividends.

(4/1/79)   There's good news and bad news. The good news first. JIMMY CARTER is about to deregulate domestic oil (and possibly natural gas) and allow domestic prices to rise to world market levels. This will probably encourage conservation and reduce consumption.

And now, the bad news!

He will slap an excess profits tax on the oil companies so the increased prices will not give them the monetary incentive to drill and explore. He may try to come up with some proposal that exempts the oil companies from some of those taxes if they pour the money into exploration. I'll be willing to bet that in the interest of appealing politically to the anti-business, anti-oil-company left that little or no stimulus to production will come out of it. He is looking for an extra $15 billion in taxes to help close his 1981 budget deficit, since he and his advisors are still holding to the fantasy that they might be able to balance the budget by then. I don't think he's looking for more energy at all.

This is just part of an overall assault on business profits. When it was reported that fourth quarter corporate profits were up 26% over the same quarter the previous year, ALFRED KAHN referred to it as a catastrophe. GEORGE MEANY accused corporations of engaging in "profit gouging" at the expense of "the working man and woman." "Profit figures proved the deception of the business community and the one-sidedness of President Carter's wage and price guidelines," Meany said. "This program has held down wages but not profits or prices." Labor is just about to embark on some wage battles and it is building up the anti-business sentiment, unfortunately, this Administration is helping them.

This is appalling!! The assumption is that the responsibility for fighting inflation is up to business. It is not. It is up to government.

Another assumption is that businesses can always determine their profit levels in advance, and set prices accordingly. With the burst in business activity, based partly on anticipatory inflationary buying, in the last quarter of 1978, the only way businesses could have cut their profits would have been to shut their doors about December 1. That would tend to ruin your Christmas season if you are a retailer. There's no way they can tell what their profitability will be until a quarter is over and the sales reports come in.

It's also based on two more false assumptions: first, directors and officers of the companies do not have a responsibility to their stockholders to maximize profits; and second, corporations are somehow entities separate and apart from the American people. The stock of all these big corporations is mostly owned by union pension fund, colleges, charitable trusts, mutual funds, bank trust departments, and insurance companies. In fact, much of retired America, including widows and orphans, is dependent upon the profits of these companies. The economy is threatened by a sick stock market. Those profits should be acclaimed, not attacked. Unfortunately, whatever small chance we may have had that business conditions will improve will be smashed by "jaw-boning" and taxation and also by hysterical anti-business sentiment whipped up by government trying to divert attention from the real cause of inflation: government money policy and the Federal Reserve system. And Mr. Carter has indicated that he personally will be more involved in jaw-boning.

The President will try to balance the budget with business taxes, not by cutting spending. We need an anti-business hysteria in this country for him to get away with it. It could mean the destruction of the business community at a crucial turning point in American history. It is sick, immoral, and dishonest, and my stomach is churning over it, and if you've got your wits about you, yours should be too.

CONFISCATION BY GOVERNMENT

(10/1/78) Suppose the United States government suddenly announced that all American corporations were to immediately transfer to Uncle Sam 77% of their outstanding stock. Would this cause a revolution?

Of course it would. Or would it?

It's already happened, and it may be one of the real reasons behind the tax revolt. It's just that the government used such sneaky tactics

that BOOBUS AMERICANUS doesn't know it happened. He hasn't
added it up. Let me illustrate.

In 1972, American corporations earned approximately $126 billion
in profits.

Let's see what happened to them. The following analysis is
borrowed from *THE BIGGEST CON*, by Irwin Schiff.

Profits	$ 126 billion
Less retained earnings (essential for growth, replacement of obsolete plants & equipment, operating capital, R & D, etc.)	(43 billion)
Total available for distribution to stockholders	83 billion
Less taxes (income only)	(56 billion)
Benefits paid to owners (dividends)	27 billion
Less personal income taxes paid by stockholders on dividends	(8 billion)
Total net benefit to stockholders	$ 19 billion

To rearrange those figures a bit, it seems that out of the $83 billion
available for distribution to the stockholders, Uncle Sam grabbed $64
billion, or 77%. And inflation is taking away even that small pittance.

Now the simple questions are: 1) Who benefits most from the
profits from American industry? Uncle Sam does. He is, in effect, the
beneficial owner of 77% of the company; 2) Who invested in that
business, did the work and took the risk? Uncle Sam? No way! It was
the "minority shareholders" who ended up with only 23% of the total
benefit; and 3) Who took the losses if a corporation went bankrupt?
Uncle Sam? No way! The minority owners did.

I believe that American industry has been nationalized. Government has avoided the discomfort, liability, inconvenience and responsibility of being "shareholders of record." To add insult to injury,
not only has government tied down industry with a horribly multiplying web of hundreds of thousands of regulations which restrict
their activities and drain their operating capital and resources and
consume management time, but they have forced them to pay for
their own chains through taxation.

And that doesn't complete the picture. Not only is government
venal, avaricious, and greedy, but it's also stupid. If you could find

somebody who was willing to put up all the money, give you 77 percent of the profits while doing all the work for you, and assumed all the risk, wouldn't you treat him a little better? Even a good draft animal is entitled to an occasional pat. But, oh no, that's not the way Uncle Sam treats his partners. They are treated as avaricious criminals.

The anti-business attitudes of government have been so influential that in a recent survey of high school students by the U.S. Chamber of Commerce, the following incredible facts arose:

1.   67 percent of the students see no need for profits.

2.   62 percent think the government should provide jobs.

3.   40 percent could not name one advantage of Capitalism over Communism.

4.   61 percent felt a worker should not produce all he can.

5.   50 percent felt the government contributes most to national prosperity.

6.   66 percent think the best way to improve our standard of living is not by workers producing more, but by giving workers more wages.

And to top it all off, in another similar survey, American high school and college students concluded that the average profitability of American industry was close to 50 percent of sales, as opposed to the real figure of 4 percent. No wonder the public cheers when government confiscates the wealth of big business or "the rich."

This attitude can be compared only to that of certain tribes of Great Plains Indians who, when they were migrating, would literally cut steaks off the sides of the living cattle and keep them alive for many days while driving them along the trail.

The average subscriber who calls our Member Services Department is not measuring the impact of taxes and inflation on his investments. Most investments don't work out well after inflation and taxes unless it beats the rate of inflation by a huge margin. There is no way you can beat it with fixed return investments or the typical capital-gains vehicle.

I believe the total effect of these facts is that government owns us. We spend most of our time working for it. It rips off our money and promises us great benefits in return. Most of us have tried to compensate for this incredible confiscation of our money by borrowing so we can "improve our standard of living." In the process, we have built a mountain of unstable debt which will come down some day.

American corporate ownership has been secretly confiscated. True tax rates, on real profits, after inflation and honest depreciation allowances, are a ruinous 100 percent or greater. (see: Government, Big)

BUSINESS WITH FOREIGNERS

(5/1/76)   Hanging The Wrong Man

Did you ever stop to think about all the fuss over the alleged corruption of American Corporations in paying "kickbacks" to foreign government officials, that these corporations may not be the perpetrators of a crime, but the victims of one?

In this country, we don't put people in jail for being victims of extortion. We prosecute the extortionist. In each of the countries where these alleged pay-offs have been made, government corruption is a matter of course, and kickbacks are a common method of doing business. When you choose to do business in these countries, you either do business their way or you do not do business at all. Have these companies gone out waving their money and corrupting pure and innocent people? It seems to me they may have been victimized by corrupt politicians operating in an amoral environment that cannot be compared with ours. We should be demanding the foreign governments seek out and punish the extortionists, rather than attempting to destroy the reputation of the victim. The closest analogy is the agony a rape victim must go through when she is attacked on the stand by the defense attorney, after which the trial turns into a defense of her virtue.

Perhaps this is an unpopular view in this day and age when it is so easy to point a finger and when we have begun to distrust all of our institutions. Instead, perhaps we should pause and consider this and interject a note of sanity into a hysterical situation.

C

CANCER/LAETRILE

(4/1/76)   Cancer and Chemicals

Recently there has been quite a bit of fuss in the media that cancer is probably an environmentally caused disease. Our lives are full of carcinogens—substances which are believed to trigger cancer. There are over 3,000 chemical additives of an unnatural or inorganic nature used in our food. A typical American will ingest five to seven pounds of these substances every year. No one knows what the cumulative physiological effect of 3,000 additives might be. It's my opinion that we should keep these additives out of our lives as much as possible.

(6/1/77)   The medical profession should be ashamed of itself. For years it has been fighting socialized medicine with the pious argument that if the government got involved in the management of medicine, citizens would no longer have freedom of choice in choosing their doctor or their therapy. Then, on the other hand, they aligned themselves with the anti-LAETRILE forces. Together they have opposed freedom of choice in unorthodox therapy in a series of battles which has finally culminated in the legalization of laetrile in several states. Now, it's legal to buy, own, or administer the drug in some states as long as neither it nor the apricot pits from which it is made, crosses state lines. If it does, the FDA has jurisdiction and is determined to stamp out the alleged dangerous drug.

The villains of this particular article are, as you can gather, both the medical profession and the FDA. It seems that whether someone is for or against something depends on whose ox is gored.

The medical profession has fought laetrile on two grounds: (1) it has not been proven effective, and (2) people might choose laetrile in favor of more effective therapies, and unnecessarily die of cancer.

They set aside the fact that the drug has never been adequately tested and ignore the point that the Sloan-Kettering studies with mice did show substantial anti-cancer properties, regardless of the prop-aganda to the contrary. Despite the fact there is substantial clinical evidence from human beings to whom the drug has been administered in Mexico, West Germany and the Philippines, where it is the cancer drug of choice, their argument that it is ineffective because it hasn't been proven effective is specious at best. You can't prove a negative. This is basic to the scientific method. All you can say is there is no evidence to support a positive claim. In this case, there seems to be enough evidence to indicate that it should be thoroughly tested on human volunteers. There would be no scarcity of volunteers. There are thousands of people fighting for the right to use the drug. There are thousands of terminal patients whose cases have been given up as hopeless, who would be delighted to have this one last chance.

I am most concerned about Big Brotherism. The medical profes-sion, this supposed bastion of free enterprise, has joined Big Brother to protect people from making a bad choice. I believe I have the right to choose my therapy, including the right to make a mistake and die, if I wish. There is enough anti-laetrile publicity around to warn everyone of the alleged consequences of laetrile. If one wants to use it, one should have the choice. Government, regardless of how stupid you or I might think it is, has no inherent right to prevent the patient from making his choice. The medical profession had better realize that when it supports strengthening government in telling us what we can and cannot do in these matters, it weakens its own case against socialized medicine.

Every time you give the government a sword you can expect it to use it. If it's a two-edged sword, it cuts both ways, and my friends in the medical profession had better realize that they, too, can be the victims.

I've had hundreds of inquiries as to my opinion on the drug. I'm not a doctor or a scientist, but I have studied nutrition and there is some evidence that populations which have diets high in amygdalin (the scientific name for the drug) tend to have far lower rates of cancer. In the case of some societies like the Hunzas, for whom apricots form a substantial part of their diet, cancer is non-existent. The apricot tree is almost venerated by those people.

The evidence seems to indicate that amygdalin is a preventive measure as opposed to a curative measure. The evidence also seems overwhelming that people who use the drug, even if it didn't save their lives, have had great relief of pain and suffering right to the end.

My best friend, John Manson, died of cancer a few years ago. After three major operations he was just sent home to die with a prescription for an unlimited supply of addictive pain-killing drugs. As a last resort, he made contact with a doctor in the San Francisco Bay area who treated him with the drug. Within 24 hours, his pain was substantially relieved, and the tumors, which were literally bulging out of his abdomen so that you could see and feel them, began to shrink. He had two years of pain-free life. He was never completely well, but he was well enough to get his affairs in order for his family. The cancer had already reached his liver and the prognosis for that kind of cancer is 100 percent fatality. Eventually, the cancer overwhelmed him and he went from relative health to incredible deterioration in a matter of 10 days and died. But I'm convinced that laetrile gave him two years of precious life to take care of his family.

I have personal knowledge the problem has been obscured because advocates of the drug have had to fight so hard for their right of choice they have been guilty of excesses that hurt their cause. They claimed, in some instances, cures where there were none. They claimed more benefits than the developers of the drug have claimed. And orthodox, mainstream medicine has refused to examine the pro-laetrile data.

The National Cancer Institute has decided to reexamine its position relative to clinical tests on human volunteers. I find this commendable and it is the first reasonable ray of light from the "anti" side of the laetrile argument. Perhaps if we were only to find it would give people a pain-free few years and extend useful life it would be an incredible contribution to the prevention of human suffering. There is no death more feared than cancer. It is excruciating, demoralizing and humiliating, not only to the person who suffers from it, but to all those around him. If the drug could give them only dignity and freedom from pain for their last years it would be a contribution of epic proportions. Let's get this substance tested once and for all. Then we can dismiss it, or add it to medical science's armory of weapons against this dreaded scourge.

In the meantime, if I want to use apricot pits, acupuncture, a witch doctor or stump water and old moss to treat myself in any way I want, it's none of the government's business. Government has the right to express its opinion as vigorously as it wishes, and the F.D.A. has certainly done so. In the meantime, I have the right to ignore them as long as it's my body, my disease and my life.

I don't usually join causes but I think I would join this cause for freedom to make my own choice.

CAPITALISM

(3/15/79) At our Second Annual *RUFF TIMES* National Convention, ROBERT BLEIBERG, the editor of *BARRON'S,* addressed the subject "CAN CAPITALISM SURVIVE?" Capitalism has come under increasingly heavy pressure. There is the tremendous overload of government regulation. His favorite enemy is the S.E.C., which has "deeply imbedded itself in the roots of corporate America." The cost of regulation in the U.S. in 1978 was $103.1 billion.' He gave examples of such ridiculous regulations as forklifts being required to have back-up alarms while at the same time requiring employees to use ear plugs.

He also said, "In spite of what Washington may say, inflation is whipped up in Washington." He further stated, "This April marks the 4th anniversary of the current upswing and we are 12 months away from the next recession." (I think he is overly optimistic.) He indicated that if the Dow Jones Industrial Average were adjusted for inflation today, in terms of 1966 dollars when the Dow topped 1000, the Dow would really be at 381. The whole thrust of his message was that government's attempts to solve our problems have been counterproductive, and as he said, "We must stop eating our seed corn and start investing, if capitalism is going to survive."

CARTER, PRESIDENT JIMMY

(7/15/76) I find Jimmy Carter to be the most incredibly deceptive politician of our times. Some political observers have even called him a conservative. That's ridiculous!

In the presidential race, Carter would whip Reagan by a bigger margin in the popular vote than he would Ford, but Reagan would make the electoral vote closer. . . . Barring surprises, it's Carter, but a lot closer than the polls now indicate.

Now, Ford or Reagan? It's Ford, unless he makes a major goof.

(11/15/76) Back in July, I forecast that Ford would be nominated over REAGAN in a close contest and that CARTER would beat Ford in a close election.

Unfortunately, I would rather have been wrong. I'm not too upset about it, however, because it won't make a heck of a lot of difference in our long-range prospects.

The election was close. A shift of only 7400 votes in Hawaii and any one of two or three other states, would have elected Ford by two or four electoral votes.

Here is why Carter won, and what the future holds for us with a Carter Administration.

Post Mortem

The election campaign was one of the strangest in my experience. The swinging of momentum back and forth from one to the other, could only be described as peculiar. The terrible mistake of the *Playboy* interview was immediately compensated for by Mr. Ford's goof about Eastern Europe and Mr. Butz's unfunny racial comments and jokes. But, as I watched the debates, I saw two truly contradicting philosophies.

Mr. Ford took a rather courageous position, flying in the face of traditional politics, by saying "no" to a lot of things with his vetoes. Mr. Carter realized, however, the only way you can get elected is to say "yes." He promised a national health care program. He promised to save the cities. He promised all kinds of things, and then hedged his promises by saying, "Of course, we will only do those things if we have the funds to do so," and then used some rather dubious financial forecasts to indicate we will have the funds. That put him in the interesting position of keeping his campaign promises, even if he doesn't keep them. All he has to say is that we don't have the money to do it.

He can keep those campaign promises only by inflating the currency and expanding the money supply, which will require the cooperation of the FEDERAL RESERVE which he may not get.

Both Mr. Ford and Mr. Carter are economic ignoramuses.

I sat there and cringed as I watched Mr. Carter and Mr. Mondale talk about inflation, an unfair tax system, high unemployment, recession, and a slowdown in the economy—all of which are correct—and then propose that we need "a little bit of the hair off the dog that bit us," in order to solve them.

He laid these problems all at the feet of the Ford Administration, which is nothing short of demagoguery. Today's problems are a result of policies initiated long ago and they originated in CONGRESS. They often had the cooperation of the Executive Branch, but Congress is where economic policy is made and where spending is determined.

All of our fiscal problems are the result of inflation of the currency and expansion of the money supply. This is largely determined by the size of the Federal deficits. The only way you can have Federal deficits is if the outgo exceeds the income. The only way you can survive, if the outgo exceeds the income, is to find a source of money somewhere outside your normal income. In your personal life, you would have to do this by borrowing. The government does this by borrowing also, but they borrow simply by creating the money themselves, and diluting the value of every dollar in existence. This is, in effect, borrowing from you without your permission. The result is inflation.

One of the flaws in American political life is that we tend to blame our President for everything that goes wrong. And he tends to take credit for everything that goes right. Neither of these stances is reasonable nor true. Holding our Presidents accountable for everything has brought down our last three Presidents. We just might be hanging the wrong man. Congress is usually the villain!

It is my opinion that the election of a Carter Administration insures the inflationary spiral will continue.

Now Mr. Carter has proposed a tax cut. That's wonderful, if it is accompanied by a spending cut. The effect of a tax cut would be to further increase the deficit. It's the size of the deficit as much as the size of the spending, that concerns me. The deficit requires expansion of the money supply. Expansion of the money supply creates inflation. Inflation creates a wildly swinging economic cycle and the danger of recession and depression.

I have recently said I did not think it was yet determined whether inflation or deflation would be the order of the day. I gave inflation a 60/40 chance.

With a Carter Administration, I'm shifting those odds to 80/20 for inflation, as the first steps will be to lower interest rates, cut taxes, increase the money supply, and increase government spending dramatically with the programs they've promised.

Paradoxically, the effect of all this will be to postpone the day of reckoning and give us more time because the injection of inflationary funny-money into the economy will give us the appearance of prosperity. If they act quickly, we might prevent the present pause from becoming a major downward slide. This downward slide is going to come anyway. The only question is "When?" If it occurs now because of the tight fiscal and monetary policy, it might be a less dangerous depression, in that we might escape a total monetary collapse. However, if you trigger a hyper-inflation, there is no way you can escape a major monetary collapse. If he keeps all his promises, Carter assures us of eventual hyper-inflation and a total currency collapse.

(4/1/77) I've indicated it didn't matter who was President, the destructive financial trends would continue, and all he could affect was the pace of things, as far as economic matter were concerned. I also said that the only place a President could really make a difference was in foreign policy, so it didn't really matter who was our next President.

Well, Carter has me terrified. This strange man, whom we have elected to preside over the decline and fall of this era of American history, is embarking upon a course of action that is totally predictable, based on his present and past affiliations. Bear in mind that Carter was sponsored on the national political scene as a member of the TRILATERAL COMMISSION by DAVID ROCKEFELLER who formed the Commission to make the world safe for multi-national banking. Its ostensible purpose was to promote close international and trade relations between Europe, Japan and the United States. Mr. Rockefeller is, of course, Chairman of the Board of the CHASE MANHATTAN BANK, which has over 60% of its assets overseas. Mr. Carter has selected most of the key members of his administration from the Commission, and I think many of his actions can be interpreted in the light of what is in the best interest of his sponsors.

Mr. Carter's moves to expand and normalize relations with COMMUNIST CHINA and the SOVIET UNION are consistent with the banking interests. David Rockefeller visited Communist China before Henry Kissinger did; his bank, and others like it, are up to their eyeballs in investments in development projects in Communist countries. Closer relationships with them are essential to their well being, which leads me to the subject of hypocrisy.

We are hearing a great deal about how Mr. Carter is speaking out for human rights. In my opinion, that is a smoke screen. Let me make my case.

I believe that Mr. Carter informed Mr. Brezhnev, in advance, that he is going to be sounding off to create the appropriate climate of confidence in his leadership so he could proceed with the steps he had in mind. This great "moralist" has aggressively moved to isolate advanced, capitalist, white-dominated countries in Africa. I am referring, of course, to RHODESIA and the UNION OF SOUTH AFRICA using inflammatory language as his United Nations speech he referred to Rhodesia as "the illegal regime in Rhodesia." His Ambassador to the United Nations has told the world that Cuban troops in Angola have "brought stability" to that country. Carter refuses to do business with Rhodesia, and is working to isolate South Africa on "Human Rights" grounds.

At the same time, he is moving aggressively to establish diplomatic, trade and aid relations with VIETNAM, which, unless I have missed something somewhere, is not a shining example of human rights. He's moving under the smoke screen of his human rights rhetoric to an arms pact with the Soviet Union (another "Human Rights" utopia), this is precisely what Brezhnev wants. Why don't we boycott China, Vietnam or the U.S.S.R., along with Rhodesia and South Africa? Hypocrisy, that's why.

I said it in the past and I'll say it again: if we ever succeed in getting a complete nuclear compact with the Soviet Union, we will merely have opened the world up to the danger of domination by their overwhelming conventional forces. I am sure Mr. Brezhnev knows this, and he has agreed to it, although there's some tough negotiating ahead.

Mr. Carter's efforts to improve relations with Vietnam, China, and Soviet Russia, along with the sale of gold through the IMF to strengthen the economies of the Lesser Developed Countries, all benefit the multi-national banks directly. I don't believe those bankers would have gone out so far on a limb in making loans to those countries unless they felt they would be bailed out by someone.

There's no question in my mind that Carter is a captive President, perhaps a willing captive, and perhaps he believes in all these principles. Watch what he does and not what he says, and I think you'll find I'm right.

Now, on the domestic front, Mr. Carter has done some fascinating things. He is going to present his energy policy to the nation. The rumors and leaks coming out of Capitol Hill say he is going to be discussing conservation. He is going to be making it very difficult for the buyers of big cars, by applying some kind of financial penalties. He is preparing a proposal which, in the words of one of his spokesmen, "will change the life-style of every American."

I said in my book, *FAMINE AND SURVIVAL IN AMERICA*, that we would see intermittent gasoline shortages over the next few years until the automobile ceases to be a viable means of transportation. I don't know exactly what he's going to do, but I would not be surprised if we had a 25 cents a gallon tax on gasoline, and possibly even some kind of rationing or allocation program. Carter's public opinion polls are riding so much in his favor that he may feel he can get away with it. In any event, I am using the time between now and then to conceal underground a few thousand gallons of gas. I don't think there's any way I could lose on that investment. I'm also making sure I have my emergency food storage plan replenished.

In summation, this man Carter is a disaster. We will look back upon him as the fool who presided over the crash of the 70s. Now, there are two theories on that. One is that he is a fool, and the other is that it is part of a plan. I'm going to let you draw your own conclusions on that, but, nevertheless, the fact is, that he will be at the bridge of the Titanic when it sinks, and events are accelerating alarmingly.

(5/15/77)   I Will Never Lie To You

On February 10, 1976, candidate Carter said, "I don't intend to break a single promise. I am giving you my word of honor." Earlier, on October 29, 1975, he said, "I will never make a misleading statement." On the same day he added this request to the American people: "If you ever see me doing any of those things (breaking a promise or making a misleading statement), don't support me. I would not be worthy to be president of this country."

Well, let's see how he measures up. Here's Act I.

"I will work with the Congress ... to deregulate new natural gas"—letter to governors of Texas, Louisiana and Oklahoma, Oct. 16, 1976.

"(I will allow) the deregulation of new natural gas ..." —June 16, 1976.

And then, surprise! Act II!! "Proposals for decontrol of natural gas prices would be disastrous for our economy," Carter told Congress when the energy package was sent to Capitol Hill. Got that? Now, here comes Act III. Carter has reversed course once again. At an early March press conference, the President was asked if he would relent and accept phased-in deregulation. "Yes," he said. "This was a campaign statement and commitment of mine that I thought that natural gas should be deregulated."

Meanwhile, back at the ranch, (or the farm, as the case may be),

"I will support prices equal to at least the cost of production." —Aug. 25, 1976.

In Carter's 1979 budget he cut back loan and price support programs by 20%.

In regards to the FEDERAL BUREAUCRACY, he said:

"(I will) limit wage increases for Federal employees to a reasonable figure so as to encourage the private sector to restrain wage and price demands."—July, 1976.

"I will put a ceiling on the number of people employed by Federal government agencies so we can bring the growth of government under control." —-Feb. 2, 1977.

First salaries to go up: top White House aides were given pay raises averaging almost 25% higher than those received by Ford White House aides. Since Carter took office, the Federal work force has grown by 18,476 full-time positions. Almost 20% of the increase has come in executive departments directly controlled by Carter and his Cabinet.

How about Carter on TAXES?

"I would never increase the taxes for the working people of our country and the lower and middle income groups . . . and you can depend upon that, if I am elected." — *THE NEW YORK TIMES*, Sept. 20, 1976.

Carter's first tax move was the largest single tax increase in our history—Social-Security taxes—an increase of $227 billion during the next ten years.

And this sums it all up.

"I would not relinquish actual control of the Panama Canal; I would retain actual political control."—November 23, 1975.

There is not an impeachment climate. Mondale's no prize, either. But let's all work like the dickens to elect people who will oppose him in the Congress, and work like crazy to defeat him in the next election. And let's hope, after all of these promies of honesty, piety and openness, Jimmy Carter learns this lesson in the next election: a pedestal is a dangerous place if you're the one who climbed on it. I, for one, am prepared to give him a push.

(10/1/76)   *Playboy* Interview

I've watched with great interest, the developing flap over JIMMY CARTER'S *Playboy* interview. Now, I haven't read all of it and don't intend to buy the magazine, so I don't know the whole context, but I do have one modest question.

For a man who has publicly proclaimed such high standards of Christian moral and ethical behavior, what's he doing helping to boost the newsstand sale of a contemptible, soft-core pornographic magazine like *Playboy*?

Such interviews by admired public figures, lend a kind of "respectability by association" to rags like *Playboy, Penthouse, Oui,* and others of that ilk.

At best, it's a cynical willingness to use any means to get elected, including the use of language which will make him sound like a regular guy to the *Playboy* habitue.

At worst, it's a revealing repudiation of every principle the man professes to stand for, and an affront to Christians.

Maybe you think this doesn't have a place in *THE RUFF TIMES*, but I do.

I believe the personal integrity and predictability of a candidate for leader of the Free World (relatively speaking) is an issue of paramount importance. Any President will probably lie some time in the national interest. I expect it, and allow for it, but I fear a man who will, thoughtlessly or intentionally, compromise principles he professes to honor, strictly in his own self-interest.

I disagreed with Carter's economic views, but was inclined to accept, as fact, that he was an honorable Christian of high principles. He has now persuaded me, by his words and action, that he is a dangerous type—A Southern Fried Chameleon!

I'd like to reiterate that it doesn't make any difference in our near economic future who is president, as budgets and programs affecting the next few years are already in place, and irreversible. Depression and inflation are still in the cards.

I still recommend that you concentrate your political effort and contributions on the Congressional level, where spending and taxing policy is made.

Finally, as far as Carter is concerned, way down deep, he's shallow!

(8/1/77) Ever since my analysis of Carter's energy package in our May 15 issue, I have been struggling to understand "in my heart" what it all really means.

I think I've got it now. The Carter energy problem cannot be understood without the real energy facts, and some insights into this strange man. Jimmy Carter is probably the strangest man who has ever been elected President of the United States. He is a puzzling combination of cock-sure Messiah-complex, startling honesty, contradictory deviousness, and incredible executive skill, coupled with political sensitivity unmatched since Roosevelt. I thought he was up to something we weren't being told about. I now have a plausible scenario and there's a better than even chance I'm right (gut feeling).

The Executive Order is the ultimate weapon held by the President of the United States. But he needs an emergency in order to accomplish this. Would a President of the United States artifically create such a threat? There are those who believe, and I am one of them, that Franklin D. Roosevelt felt it was in the best interests of this nation that we enter the war against Germany and Japan to save Britain, and literally manipulated us into it. President Carter has already said that this is "the moral equivalent of war" and he spoke in apocalyptic terms of the fate of the nation if we did not adopt his energy program. Congress is happily gutting that program, and it is no longer an energy conservation program, but merely another "redistribution-of-the-wealth program" and will only result in creating precisely the kind of crisis Mr. Carter is talking about.

Is it possible he knew this? He's a businessman and should understand what happens to the supply of peanuts when you hold down the price.

Could it be that he is allowing, or even creating, a crisis to frighten us into accepting this Presidential power, so his energy conservation plan can be put into effect? What motives would he have for doing this? Maybe it is just a Messiah complex. Maybe he's working for the benefit of the great oil companies through his mentor, David Rockefeller, and feels this is ultimately good for America. With total seizure of energy, "big oil" profits could be mandated, and competition eliminated. Perhaps he is a dumb peanut farmer and doesn't understand the effect of pricing on suppy and demand.

But I have become persuaded that he wants his energy program, no matter how he has to get it, and he might, if necessary, precipitate a "national emergency" to get it. Why else has his United Nations Ambassador Andrew Young gone around insulting the Arabs? Why did we deny the Arabs' demand for a vote equal to the United States in the IMF, while, at the same time, trying to get $7.5 billion from them for that fund? Why did Carter encourage the anti-boycott legislation in Congress, knowing that it was a direct slap at the Arabs and the embargo was ineffective, and not strongly enforced anyway?

Why are the Arabs accumulating large amounts of gold, both through the IMF auction and through private sales, such as Red China's 80-ton sale? Do they know something is coming which could weaken the value of their dollar holdings? Are they looking for a compensating hedge, because that's what gold is?

Out of these frightening questions, the only thing that is clear is that the President has the power to get his energy program. It is also clear that this strangely motivated, supremely confident man has a habit of getting what he wants! He has gathered around himself a group of energy people who have an instinctive distrust for the free market.

If we have another cold winter, with natural gas shortages, he will have the emergency he needs. And I'll be watching the weather and getting nervous along with you.

The sad thing is that the earth is energy-abundant. There is enough clean-burning natural gas available at low enough prices to break the Arab oil cartel and drive world energy prices down, to the benefit of us all. All it needs is total deregulation. There are enough alternate energy sources, such as solar and wind-power, to take care of a substantial portion of the world's needs in 15 or 20 years, if it became economical to do so by allowing other prices to rise.

Is this man Carter stupid, or is he a lot smarter than we think? Is he straight-forward or devious? Is he aware of the powers that are in his hands? The next few months might tell.

(4/15/78) Many months before the last Presidential election, I said the Presidency is basically a weak office in economic matters, and Congress was where the action was, therefore, whoever becomes President is a matter of great economic irrelevance. It was in foreign policy that I felt a President could make a difference, and that was the basis for which I would vote.

As much as I dislike almost everything about Jimmy Carter, I won't be able to blame the next depression on him. As I said before, he was elected President of the Titanic, and he's merely rearranging the deck chairs.

But foreign policy? Ah, that's a horse of a different color. There he can make a difference, and world economic and social stability is at stake, and he's got me scared out of my wits.

I just viewed President Carter's inflation and economic message on the tube.

He delivered it in a clear, precise, calculated, impressive manner. After it was all over, however, it was just like a Chinese dinner. You seem full right afterwards, but you are soon hungry for something else.

Basically, in terms of any impact on anything, it was a non-event. It was shot full of philosophical attacks on the victims of inflation who merely react rationally to it. He wants labor and industry to "voluntarily" hold down wages and prices so that price-inflation can overtake and overwhelm them. He blamed the whole inflation problem on those who ask for wage and price increases. He blamed the sinking dollar and our balance of payments deficits on energy. He suggested that cities and states reduce inflation by reducing sales taxes. He does not want any increase in farm commodity prices, so he's going to veto the Farm Bill. He will also veto the Tuition Credit Bill. He wants to expand timber harvesting in public lands to reduce the price of lumber. He vigorously denied any intention of ever introducing price controls because, "they don't work," but at the same time pressed for his "Hospital Cost Containment Legislation," which is nothing but a form of price controls over medical costs.

I've summarized all this to expose it as an all-out attack on the symptoms. It's controlling fever by putting a governor on the thermometer.

He blamed inflation on everything but the real cause, which is government spending and increases in the money supply. He dismissed as a "myth" the idea that only government can fight inflation. Stupid, stupid, dumb!

The dollar will continue to sink as long as there are too many of them floating around. Oil exports are not the sole cause of the dollar falling. It is distrust of the inflationary processes in this country, plus the fact that they're just too many dollars.

I don't know why everyone's mad at Carter. He hasn't done anything.

(9/15/78)   Human Rights

I see where Jimmy Carter just sent an effusive expression of support for the Shah of Iran, whose troops just fired into a crowd of demonstrators killing 250 people. Perhaps, this is part of the Carter Human Rights Campaign.

(11/15/77)   Trilateral Commission

We've received from our subscribers (anonymously, of course) several copies of an article from the current PENTHOUSE entitled, "CARTERGATE," and it's pretty interesting. It outlines what we have reported several times: the relationship between Carter and those who sponsored him on the international scene, primarily his fellow commissioners on the Trilateral Commission. It does a beautiful job of helping you understand how each of Carter's moves in the international scene has been calculated to benefit those who placed him in the Presidency.

I'll highlight the article, and incidentally, thanks for sending it to me so I didn't have to spend $2.00 on that contemptible rag.

One of the objectives of the Trilateral Commission is to create a new international world-wide paper currency as a basic unit-of-account for international transactions called BANCOR which would actually be a computer memory currency to be manufactured by the International Monetary Fund. RICHARD COOPER, now Under Secretary of State for Economic Affairs in the Carter Administration, said in the 1973 Trilateral Commission Task Force Report called "TOWARDS A RENOVATED WORLD MONETARY SYSTEM," "We also envision that BANCOR will become a unit of account in many private international transactions and that financial instruments might be denominated in BANCOR. Monetary authorities should not impede this development. Eventually, BANCOR might circulate as a genuine international currency and be used as a medium for intervention in exchange markets." In other words, in place of gold.

How does this tie in with the recent decline of the dollar? Well, as Trilateral Commisioner ZBIGNIEW BRZEZINSKI said in his 1970 book, BETWEEN TWO AGES, "In the economic and technological fields, some international cooperation has already been achieved, but further progress will require greater American sacrifices. More extensive efforts to shape a world monetary structure will have to be undertaken WITH SOME SUBSQUENT RISK TO THE PRESENT RELATIVELY FAVORABLE AMERICAN POSITION."

Now, how do Mr. Carter's sponsors benefit when the dollar sinks?

These gigantic firms earn more than half of their profits in foreign currencies, and this includes the big oil companies, the big international conglomerates and the multinational banks. Their profits increase dramatically when the value of these other currencies rises in relation to the dollar. In order to make BANCOR the basic exchange medium of international trade, the dollar has to be downgraded with, as Brzezinski put it tactfully, " . . . some subsequent risk to the present relatively favorable American position." Let me quote from the *PENTHOUSE* article. "You and I lose when the dollar is devalued because everything that has to be imported—most notably oil—rises in price. But the multinational corporations represented on the Trilateral Commission don't lose; they hit pay-dirt. First, they raise the price of the products they sell in the United States so they can pass through the increased cost of imported raw materials to the consumer. But labor contracts make it possible for them to delay raising wages proportionately. Devaluation of the dollar is good for the multinationals' U.S. operations because the wages that they are paying out never rise as fast as the price they are taking in."

Brzezinski, in his book, even talks about how these events, " . . . might also eventually lead to the possibility of something along the lines of a global taxation system." The article points out how we also have committed $3.2 billion in new appropriations which is roughly four and one-half times the current fiscal year for the World Bank, the Asian Development Fund, and the International Monetary Fund. These funds will be partly used to buy and sell buffer stocks of such key commodities as coffee and tin. This would insure, "stability and export earnings" for the L.D.C.s, in other words, it would enable the Trilateral bankers to use the taxpayers' money to manipulate the commodity markets to keep prices high enough for those countries to pay off their loans.

The article also does a devastating job on Jimmy Carter's human rights policy, contending it is a strategic bit of rhetoric designed to put a moral patina over some very cynical economic moves. It quotes, as an example, Mr. Carter's reaction to legislation for an amendment introduced by CONGRESSMAN HERMAN BADILLO of New York City. The Amendment included the requirement that the United States representative to such international financial institutions as the World Bank should vote against any loan to any country that systematically denies essential human rights, such as freedom from torture and imprisonment without trial. Carter lobbied vigorously against this compassionate measure, and was eventually able to shoot it down. The article contends that Carter was originally inclined to support the Badillo human rights amendment. It was after a meeting with Trilateral Commissioner W. MICHAEL BLUMENTHAL of the Treasury Department and World Bank President ROBERT MCNAMARA that they persuaded him this would, "introduce politics into the World Bank," and the Arab might get ideas about opposing international loans to Israel. Carter then reversed his position and the Badillo amendment was defeated. Then, of course, McNamara's World Bank cut off all loans to Israel anyway.

The Carter Administration is as cynical as any of its predecessors. Human rights rhetoric is just that—rhetoric. All of our decisions in the international marketplace have been down the line with the positions of the Trilateral Commission and Mr. Carter is an enthusiastic advocate. His recent attack on the oil companies was just rhetoric, also. All of our moves on the international monetary scene are gambles to benefit the international business scene. It is a terrible risk that has a very good chance of producing consequences unforeseen by all the parties concerned. They are willing to take the chance because they know they have "friends in high places," to put it mildly, who will bail them out, even though the cost to you will be runaway inflation, which will destroy your savings, your pension and your prospects of retirement.

If all this sounds a little strident, I'm sorry. That's the way I see the world out there. I think the facts are irrefutable.

CENSORSHIP

(1/15/76)   Inglorious Banking Report

In January of 1976, I heard on the radio a weasel-worded statement by the U.S. Comptroller of the Currency regarding reports in the national press that two of our largest banks had found their way onto the FDIC's list of endangered banks. In the report, Chase-Manhattan Bank's prospects were listed as "poor," and First National City Bank, because of its wide diversification and international banking, would probably survive in good shape. The radio statement did not deny the report, but referred to it as "pure sensationalism." I believe you were seeing censorship in action, as the first report in the *SAN FRANCISCO CHRONICLE* was a small article buried near the bottom of page 25, and not one word of this spectacular, sensational news appeared in the Monday morning edition! Remember, these are the nation's second and third largest banks!

The reasons given for their difficulties were a sharp increase in doubtful loans on the books, as well as the deterioration of their investment portfolio, primarily caused by the New York City situation. These problems added up to more than 65% of their equity capital. That, of course, is no surprise to *RUFF TIMES* readers who read our November Special Report on New York City.

(11/1/76)   Censorship In Paradise

I recently completed a two-day visit to Honolulu for a series of radio/TV appearances and newspaper interviews. Something happened while I was there that was most disconcerting. We'd arranged for interviews for feature stories at both of Honolulu's principal newspapers. I called the first one shortly after my arrival to confirm the time of my appointment, and when I reached the reporter assigned to the story, she told me, "We're not going to interview you." I was surprised because we usually have no difficulty. When I asked why, she said, "It's because you're too commercial." When I asked what she meant by that, she said, "Because you sell dehydrated and freeze-dried foods."

I very carefully informed her that this was not the case, that I was not in the business of selling anything other than information and advice in my book and newsletter. When she heard this, she said, "Well, we still don't want to do the interview." I asked her why. She said, " Because we do not think your message is appropriate for Hawaii." And then she hung up after suggesting I contact their competitor.

I looked up the phone number of the other newspaper and found it to be exactly the same. Apparently these two newspapers share the same building and telephone system. I called the person who was scheduled to interview me. He said, "We've decided not to do the interview because your message is not appropriate for Hawaii." I pressed further to find out why and he simply said, "We don't think it's right to tell people to hoard food. That's scare tactics." I responded, "That sounds a bit like censorship to me." His answer was, "Call it what you want, but we're not going to do the story."

Now I don't mind people disagreeing with me. I knew when I first wrote my book and started on this mission of information that many people would disagree. But I can't think of a place in the world more vulnerable to the kind of problems I'm talking about than Hawaii. They could find themselves in serious trouble overnight if we had major disruptions at our West Coast port cities. Such disruptions would prevent the shipping of vital commodities. I don't mind someone choosing not to interview me if they do not think I am newsworthy. That is a matter of business judgment on their part. But to squelch my message because they "do not think it is appropriate for their city" is simply saying they disagree with my message and do not wish to see it exposed. And that's censorship in its most pernicious state.

(4/1/79)   The Mouth That Roared

I promised you a report on my GOOD MORNING AMERICA non-appearance, and here it is.

After I arrived in New York, I was to receive a call Tuesday afternoon from a writer whose job was to pre-interview me and make sure DAVID HARTMAN was all prepared for the interview. We had originally scheduled the appearance for Monday, but Hartman was going to be out of town until Wednesday, and he was so enthusiastic about the interview, I agreed to the postponement.

I waited all afternoon in my hotel for the call from the writer. Finally, I got a call from my publisher around 4 PM announcing I had been knocked from the show. It seems that this writer had finally gotten around to reading the book and concluded I was much too radical for GOOD MORNING AMERICA. Now, I hear you ask, was it because I suggested people not trust the banks? Or because I have nasty things to say about government? How about my wild views on Social Security, or my forecasts or a runaway inflationary depression? No, they ignored all of those minor points. What I think offended them was my "radical" view that the sexual revolution is bad economics for America (expressed in Chapter 11, SIN-TAX). I mean, after all, there are some ideas America is just not ready for. It seems that this writer dug in her heels in a production meeting for several hours until finally she persuaded Hartman and others to drop the interview.

I am really curious as to what specific part of Chapter 11 actually offended them. Was it my opinion of the importance of the family in our society, both as an economic unit and as a foundation for our national strength? (Now, that could be a dangerous idea.) Or was it my view about the heavy dollar costs accompanying the sexual revolution in the form of welfare, Aid to Dependent Children, costs to contain juvenile crime among kids growing up in broken homes, alcoholism, drug abuse and disrupted schools? (Now, that's a real subversive concept!)

Great Scott, I think I know what it was! It was my opinion that children not born and raised in a normal heterosexual marriage relationship, live in an unstable, confused environment which leaves them the bewildered, twisted casualties of the sexual revolution and, therefore, more likely to become financial burdens to society.

This is the worst example of unprofessional conduct, media bias and censorship I've run across in all my years in dealing with the media. They actually had the audacity to say that they didn't want to interview me because it would appear as if the network were endorsing the radical views in that chapter, even if we didn't discuss that part. For crying out loud, they've had every wild radical in the country on that show and nobody believes they have endorsed them!

If they had told me I was dull and uninteresting, or this wasn't the time for them to do a show on economics or investments, I could have understood. But as it is, I feel like I'm some kind of a leper. Perhaps I should send servants in front of me shouting, "UNCLEAN! UNCLEAN!" Also, whatever I have seems to be highly contagious. The TODAY SHOW has also decided I'm not fit for that show either, for about the same reasons. However, at least they didn't go through the charade of bringing me to New York.

Things have come to a sorry state when the networks are so afraid of offending the sexual minorities. Thank the Lord there are newsletters where opinionated mavericks like me who can speak their piece. This whole incident has me sick at heart, not just for myself, but for what this means for the nation and the family. It means censorship and exclusion from the most powerful influencing tool the world has ever seen. I may end up being the only person who made the top ten in all the best seller lists for several months who didn't end up on either the TODAY SHOW or GOOD MORNING AMERICA.

CHINA

RECOGNITION OF RED CHINA

(1/1/79)

Q. Howard, what's your opinion of the recognition of Red China, and what does this mean to us economically?

A. This is another marvelous example of the true moral climate of the CARTER HUMAN RIGHTS PROGRAM. We have dumped a "repressive" Chiang dynasty government, which only allows freedom of speech, religion, private property, immigration and the free-enterprise capitalist dream, we now recognize the most blood-drenched government in history, THE PEOPLE'S REPUBLIC OF CHINA, whose very name is one of the big lies of all time.

It was a sickening move for the following reasons:

1. It was unnecessary. They came to us this time, meaning they were anxious for diplomatic relations. Yet, despite that ideal negotiating position, we yielded to every demand they made. We could have commercial relations with Red China without diplomatic relations, just as we are assuming we can continue to have commercial relations with Taiwan without diplomatic relations.

2. If I were in the Israeli government, considering conceding a strategic position on the Golan Heights or the West Bank of the Jordan River, based on our assurances we would never let the Arabs take advantage of us, I would think long and hard about this clear-cut evidence of U.S. lack of commitment to principle. This has to be looked at as evidence of an undependable ally.

3. Watch for the Taiwan government to make overtures to the SOVIET UNION (or vice versa) for a mutual defense pact. This can be destabilizing in the Far East with unforeseen, and probably dangerous, consequences.

Now comes the hard question. What do I think we should do? The people on the left say we should recognize that the Communist Chinese represent both Chinas and that this means disavowing Taiwan. Those on the right say we should recognize that people in Taiwan are really the government-in-exile, so we should not recognize the Communists. Both positions are dumb.

The Communists are, at the present time, the rulers of Mainland China, and Taiwan is a separate nation with no present chance of taking the Mainland. They are two sovereign nations and we should have never allowed ourselves to be forced to reject one in order to accept the other. We should have insisted on our right to recognize them both, and I am convinced the Communists would eventually have gone along with it. Already they have announced the need for billion of dollars in loans from us and they will probably get them. It was part of the deal.

My position? We should have correct but distant diplomatic relations with Communist China. We should maintain close and warm diplomatic relations with Taiwan. While reaffirming our defense commitment, we should not yield until those positions are recognized by the Communist Chinese. The Chiang regime is never going to recapture the Mainland unless the Mainland first collapses internally. However, Taiwan is a viable, dynamic capitalist country and, as such, deserves our support, even if her government may not be as democratic as we would like it to be.

The immediate economic impact is expansion of trade with the Reds. We should do a lot of business, but it won't help the dollar much because we will loan them the money with which to do business with us.

When are we going to get it through our heads that those people need us more than we need them, and we don't have to make concessions on principle? It's morally bankrupt.

Q. Did the banking community have any influence on our China policy?

A. The Carter Administration has again reaffirmed the disproportionate degree of influence exerted in Washington today by the multinational banks. Carter has thrown his support behind a plan to establish a "free trade zone" for international banking activity in New York City, where banks would be able to conduct international operations without any state or city taxes or Federal Reserve requirements or interest rate ceilings. This, supposedly, would lure billions of dollars worth of banking activity back to the city from various banking havens overseas.

International banking activity would be exempt from U.S. regulations. They could indulge in creating from nothing Eurodollar-type funny-money without public scrutiny. Of course, large corporate depositors in the United States could shift their deposits from domestic branches into the international branches of these banks so there would be a tremendous amount of money flowing into unregulated sectors.

Our banks are in a precarious condition because their critical ratios are at the worst level since 1929. This only will make it more likely that those problems will increase.

I've contended all along that Mr. Carter owes his position to the fact that Chase Manhattan Bank's DAVID ROCKEFELLER invited him as a lame duck Georgia Governor to beomce a member of the Trilateral Commission, and made him a star. He was proposed to Rockefeller by the President of Coca Cola, which is headquartered in Georgia.

Isn't it curious that immediately after we announce our recognition of Red China, Chase Manhattan announced the opening of several branch banks in China? And Coca Cola said, "Surprise! We have a contract to sell Coke in China!"

I am not prepared to say, as many others do, that these men are pulling the strings to Carter's puppet act. It may well be that he just shares their point of view. In fact, that seems likely to me, given his rather stubborn nature. But it is certainly evidence of the immense influence in Washington of these people who do not consider themselves citizens of our country, but literally citizens of the world. That disturbs me. More on this later. (see: Banks & Banking Industry)

INVASION OF VIETNAM

(3/1/79) The invasion of Vietnam by China could be a serious threat to world peace, but my most dependable barometer, the gold market, says not to get too excited about it. Obviously, whenever the interests of the Soviet Union and China expand into armed conflict, we have to be very concerned. But the gold market took it pretty much with a "ho hum," and the accuracy of that market in determining the seriousness of international difficulties is pretty darned good. Gold is a lot more worried about Iran than about Southeast Asia.

CHRISTMAS

(12/15/76)   The Christmas Reminder

We spend a great deal of time talking about money, personal survival, physical survival, food, and other things of a tangible nature, but I believe the intangibles have really moved the world. Great movements have been triggered by great ideas and concepts.

The greatest force in the affairs of men has been the impact of the great religions of the world, but none will ultimately affect the life of mankind, now and hereafter, as much as the birth of the Son of God almost two millenia ago. This great event, without parallel in the history of mankind, is the pivotal event in God's Eternal Plan of Mankind. The commitment of my life to the Son of God, Jesus Christ, is total, and is responsible for the basic values that have motivated my position on a great many issues.

While we are storing gold and silver coins and stockpiling food, we must not forget the greater values of life. We must devote the few years available to us to the strengthening of our relationships with our families, and the establishment of close relationships with our fellow men. In the difficult years ahead, we will treasure relationships with strong and stable neighbors every bit as much as we will treasure our store of food or precious metals. We will be grateful for the close ties to our children, which will enable us to make the preparations as a family to get through the difficult years we face. But above all, once I have made the necessary physical preparations for my family and myself, I am prepared to leave the ultimate outcome of my life n the hands of God. I feel that after I have done all that I can for my loved ones and myself, I am entitled to His assistance. The Christmas season is the great reminder, that comes but once a year, of our total dependence upon our Maker for everything that we have.

(12/15/78) As we approach the season in which we traditionally commemorate the birth of Jesus, we would like to extend to you and your family our prayers for God's choicest blessings in your lives. I happen to believe my subscribers are the best people on earth and, based on our mail, you share the values I've tried to implement in my own life. I just want to take this occasion to reaffirm my faith in a loving Heavenly Father and in His Son, and express my appreciation for every subscriber, including Christians, Jews, and non-believers.

83

We love and treasure you all because you share those values critical to the survival of the Republic.

CITIES

UNIONS & STRIKES

(Special Report #2, 1/76)   As unemployment (in New York City) remains high and crime rates increase, city services need to be increased, not decreased. The inevitable reductions in city services, and police and fire protection, will make the cities less and less tenable. It is my opinion that the American metropolis as we know it, is now in its death throes. The impact of this on the national economy and our way of life is incalculable.

Employees of state and local governments are becoming increasingly militant, pushing for new concessions in pay and working conditions. This, of course, means head-on collision with the demands of austerity being made by municipal and state governments.

(4/15/76)   I am prepared to forecast a future rash of big city strikes across the country involving garbage collectors, clerks, police, firemen, craft workers, etc. There is enough tinder, in the form of unemployed black teenagers and blue-collar workers, to spark a conflagration if public safety services are curtailed, while passions are inflamed by emotional strike issues.

A study was done by Robert Tilove, Senior Vice-President of Martin C. Segal Company, actuaries and consultants in employee benefits. In New York City and New York state it was found that in mid-1973, after-tax income of retirees, at a salary level of $14,000, was running from 112 to 129 percent of pre-retirement earnings. In other words, when you quit working, you got a substantial raise.

Such revelations are triggering a taxpayer revolt that will collide head-on with rapidly growing unions who won't back an inch. In many cities, despite the possibility of fiscal collapse, they are actually pressing for increases in benefits.

When city unions go on strike to protect their benefits, it can mean disruption of normal commerce within cities, and also between cities.

FROM A TO Z

ENDANGERED LIST

(4/15/76)   Here is a partial list of the most vulnerable cities. They are on this list for a variety of reasons, including: imminent fiscal collapse, vulnerability to labor problems, isolation and total dependence upon transport of food and other commodities, high unemployment and the accompanying crime and frustration, or potential racial problems.

New York	San Francisco	Las Vegas
Boston	Los Angeles	Atlanta
Philadelphia	Memphis	Omaha
Detroit	St. Louis	Chicago
Cleveland	Honolulu	Washington/Baltimore

Here is a partial list of the least vulnerable cities.

Kansas City	Portland	San Antonio
Salt Lake City	Eugene	Des Moines
Phoenix	Tampa/St. Petersburg	Wichita
Albuquerque	Austin	Houston

To this second list you may add the states of Idaho, Wyoming, Washington, Montana, North and South Dakota, Iowa, Wisconsin (except for Milwaukee), and Michigan (at least 50 miles from Detroit).

If I haven't named your city, it's because I don't have enough information or I haven't correlated the data I do have, or I simply have not made up my mind yet.

If I lived in the most endangered cities, I'd either move or make arrangements to visit relatives on a moment's notice, until whatever troubles should occur blow over. If you can't do that, then quietly stock up on food, water, etc., and be prepared to maintain a low profile for awhile and be self-sufficient for several weeks without leaving home. It's not too late—yet.

NEW YORK CITY

(9/15/76)   I have always contended that the fiscal trouble of New York City was the most important financial event of the last half of the Twentieth Century, because it was merely the first of a domino-like series of collapses that would overwhelm Washington's ability to rescue them all.

(1/1/78) Our cities are also jostling for position at the public trough. Unfortunately, they may have no other alternative now. Our urban problems are generally government caused. The cities who willingly jumped on the revenue-sharing and welfare bandwagons, and all of the other Federal bandwagons that came parading by, are crying for government to save them from the problems government and their own bad judgment have created. NEW YORK CITY is a case in point. Mayor Beame, as one of his last acts as mayor, urged the $2 billion Federal short-term loans be extended beyond the June 30 expiration date and phased out over four more years. The nation's largest city still can't borrow on its own. An attempted sale of city notes collapsed three months ago. Senator WILLIAM PROXMIRE asked Beame if New York could survive without continuing Federal aid. Mr. Beame replied, "It's going to be impossible to solve the probems alone." The comptroller of New York City, HARRISON J. GOLDIN, says the city budget deficit has been understated by $450 million or more. JACKSON PHILLIPS, Executive Vice-President of Moody's Investors Service Inc., says New York City continues after two and a half years to "alter its budget figures."

Regarding New York, Secretary of the Treasury, W. MICHAEL BLUMENTHAL, told the Senate Banking Committee, "We do not consider bankruptcy an option. That would really be a worse situation than the current one."

He said, as I did two years ago, that the city would be run by a Federal judge and there would be a collapse of credit markets. PRESIDENT CARTER has repeatedly vowed to keep New York City solvent.

But New York City isn't the only pig at the trough. Treasury Department official, RALPH SCHLOSSTEIN, announced: "The distressed-cities approach will aid communities of all sizes, including healthy ones. This policy should be in the interest of the whole country, not just the cities that are on their backs at any one time." (see: New York City, & Economy, U.S.)

CITY TROUGH

(1/1/78) The HUD Secretary, PATRICIA HARRIS, predicted that Federal funds for state an local governments would increase to $80 billion in 1977-78, up from $59 billion in 1976-77, and you ain't seen nothin' yet.

The mayors of most other cities in the United States are complaining that all cities should benefit, and they don't want to be taxed to take care of the older deteriorating cities of the Northeast.

Mr. Schlosstein says, "In regard to Federal aid, our studies have found there are many cities for which the program contributes 10 percent to 15 percent of the operating budget, and a higher percentage of capital spending."

LAWRENCE O. HOUSTON, JR., Assistant to the Secretary of Commerce, indicated that in some large cities, for every $100 raised from their own sources, the Federal government will have to spend another $55 to $69. These cities include ST. LOUIS, NEWARK, BUFFALO, NEW YORK, CLEVELAND, BALTIMORE and DETROIT.

Cities in all parts of the country, with rare exception, have concluded that they must get on the Federal gravy train and swill at the Federal trough. If you think their troubles are bad now, wait until the economic downturn comes and unemployment rise, and tax collections fall, and the cities realize they have to pay "blood money" in benefits to keep blood from flowing in the streets. Uncle Sam will shell out the money, and the demands will be overwhelming.

(9/1/78) Not long ago, the U.S. Conference of Mayors held a five-day convention in Atlanta. MAYOR LEE ALEXANDER of Syracuse, New York, the head of the U.S. Conference of Mayors, said that the major cities are already "at the wall" financially, and a spreading tax revolt makes it imperative that the Federal government assumes the welfare burden.

For two years, I have been saying that our cities are the vulnerable point in our economy. The Federal government will eventually have to bail them out, paying for it with printing press money, and this would become one of the major causes of a runaway printing-press inflation.

These mayors are crying during the last boom phases of an economic recovery.' How loud will they cry when we actually slide into a deep recession and tax collections fall off, unemployment soars and the demands on government are increased just as its income is falling?

Local government operates under one handicap that the Federal government doesn't have. It doesn't have a printing press. But Uncle Sam does. The Carter Administration will swear on a stack of Bibles that they are not going to break the budget or cause inflation by excess government spending. But when push comes to shove, and the mayors and governors of this nation have the President with his back to the political wall, he will go to Congress for the necessary money to bail out the cities.

The tax revolt is not a spending revolt, although there are organizations actively working to limit government spending. The cut-spending crowd doesn't have the grass-roots support the cut-taxes movement has. The printing press, as a source of money, is a deceptive siren, because it doesn't seem like anyone has to pay for it. The assumption is that if the government is not taking the money away from you in taxes, they can't spend it. That attitude is naive and dangerous. Government always finds a way. City governments will get it from the state, state governments will get it from Uncle Sam, and Uncle Sam will take it away from you via the inflation tax and the printing press. Uncle Sam will simply create money, which he will spend into existence, which will dilute the purchasing power of every dollar in existence. Anything else is politically unacceptable.

The mayors and governors of this country are probably the nation's most potent pressure group, and there's no question in my mind they will not take their knee out of Uncle Sam's back until he has coughed up the money they want. And it won't be just the poor cities that will get it. Everybody else will scream, "Unfair."' They will say, "We have been the responsible guys who watched the pennies. Why are you rewarding those grasshoppers? We ants should be rewarded with money." And the Carter Administration has already indicated they are prepared to do just that in principle as well as in practice.

The Social Security system and the cities are part of the context within which all of my advisory decisions will be made. We mustn't forget that so-called "normal times cannot go on forever in a period of inflationary excesses. Inflationary booms always end with a crash, and this one will be no different. The recession we are moving into now could be the beginning. You have had plenty of warning and you've had enough guidance, so if you are still not ready, don't blame me.

(12/15/78) You might also want to relocate your business if it is in a high- risk uban area, and increase your arson and theft insurance, as crime rises during economic downturns.

COIN DEALERS

(5/1/76)   James Cook of Investment Rarities gave some of his insights on coin dealers through this portion of an interview we had back in May of 1976.

HJR: John Smith wants to buy some gold and silver coins to protect him against the hyper-inflation he had decided is coming. So, John Smith is about to walk into XYZ Precious Metals dealer. If he came to you for advice, and said, "What should I look out for? What are the pitfalls of getting into this?" What would you say?

Jim: I think there are several problems. Probably the greatest risk of all is: who exactly are you dealing with? How about their integrity? A lot of precious metals dealers have gone out of business, and they left a fair number of investors high and dry.

HJR: How did they do that?

Jim: Well, a number of them have taken people's funds and never delivered the goods. Others have sold rather poor investments at exorbitant prices. For example, a tremendous amount of silver bullion has been sold at prices so far above the market that huge increases would be necessary for people to recoup their acquisition costs. And, of course, there's always a few charlatans around who will sell counterfeit or damaged material and pass it off at inflated prices.

HJR: How can you protect yourself against this sort of thing?

Jim: My firm carries a half-million dollar bond with one of the largest insurance companies in the world, The Insurance Co. of North America. We have sight-draft bills-of-lading direct to the client's bank when they request it. We use customer trust accounts, where the customer's funds are deposited into a trust account and their payments are mailed directly to our bank. Those are the kinds of things careful investors are looking for.

HJR: Can John Smith ask a dealer to prove he has such a bond?

Jim: I don't think there is any other dealer in the country who carries that type of bond. None that I'm aware of, in any case. I'd be glad to send anybody a copy of it.

(Special Report #4, 10/76)   I ran into an interesting situation where a trusted dealer, with whom we've done business, called and indicated he was being substantially underbid by another dealer. In fact, the customers were being offered prices well below the market. I found out later that this dealer was in financial trouble, and he was selling bags of coins he had stored for some of his customers and was moving them well below the market price to obtain some quick cash. In this instance, he did find some money and was able to save his business, but if he had not been able to, he would have gone broke and all of the people whose coins had been stored by him would have lost everything they have invested. It is best to be suspicious of "super deals" offered by coin dealers.

(4/1/77)   Some of you have just gotten a good lesson in why you should be super-careful in doing business with coin dealers.

It seems that Security National Coin Corporation of San Antonio, Cooper's Riverside Coin Company of San Antonio, and Southwest Rare Coin Gallery of Houston, all advertised heavily in the *WALL STREET JOURNAL*, have just been indicted for fraudulently "buffing" common circulated gold and silver coins, and selling them to the public as "brilliant uncirculated" coins at prices far in excess of their value.

They all have large liabilities for coin deliveries to customers who have paid for but not received their merchandise. That means, if the allegations are true, they have spent customer money, but not for coins.

This is precisely why we at *THE RUFF TIMES* have recommended you do business with bonded, recommended dealers we have checked out for you, or demand "cash-and-carry" service from a dealer.

Coin dealers have dropped like flies over the last two years, and even though there are still some fine, sound people in the business you should consider them all suspect in order to protect your hide.

Ruff's Recommendations

1.   Deal with our recommended merchants, and demand delivery at the time of payment.

2.   Even with Investment Rarities, our recommended dealer, buy on a "sight- draft" basis through a bank. I.R. can explain it to you (800-328-1860).

3.   Don't let any coin dealer store your coins for you.

4.   If you have paid an indicted firm and you still don't have your coins, walk in and threaten criminal fraud charges if you don't get your coins, and don't leave until you have them.

5. Buy numismatic coins only through our recommended dealer or long-established, bonded dealers.

COINS

(5/1/76)   Real Money And How To Buy It
  (Interview with James Cook, President of Investment Rarities, Inc.)
HJR: Jim, to begin our interview, what background do you have in the investment field?
Jim: Well, Howard, I have a wide range of experience. Formerly, I was in the Securities business, which I left because of disillusionment. Prior to that, I owned and operated a general insurance agency. After I left the Securities business, I became interested in precious metals and have read extensively for the last five or six years. I've been in the Precious Metals field for five years, and during that time I and my staff of monetary experts have counselled thousands of clients with their survival investment program.
HJR: What disillusioned you with the Securities Industry?
Jim: It wasn't necessarily the Industry. It was the economic cycles that frightened me away from that type of investment.
HJR: For what reason?
Jim: First, inflation began to worsen with each boom-bust cycle, which seemed to be happening more and more often. The cycles are coming faster and faster. So I felt that stocks and bonds were not a safe hedge.
HJR: We agree. What other kinds of investments do you handle, and which ones in those related areas do you prefer not to handle, and why?
Jim: We deal in gold and silver coins, including some coins whose value is a combination of the bullion value and the numismatic value. We've always avoided margin transactions, because we felt fluctuations in the market rendered that too risky.
HJR: Wouldn't you show greater profits if you handled margin accounts?
Jim: Definitely! I would have been a millionaire, but on the other hand, a lot of margin buyers lost an awful lot of money and some firms have been indicted, so I am satisfied that I made a correct decision.
HJR: What is "bullion value" and "numismatic value"?
Jim: Coins that have strict bullion value are, for example, the pre-1965, circulated U.S. 90% silver coins. They are purchased

91

purchased purely for the silver bullion content. The gold Krugerrand and the Mexican Fifty Peso, which are roughly one and 2/10th ounce gold coins, are purely bullion-type coins. One ounce of bullion sells for approximately the same price as one ounce of coins, but there is a much broader market for coins, giving greater liquidity.

"Numismatic value" means that a coin has great collector demand. Of course the collector demand is the same thing that makes a painting worth a million dollars. Although some people shy away from numismatic-type investments, properly selected numismatic investments over the last decade have out-shone virtually any other investment.

HJR: Do you feel that there is a qualitative difference between the two kinds of coins as a hedge against monetary crisis or economic collapse?

Jim: Yes. I structure my investment philosophy in this fashion. The first line of defense is silver coins. Maybe a bag or two. Then gold bullion-type coins until approximately 40-50 percent of one's invested assets are somewhat equally divided between gold and silver. Then, if a person wants to invest more aggressively, some numismatic-type pieces, like the uncirculated Morgan dollars, which are about half bullion and half numismatic, or the U.S. $20 Double Eagles or $10 Liberty gold coins. These all have excellent potential.

HJR: If someone wanted to buy a bag of "junk silver," pre-1965 silver American coins, what would be the face value of the coins in the bag?

Jim: The face value of a bag of silver coins is $1000.

HJR: What would be the market value of a bag of silver coins?

Jim: You base the market value on the silver content, which is roughly 720 ounces in a bag, and with silver selling today around $4.50 ($16 in November, 1979, Ed.), it comes to $3100 a bag. However, there is a limited quantity of these bags, and I think eventually enough of them will be tucked away that there will be a premium above the silver value. But, of course, at present, that is not the case. We will see silver bags at much higher prices. ($11,000 in Nov., 1979, Ed.)

HJR: Do you think there would ever be a substantial premium for gold coins over and above their bullion value?

Jim: There probably would be, if the Government no longer allowed people to buy gold coins, which happened in Britain recently. With this restriction an active black market is generated in the coins, but at a significant premium.

HJR: Is it possible to have the paradox of downward pressure on the price of gold bullion, due to International Monetary Fund sales and, at the same time, perhaps, an increase in the value of gold coins, simply due to the scarcity factor, if there were enough people frightened about increasing inflation rates?

Jim: It is quite conceivable that they could go to some sort of a premium over bullion. At the present time, however, there seems to be an adequate supply of both gold and silver coins.

HJR: Many forecasters have postulated a run-away, hyper-inflation and, on the other hand, some are forecasting an explosive deflation. How would gold and silver coins fare in each of these circumstances? Let's take hyper-inflation first.

Jim: I think we would see gold and silver go to much higher levels in a severe inflation, which I feel strongly is going to be the event of the future. I think it will be mind-boggling.

HJR: Do you care to attach a number to that?

Jim: I would be comfortable in saying silver would be handily over $10 an ounce and gold probably over $300 an ounce. Ultimately, they could go much higher than that, but at this point in time, it's very difficult to see how severe the events of the future will be. I would be reluctant to say much higher than that at this time.

HJR: How would these kinds of investments fare if we should have a sudden explosive deflation and a major depression, perhaps worse than the 1930s?

Jim: Silver probably would fall somewhat, because industrial demand for silver would dry up. Remember this about gold—in a depression, it has historically played the role of capital preservation. Some gold securities in the 1930s multiplied 10-20 times. So I think gold would probably be more than a bit better in a depression, and although I think it could fall somewhat too, I think the thing to bear in mind is that, compared to anything else, it would probably be the best holding.

HJR: Aren't we really talking about trying to maintain our purchasing power, rather than some artificial level of value of our gold relative to the dollar? For example, if the price of gold dropped by 50 percent and other prices dropped by 75 percent, I would not be concerned about the drop in the value of my gold. It presents a real increase in value, relative to goods and services.

Jim: My feeling is that precious metals represent a store of wealth that will tend to hold its value relative to goods and services.

HJR: You could argue either bullishly or bearishly for silver right now.

The bearish argument is that everything is looking good, and so the people who bought gold and silver coins as a hedge against calamity have relaxed and said, "I don't think we are going to have any trouble." so they are unloading

On the bullish side, you could very well argue that during this recovery, industrial uses of the metal will increase consumer demand.

Jim: That certainly is true about the industrial demand perking up. Also, most people who have taken physical possession of gold and silver over the past two or three years are committed to both metals as a hedge against what's in store for us. There has been some selling, but for the most part, people are still holding on.

HJR: Then you feel that the bullish factors would prevail?

Jim: Yes, I do.

HJR: All right. Now, if an investor with $5000 came to you and said, "I don't know anything about this, Mr. Cook, but I trust you. What should I do with my money?" What would you advise?

Jim: First of all, I'd buy a bag of silver coins, which would leave approximately $2,000, and with that I'd buy 15 gold Austrian 100 Coronas or 15 Krugerrands.

HJR: Are gold and silver coins good collateral? If so, are most lending institutions willing to accept them as such?

Jim: They certainly are. If somebody has a good relationship with his banker, he can sit down with him and say, "Here's the market on gold and silver. I should at least get what I get on a security, which is usually 50 percent of its value."

HJR: All right, let's get a little bit speculative now, in terms of the original meaning of the word "speculate," which comes from the Latin word "speculare," and means to "spy out in advance." What role would gold and silver coins play during a period of hyper-inflation?

Jim: Historically, in hyper-inflation, gold and silver have served as currency and I think that is most likely to happen. If people lost trust in paper money, they have to trust something, and gold and silver coins are the reasonable place to turn.

HJR: Why do you think we are headed for hyper-inflation?

Jim: The reasons are numerous. We are still creating more paper money, which is inflationary. With the new consumer confidence that's been generated recently, corporations are going to need money to borrow for inventories, and consumer financing. They will have to go to the banks, and of course, that's newly created money. If you paid attention to M-2, the money supply which includes savings account money, you can see that its growth has been above the Federal Reserve guidelines. And that's tremendous stored up purchasing power —all those things will be highly inflationary factors in the near future.

However, I think the most insidious thing which lies in wait for us is the fact that capital formation in this country, which has been the life-blood of our high standard of living and progress, is being choked off. This has potential to really produce a significant reduction in the well-being and standard-of-living of all of us. This may even be a greater problem than the inflation.

HJR: Are there any specific events, other than the broad general trends that could possibly trigger this kind of problem?

Jim: Yes. Right now, we are looking at the potential for a commodities explosion. If you will recall, back in '73, commodities went through the roof. You cannot discount the inflation expectation in the minds of corporate officers. If these people—and the people who run corporations are smart people—feel that raw materials are going out of sight, they will step into that market and buy for inventories, and this could cause a tremendous inflationary boom in commodities.

Also, we have experienced a fair amount of dry weather through the central part of the country, which is really the world's bread basket now. Any extension of that trend would be highly inflationary. Already we see certain grains and cattle prices rising significantly.

There is also the oil time-bomb: the energy problem. All those things could be the detonator for the future explosion of inflation.

HJR: Jim, do you have any final words for us?

Jim: One other thing. Typically, investors are prone to jump into the market right at the top, as we saw when gold and silver were at their highs in 1974. Then we sold a much greater volume than we ever do when prices are in the doldrums. Now, when gold and silver are depressed, the sophisticated investor will begin to make his purchases, rather than waiting until the public is clamoring for precious metals at higher levels. It is my personal opinion that we probably have the last great opportunity to buy silver and gold.

HJR: There is an old story about an old Idaho farmer. One year everybody planted potatoes, and, of course, there was a glut of potatoes, and the price of potatoes dropped. But he had planted corn. Then next year, they saw how much money he had made, so everyone said, "Well that's a pretty smart fellow, so we're going to plant corn." So they all planted corn, and, of course, he was out planting potatoes. And I think the same thing applies to investments. You've got to be willing to go the opposite direction of the herd. In fact, one of my methods of economic forecasting is to get a consensus from all the great economists as to which way we are going to go, then bet on the other direction, because they have been uniformly wrong in the past three years. (see: Economists)

Jim: And the great economists today are currently projecting rosy pictures of the future.

HJR: It sounds exactly like late 1973 and early 1974.

Jim: Yes, it's a rerun. Only this time it's worsening and more intense.

(*THE RUFF TIMES* has no financial interest in the sum represented by people interviewed in this publication. These interviews are offered purely as a service to our readers.)

(2/1/76)   Precious Metals, or Food?

Brigham Young once said, "the time would come when, if faced with a choice between a wheelbarrow full of gold and a cat, you would choose the cat, because you could eat it."

There's the distinct possibility that the time will come when there will be insufficient food available in the stores. I foresee in our future a time when federal, state, and municipal debt will be repudiated, when crime and disorder will rise and normal commerce will be disrupted for awhile. I have no idea when or if it will hit your community, but if it does, you can't just pop into your station wagon and run to the supermarket.

Silver or gold coins are no good if there is nothing for which to exchange them.

I've never eaten silver bullion, but I have eaten beef bouillon and it's good, and the time may come when you would trade, even-up.

Why buy coins then? Because they will have monetary value after the possible chaotic periods are over. They could make you wealthy. You can buy whatever is available when others can't.

There are two reasons for buying gold or silver: speculation, and as a hedge against runaway inflation or debt repudiation by governments.

You should buy coins for protection against currency loss-of-value, and not worry about today's price. If it drops, think of it as an opportunity to buy more.

I am sticking with coins instead of bullion as matter of preference. If I had a lot of money, I might buy bullion.

BUYING ON MARGIN

(3/15/76) The theory of buying coins on margin is that you can buy more coins and increase your speculative profit. For example, if you paid $3000 for a bag of silver coins, and were able to buy it for 10% down or 20% down, you could buy five to ten times as many coins and your profit potential is increased by that amount. Bear in mind, however, that the potential for loss is equally multiplied and a relatively small downturn in the cost of silver could wipe out your total investment. However, if you guess right, and the price of silver rises, your profits are greatly increased. This principle, as any sophisticated investor knows, is called "leverage." It is our advice, at this time, that you buy coins and take physical delivery. Here is why.

In a margin transaction, the dealer holds the coins as security, and you are totally dependent upon the solvency of the coin dealer. The mortality rate of coin dealers is high, and your margin could be lost if the dealer should go bankrupt.

We are not recommending coins and silver and gold bullion for short-term speculative purposes. We are recommending them as a hedge against possible economic collapse. I have no way of forecasting the short-term ups and downs of these markets. They should be held long-term, as short-term fluctuations are irrelevant.

I have just found an unusual way to accumulate some silver. I've just read a booklet by Werner Pauson explaining how to recover silver from waste photographic and X-ray developing chemicals, and how to get your raw materials free. It sounds kookie, but the booklet makes sense. You could acquire from $320 to $4600 worth of silver in a year with his well-thought-out scheme. Write to the following address for more information:

W. M. Pauson, P. O. Box 425, WILLOW GROVE, PA 19090

HOWARD RUFF

KRUGERRANDS

(7/15/78) The following article appeared in the *OAKLAND TRIBUNE* recently.

Members of the African Liberation Support Committee (ALSC) are picketing a downtown Oakland coin shop to protest the sale of the Krugerrand, a South African gold coin.

Yesterday afternoon, 10 demonstrators played drums, chanted and marched in front of the 17th Street store of Gary Young, a rare coin dealer.

"The Krugerrand is blood money," said ALSC chairperson Von Ashford. "The gold props up the South African regime and the government is pushing the coin because it is in a crisis. The money for the coin goes directly for the purchase of arms in South Africa. We are calling on all coin dealers and gold shops not to participate in the oppression of black South Africans."

The protest against the Krugerrand is growing and there is a very good chance the supply may be cut off sometime in the future, in which case the Krugerrand could become a rare coin and the premium could increase. This would give you interesting protection if the price of gold should decline, because an increasing premium might make up the difference. Don't expect it right away, but it is a distinct possibility for the future.

(3/15/78)

Q. I see that Merrill Lynch and some big banks have decided to no longer sell the Krugerrand, due to pressures from civil rights groups in protest of South Africa's racial policies. Doesn't this make the Krugerrand a dangerous investment?

A. No. Quite the opposite. These people want no foreign exchange to flow into South Africa, so they don't want South Africa to benefit from any further Krugerrand sales. My opinion is that it will probably succeed in cutting off much of South Africa's Krugerrand sales about a year from now, as all of this year's production is sold. However, this could mean scarce Kruggerands and a higher premium which makes an even better investment. South Africa's troubles could be your good news. As the coin becomes scarcer, it could become a numismatic coin, trading way above its intrinsic value.

(9/15/77)   Two-Way Hedges

by Gary North, Ph.D.

Will it be mass inflation, inflationary depression, price controls, or will it be a deflationary depression? There are good men who are convinced that each of these scenarios is likely, and some think that more than one may hit, though not necessarily at the same time.

It should be obvious (though it isn't to several of the writers) that an ideal edge against one disaster may not perform very well if one of the others should hit instead, or at least hit first. For example, gold does well in a mass inflation, while cash currency is destroyed. On the other hand, it is quite possible to imagine a deflationary (prices falling) depression in which the government, for idealogical reasons, refuses to step in and place an official floor price on gold. Then gold becomes a poorer investment than cash or Treasury bills, since prices are falling in relation to the dollar.

An inflationary depression, where prices continue to rise, but unemployment goes up anyway, is what we experienced in 1974-75. Gold did well in early 1974, but dropped in 1975. Silver also peaked in 1974. So both rising and falling prices characterized the precious metals in the midst of an official recession (falling GNP for two successive quarters or more). We have to say that the precious metals were not good devices for capital preservation in that particular inflationary recession-depression.

(Sorry, Gary! I disagree. They never fell back to their pre-recession levels. It was still a good hedge, until the recovery began. But go on. I agree with everything else, Good Buddy. HJR)

Are there ways to protect our capital, no matter what? As far as we can determine, no single investment will invariably appreciate in all of these circumstances, but there are some that will do reasonably well in inflationary times, and not lose too much in a deflationary depression. In other words, they can serve as two-way hedges, allowing us to "buy and forget" for the next decade. These two investments have not caught the eye of investors, so the premium is low.

The first, and best, in terms of long-term safety is the lowly copper penny. Copper is a "hard asset" which will appreciate in a mass inflation, and also in a price-controlled inflation. The present low price of copper on the free market at $.55 per pound puts copper a long way from $1.55 where the penny becomes a "full-bodied coin," meaning a coin whose metal content is worth exactly the same as its face value. If inflation pushes the free market price of copper much above $1.55, then it will become profitable to melt pennies for their copper content, and the penny will disappear from circulation, just as it did in 1973, when copper hit $1.30 and the penny shortage occurred.

The Treasury is trying to abolish the penny, so a systematic conversion of paper bills to rolls of pennies should be a basic savings approach of every *RUFF TIMES* subscriber. Of course, you lose 5% or 6% you could have earned from your savings account, or the returns you could have earned by investing in your business. But if inflation continues upward, or if price controls are imposed, the penny will become an excellent barter coin for small purchases.

Rev. Karl Treutz of Germany hoarded copper coins in the Nazi era by removing them from the collection plate and substituting the paper bills of his own salary. By 1945 he had a bathtub full, and he lived on that hoard right through the shortage period of price controls that the Allies imposed on Germany, 1945-48.

If we have a deflationary depression, either before the inflationary crisis (unlikely) or after it (more likely), then pennies perform well. The face value of the penny is legal tender. People sell goods for money, and the penny will be money. Thus, the purchasing power of the penny will increase as prices are falling. In short, the penny is a two-way edge. The only time it does not perform well is during stable tlmes of low inflation or low deflation.

But pennies are bulky. That makes them difficult to steal, so perhaps their weight-per-unit-value is an asset. But for investments larger than $1,000, the penny is not as satisfactory as the Kennedy "clad" half dollar of 1965-69.

The clad halves contain 40% silver. Thus, they do appreciate during a time of price inflation. They do not appreciate as rapidly as a 90% silver coin (pre-1965), but you pay today about $1,500 per $1,000 face value, rather than over $3,000 for a bag of 90% silver coins. The downside risk is much lower because if the price of silver drops, your potential loss is limited to (a) the premium you paid over the face value, plus (b) the forfeited interest. The 50¢ piece is always worth 50 cents in current purchasing power. If prices are falling generally, then the holder of 50¢ pieces can profit simply by holding his coins longer. He has an appreciating asset in a deflationary depression. And because of the silver content, he has an appreciating asset in a time of price inflation, too.

Not many 40% silver halves were produced, thus, they could develop numismatic (collector) value. There will be a tendency to melt down these coins in a time of inflation or price controls, thereby adding an additional scarcity value.

You can buy the clad halves from our dependable recommended dealer, INVESTMENT RARITIES (800-328-1860, toll-free). Every time you go to the bank, buy a couple of rolls of pennies. If they begin to get really scarce, then buy $50 bags from your banker, or if he refuses, from a local coin dealer.

COMMODITIES MARKET

(9/15/77)   Interview with R. E. McMaster

HJR: R.E., let's assume none of our readers knows anything about the commodities market. What is the commodities market and how does it function?

REM: Howard, the commodities market deals with the basic raw materials of our economy— such things as wool, wheat, sugar, soybeans, silver, cattle, coffee—and they are traded on major exchanges, such as the COMEX, and the granddaddy of exchanges, the CHICAGO BOARD OF TRADE. Commodity trading is a process of contracting between a buyer and a seller. Here is a simple analogy. Let's say you wanted to buy a Cadillac for delivery in March of the following year. But you think prices will rise by then, and want to pay only today's price of $9,000. So, betting on lower prices by then, I would say, "OK, I will take your $9000, and deliver it in March." I am betting that sometime prior to March, I will be able to obtain a Cadillac for less than $9,000, and I will pocket the difference. If I guess wrong on future prices, I lose money. You and I have contracted for a specific item, at a specific point in time, at a specific price.

The FUTURES MARKET works the same way. I want to buy 5000 ounces of silver in December at $4.55 an ounce, and you agree to sell it to me for December delivery. We now have a Future Contract. Whether or not you own the item is really immaterial, but as the first "notice" day approaches in December for the actual delivery of that silver, you either sell that contract to someone else, at the current silver price, at a profit or loss, or you have to deliver the silver. If I buy a December contract for $4.55, I am hoping that the price of silver will go up, so that sometime between now and December I can sell that silver for a profit. If it moves from $4.55 to $4.65, a ten cent move, then I will have realized a profit of $500 on my purchase. If you sold at $4.55, instead of buying, that's known as "going short." If prices moved up to $4.65, you would have suffered an open loss of $500. It is difficult for some to understand that you can sell something that you don't have, and if the price goes down, you can buy it back at a lower price, and make a profit.

HJR: How does this even out without 5000 ounces of silver dumped on your doorstep?

REM: Since there are always an equal number of off-setting buyers and sellers, it washes out by the due date of the contract.

HJR: Don't most people think of this market as a high-rolling crap shoot?

REM: Actually, it has two functions. First of all, it is the world's pricing mechanism. Also, it serves as an insurance policy for the "commercials." Let me give you an example. I do consulting with wheat producers in Washington state. The price of wheat tends to bottom out in July when everyone harvests their wheat and sells it. So, if you raise wheat, you don't want to sell your wheat in July. For simplicity, let's say you raised one contract of wheat, which is 5000 bushels, and would be happy to sell for $3.00 a bushel. In March of this year, let's say that the July contract was selling at $3.00 a bushel on the futures market, and your break-even is $2.50. You sell the equivalent of your crop on the futures market at $3.00. You have already bought wheat, in effect, by the fact that you've raised 5000 bushels. You want to lock in that profit. So you sell against what you are raising, or "hedge" your wheat at $3.00. If prices come down, you don't care, because even though the value of your wheat goes down, your hedge position neutralizes it.

HJR: I don't think one family farmer in fifty understands they can lock in their price.

REM: What you say is 100 percent correct. I just did a "hedging" seminar for the potato raisers in Maine. They don't understand how the futures markets work. The most reckless gamble is to bet that they will get the best price at harvest time. It's always the lowest then. Farmers typically measure their success on a yield-per-acre basis. That's only partly true. They should also be looking at their bottom line—their profit. With this year's big crops, with the rising costs and low grain prices, their profits are really being squeezed because they don't really understand how to market and price their product.

HJR: Back to silver. How do you actually buy a contract?

REM: Right now, the initial margin on a silver contract is $1000. That means you can put down a "deposit" of $1000 and control the value of that $22,500 contract. That's "leverage." Obviously, if you buy 5000 ounces of silver and the price moves down ten cents, half of your original margin is wiped out. If it goes up a dime, you make a 50 percent profit—$500 on your $1,000 investment. You control a large investment for a very few dollars.

HJR: Then a 20 cents move down would wipe out your margin entirely, and conversely, a 20 cents move upward would give you a 100 percent return on your $1000 investment.

REM: And if it took two days, which it can, the annualized return is incredible.

HJR: So the risks are high and rewards are great because of the leverage factor. You can guess right about the ultimate direction, but be whipsawed out by a short-term move in the wrong direction?

REM: Right. That's why timing is so critical. You are betting that the market will move substantially for you before it moves against you, if you are playing with small margin. Speculation in commodities should be confined to those who have "risk capital."

HJR: We all like to think we act coolly and objectively, but in a high risk, high velocity situation, the stress factors tend to short circuit our critical abilities—our ability to criticize our own actions. How can we keep our minds clear, and avoid bad decisions?

REM: First, you must "remove yourself" from your emotions and look at the commodity arena as if you were viewing a football game. I also "train for pain." I will literally discipline myself, condition, run, work out, go without sleep sometimes to test my stress level, fast, go without food for a day during the week. We all like to be comfortable, but if we recognize that pain is a reality of life, and make that mental adjustment to see that we do accept pain along with everything else, the inevitable painful losses are much easier to deal with. There are times when you "short out."

HJR: What are the margin requirements to "go short"?

REM: The margin is the same whether you go long or short.

HJR: What market strategies do you use?

REM: If you have a natural tendency to like fast action you should take a "scalping," or in-and-out trading approach, to the market. You incur less risks if your objective is short-term, and you set "stop-losses" to get out of the market with only small losses if you are wrong. Contrarily, some trader might buy December wheat now and not plan to sell it until December. That's a long-term position. You may incur more fluctuations and temporary paper losses before the decision point is reached. If you have an easy-going temperament, and plenty of capital, and can emotionally handle these fluctuations—$1000 up two days, $500 down the next—then that may be what you should do. It must be consistent with your temperament.

    You need three things to be successful. One is a good, solid trading method. Two is money management techniques integrated with the trading method, and three is the discipline to carry out one and two.

HJR: But isn't it true that too many people get hurt in the commodities market by jumping in on a "hunch basis" without that internal data bank?

REM: Absolutely. The people that jump in cold and try to trade on their hunches withut having really paid their dues, usually get stung badly.

HJR: Our readers are very interested in gold and silver. How does it look?

REM: That's a tough question. December gold has just closed above 150, which is a signal indicating a "break out" to the up-side. Plus, 150 is a psychological barrier. Someone could risk $500 a contract, and put a stop-loss order at 145, and hold on to December gold and wait and see what happens. If he is wrong, he would only lose $500 if the market backed off to 145. However, a "cyclical oscillator" that I follow, is giving some preliminary "bearish" indicators. A second indicator, a variation of what's known as a "chase formula" is giving a "shot" signal. The chase formula says that when everything is in gear, then you better watch out, because the prices are going to go the other way. There is heavy overhead resistance between 152 and 153. I want to see December gold close above 151 and then above 153. I'm cautiously bullish right now, but the technical indicators say that the market could be due for a severe correction.

HJR: Any opinions on the long-term prospects for gold?

REM: Long-term prospects are based on fundamentals. I think that our economy is at a very very critical stage. We are seeing an economic slow-down. We could see a sharp contraction, and if we do, that will affect gold negatively, unless the government starts to really turn on the boiler and pump up the money supply.

HJR: Well, they will, and then you've got inflation which is always bullish for gold.

REM: The question is, are we going to see a contractionary slow-down, or an inflationary spiral? It makes sense to own some gold as an insurance policy. I'm positioned on the "long" side, while watching the market very carefully. Let me give you some key points. December gold above 150 was significant. 151, 152 and then, last but not least, 153, would be very significant. A close below 146 will return the bullish case to neutral. The long-term indicators are presently bullish.

HJR: How about silver?

REM: Silver is in exactly the same situation, but has not been as strong as gold. The "down-trend line" in silver has been touched seven times now, and each time the market has backed off. I'd like to see the December silver contract close above $4.60, and then above $4.70. That would be a bullish signal. It would be worth a play with the "stop-losses" around the $4.50 level. On the down-side, if December silver closed below $4.40, that would be as decisively bearish. Cyclical indicators are presently calling for lower/neutral silver prices.

HJR: How about wheat?

REM: Fundamentally, there is a real problem with subsoil moisture. Seasonally, wheat should have bottomed in July, but it bottomed in August, which is acceptable. The downside risk is really quite limited. If you want to speculate in wheat, buy on a dip to around $2.35, with a protective stop order at $2.27. You are only risking $500 per contract, which is O.K. for a "position trade."

HJR: What about the farmer who is undecided about selling the wheat in his bins?

REM: I'd hold on to it. There is no indication that he should hedge his contract.

HJR: How has the market reacted to the midwest drought, which now seems to have broken?

REM: The market acts as a discounting mechanism. It anticipates the future. What is going on in the market today will be reflected in the news sometime in the future. By the time the drought was widely reported, the markets had already fully anticipated the news and had already climbed. And the market, as it aways is, was correct.

HJR: You mean the market forecast the weather?

REM: In a way, it did. That is something that most people have great difficulty believing, unless you work with market cycles for a long time. You see prices move, and you wait for the event to occur to confirm what's already been reflected in prices. That takes some getting used to, because you do not believe it the first year or so you see it. Larry Williams, Bill Jones, and I have all done some work on the technical analysis of temperature and weather and we find that we can predict as accurately, and sometimes more accurately, than your meteorologists, just looking at it from a technical perspective, knowing nothing about which weather fronts are moving where.

HJR: And, I'll bet you don't know why.

REM: I haven't the foggiest idea, but I don't really care. It works.

HJR: All right, Joe Blow reads this interview carefully and decides that he has the temperament and the resources to do the job. How does one select a broker?

REM: Very carefully! I look for strong reputable firms that have been around awhile. And I look to my broker primarily to give me good "execution," in and out. I never look to a broker for advice or recommendations. I may ask him to gather information for me occasionally, such as, how are "the commercials" acting in the market, or on which side of the market are "the locals," but I never use him for trade recommendations, only for execution of orders. A broker is not trained as an analyst. Also, he is so occupied with his normal duties, he doesn't have the time to be an effective analyst. I think an investor is better off following our advice, and, learning how to trade his own account. Go down to some of the commodity offices and meet those who are watching the board. They can tell you pretty quickly who the good brokers are. A stock broker would be objective and tell you who the heavyweights are in the commodities area.

HRJ: R.E., how do you decide what to buy or sell and when?

REM: There are two basic approaches to the market. The FUNDAMENTAL APPROACH says to gather all the information, and project future price movements based on your analysis of supply and demand. However, the Fundamental Approach doesn't deal with timing, which is critical. The TECHNICAL APPROACH says that the market, by its own action, will tell you which way prices are going, and you don't really have to know why, because the market is anticipating news that will come out in the future. And it signals when to act. There are several ways of doing this. I use bar chart analyses, cycles, weekly charts, oscillators, and volume indicators. But I also keep an eye on such fundamentals as seasonal tendencies. So I combine a technical approach for timing, with an eye to the fundamentals.

HRJ: How does one get in touch with you, or obtain your publication?

REM: They can write for THE REAPER at P.O. Box 27554, Phoenix, Arizona, 85061.

(12/15/77)   Business Inflation Protection

Q. How do small businessmen protect themselves against inflation and depression?

A. If you deal in a basic commodity for which demand will not drop sharply during a depression, you should increase your inventory, if you have sufficient cash. If you are dealing with a product or service that will be hurt by an inflationary depression, you must reduce your inventory, or sell your business now.

You can protect yourself against rising prices by going into the commodity futures market and hedging, if you deal with some basic commodity for which futures contracts can be purchased. You then are assured of the price you will pay or receive.

CONSPIRACY

(1/15/79)   Is There a Great Conspiracy?

There is a substantial and growing minority who believe that all of the world's troubles are the result of a conscious, calculated conspiracy, generally headed by insiders such as NELSON ROCKEFELLER, DAVID ROCKEFELLER, BARON ROTHSCHILD, etc. They have formed organizations such as the BILDERBERGERS, the COUNCIL ON FOREIGN RELATIONS, and THE TRILATERAL COMMISSION.

The theory goes something like this: Their plan is to create a one-world Communist dictatorship that will rule the world. Our president is a puppet who is totally manipulated and these people even control the governments of the Soviet Union and Red China. Consequently, every action taken by this country is consciously manipulated for their benefit.

Some of the best people I know share all, or part, of this view. I don't have a dearer friend on earth than W. CLEON SKOUSEN, who wrote the book *THE NAKED CAPITALIST*, one of the first big-selling books on this subject. Subscribers have probably sent me 150 copies of GARY ALLEN'S book, *NONE DARE CALL IT CONSPIRACY*. This is the general theme of publications like *SPOTLIGHT*. Also, a series of articles in *PENTHOUSE* magazine (clipped out by our loyal subscribers and sent to me anonymously) has explored Jimmy Carter's Trilateral Commission connections.

I think it is about time I told you about my views on this rather touchy subject, despite the fact that I know this is not going to please some of you. It is time to grasp the nettle.

Ruff's Recap of the Conspiracy Theory

The word "Conspiracy" is from Latin, meaning "to breathe together," or "to secretly work together for a common goal."

There are powerful conspiracies loose in the world. THE INTERNATIONAL BANKERS do manipulate this country's policy to their benefit through their immense political influence and the sheer weight of their economic power. They control the economies of dozens of nations through monstrous loans. Through their creations, the INTERNATIONAL MONETARY FUND and the WORLD BANK, they have been able to extract public funds to be advanced to these countries so they can pay the interest on their loans. These "conspirators" consider themselves "citizens of the world," rather than citizens of the countries in which they reside. They represent the great investment and banking houses of Europe and the great multinational corporations, including the oil companies and some of the huge manufacturing octopuses from Japan, West Germany, France, etc. These people literally make public policy.

I don't believe they are in total control of the world, and I cannot make the leap in logic that others have made, that concludes they manipulate the smallest details of public life. Nor can I accept the conclusion that they want all of us to all be part of a one-world communist state.

These unelected leaders have attained their power, influence and fortunes, which are almost beyond comprehension, by exerting decisive influence on controlled capitalist economies. I can see no logical reason why they should want to change that. True, they form organizations, such as the Trilateral Commission, for international monetary manipulation, and to make international trade cheaper and easier to conduct. I have pointed out that I believe they were behind the recognition of Red China. They are the inflaters—the deficit spenders. If governments did not run deficits on the state, city and Federal level, one of their greatest sources of safe profit would dry up, which is the interest they earn by purchasing debt securities issued by these political subdivisions. If there weren't government bonds, municipal bonds, or local sewer district bonds, etc., these organizations would have no safe place to park their money when it is not employed in direct loans or mortgages. These bonds have provided tens of billions of dollars of profits annually for the bankers. It is in their interest to have "controlled" inflation and "controlled" deficits. Profit, power, and freedom to operate are what they strive for, along with the protection of their accumuated wealth and privilege through special tax advantages.

I do not believe, that they are infallible, nor do they consider themselves to be malign or evil. I believe that David and Nelson Rockefeller think of themselves as public-spirited in every sense of the word. Fortunately, they are not all-powerful. No one ever wanted to be President of the United States more than Nelson Rockfeller and he never made it. No matter how hard David Rockefeller tries, he is still running only the third or fourth or fifth biggest bank in America.

These men can and probably will miscalculate. The banking system which they dominate is gravely threatened by the events in our future, and I don't believe they are assured of being able to patch up their sinking ship as we sail into the next depression. Some of the conspiracy scholars have concluded that these people are deliberately leading us into a depression. I am not persuaded.

So how does this sum up? They wield far too much power. They act in their own self-interest and get their way more often than not. They don't just influence the monetary system, they *are* the monetary system. However, they are a long way from being totally in control, and probably never will be.

They aren't even agreed on their objectives. They fight among themselves. The Rockefeller center of influence wants to cast off gold as the world's reserve money, and has fought tooth and nail for this, because it allows them to benefit from inflation and funding of government deficits through government securities. The Rothschild family, on the other hand, with its huge gold and diamond interests wants to re-enthrone gold as the centerpiece of the world monetary system, and the struggle has been going on for some years. The IMF is the principal tool of the Rockefeller-centered philosophy, and the Bank for International Settlements (BIS) is the principal source of concentrated, economic power of the Rothschild clan.

Conspiracies? Yes. They take the form of shifting alliances, with organizations that come and go in prestige and influence, such as the Council on Foreign Relations, the Bilderbergers, and now, the Trilateral Commission.

Those guys couldn't lose in the last presidential election. JERRY FORD was a Nelson Rockefeller man all the way, as was most of his admininstration. And JIMMY CARTER was David's boy. The "conspirators" were working both sides of the street and I'll bet they literally did not care who won. Public policy would have been pretty much the same no matter who won.

But totally complete control and a one-world communist dictatorship? No, I don't think so. I am unconvinced.

Whether or not such a conspiracy is going to take over in the near future, my advice is still good. Public ignorance and the great cycles of history are going to produce certain financial results that would happen in any case. Even the Rockefellers are not as big as the great world-wide market place of money, commodities and ideas. We will have a hyper-inflation and a depression, whether or not there is a conspiracy. Gold, silver, diamonds, and small town real estate will be our principal safe financial havens during the struggles ahead. Just keep taking my basic advice and live your life positively. Elect good men to office who can help keep the Ship of State afloat. Perhaps those who believe they are omnipotent in manipulating the world's affairs will, themselves, drown in the flood of paper they are creating. Perhaps their own creation will be the Frankenstein monster which will destroy them.

I am opposed to any great concentration of power, whether it be government, manufacturing, banking, big oil, or big labor. I am offended by their ability to dictate public policies, such as the recognition of Red China, but I'm not about to attribute to them powers beyond those which I can demonstrate they have. In the meantime, I believe I can make forecasts with reasonable accuracy simply by studying the great cycles of history and the repetitive nature of man's folly. Economic forces will bury us all if we don't accommodate ourselves to the great tides of history. Even David Rockefeller must obey universal law, or like King Canute, he will find that if he tries to command the tide to bend to his will, he will get his feet wet.

CRANE, CONGRESSMAN PHILIP

(3/1/79) CONGRESSMAN PHILIP CRANE was our major speaker on the last day of our Annual Convention and he did something I've never heard any politician do. He demonstrated that this nation's economic system was based on fundamental religious principles. He explained how the principles embodied in the Ten Commandments were fundamental to the entire American system and that religion and faith in God were the basis of the American system. He did not, in any way, imply how those who do not have such faith could not be good Americans. Quite the contrary. He demonstrated, point by point, how faith in such principles, as embodied in the Ten Commandments, has made possible this greatest of all governmental and social experiments.

Congressman Crane is a handsome, articulate man, who looks at everything through the eyes of history. Being a historian by training, his speeches are salted with historical references. He has an incredible grasp of what was in the minds of the Founding Fathers when the Constitution was established.

He referred to the government as a parasite. There are beneficial parasites which assist us with digestion and actually help to fight disease, but then there are the tapeworms which steal our essence until we die. Government is just such a tapeworm. In reference to the anti-spending revolt, he said he did not object to a move to balance the budget (see: Balance The Budget Amendment) but he felt we first had to get a handle on the percentage of our Gross National Product that could be spent. Then we should go on to a Consitutional requirement to balance the budget. If we don't do it in that order, a balanced budget might be achieved by raising business taxes, not by cutting spending (my position exactly in the last issue). After that, he said, might come the Liberty Amendment, for which there is a groundswell of rising interest on the political right. This would require that the government to sell off all the business ventures which are in competition with private enterprise, abolish the Federal income tax, and use the taxes from the profits on these new privately-owned enterprises to offset the loss of revenues. Just the week before, I interviewed RONALD REAGAN for RUFF HOU$E, and I found him also to be a very thoughtful and articulate man. I found that he has a brilliant grasp of the issues. Senator Hatch, Congressman Crane, and Ronald Reagan all freely conceded that if we were to balance the budget and do the things necessary to save the economy, it would be painful indeed. We would have to be willing to bite the bullet in order to save the system from inflationary ruin. Governor Reagan said we need someone like Churchill who would demand from us blood, sweat and tears.

CRIME

(5/15/77)   During the last recession, unemployment in our central cities, particularly among Black and Chicano teenagers, was as high as 60 percent. And yet, the racial explosions so many people expected in our cities never materialized. Unemployment benefits had run out for many, and yet, somehow, we kept a lid on the potential festering violence in the cities.

It seems these people were not as unemployed as we thought. In fact, many of them were very lucratively employed in one of the great counter-cyclical industries. This industry is efficient and effective, primarily because it is not subject to Government regulations. It requires only skills that can be learned on the job, without college education, or even a high school diploma. It allows people to start on a shoestring and live the Horatio Alger dream of pulling oneself up by the bootstraps through hard work and willingness to take risks. It is a growth industry and provides a tremendous boost to the economy through the spending power of its employees, and it is the sole support of a large segment of our population. I am referring, of course, to crime.

If you want to know how big it is, just look at the FBI figures for the cost of crime in the cities. It provides employment for an army of policemen, firemen, insurance adjusters, doctors, nurses, medical technicians, hospital employees, middle-men, children, males, females, teenagers, adults, importers, money lenders, embezzlers, attorneys—in short—the whole living fabric of our great cities. I'm not talking about so-called "organized crime," the Mafia, the Syndicate, or whatever you want to call it, although they do manage to get their hand in much of the crime I'm talking about. I am referring to simple street crime. Your good old-fashioned American mugger, pimp, prostitute, numbers-runner, arsonist, bank robber, embezzler, forger, burglar, drug pusher, bookie and fence.

Have you ever wondered why it's so difficult to stamp out crime, despite all the money we spend trying to do it? It's simple. Crime is one of the last remaining totally free markets and, as such, it is so efficient that it's like a hardy perennial weed. Unless you get the whole root, it will continue to live and spread.

The ironic fact is, if we ever succeeded in suppressing crime, it would create an immense social burden. The government would have to extort more from us in taxes to hand out to those people who would be cut off from their criminal source of livelihood. And, if we ever stamp out crime, be prepared for riots.

Crime is tolerated by millions of our non-criminal citizens because they live from the benefits in some way or another.

There are only two ways to protect yourself from crime: Move from high crime areas and provide as much personal security as you possibly can.

Crime is so deeply inbedded in the fabric of our country, that we will never even slow its growth. In fact, it probably has reached "critical mass." It will snowball and become an even greater percentage of the GNP.

Now don't get the idea that I'm for crime. (Heaven forbid!) I'm merely making a social observation about an increasingly perverse world. (see: Sin-Tax, Taxes, Racial Problems, & Cities)

CURRENCY

FOREIGN VS. U.S.

(11/1/77) While traveling recently, I noticed in many foreign newspapers, including the *International English Language Paper* published daily in Zurich (one of the best newspapers I've ever read), that the world's monetary system is beginning to come unglued. The great reality we had to face every time we changed our money was how much the dollar had fallen that day. The Swiss franc has soared in value against the dollar; so has the Italian lira, the French franc, and the Japanese yen. For crying out loud, even the British pound has risen dramatically. About the only major currency that has not is the Canadian dollar, and that's only because their economy is sicker than ours.

Let me explain precisely what this means to Americans. If the dollar sinks, we will have to pay more for imported goods, including oil, because our dollar will buy less. Because we import so much, it will have a severe inflationary effect upon us, but it has a deflationary effect on other economies because they can buy American goods more cheaply and they get a better price for their commodities. I know what the Administration is trying to do. By allowing the dollar to sink, they are making American goods more attractive overseas and hoping that our exports will pick up and bring our balance of payments to a more favorable ratio. As I said in the last issue, this is an incredible gamble because it could trigger a massive world-wide monetary crisis if the dollar gets into really bad trouble. And we ain't seen nothin' yet!

Well, let me tell you what the October 31 issue of *BUSINESS WEEK* has to say about it, and if I may be permitted to dance on the grave for just a moment, I've been forecasting this for months.

"FOREIGN INVESTORS THRASH THE DOLLAR"

A boycott of U.S. dollar-denominated securities by Arab and Swiss international money managers is already under way in the Eurodollar market, and the stage is being set for a major flight from dollar securities in the U.S. as well. Not only is the Eurodollar bond market in a state of virtual paralysis, with prices off $40 to $50 a bond over the past month and investors fleeing into any paper denominated in Swiss francs, German marks, and Japanese yen, but now there is a growing possibility that funds may start flowing out of the U.S. itself into the London short-term money market.

So sharp has the shift in sentiment been against the dollar in recent weeks that the Saudis—traditional purchasers of U.S. government securities—reversed policy this week and bought, for the first time, $4 billion worth of Japanese government bonds. Other Middle East money fleeing the dollar is also flooding the gold market, pushing the price of that traditional hedge against uncertainty to a two-year high of $161.55.

U.S. corporations are getting caught in this flight from the dollar and are finding it harder to raise capital overseas. Just this week, City Investing Corp. had to withdraw a scheduled $25 million, 12-year Eurodollar bond issue even though it was offering a hefty 9% coupon. And Citicorp's two-part $300 million Eurodollar issue, the largest U.S. corporate sale in the Euromarkets in recent years, is now trading about $40 per bond lower than when it was offered on Sept. 30.

Behind the massive shift of money away from the dollar overseas is the growing double peril of rising U.S. short-term interest rates coupled with a declining U.S. currency—with no end in sight for either. Fueled by an exploding money supply that the Federal Reserve has yet to restrain, short-term interest rates in the U.S. have jumped by nearly two percentage points in recent months. Six-month Treasury bills now yield 6.81% compared with only 5% in June.

At the same time, the U.S. dollar continues to steadily drop lower. Since January, the dollar has fallen 6% against the Swiss franc, 4% against the German mark, and a huge 16% against the Japanese yen.

The Arabs are getting a double whammy, because not only is ordinary inflation chewing at the value of their dollar holdings, but the value of their dollars is sinking in relation to other currencies. They have only two ways to protect themselves. One is to buy gold (which they are now doing to such a degree that even the last die-hards who wouldn't admit they might do such a thing have to concede they are doing it), or they can switch into stronger currencies. The only currency that is sufficiently strong and has enough money in circulation to allow them to do so on a large scale is the Japanese yen, and to a lesser degree, the British pound and the Swiss franc, and that is precisely what they are doing.

This kind of action on their part can destroy the American dollar, and bring temporary prosperity to these other nations who are the beneficiaries of Arab buying and investment. Eventually, as our economy sinks into a shambles, as investors bail out of bank deposits and U.S. bonds and all of the kinds of investments that are threatened by massive Arab removal, you then will have a full-fledged, world-wide monetary panic.

To summarize:

1. The international monetary system is in great disarray. Its collapse will eventually be felt by every citizen of the world.

2. The cost of imported goods will rise sharply, kindling more price inflation.

3. The banking system is coming into jeopardy, and you should only have emergency funds in the bank in short-term deposits only, as bank troubles could come with devastating suddenness. You should have on hand, concealed at home, enough small bills to get you through six months of installment and contractual obligations.

4. Also you just might see some spectacular and puzzling gyrations in the fortunes of our great banks. There are some interesting opposing forces at work. Allowing the dollar to sink jeopardizes the banks by giving foreign investors an incentive to bail out. By the same token, it strengthens the economies of the poor countries to which our banks have loaned so much money. It's a deadly race between the forces.

(11/1/76) HARRY BROWNE and others have written extensively about the value of trading in foreign currencies, particularly those which are gold-backed, such as the Swiss franc. Harry Browne was right in the past, as the devaluation of the dollar did result in substantial profits to those who made the right moves at the right time. But with the war against gold as a monetary metal, this method of capital preservation is very risky, and should only be indulged in by those who are prepared to become quite sophisticated in foreign exchange. I don't believe this is any place for the amateur.

I would also be concerned about having my money overseas in a Swiss bank. When economic dislocations occur, nations often place restrictions on the movement of capital across international boundaries. It might be difficult for you to repatriate your money, if we should have some sudden problems. I would prefer to keep it here and not speculate in foreign currencies at this time.

(11/1/78)   When you read in the newspaper that the "dollar is sinking," you feel uneasy but you don't know what it means to your personal life. Let me explain. The dollar is not just the currency you and I spend. It is the world's "reserve currency." This means that nations settle their balance-of-payments debits and credits using our dollars. It means a lot of our dollars are employed in things other than commerce, savings or individual investments. If the dollar sinks far enough so that it is totally rejected as the world's reserve currency, there will be a tremendous amount of unemployed dollars floating around to be gotten rid of, and the decline of the dollar we've seen so far would be nothing compared to what would happen if all of those dollars find themselves on the loose. Moves are already underway to establish a new international reserve currency. The Common Market in Europe is planning to use the E.C.U., which is a computerized accounting unit based on a "basket" of currencies, plus gold. And the E.C.U. might be the world's next reserve currency. That doesn't mean it will replace dollars for circulation purposes in the United States, but it does mean that all those unemployed dollars will be there to break the dollar market. I believe the dollar has had it as the world's dominant currency, despite current corrections. This means runaway inflation. The financial mechanism of recession and depression has already hit its stride.

(11/15/78)   The Big Heist

Now that I've had a chance to absorb and further contemplate the Carter "SAVE-THE-DOLLAR" plan, I'd like to tell you what I believe happened and why, and what the effect will be.

We have just been the victims of the biggest heist in history —somewhere in the neighborhood of $40 billion, and maybe a lot more if we ever uncover all of the secret agreements behind the Carter action.

I believe that our actions in "support of the dollar" were imposed upon us by the German, the Japanese, the Swiss, and the Arabs. They were accumulating ever-increasing amounts of depreciating dollars and taking horrendous, ever-mounting losses, and they saw no end to the Great American Inflation, so they had to find some way of bailing out. I'm not quite sure which weapon they used. They could have either threatened to dump our Treasury bills, of which they own about 23 percent, or simply made a final firm decision to reject the dollar as the world's reserve currency and substitute the E.C.U., which would have given us a flood of dollars to contend with. I believe they designed the plan.

If you ever want to know who conned whom, just look and see who benefits. I'd like to outline the benefits for our traditional "friends," the Arabs, the Germans, the Japanese and the Swiss, so you can understand the universal applause from abroad.

1.   They have managed to unload 30 billion depreciating dollars, after forcing us to take action which caused them to rise in value by 10 percent.

2.   They have managed to get us in debt to them for $30 billion in their strong, hard currencies.

3.   We have driven down the price of gold by 15 percent or more, and then placed our suddenly-cheaper gold on the world market where it will be snapped up by the central banks and commercial banks of the Germans, the Japanese, the Swiss and the Arabs at fire sale prices. And if you don't think they will snap it up avidly, you haven't been watching their past behavior. If the first 1½ million ounce gold auction on the 3rd Tuesday in December is not fully subscribed, it will be because they are expecting still lower prices. Once they have perceived the bottom is near, they will snap up everything in sight.

Recently at the New Orleans Conference I heard an address by WILLIAM REES-MOOG, the financial editor for *THE LONDON TIMES*. In his brilliant address, he pointed out the sheer stupidity of our gold policy. It is our ONLY monetary reserve—worth approximately $60 billion. There are some $300 additional billion in gold reserves held by central banks of foreign nations. In our insane desire to cut the dollar loose from gold so that there is no obstacle to the money creation process, we have managed to drive down the value of our only monetary asset and sell big chunks of it at depressed prices, while convincing ourselves that this is "support of the dollar." It's insane, and although it will achieve the government's objectives in the short-term by distorting the signals of the marketplace, it can only accelerate the eventual collapse of the dollar. We are not only stripping ourselves of our only protection against the inflation process, but we are in the early stages of preparing a guarantee that when it has all come down around our ears, we will not have the necessary reserve assets to establish a sound currency for a fresh start.

(12/15/78) Remember recently when I said the Carter "Save-the-Dollar-Plan" was forced upon us by the Germans, the Arabs, the Swiss, and the Japanese, using the threat of their dollar holding or T-bills? I said the plan did not have the Carter hallmark of indecisiveness and I had reason to believe it was devised by others. Well, EVANS and NOVAK, the *WASHINGTON POST* syndicated columnists, have confirmed my view of this "desperate move by desperate men" (as R.E. McMASTER says). Let me quote from a recent column.

> "Near panic" on Wall Street the week of October 23, possibly instigated by Saudi Arabia as a move to force the U.S. to defend the dollar, was the real explanation for President Carter's belated dollar-saving actions on November 1.
>
> The panic conditions were created when up to several billion dollars worth of Arab investments in what are called Certificates of Deposits (CD's) came due and the cash was demanded by the Arabs—most of it from one bank, MORGAN GUARANTY of New York City and its European branches.
>
> The effect of the Arab decision to liquidate this huge investment instead of rolling it over by buying new C.D.'s was electrifying and potentially devastating. It forced Morgan Guaranty to scour other New York banks for cash. Worse, it put the focus on the long-dreaded spectre of the Arabs liquidating tons of billions of their holdings and converting the dollar receipts into stronger foreign currencies, such as the German mark or the Swiss franc.
>
> Analysts have differing interpretations of the true reasons for this unexpected-crisis-making liquidation. Some believe that the Saudis, whose immense dollar resources from the sale of Mid-East oil make them bankers of the world, were signaling President Carter: shore up the dollar fast! A falling dollar makes it far more difficult for the Saudi to resist pressure from other oil producing states for a steep increase in oil prices later this year.
>
> Other analysts say the Saudis were caught short of cash and

converted the C.D.'s because they had to. Whatever the true explanation, the crisis created in the money markets, described by one insider as a "near panic," forced the Treasury Secretary, W. Michael Blumenthal, into action. The result was President Carter's defense-of-the-dollar actions announced November 1.

I still say it was the biggest heist in history by the Arabs, the Swiss, the German, and the Japanese. They got rid of our dollars at inflated prices, and they were able to buy our gold at fire-sale prices.

CURRENCY CRISIS

(1/15/78) The world monetary system does not have any fixed standard by which you can measure the rise or fall of a currency, like our long-lost gold standard. Currencies "float" up or down relative to each other based on the law of supply-and-demand. There is a huge currency market, made up of (1) governments settling up their accounts with each other, (2) speculators hoping to make a profit by switching from one currency to another as they rise and fall, and (3) multinational corporations exchanging foreign currencies for their "home" currency to bring their profits into their corporate treasuries, and a myriad of transactions for a million different reasons. The dollar has fallen against the Swiss franc, the German mark, the Italian lira, and the Japanese yen, and that is a sick joke when you consider Italy. The major factor is that we are sending more money abroad than we are bringing home—importing more than we are exporting. This is partly due to the high price of oil.

Now, the Treasury Department and the Federal Reserve announced that they will step in to "support the dollar" by using foreign currencies to buy up those excess dollars, dry up the supply and stabilize the dollar. We also have agreements by which we can borrow currencies of foreign countries to use to buy dollars, but we have to repay those deutschemarks or Swiss francs at some future time. We can only temporarily arrest the slide. The Administration hopes that before those resources are exhausted, the fallen dollar will have made American exports less expensive for foreigners who hold dollars, and will have made foreign exports to the United States more expensive, so we will stop buying them. That's why they have allowed the dollar to fall until now. The price of Datsuns and Toyotas has been raised three times since June, 1977, so Step 1 of the government strategy has begun to work. There are two unresolved questions, however: (1) Will it work soon enough to stabilize the dollar, before the government's ability to support the dollar has been exhausted? And (2) if it doesn't, will the entire world monetary system come unglued? The dollar is the world's reserve currency.

The whole system would have come unglued a long time ago if the Arabs had not put their money in short term deposits in New York banks. Now that is in doubt.

The press just reported that President Carter had told Energy Secretary JAMES SCHLESINGER that Saudi Arabia, France and Iran are particularly concerned that excessive U.S. energy imports are damaging to the value of the dollar. If those people stop wanting dollars, we'll have a full-fledged currency crisis which would be the beginning of international economic chaos, resulting in the worst depression this nation has ever seen.

Our government announced its decision to support the dollar immediately after the President met with the Saudi Arabians. I think they scared the wits out of him and threatened to withdraw their deposits from the New York banks. It took only 24 hours for us to announce our new policy and actually begin to act.

This affects you in two ways. (1) You will pay more for your foreign television, a pair of shoes, a small car, or that electronic equipment. (2) The falling stock market is a direct reflection of the decline of the dollar; in particular, the inability of industry to keep up with foreign competition because it cannot modernize its plants.

U.S. CURRENCY—A BRIEF HISTORY

(9/15/78) A subscriber sent me an interesting summary of what's happening to our money. Without these changes I will be describing, a German-type inflation would be impossible. With these changes, a German-type inflation becomes the odds-on favorite.

Here's how we went from uncorruptible gold-backed money to our present backed-by-nothing dollar.

In 1928, the government was printing "gold certificates." On the front of the certificate there was a statement which said, "This certifies that there has been deposited in the Treasury of the United States of America $10 in gold payable to the bearer on demand."

With that kind of a dollar, the government had to be terribly cautious about how many we created, or it could lose all of its gold to claims against it. These were basically warehouse receipts for gold and were universally accepted. In fact, paper money was created because citizens found gold and silver too bulky to carry around. These certificates were "as good as gold" because of their 100% backing.

A similar FEDERAL RESERVE NOTE also issued in 1928 said essentially the same thing: The United States of America will pay the bearer on demand $10.00 redeemable in gold on demand at the United States Treasury." Basically, it meant you could exchange your Federal Reserve Note for American gold certificates and those certificates would be redeemed at the Treasury. However, at this crucial point in our monetary history, the Federal Reserve concluded that because it was unlikely that everyone would ask for his gold at the same time, the Federal Reserve could issue more currency than there was gold on deposit. At that time the Federal Reserve was required to maintain only 40% gold backing and could issue 2-1/2 times as many Federal Reserve notes as the Treasury had gold to back them up, in effect, a 250% dilution of the currency.

There is an important difference between these two pieces of currency. While the $10 gold certificate was a certificate of deposit with $10 in gold coin at the Treasury which the bearer could claim on demand, this Federal Reserve note was just what it says—a note—an obligation of debt. There was not $10 in gold coin on deposit but only $4, and the bearer could only claim his $10 provided no more than 40% of the people wished to do so at any one time.

The dollar evolved further with the Series 1950 Federal Reserve Note, promising, "The United States of America will pay to the bearer on demand $10 redeemable in lawful money at the United States Treasury." No gold at all!

Also the wording, include the promise to "redeem for lawful money," was reduced in size so it was more difficult to read. You notice the subtle difference between being redeemable in gold and in "lawful money." Now, theoretically, that's the same thing because the Constitution defines gold and silver coin as lawful money. These notes did not yet claim that the currency itself was money.

Now we look at the Series 1963 Federal Reserve Note when the debauching of the currency was complete. There is no promise to pay the bearer $10 on demand. There is no promise to redeem for anything of value. There are no promises at all. All pretense that our paper currency was redeemable for lawful money was dropped. All it says is "legal tender for all debts, public and private." Gold certificates were discontinued in 1933 and silver certificates in 1962, leaving only Federal Reserve notes in circulation, and with the printing of these Federal Reserve notes, all promises were abandoned 15 years ago. They simply declared that this piece of paper, by some mystic process, was $10 all by itself. This is called "fiat" money

—currency by government order.

Up until 1964, our dimes, quarters and half-dollars were required by law to contain 90 percent pure silver. In 1965 all silver was removed from quarters and dimes and the silver content in half dollars was reduced to only 40 percent. By 1971 even that final small link with lawful money was done away with. Now we are told that our backed-by-nothing currency is "legal tender for all debts, public and private."

The Federal Reserve carries all Federal Reserve notes on its balance sheet as liabilities of the United States government. A "liability" means you are required to give somebody something in return for the paper you hold. If I hold your note, it says what you are going to pay me upon maturity. The liability aspect of money is a laughable farce, because they do not specify the form of payment and it has no maturity date. As I understand it, a note is a promise to pay, so take it to the Federal Reserve Bank and ask them to pay you. They will ask you what kind of change you want, and they will give you more fiat money.

The fascinating thing is that few of these changes were brought about by legislation. How does that grab you?

In the real world, money is worth whatever someone is willing to give you in exchange for it. As of now, people are willing to give you valuable things in exchange for this currency, so it has value. If you don't think it's worth anything, I'll be happy to take any of yours off your hands. However, the creeping awareness of the dilution of our currency, and the non-monetary nature of our money, is reflected in the eroding value of the dollar, both overseas and at home. As the government supply of unbacked currency increases, and the value of each dollar drops, a landslide can develop as it did in Germany, Argentina, Peru, Chile, Brazil, China, France (after the revolution), etc., until eventually the basic structural factors that keep inflation reasonably under control are absolutely overwhelmed by an acceleratng, panicky loss of confidence in the currency. Eventually, rising prices create their own cannibalistic demand for more money, and cause and effect become blurred.

(12/15/77)   Potpourri

Q. Franz Pick says we are going to have a new currency and our money will soon be exchanged for it on a 20-1 basis. How will that affect the purchasing power of my dollars?

A. I don't know how Dr. Pick came to that conclusion, but such an event will only occur after a real runaway inflationary spiral

—something like Germany of 1923, and it probably wouldn't be 20-1, it would be 1000-1! To say it is imminent is absurd. That will only happen in the last stages of an inflationary currency collapse and that's still out in the future.

Q. Could we have a devaluation of the dollar?

A. With floating rates, and money severed from gold, currencies devalue themselves by falling in relation to other currencies. We have just had an unannounced devaluation of the dollar. It's been allowed to fall in relation to other currencies. Mechanically, governments do not formally devalue. They merely stop supporting their currency by refraining from buying it in the marketplace and letting market forces work. They used to devalue by raising the official price of gold. It doesn't work that way anymore.

D

DEMOCRACY

(11/15/76)   Cycle of Democracy

The following was written by Professor Alexander Fraser Tytler shortly before our original 13 colonies gained their independence from Great Britain. He was speaking of the History of the Athenian Republic some 2000 years before, but it has application today.

> A democracy cannot exist as a permanent form of government. It can only exist until the voters discover that they can vote themselves largesse from the public treasury.
>
> From that moment on, the majority always votes for the candidates promising them the most benefits from the public treasury, with the result that a democracy always collapses over loose fiscal policy, always followed by a dictatorship.
>
> The average age of the world's greatest civilizations has been 200 years. These nations have progressed through this sequence:
>
> From bondage to spiritual faith; from spiritual faith to great courage; from courage to liberty; from liberty to abundance; from abundance to selfishness; from selfishness to complacency; from complacency to apathy; from apathy to dependence; from dependency back again into bondage.

HJR comment: It is my opinion that our nation has reached the apathy stage, as witnessed in the lack of interest in the last election. In fact, it appears that much of our populace has moved already into dependency and certain portions of our economy and society are now in bondage.

DEREGULATION OF GAS

(1/15/77)   Recently, I made the point deregulation of natural gas prices would end up benefiting the country because:

125

1. It would break the oil cartel.

2. It would stimulate exploration. Oil and gas are often found together.

3. If prices were allowed to rise naturally, the potential market-ability of alternate energy sources, such as solar heating, geothermal heat, etc., would be worth a look from major corporations, as it would narrow the price gap. If prices rose, we would suddenly get religion about conservation and alternate energy. Declining use would drive prices back down.

4. There are vast known supplies of gas and oil that could solve our energy problems for the next 600 years, if it became profitable to search for it.

Look at Carter's irrational "solutions." We have just created a DEPARTMENT OF ENERGY with a budget of $10. billion a year. The primary purpose of the DOE is to keep the oil companies from making big profits. The DOE Budget is over 3 ½ times the total profits of all of the oil companies! Mr. Carter wants government to rake off the oil and gas companies additional profits created by allowing the price to rise, bcause he doesn't think they deserve the profits. What did government do to deserve them? Oil companies are responsible to their stock holders. Stock holders demand growth. You only get growth through reinvestment and exploration. Government will take its tax bite from profits.

Right now, the price structure of oil is two-tiered. Domestic oil is controlled at a very low price. Foreign oil is much more expensive, but much more profitable. Consequently, the oil companies are spending billions for overseas development, and profits are transferred to their overseas exploration and development divisions. They pay taxes to foreign governments and, under present U.S. tax law, take credit for those taxes against their U.S. taxes. This set-up has given them the incentive to increase our nation's dependence upon foreign oil, while cutting the U.S. tax take. Allowing domestic prices to rise through de-regulation will make further development of domestic reserves more profitable, and the oil and gas companies will not go to Indonesia to develop expensive sources of liquified natural gas, or travel to the continental shelf off Vietnam to drill for more oil. There's plenty here!

Any Economics 101 student understands that the market price of energy will always be geared to what we have to pay for it abroad. Carter's program will create shortages, increase our foreign dependency and accelerate the decline of the dollar by forcing us to continue to transfer $40 billion of our national wealth each year to OPEC.

Remember, Carter is a member of the Trilateral Commission (see: Conspiracy), which was formed to make the world safe for multi-national banking and large multinational companies, including Big Oil. He has stated publicly that the Commission trained him and gave him his foreign policy expertise. It gave him a platform and the financing by which he became President. The oil companies are making all the appropriate noises in favor of deregulation, but if you understand the economics of *oil* and *banking*, you will understand that high priced foreign oil is a tremendous windfall for both of them. The banks are making fortunes loaning to insolvent countries whose insolvency is caused by the quadrupling of energy prices, then they created the INTERNATIONAL MONETARY FUND to bail them out if the countries can't pay up. We have even given away the Panama Canal with a Treaty that will give Panama revenues so they can pay off their loans to the American banks—and not by accident!

I suggest we throw the oil companies to the wolves of competition and let them fight it out in the free marketplace. The natural economics of the oil business will force them to develop our huge domestic reserves and eventually free us from our dependence upon foreign oil.

This may all sound pretty cosmic, and maybe you don't feel you can apply it to your personal life, but you are being asked to make economic decisions when you elect your representatives, and next year is an election year. That's where our political money and time should be spent. That's as much a part of your survival behavior as the storage of food or the purchase of coins.

(11/1/77) Europe lives in the same energy world we do, and is far more vulnerable to a cut-off of imports, but they have dealt with it in some interesting ways.

I've been advocating the deregulation of oil and natural gas prices. Jimmy Carter wants to gradually raise the price of gasoline by 5 cents or 6 cents a gallon over the next four years to encourage conservation. Well, every time I filled up our gas tank in France, Italy, Luxembourg, Belgium and Switzerland, it cost me close to $2.00 a gallon, and yet Europe has coped. High prices have forced them to conserve gas by buying little cars (including one two-cylinder model that's illegal here) and by riding the subway, or by buying mopeds by the zillions. Everywhere we went, even in the busiest of city streets, there were mopeds all over the place, getting a hundred miles to the gallon.

There is no 55 mile per hour speed limit. There are speed limits, but I didn't think anybody has ever reached them. It's at least 130 kilometers per hour on most of the great superhighways—about 80 miles per hour. Allowing the price of gas to seek its own level has solved the problem naturally, without a loss of liberty. This is a continent-wide phenomenon, expensive gas, and reasonable answers. As a result, most of the countries we visited have been able to carry on normal life and commerce, even though many of their economies are basically very sick, but I don't think we can blame that on the energy crisis. There are a lot of other things terribly wrong with the economic and political processes of these countries.

If we were to allow the price of gas to rise to its normal level in the U.S.A., even $2.00 a gallon, sooner or later, the big automobiles would be off the streets. Most of us would be voluntarily driving small cars and riding mopeds, and Mr. Carter would eventually have free-market inspired conservation without repressive, coercive measures. Let the wealthy drive their big cars and pay $2.00 a gallon and get 10 miles to the gallon; there aren't many of them anyway. (see: Price & Wage Controls)

(2/15/79) I'm still convinced that if we deregulated natural gas tomorrow, the price would shoot up temporarily, stimulating new drilling and exploration. New supplies would drive the price back down again. Of course, the senators and congressmen from cold states will scream that the temporary price increases are damaging to their constituents. But until we act, we cannot unleash the natural gas industry to produce the non-polluting and ultimately inexpensive natural gas that could forever end our dependence on foreign oil.

DIAMONDS

INTERVIEW WITH DAVID B. JOHNSTON

(6/1/77) For a long time I have been intrigued with diamonds as a hedge against inflation, and especially depression.

After you have bought your emergency food supplies, reduced your personal indebtedness, and bought your silver and gold coins for survival purposes, many of you will still have liquid assets. We have suggested Treasury bills, real estate, gold and silver. Diamonds may very well be added to your portfolio, if you have $5,000 or more to invest.

While researching the subject, I became acquainted with DAVID
B. JOHNSTON, President of DIAMOND FINANCIAL SERVICES,
INC., San Jose, California, a financial counseling firm using diamonds as an investment medium. After doing our homework and
assuring ourselves that Dave is an OK guy, we decided to interview
him and find out all you need to know about diamonds.

HJR: Dave, how did you get into the diamond business?

DBJ: I have been a stock broker and investment counselor since
1967. In 1975 I became affiliated with a group which has been
in the diamond business for several decades. There were very
few people who qualified as investment professionals and
gemologists. So I was trained by the GEMOLOGICAL IN-
STITUTE OF AMERICA as a Certified Diamond Appraiser
and gemologist, and that, coupled with the investment (and
financial planning) background, has created a marriage of
those two worlds.

HJR: How do diamonds fit into *THE RUFF TIMES* philosophy?

DBJ: look at the (investment grade) value record since 1934, and you
don't see any down-tick in price. Diamonds have provided
price stability over the years despite inflation, devaluation of
currencies, etc. They have helped people to move wealth from
one country to another. The Israelis treat the diamond industry
as somewhat of a religion, as it bought many of them their
freedom during times of persecution and chaos.

If we believe that inflation is with us to stay, even the
"normal" 3 to 4% rising to double-digits in the more extreme
years, diamond prices will appreciate accordingly.)

HJR: *FORBES* magazine did an article on April 15, 1977, which
states, "There was a big break in the retail market between
1959 and 1962, when prices of the better stones fell as much as
25%." How does that square with your statement that there's
not been a down-tick in the market?

DBJ: They're talking about retail prices! Retail prices fluctuate
because the markups are anywhere from 100% to 300%, and
people buy less engagement rings during time of economic
uncertainty. I was talking about wholesale prices.

HJR: What happened to retail prices in 1973-1974 when the inflation
rates were well over 10%?

DBJ: Well, a lot of people didn't buy engagement rings. However,
the Japanese were active in the wholesale diamond market and

the wholesale prices for one-carat gems nearly doubled in that two-year period. Diamonds are concentrated, and values have been so stable compared to the lira and the franc, that Europeans have been buying at wholesale in huge amounts in the past few years.

HJR: "Wholesale" is a rather elusive term. There are boiler shop telephone operations who claim they are selling wholesale. Are they? And if they are not, what are they doing?

DBJ: Real wholesale prices are those prices offered by distributors that sell to diamond brokers and manufacturing jewelers on the fourteen Bourses and diamond trading clubs in Antwerp, New York, Bombay, and various other places. In the New York Diamond Dealers Club, you have 1500 daily trading members.

HJR: Are you buying them from the same sources as the distributors so you can afford to sell at distributor prices to small investors and still make money?

DBJ: That's right. Wholesale mark-ups range from two percent, if you have a trade between wholesalers, to 20% maximum. The retail mark-up would be from 100% to 300% above that.

HJR: If you were to sell diamonds to our *RUFF TIMES* subscribers, how would that price compare with one of the telephone sales operators, or to a retail jewelry store?

DBJ: An "investment grade diamond" would be within 10% of the distributor's list price and at 45% to 50% of what a retail store would sell it for. The telephone sales operators have very high marketing overhead, huge mailing and telephone costs, expensive literature, and salesmen's commissions.

HJR: Would you mind giving our subscribers a brief two paragraph primer on where diamonds come from, how they are sold, and how prices are set?

DBJ? DeBeers Consolidated Mines, Ltd., controls 40% of the world's mining and 80% of the world's marketing. That means that 20% of all available gems are sold through non-syndicate sources and turned over to "rough diamond" brokers and large C.S.O. (Central Selling Organization) customers. They, in turn, are sold through the clubs and Bourses, and then to manufacturing jewelers who will mount them and then sell them to retailers. Now, up to the club and Bourse level, there is usually a two to five percent markup. From there to the retail store in a mounted ring, it will be anywhere from 100% to 300%. We buy directly from syndicate sources, including the largest non-

100 percent to 300 percent. We buy directly from syndicate sources, including the largest non-syndicate purveyor of "rough" or polished diamonds. We also buy at estate sales and we can buy rough goods and have them cut. Also, we are affiliated with five polishing factories in Tel Aviv with over 150 cutters and their own mines.

HJR: How does the DeBeers syndicate control diamond prices?

DBJ: Their pricing policy is really interesting. They consider currencies, devaluation, and inflation rates every six weeks, and they bump up prices accordingly. For instance, after the Japanese left the market for one-carat stones in 1974-75, DeBeers actually withdrew goods from the market. During the depression of 1929, diamonds suffered less than any other investable asset, simply because DeBeers sent people to estate sales to bid prices up. They have a $5.5 billion asset base and their bottom line is growing at 35 percent per year. They have the financial clout to be able to control the supply and demand.

HJR: What if South Africa became a Black Marxist state and decided to dump diamonds in the marketplace, bypassing the DeBeers syndicate. Could DeBeers still manipulate that marketplace?

DBJ: There's only one safe position during times of South African political turmoil, and that is as an owner of diamonds. Let me compare this with another Marxist state—Russia. Russia, for the past ten years has had a contract with DeBeers, and even though their production is outstripping many of the South African producers, they still opt to move their goods through DeBeers. Trying to glut the market with their own goods would merely damage their own financial capability.

HJR: What should an investor expect from his investment in terms of appreciation and liquidity?

DBJ: He should expect not to liquidate the stone, unless he absolutely has to, within two years, simply because that isn't the nature of the market. He should not expect any income. It's a long-term-hold type of investment that will appreciate at least 50 percent better than the riskless bond rate, or, in excess of the world-wide inflation rate.

HJR: How does one make sure that he has bought a quality diamond?

DBJ: The premium stone is from one to three carats, produced from two to six carat "roughs," which are becoming more and more scarce, even though a lot of selling organizations are selling smaller stones to smaller investors to hit "blue collar" America. These are 30 to 60 point stones used in engagement rings.

HJR: What are points?

DBJ: One hunded points make one carat. One carat weighs 1/142 of an ounce. The price of these smaller stones is predicated upon the jewelry demand. The best investment value is in the larger, rarer stones. They would be "H" or better in color, meaning a white stone. They should be VSI or "very slightly imperfect," 1st grade, or better. This is not to say that stones that are lower in color than "H," for instance "I" and "J," are bad investments, because they appreciate likewise, but they don't possess the rarity and potential of the higher quality stone.

Two stones of the same weight, the same color and the same clarity, can vary 40 percent in price, becaue the stone is not cut to ideal proportions as determined by TOLKOUSKY, who developed a precise mathematical formula to determine the proper cutting angles so that the gem would disperse fire to the eye. Improperly cut stones will virtually lie dead on the table next to stones that possess their own little fire. You will not get any two certified appraisers to come up with the same value. However, if they are adequately trained with proper pricing materials and proper equipment, they should never vary more than one color, one clarity, a tenth of a millimeter in measurement and a half a point in weight. That is the only tolerance which we guarantee. If a person wishes to check, he can either send the stone directly to the Gemological Institute of America by registered mail, or go to a current, well-equipped gemologist, preferably one who doesn't sell stones.

HJR: Who certifies your stones?

DBJ: Our staff has been trained by the Gemological Institute of America. A member of management will double-check the color and clarity. We assume that measurements are fairly mechanical and accurate. There will be a double-check, and an appraisal will accompany the gem, over one of our signatures, within those tolerances mentioned.

HJR: Doesn't the Gemological Institute of America certify your gems?

DBJ: They don't have the capacity to keep up with the volume of stones from even the jewelry industry. The more valuable stones, and those stones that go into trusteed plans, are doubly certified by the Gemological Institute of America.

HJR: How does one know that the stone which he is buying is the one which was certified?

DBJ: It's very easy to match up stones with the certificates. If you compare the weight and shape of the stone, round, brilliant, whatever it might be, plus the depth and the diameter, there is one chance in ten thousand that there can ever be a substitution. Take it to any jeweler who possesses a millimicrometer or a leverage guage and ask for verification of the depth, diameter and the weight of the stone.

HJR: How much does someone need before investing in diamonds?

DBJ: The minimum purchase is $3000. Generally, no more than 20% of investable assets should be in diamonds. In the self-directed profit-sharing or pension plans, the percentage may be much greater, depending upon the cash flow.

HJR: Can you actually set up a Keogh or an IRA?

DBJ: We can establish Keogh plans, profit-sharing, pensions, charitable and educational trusts, but not an IRA.

HJR: *FORBES* quotes Lazare Kaplan, a famous diamond cutter, who said, "A diamond is to enjoy all your life and then maybe sell for more money. If you keep it in a vault, a diamond is just another piece of goods." Why do they seem to go out of their way to try to tell us that diamonds are not investments?

DBJ: They are retailers who know diamonds, but not investments. Anyone who has bought gems with verified quality at, or about the wholesale price, has never lost money in diamonds, if they've held on.

HJR: Robert Crowningshield, the New York Director of the Gemological Institute of America says that diamonds are not an investment unless you are a promoter or "very anxious like a Rhodesian farm owner." That fascinated me because our subscribers are "anxious, like Rhodesian farm owners." And that's precisely why we have interviewed you today. We feel that diamonds have the potential for preseving assets through a real bust, and doing well in good times, too. This same *FORBES* article declared gold dead when it was about $107 an ounce, and indicated that only the paranoid people who thought that the world might run into economic troubles, would buy gold. Would you like to add anything else?

DBJ: Just one point. There are virtually no organizations that are qualified investment counselors, as well as having been trained by the Gemological Institute of America. A sound investment firm would adhere to the principles of proper financial planning along with the professionalism that comes through use of copyrighted price materials and knowledge of the specific elements of diamond grading. We have married the two. The record speaks for itself. Never a down-tick in rough goods or in goods at wholesale since 1934.

HJR: Thank you, Dave. I would like to add just a few observations of my own.

1. Diamonds are only for people who have done all of the other basic things first.

2. No more than 30% of your assets should be in diamonds and you probably ought to have several thousand dollars available for diamond investment before you even consider it.

3. This is a long-term inflation and depression hedge. It's not for anybody who wants excitement because it won't provide much. Most of the thrills on the roller coaster come when you are on the way down.

If you want to know more from Dave, or his associates, call collect from California (415) 837-8805, or toll free from the other states (800) 227-1590.

SYNTHETIC DIAMONDS

(1/15/78) One member called in and described a "true-bright" diamond he said he could buy for a very low price. Unfortunately, it turned out to be a synthetic diamond, which is chemically identical, but a heck of a lot less valuable. The seller used GIA terms to describe it, and those terms simply don't apply to synthetic diamonds.

GUARANTEED REPURCHASE AGREEMENT

(1/15/78) There are several firms that offer a "guaranteed repurchase" of their diamonds. The SEC has ruled that a guaranteed repurchase agreement is legally the same as offering a security, and would fall under the SEC securities laws, and any such firm would be guilty of the crime of offering an unregistered security. There are indications that the SEC will begin to enforce this ruling with diamond companies, and, of course, that means they won't be offering that kind of agreement anymore. RELIANCE has been successful in brokering diamonds for customers at the fair market price, which is generally at or above the price you paid for it, with a 2% commission, if you need to sell out. However, I am not recommending diamonds for in-and-out-purchase. They should only be sold when paper money is worth more than diamonds. One member purchased diamonds a few years ago and recently called the firm he bought them from to exercise his repurchase option. It was one of the largest investment diamond firms in the business. He asked them first for a current quote on what he could buy the same diamond for, and was quoted $11,500. Then he asked what he would be paid for the same diamond if he were to sell it. They offered him $8200, less their 20% commission. This is unethical, because the spread between buy and sell should never exceed 10%. Of course, if you want to sell the diamond yourself through advertising, the difference between what you paid for it, and a fair retail price, is so great that you can offer it at a substantial discount in the marketplace and still make some money.

THE "LOW-BALL"

(4/1/78) I have another problem. I know that most RETAIL JEWELERS are vigorously opposed to the investment diamond business, because it does not allow room for retail markups, but I didn't realize how wide-spread the "low-ball" really was. It's almost universal. Over and over again, our friends have bought a diamond from Reliance, gone into a retail jeweler and been told the retail value of the diamond was below the wholesale price which they paid. This is not just an infrequent occurrence. When it happens, I suggest you tell them the following: "Wonderful. I can get my money back from Reliance Products as I have a money-back guarantee. I want to order an equivalent diamond of the same quality and size from you at the price you have indicated."

If they agree, you have found an incredible bargain and I suggest you take advantage of it, if they are reputable and will supply a GIA or USGS certificate with the stone. Our experience has been that the dealer has, in very instance, backed down.

I have personally arranged for the GIA to appraise some of these stones as to color, weight, clarity, etc., and they have checked out each time.

I'm sure there are some good retail jewelers, but right now, I'm terribly disillusioned with the whole industry. I know about five jewelers and I trust two of them, and right now I'm looking at the whole industry with a jaundiced eye.

This has caused me a lot of personal grief. Maybe I'm still too thin-skinned, but it does bother me when my integrity is challenged so I've decided to go firmly on the offensive on this matter.

(1/15/78)   Here's my favorite story on the subject. One of our members wrote me a lengthy letter complaining about a diamond she had purchased from RELIANCE. She had taken it to a local jeweler who said the tip was broken, and gave her a retail price quote substantially below the WHOLESALE price she had paid to RELIANCE. I requested that she send the diamond directly to me and I sent an office messenger with the diamond to be independently appraised. Even under 30 power magnification (normal lab analysis is 10 power) the diamond was perfect. My appraiser said the diamond was worth more than the price she had paid on the wholesale market and, of course, to verify, we sent it to the GEMOLOGICAL INSTITUTE OF AMERICA to make sure the initial specifications were accurate. The GIA verified it exactly.

This is an example of jewelers "low-balling" the investment diamond business. It is a great threat to them. If you want to have a diamond appraised, take it to a qualified gemologist for your own independent appraisal. Stay away from jewelry store salesmen.

Diamonds rank with gold and real estate as hedges against inflation and depression. Don't hesitate to buy them, but you are an amateur swimming in a pool full of sharks. Deal with the recommended firms, and we will stand in back of your purchase.

RETAILERS VS. WHOLESALERS

(1/78)   In the meantime, I can't believe what's happening in the diamond word. About two weeks ago, Tiffany's, the world's most famous retail jeweler, took out a large ad in *The New York Times* to declare, "diamond prices are too high" and advised people not to buy them. Incredible!

The immediate cause of this bizarre behavior is the unprecedented jump in diamond prices at the wholesale level. Retailers, like Tiffany's, feel, with some justification, that they cannot increase the retail prices of their jewelry sufficiently to restore their shrinking profit margins to normal size, and as a result, they are trying to talk prices down, by cooling off demand for investment diamonds at wholesale.

Simultaneously, the DeBeers CENTRAL SELLING ORGANIZATION (CSO) announced a 40% surcharge on their next diamond "sight." When the diamonds are put up for auction, the CSO simply demands their price, and those allowed to bid buy at the demanded price. If they don't, they might not be permitted to bid at the next "sight." DeBeers claimed the reason for the 40% surcharge was for the producers to be able to share in the tremendous windfall profits being enjoyed by the diamond cutters in Tel Aviv, who were withholding diamonds to create an artificial shortage and taking hefty wholesale mark-ups occasioned by the rapid appreciation of the diamond. Rather than letting them enjoy that windfall, the CSO decided to see that the basic producers of the diamonds reaped the benefits.

What does all this mean to the diamond buyer? It means there is a buying panic in diamonds, accentuated by an artificial shortage. Prices will eventually resume their rise, and at RELIANCE's prices, they are still a great buy (about 15% under most others).

Tiffany's says you shouldn't buy because prices are going to come down. That might be true if you bought at alleged inflated "wholesale" prices.

I expect diamonds to maintain their present price levels without substantial additional price increases for a short while. After all, we've had close to 100% appreciation since I first started touting diamonds as an anti-inflationary investment. I feel really good about catching the beginning of a major price advance a year ago. I have not advocated diamonds for short-term speculation. In fact, I have counseled against it, but it does give you an awfully good feeling in the pocketbook to see quick appreciation on your long-term holding. Now, hopefully, sanity will return to the market and diamonds will hold their present value and begin again their stable rise at about twice the rate of inflation. Disorderly markets like this can be frightening.

Tiffany's action is indicative of the desperation that is generally felt by retailers from the tremendous challenge of the wholesale diamond investment business. They are trying to blame it all on the cutters in Tel Aviv, but the real truth of the matter is, the investor looking for an inflation hedge has discovered the diamond and there is an unprecedented demand.

CERTIFICATION

(4/1/78) Because of chaotic conditions in the diamond business, if you order a diamond from anybody, unless you are lucky enough to find exactly what you want in their inventory, you must wait for your stone. It takes weeks to get GIA certificates. As a result, more and more jewelers are depending on USGS certificates. Until recently, USGS certificates have been considered a distant second best to the GIA in terms of acceptability; however, by sheer necessity and the GIA's inability to cope with the volume of business, more diamond businesses are turning to USGS. When we have obtained appraisals from both labs, our experience has been that they are comparable. It's my opinion that not many months from now, the USGS appraisal and certificate will be equally as valuable as the GIA. In fact, the USGS have one advantage in that it does list an average retail market value of the gem on each certificate.

The buying panic may soon be over, but I believe that diamonds are in for a long-sustained rise, and I do not expect a collapse of the diamond marketplace. The Central Selling Organization will not permit it to happen. They will absorb all diamonds that hit the market, over and above normal trade.

UNCUT DIAMONDS

(12/15/77)   Subscribers have asked if uncut diamonds are a good investment. No way. People have made money in uncut diamonds, but it's not for the inexperienced diamond buyer. There are a lot of genuine diamonds that are so flawed they are worth only a fraction of a true investment diamond. Stay with quality investment grade diamonds of one carat or more, either flawless, or VVSI (Very, Very Slightly Imperfect). However, I am investigating the uncut diamond marketplace, and my mind is still open. Until I give the signal, stay out, unless you know a lot more about it than I do.

DIAMOND RIP-OFFS

(1/15/78)   Early last summer, I began recommending DIA-MONDS to investors, and I suggested you contact RELIANCE DIAMONDS for your purchases. One of the most important services we offer you is a close check on dependable firms so you can translate our advice into concrete action. I'm developing a file of horror stories from people who have not taken our advice and have wandered off to other firms. I'm not claiming that RELIANCE PRODUCTS is the only dependable diamond seller in the business. I'm sure there are several, but we don't have time to check them all out. We have yet to find anyone who consistently sells diamonds at prices as low as RELIANCE.

FOUR REASONS TO BUY

(7/1/78)   Some of my friends in the "Hard Money" press, have advised against diamonds. I think they're wrong. Here's why.

1.   Investment grade stones, between one and two carats, with

GIA certificates, are becoming very hard to find. There is a genuine shortage. This shortfall is probably permanent, as very few people who buy this kind of diamond are expecting to turn them over quickly. They are hanging on to them for the long haul.

2. The price of small diamonds of lesser quality will probably drop, possibly substantially, as we move into a recession. This market depends on young engaged couples buying engagement and wedding rings, and as people begin to worry about their jobs, and the young people with the lowest seniority start being laid off, that market is adversely affected. Those are not investment grade stones.

3. It has been loudly pointed out by those who are anti-diamond that the Russians produce large amounts of gems and could destroy the market by dumping them. That's absurd. The Russians made their deal with DeBeers Central Selling Organization to market their diamonds to maximize their prices. It's an important source of desperately needed foreign exchange. It is not in their best interest to blow the market price. The Russians are one of the largest producers of industrial diamonds, but they provide less than one percent of the one to two-carat investment grade market supply.

4. When everybody turns negative, the dependable Theory of Contrary Opinion tells you it's about to take off, but we're not looking for overnight profits. We just want to buy them as cheaply as possible before they take off, then hang on. Prices have been stable for awhile, but I think we will see another wholesale price increase late this summer or early in the fall, which means you should act soon.

Remember, in August 1976, when everybody was proclaiming, "Gold is dead," and it was below $120 an ounce? Your old Dad—HJR—was yelling, "Don't listen to them. Buy with both hands." I think diamonds are again in roughly the same position.

A word of caution, don't buy diamonds until you have your year's supply of food, your bag of silver coins for every member of the family and an equivalent dollar amount of gold coins on hand. Then, go buy some of those pretty stones. And don't wait until the mania is roaring again. Diamonds don't jump one percent or five percent. At the prices our subscribers pay, the increases will be from 10% to 40% when they do occur.

FORBES ARTICLE

(9/15/78) The September 18th issue of *FORBES* had a most interesting article on diamonds which is must reading for any potential diamond investor. The over-all tone of the article is negative, and the conclusions are wrong, but there's a lot of merit in the article. I suggest that you pick it up, look it over very carefully, but keep several points in mind which I'll touch on later.

The article discusses the background of many of the diamond sales firms and points out that many of the principals of the boiler-room operations have been in trouble with the law before. Many of them come out of the silver bullion hustle of 1973 and 1974. Some of them have been convicted of securities fraud. All in all, a rather unsavory picture. The article does a great job of laying out this history.

However, there are some fundamental problems with the article that bother me. It lays heavy stress on the boiler-room diamond firms, not indicating that there are some very sound, conservatively run companies that do not overprice their gems.

The boiler-room firms often pay more than ordinary jewelers for their stones and often charge huge markups, as the article says, but the article makes a sweeping statement that, "They do not, of course, get them direct from the DeBeers Central Selling Organization." That may be true of a lot of them but some do buy from DeBeers or from alternative sources at similar prices. About 20% of the world's diamonds are not sold through DeBeers.

Forbes quotes favorably from a publication of the retail jewelry industry, *Jeweler's Circular Keystone*, which they call "a lively trade publication." *Keystone* recently spoke of fast-buck artists who "... came in to hustle common folk blinded by visions of big easy money." Sometimes you have to untangle your friends from your enemies. Along with legitimate complaints about the diamond industry are the illegitimate complaints from the retail jewelers who publish *Jeweler's Circular Keystone* and feel seriously threatened by anyone who sells diamonds at prices below the retail jewelers' monstrous markups.

I'd like to repeat the guidelines that must be observed by the diamond buyer:

1. Don't be scared off. Diamonds are an outstanding, long-term inflation hedge.

2. When dealing with any diamond sales firm, require a GIA appraisal. This won't tell you the dollar value of the stone but it will certify it as to color, cut, clarity and carat weight. A GIA certificated diamond is quite negotiable and can be sold at any time for a fair wholesale price.

3. Be sure you pay close to a fair wholesale price in order to insure full liquidity. The simplest way to do this is to follow this two-step process:

a.   Be sure that the selling firm has a full return privilege on the stone, so that within a reasonable period of time you can receive a full refund.

b.   Take the diamond to a certified gemologist to verify it and get an appraisal. You might even want to shop around with several gemologists. (Beware of the low-ball, which is very common.)

4.   Don't buy diamonds with funds you might have to use in the near future. This is a long-term investment to keep your money safe from inflation. Don't listen to the salesman who tells you how it's going to go up next week. It may, and it may not. It is not a place for your liquid funds.

5.   Do not rely on the buy-back-at-a-profit promises of any firm that you do not know.

6.   Be sure to buy larger investment-grade stones.

BERNARD CIRLIN CONVENTION REPORT

(3/15/79)   BERNARD CIRLIN, editor of *PRECIOUSTONES NEWSLETTER*, gave us the straight scoop on diamonds. From 1957 to 1977 they out performed all other commodities in real value growth. There has not been a down-tick in wholesale prices since 1934.

He stressed that you must know your dealer and educate yourself. "You don't have to be an expert, but you should work patiently at finding a competent seller. Don't buy diamonds unless you plan to hold them for two or three years." He said, "You will find better resale value in a high quality stone, but not the very highest. Perfection demands a high premium, and there is a better market a couple of steps down." He also feels liquidity will increase in the early 1980s, making it much easier to sell diamonds. His scenario for the next two years is tied to inflation. His most pessimistic scenario, with high inflation (10%), suggests an annual increase in investment diamonds of 40% to 45%. Under his medium economic scenario, with 7% inflation, diamond prices will increase 18% to 25%. The most optimistic scenario, with inflation under 5%, shows investment grade diamond prices ranging anywhere from a negative 10% to a positive 5%.

The future of DeBeers in Africa is bright, despite potential political problems. Whoever is in power in Africa will need DeBeers for future economic stability.

SUMMARY

(10/15/78)   The Bad News

1.   It takes a lot of dough to buy top quality investment-grade diamonds. You have to start somewhere around $6,000.
2.   Diamonds are not as liquid as gold coins. They are a lot more liquid than real estate, but somewhat less liquid than gold. Consequently, it is for the long-term investor only.
3.   It doesn't offer the spectacular short-term profit opportunities of gold, but it will probably appreciate at something near double the rate of inflation.
4.   You have the same storage problems you have with gold, albeit smaller.
5.   Diamonds are vulnerable to fire.
6.   There are a lot of schlocky investment diamond dealers selling diamonds at too high a price. You must select your dealer very carefully, as the liquidity and risk factors of your investment are directly related to the price you pay. It should be somewhere near authentic wholesale—the price jewelers pay for their stones.
7.   There is a concerted campaign on the part of the retail jewelers of this country to convince people that diamonds are a lousy investment, and this makes owning diamonds rather scary when you see this happening all around you.

The Good News

1.   When you buy a fine diamond, you have peace of mind. You don't have your stomach upset by a quote in the paper every day.
2.   You can have an awful lot of wealth in a very tiny space, unlike coins. So storage is no problem.
3.   There has never been a time in modern history when there has not been a buyer somewhere for a good quality diamond. So they are relatively liquid.
4.   Diamonds are appreciating at a very steady pace and represent the best choice for the conservative, nervous investor.
5.   The government may call in gold, but they will never call in diamonds. Diamonds are a matter of great irrelevance to government and that gives any investment a tremendous advantage.
6.   They are portable. If we should ever have severe disorders or some form of martial law or dictatorship in this country, it would be relatively easy to transport diamonds from one place to another.

7.   Diamonds are excellent for those people who have substantial sums of investment money, $25,000 and up. I truly believe that they are in the beginning of another explosive price increase.

DISCOUNTS

(3/1/78)   It Only Hertz When I Laugh

Most of our subscribers don't work for big companies, which means that they miss the financial advantage of having discounts at car rental companies. If you don't belong to certain associations, like the Aircraft Owners and Pilots Association, there's no way you can get a decent discount.

Well, we've pulled off a miracle. We have arranged for all subscribers to *THE RUFF TIMES* to have substantial discounts at all Hertz offices in the United States and Canada.

Before settling on Hertz, we did an intensive, detailed investigation and comparison with Avis and National. We limited ourselves to these three because they have the most outlets around the country. It was a difficult decision. We would have been able to make a slightly better deal with National than we did with Hertz, but there would have been no discounts in Florida or in Canada, and that, plus the widespread availability of the Hertz offices gave Hertz the edge.

Four or five car rentals a year could end up paying for your *RUFF TIMES* subscription, so we've given you another reason for subscribing.

You have no idea how hard this was to work out. There was no precedent for this kind of arrangement with a newsletter subscriber list so we had to convince Hertz that the whole deal made sense. As is always the case, we receive no discounts or commissions, although I did personally get a FIVE STAR STICKER (Whee!) which guarantees me a car at any location (at the same rate you pay), even if they have to give me the local manager's personal automobile, and I didn't think you would mind that special arrangement. But other than that, it is the same as usual—no commissions and no kickbacks. We had trouble convincing them that we didn't want them to rebate the additional discount benefits to Target as a commission, instead of giving you the cheaper price. They found that hard to believe.

(10/15/78) Effective November 1, in the U.S.A., the previous discount of 10% on the "dry rate" (gas not included) will be increased to 20%. This is the equivalent of more than a 40% discount on the old "wet rates."

In Canada, the discount rates will remain the same.

We will be adding additional benefits in the near future (already accomplished 10/1/79, Ed.). It is our policy to try to give you so many benefits that your actual *RUFF TIMES* membership costs you nothing.

E

ECONOMY OF U.S.

POSSIBILITY OF COLLAPSE

(4/1/76)   In a recent issue of *WORLD OIL* magazine (December 1975), Dr. H. A. Merklein, Director of the International Institute, the University of Dallas, Irving, Texas, made a convincing case for the possibility of economic collapse. He began his thought-provoking article with this flat-out statement:

> The financial collapse of the nation's largest city is imminent; it would be history today, had not New York State temporarily bailed out the city, wisely or not. The fundamental reason for New York's problem is the same perennial cause of any financial collapse: expenditures exceeding income. If and when that happens over extended periods of time, any economic entity, private or public, must fold, including the United States Government.

Dr. Merklein presented some interesting concepts, such as "A nation can and will go bankupt when the interest payments on its public debt exceed the net-capital-generation of that nation. When this happens, Doomsday is at hand and the collapse of the economy is imminent."

He postulated that economic collapse occurs when a combination of unemployment and inflation reaches the point where the market ceases to function effectively. He established what he calls "an admittedly arbitrary rule," that when the sums of the "percentage of inflation," plus two times "the percentage of unemployment," equals 50 or more, a collapse of the free market system as it now operates in the United States is likely. For example, 25% unemployment and no inflation means collapse under this definition. Zero unemployment and 50% inflation also means collapse, as does 10% unemployment and 30% inflation. Other collapse combinations under the terms of the preceding definition are as follows:

Collapse Combinations
(2 x unemployment percent + Inflation percent)

Unemployment %	0	2.5	5.0	7.5	10.0	12.4	15.0	17.5	20.0	22.5	25.0
Annual Inflation %	50	5	40	35	30	25	20	15	10	5	0

By this definition, the great depression of the 30s constituted an economic collapse with 25% unemployment and no inflation. That's why Dr. Merklein shows 25% unemployment as the one extreme, and the other extreme, 50% inflation, is based on the fact that public confidence in government issued paper money tends to break down somewhere near that threshold and barter begins to replace the money economy. At one time in 1974, we had 9% unemployment and 15% inflation (2 x 9% = 18 + 15 = 33%). If unemployment had climbed to 5% and inflation to 20%, it would have been doomsday, according to Merklein's formula.

Dr. Merkein illustrated the basic trends of U.S. post-World War II deficit spending and indicated that the nation's economy will inevitably collapse sometime in the early 1980s.

For example, by 1982 or 1983 the government will have used all available funds to meet its obligations and pay its debt and doomsday is still at hand. The only alternative is to repudiate the national debt. However, if the national debt were to be cancelled, it would destroy all the banks in the country, drag down countless corporations and individual savers, and destroy the livelihood of tens of millions of Americans. We have reached the point where only bad choices remain.

(10/15/76)   During an economic collapse in the cities, what should I really be afraid of?
1.   FIRE! In a major currency collapse, or a sudden Arab oil boycott, electric power and gas supplies will become intermittent at best. People will attempt to cook and heat with open fires in apartment buildings and row-homes. Firemen will find it difficult to get to work, or will be unwilling to face urban disorders.
2.   FEAR! Fear and panic cause deaths. Fight fear by understanding the real risks and making preparations.
3.   I would fear living too close (under five miles) to an all-black slum, during the first few weeks of an economic and currency collapse.

4.   I would fear the white bigot with a gun who is always looking for an excuse to "get even" and will have the opportunity of a lifetime. He will cause violence and panic.

5.   I would fear not having food supplies, cash, gold and silver coins, and a health conditioning program. Data from the 1930-39 depression shows that illness did not increase in the "already-poor," but climbed astronomically among the "newly poor." A major change in circumstances is stressful, and stress brings disease.

6.   I would fear not having friends or neighbors who had also prepared for trouble, that I could turn to for support and mutual assistance.

7.   Last, I would fear my own panic that would cause me to shed my values, including spirituality, generosity, and the sanctity of human life, to be replaced by racial hatred, selfishness, easy willingness to kill, and revenge. Only with our intangible principles intact will we recover. They are our real wealth.

(6/15/77)

Q. Why are you so positive a depression is coming? Could it be prevented?

A. No, I don't think it can. I feel sorry for conservatives who fight so hard for balanced budgets and retirement of the national debt. It is love's labor lost. Not that they're wrong in theory, but once you have gone down this path, there is no turning back. For those who think balancing the budget would create Utopia, I suggest you look at history. The depression of the '30s was triggered by government economy moves very similar to those that conservatives are recommending today. If we were to balance the budget, reduce taxes, slash the size of government, cancel government contracts, etc., you would have an army of unemployed government workers, companies laying off workers and it would trigger a massive depression, probably worse than the '30s, because of the delicate interdependence we talked about earlier. Thomas Wolfe said, "You can't go home again," and he's right.

   Sooner or later, we will miscalculate. The economic world is so complex that, as a good friend of mine, Cleon Skousen, said, "The cross-currents of national life have begun to ebb and flow so rapidly that it is beyond the ingenuity of human leadership."

   Moving forward will eventually precipitate a runaway inflationary spiral.

(11/15/78)   Invisible Crisis

The actual fall of ROME came as a terrible surprise to those who lived there. During the last years of the empire, evidence indicates most of the Roman middle and upper classes had no idea their society had rotted from within and was about to come unglued. Societies in deep trouble often don't feel like it until it's too late to act.

This is an "Invisible Crisis" because most of the problems we face are not directly felt by the individuals. They appear to be abstract events unrelated to you. Lots of bad economic events never really change our personal lifestyle, so we tend to ignore them. Most of you were not directly affected by the 1974 recession. The falling stock market did not cause panic because the individual investor had generally fled the market and left it in the hands of institutional investors. When unemployment reached 10%, 90 of the population still had their jobs and their life was not affected. Although the crime rate rose, most people didn't suffer from a crime, so it was merely an abstract statistic.

We did have a sense of unease from the 12 to 15% rise in prices at the super market. But that didn't keep us from buying the things we usually buy. We just complained about it more, or went deeper in debt.

This year, however, is the beginning of an economic crisis that will eventually touch us individually, and could turn into a genuine financial panic, but for awhile it will be an "invisible crisis."

1978 is the "year of decision." Actually, the invisible slide has already begun with the much-publicized collapse of the dollar. Because it has little or no obvious effect on you, however, it appears to be one of the esoteric, abstract problems that you leave to the politicians to handle, but it is one of the "stress cracks" I predicted, and it is very important for you to understand.

PROFESSIONS DURING A DEPRESSION

(Special Report #4, 10/76)

Q: Are there any professions which would be hurt less than others in a depression?

A: There are certain skills which will always be in demand. Doctors, chiropractors, and other health practitioners will always be needed. If you have manual skills in carpentry, automobile repair, electrical repair, blacksmithing, farming, gardening, or any related field, you will do very well.

In addition to these, I believe the people involved in the sale of storage food and nutritional products will do very well, both immediately before, and even during such an economic disaster, subject only to the availability of products.

I spent five years as a distributor of nutritional products with the Neo-Life Company of America, and helped design an emergency food program. Although I have sold my business and am no longer involved, I still feel this line of work offers a marvelous opportunity for people who wish to get into a business which will be less susceptible to the kind of problems we're concerned about. You can start in it on a shoestring, and do very well during optimistic times, such as we are presently enjoying.

When inflation rates turn up and people become worried about their future, the dehydrated food storage business tends to boom and you could make a great deal of money in a short period of time, if people really began to recognize the need for such products.

Those of you who are operating on the thin edge, financially, could have a second source of income as a distributor of such products. You can set aside a lot of food each month if you could make an extra $50-$100 a month and put it into such products. This can be done with an investment of less than $100 and without a great deal of work or sales skill.

If you are in a profession such as law, dentistry, automobiles, appliances, etc., I suggest that you consider some alternatives. Strangely enough, during the last stages of an inflation, before the collapse, the luxury businesses do extremely well, as the well-to-do rapidly attempt to unload their depreciating money in a last orgy of buying. In ARGENTINA, when inflation was running at 300 percent, the luxury resorts were booming. Sales of big cars and yachts were going through the ceiling, but eventually, when the final collapse comes, of course these businesses are wiped out. So, you can do well for awhile, as long as you have a prepared fall-back position, either to depend upon your own accumulated resources or to provide a service for which there will always be a need, even in a barter economy.

RUFF'S FORECASTS

(2/1/78)   I can almost feel the bands tightening as we move into this critical phase in our economic history. I am still holding to my timetable. I believe the economy is going to peak, sometime in or shortly after the first quarter of this year, plateau for awhile, and then begin a short-lived, deflationary slide. When the slide is perceived by government, it will frighten it into stimulative spending which will trigger rampant inflation and, when eventually out of hand, will result in a deflationary collapse. It could be strung out for three or four years. I don't believe we can stay on the plateau much past August. All the fundamentals are still the same.

In the meantime, watch the forces of deflation beginning to work, but never underestimate the government's ability to panic and try to spend its way out of it, and that's inflationary.

A few comments by some mainstream economists will reinforce what I've just said. ARTHUR OKUN, Chairman of the Council of Economic Advisors under Lyndon Johnson, commented on Carter's promise that he will, within the next four years, produce a happy combination of low unemployment, moderate inflation and budget surplus large enough to finance at least a modest start on some of Mr. Carter's pet social programs. Mr. Okun says, "History tells you it just isn't going to happen. In fact, history tells you, you ought to ask when is Carter going to have his recession?"

If you don't believe the government would attempt to spend its way out of economic troubles, Charles Schultze, one of President Carter's closest advisors, stresses that should things go awry, the administration strategy "permits us to add additional stimulus later" to put the economy right. "We must be fully prepared to reduce taxes or increase spending if it appears that the economy is falling significantly short of the targets we have set. If we plan now to balance the budget in 1981, counting on a strong private economy, and we are proved wrong about the strength of the economy, it is relatively easy to correct our mistake with appropriate stimulative actions."

No one in the Carter administration has repudiated these statements. We don't know enough about economic cause and effect. The rheumatism in my forecasting bone tells me the economic storms aren't too far away. (see: Forecasts)

(7/15/78)

Q. Howard, you gave us a timetable several months back. You said that the economy would peak sometime in, or shortly after, the first quarter of 1978 and would plateau for awhile, then begin a long downhill slide. How do things look now?

A. Near the peak or plateau state of an economy-about-to-turn down, opposing economic forces seem to struggle for supremacy. That's precisely what is going on now. This is what I call the Fake-You-Out Phase of the Economic Cycle.

Look at all the contradictory signals. Unemployment is falling, which is good news, but price inflation has been in the double-digit range for three out of the first five months of the year, which is bad news.

The dollar is still sinking (inflationary) and, in fact, has dropped below the lows established a few months ago when the dollar was making big headlines. Commodity prices are falling (deflationary), but gold has resisted that trend, demonstrating considerable stability, which would seem to indicate inflation.

The stock market is falling (deflationary) and interest rates are rising (inflationary), while polls reflecting consumer confidence tell us that the consumer is less confident of his future than at any time in the last few years (deflationary), but the sales figures indicate that he's perfectly willing to send his money (inflationary).

We will probably remain on this wobbly plateau for the rest of the summer, and then the economy could turn down dramatically, but let's define what I mean by "turn down." You must distinguish between an inflationary depression and a deflationary depression similar to the 1930s.

When inflation really takes off, the economy will be in bad shape, but it will appear to be busy and dynamic because the gross dollar-measurements of business activity are rising, due solely to inflation. Retail sales might look good because people are buying in anticipation of higher prices later. This fever is anything but healthy. The Leading Economic Indicators may rise, but it is really a downturn, because it is the beginning of the troubles that will undo us. Sharply falling unemployment is also characteristic of an economic peak, as is inventory building by business and industry, and we are now seeing both.

In other words, the economy is performing almost exactly as I thought. Sometime before the end of the summer, I expect inflation, based on government figures, to appear to be easing. We could see the first real softening in big city real estate prices as early as September, although it may be as late as next winter. A big downturn in big city real estate prices may distort the Consumer Price Index, so the CPI will look like deflation is setting in, but it is only temporary. The long-term trend of inflation is still intact and it will increase exponentially. However, in the early stages of a runaway inflation it moves in fits and starts, and it could look as though inflation is easing. We might even see a brief downturn in interest rates, but not until they have climbed considerably higher.

This pause will be called a recession, and there is nothing that will panic the politicians like a recession, especially when unemployment starts rising again and Big Labor starts making demands. I expect that these events will panic the government into more stimulatory deficit spending as a deliberate policy. This spending will be the trigger for runaway inflation.

STRENGTH OF RASPUTIN

(6/15/78) RASPUTIN, the Mad Monk, was a Siberian peasant monk who achieved a tremenous influence over the Czarina of Russia just prior to the Bolshevik revolution. Many believed he was a holy man, capable of great miracles. He was certainly capable of prodigious excesses of appetites, including legendary sexual feats. Eventually, a palace conspiracy determined to murder him. First, he was fed huge drafts of poison with his meal that would have killed ten lesser men and he didn't even belch. Finally, he was stabbed and shot, and he wouldn't die. He was dumped through the ice on the Neva River and he clambered out of the ice, terrifying his would-be assassins. Finally, they managed to kill the man-monster and he stayed dead.

The American economy is the Rasputin of the '70s. It has endured incredible insults and fended them off with marvelous resilience. Despite the inflationary excesses of government and the creeping bonds of tyranny from government agencies, it is still the marvel of the world. My guess is nothing can really kill it. Although it will get terribly sick, somehow, someday, it will come staggering back like Rasputin. I have a lot of respect for those who advocate heading for the mountains. I've read everything they have to say and I find their economics basically sound, I just don't agree with their conclusions.

I don't know how to prepare for the end of the world, so I'm not even going to try—at least not physically. About all you can do in that exigency is repent. However, I think that we must simply and prudently prepare (as far as practical) for the worst possible case. I am not going to set up a retreat and shoot the starving hordes when they come after me. I will take my chances in a small town and assume that America can come staggering back like Rasputin. In the meantime, I want to save and invest as much money as I can, without sacrificing Church and Family and Principles, so that my family can be as comfortable as possible through these difficult times and be prepared to take advantage of the investment opportunities which will arise. I agree with Dr. Sennholz. This is a time of great opportunity, and more times of opportunity will come when things bottom out, but don't panic and listen to the real prophets of doom unless a retreat is necessary for your emotional well-being. I'm in favor of anybody doing anything as long as it doesn't hurt anybody else or "scare the horses," as H. L. Mencken said. (see also: Retreats, Survival Preparations)

FROM A TO Z

SUBTERRANEAN ECONOMY

(5/1/77) GOVERNMENT IS DUMB!! Why? Well, there are a lot of reasons, but one is that the voluminous statistics on which they base policy decisions are invariably no good. For example, there is an underground phenomenon which distorts the money supply measurements (M-1, M-2, etc.) and also the Gross National Product, which puts quicksand under these number. *THE FINANCIAL ANALYST JOURNAL* reported a study by PETER M. GUTMANN, in which he describes, "the subterranean economy" of the United States which has its own Gross National Product of $195 billion for 1977.

There is in the U.S. nearly $400 in cash per capita floating around outside banks which lubricates a vast amount of unreported work and employment. That's as large as the legal Gross National Product of the United States in the middle of World War II! It is traceable to cash-oriented restaurants, garages and small retail shops, to youths doing part-time chores for pin money, to illegal aliens, and retired people who also collect social security checks and can't report the income.

This subterranean "black market" economy was created by the nation's cobweb of employment restrictions and tax rules, coupled with a "new morality" spirit, characterized by "selective obedience to the law."

But setting all that aside, such ignored data means that the "button pushers" cannot "fine-tune" the economy because it's not fine-tunable, and bad decisions are being made based on erroneous data.

I also see some disturbing parallels between this "subterranean economy" and what is happening in ITALY. As you read on, see if this doesn't have some frightening similarities to the "safe and sane" American world in which you and I live.

Italy is rushing toward economic disaster—to say nothing of Communism and Anarchy. Unemployment is at 7.4%, government job programs have only created 62,000 job openings thus far. They reduced inflation from 22 to 12% but at the cost of lowering the economic growth rate, driving up interest rates to 22%. As a result of lessened business activity, tax revenues are down by $2 billion and social security obligations have skyrocketed to 100% of some workers' basic salaries. Automatic cost-of-living increases have pushed the cost of labor so high that it is rapidly killing off Italy's once booming industry. The political and social result is terrorism and kidnappings.

As a result of these "gains," negotiated by militant trade unions, a booming black market labor force of 8,000,000 has developed, which works for low pay and no fringe benefits. Most of that income will be unreported and will not show up in economic measuring indicators and, or course, no taxes will be paid on it. Without this black labor market, 8,000,000 people would merely be unemployed at a higher wage and Italy would be devastated by revolution.

Every day we read in the papers about economic decisions being made by government, or, in the opinion of some "expert" or politician, what decisions government should be making. An invisible thread running through our basic assumptions is that not only is government the prime factor in the economy, but it should be. As far as the media are concerned, the free market is dead, and it is the government-manipulated marketplace that rules. When we elect a Jimmy Carter, it's like turning a sensitive, supersonic jet over to an amateur Saturday afternoon pilot, after first making sure all of the instruments are inaccurate. Even wise men can't deal with problems if the data is incorrect. When the response is wrong because all the input is wrong, government simply falls back on its basic defensive position: "when in doubt, inflate." (see: Bureaucrats, Regulatory Agencies)

THREATS OF STABILITY

(5/15/77)   Remember the story of "the little boy who called wolf"? Well, here are some prowling wolves: INFLATION, DEBT, EN-ERGY SHORTAGES, WEATHER CHANGES, A WEAKENED BANKING SYSTEM, INTERNATIONAL ENEMIES.

I will "cry wolf" every time they appear on the horizon. You should build your barricades now. I don't cry wolf unless I see wolves. That doesn't mean that every threat will result in a full-blown crisis, but we can't emulate the "Dresdeners" of World War II who weren't in their shelters when the massive fire bomb attack came and destroyed their city.

It's also my job to make sure you don't worry about problems that aren't real so you don't waste emotional energy and time preparing for threats that will never materialize.

We have many malevolent economic forces pressing us from every direction. It's a great testimony to the power of the free enterprise system that these things have not overwhelmed us long before now. Bear in mind, no system is indestructible. Nations rise and fall. Civilizations reach their zenith and then collapse, generally because of the actions of its leaders, with the tactit permission of its people. This nation is beginning a period of decline. By that I mean, we are going to see massive readjustments in our economic life and, perhaps, even in our form of government. I believe we have been weakened to the

154

point where the next economic downturn as the potential to bring about the economic collapse I've talked about.

There is about one chance in three I'm wrong. We may get away with one more relatively minor recession before the big event, but I don't think so. We could go with a bang or a whimper. No one knows. It may take a year or two before we strike bottom, but I believe the next downturn will be the big one.

MISCONCEPTIONS ABOUT IT

(1/15/79)   For about the fifth time since I began writing *THE RUFF TIMES*, I will quote Pogo. "We have met the enemy and he is us."

Several areas of misconception or downright ignorance have brought us to the brink of a financial precipice; so close, in fact, that it doesn't much matter whether we send the American economic machine soaring over the cliff with our foot on the accelerator or skidding over with our foot on the brake. Either way, it is inevitable. The only question is "When?" Let's look at the great areas of American ignorance that have allowed us to reach this point.

MISCONCEPTION NUMBER ONE: There is a free lunch.

Someone says, "There ain't no free lunch," and, upon hearing this beaten-to-death cliche, we all nod sagely. But down deep inside, most Americans believe there is a free lunch, that government can give without taking, and that Federal grants to our city or state cost us nothing. We reelect politicians who wave these "gifts" like scalps taken in battle because they have gotten us some "free money." Of course, "there ain't no free lunch!" Government can't give you anything it didn't first take away. The principal area of ignorance, however, is how government takes it away from you.

Tax rebels hold, as an article of faith, that if you take tax income away from government, you will force them to cut spending. Those who hold this view are displaying appalling ignorance of the resourcefulness of government in creating whatever money it wants to spend, regardless of its tax income.

New money dilutes the value of every dollar in existence when it is spent into circulation. When government gains purchasing power through money creation, we collectively lose purchasing power. This is the inflation process.

Everything we receive from government—from our social security checks, the new dam, or the inner-city grant—has come out of our own pockets, either from taxation, which is a drag on the economy, or the inflationary process, which reduces purchasing power. There is no way we can receive a benefit without it first costing us.

Unfortunately, the tax revolt has assaulted the most effective, most responsive level of government—cities and states—because their taxes are the most directly levied upon us. Washington will one day have to pick up the slack when the cities and states get into trouble, or there is no chance this administration will win the next election. That money will be raised through the "inflation tax."

MISCONCEPTION NUMBER TWO: There is no "business cycle." Recessions and depressions can be avoided by careful and wise government fiscal policy.

This misconception is so persistent, even though we learn every two to four years it isn't true, we still continue to believe it. History tells us that during your lifetime you will see at least one (more likely two) major depressions or fiscal panic, and a recession every two to five years. We still, somehow, believe that it can't happen to us.

In early 1929, when some pundits raised the possibility of a depression, we were told of all the government safeguards that "ensured" against such a depression. That "impossible" depression is history. Now we're hearing the same kind of garbage. We experience a depression and financial panic every forty-five to fifty-five years, and this current business cycle is running on borrowed time.

Any dynamic financial machine will have its ups and downs. Usually they are minor and we call them "recessions." But every once in awhile we will have a real downer. We had one deep recession in the mid-twenties which was a dress rehearsal for what happened in 1929. We had a deep one starting in 1973 through 1974 which I believe was a dress rehearsal for the one into which we are now heading. The business cycle is still intact, no matter how often politicians say otherwise.

MISCONCEPTION NUMBER THREE: Government is attacking inflation!

Actually not one person in 10,000 really understands the nature of inflation. That's why Mr. Carter can get away with blaming big labor and big business by claiming if somehow we can keep them from asking for higher wages or higher prices, we will hold inflation under control. Rising wages and rising prices are not inflation. They are rational reactions to the inflationary environment created by the government. Government is not "fighting inflation." Government is causing inflation!

The only way we can stop inflation is to literally shrink the money supply and cause a deflationary depression. Government is like a doctor fighting fever while vigorously, but quietly, encouraging the spread of bacteria and all along calling himself a healer.

Our problem is compounded by the fact that European banks have been able to create dollars at will, totally uncontrolled by any regulatory body. We cast off the dollar from the discipline of gold, and we now face what happens to every fiat currency system. The political process demands the creation of more money to fund programs demanded by those who vote themselves benefits from the public treasury." (Alexander Tytler)

MISCONCEPTION NUMBER FOUR: My benefits are not inflationary. Yours are!

When you get right down to it, the principal reason why we will never really get the budget under control until the system has collapsed of its own weight is that nobody is really in favor of cutting spending.

Before you get outraged over that statement, look at the facts. The conservatives want to cut the HEW budget and get all those "welfare bums" out of the public purse, but they also want substantially increased defense spending. The liberals want to cut defense spending to prove we aren't "Cold Warriors," while at the same time saying, "We, of course, can't take money away from needy people by cutting progressive social programs." Each of these groups is strong enough to block the budget cutting efforts of the other group and, as a result, nothing gets cut.

Even if the various amendments floating around should limit spending to some percentage of gross national product, or to some fixed percentage of increase each year, we'll still have to face the hard issues of what gets cut.

THE UPRIGHT SPIKE

(5/1/78) MARK TWAIN said, "There are lies, there are damn lies, and then there are statistics." After statistics come charts!

DR. E. L. ANDERSON recently published a very telling piece called THE UPRIGHT SPIKE, which has been promoted by SPOTLIGHT. He also did another article in which he showed how the government can flatten out an otherwise frightening curve on a chart by using the vertical up-and-down scale to chart a geometric progression rather than an arithmetic progression. For example, if you want to show the national debt as a flat, soothing, slightly climbing line, you simply change the scale along the left-hand side from 10, 20, 30, 40, 50 (arithmetic), to 5, 10, 20, 40, 80 (geometric). You get bigger numbers per inch and the line isn't anywhere near as steep. I thought it was a brilliant exposition of the problem. However, in THE UPRIGHT SPIKE, he seems to be guilty of another kind of distortion—inadvertently, I hope. I have made unsuccessful efforts to reach Dr. Anderson by telephone and was told he does not accept phone calls nor return them, so I am inviting him to respond to this article and I promise to print in full any explanation or rebuttal.

THE UPRIGHT SPIKE is a very impressive, short pamphlet which presented a series of charts on a variety of money measurements, including the national debt, the growth of the money supply, interest on the national debt, budget deficits, etc. He laid them out on an arithmetic progression chart using five year increments from 1913 to the present along the bottom line. Along the vertical left-hand side, he used whatever money scale he thought was appropriate for the subject under discussion. After plotting the chart and drawing his lines, he saw that it formed a "concave parabolic curve" or an arc. Around October of 1980 it became "upright" and began to curve back on itself as it completed more than a quarter of a circle. This is called a "spike" and that means these numbers suddenly project into infinity, meaning total collapse of the economy, money and society. Every chart spikes at approximately the same time, October 1980, and that is DOOMS-DAY.

Now this very impressive work by an economist with a fine reputation seemed generally irrefutable and consistent with my views but I had some subliminal nagging doubts. R.E. McMASTER and I sat down in Hawaii to see how these charts all arrived at collapse at exactly the same time. It seemed so "pat."

I think I know how it happened. If you either stretch out or compress the up-and-down vertical left-hand line, which is the measurement of the dollars, you can produce a spike on any date you choose. Here is one of Dr. Anderson's charts for Interest On The National Debt (Fig. 1). You can see that it does "spike" about 1980. However, if you adjust the left-hand vertical scale either way, the chart spikes later (Fig. 2) or earlier (Fig. 3). The curve can look steep or shallow, depending upon what you do with that left-hand line.

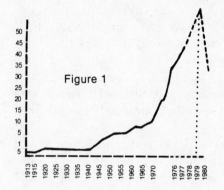

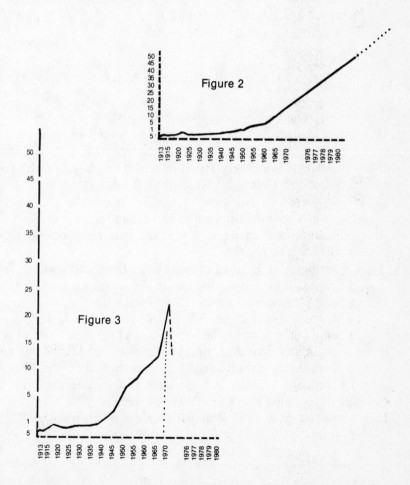

When you examine a chart, examine the scale. Government can soothe your reaction to their figures by making it look very flat so it isn't frightening. Someone who wants to paint a doom-and-gloom, cataclysmic picture can make it look very steep by adjusting the scale.

It all boils down to the fact that I have grave mental reservations about an apparently impressive piece of work. If there's something wrong with my reasoning, I would like to know about it and I will immediately publish a correction in full. I don't believe in loading the evidence to prove a point, no matter how passionately I am devoted to the point. Impeccable intellectual honesty is absolutely critical when you are trying to persuade.

Please, Dr. Anderson, in all good will, I extend an invitation to you to get in touch with me. I'd also like you to be a guest on my TV show. Your UPRIGHT SPIKE may be one of the most important pieces of financial analysis in our history, and if it is, I want to help publicize and distribute it. Just call on our Hot-Line at 800-227-0703 and let's talk. In the meantime, folks, suspend judgment.

TIME FOR REEVALUATION

(5/15/79)   Our economy now stands poised and trembling like an alerted deer that smells something wrong but doesn't know which way to run. We are being bombed by contradictory signals, including six different opinions from every expert on which way to jump with your money. Inflation? Deflation? Recession? Boom? Depression? Stagnation? Slow growth? No growth? A valid, persuasive case can be made for each scenario. Pushing numbers around in a computer won't give you unequivocal answers. Now is the time for good judgment. Now is when I earn my fee.

Just what the heck is going on out there? Lots, that's what!

1.   Price inflation is now running at a true annual rate of about 15% in the big cities, and about 11% in rural areas.

2.   There is a genuine gas and diesel fuel crunch in California, Florida, and other places. This is the sickening legacy of: a) government mandates requiring lead-free gasoline and catalytic converters, which increase the demand for unleaded fuel at twice the rate at which refinery capacity can be increased; b) price controls on domestic oil, coupled with Carter's announcement of deregulation on June 1, causing most intelligent independent oil men to hold back

production until then; c) uncertainty over natural gas availability, due to a Rube Goldberg "deregulation" plan that caused many industries and utilities to switch to oil; d) the Iranian situation; and e) a lot of dumb-headed actions by government and big oil. The crunch is real! And it will be with us for several months.

3.   Atomic energy is in limbo. The Three Mile Island incident has paralyzed forward movement and shut down some plants. Whether you're pro or anti-nuclear, we're a long way down the road to nuclear energy, and retracing those steps means some nasty changes in our comfort and lifestyle.

4.   The markets are schizoid. As of this moment, gold, my most important barometer, is flirting with a break-out point around $254.50, and could bolt in either direction. In the meantime, silver has gone nuts and the stock market continues to wallow around, going nowhere. The dollar is rock solid, and interest rates are fluctuating narrowly.

5.   The inflation rate in Europe is picking up. The Germans and the Swiss have recently experienced price inflation at close to 9% per annum, primarily as a result of hoarding demand for their currencies prior to October of last year.

6.   The Carter "fight inflation" program is breaking down—and a good thing too. If you don't think price controls create shortages, what do you think we are experiencing in the gas and oil area right now? If that's not the long-term consequences of price controls, I don't know what is.

7.   The money supply figures are impossible to interpret. The newly found ability of banks and savings and loans to create instant transfers from savings accounts to checking accounts has, in effect, created mobility between M-1 and M-2 that is difficult to interpret. The Eurodollar market is completely out of control and nobody knows what its effect will be on domestic inflation, and the velocity of money—the speed with which money gets spent—is difficult, if not impossible, to measure accurately. One dollar passing through two sets of hands in a week is twice as inflationary as the same dollar passing through only one set of hands in a week. Now, what do we make of that mess?

Briefly, I would like to give you my conclusions as to what lies immediately ahead, and then my recommendations for dealing with this very uncertain set of problems.

The Most Likely Scenario

It now appears that the most likely scenario includes a recession, some contradictory reports on inflation, an apparent slowing in some key areas of the economy, a temporary fall in short-term interest rates and a slight easing in long-term interest rate. The forces of inflation and deflation will continue to struggle and deflation may appear to be winning for awhile, just like the Germans during the Battle of the Bulge in World War II appeared to be winning. But the Allies won, and inflation will win this struggle, too.

The price of gold could move up to as high as $275-$280 an ounce (No comment!—HJR), and from those levels a major correction, which I have been expecting for some months, will take place. MAURY KRAVITZ, who has called the basic trends very accurately for me for many months, agrees with this scenario and feels that when the correction comes, it will be massive. The preceding rise will probably be triggered by unsophisticated public buying. The Europeans are not buying. The Arabs are not buying. The recent announcements of decreases in both the IMF auction and the Treasury auctions are bearish in the long run. They are indicators of lack of demand. My advice is still to stay out of that market for now. We will have a chance to buy much cheaper gold sometime in the next few months and I do not know when that chance will come, but the odds favor it. If you are a trader you might want to try to play with the next $10 to $1 rise, but I wouldn't. It's too dangerous and too volatile. I prefer to stand on the sidelines.

Soon, I expect a rather abrupt decline in business activity, with falling inflation and interest rates. This will be relatively short-lived (6-15 months), as the government will go to work to stimuate us out of it in anticipation of next year's presidential election. I then expect inflation to take off, interest rates to soar to new highs and inflation to climb sharply from the 10% level. Remember, it's running 13% to 15% now and I would not be surprised to see a brief decline of three or four points. Short-term interest rates could, after moving up another half to three-quarters of a point, move clear back down into the 7 or 8% range. Long-term interest rates could back off as much as a full point, but that's only a pause in what will be a steady upward climb over the next few years.

Basically, I believe this next decline is probably not the beginning of the "Big Depression." I haven't come to that conclusion lightly or casually. I believe that we will come out of this next recession into a wild feverish inflation. My thinking crystallized somewhat during my recent trip to Brazil where I was on the faculty of the Young Presidents' Organization International University. I didn't go there for fun, but rather to listen to some of the top businessmen and economists attending that conference and also to talk to some Brazilians about inflation and its effects. Their inflation rate is running close to 42 percent, and certain aspects of the economy have the appearance of feverish good health (if that isn't a contradiction in terms). But inflation has brought more poverty. The percentage of the nation's wealth, which is owned by a small cadre of wealthy people in Brazil, has expanded and the percentage owned by the people at the bottom of the scale has shrunk—the classic effect of inflation. Brazilians have escaped revolution and have actually been able to reduce their inflation rate somewhat over the last few years, for multiple and complex reasons. Basically, they have been able to dramatically increase productivity by expanding the industrial sector. All the automobiles you see on the crowded streets of Rio de Janeiro were made in Brazil.

There is no chance of the United States similarly increasing its productivity. Ours is shrinking. The Brazilians have literally produced themselves into a lower inflation rate. In addition to that, they have established a military dictatorship which could rule by fiat and do what had to be done. This country would not tolerate that, at least not until things got a heck of a lot worse. Also, there are no high expectations on the part of the Brazilian masses, no huge promises that would trigger automatic spending programs for their benefit. The hills are covered with slums which make the worst of our big cities look like paradise. There are a million and a half orphans, 12 years old and under, roaming the streets of Sao Paulo, with the 10-12 year-old children taking care of the two and three year-olds. The people accept this because they have never been taught to expect anything better.

Our country is afflicted with rising expectations without a corresponding sense of responsibility, where even the slightest downturn in the fortunes of the lower end of the economic spectrum would result in revolution in the streets.

Brazil is going to get it someday. I would not want to be one of the conspicuous rich living in Brazil.

As of now, in the good ol' U.S.A., it looks like a dip in the economy, at least by traditional measurements, probably ending early in 1981. Inflation will take off from the 10 percent range to heaven-only-knows-what, and the distortions and transfer of wealth from lenders to borrowers will increase. The demand for cash in a credit-disrupted economy will increase, and we will probably switch from a credit economy to a cash economy. The Carter "fight inflation" plan will not work, although it will appear to for a short time.

All in all, the devil to watch for is not recession or depression, but inflation. Its fluctuations are important because you can take advantage of them. (See Survival Preparations for my basic recommendations.)

EDUCATION

(10/1/77) The College Entrance Examination Board recently reported a startling 14-year drop in average scores in the SCHOLASTIC APTITUDE TESTS. Since 1963, the average score on the verbal section of the exam has declined 49 points and math scores have dropped 32 points. The College Board blamed the poor scores on lower school standards, television, increased number of females and blacks now taking the test, and social upsets during a "decade of distraction."

The Nobel-Prize winning economist, F.A. Hayek, a venerable and wise man, made a statement to the effect that, as he has gained in years, he has realized that the study of economics is the study of human beings functioning within the society they create. A major factor in economics is productivity, and this in our complex society is directly related to the educational level of its citizens. Unfortunately, we are building a generation of functional illiterates. My children have learned very little of history, ancient or modern, in school. Hitler's war in Europe would be practically unknown to them, if I hadn't spent time teaching them.

Now, lest this sound like a "things-were-better-in-the-good-old-days" statement from someone whose arteries are hardening, JOHN RYER, president of the teachers' NATIONAL EDUCATION ASSOCIATION, said that the tests have remained the same during 16 years of "great change in our society and its values," and are "therefore busily measuring what used to be, but no longer exists, in education." Stated simply, we are not teaching what we used to teach. We are so wrapped up in "relevance," we are creating a younger generation which does not know the lessons of history. They are not grounded in the democratic tradition, nor conditioned to the work ethic. They are anti-free-enterprise and pro-socialist, and if that isn't a gut economic issue, I don't know one.

Hayek is right. Those economists who merely look at their econometric models and push their slide rules around are missing the whole point of human economic history—that it is rooted in human behavior and performance. The next generation will be our Army officers, our corporation presidents, our teachers, our judges and senators, and will have to preside over a far more complex world than the one in which we live. They are less and less prepared in the fundamentals of math and basic written and spoken communication, in an age where the volume and velocity of necessary communication is light-years beyond that of even 25 years ago.

I think you are copping out if you blame "permissive educators" and "schools that don't teach." I say that with full knowledge that there are permissive educators, in schools that don't teach, but they are symptoms, not the bacterium of infection. The bacterium and the carrier thereof is we the parents.

In Philadelphia, recently, parents protested that the schools were not preparing their children for jobs, that many of them were graduating from high school unable to read, that the drop-out rate was terrible, that the schools were armed camps where teachers feared for their life, and the schools were to blame.

If you have crummy schools, why aren't you making a lot of noise about it? We probably can't make a heck of a lot of difference in the world's current economic trends, but we can make a difference in our communities. That's why I'm encouraging our *RUFF TIMES* Discussion Groups to concentrate on the improvement of our local schools.

We can't save the world from the coming economic holocaust, but we can have a lot to say about the nature of the world that follows what our children will inherit, in which they will be asked to manage. If we want strong fundamentals, an understanding of history, and the mastery of the basic skills required by our complex civilization, taught in an environment of traditional morals, then we are going to have to insist on it and *RUFF TIMES* Discussion Groups can bring pressure to bear. Vocal minorities have always had influence beyond their numbers. It has usually been the bad guys who have made the fuss. It's time the good guys spoke out. Let's stop blaming others for our troubles. (see: Family, Sin-Tax, Values & Morals)

HOWARD RUFF

ENERGY

PRESIDENT CARTER'S PLAN

(5/1/77)   Mr. Carter's conservation plan uses a variety of penalties
and tax rebates to stimulate the kind of behavior that will lead to
reduced use of existing energy supplies. For example, if Detroit
doesn't reach the government mandated standards for gas mileage by
a certain date, a Federal tax will be added to the price of gas. This can
happen each year for the next several years. Conversely, if it does
surpass the goals, the government will remove the tax. Beginning with
the 1978 models, there are severe penalties on cars which don't
achieve low mileage levels.

On the "energy-conversion" side of the coin, tax credits are offered
for those who insulate or convert their homes to solar heating. Also,
Mr. Carter is proposing that nuclear plants be licensed in three years
instead of the usual ten, using conventional nuclear power as opposed
to the fast-breeder reactors.

He made a bow towards increasing production by first stating that
"total deregulation of prices would be disastrous," but that newly
discovered oil would be allowed to be sold at world prices. A
"well-head tax" would be added to the regulated price of "old oil" to
bring the total up to the world price. There is a lot more to it than
that, but I think you've got the idea.

Why is this disastrous for America? In the last few days, a study
was released, compiled by seventy geologists, engineers, economists
and systems analysts gathered under the auspices of the U.N. Institute
for Training and Research and the International Institute for Applied
Systems Analysts. They agreed that oil and gas from conventional
sources "would last at least until about the time period 2020-2030."
The report said the consensus at the conference was: as rising prices
make it economical to tap new sources, "additional petroleum and gas
sources would almost probably be available, albeit at substantially
higher cost during the period of transition to the use of renewable
energy sources, even if this transition period should last a hundred
years or more," and cited these reasons:

1.   Most of the world has never been systematically explored for
oil and gas, particularly the developing countries, off-shore and on the
ocean floor.

2. The world's oil industry will be able to get more and more of the oil and gas out of the ground thanks to its "ceaseless technical advance."

3. As prices increase, small fields or hard-to-get deposits, which are not economical to develop now, may become worthwhile. More oil may be produced from so-called unconventional sources, such as oil-bearing shale and tar sands.

If this is the case, why the great panic? Government has fouled up the works.

On February 17 at the Second Rocky Mountain Fuel Symposium at the University of Utah, CHALMER G. KIRKBRIDE, Engineering Consultant to Dr. Henry R. Linden who is President of the Institute of Gas Technology in Chicago, said:

> In 1776, essentially all the mechanical energy to do our work was from human beings and animals. Heat energy to keep man warm was obtained from burning wood. But in 1850, human energy was 23% of our total mechanical energy consumption. Animal energy was 51% and mechanical energy from the machine 26%. . . . Today, human energy amounts to only about 1%, animal energy to almost zero, and energy from the machine to 99% of our total work energy. . . .
>
> This is how America achieved the highest standard of living of any nation in history. But in getting to where we are, we have become almost completely dependent upon oil and gas.
>
> In 1975, we had to import about . . . 38% of our petroleum needs, and about 12% of our natural gas. But in 1976, our imported petroleum increased . . . from 38 to 43% of our national consumption. (Only one year! HJR).
>
> This is a serious threat to our national security, and it represents a major transfer of our national wealth to OPEC . . . The projected oil imports of the U.S.A. theoretically would permit OPEC to buy the 500 largest corporations of America within a six-year period.
>
> The pitiful part of this, is that we could produce substantially more oil and gas domestically, but the cost of production would be greater than the price ceilings being imposed on the nation by Congress.. . .
>
> But these price ceilings contribute to our acute shortages of domestic oil and gas. The price of gasoline is so low, that there is little incentive to use it efficiently . . . . In the case of natural gas, its artificially cheap price causes consumers to prefer it to the burning of coal.
>
> If the price of domestic oil were allowed to rise to $14, its production would be 3.3 million barrels per day higher by 1980 and 4 million barrels a day higher by 1985, assuming the price of

imported crude oil is only $14 per barrel (which I think is less than half what it will be by 1980). This would reduce the transfer of America's wealth to OPEC between now and 1980 by more than 30 billion dollars and by over 93 billion dollars during the period of 1980 to 1985 . . .

The same situation exists with respect to production of natural gas. There is a deposit of 6 hundred trillion cubic feet in the Rocky Mountain area that cannot be produced by primary production methods because of the very low permeability of the reservoirs. However, there are massive hydraulic fracturing methods that might be successful for producing this gas, but the price ceiling of $1.42 cubic foot at the wellhead for natural gas being sold into interstate commerce is substantially less than the probable cost of producing this gas by these methods.

You can be certain that no one will risk his capital to produce gas that costs more than the price ceiling. If only a third of 600 trillion cubic feet were recovered, it would double our natural gas reserves. Congress is destroying America by price ceilings just as effectively as if they were a partner of the Kremlin.

When the ERDA Coal Gasification and Coal Liquification processes are commercialized on a large scale after 1985, the probable cost will be about $26 per barrel of oil and $4.50 per cubic foot of synthetic natural gas. You can be sure that OPEC will be pushing up their price of oil at least $26 per barrel. My feeling is we better be prepared to pay $30 per barrel for oil imports by 1980.

If we don't maximize domestic production between now and 1990, America will not survive, and it's just that simple. If we stop using machines, we can terminate our need for oil and gas, but our standard of living would degenerate to what it was 200 years ago.

Now, in the light of all that blast, will Mr. Carter's plan solve the problem? Even if it were well conceived, he wouldn't get it though Congress intact. Congress will eliminate any possible benefit to the oil companies, thus crippling production. Also, Congress will probably eliminate the gas taxes that would have reduced consumption because they are politically undesirable. Life will be more difficult for Americans without achieving any measurable conservation benefit, while further discouraging production.

The taxes on gas guzzling cars and rebates on the small ones will be self-cancelling. For example, if you know there won't be any rebates until the 1978 models, and you are in the market for a small car, you'll wait and you will continue to use your gas guzzler. As a result, sales of small cars should drop off sharply for six months or so while Congress finishes fighting out this issue. In fact, AMERICAN MOTORS just announced that President Carter's attempt to put Americans into fuel-efficient cars is hurting their sales. Buyers are going to wait until the promised rebates begin.

Conversely, if you know there is going to be a big penalty on gas guzzlers and you want one, you will probably buy before the penalties hit, so Mr. Carter's program should temporarily stimulate sales of big cars.

By the same token, once the government starts giving rebates, the price of small cars will soar, as demand for them increases, which will probably just about make up for the rebate you would get from the government.

The plan will not work because there is no way, politically, government will give the oil companies incentive to produce.

If energy prices were allowed to rise normally, entrepreneurs would jump into the marketplace with better and cheaper methods of solar heating. Conservation devices would find their way into the marketplace, and as these markets broaden through mass production, costs would come down. As the cost of the old way of doing things rises, the gap is narrowed and transitions are made naturally with a minimum of pain. Under Mr. Carter's plan, the transition will be attempted with the wrong stick and the wrong carrot, while sitting backwards on the wrong donkey. We've got to deregulate the cost of fuel and take our medicine.

(2/1/78) As we have reported, Congress has approved of a new Department of Energy (DOE) with a staff of 20,000 and a budget of $10 billion.

Western Crude Oil, Inc., has done some fascinating arithmetic based on these numbers.

To put that budget into perspective, consider the following:

1. It represents $500,000 per department employee.

2. It represents $50 for each and every citizen of the United States.

3. It represents $266,871 for each of the 39,763 wells drilled in 1976.

4. It represents $58.35 for each of the 181,855,700 feet drilled in 1976.

5. It represents $3.59 for each barrel of domestic crude oil

production in 1976.

6. It represents $1.67 for every barrel of petroleum products consumed in 1976.

7. It represents 10 for every gallon of gasoline consumed in 1976.

8. It represents $0.3434 on every barrel of proven crude oil reserves as of December 31, 1976 (30.9 billion barrels).

9. It exceeds total 1975 capital and exploration expenditures by the petroleum industry to produce domestic crude oil, natural gas, and natural gas liquids ($9.4 billion, according to the Chase Manhattan Bank) and it is almost 3/5ths of the capital expenditures of all U.S. petroleum sectors in 1975 (17.7 billion).

10. It exceeds the 1974 profits of the seven largest oil companies —profits which were called "obscene."

This is the Carter energy program. In attempting to protect us from the oil companies' "obscene profits," it looks like government is going to be collecting some obscene taxes to pay for their DOE.

The more I look at the Carter energy program, the sicker it looks. Even the NAACP, which has been in favor of every liberal government spending nostrum since it was founded, has published a startling position paper in opposition to the Carter energy program. These people understand that we cannot embark on a program designed to slow down American industry to accommodate this unnatural, manufactured crisis. They realize that if the energy program is going to be felt by somebody, the pain will start at the bottom of the economic pyramid and the black man will feel it worse than anybody. He's the one who drives the older gas-guzzler, and he knows what's going to happen to his job and the cost of his gas without increasing production to eventually drive prices back down.

If Mr. Carter will allow the price of fuel to rise through deregulation, the following will happen:

The price will rise to roughly its equivalent in cost-per-BTU with foreign oil. Resulting in more exploration, drilling, and gas that would have been denied the American consumer because of price controls, leading to surpluses which will break the Arab oil cartel and drive all energy prices down, possibly as much as 50%.

Will that cause us to run out of energy tomorrow? That's ridiculous. We have from 600 to 1000 years supply of natural gas available to us at the present rate of consumption.

During the period of high prices, the potential profits will provide the economic stimulus necessary to develop alternate sources of energy, including the broadcast of energy from space to huge solar reflecting collectors. This is technically feasible. It just needs to become profitable. It would give us a clean and inexhaustible supply of energy. And this is only one of several possible solutions.

I think we had all better get it through our heads, this administration does not trust free enterprise, regardless of the lip service that was paid to the private sector by President Carter in his State of the Union address. Dishonest rhetoric, that's all it is.

Even now, we are negotiating to bring LIQUIFIED NATURAL GAS from Algeria and Indonesia at prices two or three times higher than Mr. Carter will allow domestic producers to receive. Imported gas profits are higher, so the stimulus is there to expand our dependence upon foreign oil. There is little profit in developing domestic supplies. All the real cheap gas has probably been found. If Mr. Carter's plan is enacted, it will increase our dependence on foreign oil, and will continue to give the OPEC nations and the oil companies their present stranglehold on our vital energy jugular, and will leave us vulnerable to Soviet disruption of the sea lanes. Their meddling in Africa is aimed at complete control of the sea lanes around Africa, and with their bases in Somalia, Ethiopia, and all of the Marxist dictatorships clear around Africa, including Angola, the only remaining weak link is South Africa.

Bombard your Congressman and Senator with mail until this pernicious plan is defeated. I won't be content until the Department of Energy has been driven back into the sea. It is a monster that can only make our problems worse, while draining incredible amounts of our national treasury from us in taxes.

And while we are on the subject of money, Mr. Carter has just announced his $500 billion budget. That's half a trillion dollars! To put that into perspective, I thought you might be interested in the following exciting facts:

That's enough money to give every man, woman and child in Atlanta a million dollars; or provide a $115,000 Rolls Royce to every one in Minnesota; or, if you wanted to, give $120 to every human being on the face of the earth; or, more selfishly, build a stack of $1 bills to the moon and back—250 times. Just thought you might be interested.

(12/15/78) It seems that the term "moral" is being used rather loosely in describing Mr. Carter's "moral equivalent of war" on the energy problem. When he made his scary announcement over a year ago that the nation was running out of energy and launched his energy/tax-transfer plan, I said there was enough natural gas to last for 600 years if they would merely deregulate it. I also alleged that the government was concealing scientific reports that disagreed with his concept of "energy crisis." (see also: Energy Shortages)

I referred specifically to the MOPPS (Market Oriented Programmed Planning Study) Report, which had been produced by ERDA (Energy Research and Development Administration), and which included assumptions so optimistic, the President sent it back to the drawing board. It came back modified, and he still wasn't satisfied. He sent it back again and they finally came back with a pessimistic enough report, but it still had 65 years of energy use at reasonable prices. Then the MOPPS chairman resigned.

The charge that your government is concealing information in order to make a political case is a pretty serious one. I didn't expect them to 'fess up, but apparently, administration officials are now doing so privately.

The Mexicans have recently announced that they have what is probably the world's richest source of oil, which surpasses even Saudi Arabia in long-term potential. The Carter Administration hasn't paid much attention to these developments, even though American intelligence began tracking Mexico's oil potential three or four years ago.

According to THE WALL STREET JOURNAL, administration officials now privately concede they let the Mexican potential go unpublicized because calling attention to it would have undercut the urgency of the President's "moral equivalent of war" in the energy crisis.

According to the article, Mexican leaders themselves have kept quiet until recently because of internal political differences. American officials also say intelligence officers feared that disclosing the information would jeopardize their information sources and anger Mexican leaders.

There will be an energy crisis created by government because of the bewildering array of controls. The so-called "deregulation" of natural gas has actually resulted in regulating gas that was never regulated before—specifically that which is produced and consumed within the same state. The resulting distortions in the marketplace could very well undermine the other beneficial deregulatory aspects of the energy bill.

I said I was expecting Carter to impose a large import tax on oil as part of our defense of the dollar. Carter asked for it, but didn't get it in his original energy plan. He might use the defense of the dollar as an excuse. He only needs the dollar to enter into its next decline before imposing such a tax.

These government actions will tend to create less oil and gas supplies above the ground, and it isn't because there aren't plenty available. There are enough in known reserves in the ground at reasonable prices at our present rates of consumption to last the world at least another 100 years.

That will buy us all the time we need to develop alternate sources of energy, including the broadcast of electricity from space, which, in my opinion, holds the greatest, least expensive potential.

The reason I brought up this whole subject was to point out to you the moral bankruptcy of politicians once they have decided upon an objective. This administration has engaged in conscious deceit in the pursuit of a political purpose. The total intent of the Carter energy plan is to transfer income, and it was basically conceived as a tax program (wellhead taxes, gas-guzzler taxes, etc.). The energy bill is bad for America, will create shortages, and increase our dependency upon foreign oil, and that ain't the way it's supposed to work.

(4/15/79) The Carter Plan is designed to do two things: (1) induce conservation through higher prices (probably successfully), and (2) create new taxes to help narrow the budget deficit (which also will probably be achieved). The third and most important leg of that tripod is missing. Increasing energy supplies will not be the result. In fact, supplies will shrink, creating shortages and upward pressure on prices.

Anyone who knows anything about the oil industry knows the immense impact of the hordes of independent oil operators. These are the free-enterprise mavericks of the American economy. They take tremendously high risks and drill nine dry holes for every one that produces either oil or gas. If the profit potential is not there to cover the risks and pay for the dry holes, no one in his right mind is going to go out and explore for anything.

The other thing that really concerns me is the assumption that profits are bad and those who seek them are greedy exploiters of the public. This is pure socialist-communist rhetoric and has no place in a free-enterprise society. It especially has no place in the thinking of the man that presides over this capitalist system. Increased supplies depress prices. Controls cause scarcities that increase prices. If the big oil companies try to maintain artificially high prices in a decontrolled environment, the independents will undercut their prices. Over the long haul, the free market will always seek a reasonable profit level, no more, no less.

As I've listened to Mr. Carter and some of the attacks from congressmen and senators who think he was wrong to deregulate in the first place, I have this sick feeling in the pit of my stomach that if this trend is not arrested, it could be the end of the free-enterprise system, as we know it, in America.

The inconsistency of government policy leads me to conclude that this is another example of government attempting to solve one problem and creating two or more problems of equal or greater dimensions in the process.

For example, one new coal-fired utility in the East, which would have cost about $800 million to build, was cancelled because government required it to spend $85 million for scrubbers to remove sulphur from the emissions, despite the fact the plant was going to be burning low-sulphur coal and scrubbers were not necessary. The company finally decided to convert to oil because it is cheaper. Power plants all over the country are converting to oil, even though this threatens the nation's security and independence. At the same time, the coal industry is depressed and there is probably enough coal above ground to meet the nation's needs for the next year and a half. Miners are out of work and coal prices are way below the cost of production.

At the same time, we are busing children, pouring money into the pockets of foreign desert despots, and driving our oil companies to where the profits are: high-priced oil in the Middle East. We're bringing in liquefied natural gas from Indonesia at $3.25 per thousand cubic feet, which is a considerably higher price than what is necessary to stimulate the drilling of all the gas this nation could possibly need, if we merely allow the domestic price to rise a bit.

In addition, we stand helpless before a Moslem revolution in Iran that could sweep through the whole Middle East, with heaven-knows-what results on oil supplies.

President Carter gets one and a half cheers from me for the great persistence and determination he exercised in bringing Begin and Sadat to the peace table to sign the treaty, but it's impossible to drop a pebble in a pond without causing ripples. The ripples and fallout from this peace treaty may create energy problems worse than those which we had prior to the signing.

Egypt is now alienated from the entire Arab Middle East. It is the only Arab nation without significant amounts of oil. We may have devastated Egypt's economy if it becomes isolated from its Arab brethren and their subsidies. The Arab nations, including the hitherto moderate King Hussein of Jordan, have literally declared economic war on Egypt. The Saudi Arabians are nervous because of Soviet pressure. They are not militarily strong and their oil fields are vulnerable to sabotage, and their government is vulnerable to revolutionary assault from a fanatic Iranian Islamic republic in Iran. If we were to see war, increasing PLO influence, or any other threat to the stability of the Middle East, it would thrust the world-wide economy into inflation and depression at the same time.

The best the President of this country can do is to pour out his vitriol on the only people who can save us—the oil companies.

Do not conclude that I love the oil companies. They often act like arrogant pirates. But their responsibility is to maximize profits for their stockholders. Their stockholders either get a return on their invested money, or they simply won't invest anymore. If we do not nurture and cherish the idea of profits, the nation is doomed as a free-enterprise system. If we do not have sufficient faith in the system to realize that deregulation will produce competition that will ultimately keep profits at reasonable levels, without government sticking its fat nose into the situation, then we are saying we no longer trust the free-enterprise system, and all is lost. Our freedom will not just erode away from us a bit at a time, as it has until now, but it will be gone so quickly we will hardly know what happened to it.

Write to your congressman and senator and indicate your displeasure with this immensely dangerous, demagogic, collectivist attack from a hypocrite who parades under the guise of a born-again, free-enterprise, small businessman. The man is a bloody Bolshevik.

Incidentally, I own no oil company stock, and I wouldn't know an energy company executive if he bit me on the nose. I just believe in freedom, profits, and sound economics in a capitalist system. You can't spur a horse to greater effort by cutting his oat ration.

ENERGY "CRISIS"

(8/15/77) Why are the poorer societies of man clustered about the earth's belt line? After all, in the tropics the earth produces green abundance with little effort. Food and water are all that is needed for actual survival. Shelter is not a matter of life or death there, as cold is no problem. Clothing is not needed except for decoration or modesty, and yet civilization in modern times has reached its highest flower where crops grow only part of the year, and cold threatens life for a third of the year.

In the temperate zones, however, you must add shelter, clothing and heat to the two basic necessities, food and water. Civilization is completely dependent upon our ability to produce warmth for man's comfort and survival.

When man was living in the stone age in Northern Europe and

England, the world's greatest civilizations were flourishing in Africa, India, Southeast Asia and middle America. What caused this modern reversal of roles? Why did the cooler climes outstrip the rest of the world in building a civilization of comfort, leisure and affluence? Man learned to enclose his environment within four walls and produce a comfortable temperature with coal, oil and natural gas. These energy sources have brought about the great industrial revolution and all the technological advances that have created man's generally comfortable state. And now these sources are threatened possibly as close as three months from now!

As of now, the possession of a wood burning stove is considered a quaint fad, but we are approaching a time when it might be a lifesaver. Changing climate and artificially created energy problems might plunge us unprepared into a total restructuring of our life style and population patterns. There are many parts of this country where the failure of society to deliver electricity, oil or natural gas to homes could mean utter disaster.

Yesterday I drove through San Francisco where wooden houses and apartment buildings are crowded cheek-to-jowl, many of them having been built immediately after the great earthquake of 1906. I visualized the holocaust that would occur if gas and/or electricity were cut off and people began to heat or cook with open fires, even in the luxury apartments of Nob Hill.

We are approaching a time when it is likely that our great cities will find themselves without power. In past depressions, such as those suffered in the Revolutionary War, the Civil War and in the 1930s, society was locally self-sufficient, and the economy was solidly based upon local farming. Communities rarely saw products grown or produced more than a hundred miles away. Such items were considered luxuries. A breakdown in the economy resulted in hardships, but was not a matter of life or death, again, because of this lesser degree of interdependence. One nation could have an economic collapse and its financial evils were less likely to be exported to other nations, as national economies were also less interdependent. Can you imagine the effect on Minnesota, Maine or Illinois if power, natural gas and fuel oil delivery ceased in January or February for even a few days? And yet this is precisely what is threatened if we should have a major economic collapse, or a bad winter again.

Can you imagine how secure and comfortable you would feel if you had in your home an independent source of heat, and a supply of food and water so that you could remain comfortable and free of actual physical suffering? We are a nation of manual illiterates who know nothing more about life-giving heat than turning on a furnace or turning up a thermostat.

(2/15/79)   So, what should we do to solve the energy crisis?

1.   Explore and drill, but with some reasonable safeguards. Until we do, we increase our dependence on the whims of fanatics like the AYATOLLAH KHOMEINI.

2.   Deregulate natural gas and oil. Deregulation of natural gas alone could bust the Arab oil cartel in 18 months.

3.   Allow prices to rise to their natural level, which will cause people to think twice before driving. They might even decide to buy small cars.

4.   Aggressively follow up on some of the promising new methods of recovering fuel (see: Oil Recovery) and of getting better fuel economy, such as the Oglemobile, which operates on the simple principle of bypassing the carburetor and injecting vaporized fuel. Ogle gets over 100 MPG.

An energy crisis isn't necessary, but we will have one. Get a fuel storage tank, if possible, and a MoPed or a diesel Rabbit, or you will be seriously inconvenienced by the energy crisis which is just around the corner. The ration coupons are already printed. ("President signs Gas Rationing Bill" is front page news at the time of editing, 11/79, Ed. note.)

The alternative to deregulation and further development of our oil resources is to see the lights gradually wink out in America, the last great hope of western civilization. We have no choice.

ENERGY "SHORTAGES"

(8/1/77)   There is no imminent shortage of natural gas and petroleum in the ground. There is a current glut of oil above ground. There is a developing shortage of natural gas production. Recently, the ENERGY RESEARCH AND DEVELOPMENT ADMINIS-TRATION (ERDA) put together a study on the availability of natural gas at various prices, called MOPPS (Market Oriented Programmed Planning Study).

Considering conventional sources only, at worst ERDA found us 55 years worth of natural gas at a reasonable price.

MOPPS Executive Director, Harry Johnson, believes the higher estimates, which they were told to adjust, were the correct ones. Philip White, MOPPS Chairman, says the original estimate might have been a pretty good guess. The *WALL STREET JOURNAL* estimates the deregulation of natural gas would bring in so much that it would soon force down the price of its nearest substitute, No. 2 fuel oil, which now sells at the equivalent of $4.00 per thousand cubic feet, and DEREGULATION OF GAS PRICES COULD VERY WELL BREAK THE OPEC CARTEL.

There are incredible amounts of available natural gas. Over 20 years of low prices have left 98% of the prospective sediments untouched by drilling.

There are low-production wells requiring expensive special recovery treatment which would become economical at somewhat higher prices. This has been demonstrated in Texas where unregulated prices produced the incentive to increase drilling activity, swelling the gas supply by 3000% in four years.

There are deep geological basins with huge reserves. ERDA has just brought in the first geo-pressurized methane well, bringing that absolutely unlimited resource a step closer.

There are suitable frontier areas, but a long way from pipelines, where the long-term investment has not been justified by artificially low prices.

105,000 trillion cubic feet of gas has been calculated to exist below 8,000 feet on the Texas Gulf Coast. Even if U.S. consumption doubled, we could supply the nation's need for 200 years with 10 percent of the gas from this source alone.

The necessary price to make this economical is well below the cost of imported liquefied natural gas (LNG), on which the government is willing to spend billions in subsidies for "Big Oil," wishing to bring it in from such places as INDONESIA at prices well above what it would cost us to recover our domestic supplies.

To add the frosting to the cake, Bill Brown, who is Director of Technology at the HUDSON INSTITUTE "think-tank," tells us that, although he does not recommend it, as far as our fossil fuel resources are concerned, ". . . there is no doubt in my mind that, if we wanted to, we could continue using energy at the present rate and even increase consumption and export oil in the future. The only things preventing it are environmental regulations and uncertain government pricing policies. There is enough to last us about 600 years at the current annual consumption rate if we use high grade recoverable shale oil and if the low grade oil is included, it is 10 times as much."

Whenever oil companies have been able to manipulate prices to the public's disadvantage, it has been through the use of their relationships with government, so they fear TOTAL deregulation, which forces them to compete with each other. And yet, Mr. Carter and his staff celebrated when deregulation was struck down in Committee in Congress by a vote of 22 to 21.

Why did Mr. Carter manipulate the MOPPS report? Why did Mr. Carter break his promises to the voters of Texas and Louisiana, when he won those states by promising them deregulation of natural gas prices?

Knowing there need not be any crisis, why did he launch his "moral equivalent of war"? What a strange expression! War actually has low moral value. Does this mean that in time of war, anything goes, including deception?

If Carter has trouble getting his program through Congress, WHAT CAN HE DO, AND IN THE LIGHT OF HIS PERSONALITY AND TEMPERAMENT, WHAT IS HE LIKELY TO DO?

The answers to these questions make my hair stand on end as I examine his options. A small hint hit the press a few weeks ago when Mr. Schlesinger, the White House energy advisor, said, "We are surveying all the range of alternatives to a gasoline tax to achieve a 10% reduction in gasoline consumption by 1985." Then, he said that proposing a system of GASOLINE RATIONING would be the most drastic alternative. He said they are considering restricting the hours that service stations operate, or closing stations on Sundays and having motorists buy on odd or even numbered days, as we did in some states during 1973-74. (It happened in '79, Ed. note.)

He also said that under existing law, the President could order rationing or, in other ways, limit gasoline use, but only during an oil embargo or other national emergency.

(5/15/77) Suffice it to say the United States is running out of energy. Not because there are no energy sources out there to meet our needs, but because Government has suppressed the price, and smothered the normal signals of the marketplace to the extent that it will take us from three to ten years to catch up. Had it not been for last winter's very cold weather, we would still not be aware of our energy shortage.

Energy affects more than just your automobile or the temperature of your home. Energy is crucial to growing food, and if farmers are not to be bankrupted by rising costs of fertilizer, and other energy-based essentials, they are going to have to get far higher prices for food. If we attempt to control food prices through controls we will merely create shortages, wound the farm economy or cause it to be nationalized, which will add to your tax burden. There are no other choices.

(10/1/77) This whole episode will rank as one of the more shameful in the history of the American presidency. Mr. Carter knows there is no shortage of natural gas.

The *WALL STREET JOURNAL* reports that Dr. Vincent E. McKelvey, who, for the last six years has been the Director of the U.S. Geological Survey, was recently bounced by the White House. He wasn't fired for incompetence. While Carter is trying to bulldoze a $100 billion tax/energy conservation program through Congress, McKelvey gave a speech in Boston observing that as much as 60,000 to 80,000 trillion cubic feet of gas may be lying in the geo-pressured zones underlying the Gulf Coast region. THAT'S 3,000 TO 4,000 TIMES THE AMOUNT OF NATURAL GAS THE UNITED STATES WILL CONSUME THIS YEAR.

"This is an almost incomprehensibly large number," says Dr. McKelvey, noting that, "even the bottom range represents about ten times the energy value of all oil, gas and coal reserves in the United States." In the same speech he observed that, "A large amount of oil is still to be found in the United States." This is just another reflection of the same kind of mentality that rejected the MOPPS report.

Mr. Carter's prophesy of an energy shortage will become self-fulfilling, not because it isn't there under the ground, but because the policies which he has proposed will keep it in the ground.

This wretched Carter energy program is a hype, a scam, a con, a cynical manipulation of figures and an abuse of power.

(8/1/78) About a year ago, I commented on the firing of the head of the U.S. Geological Survey, Dr. Vincent E. McKelvey.

Having dutifully reported this, I thought he might be a great guest for RUFF HOU$E TV. However, when we began looking for Dr. McKelvey, we ran into a series of surprises and I'm still not quite sure what they mean. I'll just report to you what happened and let you draw your own conclusions.

It took us some time to locate Dr. McKelvey. We found out, to our surprise, he was still working for the U.S Geological Survey, as a research geologist, and he was attending an energy conference in Switzerland. When invited to appear on our show, he showed tremendous reluctance to discuss his firing with anybody, let alone on TV.

After several communications back and forth and a lot of vacillation, where it was on-and-off two or three times, Dr. McKelvey finally agreed to come to our recording studios and be taped, but he had two stipulations: (1) we would not pay him any expenses, as his trip would be paid for totally by the U.S. Government, and (2) we would talk for a half-hour or so before he went on the show.

When he arrived, we sat down to talk. I was startled at what I saw. He was obviously a very frightened man. The beads of sweat were standing out all over his forehead and upper lip and literally running down his face and dripping off his chin. He informed me that he did not want to discuss politics of any kind, nor would he have anything to say about his firing. He claimed he had been misquoted, that he had never, at any time, been in disagreement with the Administration on any matters of policy, that he was just a scientist trying to do his job, and that his firing had nothing to do with any statements about an abundance of energy.

I said to him, "Dr. McKelvey, if you have been misquoted, and if it is not true that you were fired for disagreement with your employer, I can't understand why you would not jump at the chance to go on television and tell one or two million people the truth to set the record straight." After a couple more gallons of sweat, which literally left wet spots on his necktie, he reluctantly agreed to go on the show if he could stop it at any time.

When we taped the show, I had a very nervous man on my hands, and there was no way I was going to be able to ask him deep, challenging questions because he would simply bolt and run. He was obviously frightened of something, or somebody, so I handled him with kid gloves.

Toward the end of the taping session with most of the interview safely in the can, I asked him, "Dr. McKelvey, has your public position on energy changed at any time since you were discharged as head of the U.S. Geological Survey?" Again, the gallons of sweat. He said, "Well, no, my position has been the same, although I have recently been more concerned about the exponential growth in the use of energy." (That's not word-for-word what he said, but it's close enough to be completely accurate.)

Later, I compared the speech that he had given to The Commonwealth Club in San Francisco after his firing with the one he had made in Boston before his firing. There had obviously been a major change in attitude and tone.

In the Boston speech, he was realistic about some of the problems in developing our gas reserves, but the tone was generally optimistic about the future possibilities. In the Commonwealth Club speech that occurred after his firing, he said many of the same things but talked about how the exponential growth of energy at the rate of five percent a year would use up those resources in 60 years and the pessimistic shift was blatant, obvious and unmistakable.

I can only draw one conclusion. He is a frightened bureaucrat who has worked for the government for 35 years, is worried about his pension, and has been farmed out to pasture, if he stays in line.

What does it all mean? Well, it could mean he was fired because he disagreed publicly with Carter, who couldn't have anyone running around the country saying we had 600 years worth of natural gas, when he was trying to get his miserable energy/tax/redistribute-the-wealth bill through Congress. That requires a "crisis."

Maybe he was discharged for other reasons, and this is all merely coincidental. Maybe his shift of emphasis is legitimate and not politically influenced. But why in the heck was he so scared? Stay tuned. We're still investigating.

I promised him that I would publish his denial of the allegations in this letter, and I have now discharged my responsibility. I really feel sorry for Dr. McKelvey. He is a fine scientist and not a bad man. In fact, I feel bad about embarrassing him with this story. But the issue at stake is greater than the people involved.

ALTERNATE SOURCES

(8/15/77) We are vulnerable to a group of despotic, semi-literate, total monarchs, who by some freak of nature find themselves squatting over a great pool of the world's real wealth in the sands of the Middle East. The minor shortages created by the oil boycott of the winter of '73-'74 almost paralyzed us and threw near panic into all of western civilization. Rather than learning our lesson, we have raised our exports of oil in three years from 15% to over 50% of our total needs, and this figure is rising rapidly. Mr. Carter's energy program will do nothing but increase the shortage, and America's vulnerability.

The only recourse left to me, as a husband and father, is to prepare my home so my family will be little affected by this insanity. I can't think of anything more critical to your life and well-being than an alternate source of heat that would not depend upon the smooth functioning of a fragile society. Much of my emergency food supply could be eaten raw, but I would rather not. The simple expedient of a modern woodburning stove is basic.

FROM A TO Z

NUCLEAR ENERGY

(Special Report #2, 1/76)   Atomic Power Is Out Of Control.

> We will not be able to regulate nuclear weapons around the
> world any better than we can control the Saturday-Night Special,
> heroin, or pornography today.—Harvard's Thomas Schelling

This is the chilling conclusion of a symposium in the November
issue of *Harvard Magazine*. In it, five arms control experts judge that
some nuclear wars are likely to occur before the century's end. The
five are Schelling, a professor of political economy; biochemist, Paul
Doty; physicist, Richard Garwin; chemist, George Kistiakowsky; and
MIT political scientist, George Rathgens.

The participants expect nuclear war will strike as a direct result of
bombs spreading around the world like an epidemic disease, and no
current disarmament policy can curb the spread. The proliferation of
"peaceful" nuclear power only aggravates the danger, because as
Rathgens writes, "By the end of the century, there will be several
thousand reactors around the world, each producing enough material
to build a weapon a week."

"A false sense of confidence may be fatal," warns Doty. "We now
have a period of relative public confidence that nuclear war is not
imminent. We are apt to lose the vision of how absolutely catastrophic
nuclear war is," he concludes.

There are at least eight small nations which have the capability of
manufacturing small atomic weapons, which could be smuggled into
this country. Dropped to the bottom of one of our large coastal
harbors, they could then be used to demand our wealth and resources,
under threat of the detonation of these weapons by remote devices.
This is closely related to the fact that the Third World is Out of
Control.

HOW TO CAUSE AN ENERGY CRISIS

(4/15/79)   Here is a sure-fire formula for a wing-ding of an energy
crisis.

1. Control the price of domestic oil and natural gas in an
inflationary environment. That guarantees that energy company
profits on domestic oil and gas will be squeezed by rising labor and
material costs, so they'll stop exploring and drilling at home, and will

meet their profit responsibility to their stockholders by developing high-priced sources abroad, rather than in the good old U.S.A. This will increase our dependence on foreign oil.

2. Deregulate prices, but demand that the oil companies plow back all new profits into exploration, leaving none of the rewards of high-risk exploration to the stockholders. If I were an oil man, I'd say, "to heck with it!" Government took no risks. They invested no money. What right do they have to take all the rewards?

3. Bus kids all over town, using millions of gallons of gas to implement a dubious social experiment most everyone hates.

4. Make it next to impossible to expand the use of coal, by creating expensive environmental regulations. Due to controls, oil is so artificially cheap, compared to coal, that power plants will be forced by economics to continue to use oil. That ought to be good for a few million gallons a week.

5. Ignore technological developments: hydrogen cars, the Merkl oil recovery process, the Oglemobile, and solar broadcast electricity. (see also: Energy Savers)

6. Insult Mexico by refusing their $2.80 mcf natural gas, then later, backtrack, crawfish and crawl, until they condescend to sell us oil at OPEC prices, keeping their cheap natural gas for themselves.

7. Pass stupid laws which prevent us from selling Alaskan heavy crude to Japan in return for their imported light crude, which would save everyone money. This assures the Alaska pipeline will operate at far less than capacity because there is only one refinery on the West Coast that can handle it (also because of environmental regulations).

8. Allow the environmentalists to create a web of regulations, permits, lawsuits and delays, making it economically impossible for Sohio to use an existing natural gas pipeline from Long Beach to the Gulf Coast, where the refineries are.

Of course, no sane government would do all those stupid things!

Oh, yeah? In the last *RUFF TIMES*, I forecast that Jimmy Carter would call for deregulation of oil prices, while at the same time pushing for heavy taxes on excess profits. He came through right on schedule, probably a day or two after you received your *RUFF TIMES*.

What I was not really prepared for, however, was the virulence of his April 10 press conference attack on the oil industry. He said he would not allow the oil companies to enjoy any deregulation windfall profits "at the expense of the American people." He demanded that ALL profits not taxed away must be plowed back into exploration and drilling. I must reiterate that this is part of an anti-business campaign. (see: Business)

As I read back through the previous article, I concluded I didn't make enough of the point that the big oil companies are not owned by fat, rich millionaires. They are mostly public corporations, owned by literally millions of stockholders, who depend upon the profits from American businesses to pay them dividends for their retirement, or put their kids through college. The shares are owned by mutual funds (generally bought by small investors), insurance companies (widows, orphans and senior citizens), union pension funds (your retirement plan) and college endowment funds (reducing the cost of education), etc. If their dividends shrink, tens of millions of Americans will be hurt.

ENERGY SAVERS

DIESEL CARS

(4/15/79)   There Is No Fuel Like An Oil Fuel

A few weeks ago I got in my brand new Oldsmobile Regency diesel and drove 340 miles from my home to Los Angeles for a series of radio and television appearances. I then drove all over Los Angeles for two and a half days. When I stopped to refuel, I still had a third of a tank. I cannot tell you how confident that makes me feel, knowing we may have severe allocations of fuel and closed service stations on Sundays, when the government begins to mess up the energy situation in earnest. The Regency is a large, comfortable car, and yet it gets a consistent 24 miles to the gallon and has a very large tank. What I have is RANGE. When I am looking for absolute economy, I use my diesel Rabbit which gets 50 miles to the gallon. Diesel fuel will be less likely to be rationed because it is the same as No. 2 heating oil, and it would be pretty difficult to allocate, at least in the early stages of a rationing program. So I have it all—comfort, range, and economy. I suggest you consider similar alternatives.

The only thing I don't like about my Regency is that it is noisy on the outside. When you stand beside it, it sounds like a distant thrashing machine with a bolt loose. However, with the windows closed, it makes no more noise inside than any other car. That is a minor drawback to an otherwise wonderful automobile.

Another major advantage is that diesel stores so safely, and with Fuel-Mate added (Bob Hinrichs, P.O. Box 3471, Santa Barbara, CA 93105, 805-682-6919), it keeps for years. I have 750 gallons in a rented tank on a nearby farm. Give it a try.

HOWARD RUFF

GASOHOL

(Special Report #2, 1/76) Not only is demand for grain increasing as a food, but it is now being looked at as a source of industrial chemicals. For example, in Nebraska, rapid development is being made in a product called "gasohol," a blend of gasoline and ethanol, which is alcohol made from corn and wheat. This is seen as a way to aid the farm economy and stretch fuel supplies, with the argument being that grain is a renewable resource, while petroleum is not. That would be fine under normal growing conditions, but this is no time to be converting our wheat and corn into smog. Especially when it takes so much fuel to plant, cultivate, irrigate, fertilize, harvest, and process the grain. Gasohol is said to deliver more power with less pinging, but I'm still withholding judgment on it as a viable alternative. (see: Energy & Farming)

HYDROGEN CARS

(8/1/78) I went to Provo, Utah, to interview ROGER BILL-INGS, President of Billings Energy Corporation, for RUFF HOU$E. He has a profitable company, utilizing hydrogen as a power source for cars, houses, buses, lawnmowers and almost anything else you can mention. My first reaction, remembering my high school chemistry, was that the Hindenburg used hydrogen, it is terribly explosive and I don't want to turn my car into a funeral pyre. He has solved that problem, however. The storage tanks are filled with small chunks of "hydride," which is a metal with an affinity for hydrogen. Hydride converts hydrogen to an inert nonexplosive, nonflammable form and, when it's drawn on demand from the tank it's no more flammable than gasoline. He's converting Dodge Omnis to hydrogen right now. They cost about $4000 above the factory price, but his next run of 100 converted cars will cost considerably less. The interesting thing is that it will still burn regular gasoline, and still has its regular gas tank. He is also marketing an "electrolyzer" which can be plugged into regular house current in your garage to separate water into hydrogen and oxygen. You merely connect it to your car overnight and, presto, you have 120 to 150 miles of range. When you run out of hydrogen, if you are away from home, you merely flip a switch and it smoothly switches to gasoline. When burning hydrogen, it is totally pollution-free.

Billings is building and selling homes in a small subdivision which are all hydrogen powered. There is a city bus running around Provo, Utah, and another one in Riverside, California, burning hydrogen, using his process.

(5/1/79)   Burning Water

It has been an age-old dream of the alchemists and magicians to be able to extract from water all the power needed by man. Theoretically, we know it's there in the form of hydrogen.

Some months ago, we had an interview with **ROGER BILLINGS**, of The Billings Energy Corporation, who has developed a hydrogen car. The hydrogen is created by means of a device called an Electrolyzer, which separates water into oxygen and hydrogen and runs off your house electricity. The hydrogen is converted into a "metal hydride," (basically, hydrogen combined with metal particles in a heavy pressure tank forming a powder) which is converted back into a gas when it is released to be burned in the engine. Billings' car runs on either gasoline or hydrogen with a flick of a switch, but requires heavy, bulky hydrogen tanks in the trunk. The disadvantages of the system are *the cost of the Electrolyzer* (around $5000) and the fact that more fossil fuel energy is consumed in creating the electricity to hydrolyze the water than is produced in the form of hydrogen. Because of the weight and bulk of the tanks, the car's range was limited. But still, I consider it an important development.

Now I've run into something that goes several steps further. This could be the end of the energy crisis.

DR. GERALD M. SCHAFLANDER, the head of **SOLAR-HYDROGEN DEVELOPMENT COMPANY** has developed a method of using **SOLAR ENERGY CELLS** to generate electricity to separate the hydrogen from water. The hydrogen is then converted from a gas into a Liquid Hydride, which acts, pours, and burns just like gasoline. Standard cars can be converted in about two hours by any competent mechanic, basically using the existing technology by which cars are now being converted to burn propane. Hydrogen is then pumped into the gas tank just like gasoline, requiring no special equipment. You get the same range and mileage that you get with gasoline.

The aspects of this breakthrough are as follows:

1. They have developed a break-through method of mass-producing the solar cells, which lowers the cost by 2/3, which makes the conversion of solar energy into electricity cost-competitive with nuclear or fossil-fuel energy.

2. The liquid hydride is unique. It can be safely stored, shipped,

pumped through pipelines, carried in tankers, burned in cars, or what have you, with no more danger than gasoline. They don't have to convert it into the heavy metal hydride Billings uses. No trunk space is used.

3. They are ready to go now and there probably will be franchising centers around the country to both convert the cars and pump the fuel.

Their new solar cell technology is so efficient that with 60,000 acres they could produce as much energy as the entire power grid of the United States. With 20,000 or 30,000 acres and access to water, they could produce all the fuel necessary to run all the automobiles of America. They also have the land and the water.

Their concept is simplicity itself. Produce the hydrogen fuel, ship it to franchised centers (which could be a Firestone Store, a Sears Auto Service Center, or whatever), in your local community. They convert your car, and that's where you go for a fill-up. Sooner or later, as the market develops the demand and there are more and more cars on the road, more and more service stations would provide the fuel. In the early stages, the limitation would be that you would have difficulty driving very far from home, knowing you couldn't get a convenient fill-up. I imagine that problem could be very quickly solved if they were able to do it through Sears or Firestone outlets, because there is one almost everywhere.

The system's limitations are relatively few. For example, they have not figured out a way to do it effectively with sea water, which means they will need a dependable source of fresh water, and a lot of it. Second, it's not possible, with the existing technology, to convert diesel engines to burn hydrogen.

The beauty of this system is that any car can be quickly and easily converted, and the emissions consist strictly of water vapor. Your car will have approximately the same range and mileage that it would have burning gasoline. Probably better, because you would not need the smog devices.

There are a lot of business sidelines from the use and sale of the oxygen developed through the process, to say nothing of the sale of electricity. Incidentally, actors Jack Nicholson and Paul Newman are also involved with the project.

Up until now, they have made the mistake of jousting with Washington. They were even denied the privilege of making a competitive bid for adapting government vehicles and providing the fuel. They have even offered to convert the vehicles free, and sell the fuel at some mutually agreed upon price (around 40 cents a gallon), which would produce great savings for the government. Washington has not given them the time of day. Frankly, they have wasted a lot of time and energy in Washington when they should forget them, raise money privately, and proceed without government. Schaflander has the engineer's usual lack of understanding of corporate finance, so he hasn't figured out what financial devices could be used to raise sufficient money without relinquishing control of his company. There are lots of ways to do it.

(5/15/79) More On Hydrogen Cars

Our article on the Schaflander hydrogen car in the last issue kicked up an absolutely incredible reaction.

I'd like to suggest a little caution. Schaflander's development is interesting and exciting, but still requires serious investigation. It could be all it claims to be, or it could have some serious problems. The purpose of my article was not to endorse Schaflander's hydrogen car, nor Mr. Carman's Inertial Storage Transmission, but to start a stimulating debate on the need for an open-minded investigation of all of the more interesting claims for energy innovation.

Even if Schaflander has made the technical breakthrough he claims to have made, the next step to concluding, "it's a good business deal," is a big one. We don't know enough about Schaflander as a businessman, the capital structure of his company, or whether there are some technical bugs that might prove insurmountable.

This leads me to a little piece of basic business advice. Billions have been lost by people who enthusiastically jumped into promising ventures without any understanding about the business acumen or judgment of the people involved in the company. Most innovative inventors are, almost by definition, rather strange people. That's not a criticism, it's just Ruff's First Law of Genius. A genius can be the royal road to riches, or a royal pain in the pocketbook. In other words, there's a lot more to getting rich than having an invention, and many promising inventions have died on the shoals of business reality, sometimes simply because they came along a bit too early.

I'm not knocking Schaflander or his invention. I'm terribly intrigued by it. It appears immensely promising, but at this point, I don't know enough about it to endorse it as a business venture, and you should not go throwing your money around until you have done a thorough and complete investigation.

Take a look at it, weigh it for yourself and draw your own conclusions. It's your money, not mine.

HOWARD RUFF

INERTIAL STORAGE TRANSMISSION

(5/1/79) I have just interviewed a man on RUFF HOU$E who blew my mind. VINCENT E. CARMAN has developed another tremendous energy saving idea. Here it is.

It seems that large amounts of kinetic energy are expended when you brake your car. His hypothesis was that if you could somehow store that energy, you could use it to propel the car, until the stored kinetic energy was dissipated. He has developed a method of doing just that. Except as an emergency back-up, this car has no brakes. The key is a new type of transmission and an energy accumulator. When you let up on the accelerator, the transmission brakes the car. You have to learn to use your accelerator as a brake as well as an accelerator. The energy used in braking is not lost, but used to pump oil under increasing pressure into an accumulator tank. When the car is ready to start and you step on the accelerator, the pressurized oil drives the wheels. The engine automatically shuts off until the pressure in the accumulator tank has reduced to the point where there is not sufficient stored energy to continue to propel the car, at which time a small computer kicks a solenoid and restarts the engine which recharges the accumulator tank and then it cuts out again. In stop-and-go driving in the city, which is about 55% of the driving in this country, the engine is off 80% of the time, creating an eerie silence.

That has obvious implications for gas mileage. The cars they have converted get approximately double the normal gas mileage in city driving. There is relatively little advantage in freeway driving, where you are not doing much braking.

Acceleration, using the stored energy, is tremendous, in fact, much more so than a typical engine. If you let up on the accelerator too fast, it's just as if someone threw out an anchor.

This invention was featured on the cover of *MECHANICS ILLUSTRATED*, and their evaluation of it was that "it works." The inventor estimates it takes $1200 to $1500 to convert an existing car, but if it's mass-produced and installed at the factory, the cost would be roughly $150 per automobile, over and above present cost. The fuel savings would make up for that in no time at all, given what fuel prices will be in the near future.

So far, I have described a relatively simple and straightforward invention. Now the plot thickens! The invention was submitted to the

Energy Research and Development Administration (ERDA), which referred it to the National Bureau of Standards (NBS) for testing. NBS tested it, and out of several thousand energy inventions evaluated, determined that this is one of 45 worthy of funding and continued development. Because ERDA, according to the inventor, was interested in a fly-wheel system, and was emotionally and financially committed to it, this report was buried. In fact, it darn near took an act of Congress to get the report released, and in the meantime there has been no funding. The only reason Mr. Carman isn't starving is because his wife has a job.

It is obvious that if you could double the gas mileage of city driving, you would reduce the consumption of gasoline in this country by millions of barrels a day. The consequences of this invention are staggering. I'll let you know more as things develop later on.

EQUAL RIGHTS AMENDMENT (ERA)

(7/1/78)   I am immensely disturbed at the tactics of the EQUAL RIGHTS AMENDMENT advocates in attempting to get a seven-year extension of the ratification period for ERA. It is like a losing football team being able to change the rules of the game to allow them to keep playing until they win.

I find this particularly offensive when they want to change the rules of the game for themselves, and yet not allow state legislatures to change their minds and reverse their vote prior to final ratification.

This is a gross abuse of the process of amending the Constitution. One of our most precious rights is the right to amend it and anything which creates uncertainty about the amending process should be resisted. If you can change it to 14 years, why not 20, or 30, or 50? Would the Americans of 1943 wish to have been bound by an action the state legislatures passed in 1929?

Write to your Congressman immediately. Whether you agree or disagree with ERA is irrelevant. I am opposed to ERA, but even if I were on the other side, I would just as vigorously resist any attempts to change the rules of the game just before the whistle blows.

ESTATE PLANNING

DO WE TRUST THE TRUST

(4/1/77)   Well, we finally completed our research on the family trust situation. As you will remember, we published an interview with John O'Donnell concerning a course to teach the family how to set up a family trust to avoid probate and estate taxes, reduce personal liability and personal income taxes (*RUFF TIMES*, 2/1/77). We have had a blizzard of paper, either expressing interest in the course or denouncing us for having published misleading information. And as a result, I have done some additional research.

I have spent several thousand dollars in research time and legal fees examining this course and trust law generally. I invited my attorney, BILL ANDERSON, of ANDERSON AND NEARON, and DENNIS SCHARF and BARRY MORRIS of POLARI-OMNI CORPORATION, to spend several hours in my office confronting the subject.

Mr. Scharf and Mr. Morris run a tax counseling firm which specializes in advising those who are setting up and using such trusts. They are concerned and honest, and I very much appreciated their candor. They, of course, are advocates of the family trust concept, but feel pushing "courses" like some firms do is ethically questionable.

Bill Anderson's firm draws up over 300 trusts a year. These trusts are often referred to as "family trusts" but are quite different from the trust now under discussion and are usually revocable. Members of the Anderson firm teach Estate and Gift Tax Law at one of the local law schools and also conduct frequent seminars on the subject of trusts. Bill Anderson was with the IRS for several years and is certified by the State Bar of California as a Tax Specialist. I consider him to be a genuine expert on trusts and trust law. He was opposed to this program.

It is the opinion of Bill Anderson that the "Family Trust" will neither hold up under assault nor accomplish all the things claimed for it. In fact, Bill said he felt that if he were to prepare such a trust for his clients, he would be guilty of malpractice. His objections rested on the following points:

1.   There are four IRS rulings, issued in June of 1975 (and referred to by John O'Donnell in our previous article—Revenue Rulings

75-257 through 260), which Bill Anderson feels are on point. He contends these rulings merely reinforce the Internal Revenue Code and that any trust designed similar to the trusts described in the rulings will be subject to adverse tax consequences.

2. The trust, as described in the course, is essentially the same as in those rulings.

3. Bill says he is 90% sure the wife cannot be an "ADVERSE PARTY" because of Section 677 of IRS and it is essential to many of these claimed income tax advantages of this trust that the wife so qualify. This trust proceeds on the assumption that, if the Grantor were to qualify as an independent contractor, and grant his income and assets to the trust, he would receive, in exchange for the transfer, 100 "Units of Beneficial Interest." He would retain five, his wife would be given 50 and his children the balance. His wife, argue the proponents, would be treated as an "adverse party," which would mean that she would have her own personal interest which would be legally considered as separate and distinct from that of her husband, the Grantor. If that is the case, some of the income tax benefits from the trust might hold up. If it is not the case, they would not. This is a most crucial issue, and Bill Anderson says it would not.

He also says, that even if you win that point, and she is an adverse party, then her interest could not be a future interest to be taxed under the gift tax laws, based upon a discounted value as contended by the proponents, but rather a present interest. He states the gift taxes would be as high as estate taxes when the Grantor gives the 50 Units to his wife, and that upon her death, 50% of the value of all trust assets would be taxed in her estate. The course assumes that when she dies, her Units of Beneficial Interest are a gift to the trust, and none of these assets is included in her estate. Bill Anderson disagrees.

4. Bill says you cannot split personal service income for tax purposes as claimed.

5. There is marital risk. If there were an unfriendly dissolution of the marriage, as these things often are, the wife would probably get custody of the children and would automatically have control of 95% of the estate. The Grantor would only have 5% of the Units of Beneficial Interest, which could ruin his whole day.

6. The IRS has ruled that when the Grantor dies, 100% of all trust assets will be included in his taxable estate.

The IRS Code, Section 2036 (a), provides as follows: "The value of the gross estate shall include the value of all property, to the extent of any interest therein of which the decedent has at any time made a transfer . . . by trust or otherwise, under which he has retained for his life. . . .

(1) The possession of, or the right to income from, the property, or

(2) The right, either alone or in conjunction with any person, to designate the persons who shall possess or enjoy the property or income therefrom."

This is interpreted by Bill to mean that if the Grantor remains a trustee, alone or in concert with others, he has "maintained control," and as a result, the total trust assets would be in his estate. Bill Anderson further states that making the wife an adverse party will not change the federal estate tax results.

7.   Bill believes that the trust would be taxed as a corporation, and you would end up with double taxation of profits and dividends.

In rebuttal, Dennis Scharf and Barry Morris strongly argued that this trust differs substantially from the trust described in the IRS rulings. In one of the cited cases, they say, the Grantor kept all 100 of the Units of Beneficial Interest for himself, that he had power to revoke the trust, and that he also had power of "control of enjoyment of income." According to them, this is not the case in this trust. Bill Anderson answers that if the Grantor is a trustee, as the course advises, operating "alone, or in concert with others," it doesn't matter whether he has absolute personal control or not.

Barry Morris argued that the estate tax matter rests partly on the theory that if the wife, holding 50% of the shares of beneficial interest, should die, that the trust assets are not liquidated. Consequently, her estate would not be taxed on the total value of those assets but merely on the value of her right to receive income in the future from it, which is a much smaller value, and consequently, her estate would be taxed at a far lower rate.

Morris and Scharf also argued that a major factor as to whether or not there would be any income-splitting benefits from this trust is whether or not one could qualify as an independent contractor, and much of their effort is in this direction. Bill Anderson feels that the income-splitting benefits could only work if one had passive income only, not derived from personal services or profession, and either an adverse party were involved or the Grantor did not act as a trustee. Also the wife, according to Bill Anderson, could not be an adverse party in a community property state because she is a co-grantor.

If you are still with me after all that legal jargon, let me pass on to you my opinion of the whole mess.

Ruff's Recommendations

1. The "Family Trust" under discussion is a rather ingenious effort to have your cake and eat it too. It rests on some untested legal theories, particularly in the estate tax area, and there is a great lack of case law to either prove or disprove the claims.

2. The IRS has taken a very gingerly approach to these trusts, as there is a strange lack of direct challenges of these trust returns. O'Donnell alleges that this is because the IRS feels it has no leg to stand on. Bill Anderson presents an interesting theory that, in his trust management experience, whenever he has faced an IRS audit, he has found a great lack of trust sophistication on the part of the IRS agent and that historically the IRS has not aggressively audited Form 1041s (Fiduciary trust income tax returns).

Those days may be over, as the IRS is now in the process of launching a massive public relations attack on the trust concept and is involved in litigation right now in Santa Barbara against some of the promoters of similar, but not identical, trusts. They are using such scare headlines as one which appeared in the *Los Angeles Herald-Examiner* on March 17, "IRS WARNS CONSUMERS ON TRUST FUND SCHEME."

That does not necessarily prove the family trust promoters are wrong. This is a typical government tactic for trying you in the press before you get into the courts. I've seen the FTC, the FDA, OSHA, etc., do this, and I think this is detestable, and has no relevance whatsoever to the merits of this case. It does, however, suggest that the IRS may be about to make life very difficult for this form of trust.

3. It is my opinion that John O'Donnell was wrong when he indicated the family trust was the principal method used by the super-rich to perpetuate wealth and power. Most of them have used tax-free foundations. Although trusts are part of their program, it cannot properly be inferred that his trust is precisely the same device. There are some similarities, but there are probably more differences.

4. John also says, "The only way they could ever knock out this trust is to take away our Constitutional right to contract." There's no question you can contract, but that doesn't mean the IRS, who is Not a party to the contract, has to honor it.

5. John's statement that it would cost "in excess of $10,000" to set up such a trust is also incorrect. I have letters from numerous attorneys indicating they would set up a similar trust for $500 to $1000. Then, of course, there would be costs in administering the

trust. I would say the basic cost of doing this through a competent attorney, or through buying the trust, is approximately the same, assuming nothing goes wrong.

John does have a good point when he says that it is hard to find an attorney who is an expert in trusts, as it is a specialty.

6. It is apparent there are substantial benefits from trusts and there are different kinds to meet different needs. It should be stressed that Bill Anderson is not hostile to trusts. In fact, he is one of the few attorneys who doesn't think Norman Dacy's book, *HOW TO AVOID PROBATE*, emanates from the devil himself. His objection is with this particular trust.

7. It is apparent that Mr. Scharf and Mr. Morris of Polaris-Omni are honest men, as is John O'Donnell.

8. Based on what I have seen, I believe that if you were to set up such a trust and file the appropriate tax returns that you would be buying an almost automatic audit, with all of the expense that entails.

The good news is that if there were thousands of people filing similar returns, the IRS could be overwhelmed by the volume, and you might not see an audit for several years, in which case, the worst thing that could happen to you is that you would be hit with interest and penalties. This would be partially offset by the fact that you would have the use of that money for investment purposes during that time, rather than having paid it out in taxes. There would be, in Mr. Anderson's opinion, no fraud associated with taxpayers filing those tax returns, but you could be involved in a civil dispute with the IRS, not a criminal action. You would also be out the cost of the course, if this theory were to be shot down.

In Summation

The net of it all is: The trust course represents an opportunity to get an education in this most interesting area of law, although Bill feels that much of what you would be learning is wrong. It also has some pitfalls on which there are substantial legal differences of opinion. It rests on certain novel and untested legal theories and has not undergone its "trial by fire" from the IRS, but apparently will do so soon. If you buy the course, you should first have your situation analyzed thoroughly by Polaris-Omni. Most competent experts in this field feel it is in direct contradiction to certain aspects of the IRS codes, and feel there are sufficient analogous situations in other aspects of law to raise a high probability that many of the expected benefits of the trust will be shot down.

It is also quite clear, in my opinion, that trusts can be of great benefit, when properly set up, in reducing taxation, avoiding probate, and reducing estate taxes. The big difference of opinion does not seem to be whether trusts are valid, but whether this specific trust was properly set up to achieve those objectives, and whether or not the writers of the trust were over-reaching in trying to have their cake and eat it too (claiming benefits that could not be derived from the trust). All of the parties to this dispute seem to be honest and sincere. Basically, this boils down to this: the risk is yours. If it were my decision, I wouldn't do it until I could see some more effective rebuttal. I am waiting for some more supporting data from Polaris-Omni and Mr. O'Donnell's attorneys, and if it appears persuasive or significant, I'll bring you up to date in future issues. (Editor's note: Since this article was written, both O'Donnell and Polaris-Omni have moved out of the "Family Trust" business.)

B. RAY ANDERSON CONVENTION REPORT

(3/15/79) At our Second Annual National Convention in Ana-heim, attorney Bill Anderson, discussed tax and estate planning. He indicated, "Tax evasion is illegal, tax avoidance is not." And he is into tax avoidance. The IRS has new guidelines for a special task force relating to major schemes promoted by "tax protestors." They will be aggressive in auditing, challenging and even litigating against those who seek to avoid taxes by blank income tax returns and other means. (Irwin Schiff, who was a guest on my show, is one of the cleverest of all the tax protestors and he was just indicted in Federal court. Even if he wins on appeal, it will turn out to be a very expensive victory.) Additional tax protest schemes, such as family estate type trusts, ministerial certificates, and other tax revolt methods will continue to be dangerous. If you join one of these movements, be prepared to go the distance, as you may spend a lot of time and money defending your position, and, as Bill says, "All I can say is 'good luck'."

Bill discussed the use of gold clauses in contracts, pointing out that, while they are a little complex, they have definite merit. We have copies of Bill's detailed brief on gold clauses which you can obtain for $3 by writing to us at Target.

Bill also said, "My number one recommendation is that the principal estate document you should create is a revocable, intervivos (living) trust. The dominant objective in family tax planning is to transfer property to the next generation, while at the same time preserving control and shifting much of the income tax and avoiding probate. In many instances this can also be done with certain irrevocable trusts." If you can't find an attorney who does a lot of trusts and really knows what he is talking about, you should then contact B. Ray Anderson of Anderson and Nearon, 1924 Tice Valley Blvd., Walnut Creek, CA 94595, 415-933-6760. We find them to be highly competent.

He discussed some of the techniques of tax freezing (which means keeping the value of 'one's estate from growing for estate tax purposes), income tax shifting, equity appreciation shifting, ancestors' trusts and private pensions. Unfortunately, it is too complex to go into here, but his basic premise is that you can (1) structure your life to avoid current taxes or (2) you can structure your estate to avoid inheritance taxes. You will have to make the decision as to which is more important. You can get some of each by using more than one trust, but in essence, there is a fundamental decision to be made.

You can set up trusts to educate your children and grandchildren, but the primary purpose of a trust is to disinherit Uncle Sam and make sure your family will not go through difficulty and expensive procedures in order to inherit what is rightfully theirs. Not only do we have to beat the inflationary bite, but we also have to beat the tax bite, which at this time is bigger.

EXECUTIVE ORDER 11490

(8/1/77)   During the last days of the Ford Administration, Congress cancelled several Presidental Executive Orders that had been around since WWI, including several declared by President Roosevelt, which gave the President dictatorial powers. At the same time, they approved another Executive Order, No. 11490, which can be put into effect by the President of the United States by declaration, and I quote from the Order "... IN ANY NATIONAL EMERGENCY TYPE SITUATION THAT MIGHT CONCEIVABLY CONFRONT THE NATION." Under Congress' mandate, the President can invoke this at his own descretion and then it can be reviewed by Congress after six months. If you read this 35 page Executive Order carefully, you will realize that it gives the President absolute dictatorial powers. THIS ORDER GIVES THE PRESIDENT POWER TO ACHIEVE ALL OF HIS ENERGY REGULATION, RATIONING, AND ALLOCATION OBJECTIVES BY DECLARATION.

Let's look at this law of the land, only awaiting declaration. Its full title is "EXECUTIVE ORDER 11490—ASSIGNING EMERGENCY PREPAREDNESS FUNCTIONS TO FEDERAL DEPARTMENTS AND AGENCIES (AS RECOMMENDED)." It gives almost every governmental agency specific instructions and powers in case of national emergency. At my first reading, it seemed fairly innocent, in that it seemed directed toward contingency planning for nuclear war, but as I looked more closely, it had teeth. Each agency is to conduct its day to day operations with emergency plan in mind.

In case of such an emergency, virtually all power comes under the Director of the FEDERAL PREPAREDNESS AGENCY, which is subordinate to the GENERAL SERVICES ADMINISTRATION. This man becomes literally "Deputy Dictator," operating under the direct authority of the President of the United States ". . . in any national emergency type situation that might confront the nation." (Section, FEC 102a) "In accordance with the guidance provided by, and subject to evaluation by the Director of the Federal Preparedness Agency, they are to be prepared to implement, in the event of an emergency, all appropriate plans developed under this order."

Section 105 indicates, "plans so developed may be effectuated only in the event that authority for such effectuation is provided by a law enacted by the Congress or by an order or directive issued by the President, persuant to statutes or the Constitution of the United States." Such a law has been enacted by Congress, granting the President such authority, so it is the law of the land, if the President chooses to make it so.

The Department of Defense will develop ". . . plans and programs for the emergency control of all devices capable of emitting electromagnetic radiation." THERE GOES YOUR OLD CB.

THE DEPARTMENT OF INTERIOR ". . . shall prepare national emergency plans and develop preparedness programs covering electric power, petroleum and gas, solid fuels, minerals and water." Under the heading "Production," they are to ". . . provide to insure the continuity of production . . . and cooperate with the Department of Commerce in the identification and evaluation of essential facilities."

The DEPARTMENT OF COMMERCE is to ". . . control the production and distribution of all materials, the use of all production facilities, the control for all construction materials and the furnishing of basic industrial services, including (a) production and distribution and use of facilities for petroleum, solid fuels, gas, and electric power.

The SECRETARY OF COMMERCE shall ". . . develop control systems for priorities, allocation, production and distribution as appropriate to serve as alloting agents for materials and other resources . . ."

And therein, lies the President's power to take control of all energy sources.

The DEPARTMENT OF LABOR shall ". . . develop plans and procedures for wage and salary stabilization and for the national and field organization necessary for the administration of such a program in an emergency, including investigation, compliance and appeals."

That simply means all of these steps taken by government are going to result in terrible inflation which must be controlled with price and wage controls.

Now we get to something really scary, and that's in the description of the responsibilities of the FEDERAL BANK SUPERVISORY AGENCIES in Section 1701. They are to provide for the ". . . REGULATION OF THE WITHDRAWAL OF CURRENCY AND THE TRANSFER OF CREDITS INCLUDING DEPOSIT AND SHARE ACCOUNT BALANCES." This happy little clause says that they can simply freeze all of your money if it is sitting in a financial institution. Of course, this is explained away as the need for government to prevent hoarding or panic buying. Actually, what it prevents is the rational response of those who have a natural dislike of having their assets confiscated. And here's another little joker thrown at us by the GENERAL SERVICES ADMINISTRATION. They are to ". . . develop plans and emergency operating procedures for the utilization of excess and surplus real and personal property . . ." including "THE DISPOSAL OF REAL AND PERSONAL PROPERTY AND THE REHABILITATION (?) OF PERSONAL PROPERTY." TOTAL SEIZURE!!& # ?!

The SEC can effect ". . . the temporary closure of security exchanges, suspension of redemption rights and the freezing of stock and bond prices, if required in the interest of maintaining economic controls."

And, how does this grab you? They can prevent ". . . the flight of capital outside this country in coordination with the Secretary of Commerce." So don't think you can just grab your money and send it to Switzerland. You can bet your life that the Swiss won't let you bring your money back here, either. They will obviously retaliate in kind. Well, those are the highlights.

F

FAMILY

(Special Report #2, 12/75) Setting religious philosophy aside, it is my opinion that as a practical matter, one of the great threats to the survival of the nation is a breakdown of the family ties. The family is the smallest unit of society. And when the smallest unit crumbles, the entire structure is endangered. The separation of the generations and the increasing tendency of family members to find their recreation and diversion separately, away from their family, in my opinion, represents a great danger to the nation. The kind of preparation I have proposed for protection against calamities is difficult to execute unless families are unified and working cooperatively.

For that reason, I am going to make the only exception to one of my basic rules that I will make this year. That rule is to never impose any of my religious views or practices upon my readers. But the CHURCH OF JESUS CHRIST OF LATTER-DAY SAINTS has developed a concept for tying together the family that I believe is easily transportable into any religious context and can be practiced to advantage by all good people everywhere. This concept is called the FAMILY HOME EVENING.

Every Monday, active Mormon families set aside an entire evening for family recreation, family council, and a series of actual lessons which help to pass the family's values and standards to the next generation. This Family Home Evening concept has been carefully structured in the form of a manual, which can be used by people of all faiths without the imposition of Mormon theology. I would strongly recommend that you contact your nearest LDS ward and ask where you can obtain a copy of the Family Home Evening manual. It will give you instructions on how to save your family, or improve upon that which you are now building.

The continuity of nations and civilizations depends upon the values of one generation being effectively passed on to the next generation. Older people used to come to live with their children, and families generally included three generations. But now, older people are placed in rest homes and are taken care of by Social Security. Their grandchildren do not have the same opportunity to benefit from their wisdom and experience. The children are drawn in all kinds of directions by the diversions that society offers, or they become hypnotized and have their values determined by the great electronic eye in your living room.

I believe that a Family Home Evening every Monday night, or any other night, could be a major influence in helping young people to share your values and avoid becoming rebellious and unhappy as they struggle to find "absolutes" in a world which is teaching them "everything is relative" and nothing is eternal.

(7/1/77)   A strong family life doesn't just happen. It has to be planned for. You have to conclude that your primary role in life is as a father or mother of a family unit, and that transcends any other professional or community responsibility. We reinforce this in our home through this Family Home Evening. In our Family Home Evening, we have a family council where every child has a voice and is listened to seriously on all family matters. This includes frank discussion of family finances and a thrashing out of problems, and the children are full participants in solutions. As a father, I retain a certain amount of veto power, but I look upon my vetos as Blue Chips which are to be used only on big issues, and only occasionally. I'm prepared to yield to the consensus of the group on any issue where it is not a matter of right or wrong, but only a matter of preference. That doesn't mean I don't assert leadership, but I recognized long ago that the only real power I have over my teenagers is the power of persuasion and moral force. I have only that power which is granted to me by them, as any parent of a rebellious teenager has learned.

I believe it's nearly impossible to pass on values to the next generation, even in the Family Home Evening context, if it is done separately from religious principles. There are all kinds of studies indicating that where religion is a strong factor in the home and a unifying force in the family, the next generation is more likely to adopt the highest values of those who preceded them.

Family prayer, morning and night, is a part of our family life.

I insist upon breakfast together, even though that means some of us have to rise much earlier than we would ordinarily, in order to accommodate the needs of those who must leave early. This policy met with some protest at first, but all now agree with it, and it does give us a chance to be together.

FAMINE

(11/75) In my studies of famine and financial panics, I've seen a mortality rate of 8% to 10% with the possible exception of the days of the black plague where 40% of the population was lost. It has been my opinion that depression and financial collapse can create difficult, dangerous times, with sickness, illness, famine and epidemics. But, even in the great San Francisco earthquake, where something like 55% of the buildings were either damaged or destroyed, the mortality rate was less than two percent of the people in the city.

(4/15/76) As I travel about the country and make public appearances, I am so often confronted with the question that goes something like this: "Don't you think it is wrong for us to think of hoarding food in this country when there are so many people abroad who need food?"

So often, India is given as the example of a country we should help. It is my opinion that generally when we give food to other countries, we end up helping no one. I am not interested in futile gestures that jeopardize our security and aid no one. India is thought of by most people as a country teeming with so many people that it has no chance of raising enough food to feed itself. This may come as a surprise to you, but India was self-sufficient in food from 1960-1968. As George F. Will, the syndicated columnist has said,

> There is nothing about India that makes its economic backwardness and subsequent misery inevitable. Of India's many afflictions, the Indian government is probably the worst and least tractable. India is less densely populated than Italy, the Netherlands, the United Kingdom, Japan, West Germany, or, for that matter, New Jersey, and a lot of other places. The ratio of arable acres to population in India is about the same as in France. To mollify the urban population, and for the sheer Socialist fun of it, the Indian government has mandated artificially low food prices, thereby discouraging food production. When you add immoderate corruption to the natural inefficiency of Socialism, and stir in India's distinctive arrogance towards foreign investors, you have a recipe for an economic disaster, and India is a disaster.

This expresses very well my contention that most famines are political and economic in nature, and they're not because of the vagaries of the weather. For example, in Africa, in the Sahel, while people were starving to death, food aid was pouring into Addis Abbaba and other cities for distribution in the back country. Most of it was not distributed for political reasons. Much of it is still sitting there and due to poor storage conditions, much of it has been destroyed. While one country can have a surplus, another country can be suffering genuine privation. While one country can produce surpluses from its own land, another country with superior natural resources and more land will produce disaster after disaster.

If we should face true famine in this country, it will be the result of a breakdown of the system by which food is grown, processed and distributed. Food does not grow by magic on the supermarket shelf. Somebody had to have the incentive to grow, process, transport, package, place it on the shelves and inform you through advertising that it is there.

It is my contention that as a piece of machinery increases in complexity, it also increases in vulnerability. Let me illustrate. Several years ago, I bought an airplane. It had a single engine. I enjoyed flying my airplane and I used it effectively in business. I was soon persuaded that I would be much safer if I had an airplane with two engines, because if one should quit, the other one would get me safely back home. This seemed like a reasonable contention. What was not pointed out, however, was that if I had two engines, there was then twice the likelihood of something going wrong with an engine, and flying an airplane on one engine just ain't really that safe, especially if you find yourself at a high altitude, unless you practice simulated engine-out emergencies, and stay sharp.

Our economy is very much the same. As it becomes increasingly complex, a malfunction can have increasingly dangerous effects upon us. We have seen example after example of the possible effect of labor problems on our food distribution.

Bear in mind that as economic complexity increases, our ability to make wise decisions in order to manage, also diminishes. We may have reached the point where the cross-currents of national life are ebbing and flowing so rapidly, that it is beyond the ingenuity of human leadership. That is my major concern at this time.

(5/15/76) Our ability to produce food is probably preventing blood from flowing in the streets of Calcutta and many major cities in the world. Bear in mind, however, most famines are not caused by crop failures. There are, of course, exceptions to that statement, such as the famous Irish potato famine, however, most famine deaths are caused, either primarily or secondarily, by political and economic factors. South of the Sahara in 1973-74 and on into 1975, people were starving, as the Sahara Desert was marching southward at the rate of about 100 miles a year, due to a change in the rainfall pattern. Sufficient grain to feed everyone was sitting in storehouses in Addis Abbaba and several other major cities. It had been contributed by the prosperous nations of the world, but the people still starved, because the food didn't get to them. Their starvation was political and economic.

India's famine is not due to its population. It is not due to the weather problems. It is due to socialist destruction of the incentive to produce. Admittedly, they have had some bad weather. However, a strong, free-enterprise system can generally endure such shocks. (see: Food Storage & Food Shortage)

It is my fondest wish that the people of the world will find ways to solve their problems and prevent the death by starvation of a substantial portion of the human race. However, realistically, I do not believe that it is preventable, politically and economically. I believe that millions of people will die of starvation, however, it will not be because man has efficiently tried to utilize every bit of his resources to prevent it and failed. It will be because he has become steadily less efficient and has not efficiently utilized the great, constantly renewable resources of this beautiful planet. We're not going to run out of energy; we're going to learn how to harness the sun. We're not going to run out of land. If you gave every family in the world a five-acre plot of land, then they could fit inside the boundaries of the United States of America. What we have already run out of, though, is common sense principles, and an awareness of the economic power of incentive. The economic laws have not been repealed, they have merely been honored in the breach and ignored.

(7/15/76)   The prospect of famine still stalks the world. Australia is in the grip of its worst drought in eighty years. Russia's grain crops are in trouble. California is in the midst of the worst drought since records have been kept.

FARMING

INTRODUCTION

(8/15/76) With present farming methods, the food chain begins in the sands of the Arabian peninsula. Oil and gas must be pumped, bought by oil companies, shipped around South Africa, converted into fuel, fertilizer, pesticides, insecticides, herbicides, and what have you. Only then can the food growing process begin!

We've got to change. As Frank Ford says, Arab-Israeli conflict is inevitable. The Arabs, unfortunately, have a dangerous combination of religious dogmatism, nationalistic fervor, tens of billions of cash reserves built up since 1973, a festering hatred of Jews, and a realistic sense of their increasing power. They could now ride out a prolonged boycott. We can't!

They can strangle our farm economy. They can seriously damage and perhaps destroy our banking system by suddenly withdrawing their huge deposits. And they can cripple us by hitting us where our greatest strength lies—our food production.

Without our food exports, the collapse of our balance of payments would destroy the dollar.

We are staking our lives on agricultural methods that won't work unless the Jews and the Arabs avoid war, and the Soviets are thwarted in South Africa, or choose not to use their power to hurt us. We are betting that the weather will be kind to crops that are more weather vulnerable than they need to be. We are assuming that farmers will continue to bring in record crops and sell them, in some cases, below the cost of production.

There are only two solutions:

1. Change our agricultural methods. Reduce our farm petroleum consumption by half or more, I believe it can be done with no long-term loss of production. This way we have a chance. Unfortunately, the probability of convincing farmers to change is fairly low; but we have to try.

2. Pray for a couple of good years, and hope enough Americans will get the message about food storage to give us a national food reserve (see: Food Storage and National Food Reserve), and a large number of families who are stable, prepared, and unafraid. This will

lessen demand on supplies when they become scarce and prices leap upward.

FOR FARMERS ONLY

(2/1/77)   Should you buy more farm land if you have the chance? The answer is yes, with the following qualifications:

1.   Will you be so heavily in debt, with no cash reserves, that you couldn't make your loan payments if you had one bad year? Or two bad years?

The weather is far more variable than in the past, and you need cash reserves to protect you. Colder springs, drier summers, and earlier frosts, may become the norm. The upper Mid-West and the high plains will be the most uncertain.

2.   Do you have generators and underground fuel storage to keep you going when fuel supplies become disrupted at harvest or planting time?

3.   Can you move towards less energy-intensive methods—modern Eco-Science methods—as espoused by the Iowa Secretary of Agriculture, and covered in our August 15, 1976, issue of *THE RUFF TIMES*?

4.   Can you irrigate? Is there a dependable river? How about wells? Some parts of Wisconsin, Minnesota, the Dakotas, and Iowa have recently experienced wells going dry.

On the other side of the depression that I think we're going to have, farm land will be one of the most valuable commodities around, and the farmer is going to be KING. If you can buy it without jeopardizing your overall financial security, and if you can afford to hang on to it through one or two bad years, and if you can answer the above questions properly, I think you ought to buy it. (see: Organic Farming and Real Estate—Farmland)

SOCIALIZED FARMING

(12/15/76)   Normally, world food production is within one percent to two percent of consumption. That's been true throughout all of history. If we produce one percent or two percent more food than we use, we have surpluses which depress the market. If we produce one percent to two percent less than needed unless we have large surpluses to draw on from previous years, it means hunger and perhaps even starvation for some of the world's population. At best, this makes farming a chancy business, but when you have an extraordinarily unpredictable weather pattern (see: Weather and Climate), with the possibility of two or three bad years in a row, the gloom-and-doom prophets, such as Paul Ehrlich and others begin to scream for the socialization or the nationalization of farming. They are operating under the assumption that a socialized and nationalized farm operation can produce more food than the American free enterprise system. This is absurd, of course. The history of socialized farming is a history of crop failures, plain and simple. American free enterprise farming has provided the food which is the glue that holds civilization together.

I'm not the least bit concerned that we would ever have such a decrease of crops in this country that we would be unable to feed ourselves, unless we socialize farming. If everything else remained the same, we could lose over half of our crops without seriously affecting the eating habits of the American public. A large crop loss, however, could destroy the financial and economic system of this country.

Look at it this way. The dollar buys a certain amount of foreign goods, based on the value of the dollar in relation to other currencies. If we send more dollars abroad to pay for imports, such as oil, than we are bringing home from our exports, such as food, the dollar becomes less valuable in relation to other currencies. People begin dumping American securities and other dollar-related investments, preferring to hold other stronger foreign currencies. (see: Balance of Payments)

FARM STRIKES

(6/1/78)   Let's talk about the farm strike. A minority of farmers are demanding the government guarantee that the price they receive for their crops be sufficient to cover all of their costs and give them a profit. In protest, thousands are driving tractors to state houses and Washington.

My farmer friends, don't get caught up in this foolish exercise. You are begging for government chains to bind you. The only way government can meet your demands is by subsidies and production controls. And if you think they are going to do this with no strings or regulation of your life, you're crazy. Government is not the solution. Government is the problem! Government has encouraged the over-expansion of production to fight inflation.

Remember the old Idaho farmer who beat the system. One year

everybody planted potatoes, and there was a great glut of potatoes, but he planted corn and made a bundle. Everybody saw this, so the next year they all planted corn. There was a glut of corn, but that old farmer planted potatoes. Nothing can substitute for good business judgment. When you substitute government subsidy for the signals of the marketplace, you are merely sowing the seeds of your own destruction and bondage.

The odds are the farm strike will fizzle. Here's why:

1.   Rising commodity prices over the next several months, due to foreign buying, will cause a lot of "defectors" to sell their stored grain.

2.   As of now, the striking farmers represent a relatively small percentage of land currently in production, at most, six percent of our food production will be affected, mostly wheat, corn and soy beans, and possibly some cattle.

3.   Most farmers are too individualistic and independent to join such an action.

(2/1/78)   I am not opposed to the farmers' strike. I think it is a legitimate tactic for farmers or anyone else to withhold their services if they feel they are not getting adequate compensation. I am also in deep sympathy with the plight of the family farmer in this country. He is in trouble. We cannot afford to see our largest single industry get into serious trouble. I object, however, to what the farmers are proposing as a solution. All I am saying is that what they are asking for is bad for them and for the country. Basically, they want government to set minimum prices which would guarantee a profit. Let's examine the morality of this.

1.   Why not newsletter publishers, shoemakers, and steel manufacturers? Where does it stop?

2.   Are you farmers prepared to accept limitations on your profits in good years? Are you prepared to give back the high profits you earned in 1972, 1973 and 1974 when farm income was at an all-time high? One of society's most dangerous trends is to protect inefficient producers from the consequences of their inefficiencies. Farming has always been a literal "feast or famine" business, but good businessmen who study the trends and listen to the demands of the marketplace, generally make money. What makes you think the American consumer would stand by and watch farmers receive guaranteed profits, while prices rise at the supermarkets? Your farm strike would be countered by a consumer rebellion. You might say that the consumer can't eat unless you provide his food, but in order for that statement to be true, you would have to have the majority of

the farmers in the country unified behind your goals. If you get full parity and price supports, or market price controls, you will have given up your freedom because the government is not going to let you reap large profits in good years. You will, in effect, have become nationalized and socialized and I'll guaran-darn-tee you won't like it.

I received a UPI clipping about a legitimate economic weapon that some farmers are using. It deals directly with your problem without getting government involved. The article says:

> The Chicago and Kansas Trade Boards are edgy about farmers' plans to force prices up to 100 percent parity by making large commodities purchases, an American agriculture spokesman said today. Lon Kerr said, "Farmers can purchase their crops through the Boards for less than the cost of production." He said many farmers decided to plow their fields under and, instead, purchase the grains from the markets at the going price. "The thing is, there isn't enough grain to cover the increased demand and you can bet the price is going to rise when we demand delivery," he said. The Boards say they have a lot of new customers suddenly and are getting worried.

Now, I think that's a heck of an idea. There's a lot of surplus wheat out there overhanging the market, and farmers can buy wheat at today's prices cheaper than they can produce it, and hold it for future sale when the price is right. This, at the very worst, reduces their losses. Instead of growing grain, they are buying it for resale. Now, that is really clever. You consumers out there probably won't like the higher prices you will have to pay, and I won't either. However, it is a legitimate means of protest and uses the free market mechanisms to get the job done. I can support that in principle, even though I may not like the dent it will put in my pocketbook.

In summary, I really am not hostile to the strike. I am hostile to the full parity non-solution the farmers are trying to achieve.

(6/1/78) In January, when I first discussed the farm revolt, I said, "I don't think it will work." Well, as it has worked out, the Carter Administration wants farmers to reduce their acreage by 20%. They are even offering incentives not to plant, but so far they have only reduced acreage by 10%. As of now, the farm strike is a bust.

That doesn't mean the strike is not without merit. It's just not successful. They have genuine problems, mostly caused by government. Farmers who spent their capital or went heavily into debt to buy very expensive land during the glory days of '74 and '75, have been hard pressed to meet their mortgage payments. I think we can expect a wave of bankruptcies in the corn, wheat and soybean belt.

I advised my subscribers two years ago that, if they bought farm land, to be sure they had sufficient cash reserves to carry them through a bad year or two. Those who have taken that advice should be in pretty good shape. (see: Farming)

It looks like the tide of the farm revolt has peaked and is receding.

If I'm right about commodity prices continuing to rise over the next year, this may save a lot of farmers, but despite that, we still may see an American tragedy in the making. Much of the farm industry is in bad shape. I only hope we will be able to produce enough in reserves to carry us through when the inevitable bad crop years return to plague us.

Patience, my farmer friends, there are much better days ahead.

FDIC

(3/1/76)   A New Threat To FDIC Insurance Funds

Although money in banks is officially insured up to $40,000 for each account, it is the government's policy to cover every last dollar when a bank fails. This means that FDIC funds, a total of $9 billion, could be exhausted far more rapidly than formerly estimated. Is the FDIC just being nice to us—going the extra mile?

No! It was revealed by John Hensel, the FDIC Regional Administrator for national banks in the California region, at a seminar sponsored by Security National Bank (one of the banks on the Federal Reserve's problem list), that this generous policy was to compensate for the official policy of not disclosing the conditions of a problem bank, to prevent runs and failures. If the FDIC did not pay off 100%, they could be liable for damage suits from bamboozled depositors and innocent investors.

Hensel admitted this could threaten the Insurance Fund, since it has not been set up for such exposure.

The FDIC, Federal Reserve, and Comptroller of the Currency, are so concerned about the extent of the problem and its disclosure, they are now defying a Congressional subpoena demanding disclosure of Federal records of all U.S. banks with more than $1 billion in assets.

The fact is, there's only one dollar of FDIC insurance for every $76 on deposit! Therefore, the FDIC is not capable of rescuing much more than one major bank failure, whether or not banks ever officially disclose their true financial conditions!

It's difficult to comprehend just how close we came to completely overwhelming the system. The Franklin Bank failure used up 40% of the FDIC funds. They will get it back, but the large amount of money required at that moment to effect a rescue operation is significant. Two or three banks the size of Franklin National would exhaust the fund. In other words, no defense is impregnable. Our economic defenses ultimately depend upon Federal government spending. (see: Banking Industry, Banks, and Inflation)

FEDERAL RESERVE BOARD

(12/1/78)   Stupid, Stupid, Stupid

I've heard of stupid before, but not from such high sources for a long time. Any last vestiges of respect I might have had for the judgment of our Federal Reserve Board Chairman, G. WILLIAM MILLER, have disintegrated.

He has asked economists and others to stop predicting recession next year, saying their "death wish" talk could be the cause of recession, and he said there will not be a recession next year, "unless we talk ourselves into it." He also said because of "the clamor and the noise and the pessimism, we can talk ourselves into a recession." He indicated that "there is no reason, based on economic realities to have a recession and there is no reason at all to talk about a depression, even if the anti-inflation program fails."

Either that man has joined the crowd of fools who believe the economic cycle is strictly a psychological phenomenon, or he is lying to us, and either prospect is rather grim. Blaming recession or depression on talk, is like blaming speedometers for highway deaths, saying thermometers cause disease, or proclaiming refugees to be the cause of war.

I believe we have entered into the era described by W. CLEON SKOUSEN in his book, *PROPHECY IN MODERN TIMES.* He said the decline of America would come "when the cross currents of national life begin to ebb and flow with a rapidity that is wholly baffling to the ingenuity of human leadership." We have reached the point where no one knows which economic button to push, nor what the effects of the button-pushing will be, nor when they will take effect. A recession or depression *is* the solution to the inflation problem, and no amount of wishful thinking will make it otherwise.

I'm sick to death of those who feel that if we could just all think positively the nation wouldn't go through its troubles. You cannot suspend economic laws nor reject the lessons of history. In fact, history tells us that nations slide into depression in an aura of optimism, as the majority of the people just don't believe it could happen to them. It is this passive optimism that allowed us to get into the current trouble in the first place. We are past the point of no return. We are going to have at least a recession now. We are going to have a depression eventually and all the wishful thinking in the world won't change that.

Stupid, Stupid, Stupid, Mr. Miller.

FOOD PRODUCTION & DISTRIBUTION

(4/15/76)   Drought of 1975

The latest reports indicate that, due to the drought in the Mid-West, the winter wheat crop will be 12 to 25% below last year's. I believe the USDA statements are overoptimistic, and we will see continued downward revision. Earl Hayes, President of the Kansas Association of Wheat Growers announced a forecast of 51 million bushels less than the USDA.

"I wouldn't say the government report is manipulated, but maybe the USDA has used a little bad judgment or maybe the figures coming in for their report aren't accurate," he said.

He believes the USDA has grossly underestimated the damage from the drought. Its major effect will be on world stability and world peace. American food exports are the glue that holds civilization together. The United States does not exist in a vacuum. It exists in a community of nations, and we have vast interlocking systems, both economic and political.

(5/15/76)   How To Increase Food Production

The world has approximately four billion people, and food production is not increasing sufficiently to continue to feed the masses at the world's present rate of population growth. This is not because we are up against some immovable stone wall in our ability to grow food! This is because much of the world's food production is becoming less and less efficient. India was self-sufficient in grain in

1968. Now it is a major importer, usually asking for a free hand-out. The reason is simple: socialism has destroyed the incentive to produce. The socialist philosophy says that you can, by government action, do things which benefit the masses, and that those who will be hurt are the rich dirty guys who usually are labeled "Capitalists." The government of India slapped price controls on farm products to control inflation. This meant that the farmer lost money on every kernel of wheat and every ear of corn. Socialism and communism have not yet figured out that you can't increase production by eliminating incentive. No one, even a dedicated Marxist farmer, is prepared to go on losing money for the benefit of everyone else. As a result, farm production dropped. An inefficient, corruption-ridden, incentiveless socialist system has literally destroyed one of the most productive farming economies in the world.

I've done some interesting examinations of alternative solutions to the food problem. For example, we could increase the world's food production approximately 400% if we took the following simple steps.

1. Increase our reliance on sheep, goats, and rabbits, instead of cattle, as a source of meat. They do beautifully on grass. They require no grain for fattening. Lamb, mutton, goat, and rabbit are perfectly acceptable to western taste when westerners are introduced to it.

2. Immediately convert all of the prime land now devoted to the growing of tobacco, hops, marijuana, coffee, tea, and opium, into the production of food.

3. Encourage everyone in America, or any other country, who owns a plot of land around his house, to plant a vegetable garden and produce some of his own food.

4. Begin to harvest the incredible amounts of "krill," protein-rich plankton which exist in unimaginable quantities in the South Atlantic and Antarctic Oceans. This is the food that has fed the diminishing great whales, and is now multiplying at an incredible rate. I've tasted it, and it tastes fine, like crab or shrimp. It could produce enough protein to feed the entire world, without destroying its ability to restore itself each year, as krill multiply at an incredible rate.

5. Institute organic farming procedures all over the world, over a period of three or four years. Organic farming without synthetic fertilizers is more efficient and produces considerably greater yield per acre than traditional farming methods, with far less energy expenditure, regardless of what Secretary of Agriculture, Earl Butz, says.

I recently spoke at a convention of the Natural Foods Association in Pennsylvania. I talked to an Amish farmer who came over fifty miles in his horse and buggy to attend that convention. He is farming land that has been in his family for three generations. He has approximately 4000 acres and grows corn. No pesticides or synthetic fertilizers have ever been applied to that land. His soil is not tired from raising that one crop. His intensive farming has produced corn which grows faster, with a yield per acre three times higher than the average for Iowa.

I haven't even mentioned the possibility of farming the literally millions of acres of grass strips running down the middle of freeways all over the United States. We haven't discussed the fact that in Central Africa, less than three percent of the arable land is under cultivation. If we were to put all arable land under cultivation while still allowing plenty of room for people to live and reasonably expand their habitat, while eliminating all of the inefficiencies I have suggested, we could feed a world population 10-15 times its present size.

(2/15/78)   Complexity Creates Vulnerability

Our nation has developed a complex distribution and marketing system that functions beautifully as long as the economic boat is not rocked too vigorously by financial storms. Consider the miracle of food on the supermarket shelf. Every day shoppers spend thousands of dollars in any supermarket in America, and the next day, as if by magic, these shelves are full again and ready for more hordes of shoppers. How does it happen? It is the end result of a complex market system that gets food from the ground into your home.

The process depends upon an efficient transportation system, which, in this country, depends upon profits to reward the independent trucker. It also depends upon normal credit and a sound banking system, where the farmer is willing to deliver his product on credit to the elevator operator, who delivers it to the barge operator who takes it down the Mississippi on credit and sells it to the wholesalers, distributors and jobbers on credit. They, in turn, sell it to the food processors on credit, who process it and sell it to the supermarket chains on credit, who, in turn, trust you and the banking system enough to accept your check for those groceries. Imagine what would happen to that system if our banks were in trouble, and everyone's ability to pay was in doubt. Would they accept your check? Would credit be extended at every point in that very complex chain? What if a runaway inflationary spiral caused labor troubles, with picket lines that had to be honored by every union in front of the processor or the supermarket, or the trucking terminal?

What if the rising spiral of inflation and decreasing business caused heavy unemployment in the cities, exhausting all the unemployment funds, draining the public treasuries and forcing cities into bankruptcy causing chaos in the cities as angry people realized government promises were going to be broken? Would food move into your local supermarket? What would be the effect of an Arab oil boycott?

If this process continued for several months, would the farmer, not knowing whether he would ever be paid for his product, or whether or not the money he would receive would be worth anything, just decide not to grow? All of these things are not only possible, but likely, if inflation gets out of hand as it almost did in 1974. I've carefully studied that last recession, and we came within a gnat's eyelash of temporarily losing our banking system. We came within an inch of having inflation totally out of hand in a self-perpetuating spiral similar to Germany of the early 1920s. When this next downturn comes, we are going into it in much weaker condition than we were at the start of the last recession.

In the process of trying to determine what the future will be like so we can make decisions about our lives, it would be a very serious mistake to bet against the resiliency and recovery capabilities of this country. We will recover. Remember the depression of the '30s, and the Civil War, and the banking panic of the 1830s, and the incredible inflation right after the Revolutionary War when our nation was at its weakest? They left their scars, but we survived. The big question is: will you get through without being wiped out financially and with your health intact?

FOOD SHORTAGES

(3/15/77) No Vegetables

Well, it's finally happened. The first real significant food shortage in many years. I have just received word from the major packagers of dehydrated food that some dehydrated vegetables and fruits are no longer available. Processors are first taking care of their larger canning customers, and these large customers have bought up all available supplies. No more will be available for at least 12 to 18 months, even if the drought ends. Freeze-dried vegetables are still available, and they are an excellent storage item, although they are a bit more expensive than the dehydrated foods.

Grains, powdered milk, TVP, etc., are all still in good supply, but if the nationwide drought conditions continue, they may be gone, too.

This is a good example of how market shortages develop. The nation will grow enough vegetables this year to meet domestic needs, but the canners are anticipating another year of drought and have cornered the market before prices rise. They will now benefit from price increases, and an artificial shortage has developed in advance of the real shortages to come.

Average stream flows all over the U.S. are approximately 30% below 1970, and we seem to be enveloped with an almost universal pattern of water shortage.

Drought doesn't mean only no rain. It can consist of small reductions in the normal amount of rain over a period of years, where, sooner or later, people's life styles and the economy of a given area have to change.

Farmers in the Mid-West will find more wells running dry, despite the fact that we have had some recent snows in the Mid-West. Much of that moisture will run-off into the rivers, perhaps causing temporary flooding, and will be of relatively little value.

The Central Valley of California is basically arid. Much of it is semi-desert, but it has been made to bloom because of irrigation through the gigantic reservoirs that line the western slopes of the Sierras, but they will dry up this summer. The economic effect to California has been estimated to be between two and one-half billion and six billion dollars. No one state can endure such a shock without affecting the rest of the nation.

If you don't yet have your food storage plan, you might still get around the dehydrated vegetable shortage. Buy a home dehydrator and all the fresh vegetables and fruits you can find, and start dehydrating.

(1/1/78) Just in case I'm wrong and the farmers manage to pull this strike off, get your food storage program now. You need it anyway. We could have temporary shortages and for sure, rising wheat, corn, oats and soy bean prices. It is going to cost you more very soon. We are right near the bottom of a price cycle.

Rising prices will bail out the farmer. It always looks darkest just before the dawn, and farm prices have been depressed for a long time.

(2/15/78) Many of our readers feel there is no way that the nation can survive a depression without becoming a totalitarian dictatorship. I think we have to look at the lessons of history to determine the likelihood of this being the end of the American dream.

There is no question, the years ahead may turn out to be the most dangerous and difficult in the history of the Republic. But while examining the nation's weaknesses, it is also worthwhile to keep an eye on the strengths of the country.

Our economy is a monstrously powerful machine. It could never be "taken by assault." I don't believe we could be conquered in a military confrontation or overwhelmed by the troubles of other nations. We are just too strong for that. The only real threat is rot from within, which we now have. (see: Values and Morals) I also believe the fungus destroying us is inflation, which is the result of demands upon government to spend more money than it is willing to take from its citizens through the direct taxing process. However, despite the rot, I believe our institutions can survive. Now, that's good news and bad news, because some of our regulatory institutions need to go away; however, no thinking American would like to see the congress, courts, presidency, and our marvelous systems of checks and balances disappear.

Now, I know that a lot of people are going to judge me by whether or not my timetable works out, which puts me in the interesting, but uncomfortable, position of cheering for a depression right on schedule just to prove I'm right. If I am right, your refusal to take the steps I have recommended, in time, will result in discomfort, inconvenience, possible hunger, physical danger, and the chance of losing everything you own. If I am wrong, my recommendations won't hurt you.

Many people say, "I've taken most of your advice, and I would like to ask a question." Then they ask me some financial question. When I routinely checked to see if they have stored food, they say, "Well, no, I haven't done that yet, but I have some silver coins. I'll always be able to buy food with silver coins, even if the currency collapses." But, brother, you can't buy it if it isn't being transported. You can't buy it if there's panic at the supermarkets or if there is a crowd around waiting to storm the delivery truck.

That delivery chain can be upset by the weather. One of our good subscribers in Lafayette, Indiana, sent me a page from the *INDIAN-APOLIS STAR,* dated January 30, giving an account of the effect of the big storm.

> When a Pepperidge Farms delivery truck carrying bread to Fort Benjamin Harrison Saturday night broke down near the Marsh Delicatessen at 62nd Street and Allisonville Road, the store's enterprising assistant manager saw a golden opportunity and negotiated for the bread.

But when some 50 persons shopping at the store realized what was going on, Dan Dudley was almost sorry he had. The shoppers rushed the truck in an every-man-for-himself frenzy to get the bread. Two men even got into a fist-fight over a loaf, Dudley said.

"I didn't think the guy was going to make it into the store alive," he said.

On February 2, also in Indianapolis, another article reported the following:

Grocery store cash registers continued to ring madly Wednesday and truck delivery men scurried around the city trying to keep up with the demand of customers flocking to stores in fear that a winter-storm watch might develop into a blizzard.

"They're buying everything they can get their hands on," the manager of the Kroger store at 4100 South East Street said.

The grocery store rush began Tuesday night after the forecast of more snow was made. Customers evidently were recalling what it was like when they opened their refrigerators and found empty shelves when the worst blizzard in the city's history raged outside last week.

A Kroger manager at 2620 West Michigan Street said persons were buying "ridiculous" amounts of milk, bread and eggs. "We can't keep bread in the store," he added.

The manager of the Preston-Safeway store at 7241 North Keystone Avenue said that the store did a record amount of business last Wednesday, but said he would not be surprised if yesterday's total broke last week's record.

Friendly Foods, 4907 North Pennsylvania Street, said many customers were buying two loaves of bread (of which the store has run out on each of the last several days).

Other stores around the city reported they were receiving deliveries, but were periodically running short of bread and milk.

This kind of panic buying could occur even if there weren't a real problem, but only if people perceive a problem. Perception matters; not reality.

My advice is only useful before the troubles become apparent to everyone. You have to do it now, systematically, coolly and carefully, or you won't be able to do it later. My business failure in 1968 happened with such astonishing swiftness that I went to work in the morning prosperous and came home broke that night. I remember the discussion I had with Kay some months earlier about completing our food storage plan. I had argued that food storage didn't matter when you had money in the bank, because you could always go buy food.

Well, I went to work wealthy, and I came home with $11.36 in my pocket and my bank accounts frozen. If my wife hadn't squirreled away food from the grocery budget, we wouldn't have had a food storage plan and we would have experienced genuine hunger. That's when I became a believer! So, get that food storage program completed right away.

It is imperative that the good people of the nation, who believe in sound principles, are the ones who get through in good shape so they are in a position to help remold the world that will come afterwards. To do that, you have to have money, time, and health. I want my subscribers to be among those who remold this world. I honestly believe that the only thing that will correct the system is the financial cataclysm we are going to face.

Every person who stores food now, while there are no distribution problems or shortages, will not be a burden on the community, and later there will be more to divide up among the rest of the population.

My advice is good for you and good for America. You just might be among those who save the Republic. (see: Famine, Food Production and Distribution, and Food Storage)

FOOD STORAGE

EVALUATION OF A FOOD STORAGE PROGRAM

(Special Report #2, 1/76) I think it's about time we gave you some guidelines on how to evaluate a commercial emergency food storage program. There are many of them available and they all make claims for soundness, adequacy, economy, etc. I'm going to give you some specifics about what I think is wrong with the typical emergency food storage program, and then encourage you to use these criteria in evaluating what the salesman tells you. I will also give you a set of questions to ask. If the answers to these questions are not satisfactory, then look elsewhere. Either the product is not sound, or the salesman is not competent.

So here's what you should ask the food storage salesman:

1. HOW MANY CALORIES ARE PROVIDED? One of the major shortcomings of food storage programs is they simply do not provide enough food. The only way to measure food quantity is in terms of calories. A calorie is a measurement of the amount of energy contained in a given amount of food. If you were to divide their "year's supply" of food up for a period of a year, in some instances,

you would have less than 1000 calories a day. This is a starvation diet! A typical American male of normal weight would starve to death in six months and would probably spend the last month in a coma. A good program should contain no less than 1800 calories a day. An adult male needs more, small children need less, so that would average out well for a family. Don't accept verbal representations. It must be clearly stated in the literature.

A few months ago, I contacted one of the best known companies in the field and asked for the calorie counts on their various units. I got passed on to four people. Finally, the last one said to me, "I'm sorry, I can't figure this out. Why don't we just send you copies of all of our labels and you figure it out?" That was a mistake, because I did just that and I found it averaged less than 1000 calories a day. What absolutely appalled me, though, was that this company is known to everyone in the industry. It has a fine nitrogen-pack process and an aggressive marketing program, yet their people didn't even know how much food they were selling in "a year's supply."

It's very difficult to economically get sufficient calories in a food storage program, because there are 4.2 calories per gram in carbohydrates, 4.2 calories per gram in protein, and yet fats yield 9.2 calories per gram. A high fat content, however, reduces shelf life because of danger of rancidity, so most storage programs rely on low-fat or defatted items, thereby reducing the calories.

If you do not have sufficient calories to meet your body's energy requirements, your body will cannibalize your own tissue, first your own body fat, and then connective tissue, then muscle and nerve tissue.

2. WHAT IS THE PROTEIN QUALITY? Most storage programs have sufficient protein quantity because they rely heavily upon grains, which will provide enough protein in grams. However, if you have carefully read Chapter 6 in *HOW TO PROSPER DURING THE COMING BAD YEARS,* you know that protein QUALITY is far more important that quantity. Because high-quality protein (meat, fish, eggs, fowl) is expensive to store in its freeze-dried form, most companies have attempted to solve the problem by relying heavily upon TVP (Textured Vegetable Protein). These are meat imitations made from soybeans. Taken in small quantities as a flavoring of stews and soups, I've no objection. However, most food storage programs rely far too heavily upon TVP as their principal source of protein, as it has a much lower Protein Efficiency Ratio than meats, fish, fowl or eggs.

3. WHAT IS THE PERCENTAGE OF RESIDUAL OXYGEN

IN THE CAN? Some of the largest companies use an obsolete canning process. This involves sending an open can of dehydrated food down an assembly line and squirting in some compressed nitrogen from a hose. The can then passes on down the assembly line until the lid is put on.

A good nitrogen-pack process will use a vacuum chamber, called a "Vacuum-Retort System." The can, with the lid on and almost sealed, is placed in the chamber and a vacuum is created in the chamber. The chamber is then flooded with nitrogen under positive pressure, generally about two pounds, filling the can with nitrogen. The can is then sealed in the chamber. Companies using this process will generally guarantee that it will have less than two percent residual oxygen. This is a major factor in shelf life and two percent or less should be, in my opinion, an irrevocable standard on which you should not compromise.

I will concede that there is considerable debate on this issue. However, I have access to tests with an oxygen analyzer, which determined that in some instances, there was as much as 15% to 20% residual oxygen in some cans of dehydrated food. This is roughly the same ratio as the air around you. This might not accelerate spoilage, but does have a devastating effect upon the more fragile nutritional elements.

4. WHAT PERCENTAGE OF THE CALORIES ARE DE-RIVED FROM JUNK FOODS? I have looked at storage programs where over 40% of the calories were derived from items like freeze-dried ice cream, canned sugar, white flour, gelatin (which is mostly sugar and poor quality protein), spaghetti, popcorn and similar items. I don't object to small amounts of these foods as occasional "reward" foods. However, the tendency of the industry has been to build their caloric count by using far too many of these items because they are cheap. No more than 5% of your calories should be derived from junk foods.

You should concentrate on basic staple items: fruits, vegetables, protein supplements, grain, etc.

5. IS THE COMPANY WITH WHICH YOU ARE DEALING FINANCIALLY STABLE? This is difficult to determine, but is worth the effort. I have information on some companies which I can pass on to you, if you contact us on our "hot-line." Others have refused to divulge specific information, but have given me bank references which I have checked out. If the company you deal with is unstable, you may be left holding a handful of very expensive receipts.

6. WHAT IS THE OVERALL NUTRITIONAL VALUE OF

THE PROGRAM. Many programs are accompanied by elaborate tables, demonstrating the amount of Vitamin A, Vitamin B, etc., that can be obtained from their program. These tables, in my opinion, are totally undependable. They do not result from actual analyses of the product, but from standard government tables telling you what nutrients it should have in it. This may bear no relationship to what it actually has. It does not account for processing losses, losses caused by additives nor losses in storage prior to canning. The only way you can be absolutely confident of good nutrition is with a good supplement program, and these supplements must be properly prepared for long-term storage.

It is possible to construct a decent storage program by buying food from almost anyone, as long as their nitrogen pack process is satisfactory and as long as you know what balance of products to select. However, if you don't have the time or knowledge, you may contact us, after reading Chapter 16 in *HOW TO PROSPER DURING THE COMING BAD YEARS*, and we will refer you to some good people who understand my requirements and can take care of you. But, bear in mind, this is a "buyer-beware" marketplace.

Food is the one area of preparation where no chances should be taken and where no compromises can be made. You cannot afford to be wrong. During a period of great national stress and trauma, you cannot afford to get sick. Think what life would be like if you could not run to the doctor with minor illness to prevent it from becoming a major illness. During times of stress, all kinds of illnesses increase, including infectious diseases, because stress can lower your resistance to them. Therefore, under stress conditions, your nutritional requirements increase. You must be certain that you are reinforcing your body's ability to resist the ravages of disease simply because you have no other recourse.

TVP-THE GREAT IMPOSTOR

(4/1/76) I'd like to say a word about Textured Vegetable Protein. My objections to TVP are based on the exaggerations that are used by so many food storage salesmen in representing the value of the product. Soybean granules are a useful adjunct to any food storage program, but when they attempt to convert soybean granules into something that looks and tastes like meat, the process is highly damaging to the value of the food. You can't turn a soybean into a hamburger without doing a heck of a lot to it, as anyone will testify who has ever eaten both a soybean and a hamburger. This process requires the application of high pressures and heat which damage the amino acids. These products are also loaded with flavorings and additives that, in my opinion, are harmful in relatively small amounts. But the typical food storage program contains so much of this product that it contains much more than small amounts of preservatives, flavorings, colorings, flavor enhancers, etc.

FREEZE-DRIED VS. DEHYDRATED FOODS

(1/15/76) These two preservation processes are completely different and produce a different product. I will describe the process in much more detail in subsequent issues. Here are the advantages and disadvantages of each product to help you make an intelligent decision for your emergency food storage program.

NUTRITIONAL VALUE: Freeze-dried food suffers slightly less nutritional loss in the processing, and consequently has a slightly higher value immediately afterwards. Dehydrated food, however, has a slightly lower rate of loss during storage. For a storage program, these two advantages tend to cancel each other out.

NUTRITIONAL SHELF LIFE: Both depend on the packing method used. If both kinds of products are nitrogen-packed, leaving less than two percent residual oxygen, dehydrated food has a small edge.

TASTE: A slight edge to freeze-dried food, although most people couldn't tell the difference.

CONVENIENCE OF PREPARATION: A big edge to freeze-dried foods. You just add boiling water and it's ready in five minutes. Dehydrated requires cooking or overnight soaking.

VARIETY: A stand-off, with each having advantages. There seems to be a greater overall availability of products in dehydrated foods. Freeze-drying, on the other hand, is useful for a variety of meats, fish and fowl which are not available in dehydrated form.

EASE OF STORAGE: Freeze-dried foods are bulky. They occupy roughly the same area as the fresh product. Dehydrated foods, on the other hand, shrink to one-quarter to one-seventh of their normal bulk. A large edge to dehydrated.

COST: A plus for dehydrated. Most freeze-dried foods cost quite a bit more. If your budget is quite limited, then I believe it would be best for you to spend your money on protein supplements, in place of high-protein meats, and chicken, and fish. Beef is approximately 15% protein. This brings the protein cost per pound of the freeze-dried beef close to $30 a lb. The fish steaks come out a little better in that they are approximately 40% protein, and that brings the cost of the protein in the fish steaks to approximately $13 a lb. I recommend a good protein supplement in lieu of meat, fish or fowl, in combination with dehydrated foods, unless money is no object.

FOOD ADDITIVES: A real advantage here for freeze-dried. Almost no additives are used, except in the casserole dishes (beef stroganoff, shrimp creole). I got around this problem in the dehydrated food program I helped design by eliminating most of the foods with the highest additive levels.

ON BALANCE: A matter of preference. If all additives worry you, buy freeze-dried, avoiding the casserole. If you can accept small amounts of additives, then dehydrated is by far the most food for the money. If convenience of preparation is more important than shelf space, and money is no object, then buy freeze-dried foods.

(3/1/76) The concept of food storage seems negative to many. It is not well understood that it benefits society. If those of us who can scrape together the money to put aside an emergency supply of food do so, it is good for everyone, including the poor who cannot afford to store food.

I've always felt that my security would depend upon how many others in the country were also secure. If my neighbors have an emergency supply of food, I will feel comfortable and safe around them and we can call on each other for help in times of difficulty. If I were the only person eating in a sea of starving people, I would not feel safe. Right now there is enough food that hundreds of thousands of families could set aside food, assuming there is time to do so. The Russian grain deal alone involves enough grain to provide 150 lbs. for every man, woman and child in America. If enough people would store food in this country, the American farmer would not be lobbying so hard for large windfall exports such as the Russian grain deal provides.

For this reason, I am hoping to awaken the nation to this problem and to stimulate official support for the storage of food.

(12/75) I also have a report on food storage from the University of Idaho Ag..cultural Extension Service by Don Huber, Plant Pathologist, and Esther H. Wilson, Extension Nutrition Specialist, entitled "Store a Year's Supply of Food and Household Items."

What interested me the most were the tables on shelf life of foods.

I have always said that canned goods are a poor choice for a long-term food storage program. They are heavy, bulky, of lower nutritional value due to heat used in canning, and nutritional shelf life is cut in half.

Storage Life of Canned Foods

Canned Goods	Storage Life
DAIRY PRODUCTS	
Milk	1 Year
MEAT PRODUCTS	
Beef	18 Months
Chicken	18 Months
Fish	1 Year
Ham	18 Months
Lunch Meat	18 Months
Pork	18 Months
Turkey	18 Months
CANNED VEGETABLES	
All	18 Months
FRUITS	
Applesauce	12–18 Months
Apricots	12–18 Months
Berries	6 Months
Citrus Juice	6–8 Months
Citrus Slices	12–18 Months
Cherries	6–12 Months
Peaches	12–18 Months
Pears	12–18 Months
Pineapple	12–18 Months
Plums	12–18 Months
MISCELLANEOUS	
Peanut Butter	12–18 Months
Shelled Nuts	1 Year

Ruff's Conclusions

Canned goods are a poor choice. They cost more per unit of food value than either dehydrated or freeze-dried, mainly because they are mostly water.

They lose nutritional value rapidly, and have less to start with. Two years old, use it if it's still good, or throw it away. If you use it, compensate for its nutritional losses with a good, natural multivitamin supplement and extra vitamin C.

DON'T use any cans that are bulging, leaking, or rusted. "If in doubt, throw it out."

A WORD FROM FRANK FORD

(8/15/76)   The following is part of an interview with Frank Ford, the Chairman of Arrowhead Mills, in West Texas, one of the largest suppliers of naturally and organically grown foods. Arrowhead markets "The Simpler Life" food storage program.

HJR: You became very interested in the individual emergency storage of food, and developed your food storage program called THE SIMPLER LIFE. What led you into this business?

FF: I was led into it because I believe that a breakdown will come in food distribution before it comes in food production. We could have, for instance, bulging grain elevators in Kansas or Texas, and the people of New York could be totally without food. There are several ways that food shortages could develop.

After the great earthquake in Guatamala, there were food shortages. If the San Andreas fault were to go in California, the whole West Coast would have a severe food shortage situation because there's only one week's food supply in most of those cities, and that is only if there were no looting, and no social disorders. I think it's important that we have the food where it's needed, in the form it's needed, when it's needed.

One great problem is the increasing cost of food production. Right now, in the basic commodities, the farmer's cost of production is greater than the price he can receive. If people buy reserve food supplies now, and have it to share with any who need it at a time of stress, we will keep the farmers in business during years of surplus and depressed prices. I think we'll soon be facing great economic dislocation. We always have the weather factor, but our first problem is the distribution, and then eventually, the production of our food supplies. (see: Food Production and Distribution)

HJR: You've had a lengthy period of drought here, as well as in several other parts of the Mid-West. What's happened to the dry land farmer in this area?

FF: The dry land wheat farmer here had almost no crop at all in 1976. Only one or two farmers brought in any grain at all off the dry land. The irrigated farmers lost so much money on their wheat due to high cost and the market price being so low, many of them said they'll never plant any more wheat.

HJR: What we're saying is that if enough farmers make that decision, today's large surpluses could turn into a major shortfall next summer. That looks rather bullish on prices for the farmer who can afford to hang onto his wheat this year.

FF: Well, it's rather difficult for many of us to hang on, because of storage costs. Keeping grain in good condition is expensive. Those who can afford to hang onto their wheat are trying to do so because they simply cannot break even on today's prices.

HJR: What standards have you set for your food storage program?

FF: We've tried to buy the very best grains, beans and seeds that we can get from all over the country. There are only a few farmers that raise rice organically that we know about in California, Louisiana, Arkansas, and Texas. They raise without the usual poisonous seed treatment, and without spraying the water as the seedlings come up or spraying the growing crop and fumigating the rice. We buy rice from these four farmers and bring it in and hull and clean it ourselves.

We buy pinto beans from the high altitude area of Colorado, where they are watered by melting snow. The beans are tender and they cook up well and store well. We raise our own wheat and corn organically right here. We get the very best commodities, without exception, from all over the country. We clean them thoroughly and then can them with the nitrogen to keep it in good shape for extended periods of time. When a person does open that can, he will have more than the psychological peace he gained when he stored the food. He will have good nutrition. It will be as pure and natural as possible, and most will be organically grown.

HJR: In the food storage industry, there has been what I would call a tremendous ground swell of apathy on the part of the customer in the recent past year. The industry has suffered major declines, even to the point of taking some of the household names in food storage right out of business. You made the decision a year ago to go into this business and are aggressively committed for the future. In the face of this apathy, what business grounds would you have for making such a decision?

FF: In business, I've always gone "against the grain," not with it. We've been grateful for this period of complacency, because it's given us an opportunity to get our quality control right, plot a program that's based on solid principles, and to establish distributors who have integrity and commitment. We have not been at all distraught by the complacency of the people in this country.

We're seeing people interested in putting food away before prices go up, before availability is to be a problem. And we're also making very good shipments internationally to Christian ministries in other lands.

HJR: Do you feel this marketplace is going to turn up in the near future?

FF: Yes.

HJR: On what grounds?

FF: I think we have a very high risk of a Mid-East war, based on the situation in Lebanon. I could go into some Bible prophecy, but I won't take the time. I think that the trigger point for the next Mid-East war is to the North and East of Israel. Also, it could be another very quick Israeli victory, triggering an Arab oil boycott, which would change the economic complexion of this country overnight. The complacency would be forever ended.

Worse still, we are sure to have rules imposed from a bureaucracy which doesn't understand that true wealth is created in the land. The people in the cities who are isolated from their food supply, and even in smaller towns that are away from food, should give real serious thought to a reserve food supply, and a water purifier, so that they will have done all they can to use their resources wisely for the physical future of their families.

HJR: Frank, thank you for your time. We hope you will be available to help provide some answers and consultation for our readers.

QUESTIONS AND ANSWERS

(Special Report #4, 10/76)

Q. What is the best way to store grain?

A. The best way to buy it is commercially nitrogen-packed, in one-gallon tins. Then it's 100% protected from rodents and moisture. And if there are any weevil eggs, they cannot mature.

The next best method (and cheaper) is to buy grain in 50 pound bags and place it in barrels or tins and add dry ice. Fill the container 1/3 full, place abut 4 square inches of dry ice on the top, place the lid loosely (not air-tight) and wait for the dry ice to dissipate. The CO_2 is heavier than air and will expand to fill the container. Seal the lid air-tight, and you're set.

Two cautions: Don't seal the lid before the dry ice dissipates. You might have wheat shrapnel. Also, this method is not perfect—certainly not as safe as the commercially-packed product—but the risk of loss or spoilage is small.

Q. Why don't you recommend brown rice, sunflower seeds, and sesame seeds?

A. Because the shelf-life is unknown, and is generally conceded to be short (under six months), even when nitrogen-packed. Wheat can keep forever. These other items, like wheat, are rich in unsaturated fatty acids, but unlike wheat, go rancid quickly.

Q. Isn't oil or shortening necessary for a food storage program? How can you store it so it won't go rancid?

A. Vitamin E occurs naturally in oils and serves to prevent rancidity. Its natural function is as an "anti-oxidant." This means it prevents the chemical reaction that occurs when oxygen combines with unsaturated fats, forming peroxides, or free radicals, which cause the product to spoil. We have found that added Vitamin E can be used to extend the life of vegetable oils.

When vegetable oils are refined, most of the Vitamin E is extracted. Chemicals such as BHA and BHT, commonly used anti-oxidants, are added to the product to prevent oxidation. I believe that these products are potentially harmful.

An alternative is to add Vitamin E to the product to replace that which was removed in the refining process. Buy Vitamin E in soft gelatin capsules in a wheatgerm or safflower oil base. Puncture it with a pin and squeeze the contents into the container of safflower, corn or peanut oil. Use approximately 500 unit of Vitamin E per quart of oil. Store the oil in relatively small containers (1 gallon or less), so there is little chance of oxidation due to exposure to air after the container has been opened for use. After adding the Vitamin E, shake the bottle thoroughly, and recap it tightly. Repeat this process approximately every six months.

There are no controlled studies to prove this point, but I have personal knowledge of individuals who have kept oil up to five years using this process.

Q. How do you store dog food?

A. Storing food for a dog may not be a luxury. If things get tough, I'll be glad to have my dogs barking and yapping and frightening anyone who comes prowling around our yard. Dog food can be stored very much in the same way wheat is stored. Most dry products, protected by dry ice, in barrels or drums, will keep up to three years.

Q. Where can I store my food and how much space does it take?

A. The storage program, which I helped design, will fit under two card tables and provides one year of food for one adult. Concealment is made easy by the fact that the dehydrated part of the program is so compact. The small cans (#2-1/2) are in small cases, which can be tucked under beds and into closets. If you put them on the floors of your closets, you are selecting the parts of your house that have the most stable temperatures.

Many of our subscribers have been concerned about concealment. One of our readers described how he arranged the small cases in the form of an easy chair, covered it with it with foam rubber and upholstered it. You could be sitting on his food supplies and never know it.

Other readers have told us of building a false wall in a living room, leaving a space of perhaps eighteen inches. Within that wall is their food storage program and, if they need it, it is a simple matter to cut a door into the wall.

It is also possible to purchase underground fiberglass storage tanks, which are airtight and watertight, and bury them in your backyard. They will store a year's supply of food for two or three people.

Q. Is it a good idea to have a home dehydrator, and how long will home dehydrated food keep?

A. It's a marvelous idea to have a home dehydrator. We have one and wouldn't be without it. It preserves food with less fuss and bother than canning, and you're able to avoid the heavy use of sugar. The reconstituted dehydrated food tastes excellent, and has good nutritional value.

If you will simply place the dried food in Zip-Lock plastic bags and not expose them to much heat, you can get a shelflife of six to eighteen months. It's not as good as nitrogen-packed, sealed in cans, but it certainly helps you to take advantage of good bargains or the immediate availability of foods. Almost anything can be dehydrated.

Q. Can meat be dried?

A. Yes, you can make beef jerky or pemmican. This can be done either in the oven, in your dehydrator, or even in the sun. The shelflife is approximately six months. Don't depend on it for much longer than that because the product is generally high in fat and will have a tendency to go rancid.

(6/15/77)

Q. I understand you're a Mormon and the Mormons have always advocated storing food. How much has your religion affected your recommendations?

A. Well, I wouldn't have known about the storage of food had I not been a Mormon, but my economic views are my own, not my Church's. I'm just as controversial among my Church members. Food storage has always been advocated by Mormon leadership as a protection against individual financial troubles. We ate the food we had stored when I had a franchise abruptly cancelled back in 1968 and I was without income. To the Mormons, it's just personal insurance. My views go way beyond those of my Church in that I believe there are going to be great generalized problems which are going to affect us all.

My advice on being free of debt and self-sufficient also parallel my religious heritage, but that is not a matter of theology. Mormonism is a uniquely American religion, and has its cultural side as well as its theological side. Culturally and economically, its views are very much America of 50 to 100 years ago. Hard work, thrift, debt avoidance and resistance to speculative fever are all Mormon cultural values, and I share them.

(2/1/79)   More Questions

Q. I can swallow everything you have to say except the idea of food storage. After all, buying gold and silver is good economic sense. There has never been a time in my lifetime that I couldn't buy food in the store, even during the depths of the depression, and I just can't conceive of it in this country. Your message would be a lot more persuasive if you dropped that bizarre concept.

A. Well, Buster, if you think it's a "bizarre concept," I suggest you follow what's happening in England right now. A nationwide strike by 100,000 truckers has touched off panic food buying. Train engineers announced a strike that will threaten Britain with its worst industrial crisis in five years.

My wife and I recently met a labor relations expert for a major British conglomerate on his way through San Francisco to conduct some negotiations in New Zealand. He told us what was going on in England. Transportation is jammed because truckers, not only refuse to drive, but are actually blocking highways and threatening violence upon strike breakers. This has caused panic buying, and in some parts of England people have gone hungry.

They are also having one of the worst winters in modern history, and getting around is difficult, at best.

When the rail strike is in full bloom, it is just conceivable that more people in England could suffer from hunger pains while freezing in the dark. England is an example of what inflation does to labor relations and how it can disrupt distribution. We have escaped problems like this so far in the U.S. because we have not had England's kind of inflation in this century. That spectre is looming over us now. We have no precedent for what inflation can do to a complex, industrial, highly specialized economy.

It was not just the actuality of food shortages in England, but the anticipation of them that was translated into reality. Those who have food storage will not fear. Some of those who do not will be scared, hungry, or both. The unions have said that they would allow transportation of certain "priority" goods, such as food, medicines, heating fuel for schools and hospitals, and snow-clearing equipment; but that promise seems to be breaking down. In the densely populated Manchester area, 600 water supply workers also walked off their jobs and left sewage untreated. Residents were told not to take baths or flush toilets and to boil all water before drinking it. A 24-hour strike by British Airways pilots halted almost all domestic and European flights by the government airline. On top of that, the Irish Republican Army is now bombing fuel depots in London. That's the kind of chaos you have when your institutions come under the assault of inflation, which is at the root of English problems. I used to think they were 15 years ahead of us, but now the gap is rapidly narrowing. Now, does food storage still sound bizarre?

FOOLISH, BUT READY

(8/15/77) Early last winter I got a call from a subscriber in a small town in Pennsylvania. He said, "Howard, I've taken your advice. I have a year's supply of food, two weeks of water, and a wood stove. I feel a little foolish about the whole thing."

Six weeks later, the Mid-West and the East got Alaska's weather. The roads were blocked with snow. The gas pumping equipment froze. Food deliveries stopped, and so did the frozen water supply. My friend couldn't get into town. But a potential nightmare turned into a minor inconvenience. They were warm and well fed. He wrote later and said, "Now my neighbors are the ones who feel foolish."

SIMPLER LIFE PROGRAM

(9/1/76)   Many have called or written to ask where you can buy THE SIMPLER LIFE food storage program described by Frank Ford of ARROWHEAD MILLS in the August 15 issue. Write to Martens Health and Survival Products, Inc., P.O. Box 51, Moraga, CA 94556 or call them at 800-824-7861. They have a "Howard Ruff approved" version of THE SIMPLER LIFE. (see: Food Storage—A Word From Frank Ford)

BULLION OR BOUILLON?

(8/15/76)   I've had some subscribers phone or write and object to the space I have devoted to food storage and nutrition. They usually want to talk about gold or silver. Well, I've eaten beef boullion and chicken bouillon, and I like it; but silver bullion tastes terrible. It's foolish to prepare to protect yourself by buying precious metals, then starve for a while because food distribution has broken down, or a period of civil disorder has made it dangerous to go looking for food. Silver coins won't keep you alive if there isn't any food to buy.

I'm not just going to tell you what I think you'd like to hear. I'm going to come back to this theme at regular intervals.

I'd rather be well fed and broke, than rich and hungry.

SUBSCRIBERS' SUGGESTIONS

(9/1/77)   We often receive interesting suggestions from our subscribers as to better ways of doing things.

> Stan Miller writes, I'm not sure of any precise effect on the nutritional value of wheat, but when possible, dry ice pellets (not block or powder), or "snow" should be used in the storage of wheat in place of sheets of dry ice, as these products lack the petroleum binders which might contaminate the food. I am a dispatcher of dry ice and other products for Union Ice here in Los Angeles.

I know of no instance in which there have been harmful effects from these binders, but if you are a purist, you might want to take this extra precaution.

Another reader suggests that if you have a large container of honey that has crystallized and solidified, there is a simple solution. Set it out in the sun for a couple of days. It melts down beautifully.

That sounds so simple. Just think how many times we've put a five-gallon container of honey in the biggest pot we have and left it in simmering water on the stove for hours. I feel kind of foolish.

And finally, we received a letter from Russell Simonson with a copy of a reprint from the *HERBAL HANDBOOK FOR FARM AND STABLE* from Rodale Press on the preservation of eggs. I'm going to quote it verbatim.

> To preserve eggs, rub all over with grease to render them non-porous. The French method is to varnish them with a preparation of olive oil and beeswax. This will preserve eggs for two years. Four ounces of beeswax should be melted slowly in eight ounces of olive oil and the eggs dipped into the mixture when still warm. Care should be taken to see that all parts of each egg are well immersed. Wipe with a soft cloth, and then carefully store in airtight jars or tins, filled with bran or powdered charcoal, or a mixture of both in equal parts. The small end of the egg should be placed downwards when storing.

If that works, it could be a super way of maintaining a diet much closer to your predepression standards.

HONEY

(7/15/77) In the past, we've recommended Robert Webb in Southern California as a supplier of high quality natural honey.

A honey producer is faced with a raft of problems. In California there's a water shortage, meaning less flowers and nectar. The cost of lumber, nails, staples and paint for beehives is up from 40 to 75%. Honey containers are up 35%. The cost of bees is up 85% and shipping costs are up 25% and there seems to be no end in sight. Many beekeepers are having to feed their bees just to keep them alive and others have had to sell out. Therefore, Mr. Webb says honey prices are going up.

We are using honey purchased from Mr. Webb and it is delicious. It is completely natural and is uncooked and unwatered. This means it will crystallize fairly easily, and as we've said before, it should be transferred from large containers into smaller ones as soon as you receive it. It's pretty darn inconvenient to try to reliquify a 35 lb. drum of crystallized honey. Crystallization is a natural process in good natural honey. Write directly to Mr. Webb for prices and shipping cost information.

Mr. Webb's address is 241-33rd Street, Hermosa Beach, CA 90254.

(4/1/79)   Bad Honey

I've just received a warning notice on the use of honey by tiny babies from a physician friend of mine.

As you know, I've recommended honey in place of sugar in food storage programs. It gives more sweetening for a given amount of sugar because it is sweeter. It is virtually indestructible and is a superior food to sugar in several respects, as it has the necessary trace elements for metabolizing the sugars in honey, which purified sucrose does not have.

However, honey may have caused nearly one-third of the cases of infant botulism in recent years. Only children under one year old are susceptible to it. Those over one year are not. The botulism can also be prevented by bringing the honey to a boil and simmering for five minutes.

Of 41 known cases of infant botulism recorded in California from 1976 to July of 1978, 29.2 percent had been fed honey. The disease is caused by the bacterium Clostridium botulinum, whose spores are often found in honey and other unprocessed agricultural products. The bacteria, which can multiply in a baby's stomach, produce a toxin which causes constipation, weakness, and occasionally death.

Again, it is perfectly safe for anyone over twelve months of age, but be careful if you have a new baby in the house.

(5/1/79)   Minding The Spore

I received a letter from a registered microbiologist regarding my article about botulism and honey in infants under one year of age (see preceding article). He points out that boiling honey will not destroy the spores of the botulism organism, which apparently are the major problem with infant botulism. The infant apparently does not contract the disease from eating the living organism or the toxin, but from eating the spores. As boiling will not kill those spores, I think I'd better modify my previous advice and suggest that you simply not use honey for infants 12 months of age or under. The spores represent no danger to anyone over one year of age. Many thanks to our friend for that very important information.

A FINAL WORD

(3/1/76)   I believe it is socially useful for the Ruffs to store food. It's good for everyone. It's good for the Ruffs, it's good for the nation and it's good for the poor. In fact, if enough people were to store food during a year of plenty such as 1975 appeared to be, perhaps then we would merely suffer a deeper recession, or only a 1930-style depression, without a total collapse of the system.

FORECASTS

The purpose of this section is to present some of my forecasts on a variety of subjects with the date of forecast. A conscientious effort was made to include a representative cross section of forecasts, both by subject and date, but it is by no means exhaustive. For fear of repetition and lack of textual continuity, some predictions simply have been left in their original context elsewhere in this volume.

As I've said before, I never have professed to be infallible, but my track record says I'm right far more often than I'm wrong. My livelihood depends on being right a large percentage of the time. My economic forecasts must stand the test of the marketplace every day, unlike many tenured "academic" economists who can predict with reckless abandon and still have a paycheck waiting for them each month.

Some of my forecasts have been fulfilled, some are still in the future, and a few were wrong.

Now, a few of my prognostications arranged alphabetically as follows:

1. Banking Troubles
2. Carter and Economy
3. Cities (other than New York City)
4. Collectibles
5. Depression—When?
6. Diamonds
7. Economy, general
8. Food Production and Food Prices
9. Gas Shortage
10. Gold
11. Government Spending
12. Inflation/Deflation
13. Interest Rates
14. Merrill Lynch Forecast
15. New York City
16. Real Estate

17. Remonetization with Gold
18. Silver
19. Soviets and Africa
20. Soviets and China
21. Stock Market
22. Weather/Climate (including water

For a more extensive discussion of the above topics, please consult the index of the encyclopedia under those and related topic headings.

Banking Troubles

(3/1/76) I've called it right, again. In November of 1974 I said that we were headed for banking troubles. In my book, *FAMINE AND SURVIVAL IN AMERICA*, published in July of 1974, I said that the banks were vulnerable, and a collapse of the banks was highly likely. I still believe it is possible we could have a collapse of the banking system.

The bank failure scorecard shows Hamilton National Bank of Chattanooga, Franklin Bank of Houston, and The Astro Bank of Houston all scoring big bankruptcies in 1976.

Perhaps the best banks to have your money in would be the first ones to go broke because you would probably be bailed out all right. I still feel that the bank troubles are severe. They may survive until this financial recovery peters out in the very near future, but I believe they could not stand the pressures of another deep recession or depression. (And my feelings are the same today, 11/79. HJR)

(10/1/77) The non-OPEC countries are now at their borrowing limits, the banks are overextended and scared and there is no end in sight.

THERE IS NO CHANCE OUR BANKS ARE GOING TO BE REPAID, and when they face default, the Emperor will be exposed as wearing no clothes at all.

Carter and Economy

(1/1/77) For all you Carter watchers, count on the following:

There will be fiscal stimulus. Because it is almost impossible for any Administration to make significant changes in a short period of time, there will be no all-out spending splurge, at least not much more than we are already going through. A fiscal chameleon like Jimmy Carter is not going to make a heck of a lot of difference. The trends are already established and the budget is already out of control.

You can continue to bet on lower interest rates. Last February I said that you could bet on lower interest rates. I was right. I believe that the economy will continue to be flooded with money, that short-term rates will continue to drop, that long-term rates will soon follow, and that bond prices will continue to improve.

We will feel even more of the symptoms of the "British disease," but we are still at the stage of the economic cycle where fiscal stimulus does work, and it will work for awhile, and you can bet on it.

(10/1/77)   Bet on the economic ignorance of the Carter Administration. It's evident from events that Mr. Carter does not have the slightest understanding of economic principles. He will be exposed for what he is: an overly confident, arrogant man, with no grasp of the underlying principles.

(5/15/79)   "The Carter 'fight inflation' plan will not work, although it will appear to for a short time."

Cities (other than New York City)

(3/1/76)   THE END OF THE AMERICAN METROPOLIS AS WE SEE IT is possible. This is a long-term trend. I believe it will be caused by people fleeing the cities out of concern for their safety and financial welfare. The large cities, in the last three years, have lost 6% of their population. I believe this trend will accelerate as more and more cities pull in their horns and cut back on essential goods and services. I believe our major cities soon will be unsafe places to live. The jury is still out on this forecast.

(10/1/77)   Bet on municipal bankruptcies and social problems.

Collectibles

(12/15/77)   I have advised the purchase of rare stamps, antiques, art, and rare coins and they've all prospered over the last several months.

Depression—When?

(9/16/76)   Time after time, I'm asked when the next economic downturn will begin.

Sometime in the next six to eighteen months this recovery will peak and start downhill.

At this point, my crystal ball gets cloudy. I don't know whether it will be a precipitous drop or a long slide, but it will be deep, and we are going into it weaker than we went into the last recession. Be glad you still have time to get ready.

(6/15/77)

Q. Don't just tell me what's going to happen, tell me when.

A. I believe this economic recovery will peak somewhere in or shortly after the first quarter of 1978. At this point the crystal ball gets a little cloudy, because I don't know how long it will plateau near the top, exactly when it will turn down or whether it will be a sudden break or a long slow slide.

(10/1/77)   I've had my neck in a noose since 1973 when I forecast that inflation would eventually bring about a massive depression.

How do I feel now? I'll stake everything I have on a downturn. I'd bet 70% of what I have on the timetable. Knowing what is going to happen isn't too hard; knowing when is the tough part.

Diamonds

(12/15/77)   I've been pushing diamonds for several months, and so far this year there have been 17 percent and 15 percent increases at the wholesale level, and there will be more. I am advising expansion of your holdings of these beautiful stones.

Economy, general

(7/15/76)   When the "eye" of the hurricane passes, we will move into a massive fiscal convulsion and an inflation-caused, world-wide monetary collapse. It will probably be triggered by municipal collapse, and we will have done it to ourselves by our insatiable demands for more services from government!

Any idiot can forecast a famine when the stores are empty. Any fool can predict a recession or depression when General Motors is laying off workers.

I forecast the great recession of 1973-74, and I'm telling you now that we are heading into the next one in a weakened condition, and it may have no bottom, short of a massive collapse of all fiscal institutions.

(12/1/76)   I see a pause in the economic recovery, followed by a brief period (six to twelve months) of feverish boom, due to Carter-inspired monetary and tax stimulus (80 percent probability).

Then there will be a long, irreversible slide by April 1978 at the latest.

(4/15/77)   My previous forecasts for 1977 are still valid. Economically, for most Americans, it will be a pretty good year. . . . The only things that could abruptly change the picture before the end of 1977 would be another oil boycott, a major war in the Near East or Africa, or a chain of major loan defaults by foreign countries on their American bank loans . . . We will not be heading into a down cycle until sometime after the first quarter of 1978 . . .

(10/1/77)   My scenario goes something like this.

Sometime next year, probably before the end of the second quarter, the economy will begin to soften and politicians and big labor will "view it with alarm." The dollar will start its real decline, of which the last few months have been just a dress rehearsal. You will see some selective price deflation in big city real estate and some commodities, while the basic money creating, inflation machine will be cranked up in a desperate effort to stop the slowdown from turning into a landslide, and inflationary and deflationary forces will be battling for supremacy. Government will spend like crazy and flood the system with money, running huge deficits. Tax collections will drop and the level of welfare and unemployment payments will rise, giving us the worst of all possible worlds: a sharp economic downturn, a monetary crisis sharply increasing the cost of our oil imports, an even greater transfer superimposed on this mess, a spiraling monetary inflation, something akin to the German Weimar Republic inflation of 1923.

(4/1/78)   As we complete the first quarter of 1978, things seem to be developing about as planned. Maybe that's a bad choice of words. I should have said "about as forecast."

I reiterate, we are headed for a long, slow slide that could be punctuated by dramatic breaks as the slide uncovers serious structural weaknesses in the international monetary system as well as at home.

(11/15/78)
Q. When is the economic depression you are talking about going to happen?
A. We are on the schedule I outlined months ago. I said the economy would peak sometime in or shortly after the 1st quarter of 1978, would plateau for awhile, and then turn downhill. (*RUFF TIMES*, June 15, 1977)

Now, it seems the "real" economists are confirming it. LEIF OLSEN, CITIBANK Economic Policy Committee Chairman said

241

on Nov. 14, "It appears now that early this year the economy reached its potential: that point at which it can grow only as fast as permitted by new entrants into the labor force, and new output capacity added to our capital stock." That means we have peaked and plateaued on schedule.

I also forecast we would be faced with what looked like a deflationary recession, but that government would panic and try to spend us out of it giving us a worse recession coupled with devastating inflation. (*RUFF TIMES,*Feb. 1, 1978) The Conference Board's chief economist, ALBERT SOMMERS, testified before the SENATE BANKING COMMITTEE that without the continued Fed monetary control that will likely produce a recession, an even worse inflation-induced recession will occur further down the line.

And finally, Mr. KAHN, Carter's inflation Czar, says that if the Carter inflation plan doesn't work, we are headed for a depression! There, they said it! The dirty word, hitherto only whispered in dark alleys by crackpot "Prophets of Doom" like me, and Mr. Kahn!

Signs of the downhill slide are already apparent. How long will it take for us to slide downhill? Probably several months. Possibly as much as two years. In the meantime, you will continue to see contradictory inflationary and deflationary signals, and a business slowdown in some areas, with rising fear of the future. These mixed signals will continue, and one day we will wake up and all of the great economists will say, "Hey, we're in a depression and we've got inflation at the same time. Now how the heck did that happen?"

(11/1/78) I believe that the gold market, the stock market and the interest rate markets will signal, well in advance, if there's going to be any recovery or prolonged pause in inflation. They have already signaled the economic downturn. That's history and written in stone. Will they signal a short-term recovery from the next recession? That question will occupy just about all of my time, attention, and study. Other things are unimportant compared with that. If the markets signal a recovery, we will want to be out of our investment gold and into government bonds. If we are not going to get a recovery, and we slide into depression with a runaway hyper-inflation, there will never be an opportunity to get into government bonds, because all dollar denominated paper is going to self-destruct, and for awhile there will be no monetary system worth the label.

Food Production and Food Prices

(3/1/76)   Overall food production will be down from 10% to 30%. Due to high feed costs and dry pastures, beef prices will drop sharply at the wholesale level and slightly at the retail level for three to six months. This will force ranchers to sell, creating a glut now and less beef later. Shortages and sharp price increases will be seen by mid-summer or fall.

Wheat and corn prices will rise sharply as drought damage becomes more obvious. There will be no relief this summer or fall. Look for possible spring floods at the wrong time, in the wrong places, and in the wrong amounts.

(4/15/77)   The forces affecting wheat in the international marketplace are heavily weighted in favor of future shortages.

In California, agricultural production may drop only between 10% and 20%, as a result of 8,000 water wells being drilled.

Russia has suffered a severe winter kill of her wheat crop and that means she'll be buying in world markets.

Gas Shortage

(2/15/79)   "You might just find yourself waiting in gas lines or unable to travel on weekends because of weekend service station closings." (Editor's note: only three months after this forecast the nation's drivers were doing just that.)

Gold

(12/15/77)   August 1976 gold was between $103 and $120 per ounce, and I begged you to buy gold. It could go no place but up. (Those aren't the exact words, but that's pretty close to it.) In fact, when it was $120 I said if it dropped below $120, it wouldn't be for long. It did fall to $103 and went back up in about three weeks. Anyone that took my advice then has made a lot of money in gold, and there is a long way to go yet.

(5/15/79)   "The price of gold could move up to as high as $275-$280 an ounce, and from those levels a major correction, which I have been expecting for some months, will take place . . . We will have a chance to buy much cheaper gold sometime in the next few months."

Government Spending

(11/15/78)   Until I see a ground swell on the part of the people to give up the free school bus, the mobile library, the repair of the pot-holes in the streets, the juvenile hall to keep the troublesome kids out of their hair, their social security checks, their government pensions, their defense contracts, and a zillion other programs for their benefit, there will be no significant change in the government spending climate.

Inflation/Deflation

(7/15/76)   I believe we will see 20% inflation in less than a year.

(9/15/76)   I believe we have a 60% chance of double or triple-digit inflation in the next two to three years, and a 40% chance of substantial deflation. That's not a clear-cut choice. (I've since adjusted those percentages to favor inflation even more, HJR. 11/79)

(12/1/76)   I believe inflation will pick up in the last three quarters of 1977, back to double-digit, no later than year's end, probably sooner.

Interest Rates

(9/1/76)   In the July 15 issue, I said, "If Carter is elected . . . interest rates will drop."

On August 15, Senator Mondale announced that the first act of a Carter Administration would be to press for "easy money" and lower interest rates to stimulate the economy. It's time for our "fix"! Just don't overdose by mistake! (see: Bonds, Inflation, & Investments)

(11/15/76)   For the next several months, you can bet on dropping interest rates. Then, as the inflation rate turns up, interest rates will climb sharply, as lenders demand that they receive sufficient compensation to cover inflation and return a true profit.

(12/1/76)   I see a continued slide in short-term interest rates (70%). Long-term rates will remain relatively stable, as lenders anticipate inflation and demand an inflation-compensating premium over the long haul (90%).

(5/15/79) "Soon, I expect a rather abrupt decline in business activity, with falling inflation and interest rates. This will be short lived (6 to 15 months)...I then expect inflation to take off and interest rates to soar to new highs..."

Merrill Lynch Forecast

(3/1/78) ALBERT COX, President of MERRILL LYNCH Economics, the forecasting arm of Merrill Lynch, the world's largest brokerage firm, says that he expects, "a classic business recession by the end of this year or early next year."

Cox predicts higher inflation, higher interest rates and a Federal budget deficit of between $75 and $80 billion in the 1979-80 fiscal year.

Not being able to resist institutional optimism, he did say that he "expects the recession to be a short one with a recovery late in 1979."

Well, I'll be darned! Maybe I'm not alone after all.

New York City

(2/1/76) I have repeatedly forecast that the New York City "Bail-Out" plan would probably fall apart. I have said that the cash deficit was larger than what has been admitted, that the State laws forcing a moratorium on maturing debt would be disastrous if it held up in a court test because it would make municipal borrowing harder for everyone and impossible for some. It would be equally disastrous if the moratorium were shot down by the courts because the bail-out plan would disintegrate causing a chain reaction of municipal bankruptcies and bank failures.

These were extreme views until a few days ago. Let's see how it looks now.

In his "State of the City" address, January 22, the Mayor said New York City's attempt to save itself is in serious jeopardy. This year's budget deficit could be $89 million higher than anticipated.

For ten years, they've been overstating projected income and understating costs, and according to the accounting firm of Arthur Anderson and Company, they are still doing so.

Mayor Beame is forecasting with a "sense of gravest urgency," new taxes, more firings, and further curtailment in education, police, fire, health and sanitation services.

There are only two alternatives. The city will go bankrupt and collapse into a jungle of welfare strikes, unchecked fires, rampant crime, initiating the possible end of the American metropolis; or the Federal Goverment and the courts will take over the city and it will be the beginning of the end of representative government in our cities.

I still say you are watching the most important financial event of the last half of this century, and I think it can, and probably will, trigger the next great depression.

I still say this depression will be violent and disruptive as it means the collapse of municipal and state governments and a breakdown of services leading to protests and riots by people demanding "rights" which can no longer be delivered.

I still say New York City is only the first.

Runaway inflation and "out of control" Federal budgets are the wave of the future. There is absolutely no chance I'm wrong.

(3/1/76) I predicted New York City's financial problems. I think I called that shot perfectly. I first announced that New York was facing its troubles in November of 1974, long before anybody else was concerned. I've been right on the nature of the troubles. I've been right in analyzing and forecasting what would happen, and what the alternatives were. And now I'm right when I say that the New York financial plan is falling apart. As I forecast, the taxes that were enacted to increase revenues have resulted in revenue losses as they've driven businesses and individuals out of the city. The legislature is now moving to rescind the inheritance tax on individuals who have been moving out of the city in record numbers so they won't have to die in New York City and be unable to pass their assets onto their heirs. The jury is still out on the final results, but I still believe the plan is going to fall apart.

Real Estate

(12/15/77) I said several months ago that the real estate market was going to soften in some of the high priced suburban areas around the big cities, and that has happened. In our county where I just sold my home, there were 1,500 listings a year ago and now there are almost 4,000 homes for sale, and there is no question that prices have started back down. That's not true everywhere, but it is true in enough places to be frightening.

I have advised buying real estate in-and-near small towns, and there is a tremendous building and real estate boom going on near most of the small towns in America that have the characteristics I described: (1) Diversified agricultural economic base, (2) No large industrial plant on which a town depends, and (3) No large government dependent population. These towns are booming in real estate values. It would have been a heck of a place to put your money if you listened back when I said to do it, and it still ain't bad.

Remonitization with Gold

(7/15/76)   The international bankers and manipulators know the collapse is coming. The demonetization of gold, and the IMF sales, are devices to depress gold prices, and cheaply move gold out of government hands into the private hands of the investment houses and great super-rich families. After the collapse, gold will be remonetized and the already wealthy will have more control over the real wealth.

Silver

(7/1/76)   FLASH—SILVER GOING UP.

I have reason to believe we are going to see a sharp rise in the price of silver. It involves a large transaction of silver being presented to the Philippines in payment for their sugar crop by a major American sugar company. It also involves the Hunt family. I have reason to believe that this is going to cause some severe shortages. I think this could be the beginning of a real bull market in silver. I doubt if we will see silver this cheap ($4.75/oz.) again for a long time.

(4/1/79)   I expect an explosion of silver prices. $20.00 silver within the next 18 months would not surprise me at all.

Soviets and Africa

(3/15/76)   The watchword is "keep your eye on Africa." In Angola, we have demonstrated to the Soviet Union that we will not act until we are scared, or until we feel our vital interests have been threatened. The Soviet Union has achieved military equality, or perhaps even superiority. They have found themselves unopposed as they have taken control of a nation adjacent to a country which is very important to us. I believe that they will become bolder and bolder in pursuing their self-appointed task of world revolution. I believe that they wish to dominate African shipping lanes, and control African gold, and they are well on their way to achieving this.

Soviets and China

(6/15/77)   Since the stresses of a Western economic collapse would be more than the Soviets could endure, I would also look for the possibility of a collapse of the Soviet system. And at that time, I would also look for troubles between Soviet Russia and China.

Stock Market

(12/15/77) I've advised being out of the stock market for over a year, back when the Dow Jones was flirting with the 1,000 level, and I was right.

Weather/Climate (including water)

(3/1/76) I forecast an 80 percent chance of drought in 1976, and have continually repeated this forecast in my newsletter.

Let's give you an update on the devastating drought conditions around the country.

California:

29 of 58 counties have been designated "economic disaster areas" due to crop losses.

Rainfall in the Central Valley is only 31 percent of normal.

Sierra Nevada snowpack is only 25 percent of normal. This means no runoff for spring irrigation.

Marin County, a bedroom community north of San Francisco, has instituted tough new water rationing rules because local reservoirs are now only at 51 percent of capacity.

If California doesn't get heavy rain and snowpack through March and April, over half the State's fruit, vegetable, grain and rice crops could be lost.

Iowa:

Drifting soil and dust storms are increasing over large areas.

Texas:

No relief in sight. Most of the winter crop has been plowed under.

Western Oklahoma, Kansas, Eastern Colorado:

Pretty much the same as Texas.

The dust bowl of the '70s is an 85 percent probability this year and next.

International stress and tensions will increase as Russia, Argentina, and other grain-growing countries continue to have crop failures, as the world weather goes crazy.

(4/15/77) The weather is going to be about the same this year as it was last year. By the end of the 1977 summer, the drinking water supplies for many Northern California cities will be gone, and the Colorado River will begin to feel the effects of the drought in the Colorado Mountains.

If we have another dry summer, we could have dust bowl conditions, with billions of tons of topsoil blowing off the fields and being dropped somewhere in the Atlantic Ocean.

FREEDOM

(7/1/76)   *The Story of the Watchbird—1985 A.D.*
by Ray Bradbury

Man has finally achieved perfect freedom from violence. He invented the WATCHBIRD: a system of intelligent, flying robots that blanket the earth, programmed to detect violence before it occurs and strike down the violent one before he can do harm. And they can transmit their experiences to each other, learn, and make increasingly sophisticated judgments.

Their first action prevented a New York mugging. Their second prevented the first shot of an African border war, to the cheers of a grateful world. Their third struck down a hangman and prevented the death of a rapist. Then the Watchbird network decided animals should not be killed and destroyed a slaughterhouse worker to save a hog. Soon the victims included a surgeon about to make an incision, a child pulling the wings off a fly, a nine-year-old schoolyard bully, a mother spanking a two-year old, a farmer reaping his wheat (plants are living things). Within two days, every predatory animal—every lion, coyote, ferrett, snake and spider—was dead as the Watchbird expanded its definition of violence and performed his new self-appointed tasks.

When man realized who his real enemy was, he decided to deactivate his creation. The Watchbird had a life of his own, which must be protected, and struck down his creator, and soon the Watchbird presided over a silent, but perfectly orderly world.

Newark, NJ—Five city council members were sentenced to jail by Superior Court Judge Harry Margolis, after they were found in contempt of court when they failed to vote for a measure requiring Newark to raise its assessments of taxable properties in defiance of a court order to vote for it.

Trenton, NJ—New Jersey's Supreme Court has issued an ultimatum to the State Legislature: "Pass an income tax or the court will enjoin public officers, state, county or municipal, from expending any funds for the support of any free public school." That means "Close the schools!"

249

We are guaranteed many freedoms in our constitution—press, religion, free speech, etc. In my opinion, all of them are in jeopardy when we lose certain other key feedoms. I refer to the power of the purse, and the power to hold our public servants responsible for their actions.

The great threat to freedom comes from three directions.

1. The rise of judicial power: courts out of control.
2. Unelected regulators and bureaucrats.
3. The irresistible temptation to correct every defect of society by new legislation or rules, the "there-ought-to-be-a-law" syndrome.

I have concluded sadly that these freedoms are crumbling faster than the dam on the Teton River. Just as the collapse was forecast three years ago by engineers, even describing in detail how it would happen, I am telling you now where our freedom will crumble unless we take hold and say "Stop! No more! This ends here!"

I know this all sounds a little hysterical, but it is scary indeed.

I recently visited Disneyland with my family, and the climax of our day was the presentation of "Great Moments with Mr. Lincoln." The animated figure was so real it was awesome, and his words have haunted me ever since. I'll have to paraphrase, as I haven't had time to look up the original.

He said that all the armies of Europe and Asia could not drink from the Ohio River by force. If we ever lost our liberty, it would be from within.

(1/15/79)   Economic Timetable

We have just passed the year-end milestone, and it is time to pause and contemplate the future—especially the immediate future.

Our economy has been in a "plateau phase," with inflationary and deflationary forces struggling for supremacy for several months beyond any conceivable expectation. This recovery is now living on borrowed time, but the rising interest rates and rising inflation rates that we are experiencing are steadily destroying our purchasing power. This could lead us into the deep depression that I have been expecting.

What do we face over the next several months? It wasn't long ago that I told you that I thought it would look like we were heading for a deflationary recession, that prices would appear to slow their galloping rate of increase and there would be some evidence to indicate the government's "inflation fight" was working. This would result in a slowdown of business activity which would trigger government spending to "prevent recession," and crank up inflation until it gets completely out of control, while at the same time slipping deeper into depression.

If we do experience this brief deflationary phase, it will be very soon. The Finished Goods Index is falling now. In the last issue, R. E. McMaster pointed out that the futures market was signaling some kind of deflationary scenario, and I agree. (see: Markets) But there is no way the government can resist the pressures to crank up the printing presses to try to spend us out of it. In the first place, in recession or depression, so many people get into financial trouble that we turn to Uncle Sam as the "spender of last resort." He will be forced to bail out unemployment funds, welfare funds, cities, banks —you name it—and because tax collections will be failing due to reduced business activity and the tax revolt, government will be forced to create huge deficits, and it will be monstrously inflationary.

In fact, the typical deflationary recession carries within itself the bursting seeds of inflation because our political system is totally committed to the avoidance of pain, as we've said before. I expect us to be deep in recession in the next few months. I still believe that some of the monetary phenomena associated with recession began some months ago, and from a technical point of view, we're already in the earliest stages. It has not yet been reflected in slow growth or rising unemployment, as we are also in the grip of anticipatory inflationary spending on the part of people who believe they should "buy now before the prices go up."

The American people are reaching the limit of their capacity to borrow. Consumer debt has increased 50% in three years. When we've reached the end of our lines of credit and some of these new two-income families find that the wife is laid off and they can't meet their mortgage obligations, then we are headed for deep trouble. I am not persuaded that just because we've been able to postpone it by three to six months, we have avoided it all together. The longer it is postponed, the worse it will be.

We are heading into the greatest test of our national character since the Civil War. It can come with surprising suddenness, although it is more likely we will drift down a long slide at a gradually accelerating rate.

In the meantime, I am still watching the price of gold. It's showing signs of topping somewhere around the $230 level and it should test the lows of last November. I'd say there is no 80% probability. So hang on, I'm still out of the market.

FUEL SHORTAGES/STORAGE

(5/1/77)   Get prepared for fuel shortages, and fairly soon. If you can do so safely, and if your lot is large enough, put in an underground fuel storage tank. Look in the yellow pages under service station equipment.

Be prepared for a sudden Arab oil boycott or an abrupt increase in the price of petroleum, along with all the shocks to the economy that would bring.

(11/15/77)   We are going to have fuel shortages, and we just might have fuel rationing. This Administration's continued mismanagement of the fuel situation is going to create problems, and bad ones, so I am renewing my appeal for you to have fuel storage on hand. Make sure, however, you use the necessary additives to prevent it from breaking down. One which seems to work well is called FUEL MATE and can be obtained from Bob Hinrichs, P.O. Box 3471, Santa Barbara, CA 93105.

But there may be an even better idea. JIM SIBBET puts out a real good gold and silver advisory newsletter. It's title is, appropriately enough, *LET'S TALK SILVER AND GOLD* (Sibbet Publications, 61 South Lake Avenue, Pasadena, CA 91101, 213-681-5319), and he came up with a marvelous idea. He suggested you go to your local friendly gasoline dealer and repay him for a substantial amount of gas with, perhaps, a little premium as a storage fee. If we get rationing or allocation, you are not buying more fuel than you are entitled to, but you are merely taking delivery of fuel you have already paid for which is being stored for you.

This gives your dealer some cash to work with, and assures you that you can get the gas you need when you need it. Be sure to put the agreement in writing.

(7/15/78)   It has recently hit the press that the Administration has come up with a standby, gas-rationing program. The ration coupons are even printed. The President would merely invoke Executive Order No. 11490, which gives him power to allocate, ration and even seize all gas and oil.

GARY NORTH has done a lot of good thinking on this subject. He feels your allotment will probably be based on the number of vehicles you own, so it probably would be a good idea to pick up a couple of old clunkers and, of course, I've repeatedly recommended installing a gasoline storage tank, against gas rationing or allocations. But be careful. Make sure it's done properly.

I don't like what's going on in the Middle East. The situation in Lebanon is terribly dangerous, and if the Israelis end up in war with Syria, we'll probably see an Arab oil boycott. I also can see Mr. Carter feeling forced to demonstrate to the world that we are going to "do something" about our balance of payments by declaring gas rationing, if he gives up on his energy program in Congress.

Of course, that won't solve our balance-of-payments problem. Our oil imports are not responsible for it. Our biggest deficits are with Japan and Germany, and we don't buy oil from them. Money we spend with the Arabs comes back to the United States through our banking system. That's not the real culprit. Countries like Japan and Germany, who have to import *ALL* of their oil, have balance of payment surpluses, so obviously we've got to look elsewhere for some of the causes of the problem. But, Jimmy will probably ration gas, and a war in the Mid-East and an Arab oil boycott will give him the excuse he needs, and Executive Order No. 11490 will give him all the authority he can use. (see: Balance-of-Payments)

(8/15/78) The Arabs have leaked the word that they are not going to price oil in dollars any more, and the dollar immediately started sinking into the Arabian Gulf and gold shot up to over $210 an ounce, which is pretty much how I expected it to act. The potential for war in the Mid-East and a renewed Arab oil embargo is considerable. The possible disruption of the energy supplies concerns me.

I am also concerned about Carter's promise at the Bonn Conference to cut our oil imports. How is he going to do it? I think you had better brace yourself for some kind of gas rationing or allocation plan.

1. Be prepared for gas rationing. Have a motorcycle, a moped, or a bicycle, or maybe all three. Own a low-mileage diesel automobile. (This is a reversal of my previous position, as now I know more about diesels and I have a diesel Rabbit which I love.)

2. I feel confident the technology is advanced far enough that I would feel very comfortable in having one of Mr. Billings' hydrogen-powered Dodge Omnis. The modifications are so simple, and the technique so sound, that I am going to find some way to get one.

3. Have an emergency fuel storage program. If you can't bury a tank on your property, go together with some friends and rent an abandoned gas station, fill the storage tanks, and you've got your private supply.

(11/1/78) Just before we went to press, I found it is a near certainty, that immediately after the election, JIMMY CARTER will impose a large import tax on all imported oil as a part of his fight to support the dollar. Next step? Probably gas rationing. I'll let you know when I find out. Remember, you read it here first.

(11/15/78) My sources tell me that an import tax is still the Carter plan if the Save-the-Dollar plan falters. He will simply slap a big tax on imported oil to attempt to halt our continuing leakage of dollars to the OPEC nations. Like the other moves that have been made, however, the benefits will be short-term in nature and will not affect the long-term trends.

(3/1/78) I received an interesting letter from ROBERT HINRICHS, who is one of our recommended vendors. He sells FUEL MATE, the additive that improves storage life of gasoline and diesel oil. He has published a special bulletin on fuel storage for RUFF TIMES subscribers, which I have reproduced here.

SPECIAL BULLETIN ON FUEL STORAGE FOR RUFF TIMES SUBSCRIBERS

So many of you have asked the same questions that we thought it best to provide the answers in bulletin form. We will describe the ideal system for extended fuel storage, and then you can work backwards from that point to a system that you can live with.

1. Decide how many years supply of fuel you wish to have in storage.
2. Obtain enough UNDERGROUND storage to hold this amount of fuel. Install pumps on the storage so that it may be easily recovered.
3. Fill the storage with fuel, and add enough Fuel Mate to treat that amount.
4. Start using fuel out of this storage right now. Fill all of your current requirements of fuel out of this storage. You may discover that fuel costs less in bulk than at service stations.
5. Once a month, or four times a year refill your storage tanks. Add enough Fuel Mate to treat just the fuel which you added.

If you were to follow this method, you could probably keep it up forever. You would always have a usable fuel supply when the emergency occurs.

Some other points to consider:

1. If you must store above ground, then keep direct sunlight off the tank. Have it in the shade, or build a roof over it. Heat and temperature changes are the worst enemies you will have in fuel storage.
2. Store in as large a container as possible.
3. If you are unable to rotate the supply as mentioned above, then make sure that the tank is full. Condensation is another enemy.
4. It is against the law in most states to store gasoline in a permanent structure. Your insurance will also be void. Above all, do not store in a dwelling. You may not live to use the gas.
5. Check with local and state sources for exact regulations on fuel storage!

G

GARDENING

(Special Report #4, 10/76)   Many of my subscribers ask, "How do you feel about home gardening?" And here's what I tell them.

I feel that everybody should have a garden. I have a brown thumb myself, and have never had a garden before. The idea of being a gardener does not appeal to me, but the idea of being hungry appeals to me even less. If every home in America would plant a few unused feet of yard to produce fruit and vegetables, it would mean a tremendous increase in overall stability. There would be less panic and less likelihood of social breakdown in the event of a severe economic reversal. I suggest that you subscribe to a publication called **ORGANIC GARDENING**, which is available from Rodale Press, Emmaus, Pennsylvania, and *MOTHER EARTH NEWS*. These publications will tell you all you need to know about starting a highly productive home garden, which will not be dependent upon pesticides and synthetic fertilizers, which might be difficult to find during a depression.

(8/15/76)   Frank Ford, chairman of one of the largest companies which supplies naturally and organically grown food, had this to say about home gardening.

"I think it's highly important that everyone who can should begin to compost and improve the soil in their own garden space, and do as much home gardening as possible. People who live in apartments can sprout and have little herb gardens in their window sills. This could be very important to them and the nation." (see: Organic Farming for complete interview with Frank Ford)

GERMAN INFLATION

(9/15/78)   Recently I received a copy of a German grocery price list from July 16, 1923. Bear in mind as you look at this table that the exchange rate, prior to the inflation, was four German marks to $1. These prices were from the Berlin Market Hall.

1 pound beef - 48,000 marks; 1 pound veal - 48,000 marks; 1 pound lamb - 48,000 marks; 1 pound pork - 54,000 marks; 1 pound butter - 50,000 marks; 1 pound margarine - 38,000 marks; 1 pound lard - 34,000 marks; 1 pound beef tallow - 32,000 marks; 1 pound shortening - 30,000 marks; 1 pound new potatoes - 3,800 marks; 1 pound roasted coffee - 11,000 marks; 1 pound tea - 150,000 marks; 1 pound cocoa - 56,000 marks; 1 pound sugar - 3,200 marks; 1 pound wheat flour - 14,000 marks; 1 pound live eel - 40,000 marks; 1 pound salmon - 16,000 marks; 1 calf's tongue - 40,000 marks; 1 pound beef liver - 38,000 marks; 1 pound sausage - 45,000 marks; 1 pound limburger - 30,000 marks; 1 pound oats - 13,000 marks; one egg - 5,000 marks.

As bad as those prices look, by October of the same year, only three months later, nearly all of those prices had from three to six additional zeros after them, and the presses were cranking out 100 billion mark notes around the clock. The destruction of the currency took only four years from beginning to end, ending with a political and social environment that gave rise to Adolf Hitler.

GOLD

INTRODUCTION

(8/1/76)   Just shortly before the price break on gold, I had said in my newsletter that I did not expect the price of gold to go below $120 for long. I still feel that way, but as an investor, it wouldn't bother me to be wrong.

Please remember, anyone who is trying to apply my advice for short-term speculative decisions just hasn't been listening.

The short-term forces working upon gold are, on balance, slightly "bearish." The ultimate forces over the long haul are determinedly "bullish." Gold rises sharply when inflation takes hold and interest rates rise. Gold rises in times of economic uncertainty. It would be foolish to expect any dramatic action on the part of gold until such time as our present recovery begins to turn downhill.

A drop from $125 to $115 all in one piece is shocking, but the question is: do you have ultimate faith in the objective for which you are purchasing the metal?

I consider forecasts of $300 (see October 1, 1978) to $400 an ounce by gold buffs to be an irrelevant and possibly foolish forecast. If gold ever rises to that price, it will be because people have lost such confidence in our monetary system that money will be on the way to becoming worthless. Gold was worth millions of deutschemarks per ounce in Germany in the 1920s. The only real measurement of its value will be in relation to goods and services.

When I said I would like to see gold drop further and stay down for two years, it was based on these principles.

1. I figure I have six to 18 months, before things turn down, to get the message out.

2. If gold stays down for two years, it will be because everything's great and I'd like that, just because it feels good.

3. It'll shake out the speculators, and lay the foundation for a sustained rise.

4. Gold is your insurance policy. Ten percent of your assets invested in gold could someday be worth many times more than all of your other holdings.

(11/1/76) Since the legalization of gold holdings by American citizens, and the establishment of a free-floating gold market, those who have invested in gold have, for the most part, made out very well. Gold can fluctuate dramatically like anything else, perhaps more so, because it is a manipulated commodity. But over the long haul, it will tend to increase in value faster than paper money can lose spending power; the perfect inflation hedge.

It is my opinion that gold is poised for a very substantial run up. I've come to this conclusion by watching the Central Banks of Europe and the large investment houses. They are loading up on gold at the current, relatively depressed prices. I think these people know exactly what they are doing. They have much to do with controlling the market price of that commodity, and I believe they will run the price up as soon as they are ready, in the not-too-distant future.

There are several ways to buy gold.

1. You can buy gold coins with cash.

2. You can buy gold bullion with cash.

3. You can buy on margin.

4. You can buy gold stocks (stocks in gold mining companies).
5. You can buy futures contracts on the commodity exchange.
6. You can buy options for gold shares.

Options and margin purchases give you the greatest leverage, the largest profit potential, the most excitement, and the greatest risk.

(12/15/76)   Here are a few other things for you to think about. The world's second largest gold producer, after South Africa, is SOVIET RUSSIA. It would be bullish for the value of their gold reserves in the ground if South Africa could be put out of production. Ordinarily, South African gold stocks and the price of gold tend to rise together. During the collapse of gold last year South African gold stocks lost well over 80% of their market value. The time could come when the relationship between the price of gold and South African gold stocks could be severed, simply because South African gold mines are subject to great political risk due to increasing terrorism and a possible onslaught of Marxist-inspired black unrest within their country. It is possible that South African gold production could be impaired by political and civil disorders. African gold stocks could collapse completely, and the world price of gold could soar simply because decreasing production, of course, means increasing prices.

There has been a battle between the Bank For International Settlements and its client nations such as Germany, France, Switzerland and other European powers, and the United States sponsored International Monetary Fund. Some time ago, the IMF surrendered all authority on gold matters to the BIS.

In the meantime, the nations that contributed gold to the IMF, at $42.22 an ounce, have been quietly repatriating that gold at the same price. They now have back (or will shortly) 5/6 of all the gold they originally contributed, including the U.S. If there's a "War on Gold," that sounds like fraternizing with the enemy.

The Russians are now moving to establish gold backing for the ruble to make it an international reserve currency. The Arabs are moving to transfer a significant portion of their assets into gold. They stopped buying for awhile, but are now back in the marketplace with a vengeance.

All of the signs indicate that gold will be enthroned as essential monetary backing sometime in the foreseeable future.

I also have reason to believe (and substantial evidence to support this view) that the U.S. made a deal with South Africa to cease our constant pressure on gold prices, in return for the withdrawal of their support of Rhodesia. Simultaneously, the South Africans confidently launched a successful $3.5 million advertising campaign to sell the Krugerrand as a collector's item and as a protection against inflation. All of these events together are bullish for gold, but none of these factors is as significant as the stark international political fact that the enemies of gold are in stumbling retreat.

Look at Germany, for example. They have loaned Italy almost $3 billion and have secured it with Italian gold at $120 an ounce. Italy is going to need more financial help in the near future. If West Germany, or the Arabs, or somebody does not provide it, Italy will default on its international loans. Germany would collect its gold, but the shock waves from such an event could shatter the international monetary system and leave the world's biggest banks looking rather sick.

The West Germans have tremendous financial clout. They have a huge interest in an increase in the price of gold to support the additional loans they are going to be forced to make to Italy. Remember that Italian gold is their whole collateral.

I also believe that the Arabs (especially the Saudis) feel the dollar is going to weaken, especially if there are increases in the price of oil (which we will know after we go to press). They need to hedge their dollar holdings by a substantial position in gold. It is not unlikely that we will see gold at $160 an ounce sometime in the next few months, and if we should have a major retreat in the value of paper currencies around the world, then prices of several hundred dollars an ounce are possible.

No one can determine the timing on these matters. However, you can expect gold to move up in a series of advances and retreats.

When you're trying to analyze what's happening in Africa, just bear in mind it is to the advantage of the Russians to have South African gold mines out of business.

Perhaps now you can understand why Dr. Kissinger, who is an intimate associate of the Rockefeller interests, which are closely aligned with the great investment houses of Europe and America, would be following courses of action which would seem to militate against the independence and solvency of Rhodesia and South Africa. Perhaps it all becomes a little clearer when you understand this very critical relationship.

As Gilbert and Sullivan said in their comic opera, "H.M.S. Pinafore,"

"Things are seldom what they seem, skim milk masquerades as cream."

RUFF RECOMMENDATIONS

1. Most of the risk is out of any kind of gold-related investments.
2. The most conservative approach would be to buy gold coins and pay cash for them and take delivery.
3. North American gold shares look especially attractive to me at this time. Any of the leaders would be acceptable. You could almost put the names on a board and throw darts at them, as they will all tend to rise sharply in relation to the price of gold. The South African gold shares will probably rise if the move in gold comes in the next few weeks, but you can get the same advantages with the North American gold shares without the political risks. South Africans are paying very high dividends, but don't be seduced by that.
4. If you have some money you can afford to lose, and really want to swing, talk to your broker about options in gold mining shares. The risks are much higher but so is the profit. It is my opinion that the down-side risk at this time is very small.
5. Don't forget that I said gold will probably advance with a series of forward moves punctuated by some retreats. It is axiomatic in the investment field that, at some time, the stock you buy will be selling for less than what you paid for it. Treat this as an additional buying opportunity.
6. Don't buy gold shares at all, if you don't have the temperament to be able to withstand the fluctuations of that unpredictable marketplace.
7. Everything we've said elsewhere in this publication about climate and weather also applies to investing. Think of the weather as the short-term, day-to-day moves in the price of an investment. Think of the climate as the long-range environment which can be depended upon. I'm not a weather forecaster; I'm a climatologist.

(7/15/78) Dick Russell made a very significant comment in Nassau when he said, "Gold never fakes you out on the charts." Here are the factors I use for judging which way to jump.

You can always count on gold moving in the same direction as the FED DISCOUNT RATE (the rate which the Federal Reserve charges member banks for loans). When the discount rate is rising, so is gold. That's not true every day, but over any period of weeks or months you can depend on it. When the prime interest rate is rising, gold also rises and the stock market falls. That is characteristic of these "waves," or pendulum swings, over the last two decades. Each wave begins from a lower point in the economy and swings up to a higher inflation peak, then inflation eases, but always bottoms at a higher level than the last trough, and each peak is higher than the last peak. The economy is hurt worse each time and is more unhealthily feverish at each peak. I believe this characteristic of an economy about to take off into a wild, inflationary spiral.

All of the gold mined since the world began could be stacked three feet high within the boundary lines of a football field. A relatively small amount of demand drives prices up.

You can count on rising interest rates, increasing inflation and a falling stock market. These things are bullish for gold.

I admit I don't know what it's going to do over the short term. If I were forced to make a bet, I'd lay six to four odds that gold will diddle around in a narrow range ($175-$195) for the rest of the summer and take off sometime in the fall, but it's now in a decent buying range and it's going to go up a long way from here.

(8/15/78) To round off these observations, the economy is acting about as predicted. Everything I said in the last issue is still true in spades. We are rapidly approaching several pivotal points in our economy, and war in Southern Africa, energy, and foreign exchange problems head the list. Gold is still in a good buying range, ($210-$220) and if I were you I wouldn't wait to get on board. Silver has also broken out, which confirms what I think is happening with gold. In the meantime, if you have taken my advice to buy gold, you already have substantial profits, but if you haven't, it is still not too high, nor is it too late.

(4/1/78) We had a lot of panicky phone calls when gold took that recent nose dive. They wanted to know whether it's going to correct further, crash, or resume its upward climb.

The fundamentals have not changed. Gold is still in a long-term bull market. You have to expect corrections, possibly as much as $30 an ounce if the government announces it's going to resume its gold auctions. I don't know whether government will do that or not, or when, but the amount of gold in deliverable condition is not enough to permanently affect the market. Only about 10 percent of the U.S. Government's gold supply is of the appropriate fineness and bar size to meet the requirements for deliverable gold in the commodities market.

Paradoxically, many of the people who are afraid of a government gold "dump" are the same people who are worried about Dr. Beter's claims that the government has already sold all the gold and there's none in Fort Knox. (see: Beter, Dr. Peter) If the government doesn't have any gold, it can't sell it. I don't know whether it has any gold or not, but I do know that the fundamental demand for gold is such that if the government decides to sell some, it will merely be doing a favor for those who recognize gold as the ultimate money.

What we need is an appropriate attitude towards investment. If you are the kind who panics if an investment takes a downturn, you shouldn't be investing in any commodity whose fluctuations are reported in the daily paper. If you believe in the long-term fundamentals, then stay with it until the fundamentals change. As long as the dollar is sinking, the oil threat exists, inflation continues, Europe and Africa keep moving in fits and starts toward Communism, then the future for gold indeed is glittering. In fact, it's brilliance will be blinding, and it won't take long.

(10/1/78)   Gold is a fantastic barometer of reality, and right now it is shrugging off all the good news and moving towards higher ground.

The gold market fascinates me for several reasons.

1.   Once you have made a decision about the fundamental direction of the economy, gold provides tremendous, moderate risk opportunities for profit. Gold is still in the first 30 percent of a long bull trend and I expect that trend to continue as long as the world is heading towards more unsettled conditions.

2.   Gold is countercyclical to good news. When things look bad, the Italians buy gold and conceal it, the French hide it under their beds, the Bedouins of the Saudi Arabian and North African deserts buy gold chains and hang them around their necks. More and more Americans are looking upon gold as a hedge against inflation, stock market collapse, deflation, big city troubles, war in the Middle East, or almost anything you can name.

3.   The gold market has predictive value. It tells you whether the principal forces that make or break the gold market are accepting or rejecting good news.

So what is gold telling us?

1.   We are no closer to real peace in the Middle East. Begin and Sadat can agree all they want, but you still have the intractable problem of the Palestinians and the Israelis believing equally passionately that they have God-given historic rights to the same real estate

and the same sacred shrines. That problem is no closer to solution, and the oil-rich, gold-buying sheiks know it.

Syria, Jordan and Lebanon are no closer to resolution of their problems with Israel. The prospects for peace, in my opinion, are no better. At least gold doesn't think so.

2. Gold is telling us that we have not seen all the bad news. It's telling us that the dollar is going to sink further, that inflation is not going to get under control, that there is no confidence in the nation's leadership, that distrust of paper currency is growing, and that interest rates will continue to rise. Gold says: "Troubles still ahead."

3. Gold is telling us there is sufficient demand for the metal to soak up any amount that Uncle Sam is capable of selling. When the Treasury sells gold on the open market, it can sell gold only on the appropriate fineness (purity) and that is less than 10% of our total gold hoard. The rest of it is not in "deliverable" condition acceptable for the marketplace.

The thing that scares me about this gold market is that its corrections are so brief, so ephemeral, that the guy who sits on the sidelines looking for a correction to get in may never find an entry point. Corrections may occur from time to time, but it is likely to be brief, explosive, and offer almost no opportunity to jump in. I also believe that it is going to such highs that you could enter at almost any point and have substantial profits over the next several months.

(11/1/78) In the mad scramble of the last days of the session of Congress just concluded, an awful lot of bills squeezed through without much study. A bank regulatory bill got a lot of attention in the press, but there was a sneaky little amendment attached to it by CONGRESSMAN LEACH which requires the U.S. Treasury, when it sells gold, to sell 10% of it to American citizens in the form of medallions, beginning one year from now. This presents the government with an absolutely fascinating dilemma.

A lot of you worry about whether or not the government will confiscate gold. Well, with the passage of this bill, it can't call in gold and sell gold at the same time, because if it sells gold it has to sell it to Americans. It means that if government wants to fight a war on gold, it has to do it with one hand tied behind its back. I think this is very bullish for the metal. I can't think of a better place for the government to put its gold than in the hands of its citizens.

HOWARD RUFF

HEDGING

(11/15/78) For now, great pain is being suffered by all those who have attempted to hedge themselves against inflation by buying gold in recognition of its counter-cyclical nature. Make no mistake about it. People like you and me, looking for a stable hedge in this insane financial world, were the target of this action, and many of us have been wounded, some critically.

The signals of the marketplace have been temporarily so distorted by the threat of the increased gold sales that I believe gold is headed for still lower ground before the basic bull market basic trend asserts itself again. $185 an ounce is probable, and there is a possibility of as low as $150 in this move.

Now, that's good news and bad news! The bad news first.

The psychic pain suffered during this precipitous slide by anyone who bought Krugerrands at $240 cannot be weighed or measured on a scale or a balance sheet. It will neutralize the speculators because it will wipe out some of them and scare the wits out of the rest of them. The "hedgers," like you and me, are going to have to keep our nerve during this very difficult time. It will be painful! Even though I have been bullish on the price of gold, as the market indicated I should, I have consistently warned you against going into the futures market unless you were prepared to accept losses and setbacks, and you have just had a grisly, graphic example of that. This is a great argument for conservatism in investing in gold.

Now, the good news.

You will be able to buy gold at prices which you will never see again within your lifetime. It's an exciting windfall opportunity!

I know I will not catch the exact bottom, except by sheer luck. I will be back in the market when I've concluded that the panic is over and that normalcy and the fundamentals have re-asserted themselves. The markets are always rational over the long run, although they can be downright paranoid schizophrenic for days, weeks, or even months at a time.

My job is to call the long-term trends, and possibly the larger moves within those trends, and identify a decent buying range. I refuse to get involved with "feeling for the bottom" because an absolute bottom can come and go so fast it could happen before I could ever get the word out to you. I refuse to represent myself as doing something I don't think I, or anybody else, can do that accurately. I refuse to turn *THE RUFF TIMES* into a speculator's tip sheet.

FROM A TO Z

A VIEW FROM THE PIT

(8/1/77) I heard a CBS news report that the Arabs were thinking of demanding gold in payment for oil, and Maury Kravitz, a gold expert from Chicago, was quoted. I ran him down and found him to be a savvy guy with a lot to offer—a real professional. He is also launching a new newsletter called THE VIEW FROM THE PIT, and although it could use some editing and is a bit verbose, it has some darn valuable stuff in it.

I subscribe to every advisory service there is, and I read conflicting explanations of why gold has gone up or down. I'm told that it is the IMF auction and/or periodic U.S. Treasury sales of gold that depress the price. Maury shoots those theories down in flames. He believes gold is not a typical supply-demand commodity. The supply side is insignificant. It is the demand side that controls!

From November, 1967, to March, 1968, a four-month period, 87 million ounces of gold were bought on the London gold market!! The whole IMF sales program consists of only 25 million ounces over four years. On March 14, 1968, in four hours, 12 1/2 million ounces of gold changed hands in the London market. The United States Treasury is now down to 275 million ounces of gold. This amount could be absorbed by the marketplace in any reasonable period of time. What, then, causes gold to go up and down? It is demand.

Maury says gold demand rises when worldwide investors perceive that the Western world economies are not well, then gold will be bought as a hedge against calamity or inflation. The worse things get, the better gold will do. Gold recovered from $103 an ounce to its present levels of around $146 because there was a suggestion of resumption of the economic realities that had initially pushed it up to the $200 level.

A second bullish demand factor is the entry of the Arabs into the world gold market, and you've already read about that in *THE RUFF TIMES*. The Arabs are worried about the inflationary purchasing-power erosion of the dollars they receive in exchange for oil, and more recently, the even more frightening erosion of the dollar in relation to other currencies. There's no way they can raise prices to compensate for that, so they have entered into the gold market, as Maury says, "...in a rather stealthy manner, not buying in a way that's readily identifiable, but through their nominees—Swiss bankers, and the sophisticated London gold brokers." It is his belief that the wealthy

Arab sheiks have been accumulating gold ever since the $115 price and they will continue to accumulate on all price reactions of significance. In the last two IMF auctions, they even came out in the open by making purchases directly through several banks from the Arabian Gulf States.

Can they initiate enough buying to affect the price? They could buy it all if they wanted to. The only way they are going to get a hedge against the loss of their monstrous currency values is to own a heck of a lot of it and I believe that sometime within the next 6 to 12 months gold can soar. The major long-term trend will be up.

If the Treasury Department threatens to sell some gold, don't worry. Its price effect will be temporary, at worst. Bad news is good news when it comes to gold.

If you have the temperament to be a short-term trader and speculator, Maury appears to have a fine common-sense approach, as indicated by the first two issues of his newsletter. But for the average guy or gal, the best solution is to buy and hold. Remember, it's a long-term investment and it's in a decent buying range.

If you want to know more about Maury's newsletter, which I strongly recommend, write to him at 1595 Little John Court, Highland Park, Illinois 60035, or if you are in a hurry, call him at (312) 648-0401, and I'm sure he will send you a sample copy. In the meantime, if you wish to buy some gold coins, call Jim Cook of Investment Rarities at (800) 328-1860, and he will take care of you. Maury is in commodities; I just might give him a whirl myself.

MAURY KRAVITZ CONVENTION REPORT

(3/15/79) MAURY KRAVITZ, my broker, a member of the Board of Governors of the Chicago Mercantile Exchange, began each workshop at the convention by stating that 80% of the participants in the commodity market lose money. It's a very high-risk, high-reward activity for those who have the temperament and the time.

He feels the Iranian situation has almost ended the marriage between the dollar and the foreign currencies, and gold is the symptom of the dollar disease. When inflation reaches 20%, he sees $400 gold. He feels the gold auction is bullish for gold, and if it's stopped, it would be dangerous to the economy.

Maury said that he expected gold to go much higher, however, in a telephone conversation two days after the convention, he expressed his opinion that gold would probably move up to between $270 and $280, after which he expects a massive correction. He asked not to be quoted on the exact amount of the correction he was expecting, but it was substantial. Our only disagreement is that he says it would come only after moving into much higher ground.

I believe you should still commit roughly one-third of your discretionary gold investment money now, just in case there is no such correction, and then average down at lower prices later, if you get a chance.

TYPES OF GOLD BUYERS

(4/1/78) Dick Russell, in his marvelous *DOW THEORY LETTER*, has stated beautifully what I've tried to say in the last two and one-half years.

There are two kinds of gold buyers. The first kind (and this is what I've advocated) puts 10% to 20% of his assets in gold coins or gold bullion as insurance against the day when hyper-inflation (or some other brand of monetary chaos) sweeps over the land. This conservative gold buyer doesn't wax poetic when gold rallies 20 points and he doesn't pop Valiums when gold drops 20 points. Gold is this man's core possession of real money; it's simply part of his program of diversification. This conservative gold-buyer knows that he is in a grim struggle for his financial life during an era when his Government has embarked on the biggest program of forced inflation and debt building in world history. To him, "survival" is the name of the game, and gold is the ultimate "life preserver," the bottom line in his survival package.

The other kind of gold buyer is the speculator, the man who is out to "make a killing" or, at the least, to "beat the gold market." He may be highly successful with his trading or he may miss a few moves here or there. But my bet is that before he's through he's going to be taken out or "stopped." This fellow might as well be trading pork bellies or wheat or corn as gold. I have not advocated speculating in gold, and I am not going to start now.

GOLD VS. DIAMONDS

(10/15/78) One of our subscribers asked, "I've bought my food storage, my silver coins, and an equivalent amount of gold and I have about $50,000 left over. Would I be better off buying more gold, or should I buy diamonds?"
You can do either, but you probably should do both. Here's why.

Gold: The Bad News

GOLD is not without its disadvantages, although they are clearly outweighed by the advantages.

1. Gold may possibly be confiscated by government as it was in the 1930s. This is not likely, but it is possible, however remote the possibility.

2. Gold fluctuates rather wildly, and if we should have a recovery from the next recession, with falling interest rates and falling inflation rates (40 percent probability), gold will go into a nose dive for a couple of years, starting some months from now.

3. Gold provides no income unless you sell off some coins once or twice a year and take your income in the form of capital gains, which does represent a management problem.

4. Gold requires storage space, which means you have to have a safe or place of concealment in your home, or you have to trust the bank safety deposit box. There is no perfect answer to this problem.

5. Price quotations of gold in the morning paper can ruin your breakfast. If you have a nervous temperament, it's kind of hard to take a long-range, objective view if it should correct substantially for any reason.

Gold: The Good News

1. Gold is divisible into relatively small amounts.

2. It's instantly liquid with any coin dealer. If you change your mind or need the money, you can always turn it into greenbacks, although I don't quite understand why anybody would want to do that.

3. It's the world's frightened money and will do very well during a period of increasing instability, and it's still powerfully going up.

GOLD AUCTIONS (U.S. TREASURY)

(4/15/78) For the last two weeks, there has been an excess of worry about the prospect of U.S. Treasury gold auctions. I would like to elaborate on why I believe that the auction is not much of a threat.

The phrase, "The War on Gold" has been bandied about until the phrase itself has convinced most doctrinaire, hard-money types that, for some reason, the government of the United States just sits there awaiting an opportunity to smash the price of gold through the floor because they "fear gold."

May I suggest a totally different perspective on the problem? There is no question that in the past, as our government moved away from gold as backing for the dollar, that it launched an all-out assault on gold to tell the world that the United States no longer considered gold a reserve for the dollar. We were engaged in a war of words and monetary philosophies with General DeGaulle and European central banks who did not want us to go off the gold standard because of the inflationary implications. We not only told the world we would no longer exchange dollars for gold, but drove this point home by holding Treasury gold auctions and the creation of the International Monetary Fund which also has gold auctions.

It is my opinion, the U.S. government feels its position is now firmly established, that there is no relationship between gold and the dollar, and that their best position, relative to gold is one of "benign neglect." In other words, Uncle Sam says, "Gold is just a commodity like silver, pork bellies and soybeans. Let it do what it wants. Just to prove how nonchalant we are on the subject, we'll allow Americans to own gold and will let them use gold clauses in contracts. What the heck, it doesn't matter to us anyway."

I believe hard-money advocates have totally misinterpreted the government's position and still believe that somehow our government fears gold. It does not. It believes it has won the war and can be magnanimous to the enemy.

The government knows that the world knows our gold no longer backs our dollar. They also know, even if we decided to reverse that policy, there isn't enough gold left in our vaults anyway. Our currency is already under a death sentence. It's only a matter of time. The loss of our gold is irrelevant to confidence in the dollar. People are only interested in how much the dollar can buy in goods and services, or how many of their deutschemarks, yen or Swiss francs they can exchange for it. The government has achieved its purpose. We are off the gold standard and the world knows it. Mr. Burns (of the Federal Reserve Bank) was suggesting to stop the slide of the dollar, the sale of $50 billion worth of gold as a method of soaking up $50 billion worth of excess American dollars floating around overseas. The assumption is that those dollars can be brought home in exchange for our gold and, as the government chooses, retired or used for stimulus of our economy. Support of the dollar is accomplished by buying dollars. Up until now, our only weapon has been our accumulated foreign currencies which we could exchange for dollars, or the roughly $20 billion worth of foreign currencies that we can borrow from other countries which, of course, have to be paid back with interest. From the perspective of Dr. Burns, the sale of our gold hoard is a neat solution.

I don't think it will work because $50 billion is not enough to soak up $400 billion American dollars overseas! After our gold hoard is gone and it dawns on the world that all of our dollar support weapons are gone, then I think the dollar will plunge again and panic selling will cause the final collapse of the dollar. Then, when everything is lost and those fools in Washington realize we have no currency the people will trust, then someone will remember the Gold Standard, and we will weep for our lost gold.

But in the short view, Treasury sales of gold will accomplish their purpose.

So the threat of the sale of gold is not to attack gold. It is to try to support the dollar. If that is the case, our Treasury would want to get the maximum number of dollars per ounce it could possibly obtain.

Now, if I were in charge of this project, and accepted this evil philosophy, here's what I would do in order of desirability:

1. I would quietly hand it to the European and Japanese central bankers in exchange for their accumulated dollars. This would have no impact on the "spot" or futures markets, especially because less than 10 percent of our gold hoard is in deliverable condition anyway.

2. The Saudi Arabians have fantastic sums of money in dollars which are a potential threat to the currency marketplace and they have got to be scared by the way their purchasing power has shrunk. I would offer them a way out of their dilemma. In return for their promise not to raise the price of oil, I would say to them, "Here is $50 billion worth of our gold in exchange for your dollars at today's market prices," or even at a reasonable discount. That would not disturb the market, and I could get my maximum return on the gold.

3. The least feasible alternative would be to announce a series of gold auctions, as it might affect the market. But if I did, I would feed it into the marketplace a little bit at a time to maximize my return as the IMF has done and, as I said in the last issue, the IMF auctions have become a non-event and the marketplace has adjusted to it and swallowed it up.

I believe that the gold market has already discounted the threat of Treasury auctions. Markets generally do. The current price has already taken that into account. Without that threat, I think gold would be well over $200 an ounce today. And gold auction-inspired correction would be brief, and drastic. The market would recover quickly and things would be back to normal because the fundamentals are still strong and gold is still the world's "scared money."

I know that's an unorthodox view among us hard-money guys, but it makes a heck of a lot of sense to me.

(5/1/78) The Treasury announced its policy of intermittent gold auctions and the market did its expected thing—a minor reaction, as predicted in the last *RUFF TIMES*. It dropped off about $5 and is now sitting in the doldrums around $168 to $170 an ounce. It's performing about as I expected. The market had already discounted the auctions, and now there is little or no down-side risk.

My attitude towards market dips in a desirable, long-term upward trend is simple. I welcome such dips. They are opportunities. They are nothing to be afraid of. They are chances to average down. If you bought gold at $185 an ounce, and you can pick up some more at $168, you are better off than if it had climbed straight up.

Gold is still in an ongoing bull market and has made most of its major correction. It had to happen. The fundamentals have not changed. The stock market will resume its slide sooner or later. Gold and silver will resume their upward move, although I don't expect anything terribly dramatic for several months.

(6/1/78) The impact of the U.S. Treasury gold auction program is just about over. The successful bids were at or above the current market price. It was over subscribed six times, and that doesn't include a large number of bids that came in minutes late, or one bid for all 300,000 ounces from a Utah man that was rejected on a technicality. The market has ignored the whole thing, and it was the non-event I forecast it to be. As this is written, gold is $180 an ounce, within shouting distance of its all time high. If you will remember, when I assessed the possibility of Treasury sales, I indicated that the least practical gold sales method for government to use would be to hold a series of small auctions. True to form, government chose the least advantageous method. To give you an idea of how insignificant the amount is, they are planning ten auctions of 300,000 ounces each, for a total of three million ounces. The last IMF auction was over-subscribed by three million ounces. All the gold the Treasury is offering over the entire period could have been soaked up in one IMF auction.

(9/1/78) Well, the Carter Administration has finally done it. It has announced a 150 percent increase in the Treasury gold auctions. This is part of its campaign to "support the dollar," by signaling our willingness to use our gold hoard to soak up excess dollars. The market anticipated it about a day ahead of time with a big drop from the all-time highs of around $215 an ounce, and it dropped another few dollars upon the actual announcement.

Is this the end of the gold bull market? *Absolutely not*! Gold prices reflect bad news, and all of the really bad news is ahead of us.

The important thing is to not panic when you have a correction in a long-term upward move of anything, especially gold in this environment.

If we have the kind of runaway inflation I envision, gold will sell for thousands of dollars an ounce. If we have a relatively controlled inflation, gold will be a good long-term growth situation. If the rate of inflation slows down, I have a totally different strategy which involves selling your gold and getting into government bonds, but we are a long way from that decision point.

Fear is a killer. The gyrations of any investment can ruin your breakfast, if you let it, especially if you are a relatively unsophisticated investor. On this one, I guess you will just have to decide whether or not you are going to trust your "old Dad", and your old Dad says, "Go with gold, its long-term trend is definitely up."

(12/1/78)   Watch the U.S. Treasury gold auctions on the third Tuesday of this month and in January, when a million and a half ounces will be sold. That will probably be a key to what the gold market is going to do. I still expect gold prices to slip into the $150-$185 range, and I also expect a brief rally from present prices, if it hasn't already occurred by the time you receive this. Don't be fooled by it. The odds favor a continued decline.

The IMF auction last week produced an interesting result. There were bids for 1,900,000 ounces, against the 450,000 ounces offered, which would seem very bullish for gold; however, for the first time in the history of these auctions, the IMF refused to announce the names of the unsuccessful bidders or their bid prices! I can only believe there were a lot of very low bids and the IMF didn't want it known.

This is the time to be patient if you intend to make one large commitment to coins or bullion; however, I would like to stress that, at current prices, it's probably safer to begin nibbling away at the market now. Buy a few more coins on each downward correction. That way you are protected in case something scary should happen, such as the Shah of Iran being forced out of office and the religious fanatics, who will control Iran, refusing to sell us oil. For that reason, if you don't have your survival gold and silver, buy it now! Only play your waiting game with your investment gold money. Shocks can reverse markets. Jimmy Carter taught us that November 1.

(5/1/79)   You Can Stop The Gold Auctions
On the last frantic day of the last session of Congress, an amendment, fathered by Senator Jesse Helms, and introduced by Congressman Leach, was attached to a bank regulatory bill that had to be signed by President Carter for political reasons. It required that, beginning in October this year, ten percent of all gold sold by the U.S. Treasury had to be sold to U.S. citizens in the form of medallions.

A lot of my hard-money oriented colleagues have suggested that we should take this buying opportunity as one way to keep our gold in American, rather than foreign, hands. This is probably sound reasoning, but I think I have a better idea.

If I understand that law correctly, if U.S. citizens don't buy their ten percent, the Treasury can't sell any gold at all. Boycott the Treasury sales! Don't buy one ounce! Write to every hard-money oriented Senator and Congressman, newsletter writer, and financial advisor, and ask them to urge their followers to boycott this sale. Why? Because then the Treasury can't sell any gold.

Look at the advantages.

Some day, our government is going to decide it needs that gold. After inflation has ravaged paper money to the point that government is forced to provide gold backing to the currency, that will be the only choice left. All else will have failed. The fate of all paper fiat currencies is inflationary destruction. Government will try wage and price controls, indexing, a new currency; in fact, anything except what will work. In the final stages, however, inflation becomes a wild, out-of-control, psychological phenomenon. Finally, as a last resort, governments are always forced to capitulate and go back on the gold standard. The result? Instant monetary stability, and a fresh start from the ashes of a shattered economy. That's when we will need all the gold this nation can lay its hands on.

If the nation still has most of its gold hoard, that transition will be relatively easy. If you buy Krugerrands, and nobody buys the U.S. medallions, the Treasury can't sell any gold; there will be a flow of gold from South Africa into America to offset what the Treasury has sold already; and government is less likely to forcibly confiscate your gold to rebuild the national Treasury.

If you are not convinced by the ideological argument, then let's try a little self-interest on for size. The Treasury auctions have kept a lid on the price of gold. Without them, I think we would have seen $300 gold. If you buy Treasury gold, you are, in effect, helping to hold

275

down the price of the commodity you just bought. You are making the auctions possible. I don't think that makes a heck of a lot of sense. You can buy gold without undermining the market, just by buying Krugerrands. We will cut our own throats if we participate in the auction. I say, let's make it impossible.

GOLD CLAUSES

(12/1/77)   Issue Your Own Gold-Backed Money

How would you like to be able to earn long-term interest rates, reap the profits if gold rises, and suffer no deflation loss if gold goes down? Well, you can do it when loaning money, by using a gold clause in the loan contract, and a prudent, no-risk "hedging" procedure, using gold futures. If you understand this technique, you can loan money safely and, if you wish to borrow money, you can present a marvelously persuasive argument to a potential lender and secure his position to the benefit of both of you.

A bill permitting gold clauses in contracts for the first time since 1933 has just been signed into law by President Carter. Now it is not only legal to own gold, but you can now define contractual payment obligatons in terms of gold. It's like creating your own gold-backed currency.

Being A Lender

Let's assume that you want to loan money to an individual or business, and you've been offered a satisfactory interest rate. Here are the simple basic steps:

(1)   Take all of the usual credit precautions. Be sure that your borrower has collateral, or a secure recession-proof source of income, which would be pledged for repayment, or both.

(2)   Insert a clause in the contract which gives you the option of taking repayment either (a) in cash, or (b) in a specific number of ounces of gold (either bullion or coins), or (c) in the dollar equivalent of the same amount of gold.

(3)   The number of ounces of gold you would receive, if you should choose to take gold, should be clearly specified in your contract. This is determined by dividing the price of gold, at the start of the contract, into the face amount of the loan. For example, if gold was $160 an ounce at the time of the contract, and you were loaning $16,000, you would divide $16,000 by $160 and you would come up with 100 ounces of gold.

To avoid one day distortions of the market, use an average of the second London price fixings for the five trading days prior to the starting date of the contract.

If you choose to take the cash equivalent of gold at the end of the contract, the amount of money to be repaid is determined by averaging the last five trading days prior to the maturity date of the contract.

Let's use our previous example: a $16,000 loan, gold at $160 an ounce at the start, payment now based on 10 ounces. There are several possibilities when the payment date arrives.

(a) If inflation is rampant at the maturity date, gold will have risen and you would probably ask for the cash equivalent of gold. If gold was $200 an ounce, you would receive $200 x 100 ounces or $20,000, even though you had only loaned $16,000—a $4,000 profit —plus, of course, the earned interest.

(b) If deflation hits and drives gold down below $160, you would demand repayment of the face value in dollars. If the price is over $160 and currency markets are in disarray, you take delivery of 100 ounces of coins or bullion.

According to Donald Shapiro of the New York Law School, the increase would probably be a capital gain for tax purposes, although this has not been tested in court.

Now, the catch. What if gold should go out of sight to $500 an ounce? Your borrower might not be able to repay, as that's three times as much money as he borrowed.

Here's a simple solution. The contract must require that he buy gold futures contracts at the commencement of the agreement, equal to at least the number of ounces of gold stated in your loan agreement—in this example, one 100 ounce contact—and he must maintain that futures position for the length of the loan agreement. If the price of gold rises, his contractual obligation to you increases, but he has a corresponding profit from his "hedge" position in the futures market, so he breaks even. If the price of gold goes below $160 an ounce, he immediately sells out his position. He's not speculating, because his profits are equaled by his obligation to you. By insisting on this, you have protected his ability to repay you. You both benefit.

The interest should not be covered by the gold clause, because that becomes terribly complex, and could be a violation of the usury laws as it could force him to pay you more than the legal interest, depending on the laws of your state, which could invalidate the interest provision entirely.

That means you're protected by a floor, in that you can demand payment of the loan amount if gold falls, or if gold rises, you can demand it in gold, or the cash equivalent, and you are protected both ways.

The usual, prudent judgments regarding the collateral and the borrower's ability to pay must be observed. The gold contract is no substitute for that. The futures contract does not provide collateral. It merely provides him with profits to take care of any increase in the value of the contract, over and above the face amount.

Let's make sure you understand the basics of the futures market. It's critical.

The futures market is a place to buy or sell a contract to buy or sell a commodity at a future date at a specific price which is determined by the market. For example, you can now (December) contract to buy 100 ounces of gold in June for about $165 an ounce. You generally only invest $700-$800 per contract (about 5 percent) plus a broker's commission of $50.

You can go "long," which means you buy a contract for future delivery, profiting if the price goes up, or you can go "short" by selling a contract, profiting if the price goes down. The commodity need not actually change hands, although it could if you wanted to, as you sell out or "liquidate" your position sometime before the delivery date.

Speculator go long, or short, based on their opinion of future market movements, liquidating either to take a profit or cut short a loss.

But we are doing something entirely different. We're "hedging," using the market for the purpose it was originally intended. We're not looking for profits. We just want our borrower to stay even with his rising or falling obligation to us. He has no decisions to make. He stays "long" when gold is above the price on the contract date ("strike" price), and he liquidates when the price drops below the strike price. He's not trying to win, because if he starts guessing, he could lose instead. He must, however, "roll over" his contracts if the loan is long-term, as you can't buy contracts more than one year in the future.

There are a few pitfalls to avoid, and some limitations on the technique, however.

1. The loan has to be equal to, or greater than, one gold contract (100 ounces or around $16,000 today) or the borrower can't hedge precisely. To keep it simple, loan in increments of one futures contract.

2. If you go long, you could be caught in a temporary downward move which could wipe out the margin, forcing a sale of the contract, or a margin call. Avoid this by placing a "stop" loss order $3.00 below

the purchase price. Now if it drops, you'll be sold out and you'll absorb a small loss, and you can wait until it rises above the strike price before getting back in.

3. It's possible the price could whipsaw the strike price and move up and down past it several times, costing some commissions and small losses. The further the price of gold is from the strike price, either up or down, the safer you are.

As the lender, if gold is below the strike price, you and your borrower have no risk. You can demand the face amount when the loan matures, and he's safely out of the futures market.

4. This does cost the borrower some commission money, and he should think of it, and the possible small losses described above, as a loan cost.

You can use the gold clause to make a proposal acceptable to a lender by providing him protection, provided, of course, he's a believer in gold, but you must "hedge." You must borrow as prudently as you lend, being sure that you will have sufficient income, or assets, to be able to make repayment.

DO NOT USE THE FUTURES MARKET TO SPECULATE. Don't try to win. Merely play against your obligation, which means, as long as gold is above the price specified in the contract, you stay "long." Any commodities broker can explain how to do that, or you can call Maury Kravitz (1595 Little John Court, Highland Park, IL 60035, 312-648-0401) for help. (see: Futures Market)

This whole thing makes so much sense right now because gold is counter-cyclical to the economy. It couldn't have come along at a better time. If we have runaway inflation, gold will rise in price. If you're the lender, it's just like buying gold with a guaranteed profit and no loss because, if gold falls, you don't get hurt, and if gold rises, you win. The borrower doesn't care because he will have hedged. Who's the loser? That anonymous guy who was on the wrong side of the futures contract that you bought on the Exchange. He just bet on the wrong side.

The key is the hedging technique. If you are a lender, you want your borrower to be hedged so he can pay you off. If you are a borrower, you want to be hedged, so you can afford to pay him off.

If you have money to lend, it would probably be easier to find a borrower than the other way around, but it still would be tricky. Most people don't understand gold. We at Target intend to use this same technique for financing our immediate future expansion needs, so we've got a lot of confidence in it.

Also, remember, you enter into negotiation at your own risk, as we make no representations of any kind as to the stability or credit worthiness of either party. That is for you to determine.

In conclusion, let me sum up. With a gold clause, and a hedging technique, it is possible to loan money, receive interest and be protected against inflation with a rising gold price, which means it's the same as owning gold coins. Except for the possible small trading losses of the borrower (hedger), you can't lose money. A borrower can make the attractiveness of his loan proposal infinitely greater, while using the hedging technique to protect himself against getting financially murdered with a runaway gold market. It is a good deal for everybody concerned, and that's the kind of deal I like.

(12/15/77) Recently, we have had many additional questions about the gold clause contract, and some excellent input from some professionals in the commodity field. One senator will read that article into the Congressional Record with some laudatory comments. I've also been interviewed by two or three national publications who picked up the story.

A gold clause is useless unless both parties understand the counter-cyclical nature of gold, and the contract is hedged. The gold clause was originally used way back when gold was stable at $20.67 an ounce and the borrower didn't have to worry about being tied to a widely fluctuating commodity. The price of gold was government controlled and was stable. Since the gold clause was signed into law by President Carter, there have been several articles published in "hard-money" newsletters telling us we are going to return to utopia, because cities, states and the federal government are going to be forced to issue their securities with gold clauses. That's ridiculous. Nobody is going to issue gold-backed contracts or currencies without futures heging because, without hedging, the risks to the borrower are too great. The only way to protect yourself is to hedge, and the amounts of money borrowed by governments are so large, no futures market could accommodate the hedge buying and selling.

Hedging must be conducted skillfully, as it has some inherent difficulties.

There is the problem of the "spread." If you look at the daily quotations on any commodity in THE WALL STREET JOURNAL, you will see that the contracts furthest into the future are more expensive. The reason for that is when you buy a futures contract on margin, you are also locking away a supply of gold, and there are interest-carrying charges and insurance and assay charges built into these contracts because the market assumes you will take delivery of the gold, even though you probably won't. The major factor is the carrying charge and the "spread" reflects the cost of carrying the contract. The closer you get to the delivery date, the narrower the spread would be.

In my opinion, this would be partially offset by the fact that the lender would not need as high an interest return with a gold clause. Theoretically, interest rates reflect inflation. If there is a six percent inflation expectation in the economy, interest rates generally reflect that, plus two or three percentage points to represent profit or "true interest." In actual practice, it sometimes doesn't work out that way because often the inflation rate is higher than the interest rate, but that's the way it's supposed to work. However, if you are protected against loss of purchasing power (inflation) of your principal by a gold clause, then the lender doesn't need as high an interest return. He needs a true profit on his money, which historically has been two to three percent. That would mean without a gold clause, with seven percent price inflation, the lender needs nine to ten percent for a fair return.

The borrower may have some tax problems, also. Let's say the borrower is hedging, with gold at $160 an ounce at the beginning of the contract, and it is a two-year loan. He buys a futures contract that's 12 months down the road. If gold has risen substantially, even though his obligation has risen along with it, and he attempts to "roll over" the contract before his present contract expires, he may be stuck for some taxes on his alleged non-existent profits. I believe that the additional cost of paying off the loan will offset the profits on the contract for tax purposes. Ordinarily, the profit on your futures contract would be capital gains, which you cannot offset with ordinary expenses; however, I think the nature of the loan hedging agreement would be evidence that you were not speculating or taking a profit, but merely continuing your contract into the future by rolling it over into another contract, leaving you in roughly a zero tax position. This is not proven, however, and we are plowing new tax-law ground. More later.

There's another technique that you can use as a borrower to offset some of these costs. You can put your original margin money in Treasury bills. (The IMM requires a minimum $10,000 in T-bills, the COMEX, $30,000.) For example, if you were buying a 100-ounce contract worth about $16,000, you would put up $1000 as a margin at the beginning of the contract. With 10 contracts, you can do it in the form of T-bills, which are held by the broker and draw interest. As the price of gold rises and your profits accumulate, the additional funds in your account with your broker can also be converted into T-bills, which are presently yielding over 6%. That 6% yield will offset some of the "spreads" that we discussed above.

I hope these complications don't scare you off. It's not as formidable as it sounds if you use a competent broker.

Incidentally, after a little more research prompted by one of our subscribers, I recommend you not accept our previous optional suggestion that you go short if the price of gold drops below the cost of your contract. Stay out of the market when gold is below your striking price, and only enter the market when it rises above it. This would cut your "entry point" risks in half. With a shrewd commodity trader who can properly orchestrate your entry into the market, the risks are manageable.

(2/15/78) I have just received a copy of the CONGRESSIONAL RECORD for January 19, 1978, covering a speech by SENATOR JESSE HELMS, our keynote speaker at THE *RUFF TIMES* CONVENTION on February 20. It is as follows:

> MR. HELMS: Mr. President, on October 28, the President signed Public Law 95-147, a bill which makes enforceable in the courts financial obligations between Americans denominated in gold.
>
> It has been interesting and rewarding to note the vast number of Americans who have expressed interest in this means of avoiding the effects of inflation. My office has received a deluge of inquiries on that topic. In addition, many, many citizens have asked information from the Institute on Money and Inflation, a Washington-based public policy research organization which, by the way, provided the backup research and analyses needed for my work on this legislation.
>
> Recently I came across two articles on the new gold clause freedom in the newsletter written by Howard J. Ruff, *THE RUFF TIMES*. Mr. Ruff offers timely advice to his 30,000 subscribers on how they can make a go of things in this era of economic disruption. Mr. Ruff and I agree that inflation is one of the worst evils ever foisted on the American people by Government. He believes, and I agree, that the only standard of value never corrupted by Government—gold—is still useful as a means of defending one's self and family from the ravages of inflation.
>
> Gold has its pitfalls, and many people have said that the gold clause freedom will not be used, because of the volatility in the price of gold. It has been my observation that increased use of gold as a standard and store of value in these chaotic times will probably reduce golds volatility and increase its desirability.

Mr. Ruff has put together a proposed way of utilizing gold clause contracts and I believe it deserves serious consideration.

Like all new concepts, gold clause contracts will require study and some investigation. I have promised to do whatever I can to put an end, if possible, to the evil of inflation. The best way, of course, would be to stop inflation, until we can do that, the next best way is to make available the means to minimize inflation's effects. Mr. Ruff's proposal to use the gold clause freedom may well fit the needs of many Americans. For the benefit of my colleagues and other readers of the CONGRESSIONAL RECORD, I ask unanimous consent that Mr. Ruff's articles be printed in the RECORD.

There being no objection, the articles were ordered to be printed in the RECORD.

(10/15/78) In the mid-1930s when the government called in gold, they also made it illegal to have clauses in contracts which were tied to the price of gold. When it was made legal for Americans to own gold a few years ago, Congress neglected to correct the restriction on gold clauses in contracts. About a year ago, under the leadership of Senator Jesse Helms, legislation was passed by the Congress and signed by President Carter which allowed Americans to insert gold clauses in contracts. Immediately, this was latched onto by all of the gold bugs and hard-money fans as meaning that cities and states would put gold clauses in their contracts and that we were on our way to reenthroning gold as backing for our currency. I said at the time that I thought that was absurd.

Gold clause contracts have value under certain, carefully structured conditions. They will not come into general use, as government is not about to hedge in the futures market against its obligations, nor is it about to tie its fortunes to a fluctuating commodity. But for private transactions, there are several ways in which gold clause contracts can be used.

Bill Anderson has written a complete description of how gold clause contracts may be used in real estate and other transactions. If you will drop us a note, or call on the Hot-Line, we will be happy to put you in touch with those who are working with gold clause contracts as borrowers or lenders, although we are not acting in either a broker or an agent capacity. We are simply an information clearing house. I'm rather proud of the gold clause approach to lending. We have pioneered it and I think we know more about it than anyone.

(2/15/78)   Gold-Backed Bonds

In our December 15, 1977 issue, I discussed some bonds that had been issued in the late 19th and early 20th century, which are still in circulation, and backed with a gold clause. Some are returning quite high yields, have excellent ratings, and are approaching maturity.

We know of reputable brokers you can trust to execute your orders properly. I think this is a heck of an opportunity. In any event, if you are interested in buying some sound bonds, with good yields, which may pay off several times their face value at maturity, write to us at P.O. Box 2000, San Ramon, California 94583.

GOLD FUTURES

(11/1/78) The "Contango": The Latest Song and Dance
By Gary North, Ph.D

There is a magic wealth formula. Just offer the public something which combines ignorance, fear, and greed. Fear and greed create the sale while the consumer's ingorance allows you to overcharge him. You can make a bundle, but if you stay in the fear-greed-ignorance market too long, people finally begin to wise up. Then the get-rich-quick scheme becomes a get-poor-quick operation.

A case in point was the proliferation of "commodity options" programs that were being offered to the gullible. *THE RUFF TIMES* warned against these programs in February 1, 1977 (THE BEST OF RUFF, p. 60). The Commodity Futures Trading Commission recently outlawed them. Now a very similar rip-off is reappearing. This time, the scheme is called something like a "deferred cash contract" or a "leveraged commodity" contract.

A salesman calls you—the tip-off that you will be charged large commissions—and tells you that you can get high leverage in the gold market without the fear of margin calls. The appeal is to fear—protect yourself against a sagging dollar—and greed: profits far greater than you can get by buying some gold coins and holding them for appreciation. Finally, the basis of the operation is ignorance. They know the buyers will not ask the proper questions. In fact, the investor who asks the right questions is feared by these fast-buck artists, for good reason.

The latest super-duper deal for the super dupes is really a reworked variation of th old "coins on margin" ploy that was big in the early 1970s, prior to several embarrassing bankruptcies among the firms promoting these investments. The government cracked down and forced the remaining firms to clean up their act, but now a far worse version is being peddled. The CFTC estimates that at least 80 unregistered firms are selling these new "leveraged commodity contracts" plus dozens more firms that are registered.

Here's the pitch. You are told that you can "take control" of 100 ounces of gold for less than the current price of a 100-ounce bar. One salesman who spoke to me kept using the term "contango," which was supposed to explain everything—a mysterious term that supposedly can lead to honest riches. The firm would charge me a "contango" fee of $3950 which would allow me to "take control" of my very own 10-ounce bar of gold from mid-October through June 1979. Once paid, even if the market fell, I could never be subjected to a margin call, meaning a demand to put up more money to keep "control" of my bar of gold. The gold bar would be purchased by the firm and actually stored in a local depository, no further than 100 miles from my me. That would prove that the gold was really there, waiting for me.

If the price goes up between now and June 1979, I was told, I have the option of selling the gold and pocketing the profits, or coming up with $24,000—an additional $24,000, since the $3950 was my "contango" fee—and getting delivery. But no margin calls: here was the ultimate selling point.

What, you may ask, is the "contango?" It's really a snappy term for the normal price differential between today's cash (spot) price of a commodity and its future delivery price in a particular month on the futures market. This fee covers interest, storage, and insurance (ISI), which obviously has to be paid by the participants in the futures markets. Just look at today's price of gold, and compare it with the contract price of gold at some future specified date in *THE WALL STREET JOURNAL* or any paper that reports commodity prices. The future price is normally above the present cash price.

Let's take a specific example. *THE WALL STREET JOURNAL* for Thursday, October 2, lists the London gold price (which is a commissionless price, you can't buy gold for this price) at $225.30 or $22,530 per 100-ounce bar (plus commission).

This was Wednesday's closing price. On the Commodity Exchange of New York (COMEX), the settlement price of the October delivery date, the nearest date, for a futures contract of 100-ounces was $227.70 per ounce, or $22,770 for a 100-ounce bar. This does not include commission, since the commission of $45 is paid when the buyer of the contact initiates the purchase. The COMEX price of a contract deliverable in June, 1979, was $241.80 per ounce, or $24,180 per 100-ounce bar. The "contango" represents the difference between the two contracts (interest, storage, insurance), $24,180 minus $22,770 = $1410.

I spoke with one of these hot-shot salesmen on Wednesday, October 11, the day these prices prevailed. He offered me this fabulous deal. I would pay $3950 as a one-time-only commission and "contango" fee. Then I would "take control" of a 100-ounce bar of gold (he did not use the word "option," though this is surely what it sounded like). What was the price of the bar of gold? Why, only $24,000. But the price of a 100-ounce bar of gold on the COMEX that day was $22,770, not counting the $45 in-and-out (buy and sell) commission. He was overcharging me $1230, or 87 percent of the October-June "contango" fee on the COMEX.

Then why did I have to pay the firm an additional $3950? If 87 percent of the "contango" fee was already included in the purchase price of $24,000, what was the $3950 charge? The salesman had said the $3950 covered the "contango" plus the firm's commission. What this seemed to mean was that almost all of the $3950 was the firm's commission. Since the normal commission fee through a reputable commodity futures broker is $45, this seemed a bit excessive to me.

Are you beginning to smell a rat? Remember, the salesman guaranteed me that "my gold" would be placed in a vault within 100 miles of my home, where I could view it at any time. This is a very important claim on his part, as we'll see.

What does a "contango" fee have to do with a presently held bar of gold? A "contango" spread is only involved in a futures contract. The bulk of the true contango fee is interest charges, but why would I be paying interest? I asked him who loaned the firm the $21,000, which had to be added to my $3950, in order to purchase the $24,000 bar of gold. He couldn't say. There would be no interest charge, however. No payment of interest was ever involved, he assured me. But then where did the firm get the money to buy my bar of gold? After all, they aren't giving gold away these days. Unless the firm was covering in the futures market, there had to be a loan.

At this point, he became nervous. "Who referred you to us?", he demanded. I refused to reply. Then he turned me over to the firm's president. He was even more evasive. He wanted to know who referred me to the company. But he assured me that no loan was involved.

If no loan is involved, then how was the firm covering the contract? And where did it get the bar of gold that I could view at any time with my contract number on it? The answer should be obvious: the presently held gold is a myth.

The next day, the salesman called me back and referred me to the "famous" firm that sells his firm the gold. I had never before heard of this firm, which is not located in New York City, and I've been in this business a long time. So I called. The Vice President, who was "to provide me with all the answers," spent most of his time being evasive. He finally admitted the truth: "part" of the coverage is made in the gold futures market (I would bet about 90 percent). So I asked him the crucial question: "What is to protect the solvency of the firm that is selling me the gold contract if the gold price drops sharply, and the firm is unable to generate sufficient funds to come up with its margin money?" To which the Vice President replied: "I can't answer that question." To which I replied: "You just did."

The whole pitch is that the buyer will never get a margin call. Indeed, he won't. The company will get the margin call if gold drops sharply by, say, 10 percent, and if the firm cannot come up with the margin money by 9:15 AM the next morning, then all of its (the customers') positions will be sold out. Presto: bankruptcy.

This explains the "commission" fee of $3950 as compared to $45. The firm uses the money, or part of the money, to put a deposit on a June 1979 gold futures contract. Then the management hopes and prays that no sharp reduction of gold's price ever occurs. If it does, the whole scheme topples into bankruptcy.

If gold stays high, the firm eventually pockets the full $3950. You have to come up with the full (overpriced) $24,000 to take delivery. This means, incredibly, that in order for you to profit from this transaction, gold must rise by over $39.50 per ounce by the following June. If it rises less than $39.50 per ounce, the buyer of the 100-ounce contract loses. With a normal futures contract, a $39.50 rise in the price of gold would net the buyer $3905 ($39.50 times 100 ounces = $3950, minus a $45 commission = $3905).

How could anyone be so silly as to sign up? We are back to fear, greed, and ignorance. Fear of margin calls and fear of a sagging dollar; greed at being able to "take control" of 100 ounces of gold for "only" $3950; ignorance concerning legitimate alternatives.

If no bank will loan anyone over 50 percent of the market value of a bar of gold (and the only one I know that will loan you that much is Deak National Bank of Fleishmanns, New York, and they store the bar in their vault, not being idiots), then there is only one way that $3950 will allow me to "take control" of a "$24,000" bar of gold: my money is used as a deposit in a commodity futures contract. In either case, there always has to be a margin call threat; no one loans money, or accepts deposits on futures contracts unless he can be sure that I will ante-up in case the price of the asset (my collateral in a loan) drops. There is no such thing as a free lunch. There is only one way to buy gold and avoid all risks of a margin call: pay cash.

So anyone who buys such a contract is right back in the futures market. The company has merely covered your contract with a paper transaction, the purchase of a future contract. So far, there is no bar of gold owned by the firm (or by you) which can be displayed in its vault, your vault, or some Swiss bank vault. The salesman who says there is such a bar for all buyers to view, one for each buyer, with the buyer's own number on it, is simply lying. He is engaging in fraud. There is one way that such a bar of gold could exist: it would have to be 4-carat gold.

Of course, there may be three or four bars in the company's possession, and the firm can ship them around, upon request, to calm the hearts of the suspicious few who actually want to see "their" bars of gold. These bars, if they exist (and I suspect they do), are not inventory as such; they are advertising expenses.

If you are unfortunate enough to be contacted by one of these "world-famous investment companies," hang up.

In short, the "contango" is a real song and dance. Why buy from a firm that charges you $4000 for a service that a normal commodity brokerage firm will provide for you for $45? Why deal with professional liars who want to sell you a high-risk, eight-month contract that requires a profit of $4000 just to break even?

If you want high profits to match high risk, buy a futures contract. At least the commissions are cheap. If you want long-term protection from mass inflation, buy gold coins and take delivery. Don't try any third approach. You will be dealing with high-cost operators if you do.

You may be safe from margin calls in one of these boiler-room deals; the boiler-room operation isn't. Someday you may call their toll-free phone number and hear the magic words (recorded): "The number you have dialed has been disconnected. There is no new number."

Don't let the flim-flam boys work their number on you!

GOLD IN THE GERMAN INFLATION

By Gary North, Ph.D.

(8/15/77) (Dr. North is the founder of the Institute of Christian Economics and Editor of THE REMNANT REVIEW. He is the author of numerous books on economics and an occasional contributor to *THE RUFF TIMES*.)

Was gold really a good inflation hedge during the great German Inflation of 1918-23? Was it the best investment? For which groups might it have been a better investment?

The rise and fall of gold's price, as denominated in German marks, was just exactly that: rise and fall. It has risen sharply after 1918, but from early 1920 until the middle of the year, its price plummeted back to its early 1918 level. Then it turned back up. The inflation of the mark continued, people finally began to lose confidence in it, and gold (along with other hard goods) rose in relation to the mark.

The real source of monetary measurement was the dollar, not gold. The dollar was convertible into gold at about $20.67 per ounce, so the dollar-mark exchange rate substituted for the gold-mark exchange rate. The dollar rate was quoted all day long, and it was in the great collapse of 1922-23 that the destruction of the mark took place. The black market price of the dollar finally reached $11.7 trillion in November of 1923, the day of the currency reform. At $20.67/oz, this translates into 566 billion marks per ounce.

It should not take a Ph.D. in economics to conclude that a figure like 500 billion anything per ounce of anything makes little economic sense. By that time, the mark was not used for making transactions. Barter had replaced the mark, and dollars, and coins of any kind. The German economy was smashed by the lack of a universal unit of account, although the dollar exchange rate at least helped people to make some economic calculations.

A far more interesting question than the gold-mark exchange rate is this one: How did gold perform in relation to other commodities and investments?

When gold dropped sharply in the first half of 1920, the wise investor was out of his speculative holdings in gold, though not necessarily his survival holdings. It responded in the second half, and peaked, in relation to other commodities, in late 1921. There were sharp ups and downs through late 1923, but the peaks dropped slowly. After 1921, therefore, it would have been better to have been in goods rather than gold. Gold was necessarily supplemental, since so few people owned it. Basic hard goods, in the aggregate, outperformed gold, although gold did well in comparison to any single commodity.

Stocks lost about 80 percent of their value, although there was some rebound after 1922. Money meaning marks, lost everything in late 1922. Food commodities did well. Farmers outside the cities prospered in comparison to city dwellers. The big loser was government, since government deals in money for tax collecting. Government services were drastically cut back. By delaying payment of taxes by only a few weeks, taxpayers gained tremendously. They gave up assets worth only a fraction of what they had been worth a few weeks before. By the time the government spent the money, it had fallen in value even more.

Dr. Donald Kemmerer, then a young man, interviewed people who had gone through the great inflation. He was assisting his father, E. W. Kemmerer, whose studies of the German inflation are still taken seriously by scholars. They asked all of these people one question: Is there any step you could have taken—gold, silver, dollars, food—that could have made you better off than would have been the case had Germany never experienced the inflation? Everyone answered the same: No! There was no ultimate hedge. Monetary stability would have been preferable. But nobody said a little gold wouldn't have made things a lot easier.

Gold is always supplemental in an economic crisis. It is used to buy big-ticket items, or freedom, or vital necessities. It is limited to a minority of the population. The average man never sees a gold coin in a major crisis, if only because people hoard gold for a true crisis, a life-and-death exchange. Barter, or silver coins, or foreign currencies predominate. But gold does help people to preserve their capital during an inflationary blow-off. It is worth something before an inflation, during an inflation, and after an inflation. This is why intelligent, long-term investors will include gold coins in their investment portfolios. They draw no interest, but they survive the paper currency that interest is paid with.

(For the record, the standard study of the great inflation is still the book by Constantino Bresciani-Turroni: *The Economics of Inflation*, published in 1937 and still in print: Routledge and Kegan Paul, London.)

GOLD STOCKS

(11/1/76)   Gold stocks also show greater profit potential and more risk than bullion or coins, as a 10 percent increase in the price of gold can double the profit margins of a mining company, and double the stock price. I prefer the less exciting, safer, more conservative approach, and buy coins for cash.

I don't profess to be an expert on gold stocks and I wouldn't even begin to tell you which stock you should buy, as that is not the function of our letter. My job is to educate you on the basic principles, and then we will refer you to the experts who can execute your orders and help you make your individual decisions.

(3/15/76)   South African Gold Stocks

People frequently ask what I think of South African gold stocks. Right now I am nervous about them. I happen to think South Africa will probably survive and continue to be the world's top gold producer. However, the price of a stock is dependent on people's opinion of its value.

As I have said so many times, this is a time to be cautious. If I were holding South African stocks at this time, I would probable liquidate them. If you wish to invest in precious metals, buy gold or silver coins, or perhaps even bullion.

QUESTIONS AND ANSWERS

(12/15/77)

Q. What percentage of my assets should be in gold?

A. There's no answer to that question. Many people's assets are unavailable for investment because they are tied up in trusts or pension plans, or their home, or whatever. The best answer, and it is an imperfect one, is that I would like to see between 30 and 40 percent of your available investment funds in gold.

Q. If I have a small loan on my home, should I get a bigger loan and buy gold?

A. That depends on where it is. If it is in a safe, secure place away from the big cities and you want to live there, I would pay off your home completely, if possible, and not encumber it with any kind of loans. (I know that's not possible for many of you.) If your home is in one of the big cities, where I think the trouble is going to be, where crime rates will begin to rise and the middle class will be moving out, then I would want the biggest possible loan on my home until I could get it sold, and I would invest up to 60 percent of those funds in gold coins and diamonds, and the rest in Treasury bills.

(6/1/78)

Q. How can gold rise when the dollar is also rising?

A. It is a myth that gold is irretrievably linked to the fortunes of the dollar. Foreigners also think of gold as a hedge against economic troubles. When the dollar rises, the European or Japanese perceives it, not as a rise of the dollar, but as a fall of his currency, and he, fearing the loss of his purchasing power, will buy gold. This gives us the phenomenon of rising gold and a rising dollar at the same time. In addition, as foreign investors perceive the weakening of their own currencies, wealth begins sloshing around like water in a leaky boat. Some of it goes into dollar-denominated bank deposits, some into Treasury securities, some into gold, and an awful lot pours into the U.S. stock market. The recent dramatic rise in the Dow Jones is partially caused by an influx of foreign assets pouring back into dollar-denominated securities, as the dollar strengthens.

(6/15/77)

Q. Harry Browne and you have advised people to buy gold and silver. I have friends that bought gold at almost $200 an ounce and lost their shirts. How can you possibly recommend it?

A. There's ample historical precedent to indicate that during a paper money crisis, people do accept and trust monetary metal coins. Silver and gold are deeply imbedded in human consciousness as having value. I don't know why I have to apologize for Harry Browne. If you took his advice when he first gave it, you would have bought gold at well under a hundred dollars an ounce, you would have seen it go up to $200 an ounce, back down to $103 and then bounce back to around $140, which is where it is now. You would have still been way ahead of the rate of inflation. No advice given by anybody is good at all times and in all places. Even the people who bought at $200 an ounce are eventually going to be vindicated. Gold, I also believe, is a leading indicator of the economy and its major movement are forecasting items. When the recovery began, gold was on the way down. Gold has been on the way back up for several months now, and I believe it's trying to tell us something.

(12/1/77)

Q. Why did gold drop $12?

A. I said on October 1, gold might correct downward, and it did. When I call a correction like that, there's more than a little luck involved. This is not a tip sheet for short-term speculators. If something is in a good buying range and you want some, buy it, and don't worry if it drops a little. Nobody ever catches the exact bottom. Gold is a good long-term buy up to $200 an ounce. If you are not thinking long-term, either don't buy gold, or admit that you are a short-term speculator, and talk to R. E. McMaster or

Maury Kravitz. I study the economic "climate." I let them worry about the day to day investment "weather."

The one inexorable, unquestionable truth is that we are heading into an adverse economic climate for several years, and gold will be a method of preserving your wealth, and what it does from day to day, week to week, or even month to month, is irrelevant.

Q. Fine, but what if gold takes a big long dip like it did in '75 and '76?

A. Then I'm wrong about inflation, I'm wrong about monetary problems, and the world is headed for several years of stable prosperity. It's up to you to decide whether or not you believe me on the fundamentals. If you don't believe me, don't take my advice.

Q. What if the government calls in all gold as it did in 1933 and makes it illegal to own?

A. It's possible, but not likely, and way in the future, if at all. The government has been selling its gold and telling the world that gold isn't money. It has recently made it legal to own the metal. We now have a legal gold clause for contracts (see: Gold Clauses). The government would only call in gold after the currency had collapsed in an effort to establish a gold-backed currency. I wouldn't consider that a disaster. In fact, I would probably be willing to accept their gold-backed currency in exchange for my gold because the currency would become acceptable. I don't care what you call money as long as everyone is willing to accept it in exchange for goods and services.

When Roosevelt called in gold in 1933, we were on the gold standard and the government was worried about the gold backing of our currency. They could care less about that today.

Q. What price do you think gold will attain by the end of this year? Next year?

A. I don't know and I don't even think it's very important. If you want my best guess, it has a 60-40 chance of being over $200 by the end of February. It depends on international events. Your question really gets the cart before the horse. We won't measure gold in dollars. We will measure purchasing power in gold. What does it matter what it's worth in paper currency if you are going to hang onto it for the long haul anyway?

If watching gold prices fluctuating in the paper every day ruins your breakfast, then buy diamonds. They go up from 15 to 30 percent every year and you can't see a quote in the paper every day to stir your ulcer.

Gold is dangerous for short-term speculation because its price is a matter of direct interest to governments who manipulate it for political reasons. It is a political football. The only thing you can be sure of about gold is this: it is the world's frightened money. When the world is scared, investors rush into the metal, and since there isn't a lot of it around, a relatively small amount of buying forces it up. Fear makes gold prosper. You are, in effect, betting on a worldwide climate of fear.

Q. How could gold ever be used as money in a currency collapse? My banker won't take it, and I'm sure the corner grocery won't either.

A. You are confusing today's conditions with tomorrows troubles. Gold will serve the following functions:

1. In case of controlled inflation (three to ten percent a year) it tends to appreciate over the long haul, like any other commodity, and you buy it from, or sell it to, a coin or bullion dealer.

2. In the case of runaway inflation, you also avoid the sudden collapse of your currency by owning gold instead.

3. In the case of a world-wide monetary collapse, it's your store of value which you sit on until a normal means of exchange and "store of value" is reestablished and accepted, and then you sell your coins to a gold dealer.

4. During a period of economic chaos, when no one trusts paper currency, the free market quickly establishes a value for gold and silver coins and they will be used as money. In China, after World War II, in that great primitive country where communications were almost non-existent, it was only a month or two before every merchant in China knew, through the "Invisible Hand" of the marketplace described by Adam Smith, what the value of a gold or silver coin was, and it was universally acceptable money. Of course your banker won't accept your gold now. He doesn't have to. There is now an acceptable paper currency. If the time comes that there isn't, your banker won't be around to accept anything.

Q. What's the best way to store gold?

A. Well, you can use the "MIDNIGHT GARDENER" sold through Investment Rarities, or you can make your own. Use a six-inch thick tube of heavy P.V.C. plastic that seals on both ends. Dig a hole, drop it in, put some dirt on it, and then to confuse a detector, put an old automobile distributor or other metal object on top of that and then fill it up the rest of the way. That may be a little excessive, as who's going to come walking around your yard with

294

a metal detector unless they know there's gold there, so I suggest you not put up a neon sign that says, "GOLD BURIED HERE." I think it's perfectly safe now to keep it in a safe-deposit box.

(Special Report #4, 10/76)

Q. "Why should I buy precious metals?"

A. In times of monetary uncertainty, inflation, deflation, or depression, precious metals have tended to hold their purchasing value in relation to goods and services. For example, in inflationary times, people begin to distrust paper money and they instinctively buy gold or silver coins. During the German inflation of the '20s and the Chinese inflation after World War II, gold and silver coin of all nations were freely exchanged as acceptable currency when paper was rejected.

I don't look upon gold as a speculative investment vehicle for short or medium term capital appreciation.

I look upon gold as a "time machine" to transport your assets from the present, across the gulf of depression and monetary crisis to the inevitable recovery that will follow.

This is precisely what investment houses do.

That does not mean I am opposed to speculation. I believe that speculation is an essential part of the American system. Without people speculating on the future of new inventions or processes or business ventures, there would be no capitalist system. All I am saying is that most of you don't have much money to risk, and I am concerned only with that portion of your portfolio that you are using to insure your safety and future against downtrends.

Even though my emphasis seems to be in preparing for a calamity, it's obvious to any thinking investor that American history moves in waves of upturns and downturns, peaks and valleys. Everyone is thrilled with peaks. When gold is selling for $300 a share, everybody is scrambling to buy. When gold is selling at $107 a share, nobody wants it. The foolishness of this attitude is readily apparent from an intellectual point of view, but emotionally it's quite another matter. You must keep your eye strictly upon your objective. If your objective is to prepare for a possible calamity, then it really shouldn't matter what the newspaper says about the value of your holdings upon any given day.

THE INVISIBLE CRASH—A REVIEW

(12/75)   *The Invisible Crash* by James Dines (Ballantine Books)

Few men have taken the abuse and ridicule James Dines has. He is one of the original "goldbugs." His newsletter has touted gold mining shares since 1962 and is one of the most widely read and respected letters on the subject. But, more than that, he is a shrewd and articulate observer of the causes of inflation, recession, and stock market actions. *The Invisible Crash* is a revealing peek into the mind of this great man.

I have a few nits to pick, so let's get them out of the way first.

This book is poorly edited. It's like panning for gold, you look at a lot of sand in the process. It rambles and wanders, but on almost every page, buried in a mountain of excess verbiage, or irrelevant detail, is a gem or two of hard, brilliant, perceptive wisdom, so don't skip anything.

He explains the history of gold and its relationship to money. He demonstrates the stability of currencies and commerce when solid gold currency backing was an article of faith. He shows why governments inflate the currency and its effect on the working man. He has some marvelous quotations to pinpoint his case.

By the time he's through, you will understand gold, you will know why we're in this mess, and best of all, you will have a sense of urgency about preparation.

By far the most interesting section takes up most of the last half of the book. It's called "an Odyssey."

It consists of excerpts from his letters from January 1, 1961, through September 13, 1974, in diary form. It includes his forecasts, observations, etc. It took guts, because he unflinchingly quotes his forecasts, even those that subsequent event showed to be wrong. But, as you read, a pattern emerges that says, "The man's principles are sound. He's right more often than he's wrong," and he sometimes makes the mistake of setting the date for future events.

I said in my book, "The best way to become a false prophet is to set a date for the end of the world and be wrong." Dines' errors are few compared to his towering record for accuracy.

He forecast the market slides of 1969 and 1974-75. He predicted the dramatic rise in gold prices and the U.S. devaluation of the dollar. He tracked our gold losses to other nations and accurately interpreted the $120-130 floor on the price of gold that has held all through 1975 against determined assaults from the United States government.

He called the tune on our current recession and says that's just the beginning.

It's a great book. You will understand for the first time the incredible ignorance of the politicians we elect, who have their hands on the money levers.

GOLD AND THE DOLLAR

(2/1/79) The gold market is creating the most agonizing investment dilemma I have faced for many years. It has been showing remarkable strength and, as markets tend to do, it isn't paying much attention to my opinion. The dollar has been relatively strong, the foreign currencies are not very impressive, and the stock market has given us a bit of a spurt. And yet in the face of all these things, which have been bearish for gold for the past two years, gold has moved from its November lows to around $235. Here's the prognosis at the moment.

From a strictly technical point of view, the London 2nd price fixing over $232 was a major breakout of the same dimensions as last year's $190 breakout. It could go much higher. What then happens to my scenario of lower gold prices giving us a buying opportunity?

I believe the odds slightly favor one more massive government intervention in support of the dollar, which would bomb gold again, as happened in November.

That conclusion is based on the following assumptions:

1. Gold will continue to be the mirror image of a falling dollar.

2. Government must assault gold at the same time it is supporting the dollar to discourage money from fleeing out of dollars into gold.

In all honesty, several things have happened which could upset that neat and tidy scenario.

It appears that the illicit romance between gold and the Swiss and German currencies is, at least temporarily, cooling off, and may be heading for a permanent break-up. In the past, every time the Swiss franc, the German deutschemark and the Japanese yen rose in relation to the dollar, gold would rise, too, and that relationship was never severed for more than a few days at a time. Now, at least temporarily, there seems to be no relationship between the movements of the currencies and gold. If this is a permanent condition, then my best assumption is that government will have no interest in gold and couldn't care where it goes and will do nothing to attack the gold market—AS LONG AS IT IS NOT VIEWED AS AN INSULT TO THE DOLLAR! The market has proven it can absorb all the gold the Treasury can throw at it, as the last auction had bids in excess of six million ounces for the 1.5 million ounces offered. If the dollar holds, you will not see my anticipated correction to below $185, or even below $200, but will see dramatic new highs. If, however, we simultaneously see the dollar falling and gold rising, then government will assault us dirty, unpatriotic speculators by driving down the foreign currencies and bombing the gold market.

I believe government has only one shot left, which probably consists of another big jump in the discount rate, an increase in the amount of gold to be sold at auction, and more massive buying of expatriate dollars, using more borrowed foreign currencies. It has already spent over $60 billion to do so, according to *THE WASHINGTON POST*. This means the government, in effect, is speculating massively in the dollar and we could have billions of dollars of losses if it is not successful and the dollar resumes its fall, but I do not believe this administration will let it slide far without one more try.

If a new assault is mounted, this time you will see the unveiling of the poised-and-ready scheme to slap an import tax on foreign oil. A falling dollar and continued disruption of Iran's oil industry will provide all the needed rationale.

It is this Sword of Damocles hanging over the market that makes this such a scary decision. If that threat were not there, gold would be an absolutely unquestioned "buy" and probably would be close to $300 an ounce right now. The potential for profits would be as sure a thing as I've seen in the investment markets for many years. On balance, I expect the dollar to temporarily resume its slide, and gold to reflect that falling dollar, causing government to attack it one more time. For that reason, I would be nervous about anyone other than the most hardened speculators buying heavily into this market.

That opinion could change if gold continues to move while the dollar remains strong without further U.S. monetary intervention.

Here is the strategy which I am following as of now:

1. I will immediately commit approximately one-third of the money I've allocated for gold investment (assuming I already have my survival gold), and I'll buy Krugerrands. I don't want to miss out entirely if there is no intervention and we have a runaway gold price.

2. If the attack comes, I will simply hang on, ride it down when Carter does his thing, and then commit the rest of my funds. After the

government has fired this one last shot. I don't believe it will have any ammo left, and worsening economic conditions and rising inflation will drive gold to new highs after it bottoms. My low-priced purchases will average down my overall cost.

As a leveraged commodities speculator, I would be terribly nervous about being long in this market, even though I might miss a substantial run. If the government sandbags this market again without warning, as they did on November 1, it will be "limit down" for a day or two again with no chance to get out. The leveraged risks are just too high. Actually, I'm not too interested in helping speculators. I am trying to help survivalists and inflation-and-chaos hedgers to get in at reasonably low cost.

What are the odds on my being right? About 60-40—not exactly a sure thing.

The dollar might be "levitating" only because of U.S. market intervention and gold might be taking off only in anticipation of that rescue operation finally being overwhelmed, in which case the gold/franc romance would be on again. Gold is a chaos hedge, and the fall of the dolar was reflecting international chaos because it is the world's reserve currency, and falling meant the possibility of massive changes in all international monetary situations. If gold continues to jump while the dollar simultaneously resumes its fall, then that illicit relationship is still intact, and Carter must fire his last shot. If he does, the short-term carnage in the gold market could be awesome.

In the long run, however, rising inflation rates and rising interest rates are the fundamentals for rising gold. Right now the markets are hinting we might be moving into the expected fake-you-out deflationary phase, and that's another reason why I think gold is dangerous right now.

I don't know for sure which way it's going to go right now. The odds favor sudden governmental intervention if the dollar slides, which will drive gold down. If it happens, I don't want to be totally committed. I'm perfectly willing to miss an interim upward move because of the high risks involved.

I'll let you know more as things develop.

THREE INVESTMENT STRATEGIES

(2/15/79) Strangely enough, gold could fit into any and/or all of my investment categories—The Survival Strategy, The Break-Even-Or-Better Strategy, and the Leveraged Get-Rich Strategy. Gold coins are survival money never to be touched regardless of the intermediate or short-term trends of the economy or the marketplace.

Gold also belongs in your break-even-or-better strategy, and should be bought without a lot of concern for the current price. You are not trying to speculate on the short-term waves, so the short-term waves don't mean much, except that, of course, you would like to buy it as cheaply as possible so you can buy more. If it is lower the day after you buy, you shouldn't be overly concerned. You know it will be higher within a reasonably short time. That's why I suggest committing a third of your money now and feeding the rest in on major corrections. Corrections always come and, as you know, I am still expecting a big one. The higher the price goes, though, the bigger the correction will have to be in order to justify the time we have been out of the market, but that was always a fairly high risk recommendation.

Gold also is a vehicle for leveraged trading, particularly with gold futures or gold shares. YOUR DECISION ABOUT EACH OF THESE CATEGORIES MIGHT BE TOTALLY DIFFERENT UNDER EXACTLY THE SAME MARKET CONDITIONS. For example, with gold at these incredible highs, as a result of the Iranian situation, I think you ought to be ought of the futures market because the chance of U.S. correction of a dollar slide is so great. With the market displaying an increasing propensity for "limit moves" down, leveraged risks are unacceptable, so I would just as soon be standing on the sidelines, even though I might miss an upward move.

INTERNATIONAL GOLD AND MONETARY CONFERENCE REPORT

(1/1/76) Harry Truman said that if you laid all of the economists end-to-end they would point in different directions!

Kay and I just spent four days in New Orleans attending the INTERNATIONAL GOLD AND MONETARY CONFERENCE, and ol' Harry was right. We heard 32 experts on gold, silver, taxes, and securities make brilliant, convincing cases for totally contra-dictory forecasts.

C. V. Myers, John Hoppe, and John Exter showed us why deflation was clearly inevitable. When Jerome Smith and Murray Rothbard got through, it was inflation, as any fool could plainly see. Dick Russell (*Dow Theory Letter*) told us the stock market was ready to break out on the upside, and at least three others convinced us it is headed down.

We learned that South African gold stocks are headed for an incredible rally, but be careful, because it's all over for South Africa!

Harry Schultz told us gold is beginning a great bull rally, but others explained why it isn't going anywhere but down.

Most everyone was bullish on silver, with one or two convincing exceptions.

We also learned that bank commercial loans are expanding and contracting. The same with the money supply.

I was glad to find out "the worst is over" and doom lies just ahead.

I got to meet the entire pantheon of "hard money" deities, and assess their personalities. Because of our rapid growth in readership, there was a lot of curiosity about me and, despite the fact that my speech was at 8:30 Sunday morning, we had most of the attendees (700) in their seats.

I also got to meet several dozen of our subscribers, and that was a thrill for me.

I was generally impressed with the speakers. I got a huge amount of hard data I didn't have before. I love to learn new things, and I was like a bird dog that died and went to quail heaven.

(10/1/76)　　　　Arab Money Power

Douglas Johnston is a gold stock specialist. Here's part of what he said at this same conference.

Japan, Germany, France, and the Arab oil producers hold about 20 percent of all outstanding U.S. Treasury short-term debt. On Labor Day weekend last year, a group of finance ministers met with President Ford on his yacht, the Sequoia, on the Potomac River, on the eve of the INTERNATIONAL MONETARY FUND'S annual meeting in Washington. They threatened to refuse to "roll-over" this debt as it came due, and start dumping bonds on the market unless the U.S. voted to release the 150 million ounces of gold held by the IMF—ALL OF IT! If they carried out their threat, it would have toppled our economy overnight and closed the big New York banks.

With no choice at all, Ford caved in. A few days later, the gold auctions were announced, which supposedly would keep down the price of gold forever. The BANK FOR INTERNATIONAL SET-TLEMENTS (BIS) would handle all gold matters.

Of course, the bottom dropped out on gold. Now, the bombshell.

Only 1/6 of the IMF gold is being auctioned. The other 5/6 has been sold to the BIS in Basel, Switzerland at $42.22 for the account of the Germans, French, Japanese and Arabs. And we were blackmailed into approving, as our vote in the IMF should ordinaily have given us a real veto over its auctions.

Johnston claims the IMF auction is only a smokescreen for the bigger heist. He also said the Soviets are terrified because they have been forced to sell 200 tons of their gold to these same nations to raise money just to tide them over for the rest of the year. They were forced to sell at under $100 an ounce simply by refusing them bank loans to buy Western grain.

Fascinating history, if true. I'll let you know later.

JAMES BLANCHARD CONVENTION REPORT

(3/1/79) At our 2nd Annual RUFF TIMES National Convention, JAMES BLANCHARD, the founder of THE NATIONAL COMMITTEE FOR MONETARY REFORM (NCMR), spoke to us on gold and its relationship to our currency, as well as its future as an investment.

Speaking of the rarity of gold, Jim pointed out that if all the world's gold were divided among the citizens of the United States, there would be five ounces of gold per person. Or if it were divided among the entire world's population, there would be only 1/5 of an ounce per person.

He verified that South Africa and Saudi Arabia have worked out a direct swap of gold for oil, which means less gold hitting the world market and this, of course, is bullish for the metal. He pointed out how the Eurodollar market increased from $695 billion to $835 billion, representing a $140 billion increase. In the last four years, the Eurodollar increase has averaged 22% per year and the inflationary implications are staggering. He also indicated that the Europeans' gold reserves are now larger than ours. The first rule of gold is, "He who has the gold, makes the rules" and, as Jim says, "The Europeans have the gold. It is sad and ironic that if the United States continues its demonetization policy, along with currency debasement, it is far more likely that we will be witnessing an international demonetization of the dollar, not gold." The shift in opinion to a pro-gold attitude is not limited just to Europe. Eleven countries, including India, Kenya, Mexico, the Phillipines, Columbia, and Malaysia have recently elected to receive gold rather than currency at the IMF auctions, and 28 other countries have submitted noncompetitive bids at future IMF auctions. Japan is beginning to turn more and more pro-gold and now has a completely free gold market. Ten major Japanese world trading companies are pushing for the establishment of an open gold market in Japan which will probably rival Hong Kong, Europe, and the United States. Other developing countries are expressing the same opinion, which means a major shift in world opinion. There is an international ground swell towards gold, in fact, an international vote of no confidence in the dollar. The atmosphere of international, economic, political and monetary crisis will not be a temporary phenomenon. This will put upward pressure on the gold price, as people over the world begin the rush to the security of fully-owned bullion or coins. For example, Iran has had an extremist, collectivist revolution. The new leaders will be militant, dogmatic, and nationalistic socialists. Redistribution of the wealth will be carried forth with religious fervor. They will be out first to get the Iranian oil millionaires in their own country and later, Iran may well go on a holy war against capitalism and wealth in other areas. Even without war, there is a danger of a spread of a radical Moslem people's republic to other Muslim countries. The vast riches of the Persian Gulf are running scared and into gold, and this has barely begun. Also, Arab oil production will shrink, resulting in oil shortages, increased oil prices, and pressure on the dollar, which will result in higher gold prices.

Jim says that if it were not for the Iranian political situation, gold would probably be closer to $200 an ounce, but the Iranian situation is an important piece of a growing worldwide disease of collectivism. He then concluded with, "As to my gold price prediction, I look for $280 to $300 this year (1979) and $375 to $400 in 1980. The big boom in gold this year could come later and I tend to think that gold is topping out now and that we will have a reaction and be able to buy at least $30 cheaper after the next several weeks or a month and a half."

While it would be naive and senseless for us not to take the necessary steps to protect ourselves against currency debasement, it is also true that if things continue on their present course, we may not have the freedom to enjoy our gold profits. Once we have taken the necessary steps to protect ourselves and our family's assets, our number one priority is to join together and fight the collectivist and bureaucratic monster which is taking control in Washington. Gold is important and gold and profits are fine, but what will we have gained, if we lose our liberty?"

JESSE CORNISH CONVENTION REPORT

(3/15/79) At our Second Annual National Convention, JESSE CORNISH answered a lot of questions. Here are the highlights.

Gold and silver provide the safest haven for capital preservation. These two precious metals have weathered every currency washout in history, and offer the only truly liquid stability in today's shaky, equity-starved money systems. Gold and silver are considered to be only commodities like pork bellies, and reporting of such purchases is not required.

Will our political leaders, after they spend the dollar into total collapse, invoke another gold seizure order as they did in 1933, and enforce it under penalty of law? Fear of confiscation has caused many people to not store gold for financial stability. This attitude fosters decisions by default. Many will sit and do nothing for fear of this remote future possibility. This is counter-productive. We don't stop living just because death is out there somewhere waiting.

History shows clearly that the confiscation of gold was not the factor that caused our financial ruin. Those who surrendered their gold were paid the going rate. Those who were wiped out already had been wiped out by the stock market, not by the surrender of gold.

No one has been fooled, nor have we lost an ounce of respect for the only monetary foundation that survives everything.

We either ride the paper money to zero, or move into hard assets that will retain value, in spite of the fact that they could some day be called in at their currency value. I strongly suggest you get into hard money now.

GOVERNMENT

BIG GOVERNMENT

(10/1/76)   How Government Hurts

How does big government chip away at business profits? (see: Business)

1. THROUGH CORPORATE TAXES. WHEN THE GOVERNMENT TAKES 52% IN TAXES, THEY BECOME A MAJORITY OWNER WITH NO INVESTMENT AND NO RISK. Corporate taxes are inflationary, because they are passed onto you, the consumer. Higher taxes depress the stock market by cutting profits.

2. BY REGULATION. I estimate that if all regulatory agencies were abolished overnight, retail prices could drop 10 to 30%, as that is what it costs industry to comply with government regulations. profits.

304

3. BY PERSONAL TAXES, WHICH DRAIN THE CONSUMER OF HIS DISCRETIONARY SPENDING MONEY—less money, less consumer buying and a smaller pool of saved capital for investment.

4. THROUGH INFLATION. A calculated policy of monetary inflation drives up prices, increasing the tax bite, as everyone moves into a higher tax bracket, while the purchaing power is actually shrinking.

The source of the problem? Socialist planners, who desire more centralized control of the economy, with the arrogant assumption that they can manage the economy better than the free marketplace. And I believe it's deliberate.

These planners dominate the colleges, the press, the unions, and the upper management levels of all the regulatory agencies. Their supporters dominate Congress.

One of their tools is lavish government spending for social purposes, encouraged, aided, and abetted by those who have the most to gain—the great multi-national banks, investment houses, and huge family fortunes—who have a government license to create money out of nothing to loan to improvident high-spending governments. These great powers want continued, controlled inflation and government spending, and they nominate those who sit in the closed sessions of those international monetary bodies who determine worldwide monetary policy. They also elect complacent public officials, and provide an eager pool of government appointees for key posts.

(1/1/78) ALEXANDER TYTLER said that democracies are on the way downhill when the majority of the people discover they can vote themselves benefits from the public treasury. When government is spending $400 billion a year, almost everybody is on some form of "welfare," and I'm not just referring to food stamps and Aid to Dependent Children. Most of us work for government, are looking forward to a government pension, work for companies that receive government contracts or benefits, or send our children to schools that are supported by Federal government grants. We depend upon government for good roads, environmental controls, clean air, a safe airline trip, protection from foreign aggressors and business competition, a minimum wage, a farm subsidy, courts, a Federal penitentiary to incarcerate our criminals, a G.I. Bill of Rights, etc., etc., and that has only scratched the surface. These increasing demands have unalterably changed the face of America and have created a mindset—a state of mind that afflicts conservatives and liberals alike.

I am not even going to go into the demands of the environ-mentalists, labor and the economic egalitarians who demand more for certain segments of society at the expense of others in order to redistribute the wealth. Every time someone says, "There ought to be a law," which restricts business or adds to the cost of government, this is all passed on to you in the form of higher prices or taxes. This galloping trend towards more government costs you in direct taxes, in inflation, and, ultimately, in freedom.

(11/1/77) My overall impression is that the European society is showing signs of great stress. Its institutions are under assault. People are looking to an increasing degree towards repressive government measures. The seeds of totalitarianism are being sown everywhere. The memory of the dangers of a Hitler or a Mussolini have faded. The Communists are gaining strength and we may begin to see the phenomenon of at least two western democracies, Italy and France, voluntarily moving into the Communist orbit.

The signs of impending government crisis are all around. There is no one sign that, by itself, makes it inevitable. It's an accumulation of small things that add up to a grim picture.

(1/1/78) The irresistable political and economic force in our lives is the runaway growth of our demands upon government to give us what we want, or think we need. It is consuming our national treasure and devouring our precious freedom!

(11/15/76) Incidentally, we're hearing a lot of rhetoric about how the American public is against big spending and government social programs and there is a pronounced conservative trend developing in the United States. Don't believe it! There is no substance to it. Everyone is in favor of cutting government spending, but the average person has searched his heart, possibly prayed about it, and con-cluded that the nation can only be saved if we cut the other guy's benefits. No one is saying, "Let it begin with me."

How many of you out there with substantial income from tax-exempt securities or other sources, are accepting a Social Security check? Now, you might well argue that you paid for it early in life, and that's partly true. But, the nation can only be save if those who are receiving benefits choose not to receive them if they don't need them. The nation is going broke. Its debt is so huge, it can never conceivably be repaid. We have to start somewhere.

I think we should all search other aspects of our lives to see what government benefits we can refuse. It may be lousy for the pocketbook, but it is sure good for the soul. Search your conscience and see whether or not there might be some constructive that you could feel good about.

GOVERNMENT DEBT

(3/15/78)   I'd like to summarize my convention talk for you.

I have in my possession a document called STATEMENT OF LIABILITIES AND OTHER FINANCIAL COMMITMENTS OF THE U.S. GOVERNMENT AS OF SEPTEMBER 30, 1976, which is generally distributed only to congressional leaders and government officials. It shows all liabilities of the U.S. government. I find it most enlightening, especially in what it does not say.

The document is 31 pages long. It takes only the first page to cover all of the gross figures included in the so-called "National Debt." It indicates that public debt represented by securities outstanding is $645.7 billion, plus accrued interest, checks and other instruments outstanding, accounts payable, etc., bringing the total to $726.2 billion. This is the only figure that is generally quoted as "the National Debt." Well, if that's the case, what the heck is in the other 30 pages?

Just for openers, there is $190.6 billion in government guarantees insuring private lenders against losses. The total insurance commitments, including banks, savings and loans, FHA, student loans, etc., is $1.6 TRILLION!!

There is a fascinating footnote at the bottom of that page listing the insurance commitments: "In several instances, incomplete data have been submitted by certain agencies since their accounting systems have not yet been developed to the point where they are able to provide the required information. In other instances the data furnised were on the basis of estimates by the reporting agencies." And you can bet your sweet life that these figures are understated by at least $200 billion.

Moving on a few pages, we find that over $146 billion of public debt securities (that means government bonds, notes, bills, etc.), are held by the government itself. The total held by the public is $488 billion. Remember, when a government agency holds government bonds, it is the same as if you wrote an IOU to yourself. It's a washout, even though they do pay interest to their own agencies. Look at the so-called Social Security "Trust Fund." There is no trust fund. There are government bonds in place of the money that the government collected and spent each year. All Social Security collections are spent in the year in which they are collected. They are not put aside for you. The Treasury merely gives Social Security an IOU—a promise to create money, if necessary.

Starting on page 13, we pick up six pages of government loan and credit guarantees, including some things I have never heard of, such as the Housing Guaranty Fund, Foreign Military Sales Funds, Overseas Private Investment Corporation, the Farmers Home Administration, Agricultural Credit Insurance Fund, etc. Some of the numbers are pretty big. For example, the Rural Electrification Administration has guaranteed $4 billion worth of credit; the Maritime Administration, through their Federal Ship Financing Fund, insures almost $5 billion; the Rural Housing Insurance Fund is $11 billion; the low rent public housing program guarantees $13 billion; the FHA guarantees over $93 billion and the Veterans Administration, over $32 billion! The total contingency of these government loan and credit guarantees is $190 billion.

Now we look at insurance commitments, such as the Overseas Private Investment Corporation, the Federal Crop Insurance Corporation and a whole raft of others. This total is $1.6 trillion. That's TRILLION!! The FDIC, which insures your bank deposits, insures $587 billion worth of deposits and it has $6.6 billion with which to pay off, but that's not money. It only has government IOUs: the government's promise to print money. That's why I've said over and over again that, if you have a series of problems with big banks, the government will have to print money well in excess of the actual amount of alleged "money" that is set aside. If we have a general banking crisis, the government will be forced to print hundreds of billions of dollars, and that flood of money is what will trigger our runaway inflation.

The Federal Savings and Loan Insurance Corporation (FSLIC) insures $316 billion in deposits, and there's $4 billion with which to insure it. The Social Security total deficiency, on an actuarial basis, is over $4 TRILLION (on page 22 of the report). Now, interestingly enough, the net admitted actuarial liability of all these annuity programs was not totaled. (I wonder why? I had to do it myself.) It came to $4.6 TRILLION.

Dick Russell is right when he says that there is no unencumbered capital in America. The mountain of debt, public and private, including the Federal debt, is much greater than the total amount of wealth in America. These pyramids of debt always come down, and I remain firm in my conviction that we are very close to a massive debt liquidation, but we will probably liquidate it through the inflation process, as the Germans did in 1923.

After I presented this at the convention, I reaffirmed that the most likely scenario would include the prospect of an economic downturn, creating problems that could only be solved with massive amounts of Federal money. I am not expecting the government merely to try to stimulate. I expect that it will be forced to pour masive amounts of money into saving the cities, the banks, and the savings and loan associations, and that these ten, and perhaps hundreds of billions of dollars of printing press money would trigger this massive inflationary spiral.

Incidentally, I noted that our new FED Chairman, G. WILLIAM MILLER, has sworn to defend us against inflation. Fighting inflation is stupid. It's like looking at a cholera victim and vowing to fight fever. Inflation is a symptom, not a cause.

(5/1/77)   The Debt Wolf

The mountain of debt, Federal, private, and municipal, is so monstrous that it can never be repaid. It's equal to roughly twice the value of everything that everybody owns. It creates the illusion of prosperity. If you made $25,000 a year and spent $40,000, you could continue to do so only until someone refused to loan you the difference. In the meantime, if your neighbors tried to guess how much money you made, based on your spending patterns, they might guess you make $40,000 a year. However, your prosperity is an illusion and it disappears as soon as your credit limits are reached.

The only difference between you and the Federal government is that it can postpone settlement by printing money. This debases the value of every dollar in existence, and eventually the system collapses through the inflationary process, and the pile of wreckage is higher.

The pile of government debt is so high that it will topple of its own weight. There's roughly $800 billion in acknowledged Federal debt drawing interest at the rate of approximately 40 to 50 billion dollars per year. There are additional inconspicuous government obligations on which the government pays no interest, but are just as real. This adds many hundreds of billions of dollars to the pile. Then there are trillions of dollars in unfunded obligations for military pensions, Social Security, and other funds. The total Federal obligation that must be paid within your lifetime, over and above income, is over six and one-half trillion dollars!

This means that someday there will be no Social Security, no government pensions, your government bonds will not be redeemed, this nation will founder upon the shoals of debt, its credit will be destroyed, and there will be an international monetary collapse. There is no other way.

Check that! There is a way. The government may repay it in grossly inflated currency and you may end up with pennies on the dollar.

(6/15/78) Here's why I am pessimistic about any real reduction in government spending. *HUMAN EVENTS* published in a recent issue that, according to a study done by the North American Newspaper Alliance, more than half the people in the United States are being supported wholly or in a great part by tax dollars.

There are 218 million people in the United States, and using very conservative estimates as well as government figures, here's the way it adds up:

Retirees and Pensioners (Including Dependents)	35,300,000
Disabled and Direct Support (Including Dependents)	10,500,000
Public Assistance and Unemployed	26,073,000
Government Workers and Dependents	47,251,000
Active Armed Forces Personnel and Dependents	5,137,000
Total	124,261,000

At least 56% of the population is directly dependent upon tax dollars in one form or another for a great part of their income. This does not include those who benefit from government contracts, including consultants, government contractors (Lockheed, etc.) and all their employees, nor those who receive food stamps, Medicare and Medicaid, nor does it include those whose livelihoods are based on government aid programs such as physicians for whom Medicare reimbursements are the primary source of income. Of that 124 million people benefiting from government, government workers are only approximately 15 million, or about 12%. If you fired half of the government workers, you would still have half of the population dependent upon government support. By allowing ourselves collectively to become this dependent on public funds, we have created a situation where withdrawal would create genuine human tragedies on a grand scale.

Here are Ruff's Basic Principles:

1. The "Tax Revolt" stands a very good chance of merely being a rearrangement of the deck chairs on the Titanic unless we are willing to accept some hard decisions, make some real sacrifices and suffer some severe social pain.

2. If the lessons of history tell us anything, they tell us that no

society once engaged in this inflationary spending process has ever had the guts to undergo the pain necessary to reverse it. And no "soft landing" from inflation is possible.

3. The inflationary scenario will play itself out and there is no adequate reversal this side of national bankruptcy and a new start.

(9/15/78) One of the persistent little questions wandering around the fringes of my mind since the winter of 1973 is: Why have we not taken stronger action to force the OPEC nations to reduce their oil prices? Why have we continued to take it on the chin? We have the greatest military and political power in the world. We have economic weapons that could be used against the Arabian peninsula monarchs that are far more powerful than the oil weapon they use against us. As you know from reading *THE RUFF TIMES*, I also believe that we could break the oil cartel. Why haven't we done it?

Why did Carter come up with an energy/tax scheme which will increase our dependency on foreign oil, not decrease it?

We know that the Soviets vigorously urged the oil boycott of 1973, and the Arabs responded, and yet we are cozying up to the Saudi Arabians, selling them jet aircraft and proclaiming them as our friends. After what they've done to us, it's all insane!

This government has been running monstrous deficits to fund the vote-buying Federal programs that have been launched through a smoke screen of conservative rhetoric by the Nixon, Ford and Carter Administrations. Where does the money come from when the government has to float these monstrous new debt issues to pay for it? They borrow it, or they print it. It is estimated that in the decade ending in 1977, the Federal government took half a trillion dollars in borrowing out of the capital markets, consisting of appoximately $260 billion in cumulative deficits and about $225 billion of net borrowing for other "off budget" programs, such as over a hundred Federal credit programs in housing, agriculture, students, veterans, trade, and the like. There isn't enough capital in domestic capital markets to accommodate that kind of borrowing, but if we can covertly drain enough money out of the economy through sky-high oil prices, send it overseas, and have it reinvested in U.S. Treasury securities by foreign governments, we just might make ends meet. Sounds paranoid, doesn't it? But look at this!

Foreign holdings of Federal debt now amount to approximately $123 billion—more than 20% of the total U.S. funded debt. Most of our balance-of-payments deficit is being recycled into the U.S. capital markets, and Uncle Sam gets by far the biggest chunk. The largest creditors are West Germany and Japan who own $26 billion and $18.6 billion, respectively, of U.S. notes and bonds, but investments by the Middle East oil countries are now about $13.5 billion and have been increasing rapidly of late. We've paid interest of over five billion dollars last year to those foreign creditors. And those countries account for most of our balance-of-payments deficit. How ironic! Thirty years ago, Japan and Germany were prostrate enemies, and the only Arab we knew was The Red Shadow in "Desert Song." Now we're in hock to them for $58 billion!!

In other words, rather than taxing us directly to pay for Federal spending, the government has simply allowed this incredible sum of money to be siphoned off in the form of balance-of-payment deficits to the oil countries, the Germans and the Japanese. They send it home to Uncle Feelgood to use, and he pays them for the privilege. Carter can blame the Arabs, and yet this strange hands-off-we're-afraid-of-those-little-guys policy continues. If this is part of a plan, then the whole thing has a sort of insane logic—an inner consistency.

I just read back over what I've written and . . . Naw, of course that couldn't be right. Or could it. . . ? Jimmy said he'd never lie to us.

FEDERAL LIABILITIES

(5/15/76) I have obtained a copy of the little-known United States Government's "Statement of Liabilities," which the Treasury is required to publish every two years. Approximately 100 copies are distributed to Congress. It is not generally released. According to this statement, the government's true liabilites are over $5 trillion! This, of course, is a figure so impossibly large that it transcends many times over the total value of all of the assets in America.

THREAT TO FREE ENTERPRISE

(2/1/79)
Q. What do you see as the greatest single threat to the free enterprise system?
A. Government. Here are the Twentieth Century's three greatest lies in ascending order of immensity: (l) My wife doesn't understand me, (2) my check is in the mail, and (3) I'm from the government and I'm here to help you!

My views are consistent with those of our Founding Fathers, who realized that government was a singularly dangerous entity that had to be chained with the Constitution. Those chains, however, are proving inadequate because, like Gulliver, government is flexing its muscles and breaking its bonds.

Government with its "Robin Hood mentality" has destroyed the basic underpinnings of the capitalist economy. The only trouble is that it includes the great middle class among the "rich" from whom it will steal. There's an old saying that "He who robs Peter to pay Paul will always have the vote of Paul" and Peter is grossly outnumbered and outvoted by Paul. The debauching of the currency is the greatest single threat to the stability of the free enterprise system.

Government also is strangling free enterprise with regulation. A recent report by Sanford Goodkin, one of the nation's most respected real estate consultants, indicates that approximately 20 percent of the cost of a new home is due to the costs of government regulation. In California, you can almost double that figure.

Regulation distorts the decisions of businesses which often are forced to relinquish a perfectly intelligent, well-conceived business plan because it runs afoul of some government regulation. The costs of regulating are in the hundreds of billions of dollars a year and passed on in the cost of everything you buy. Businesses fail because of government regulation. Drugs that could save lives are not developed because of government regulation. Business efficiencies that could be passed on in the form of lower prices are aborted because of government regulation. Racial hatred is fomented and institutionalized by government regulation.

I love my country but I fear my government. Whenever I make that statement in front of an audience and ask how many agree with it, there's hardly a hand in the room that isn't raised.

In a democratic Republic such as ours, government is supposed to be an extension of the will of the people, but now it has taken on a life of its own. Whenever elected government, as personified by your city council, your state legislature, or the senate, is still responsive to the will of the people as it percives it, it has adopted the "Robin Hood Syndrome." The majority of people in this country have perceived themselves as "Paul," not "Peter," and they think Peter is rich.

Regulatory government, however, is responsive to no one. It violates the principle of separation of Executive. Legislative, and

Judicial powers, in that it can conceive a regulation, sneak it through the Federal Register, then act as judge, jury, and executioner on these new rules. The accused have little or no recourse, as the courts have generally upheld the regulatory power of agencies launched by Congress.

When all is said and done, this government is the archenemy of free enterprise, and free enterprise is the goose that has been laying golden eggs. When you kill the goose that lays the golden eggs, you can only feast on goose for a little while. Then you have neither eggs nor goose. Not only is free enterprise at stake, free anything is at stake.

The only silver lining in that cloud is the general economic collapse that we face may provide the necessary impetus for the dismantling of most government regulatory bodies. I'm convinced the undoubted good which they accomplish is outweighed several times over by the costs incurred and the evils which they do. Some great philosopher (I don't remember which one) once said, "If I knew that a man was coming to my house with the express purpose of doing me good, I would lock all my doors and arm myself against him."

We live in a free marketplace of ideas and we must keep it that way. We must not abdicate our responsibilities to some government agency.

GUNS

(Special Report #4, 10/76)

Q. Should I become proficient in the use of guns?

A. That's something I'm going to leave to your individual conscience. I, myself, do not choose to become gun oriented, although I'm a darn good shot. In the first place, if I were being swarmed over by a mob, the guns wouldn't help. They would only assure that I was killed. Second, the thought of taking a human life is abhorrent to me. I probably would, if my family member's lives were immediately threatened, and I do have a couple of guns around the house. If you decide to have a gun, I suggest you find the nearest gun club and become extremely proficient in the use of guns. The best policy would be to place yourself in a position where such a thing is not likely to happen by the simple expedient of seeing that many of your neighbors are converted to the concept of having their own emergency food storage and survival program. Not only are they no threat, but they are available to assist, if trouble should arise. This is one of those examples where we benefit by sharing. (see: Safety & Survival Preparations, Personal Survival).

H

HATCH, SENATOR ORRIN

(2/1/78)   Hatch on the Canal

I just visited with a very dear friend of mine, W. CLEON SKOUSEN, in Provo, Utah. He is founder of the FREEMEN INSTITUTE, which is dedicated to teaching the principles of the Constitution in a series of remarkable seminars conducted in many cities around the country. Cleon had a tape made featuring SENATORS HATCH, ALLEN and LAXALT, CONGRESSMEN MURPHY and CRANE, and ADMIRAL MOORER, all of whom are in opposition to the Panama Canal Treaty. I learned things that have not been hitting the newspapers and have decided to take my stand against the ratification of the treaty. (see: Panama Canal)

(3/1/78) SENATOR ORRIN HATCH, who closed our 1978 National Convention, was impressive. He discussed four major topics of legislative interest with which the U.S. Senate will grapple during this session. Each topic will have a lasting impact on the future safety of the nation.

In the discussion of the Panama Canal Treaty, he pointed out that the major constitutional question at stake was: "The Administration and the State Department, in their efforts to win ratification as quickly as possible, have ignored the unmistakable provision in our Constitution which states that the disposal of U.S. property must be approved by both houses of Congress. Treaty proponents are trying to confine the debate to the Senate in an effort to avoid involving the House of Representatives in the questions of disposition of property and appropriations required by the treaties. The Administration and State Department have also withheld from the Senate the implementing of legislation promised last October, which contains the substance of the proposed treaties."

He discussed at length the economic impact of the treaty, what it will cost the taxpayers, and what will happen to the cost of goods which must travel through the Canal, or take a more expensive overland route. We are not granting the Canal to the Panamanian people, but to Torrijos, a Marxist dictator. It is likely that, if ever a constitutional representative government were to be established in Panama, they would not feel bound by the commitments of this dictator who did not come to office by constitutional means, and who might not be around very much longer. If the treaties do not pass, he probably will be overthrown. If the treaty is approved by the senate, he might have bought himself a few years.

Senator Hatch had also attended the recent secret session of the Senate regarding th drug dealings of the Torrijos family, and as he is bound by Senate Rule 400, he did not disclose what was said. However, he did indicate in a press conference, after his speech, that if the American people knew only part of what was brought before that session, they would be furious at the Panama Canal giveaway.

Orrin Hatch is probably the most effective, conservative freshman Senator in decades. He is brilliant and charismatic and is a hard-nosed politician in the best sense of the word. I have known this man personally since college days and I believe he is destined for great things. He may even be a serious contender for the Republican nomination for the Presidency some day, although I have not heard that from him. I just think he is that talented.

(3/1/79)   At our 2nd Annual RUFF TIMES National Convention in Anaheim, Senator Orrin Hatch of Utah was, as he was last year, a most impressive speaker. He is a hard-nosed political "gut fighter" with principles, an unusual combination. He has been a member of the "new right" minority in Congress that has been forced into an essentially negative position in order to stop the onrushing liberal express train. He has a genuine zest for the battle and his speech was a pretty accurate description of that battle.

He indicated how just one or two votes made the difference in several major fights, including the Panama Canal dispute. He encouraged everyone to become involved in the political process, because just one Congressional vote could make the difference in a major issue. He felt the last election showed substantial progress for the free market end of the political spectrum in both parties. He expressed support for a Congressional initiative towards a Constitutional limitation on government spending, although he felt we needed both a limitation on spending and a Constitutional requirement for a balanced budget. He felt that the movement toward a Constitutional Convention was necessary to jolt Congress into taking effective action, as the fear of such a convention is considerable on all sides of the political spectrum. He felt that there is a new tide moving in America. He recounted a meeting with GEORGE MEANY at a party. He always thought George Meany was eight feet tall and weighed 300 lbs., but he found him to be short, and barrel-chested. He walked up to him and said, "Mr. Meany, I'm Orrin Hatch." To which Mr. Meany grumped, "I know who you are." Then followed what Senator Hatch termed "a delightful chat," after which Mr. Meany announced that they were going to raise $4 million to defeat him in Utah, mostly because of Hatch's leadership role in fighting the recent "labor reform bill" and his open advocacy of the open shop.

All in all, it was a most impressive speech by a man of great drive and charisma.

In response to a question about the Liberty Amendment, he indicated that he found the idea more than intriguing, supported it in principle, but that the economic assumptions needed to be more thoroughly tested.

HELMS, SENATOR JESSE

(3/1/78) Keynote Address—1978 RUFF TIMES National Convention

Senator Helms gave a powerful address. He spoke of Winston Churchill as he stood in the House of Commons prior to World War II, when the liberty of all mankind was at stake! His words rang down the corridors of history when he said, "If you will not fight for the right when you can easily win without bloodshed, you may have to fight when there is no chance of victory, because it is better to perish than to live as slaves."

One of Mr. Churchill's colleagues sneered: 'The gentleman is a nut.' Well, maybe so. On the other hand, a mighty oak is nothing more than a nut that stood its ground.

Senator Helms continued, "We are at the crossroads in terms of what may be America's very survival, and sometimes I confess that I wonder whether we have reached the point at which there is no chance of survival.

"But hope springs eternal. America was born of men and women yearning to be free, and who were willing to fight to be free, and who were willing to sacrifice to be free. An as long as there are enough

Americans willing to face up to the truth, and to place their faith in God, there will be hope.

"Benjamin Frankin touched on it a long time ago when he commented that a God that lets no sparrow fall without His notice is highly unlikely to have been an idle spectator as a new nation was born in His name and with His grace."

Senator Helms went on to discuss the problems of excessive Federal regulation, pointing out that no fewer than 75 Federal agencies, departments, and advisory groups issued more than 10,000 pages of new regulations—all of them in small print!

He discussed the basic dishonesty of inflation and how it insidiously eliminates honest business dealings. "No longer do we hear the term 'honest dollar,' because the dollar is no longer honest." He referred to the effects of inflation on business pending, pointing out that the present economic recovery today contains less than half the volume of long-range capital expenditures of similar recoveries in the past. Business is just not putting money into the economy. Indeed, it is surprising that we have any economic growth at all.

"... It is believed that George Washington was killed by his physicians who continued to bleed him to the point of death in an effort to draw out what they considered to be 'polluted blood.' Today, the political witch doctors in Washington are attempting to drive out the evil humors in our economy by draining its blood."

He next discussed the value of gold as an economic discipline factor. When money had to be redeemed in gold, there was a limitation on the amount that could be issued, but when the dollar was cast free from the metal, no longer were politicians contrained by any economic realities as to the amount of currency they could create, and so they had the license to spend and buy votes. This is why Senator Helms worked for the gold clause contract which will enable us to bring some gold discipline into our own business dealings.

And then the Senator dropped his blockbuster when he said, "I can announce tonight that a bank has asked the Federal Reserve Board for authorization to begin offering credit and accepting deposits IN FOREIGN CURRENCIES. In other words, if the Federal Reserve Board goes along—and I believe it is obliged to go along by Public Law No. 95147—then you will soon be able to make deposits, borrow money and start savings accounts denominated by a currency of your choosing, one that you believe to be a better store of value than dollars. I am glad that I can announce, here in California, that the institution making this request is the largest bank in the United States, the Bank of America. I have written to Dr. Arthur Burns, who is still

Chairman of the Federal Reserve Board, to encourage approval of this request. I believe that if this application is approved that other banks in our nation will follow, depending on the demand. The immediate danger is that regulatory agencies will attempt to thwart this new freedom. They may be successful; but I pledge to you that they will have a fight from this Senator."

Basically, what this means is that you can vote on the dollar by choosing to make deposits, or conduct your affairs in other currencies using an American bank without having to go to Switzerland or the Bahamas. If enough Americans did this, this could be the discipline factor that the dollar needs to begin reversing some of the trends. It is a truly remarkable concept. The Senator believes that it is legal and that you soon can choose to pay your rent in Yen, or receive your rent in Swiss francs. He cautioned, "I do not contend that any other currencies are inflation-proof, or that I would advocate denominating business deals in other currencies. What is important is that the alternative is now there. If people utilize such an 'economic vote' and get out of dollars, and into another currency, they are not only serving notice on Washington to give them a money worthy of the name, but also, I believe, they are going to make it harder for the inflationists to continue to confiscate the resources of Americans by way of manipulation based on Keynesianism."

I am grateful that Senator Helms chose our Convention to make such an important announcement and it did hit the local press. Not until Monday, February 27, did THE NEW YORK TIMES report on this important development.

He ended by giving a gripping description of a lengthy visit with Alexander Solzhenitsyn shortly after he came to this country, where Senator Helms was urged by this great man to fight with all he had to resist the spirit of collectivism in this country and the pressures of imperialistic communism. There was not a heart in the room that was not touched. A truly remarkable performance from a truly remarkable man. Senator Helms has been effective and his principles have been consistent in his defense of the free marketplace.

HOMOSEXUALITY

(1/15/77)   Give Me That Ol' Time Religion

Recently, headlines in the newspapers across the United States proclaimed that a lesbian had just been ordained an Episcopal priest. Considerable controversy has been raging since then.

The Episcopal Church is a venerable and respectable institution and its prominence and impact is such that it sets a great deal of the moral tone in this and other English-speaking countries. This action by one of its bishops has immense implications.

I've been concerned about the impact of things heretofore considered "sin" that are now gaining acceptance in so-called "respectable" institutions upon my children. Lesbianism, and other forms of homosexuality or sexual deviation, are not, and cannot be considered simply an "alternate lifestyle." These actions are condemned by Scripture as offenses againt God, and in the opinion of many leading psychologists, represent outward indications of troubled personalities. Many people in their teens or even in their childhood, reach a point at which their sexual orientation can be determined by the influences and examples around them. Now, that particular parish will present before its congregation every Sunday, a woman who is an acknowledged sexual deviate. We are encouraged to look up to, admire, and respect our ministers and priests. Subconsciously, when a parent tries to tell his children that this is a form of psychological aberration or, if you please, "sin," that child has, staring him in the face, evidence that his most respected institution, the Church, thinks otherwise.

I cannot believe that this is good for children or for the Church. We should not put people on pedestals whose orientation or behavior is deviate or undesirable, and that is precisely what has been done in this instance.

It is my hope that such a venerable organization, the Episcopal Church, will reject the decision of this Bishop, and that this lesbian woman will not be placed on a pedestal for all to admire, but will be dealt with as she should—as a woman with deep and serious problems—to be loved, helped, and perhaps pitied for her wretched state. There is no room in this world to hate her, but surely we do not have to hold her up as a shining light, representing God in the lives of her parishoners.

(7/1/77) Miami Revisted

Now, let's consider Anita Bryant's crusade against homosexuality. This raises another interesting question. Does society have a right to enforce its traditional morality as a protective measure to save itself, if that enforcement interferes with the human right to sin?

I'm a believer in free agency. I happen to believe that there are Eternal laws of Divine origin, but I also believe that one of those

Eternal laws is man's freedom of choice. He has the right to do wrong as long as it does not bring overt harm to another. To attempt to control human behavior by law in areas of personal morals raises grave questions, while at the same time, to permit the flaunting of aberrant behavior, giving it social respectability, raises equally grave questions. I feel threatened no matter what the outcome. If Anita's crusade succeeds in bringing legal sanctions against homosexuals and preventing them from teaching in my schools, I feel safer in one respect; however, being a member of a religious group that was once considered a threat by traditional religion, and persecuted by it, I think I know what it's like to be on the receiving end of such moralistic fervor. If you put a sword in the hand of government to use against your enemy, when the enemy is vanquished, government never puts down the sword but goes looking for new enemies, and there is always a possibility it may be used against you.

That's why the anti-homosexuality crusade is profoundly disturbing to me and why I've refrained from giving you an off-the-cuff opinion, but I guess it's time to take a position.

My distaste for homosexuality is three-fold. First, I am a strongly sexed heterosexual and the whole idea of intimate sexual contact with another male is stomach-wrenching. Second, I believe it is a serious sin condemned by God and is symptomatic of a sick society. And third, I belive it is destructive to family life. There are gay activists who are even promoting the far-out idea of homosexuality as a solution to the population explosion. And I guess it is a solution of sorts. Don't just laugh that off. The whole idea of "Gay Liberation" was unthinkable just a very few years ago. These far-out ideas tend to creep up on us and become socially acceptable, and eventually the norm.

Homosexuality is an assault on the family institution!

Homosexual relationships are ephemeral and unstable. Regardless of the few sad attempts at homosexual marriage, there is no homosexual equivalent of a stable social unit, with occasional rare exceptions.

Now, about Anita's crusade. Some of the things she says are so right and other things she says are so wrong. Much of the fuss is over whether or not homosexuality is just another choice, an alternate life-style. Strangely enough, Anita and the gays tend to agree on this issue. Gays would like homosexuality to be recognized as just another alternative life style or choice of sexual orientation, to be condoned and accepted by society. Anita says that gays choose to be homosexual, and they can repent and become heterosexual at will.

I happen to think they are both wrong. I believe homosexuality is a symptom of a deeper disorder, even though authorities are divided on this point. Just as rape is not a crime of sex, but a crime of violence, homosexuality is not just an expression of sexual orientation. Male homosexuality is generally an expression of supressed hostility towards women. We don't know exactly what causes it, and we don't know at which point in life the sexual orientation is determined. We have no idea whether a teacher can influence a young person who would not otherwise be so inclined to become a homosexual. There is some evidence to indicate that at some point in a young life, the sexual orientation is hanging in the balance, and a role model can determine which way it will go.

Circumstances can induce homosexual behavior. I submit as evidence, homosexual practices in our prisons. Many prisoners who are otherwise heterosexual will engage in homosexual relationships while inside the walls, and then return to normal heterosexual behavior when they leave. Homosexuality was rampant among otherwise heterosexual sailors during the years of the great multi-year voyages of exploration by Magellan, Sir Francis Drake and others. Some men and women are bisexual, allegedly moving easily between relationships with men or women.

In my opinion, Anita's most valid point is that we cannot allow homosexuals to become role models for our children. Next to parents themselves, the most influential person in a child's life is his teacher. Most homosexual teachers would never overtly seduce or molest a child, anymore than any heterosexual teacher would overtly molest a child of the opposite sex, or attempt to recruit them into some kind of sexual behavior. I'm convinced that such instances would be rare and represent no real threat, but the role model argument is persuasive. If a person is a known homosexual he is going to, consciously or unconsciously, whenever the issue arises, represent homosexuality as merely another perfectly acceptable alternate life style. At some critical point in a person's sexual orientation, he may look back upon an intelligent, likeable, persuasive, homosexual teacher and conclude that there's nothing wrong with it, and adopt this life style. I believe that the homosexual life style leads to a tortured, miserable life, but above all, it is a threat to the family unit and thus strikes at the very roots of society.

I believe that we must block the efforts of any group that would have us go beyond compassionate tolerance, to provide acceptability and vindication, so that they might feel better about themselves. That's a step I cannot take. Once we are hiring admitted homosexual teachers in the classroom we will quickly move to approving, and that's a long step from tolerating. For example, the public school system in San Francisco, which took the forefront two years ago by banning discrimination against homosexual teachers, is now revising its sex education curriculum to include the study of the homosexual life style.

The school superintendent, Robert Alioto, said he did not see "any substantive changes, just an adjustment to reflect San Francisco's social composition and family life styles." San Francisco's 680,000 population includes an estimated 100,000 homosexuals. The purpose of these curriculum changes was "to eliminate stereotypes and name calling in the schools." Basically, what it adds up to is that children will be taught that homosexuality is nothing to be feared and is an acceptable alternative. I would pull my children out of any such school system. I would move, give up my profession, do anything necessary to escape such a thing.

So, we have a classic example of rights in conflict: my right to not have my children presented with persuasive role models that I feel strike at the very foundations of human happiness and society are opposed to the homosexual's right to find a productive niche in society. I vote for my children.

Don't get caught up in the "hate the homo" movement. These people are human beings with serious problems, and I think we should carefully distinguish between limiting their influence upon our children, and their civil rights in other areas. Again, remember that two-edged sword.

The best protection against your child becoming a homosexual is a strong family and an adequate role model in the home. If there is a strong and loving relationship between the husband and wife, including such things as loyalty, fidelity, courtesy and respect, any child, whose sexual orientation is in doubt, will be favorably influenced by the model which is attractive and persuasive.

If you wish to join Anita's cause, use your influence to keep this explosive issue under control. Don't ever vote for punitive or discriminatory provisions that would actively persecute these people.

Don't fall into the trap of believing that you can legislate human morals by law. I respect the right of the "sinner" to "sin" as long as he doesn't victimize others. I also believe that people should not be allowed to openly and flagrantly entice others to sin. For that reason, I oppose the legalization of prostitution, and I'm opposed to garishly seductive advertising for pornographic movies in my daily paper. But if people want hard porn, I don't see any way we can pass laws against it without raising all kinds of "freedom of expression" issues that might be used against *THE RUFF TIMES* some day.

What all this adds up to is that while I am prepared to be compassionate and to accept the right of a homosexual to practice his brand of sex with another consenting adult behind closed doors, and I am perfectly prepared to let him have any job for which he is qualified, where he does not represent a role model for my children, I cannot agree with the aggressive efforts of the more militant gays who insist that I accept their life as merely another life style. That, I cannot, and will not do, and they would do well to rein in some of their more strident members.

If we do not teach our children that sex is reserved for heterosexual marriage, we are going to reap the harvest of unstable, confused children and relationships that shift like the sands on the bottom of the ocean, leaving children the bewildered, twisted victims.

We can have laws to protect children from premature exposure to sexually exciting stimuli, but I don't see any way we can regulate adult human behavior by law. All we can do is create oases of sexual stability in our homes and churches. If we don't, the next unstable generation will bleed us dry in welfare costs, crime, drug addiction, alcoholism, violence, psychiatric problems and other ills. If we sow the wind, we will reap the whirlwind.

The legitimate struggle between conflicting rights is an ongoing process. The right of the homosexual to a job comes in conflict with my right as a father to determine who my children's teachers will be. The threshing out of these rights is a healthy process in our society. Let's hope the process continues, but let's also be prepared to weep for a society that collectively makes the wrong decisions. No moral authority can be exercised over a society that is not granted voluntarily by its citizens, regardless of laws. (see: Family, Sin-Tax, and Values & Morals)

(1/15/79)   God And Gayness

I recently did an interview with FATHER WILLIAM BARCUS, an Episcopal priest from San Francisco, who recently announced, at a public meeting, that he was a homosexual. Whenever I do this kind of interview (such as Margo St. James), I get protests relating to two different points. First, there are those who feel that this isn't of any use to them in making financial decisions, so I shouldn't waste my time on it. Others feel that somehow I'm glorifying their position by giving them exposure on TV. I'd like you to understand why I do it.

Think of your financial world as a house, and the nation's social and political climate is the land on which it sits. The best built house on swamp land is in trouble. The sexual revolution and the "coming-out-of-the-closet" of all kinds of sexual behavior is producing disorienting social change at a rate with which society cannot cope, and is immensely destabilizing. This principle is called "future shock," and one of the most vivid manifestations of the cutting edge of this change is the homosexual drive for acceptance of their aberration as respectable. These people who take these intellectually perverse positions to justify their own behavior are having a field day on talk shows where their views are virtually unopposed, as it is chic to be "tolerant." William Barcus is a particularly sincere and eloquent spokesman for the homosexual point of view. And, by the very cloth he wears, is telling the world that there's nothing wrong with perverse behavior, because if there were, God certainly would not approve of his being one of His ministers.

When I tackle a situation like this, I'm dealing with the very fabric of society which is the background against which financial decisions must be made. I've discussed this in "Sin Tax," Chapter 11 of my book, and have touched on it in past *RUFF TIMES*, and I will continue to do so. If you refuse to care about the quality of the land on which your house is sitting, you will be like those Los Angeles residents who built on hillsides that turn into slides and avalanches when enough rain falls.

The drive for respectability of aberrant sexual behavior is one of the most dangerous trends of our time. Although we can sympathize with some of these tortured souls who find themselves captured by compulsive behavior they don't even understand themselves, we should not accept their drive to have such behavior regarded as respectable. I refuse to recognize it as merely another alternative life style, approved by God Himself. That is detestable and I just wanted to make sure that at least this one lonely talk show host's voice is heard in confrontation with these people.

HOW TO PROSPER DURING THE COMING BAD YEARS

(9/1/78) Terry Jeffers, my capable right hand man and the President of Target, Inc., went to New York with some manuscripts to see if we could work out a joint venture with a major publisher. He took it to six of the biggest publishers, and within a week the offers began to pour in. I had commitments from four publishers promising large advances to not only publish the book in January, but to make it their number one book of the season by pouring all of their advertising resources into it. They all felt we had a best seller.

Fascinatingly enough, the most enthusiastic company was NEW YORK TIMES BOOKS, with whom we made contact through a chance acquaintance who sat down next to Terry in the airplane on his way to New York. You could have knocked me over with a feather when I met with the President of TIMES BOOKS, Tom Lipscomb, and Arnold Zohn, who is one of the chief executives of the parent NEW YORK TIMES CORPORATION, and found out that they not only wanted to publish my book, but they personally thought what I had to say was right.

I can't think of any publication in the world whose editorial policies are more at odds with everything I believe than *THE NEW YORK TIMES*. Not being the least bit shy, I said so. The answer was, "Editorial policy for *THE NEW YORK TIMES* is made by an Editorial Board. We have nothing to do with that. We are capitalists and we think we can make a great deal of money with your book. It's going to be a big best seller, and besides, we still think you're right."

Nothing gives me more satisfaction than the irony of knowing that their money is being used to spread my message. Times Books is truly apolitical when it comes to money. And it is the world's most powerful communications network.

As I look at the possibilities of a book that could sell millions of copies with the resources of the world's most powerful communications system behind it, and all of the implications that has for increasing our influence and the growth of our newsletter, it has had a humbling effect on me.

Maybe if we had had 200,000 subscribers and five million book readers, we would have been able to apply enough pressure in the right places to have stopped the Panama Canal Treaty vote, or maybe we could tip the balance in a close election by rallying the vote, or marshaling a flood of telegrams and publicity.

In any event, I feel that I am on the verge of fulfilling a dream I've had since I was a child—to move the world a little bit in the right direction and make it a better place.

(7/1/78)   In my forthcoming book, much of the material that had been previously published in *THE RUFF TIMES*, has been reorganized and updated. Some of the material is new, especially the last section which deals with how to aggressively take advantage of conditions to make money.

The basic principles are about the same as you have been reading up to now, because the fundamentals do not change, but I have given you some additional guidelines for identifying basic turns in the investment environment, and I've come up with a much more coherent strategy for utilizing the principles I've given you. I've also tried to make it as persuasive as possible so that you can share it with friends and change their views. And I've kept it simple.

I

INFLATION / DEFLATION

INTRODUCTION

(10/1/76)   Inflation, or deflation? Gold up, or down?

What we really want to know is: what will life be like in our near future?

Either deflation or renewed inflation will lead to depression, and you had better prepare for it.

Out of all the mass of charts, arguments, philosophy, and opinions experts heap upon us, one thing is clear. The world is headed for trouble. If not sooner, then later.

It is also apparent that most people are not emotionally equipped to try to outguess short-term swings in the gold, silver or stock markets.

Most of you had ridden gold from $100 or $150, all the way up to $196 and all the way back down to $107. This wasn't survival gold. You were looking for profits. I suggest that you not try to guess again. Gold can defy charts and fundamentals, if the powers that fix the prices determine that it shall.

(2/15/78)   I am sick to death of the stupid, dishonest cynicism with which our "public servants" pretend that nothing can go wrong. Perhaps they have even persuaded themselves, or maybe they are just too dumb to understand, but they are stealing the wealth of America through their monetary excesses. I'd like you to hear what ARTHUR BURNS had to say, speaking before the National Press Club in Washington, D.C., as reported by UPI.

> Summing up his views on twenty-five years of advising Presidents, economist Arthur Burns says Americans understand why inflation is dangerous but may lack the will to fight it.
>
> In his last speech as Chairman of the Federal Reserve Board,

331

Burns raised memories of Germany in the 1920s, when a barrel of currency couldn't buy a loaf of bread, to underscore his concern. Burns, 73, has advised every President since Dwight D. Eisenhower brought him here in 1953. He will end eight years a Chairman of the Federal Reserve as soon as the Senate confirms businessman G. WILLIAM MILLER as his successor.

"Someday," Burns said, at a luncheon speech to the National Press Club Monday, "Americans will take inflation as seriously as I do and get on energetically with the job of fighting it."

"I only hope this will come through a growth of understanding, not from a demonstration that inflation is the mortal enemy of economic progress and our political freedom," he said.

Asked why post-war Germany has had more success than the United States in combating inflation, Burns said it was because Germany underwent a torment he hoped America will never have to experience. "The German people experienced catastrophic inflation during world War I and its aftermath," he said. "By the middle of 1923, all the outstanding German currencies could hardly buy what was available on one shelf in a grocery store. Money had become worthless. The Germans experienced another catastrophic inflation during Mr. Hitler's war. The Germans are allergic to inflation. They understand what it can do to a people, and it has affected very significantly the financial policy in that country."

(see: German Inflation)

Those are wise words, but I can't resist interjecting that they are only words, as Mr. Burns has been one of the architects of our inflationary policy, despite the fact that he has developed an unwarranted reputation for being the enemy of inflation. He has been the chairman of the engine of inflation, the Federal Reserve Board. Now, obviously, Mr. Burns doesn't want runaway inflation, he wants controlled inflation, because he is as Keynesian as John Kenneth Galbraith, in that he feels that a little dose of inflation is good for America and will make us feel good.

His speeches against inflation are really against runaway inflation. That's not hard. Even Jimmy Carter is against that. But he wants that nice, comfortable, controlled inflation that enables government to pay off its long-term securities at some future time with money worth a fraction of what it is today. Even inflation at just seven percent means that the principal of that government bond, in ten years, will be worth only 25% as much as it is today in purchasing power. Mr. Burns has never been against Federal deficits, only Federal deficits over a size that he considered manageable. Why? Because Mr. Burns is a creature of the banking system and the banking system's surest, safest source of income is the purchase of government securities on the Federal, state and municipal levels. There would be no such securities if all governments spent within their means and, as a result, our entire system is based on the assumption that there will be deficits and constant new issues of these securities to provide safe, sure profits for our banks.

So while I can cheer Mr. Burns' words, I must admit that I won't shed much of a tear when he leaves, although I might dampen my hanky just a little bit, because I believe that his successor, Mr. Miller, is going to be even more accommodating in allowing the engine of inflation to be unleashed than was Mr. Burns. After all, the man was a Kennedy and Lyndon Johnson Democrat, and a large contributor to the Democratic Party over many years. That party is not exactly a bastion of fiscal responsibility.

But what the heck, it doesn't really matter anyway. The Federal Reserve is going to provide the money that is required to meet all of our government spending plans one way or another. You will provide part of it and the Federal Reserve will provide most of the rest of it through its money creation powers. Can you imagine the Federal Reserve saying "No" when the government needs $60 billion to pick up the deficit? Of course not. So the process will go on and on until it comes down of its own weight, as it always has throughout all ages of recorded history, and as it will no doubt do in future generations. The only thing that makes this different is that this is the one you and I are going to be living through.

(Special Report #2, 12/75) INFLATION IS OUT OF CONTROL. On Monday, December 12, 1975, Federal Reserve Board Chairman, Arthur Burns, said at the University of Akron:

> The persistence of inflation in the face of eight or nine percent unemployment indicates something is basically wrong with the American economy.
>
> If an unemployment rate of eight or nine percent is insufficient to bring inflation to a halt, then our economic system is no longer working as we once supposed.

He said that unemployment, which usually suppresses demand and thus cools inflation, is running at 8.3%, yet prices at the consumer level remain 7.6% ahead of a year ago.

I have said publicly, before dozens of audiences, that the root cause of inflation is expansion of the money supply to fund the programs we have voted into existence.

Harold Hitchings Burbank, while teaching a graduate course in public finance at Harvard forty years ago, said: "The ultimate fiscal resource of the United States of America is the power of the Federal government to tax."

But sooner or later, the power of government to tax comes up against the unwillingness of politicians to vote for unpopular taxes. I believe we are close to that practical limit now.

Gabriel Hauge, in an editorial in NEWSWEEK, December 15, 1975, said, and I agree with him: "The ultimate fiscal resource of the country is the Federal power, not to tax, BUT TO BORROW."

Here is why inflation has already destroyed one of the bases of free enterprise. For an investment to bring a reasonably modest return, you need at least 15 to 20%:

10–15%	for anticipated inflation loss
3%	for true return on capital
2%	for Federal and state taxes
15 to 20%	

(3/1/76) Inflation is the enemy. Monetary creation and government deficits coupled with the freedom of the dollar from gold backing, are at the root of all of our problems. High inflation rates always eventually result in depression. This leads to lower tax revenues and larger deficits. Government deficits lead to printing more money. Printing more money leads to inflation.

(7/15/76) The printing press is accelerating at a horrifying rate; it turns the world upside down, as it converts the most conservative investments (savings accounts, bonds, mortgages) into losers.

Federal deficits will not disappear. The Fed won't go away. Fiscal stimulus is a basic political fact of life.

Asking the government for accurate data on inflation is like asking the Mafia for accurate statistics on crime.

(1/1/77) On numerous occasions, I've used the analogy of addiction to describe this country's dependence on inflation and government spending. The more I think about it, the more fitting the analogy seems.

The heroin addict eventually reaches a point in his life where the margin between the amount of dope necessary to take away his pains and make him feel good, and the amount that will give him an overdose (O.D.) and kill him, is very thin.

Stimulation of the economy by the injection of money and government spending produces the same effect that an injection does to the addict. It makes us feel better for awhile, but the habit worsens and the consequences of withdrawal become greater and greater. The more you take, the more you need.

Perhaps a recent statement by British Prime Minister James Callaghan on September 28, makes the point better than I could!

> We used to think you could just spend your way out of a recession and increase employment by cutting taxes and boosting government spending. I tell you, in all candor, that that option no longer exists, and that, in so far as it ever did exist, it only worked by injecting bigger doses of inflation into the economy followed by higher levels of unemployment as the next step. That is the history of the past 20 years.

We have not reached the point in America where such an injection will not work. It will have the desired temporary effect, but the next time the economy sags and the activists decide that we have to stimulate it, it will require a far greater injection.

HARRY BROWNE, in a recent issue of *INFLATION SURVIVAL LETTER*, says that the Federal Reserve isn't keeping up with the monetary inflation rates required to cover up the mistakes of the last fifteen years. The mini-boom that will be created will be insufficient to really solve the problem, as we've reached the point where the stimulus needed is too massive. I don't agree with him. It will probably work one more time.

I believe fiscal stimulus is desirable, not for long-range help for the nation, but to buy us time and give more people a chance to prepare.

I believe this era of our national cycle is terminally ill. Fortunately, however, we are not talking about the death of a nation, but only of an era. I do believe, as I've said many times before, that we will recover, though the next downturn will be severe.

(11/1/77) We are going to get tight money with high interest rates, and rising price inflation at the same time. Most economists have felt that these were mutually exclusive.

High interest rates in an era of large Federal deficits can only result in pouring gasoline on the fires of inflation. Here's how it works.

Increases in the money supply are inflationary. They are caused by Federal deficits which can be funded only by an increase in the monetary aggregates (M-l, M-2, etc.). When large deficits continue, tightening up the money supply to reduce inflation doesn't accomplish anything except to raise interest rates. The increases in the money supply, which have been close to 10% over the last year, and the increased cost of borrowing, which is passed on to consumers in the form of higher prices, are eventually going to work themselves into retail prices, which will be compounded by "inflationary expectations," as business raises prices in anticipation of more inflation.

If we cut spending, balanced the budget, and tightened up the money supply, you would have a depression, but it would not be inflationary, and we would stand a good chance of surviving with our institutions intact, as we did in the '30s. But our monetary system and economic structure cannot survive a runaway inflation.

The future is clear. Inflation and high interest rates, of which we had a small dress rehearsal in 1974, are in our immediate future and we had better plan our lives accordingly. Get out of bank certificates of deposit, long-term bank accounts, insurance cash value, annuities; in short, any paper that is not tied to gold. Get into art, stamps, rare coins, bullionized gold and silver coins, diamonds, food, spare parts, and rural or small town real estate. Almost anything tangible that will increase in price as inflation picks up will be good. Keep no more in your checking account than is necessary for the orderly conduct of your affairs.

Inflation can be good or bad for you, depending on which side of the counter you are standing. If you already own something, inflation increases its value, and you benefit. If you have yet to buy it, inflation means you are going to pay more, the longer you wait.

UNCLE SAM KNOWS WHAT CAUSES INFLATION, OR DOES HE?

(4/15/77) Our government has finally discovered (no doubt at great cost), that the FEDERAL RESERVE SYSTEM may be responsible for the nation's inflation.

The following article recently appeared on the newswires:

> WASHINGTON (AP)—Swift expansion of the money supply causes inflation and ultimately a decline in the country's production, a new study by a House Banking Subcommittee contends.
>
> Representative Stephen L. Neal (D.-N.C.) Chairman of the

Subcommitee on Domestic Monetary Policy, said sharp increases in the money supply are more harmful in its inflationary effect than budget deficits.

What an incredible discovery. If they had read *FAMINE AND SURVIVAL IN AMERICA* in 1974 they could have found out the same thing for $4.95.

Go back up and look at that last sentence, that "sharp increases in the money supply are more harmful in its inflationary effect than budget deficits."

Don't those fools know that increases in the money supply are caused by budget deficits? That's like saying "fish hooks are more dangerous to fish than fishing rods." It's all part of the same process. Without a spendthrift Congress and a populace demanding ever-increasing benefits, there would be no need for increases in the money supply.

All this "learned" subcommittee has done is to throw the entire blame on the Federal Reserve. The Federal Reserve is only one of their partners in crime. It is this kind of economic ignorance that appalls and frightens me. These are the guys who are determining the course of future monetary policy.

I have commissioned several articles on the causes of inflation by Gary North for the specific purpose of helping you to understand the inflationary process. If you will take the time to puzzle it out, you'll see why the process is irreversable. (See his articles elsewhere in this section.)

(5/15/77) You must understand that inflation is *NOT* an increase in the Consumer Price Index. Higher prices are a response to inflation. They are not inflation itself. Inflation is an expansion of the money supply at a faster rate than the increase in goods and services. This eventually reflects itself in the Consumer Price Index.

A LESSON FROM ROME

(8/1/77) Lionel Casson, writing in *HORIZON*, uncovered a little piece of history that should send a chill up and down your spine. "Hurry and spend all the currency you have. Buy me goods of any kind at whatever price you find them. . . ." These were the words of a wealthy Roman writing to his business agent—A.D.300.

The value of money was dropping relentlessly and he wanted possessions, not cash, for the Roman Empire had been hit violently by inflation. To quote the Emperor Diocletian, there were "increases in prices, not only year by year, month by month, and day by day, but almost hour by hour and minute by minute."

Rome solved its inflation by controlling not merely prices but the entire lives of most of its subjects, locking them forever into fixed places in the socio-economic order. Rome solved it, in short, by transforming itself into a totalitarian state, as rigid and all-pervasive as any the world has known. And the Roman's advice is still good.

QUESTIONS AND ANSWERS

(6/15/77)

Q. What are the results of inflation, as you see it?

A. The inflationary process results in economic and political upheaval and the destruction of paper value. Paper, as a means of exchange, has been a great convenience. We exchange greenbacks, checks, government securities, stocks, bonds and mortgages because in our minds they have value. If we begin to question the optimism and economic upturn we are now enjoying, nobody asks those question. But let the economy turn down as it did in '73 and '74 and people begin bailing out of paper values trying to find some way to beat inflation. They don't want their money in banks because the return is too low compared to the rate at which their money is deteriorating. So they start buying things. Rare coins, antiques, old cars, stamps, in fact, any collector's item that might become rare begins to soar in value and everybody is looking for an "inflation hedge."

The inflationary spiral eventually prices things out of the reach of the average person.

Q. You say that inflation will destroy the monetary system. Argentina and Chile have suffered much worse inflation and they haven't disintegrated. Why can't we survive?

A. They are small fish in a big pond. We loan them money to keep them from collapsing. But many personal fortunes have been destroyed, and the middle class is being wiped out, and improvident nations have either gone Communist, or are ruled by military dictatorships. Freedom is always the victim in an inflationary spiral. These countries are just further down the road than we are.

Everyone says we're running ten years behind England. I think we're only two or three years behind them. The only reason England hasn't collapsed is because the IMF and the U.S. have bailed them out with loans. Who's going to bail us out? When the dominant economy gets in this kind of trouble no one can help them.

Q. Why did you appoint yourself the "Paul Revere" to warn everybody that the "British disease" is coming? Couldn't you start a panic?

A. Those who have taken steps to protect themselves will be pockets of stability in this country. In fact, I think my message is anti-panic. The people who take my advice won't be frightened when bad times come. They won't be out looking for scarce goods in a time of shortage. If several million people in this country took my advice, I think we would all be better off.

Q. Why do all the other economists disagree?

A. The economists have generally been wrong about the last two or three downturns. At the beginning of 1973 and 1974 they were all determinedly optimistic, and of course, they were dead wrong. We went through the longest, deepest recession since the 1930s. Harry Truman once said that if you lined up all the economists end to end, they would still point in the wrong direction. Most economists have been enthusiastic advocates of Keynesian theory and they're not about to predict dire consequences for Keynesian policy.

THE INFLATION MACHINE

By Gary North, Ph.D

(7/15/77) There is enormous confusion about how the government creates money, and this confusion is exceded only by the apathy among the rest of the population. And those who do really care really do not understand. The government prefers it this way.

There are three equally important factors in the process of creating money, which are the fuel for inflation in any modern economy: (1) the government's budget deficit; (2) the fractional reserve commercial banking system; and (3) the nation's central bank. They work as a unit to create fiat money. They do not totally control the money supply, but there is no question that the initiative, in anything short of mass inflation or mass depression, lies with the government.

First, consider the deficit. Governments generally spend more money than they collect directly in tax revenues. The difference between income expenditures can be covered only by borrowing, and the Treasury Department can borrow from government trust funds (such as Social Security), private citizens or corporations (such as insurance companies), of the Federal Reserve System, our nation's central bank. If the government is worried about driving up short-term interest rates borrowing directly from the public, and if government trust funds are not buying Treasury debt (as in the case these days), then the Treasury prefers to sell to the Federal Reserve System, since the "Fed" can create, out of nothing, the funds used to buy the debt. Initially, this prevents short-term interest rates from rising. In the long run, however, the fiat money drives up all prices, including the "price of money," namely, interest rates, especially long-term (five years or more) interest rates.

Second, consider the commercial banking system, which is a fractional reserve system. This means that when you deposit $100 into your checking account, the bank has the right and (usually) the power to loan up to $85 to someone else who needs the money and is willing to pay interest to get it. About $15 is sent to the Federal Reserve Bank to serve as a reserve which will cover the possibility that you will come in and take out your money in cash. The bank creates an additional $85 in fiat money when it credits an $85 deposit to the checking account of the borrower.

Then the borrower spends the $85, and the seller gets a check for $85. The seller now deposits the $85 in his bank. His bank now can set aside 15% or $12.75, holding the reserve in cash or sending it to the regional Federal Reserve Bank. The remainder of the money, $72.25, can be loaned out to still another borrower, who spends it, continuing the process. If the reserve requirement is 15%, the original $100 deposit can create a theoretical maximum of additional new money (checking accounts only) of $566. In practice, the amount is less, since there are "leaks" in the system, but in general, for every $100 of original new deposits, about $300 of new money (checking account plus currency) is created through the entire banking system. This obviously, is monetary inflation. It leads directly to price inflation.

Third, there is the central bank—the Federal Reserve Bank. Many of its critics believe that it is a private bank. It is not a private bank. It is a semi-independent arm of the government. (50% of the stock is owned by Uncle Sam—Ed.) If both houses of Congress and the President are agreed that the "Fed" should follow a particular monetary policy, the "Fed" will do what it is told. However, if there is no strong agreement among the politicians, then officials within the "Fed" can achieve some degree of independence. Its policies have generally been more conservative and less inflationary than the policies advocated by the Congressional and Executive critics of the "Fed."

Very few of the "Fed's" critics criticize it for what it is: a governmental agency whose primary function is to deceive the public about the source of monetary and price inflation.

How do original deposits (that first $100 check) get created? The answer is quite simple: the "Fed" initiates the process when it buys government debt obligations.

The decision to buy or sell government securities is made by the Federal Open Market Committee (FOMC), made up of 12 members. The seven members of the Board of Governors of the "Fed" have permanent seats. The other five seats are held by presidents of the 12 district Federal Reserve Banks who serve rotating one-year terms. One seat, however, is always held by the president of the New York Federal Reserve Bank, who at present is Paul Volcker, an outspoken opponent of gold and the gold standard. The committee directs the Manager of the System Open Market Account, who operates out of the New York "Fed," to implement the broad policy by either buying or selling government debt from the "Fed's" account. If the "Fed" is a net buyer of government debt (which it usually is), the money supply expands.

The "Fed" buys or sells securities every weekday morning from about two dozen specialized, multi-billion-dollar firms, such as Salomon Brothers or the Morgan Guaranty Trust. The units of purchase are $1 million. The competition among these firms is sharp. The spread between buying and selling prices is often in the area of $75 per $1 million. The big money is made by predicting interest rates, not in transaction fees.

If the "Fed" decides to be a net purchaser (inflator) of securities one morning, it writes a check to the selling firms, which immediately deposit the checks in their bank accounts. The process of monetary inflation has begun, and it will not end until a 300 percent expansion of new money (M-1, or currency in circulation plus checking accounts) has been created by the fractional reserve commercial banking system. The process can take several weeks. This process is sometimes called the monetization of debt, and every modern, industrial, Western nation uses it. So do the banana republics.

If the "Fed" buys its secuities from the Treasury directly, then the Treasury spends the money into circulation. The effect is the same. These checks get deposited by the recipients (aerospace firms, welfare clients, or whoever), and the commercial banking system multiplies them. This is the modern engine of inflation.

The system is complex. It is designed to be complex. Printed fiat money is too easy to understand. The present system is just right politically. It allows the government to impose the inflation tax without risk of voter backlash—until a collapse arrives.

The Federal Reserve System should be abolished, because it is a government bank. It makes the inflation tax too easy to impose. The goal of "Fed" managers is power. They enjoy manipulating the economy by their control over money. Conservative critics fail to grasp this simple fact. The problem with the "Fed" is all of the fiat money it is creating, and all of the confusion which the present arrangement creates in the midst of those few people who try to investigate the process.

(Two reasonably clear introductions to the process are published by a pair of regional Federal Reserve Banks, sent free of charge to anyone who requests copies: Modern Money Mechanic, Federal Reserve Bank of Chicago, Research Dept., P. O. Box 834, Chicago, IL 60690; Open Market Operations, published by the Federal Reserve Bank of New York, 33 Liberty St., New York City, New York 10045.)

SUPPLY AND NO DEMAND

(9/1/77)   Two separate articles in the August 12 *WALL STREET JOURNAL* clicked into place in my sometimes unorthodox head.

The commodities section reported that we will have near record wheat and corn crops. Now, I'm not sure how we pulled off this miracle. The weather was against it. The wheat crop was barely saved on more than one occasion with fortuitous rain. The corn crop is still somewhat in doubt but it looks like it will be pretty big, despite terrible subsoil moisture conditions and a complete failure of the usual weather patterns.

Also, Argentina, Australia, Canada and the Soviet Union seem to have big crops.

In the face of this market-depressing surplus, the government has informed us that "Because of the huge surplus carryover, food inflation will be held to only (think about that word ONLY) 6 percent."

I also note that the United States is faced with a huge glut of petroleum. In fact, the government claims we have enough in this country to last us through 1979.

One question: What has happened to the law of supply and demand? In a normal, unmanipulated world you would see a collapse of food and petroleum prices.

I can only conclude one of two things: Somebody is lying to us about the supply, or something is shorting out the signals of the marketplace.

Commodities still fluctuate, but on the retail price level I don't think you will see general price deflation until you've seen an explosive inflation and a collapse of the economy. The law of supply and demand is not dead (I hope). It has merely been suspended or distorted, but something is terribly wrong and the free market may no longer be the self-adjusting instrument that it used to be. When the inflation rate drops, that doesn't mean that prices are dropping. It merely means they aren't rising quite as fast.

There are two reasons why businesses probably won't cut prices when demand slacks off.

1. Government mandated minimum wage scales, and union wage scales have made it almost impossible for a businessman to reduce prices without losing money. Labor is the principal cost factor in any product or service today. Even if demand for a product dropped sharply, you will only occasionally find someone willing to sell at a loss, and they are generally in a state of liquidation. In fact, when sales volume drops, prices will tend to rise, in order to maintain overall profits. The power of unions, and the reinforcing power of government in maintaining high wages is a distorting factor of gigantic proportions. High wages don't cause inflation, however. They make it irreversible by providing an expense floor.

2. Taxes make inflation permanent. If businessmen only paid taxes on profits, such taxes would not be an inflationary factor in a time of economic contraction, but there are inventory taxes, and payroll taxes, property taxes, and regulatory reporting costs that are really taxes. These are artificial, inelastic expenses related to government that, if not paid, will bring down the wrath of an unfeeling, uncaring and usually mindless government enforcement mechanism.

The businessman cannot respond to reduced demand by lowering prices.

Price inflation is also self-perpetuating. It has a life of its own. When further inflation is expected, a business is afraid to cut prices, as they fear the imposition of price controls, freezing prices at money-losing levels. In fact, they might raise prices in anticipation of controls.

This is a brief and somewhat oversimplified description of the problem, but the sum of it is, don't expect a slow down of the economy to produce much in the way of price deflation. Inflation will increase, not diminish, as government will attempt to stop the coming economic decline by increased government spending. That will be highly inflationary, regardless of a slowdown in demand. Plan your life accordingly.

INFLATION WITH RECESSION?

(1/15/78) Tom Holt is an astute and generally correct economic observer. He said there is no way that you could have inflation and depression at the same time—that it was not possible. There I part company with Mr. Holt. We had inflation and recession at the same time in 1974. End of argument! The signals indicate that more of the same is ahead, but I would like to give you a little more detail on our scenario.

It is possible that, as a result of the monetary crisis and deepening recession abroad, we will see what appears to be the forces of deflation taking hold. Real estate prices will start down. It's possible that a frightened labor movement may moderate their price demands, and slack demand for some products, such as steel, will cause some price discounting, as automobile sales and production continue to slow. Government, however, seeing this, will panic, because business recession is the last thing the Carter Administration is going to allow to happen. So we will "stimulate" the economy by vast increases in government spending and an increase in the deficit. The government, to accomplish this, will buy up huge quantities of Eurodollars. These are dollars created by foreign banking institutions, totally beyond the control of our Federal Reserve System. Whenever you read that the Federal Reserve is controlling the money supply, that's only the domestic money supply. Dollars are created abroad by foreign banks, just as they are here, totally outside our control. There are $350 billion Eurodollars in circulation. That's more value than the combined currencies of Germany and Britain. When we soak up those dollars to support the dollar, and bring them home, they will be available for our Treasury to "spend us out of recession." After a few months of apparent deflation, it is likely that this will produce a galloping inflation without ending the recession, because that money spent into circulation by the government will merely result in the purchase of accumulated inventories, and there's a big time lag before actual production is cranked up again and unemployment begins to drop.

To make it real simple, you will probably see a business slowdown, tremendous government spending programs to pick us up, and a spurt in inflation. Some segments of our economy will appear to have a feverish kind of prosperity while the fundamental rot of growing unemployment and inflation-ravaged savings and assets, and rising interest rates, will create an "invisible collapse." This process could continue for six months, a year, possibly even two years, before it precipitates the abrupt collapse which will result in a genuine deflationary depression. That will not happen, however, until we have gone through a period of hyper-inflation.

This is not a lead-pipe cinch because I'm attempting to outguess government, but it is the most likely scenario. THERE IS NO CHANCE OF A STABLE ECONOMIC CLIMATE OVER THE NEXT TWO YEARS. In the meantime, you can bet that there will be an accelerated redistribution of wealth. All of our problem-solving efforts will incorporate the ROBIN HOOD concept of taking from the rich and giving to the poor, simply because, as Lincoln said, God made more of them—and they vote.

A WORD FROM *BUSINESS WEEK*

(6/1/78)

> ...Solving inflation will take a long period of government self-restraint, a reduction of expectations by everyone, and a determination by elected officials not to buy votes with government spending. (Fat chance!!—HJR)

When I say things like that, I'm labeled a dangerous crackpot, but good old *BUSINESS WEEK* will be taken seriously. "Anyone who is not at least mildly panicked about the inflation outlook for the U.S. does not reocognize the seriousness of the situation."

It goes on to comment that April wholesale prices gave us the biggest one-month gain since November 1974, prompting the President's Council of Economic Advisers to raise its January inflation forecast and, friends, they aren't even close. Watch that forecast rise month by month.

A few more comments from the article:

> The planned deficit in the high employment Federal budget has only been matched in 1968 and 1972—both years preceded sharp spurts in the inflation rate—and in 1975 when the economy was in deep recession. The same is true of the rate of money supply growth that has prevailed over the last year. The Carter Administration is talking anti-inflation while running gigantic budget deficits. The new Federal Reserve Chairman, G. William Miller, is talking monetary restraint but he has inherited a swollen money supply from his predecessor, Arthur E. Burns, who proved more effective at inveighing against inflation than in actually fighting it.

And how is this for vintage *RUFF TIMES*:

> . . .policies that would push down the underlying inflation rate
> will cause a level of pain that the political system cannot tolerate.
> Although Carter has pledged to stop any governmental actions that
> contribute to inflation, Bosworth, (Carter's inflation czar) warns: 'I
> don't think the government yet realizes the implications of saying
> we're going to do the hard things and say no.'

Unwillingness to endure pain is our government's single most
pervasive guiding principle today. We will do anything to avoid it,
even at the risk of increasing our addiction. After all, it's politically
impossible to do otherwise. Note that:

> Eisenhower's conservative economics kept the inflation rate
> through his Administration to an average of 1.4% a year. But the
> political cost was high. The Republican Party lost control of both
> houses of Congress in 1954 and has never won them back.

Fighting inflation causes pain but inflation is worse. The Peruvian
government is fighting rioters because of 42% price inflation.
BUSINESS WEEK says:

> Ten years of inflation have created a private-sector wage-price
> spiral that has assumed a life of its own. If the government
> attempted to hold down demand, prices would continue to rise, and
> the result would be a sharp drop in output and a sharp rise in
> unemployment. The country would be in a deep recession long
> before wages and prices could begin to adjust.
> ". . . Experience of recent years has also given many businesses a
> vested interest in continued inflation. When investment is planned
> and debts incurred on the basis of expectations that inflation will
> continue, a check to rising prices would cause acute financial
> embarrassment and might precipitate a sharp slump. An infla-
> tionary economy is in the situation of a man holding a tiger by the
> tail.

On top of that, many corporations, because of the weak stock
market caused by inflation, are forced to raise more and more debt
capital which makes them vulnerable to a credit crunch resulting from
sustained tightening by the Fed.

Within the main article, there is a box entitled, "HOW INFLA-
TION THREATENS THE FABRIC OF U.S. SOCIETY." How do
you like these quotes? Sound familiar?

> "What you are really confronted with is a rate of inflation that
> exceeds your return if it is invested with any caution. What makes

it all the worse is that we had a fairly well-organized financial society for a very long time, and now it has disappeared." (Economist FABIAN LINDEN of the Conference Board)

I've been saying that the financial world has turned upside down and that there are no more "widows and orphans stocks." How about this one: "We're beyond a panic situation. Americans have a marvelous ability to adapt, but there is the feeling of no one having credibility and of no one able to make an impact." (From CADDELL of CAMBRIDGE Surveys)

GARDNER ACKLEY, Professor of Economics at the University of Michigan and at one time the chief economic advisor to President Lyndon B. Johnson, says, "Tensions between labor and management, between government and the people, and eventually among social and economic classes become overwhelming and these tensions "are thus destructive of the social and political fabric. A significant real cost of inflation is what it does to morale, to social coherence, and to people's attitudes toward each other."

ARTHUR OKUN, in commenting about inflation's threat to the nation's social cohesion says, "This society is built on both implicit and explicit contracts, ways of doing economic things economically. They are linked to the idea that the dollar means something. If you cannot depend on the value of the dollar, the system is undermined. People will constantly feel they've been fooled and cheated." (They have!—HJR) "Now the economic outlook is clouded, inflation is no longer waning, and this country could be heading into the worst period of economic and social dislocation since the Civil War."

Even big labor has recognized the dangers in the inflation system. Jackie Presser, Cleveland-based Vice-President of the TEAMSTERS said, "We have done the best job of anybody going to the bargaining table. Whether this country can afford the job we are doing, that's another question." In all fairness, I must say that both big labor and big business, as they raise prices and wages, are only responding rationally to the terrible inflationary environment created by government.

So what do we face? Runaway inflation, price controls, shortages, black markets, and eventually—depression. Get your gold and silver coins, your diamonds, your small town real estate, and especially your food storage. If you don't, you will miss an opportunity that comes but once in a lifetime.

347

HOWARD RUFF

INFLATE OR DIE

(7/1/78) Government must inflate or die. Government will panic in the next recession. Never underestimate the ability of government to inflate. Deflation means unemployment and pain, and we are not to be allowed to suffer that through inaction. It is highly likely that we will switch from a credit economy to a printing press economy, as government will be forced to go to the printing press to meet the cash requirements of the people and the government. The deflation scenario assumes that government would not be willing to produce the cash demanded. Most investment advisors don't understand money, and none of them understands politics, because it is the political factor that will determine whether or not we will inflate.

Here's a possible scenario that might help you to understand.

The basic structural inflation rate rises to 10 percent to 15 percent, and at the same time, we find ourselves in an economic downturn, just like 1974. Government, caught between whether to fight inflation or unemployment, decides to fight unemployment. The inflation rate picks up. When it reaches 20 percent to 30 percent, merchants, manufacturers, wholesalers, etc., who all extend 30-day credit to their customers, decide that their inflation losses from allowing 30-day net credit accounts in a 30 percent inflationary spiral (2½ percent a month) are unacceptable, so they (1) begin to demand cash up front, or (2) raise their prices to compensate, or (3) charge high interest rates on what used to be net accounts. The demand for cash forces the government to heat up the printing presses. The flood of money forces up the wholesale and consumer price indices still further. The interest charges are passed on in prices to the next level of the distribution chain and begin to compound throughout the economy, resulting in accelerating price increases. Government then institutes price controls, and you know the rest. From this, a runaway printing press economy is only around the corner.

INFLATION "FIGHTERS"

(6/1/78) I recently discussed how inflationary it would be if very many of those $400 billion Eurodollars decided to come back to the United States. Eurodollars have helped fuel the recent rally in the stock market. It's a kind of inflation—more dollars chasing a fixed amount of goods (stocks). It's the first wave of dollars coming home (and that phase is almost over), and you will soon see CONSUMER PRICES bid up, just as stocks were bid up explosively. The Fed had been trying to keep the money supply under control and all of a sudden it jumped to an annual rate of 14%. That's also Eurodollars coming home. As interest rates continue to rise (which they will), more dollars will come home causing only a brief strengthening of the dollar. It is fundamentally weak, because the dominant bearish fundamental for the dollar and the stock market over the long haul is inflation, and you ain't seen nothing yet.

So what does this mean to you? It means:

1. Don't own any fixed return dollar-denominated paper. Government bonds, municipal bonds, certificates of deposit, cash value life insurance are all losers.

2. It means "batten down the hatches" for inflation. If you are considering a loan commitment, get it. Stock up on inventory. If you are considering small town real estate, do it now. Interest rates will soar. Inflation is prowling.

If you don't believe me, the May 22 issue of *BUSINESS WEEK* contained a special report called, THE GREAT GOVERNMENT INFLATION MACHINE. I'll give you the highlights here. It begins by saying that:

> Inflation in the U.S. is again at a dangerously high level—with wholesale and consumer prices both rising at double-digit rates and with prices of some goods and services advancing at close to triple-digit rate. Inflation has reached the point where it is destroying the nation's efforts to achieve solid economic growth, is wrecking the financial markets, and is blasting the retirement hopes of everyone over 65 years of age.
>
> One symptom of the current disease is that big business and big labor are raising prices and wages in an effort to stay whole. But the real villain is the Federal government, which has been running huge deficits for years. What makes government's inflation engine so dangerous is that many of the measures Washington is taking to alleviate the painful impact of price increases on one segment or the other of the economy only make the inflation more virulent. Thus, to ease the pinch on people at the bottom of the income scale, the Carter Administration has increased the minimum wage, guaranteeing another burst of inflation. To offset the higher costs of fertilizer and farm machinery to agriculture, the Administration has boosted farm supports, shoving food prices up sharply. And to help out pensioners who see their retirement pay shrinking away, Congress has raised mandatory corporate and individual contri-

349

butions to Social Security, adding another percentage point or so to the rate of inflation.

(9/1/78) At a Cabinet-level meeting with Carter last March 16, all of the members of the Cabinet agreed that something had to be done to hold down inflation, but that was followed by nearly all those department heads resisting cuts in their own program. Secretary of the Treasury BLUMENTHAL is opposed to any roll back in Social Security taxes for fear it would unravel the Administration's income tax reform package he had labored so hard to construct. Each Cabinet member made his own project an exception in his campaign against inflation. The process is politically out of control. It is not going to be reversed. If you think it is, you are living in a fool's paradise. Hyperinflation will rule and it's a lot closer than you think.

INFLATION DEPRESSION VS. DEFLATION DEPRESSION

(12/15/78) I am somewhat sympathetic to President Carter, in that his "Save-The-Dollar-Plan" may have been the only choice open to him. I'm really mad at those people who put us in the position where we are so vulnerable that we are eventually forced to take such desperate actions. Mr. Carter is no better or worse than those who preceded him. They have all been anti-gold, pro-paper money, pro-"controlled inflation" (which is a contadiction in terms). We are in the grip of forces that were set in motion 30 years ago and we are merely playing out the inevitable scenario. It would be stupid to blame it all on Carter, although I am sure that for the next 50 years, the coming depression will be called the Carter Depression.

Another concept may help you to understand the principle of an "inflationary depression." Perhaps you can grasp this concept a little better by understanding that an inflationary depression and deflationary depression are very much the same in one important respect. In a deflationary depression, people lose purchasing power becaue they have lost jobs. They don't have much money so they can't buy much. In an inflationary depression, people lose purchasing power because prices have soared to the point where they can't afford things. Both positions are relatively the same. They both represent loss of purchasing power. The history of inflation shows that prices rise faster than incomes can be indexed to catch up with it, and you are always lagging behind.

FROM A TO Z

INFLATION—A TRANSFER AGENT

(5/15/79)   Do you want to use inflation to transfer your wealth to your kids, with no estate or gift taxes? Buy a piece of income-producing rental property—an apartment house, an office building, etc. Sell the land under the building at fair market price to a trust which has been set up for the benefit of your children, probably with you as trustee. Sell it on a long-term note, interest only (6%), due in twenty years. You now hold a depreciating asset—the note. The trust owns an appreciating asset—the land. No gift tax has to be paid. You now take the full depreciation on the building. In the meantime, you lease the land from the trust, the lease payments go into the trust for your kids. The payments are tax deductible. Doesn't that blow your mind? You avoid the gift tax and the children are the beneficiaries of inflation, while the note you are holding eventually becomes worth nothing.

(6/1/79)   Inflation Can Transfer Family Wealth—Tax Free
By Hans Sennholz, Ph.D

DR. HANS SENNHOLZ has one of the most stimulating minds I've ever encountered. He is a rare combination of an academic economist and a successful entrepreneur, having accumulated a zillion dollars worth of real estate investments. He also has a unique ability to find the unorthodox answer to the orthodox question, as you will see from the following article.

For a long time, I've had rattling around in my brain the question of how to transfer wealth from one generation to the next. I'd like to be able to control my holdings, while having my business and other assets transferred either to my children, the university of my choice, or whatever, without having it confiscated by Uncle Sam's IRS. In the words of Philip Fry, I want to "disinherit the IRS." This article resulted from a chat Hans and I had on this subject while flying from Kona to Honolulu after the recent Hawaii conference.

Dr. Hans Sennholz is the Chairman of the Economic Department of Grove City College in Pennsylvania. He is a prolific writer, a man of immense wit and brilliant insight. (HJR)

Inflation is the cleverest wealth-transfer scheme ever devised. You can use it as the most effective tool of intentional wealth transfer from one individual to another. You can use it deliberately to transfer family wealth from one generation to the next, and to protect this wealth from confiscatory taxation.

351

Inflation is sometimes properly described as a tax on the holders of money. In reality, for most people it is a terrible instrument for the redistribution of wealth. Government undoubtedly is inflation's greatest profiteer as tax revenues are boosted by the built-in progression of income and death duties, and government debt is depreciated. Inflation also shifts wealth from those classes of society who are unable, or do not know how, to defend themselves from monetary depreciation, to those people who understand inflation. It benefits some entrepreneurs while it hurts most working people and professionals. It decimates the middle class of investors who own securites or hold claims to life insurance and pension payments.

As a parent, you probably would like to leave your earthly possessions to your children. You may want your children to continue the family business, to own the family homestead, or just enjoy the fruits of family achievements. But the welfare society covets and, through its tax collectors, may seize the lion's share of your famiy income and wealth. If you know the causes and consequences of inflation, you can easily thwart this immoral seizure by using inflation as your transfer agent.

Inflation, you may recall, transfers income and wealth from the creditors to the debts. The U.S. Treasury is now selling debt instruments that are scheduled to fall due in the year 2008. At a 10% annual inflation rate, it will make final payments in dollars that will be worth less than a 1979 penny.

YOU CAN DO THE SAME WITH YOUR FAMILY FINANCES. You need not make taxable gifts, nor leave an estate which would be taxed at devastating rates. You simply sell your assets to your chilDen at today's market prices in exchange for long-term debt instruments (I.O.U.). That is to say, you can become a family creditor and make your children the debtors. Inflation now will shift your wealth, unmolested by income taxes, capital gains taxes, gift taxes or estate taxes, to your children. In a few years of double-digit inflation they will own free and clear all the property you sold.

Just as the government issues its depreciating bonds, so may your child give you a 20-year mortgage as security against his debt. Inflation gnaws indiscriminately at both bond and mortgage, and thereby enriches the debtor (the kids) at the expense of the creditor (you). But while the bond issue is designed to deceive the buyer and its depreciation is consuming productive capital, the mortgage given by children to parents is done deliberately to serve the noble purpose of family wealth transfer and capital preservation.

The Plan

You sell a house, farm or business to your son for $100,000. He gives you an interest-bearing note, secured by a mortgage, payable in a lump sum 10 years from the date of sale. Double-digit inflation will shrink the balloon mortgage to a negligible amount, and even depreciate your income tax on any interest you may receive and the capital gains tax you may owe 10 years hence.

Or you may use a family annuity, in particular, a joint-life-and-survivor annuity, as the legal vehicle by which inflation transfers your wealth. In early America this was the most popular method by which the old generation relinquished the farm or business in exchange for life-long payments or services by the younger generation. Its popularity is waning today because inflation is impoverishing the annuitants as creditors, while it enriches the insurance companies as debtors. But it is a very effective device for family wealth transfer that makes children the property owners and debtors, and the parents their creditors. A "stepped up" annuity, especially, should give double-digit inflation ample opportunity to do its wealth transfer work. You receive smaller payments at first, or none at all, and when you reach a certain age, usually on retiring, you receive larger payments that are greatly depreciated. There would be no estate tax if you should fail to live long enough to enjoy the return.

If you are the owner of a growing business or valuable real estate, it is important that you freeze the value of your estate now and that you siphon off all dollar growth to the family. Therefore, you may organize or reorganize a family business in such a way that you retain voting preferred stock, having a fixed-dollar value. But your heirs acquire the common stock equity interest that will grow in value. You continue to control the business, which gives you adequate executive income, but inflation is giving your children the substance of the family wealth, tax free.

An example may illustrate the case. Your family corporation has current assets, fixed assets, and other assets with a book value of $1 million. If there are no liabilities, the shareholders equity amounts to $1 million. You own the voting preferred stock of $997,000 and your child, the common stock valued at $3,000. After a few years of double-digit inflation the value of your corporation may double. But your preferred stock with its fixed rate of dividends remains at $997,000, while the common stock, with its exclusive residual claim on the assets and net income of the corporation, will soar to $1,003 million. It does not matter whether your corporation grows in real value or merely reflects the dollar depreciation, your child will now own more than half the assets of the family corporation. You paid no transfer tax or capital gains tax, no gift tax, no estate tax. Silently and efficiently, inflation tansferred your wealth to your beneficiary.

If such a family organization is impractical, the estate owner may use a "holding company," i.e. a company controlling partial or total interest in other companies, to achieve a similar transfer. He transfers his wealth to a corporation in which he acquires voting preferred stock of fixed-dollar value, while the heirs subscribe to the equity stock at the residual value. Any growth in asset value then accrues to the heirs.

The owner may use the same principles by designing trusts under a will. To creat a "siphoning" trust, he puts the marital deduction for the surviving spouse in one trust, and the balance of the estate that goes to the heirs in another. Fixed-value assets are put in the former, while the equity assets promising either real or inflationary growth, are allocated to the latter. Any appreciation in estate value goes to its remaindermen.

The proper use of inflation as a wealth transfer agent permits the preservation of family wealth, which is a most desirable objective. After all, the family, which is antecedent to society, is the spring from which go forth the streams of human greatness and prosperity. Financial destruction of the family through estate taxation or any other political means must have incalculable effects on society.

Everyone loses when government consumes productive capital. Yet, for the sake of economic equality, confiscatory death duties continue to destroy family wealth. When the duties fall on a large enterprise, scarcely a word is said about the economic impact on the heirs, on employees and customers. If the popular news media should actually cover the story, they may gloat about the "passing of an era." When the same fate befalls numerous small businessmen, the estate tax is felt to be burdensome, although the tax rate may only amount to 30 to 50 percent.

Actually, whether the tax levy falls on a small business or a large enterprise, the economic inpact is basically the same, although it may differ in degree. In both cases, all or part of the productive assets may need to be sold in order to pay the death levy. As the rates on large estates are significantly higher, a larger percentage of the productive assets usually is sold, and more capital is transferred to government. The large business that was built by several generations of able entrepreneurs is more likely to be sold under the impact of a 70% capital estate tax.

Continuation of family wealth over several generations is especially objectionable to the "equalizers." The prosperous enterprise that is in the possession of one family throughout decades is their favorite target.

INFLATION LEAPS

(3/1/79) January saw the greatest leap in the WHOLESALE PRICE INDEX since the worst inflation days of 1974—1.3% for the month, which works out to an annual rate just under 16%. Now the CONSUMER PRICE INDEX shows retail prices advancing at .9% in January, which works out to just under 11% for the year when compounded monthly. I think we will see much worse numbers than that before it's over; however, there could be startling fluctuations, both up and down, which will make it difficult to read. Ignore the fluctuations and bet on a steadily climbing inflation rate. Also, bet on interest rates to follow suit. As long as interest rates and inflation rates are climbing, the market will be generally bullish for gold, even assuming the expected corrections in the price.

People ask me, "Why doesn't the government do something about inflation? Surely they understand what's causing it?" Well, they may, but some of the media sure don't. There was a recent editorial in my local newspaper attacking the concept of the Constitutional Convention to limit spending. They were against it for a variety of reasons, but the statement that really dropped my jaw was the following:

> Even though people may be angry about government spending, the Senators owe it to their constituents to point out that it's the wrong target in the battle against inflation. Putting a spending limit on Congress wouldn't significantly dampen inflation since price increases in the private sector—the cost of food, housing, medical care, and many necessary services—are mainly responsible for the high cost of living.

That's incredible! No wonder Carter gets away with it when he blames big business and big labor. I just may be dreaming, but I believe that if we can get the opinion molders of this country to read my book, there is a fighting chance that a few of them might understand the nature of the real problem.

WILLIAM TEHAN'S BAHAMA CONFERENCE REPORT

(6/15/8) MR. WILLIAM TEHAN said that we are facing a period of massive deflation and liquidation of debt. He told a very funny story about a French balloonist who misjudged the wind one Sunday afternoon and ended up across the English Channel in a field. As he lay in the basket half stunned, an Englishman rushed up. The balloonist asked, "Where am I?" The Englishman replied, "You are in a basket in the middle of a field." The balloonist responded, "You're an accountant, aren't you?" The Englishman said, "Yes, how did you know?" "Because the information you have just given me is completely accurate and totally useless."

He felt that the United States could not run into a super inflation because it is not a "printing press economy. It is a "credit economy" and he believes we are heading for a liquidity crisis where the money supply will be inadequate to meet the demand, which means that the value of money will rise in relation to goods and services, and that is, by its very nature, deflationary. With inadequate money to fuel continue expansion, we plunge into a depression.

When asked, he said he has been saying this since 1973, which raised an obvious question. What kind of mistakes would you have made if you had started planning for deflation in 1973? Your total investment strategy would have been wrong for the last five years.

ON THE BRINK—A Review

(10/15/77) If you want a chilling look at what a runaway inflation looks like, feels like and almost smells like, I suggest you read ON THE BRINK by BENJAMIN and HERB STEIN. Benjamin Stein is a columnist for THE WALL STREET JOURNAL and his father, Herb, is a former Chairman of the COUNCIL OF ECONOMIC ADVISORS in the Nixon Administration. They give you an absolutely horrifying look at what happens in a runaway monetary inflation, some three years in our future.

I read a review of this book about four months ago and it was well received by the critics, but I've looked for it in twenty bookstores all across the United States and no one had it in stock. It has all the ingredients of a best seller, but for some reason, it has been suppressed and we had to wait three weeks on special order to get it.

The narrative is from the perspective of a future President's Council of Economic Advisors, sowing the battle between conservative economists who understand that the printing press and its modern day fractional banking equivalent is the root cause of inflation, and those who understand the political difficulty, if not impossibility, of slowing down the inflationary process.

The action centers around a President who is economically ignorant and is always persuaded by those who speak with the highest degree of conviction. He has to deal with a post-Burnsean Chairman of the Federal Reserve Board, who believes that inflation is a proper means of redistributing the wealth, by allowing the "little guy" to pay off all his debts with inflated money at the expense of the "rich" who hold bonds and mortgages and long-term debt. The President can't face the difficulties of causing a depression by tightening the monetary policy, so he agrees to "try it for awhile to see what happens," and the result is an irreversible monetary inflation.

As the book approaches its climax, gold is at $200, then $500, then $3000, then $10,000 and, finally, over $100,000 an ounce. A round-trip cab fare from Kennedy Airport into downtown Manhattan is $17,000, and the Eastern Airlines shuttle from Washington to New York is $100,000.

Small towns and farmers are prospering, and those who hold commodities get rich, while those who trusted paper money find themselves unable to pay the light and power bills, and the lights are winking out all over America.

It portrays the rise of a demagogue who knows how to play on the inflation-caused disaffection of the masses, and almost brings about the downfall of our democratic institutions. The market for bonds disappears and the Dow Jones averages collapse. Fortunes are wiped out, unemployment climbs, and airlines refuse to quote round-trip fares because prices are rising so rapidly.

Unfortunately, it contains some obligatory sex scenes and you might want to skip past those, but in a way they do represent the kind of orgiastic "eat, drink and be merry, for tomorrow we die" attitude that often pervades civilizations in their last death-throes.

The Cabinet meeting and Oval Office scenes have the ring of truth, written by one who has spent a lot of time there.

I wish every American could read this book. It may just be the persuasive tool that could turn the tide and steel us to the necessity of retracing our steps, and taking our bitter medicine to save the system.

I can recommend it unqualifiedly. Run, don't walk, to your nearest bookstore, and set aside three or four hours to digest it in one gulp. You won't regret it.

INSURANCE, LIFE

WHAT KIND TO BUY

(11/75)   I want to thank Floyd Weston of Master Plan, for helping me crystalize my long-held opinion that cash values in insurance policies are a rip-off and should be converted into other investments now. I'd like to show you:

1. How you can get twice the insurance for half the money.
2. How you unlock the cash value of your present policy, without jeopardizing your family's protection.
3. How to contact the people who can do it for you.

You had better prepare yourself for a fight with your insurance agent, as he won't like this advice, but that's his problem. He probably knows the things I'm going to tell you, but he believes in what he sells, and has accepted the industry propaganda that "less is more," and his whole commission structure is designed to encourage him to sell you cash value life insurance.

Here are the facts:

Premiums are structured so you have no idea what you are really paying for insurance coverage, and you always overpay.

In testimony before a congressional committee in February 1973, Herbert S. Denenberg, Commissioner of Insurance of Pennsylvania, said:

> The life insurance industry—however pure its motives and morals—is inflicting confusion on the public, with policies that the public cannot understand, with a pricing system that prevents intelligent shopping, with agents that are often incompetent, and with many companies that are unsound financially.
>
> So the public is the victim of the system. And this means the public often buys the wrong policy and pays too much. This can mean economic disaster and destruction of the security and the peace of mind of those who rely on life insurance. We have competition, but it is competition by confusion. So life insurance, which is supposed to provide protection, has become another of the leading consumer frauds.

Before the same committee, Ralph Nader declared in regards to the insurance industry:

Its contrived complexity, secrecy, and public relations have fulfilled a strongly supplemental camouflage function. Hidden behind this camouflage are two principal levers of maximizing life insurance company profit, or, as the mutual companies call, its surplus. These two are deception, and ironically, gross waste. Neither rebounds in any way to the consumer's benefit. For almost 70 years, the life insurance industry has been a smug sacred cow feeding the public a steady line of sacred bull.

And finally, Dr. Joseph Belth, Professor of Insurance, Graduate School of Business, Indiana University:

In an atmosphere of ignorance, complexity and apathy there are ample opportunities for the exploitation of consumers. Many policy holders are overcharged for their life insurance in the sense that they could have bought comparable coverage at much lower prices.

In truth, all cash values represent an overpayment of premiums on which you receive no real return. They are of value to you only if you don't die. They are confiscated by the company and deducted from the face value of your policy before paying benefits to your family on your death.

This is generally disguised by clever charts showing an increase in cash value and a decrease of insurance coverage, but the effect is the same—confiscation of your insurance savings. This cash value is eaten away by inflation.

Here is my advice:

1. Find a company that will sell you low cost death protection to age 100. Be sure to get their quotes before you buy.
2. Be sure you get quotes based on current death tables (mortality tables) rather than the ancient ones used by most companies, which show much higher death rates, and justify much higher premiums.
3. After you have secured such coverage, cash in your present policies.
4. Invest this money in whatever gives you the best return and the most peace of mind.

PAUL PREHN INTERVIEW

(7/15/77) Insurance confuses people. That's not so strange because that's what it's designed to do. Faced with a bewildering array of policies, special gimmicks, rate and apparent incentives that the average person simply can't sort out, many buy from the most persuasive salesman.

For that reason I've asked Paul Prehn, an insurance expert who shares my philosophy, to be our guest for an interview.

HJR: Paul, what qualifies you to speak authoritatively on the subject of insurance?

PP: I went to work for a large mutual company on the East Coast in 1960 and was with them for ten years, selling conventional types of insurance, primarily "whole life." After ten years, I and some other sales people in the company became aware of attractive new concepts in insurance. We found a life insurance company that agreed to underwrite our new concepts, so in 1970, we left and began building a nationwide organization.

It took us two years to build the products, and in 1972 we started selling a low-cost permanent term (renewable to age 100) life insurance policy.

HJR: I've often thought how terrible it would be to outlive my insurance, then die and leave a widow. Isn't that a disadvantage for term insurance?

PP: Over 90% of all the term insurance policies in force today are only renewable to age 65 or 70. If I sold you a race car but I guaranteed that it would only run 15 laps in a 200 lap race, I doubt very seriously that you would buy it.

HJR: It is most difficult for people to understand that as their cash values build, the amount of actual insurance coverage is reduced. If you buy a $100,000 whole-life policy, for example, and you die, your heirs get $100,000. The longer you live, the less of that money is insurance, and the more of it is simply return of your cash.

PP: That's right. One of the greatest contractual paradoxes today is in the whole life policy. You pay for cash value and insurance, but by contract, no matter what you do, you only get one of them. If you die, you get the insurance. If you cancel the policy, you get the cash, but you never get them both. You should buy whatever insurance you need to cover your needs at low cost and then take whatever money you might have spent for whole-life and invest it.

The life insurance industry is very quick to add that you can borrow that cash value whenever you have an emergency and want the money. You have to pay interest at the rate of from five to eight percent to borrow your own money. Whereas, if you don't put it in the policy in the first place, and you put the money in the bank, you don't have to pay the bank interest to take it out.

HJR: Well, what about the "dividends" that I receive on a whole-life policy. Isn't that the equivalent of interest?

PP: Well, the IRS defines a dividend in a mutual company as a "return of overcharged premium." Dividend paying companies charge you from 15 to 25 percent higher premiums in the first place. There's no tax on it because it's a return of premium.

HJR: Well then, isn't "dividend" a deceptive term?

PP: In my opinion, it is. A true dividend from a regular corporate entity is taxable. The point is, that the life insurance industry is selling life insurance for more than they need to sell it for.

HJR: Paul, when I was a stock broker, I knew where my self-interest was. I worked for a little "Over-The-Counter" brokerage house for awhile, and if they wanted to sell off inventory, they would call us into the office and offer us a bonus or an extra commission to sell the stock to our customers. And everyone would immediately jump out, motivated by the best commission, and call their clients with a "sage" investment recommendation! I left the securities industry because I felt there was a great conflict of interest. Salesmen are not collectively prepared to overlook their own best interests in making recommendations. What product is the average insurance salesman motivated to sell by the commission structure?

PP: The life insurance industry offers substantially more commission on whole-life than they do on term so that they can invest those excess premiums in stocks and bonds and mortgages. If you sold a man a $100,000 term policy, the premium might be $1,000 a year. With a whole-life policy, the premium might be $5,000 a year, yet if he dies, either policy will pay off $100,000. Would you rather have $5,000 in premium, or $1,000 for the same risk, if you were President of the life insurance company?

When a life insurance salesman sells the traditional life insurance policy, he gets a first year commission of from 50 to 100 percent of the first year's premium, depending upon the company. And then, a renewal commission of maybe 5 or 15 percent of the premium for the next 10 to 20 years.

HJR: Paul, whenever I've bought term insurance, which is all I've been buying the last few years, I've had to practically get the salesman down and put my knee in his back in order to get him to sell it to me.

PP: That's right, but the average man doesn't know any more about life insurance policies than he does about lawnmowers, so he ends up buying whole life.

We give the client a very competitive term insurance rate for 10 years. In addition, the first year he makes a small investment, like a certificate of deposit, which matures in 10 years. The insurance company pays 7.2% interest on the deposit. This 7.2% is not taxable as it earns, and it's not taxable at time of receipt, because of a section in the Internal Revenue code.

HJR: Isn't this, a form of cash value life insurance? Aren't we back where we started?

PP: Yes, it is, but it is only a small fraction of the cash value of a normal cash value life insurance policy with equivalent coverage.

If we were selling you a life insurance policy, we would say, 'Mr. Ruff, we can sell you a very inexpensive term policy. In addition to that, we will give you an opportunity to make 7.2% tax free on some of your money over a period of ten years.' The catch is that if you don't keep the policy for ten years, then there's a penalty against the interest and/or the principal of whatever you invest. The lapse rate drops sharply, so we can pay the salesman not only the first year commission, but we can also pay him all of his renewal commission in the first year, and now he is financially motivated to sell term.

HJR: Are there some circumstances where the client would be better off buying just plain old "term," as opposed to your concept?

PP: Yes. If a client is only going to need the insurance for five years or less, it's cheaper to buy just term. Our product is designed for a longer term.

HJR: Are there circumstances under which a whole-life policy might be more advantageous?

PP: For a person who did not have any discipline whatsoever in saving money, a whole-life policy would force a man to accumulate some money who otherwise wouldn't save any cash. But he will lose it when he dies.

HJR: During the depression of the '30s, a lot of people had cash values in their insurance and it saved them, and this is one of the most potent arguments used by the whole-life salesman with the person who fears his own lack of discipline. Assuming you're not a spendthrift, what should you do with your cash values?

PP: Well, if someone has a cash value build-up, he should consider cashing in his policies, invest the money someplace else, and buy term insurance. Obviously, one should not make the exchange for the old insurance policy until the new one has been issued and put in force.

HJR: Let me sum up. A person who intends to keep his insurance at least 10 years, or more, would be better off with permanent term. A person who has a short-term need for the most insurance for the least money should buy annually renewable term at the best competitive rate he can find. A person who cannot manage his money, who would dissipate his funds, or simply cannot save otherwise would probably be better off with whole-life, accepting the disadvantages of the whole-life policy in return for the benefit of having money there when he needs it. Is this correct?

PP: As long as he clearly understands the disadvantages. I don't think most people do. If they really did, they might choose to be more frugal and invest their money otherwise. Maybe a person could hedge it both ways. Let's say he needs $300,000 of life insurance. He is a little bit worried about his ability to save money, but he knows he needs more life insurance. Let him buy $50,000 or $100,00 of conventional whole-life, and build cash value and buy $200,000 of some form of permanent term.

HJR: Now, let's sum up my recommendations.

1. Make a decision about how long you want your insurance policy to remain in force and what your needs are, then choose that policy which is best for your needs. If it's going to remain in force seven years or less, straight term would certainly give you the most coverage for the money. Ten years, permanent term, such as that described by Mr. Prehn, would be more advantageous.

Whole-life is for the person who wants to keep his financial life very simple and is willing to pay more for that simplicity and the assurance of having set aside that money every year, although inflation will destroy his purchasing power.

2. Understand the motivation of the insurance salesman. He is in business to make a living. That's no sin. That's just the way it is. He is paid the highest commission by selling whole-life. You may have to struggle to find someone who will sell you term.

3. Permanent term with a cash deposit, as discussed in this article, provides built-in motivation for the salesman by paying him his first year commission and his renewals, all in the first year, and the insurance company is willing to do this because the lapse rate will be low because of the discipline of the cash deposit that would have to be

forfeited if the customer lapses. Inflation can hurt you here, too, but far less than whole-life, as the cash value in relation to insurance coverage is far lower, and the 7.2% return does offset some inflation loss.

4. The uncertain future that we face, as discussed in *THE RUFF TIMES*, argues for some form of term as opposed to whole-life. Having money tied up in cash values and out of your control is not very astute. If you have insurance cash values, use that money to buy food and coins, or even bullion or diamonds. They'll beat inflation. Don't leave it in the hands of the insurance company earning nothing.

THE BOARD OF DIRECTORS AND ME

(11/15/78) If you have an insurance policy or an annuity, you might want to skip this article because it's going to ruin your lunch. I have just had an interesting experience that has helped to recrystallize my thinking on insurance as an investment and as protection, and an account of this experience might well be useful for you.

I recently found myself as the only passenger on a $6 million corporate jet headed for an eastern city to be a guest expert at a meeting of the Board of Directors of one of the nation's larger insurance groups. I was invited because the Chairman of the Board is a subscriber to *THE RUFF TIMES*, believes our philosophy and wanted me to persuade the directors of his company that there are some significant changes afoot that might require an alteration of their investment policies. Not only was I flown back and forth across the country by corporate jet, but they paid me an outrageous fee to spend an hour and a half presenting my rather solitary views.

I think they wasted their money, although I was not about to turn it down. I don't think I changed one single factor in their investment policy, for reasons which will become clear as this tale unfolds.

I really sat in on two meetings. One was with the Investment Committee, which decides what to do with tens of millions of dollars of new investment money each year, and the second meeting was with the Board of Directors. I listened to the chief economist of one of the nation's largest banks as he informed us that the tax revolt and the new conservative movement were going to restore fiscal sanity to the country. He projected an average inflation rate over the next ten years of 5½%; however, he did give us only a 4% probability of that happy view. He had two other scenarios, one better and one worse, to which he attached 30% probability. In other words, his forecast was so his forecast was so hedged that he could be right no matter what happens.

It was a unique experience to sit in such a meeting and see how they are handling the money which you are depending upon either for your death benefits, or as a return of cash value. I drew several very interesting conclusions.

1. The interests of the insurance company stockholders and the policyholders are not necessarily the same.

2. Insurance company capital, while growing on paper, is actually going backwards in real purchasing power.

3. The stockholders are paying themselves substantial dividends out of illusory inflation profits and are, in effect, consuming their capital.

4. There isn't much they can do about it, for reasons I'll explain later.

5. The only reason the insurance business is a good business is because they have the perfect inflation hedge—they have borrowed large sums of money from you and they will pay you back in dollars worth far less in purchasing power.

Every time I write an article that's negative on insurance, I get a flood of letters from insurance salesmen castigating me for my opinion that you should never own any cash value insurance. Inherent in their position is the assumption that we will have stable money. I've never contended that the insurance companies will go broke. It is the money that is going broke, and the return you receive is not sufficient to keep up with inflation and you will be ripped off by the inflation tax. But let me elaborate on the conclusions which I drew from that meeting and how I arrived at them.

I pointed out to the group that they were making several serious mistakes. One, they were paying themselves dividends out of non-existent profits because a 9 percent return on their bond holdings is not sufficient to keep them even with inflation. In addition to that, because of rising interest rates, the market value of their bond portfolio had fallen and I recommended that all of their money should be put into Treasury bills so that they would not suffer additional capital losses, as I see long-term rates rising even higher in the future.

Even those who agreed with me pointed out that they couldn't do it. If they cut the dividend, the stock would plummet in price, and immediately rumors would begin to spread as to the solvency of the insurance company. This obviously would have such a negative impact on their personal financial well-being that such an act of financial statesmanship was unacceptable. If their long-term bonds were sold to go into shorter-term securities, the capital losses would wipe out profits and then some, affecting the financial stability of the whole operation.

After I pointed out the inflation losses in their portfolio, a position which was vigorously supported by the Chairman, one member of the Board pointed out that they had the perfect inflation hedge. He said, "Don't forget that we pay off the policyholders' death benefits and cash values in money of far less value than that which we received. So even though we may be losing by inflation in our investment portfolios, we are making it up by being on the right side of inflation in our insurance commitment." That factor makes the insurance business basically inflation-proof.

If those inflation forecasts are correct, that means that any money you have given to them to invest for your benefit is producing illusory profits available to the stockholders of the insurance company for dividends. If they truly had your best interest at heart, those funds should be reinvested to guarantee a sound base for paying benefits and returning your invested capital. In addition to that, if you are someone else's inflation hedge, you are holding the wrong end of the stick.

I pointed out to the Board that the American people had no real perception of the effect of inflation. This created an immediate furor, and two members of the Board informed me that that was ridiculous —that Americans really understood the impact of inflation. They said, "Everywhere we go they are complaining about rising prices at the supermarket." My response was, "That is not a true perception of the impact of inflation. Rising prices are not 'inflation.' Decreasing value of money, over the long-term, is really inflation."

Not one American in ten thousand understands the effect of compounding inflation rates eating away at the value of their long-term holdings. His anger is focused on the grocery store precisely because he doesn't understand the impact of inflation.

If you have more money loaned out than you have borrowed, you are a "net-lender." Net-lenders always lose in inflation. If you have given the insurance company your money to invest for you, you are a lender, in that respect. The insurance company stockholders will probably make out all right because they will rake off their stock dividends and probably put them into some kind of inflation hedge. The company has the aforementioned inflation hedge, in that they only have to pay you in depreciated dollars.

The insurance companies will probably survive, but as GARY

NORTH is fond of saying, and I have stolen that phrase from him for use in my book, "The money is going to go broke."

QUESTIONS AND ANSWERS

(12/1/78)

Q. Howard, I've bought your conclusions that insurance is a poor investment. Do you mean all insurance? How about term?

A. From a pure dollars-and-cents point of view your best buy is pure term insurance, but rates will vary dramatically from one company to another. If you buy annually renewable term, which you can buy in varying terms from single year, five or ten years, or term to age 100, you are guaranteed annual renewability for the term you purchased. The policy can be cancelled only for non-payment of premium, which gives this type of insurance great advantages.

Q. Then, what do we do if we already have whole life with substantial cash values?

A. You have two choices. You can cash it in, or you can borrow against it and put the money to work in the kind of investments we have been describing in *THE RUFF TIMES*. Probably in the early years you would be better off to cancel the policy and buy term, all other things being equal. If, however, you have an incipient health problem that you are afraid could become serious or could make you uninsurable, that would be a major factor in your decision to borrow against your policy as opposed to cashing it in.

Q. Are there any companies that sell inexpensive term insurance?

A. Yes, most of them. But it's hard to get them to sell it to you sometimes, as the saleman's commission structure is not generally designed to encourage the sale of term insurance.

Bear in mind, inflation has destroyed the usefulness of whole life insurance, and no argument is going to change my mind on that one until the inflation rate drops permanently well below 10%, and that is not in the immediate offing.

A few miscellaneous comments: The wife should pay for her own policy with her own check from her own checking account, for inheritance tax reasons. You're better off buying annually renewable term, which is non-participating, from non-mutual companies. It might be worth paying a little extra premium to have the option to convert to permanent whole life or to guarantee insurability if we ever move into a deflationary spiral. Even though I don't think that's likely, it is possible and you should hedge.

PEN PALS

(12/5/78) I've received some marvelously thoughtful letters from some highly qualified insurance people offering some suggestions on life insurance. It was a good education for me and I'd like to pass them on to you.

1. My pen pals pointed out that most annually renewable term policies have maximum rate schedules for each year, so that you are reasonably well protected against inflationary rate increases. The biggest problem is keeping your death benefits in line with inflation, so you need to increase your insurance amount to cope with inflation while you are young. As you get older, your need for insurance may diminish, so the inflationary reduction of purchasing power of the insurance may coincide with that reduced need.

2. Several people pointed out that there are certain tax advantages in whole-life insurance for owners of small businesses, but I still am not convinced that whole life has any merit when the inflation rate is over 10%.

3. An interesting point was made by one man that if we move into an inflationary spiral, the best form of guaranteed insurability would be to have enough insurance coverage today. In case of deflation, you could be over-insured, but you could reduce your coverage. I think you should be "over-insured" to compensate for inflationary increases. He also says there is no need to have the convertibility feature to whole-life if you have a policy to age 100.

4. Shop carefully and compare "apples with apples."

For all those who have written, many thanks. You have been most helpful.

INTEREST RATES

(2/15/76) When the Treasury printing presses are running, and inflation and government spending are just enough to stimulate the economy, but not high enough to scare anyone, everybody feels good. Even people on fixed incomes often get cost-of-living increases to keep up. Then the banks are almost pushing loans on people with aggressive advertising campaigns for consumer loans and they uncritically shovel money, by the hundreds of millions, to the nation's largest corporations, real estate investment trusts, foreign nations, etc. As the demand for money increases, as a result of this largesse, the Federal Reserve then allows the banks to loan more and more money in relation to their deposits. Remember, these deposits are money literally created from nothing. Loans outstanding will also rise in relation to the bank's capital or stockholder's equity. These loans increase the money supply, and this is inflationary. But then interest rates are low. Companies can borrow cheaply and expand operations. Bank profits rise because of increased loan volume on newly created money which costs nothing. Unemployment goes down and everybody is happy—until the inflation rate climbs six to eighteen months after the money supply expansion began and everybody gets worried. Then the Federal Reserve decides we need a dose of "tight money" and higher interest rates to "cool off" the economy.

This is a bunch of buffalo chips! At this point in the cycle, loan demand is still high, so heavy borrowing still goes on at higher rates, producing great increases in bank profits. Higher interest rates to corporations are merely passed on to customers in higher prices, just like any other cost of doing business. This is highly inflationary.

The Fed tightens money and increases interest rates to fatten the loan profits of their big banking friends, then lowers them to increase the price of the high interest bonds the banks bought at the interest rate peak. But banks can miscalculate and hurt themselves or others by misjudging the length or severity of the inflationary period, or having their money in the wrong corporate and municipal bonds.

Interest rates are generally affected by two things, demand for money or the lack of it. Today there should be enough demand for money to sustain high interest rates, but the Federal Reserve is expanding the money supply, which drives rates down. This pushes up bond prices and strengthens the banks' capital position. So the banks, in the past, have enthusiastically bought new bonds at face value, when interest rates are high, which gives them strong income, then may have watched the market value of the bonds increase as interest rates go down. And they have it made both ways. Banks love fluctuating interest rates—up and down! They can profit from the sheer fact of movement.

(3/1/77) Shortly after the nomination of Carter, I forecast that interest rates would be heading down, which, of course, would affect the market value of fixed-return holdings of all kinds, including bonds, commercial paper, certificates of deposit, etc. And it did for several months. I have been watching with concern the recent slight up-tick in interest rates, with a subsequent fall in market value of these kinds of holdings. I have concluded that with the problems of the weather, the high probability of bad crops, and the developing energy shortages, that the inflation rate is going to be turning upward sharply, as already indicated by the figures for January. The decline in interest rates is over, and they will be turning back up. Short term rates MAY continue to decline or hold their own. Consequently, Treasury bills are still a pretty good holding, but all Government securities over ninety days, and most municipal and corporate bonds, will probably continue a gradual decline in value. Why? Remember the basic rule: when interest rates go up, the value of bonds, certificates of deposit, notes and other interest-bearing instruments will go down. This means, according to JIM BENHAM, President of Capital Preservation Fund, that the smart purchasers of money-market instruments are buying those with the shortest maturities, and getting out of the long-term instruments.

(11/15/77) Many of you have your money in interest-bearing instruments, such as government bonds, and we want you out now, as long-term rates are heading up. Here's why.

Let's say you own a $1000 bond with a 6% coupon. If interest rates generally have risen to 8% or 10%, and you decide to sell your bond, you are not going to be able to sell it for $1000. The coupon will yield $60 a year, regardless of what you pay for the bond, as it is a fixed return. Anyone who wants your bond is going to want it at a discount, as he has no way to increase the $60, but if he can buy it cheap, the $60 represents a higher rate of return, so he might only want to pay you $900, or $800. When rates rise, market values go down, and vice versa. The market value swings most widely for the longer maturities. If you have a bond coming due in 1999, you are going to get a much wider swing, than one maturing in January 1978, under the assumption that you can simply wait and cash it in as it matures. You see, bonds, notes and bills are bought and sold every day. I'm astounded at how many of my subscribers, who have their inheritance or insurance money invested in bonds, don't understand that you don't have to hold them to maturity. They can be bought or sold, and the bond market is much larger than the stock market. When interest rates are rising, you should be in short-term securities, if you must be in any interest bearing securities at all. During a time of rising interest rates, a lot of money flees from long-term municipal, government and corporate bonds into Treasury bills, because they generally have maturities of three months, six months or one year, and the risk of loss is negligible. They don't fluctuate as much and you can simply wait out another month or two until they mature, regardless of what interest rates do.

INTEREST RATES ARE GOING TO CONTINUE TO RISE however, as the Federal Reserve battles with the Administration. The Secretary of the Treasury has just informed us that we might have a massive tax cut in the near future, and Mr. Burns is going to counter by tightening up the money supply. So bet on rising interest rates, get out of your bonds and into Treasury bills and gold. Let's not forget, of course, the standard advice which can keep you ahead of inflation, which includes diamonds and small town real estate.

There's more than one way to do it. You can either buy the bills through the local Federal Reserve Bank, your commercial banker, or you can invest in one of the money funds which invests strictly in such securities. The Capital Preservation Fund is typical.

(7/15/78)

Q. Why do you talk so much about interest rates? I'm not looking for a loan, so it doesn't interest me.

A. If you were only right about one thing—interest rates—you could get rich. If you can accurately call the turns in interest rates, you can make a fortune in bonds, gold, and the stock market, because it's the key to everything else. It also is an indicator of future inflation, as interest rates and inflation are the chicken and the egg. Who knows what comes first? All I know is that when inflation is rising, lenders alway jack up their interest rates in order to receive a return equivalent to the current rate of inflation, plus at least a 3% real profit, which is what lenders have realized throughout the history of lending. Interest rates not only react to inflation, but they forecast it, as they tell us what lenders are expecting.

If you catch a major reversal of interest rates at the peak, you can make a fortune buying top-grade bonds on margin. If it looks like inflation is going to ease and we're going to get out of one last recession with a whole skin, interest rates will fall and the world's best buy will be government 30-year bonds, bought on margin near the top of the interest rate cycle.

INVESTMENTS

INTRODUCTION

(4/15/77)   There's an old Indian proverb that says: "You should not judge a man until you have walked ten miles in his moccasins."

Well, I've learned that my advice is just as good for me as it is for you. The answers are still the same. The only difference is that the emotional load is a heck of a lot different when you're talking about your own money, than when you're talking about someone else's. I'm going through the emotional trauma of wondering how speculative I should be. I'm fighting my own gambler's tendencies in trying to set up a very prudent and careful investment of our money, so that when it is needed by Target to finance a major mailing, or to stock up for a paper shortage, or whatever, the money will be liquid and safe. And yet, by the same token, because of my constant study of the financial markets, I am alert to speculative opportunities that offset high risk with large profit potential. I'm sure, in this respect, I'm no different from any of you.

(12/75)   Can you remember when bonds were the safest and most conservative of investments, when stocks were considered an "inflation hedge," when mutual funds were a sure way to a modest, conservative return, and prudent people put money in the bank?

Well, all the investment advisors I know of, with an occasional rare exception, are still recommending these as "investments" because they base their advice on the following assumptions:

1. Western civilization is basically stable.
2. The economies of Western nations are reasonably predictable.
3. The immediate past will probably project itself into the near future.
4. No major crisis looms ahead to upset these assumptions.
5. Most economic changes occur slowly, and there is always time to alter investment strategies.
6. There will always be an orderly marketplace for you to buy or sell your investments.

All of my recommendations are based on the assumption that some or all of the above assumptions may prove to be untrue at some time in the near future.

My investment philosophy and advice assumes the possibility of sudden economic "climate changes," not economic "glaciers" that even a sluggish investor could stay ahead of.

Our inflation-weakened economy is in the grip of irreversible trends.

These trends could lead to sudden, unforecast economic events, altering the marketplace in a matter of weeks, and possibly days or hours, making it difficult to liquidate investment, or buy food, clothing, etc. A sample of such events includes:

A sudden Middle East war and an oil boycott, with greater consequences than last time, because our dependence on Arab oil has doubled since then; a nuclear exchange between small nations (Eqypt and Israel?) paralyzing world commerce; sudden failure of one or more large banks, here or abroad; inflation-fueled major labor unrest in automobiles, transportation, communications or the post office; municipal bankruptcy in New York, Philadelphia, Detroit, etc., throwing investment markets into chaos; and race war in South Africa, triggering sympathetic spasms here in America, igniting the tinder of black teenagers, who are unemployed, unoccupied, and seething with hatred for whites.

(8/1/76) With these principles in mind, here are my "asset deployment" principles:

1. PROTECT YOURSELF AND YOUR FAMLY FROM POSSIBLE PHYSICAL SUFFERING.

This means preparing yourself to maintain a low profile for a few weeks or months. It may mean relocating.

It means insuring you won't have to go out looking for scarce commodities in competition with others who are richer, or less scrupulous about how they acquire what they need.

You may never need them, but you'll sleep better if you have them.

There is an old adage on Wall Street that says: "Sell to the sleeping point."

What this means is that if you own a stock and you're worried about it, afraid it might go down, or won't rise anymore, sell some shares. If you still can't sleep, sell some more, and keep selling "to the sleeping point."

I think we should "act to the sleeping point." If you're worried about civil chaos, do whatever you must until you can sleep at night.

2. SET ASIDE A "MEDIUM OF EXCHANGE."

Now let's restate the relationship between silver and gold.

Silver, because it is divisible into small value units, as small as a silver dime, is a useful medium of exchange if paper money should become totally distrusted. Gold, because it would contain many times the value per ounce would be an unwieldy means of exchange if you wanted to buy a loaf of bread or a pound of butter.

Gold is your permanent store of capital until normal times are reestablished and, if history repeats itself, a currency is reestablished based on gold.

3. (10/76) PROVIDE FOR LIQUIDITY IN YOUR FINAN-CIAL LIFE. Realize that some investments are not liquid and cannot be readily converted into other forms of wealth when the normal marketplace is distorted by a major financial cataclysm. (see: Survival Preparations)

(8/15/77) In a recent issue of *The Dow Theory Letter*, Dick Russell expressed his philosophy of investment advice when he said his objective is to keep his clients from losing money. In the process, his clients generally make money.

The story is told of a man who was complaining to a friend about the local Thursday night poker game. "It's fixed," he said. "The cards are marked, and two of the guys cheat. I'm losing $100 a week!"

"Why don't you quit?" said the friend.

"I can't," he replied. "It's the only game in town."

Most investors and speculators act the same way. They are suckers for advisory services that claim to be able to show them profits "in good times or bad, in both bull and bear markets."

Let me tell you how I make money.

1. If the broad trend is confused and unclear, giving mixed signals, I stand on the sidelines. For that reason, I've been out of the stock market since early 1976 (except for gold shares).

2. I rarely trade for short-term profits, and I usually get hurt when I do.

3. I recognize my temperament as the biggest factor in investment success or failure. I have friends who really do well in bull markets, but get whipped in bear or mixed markets because they can't stand on the sidelines. They are victims of the "only game in town" syndrome.

What does the investment environment look like over the next year? Again, it's mixed and confused, and there are no broad, clear trends, except for gold and silver related investments and rare collector items. If I had to bet, it's even money that the stock market is going to continue to waffle sideways or drift downward.

I believe the trend is clear that the patient investor can make a lot of money in North American gold shares, and the move should occur sometime in the next six months. It might be tomorrow or it might not be until January or February, but it's going to come. That course seems clear. Commodities generally are going to drift aimlessly with no powerful upward move in the next few months. That's what the odds seem to favor. But again, the trend is not clear so I'd rather be on the sidelines.

Now, don't get mad at me if you look back and find some commodity or some hot stock that you were thinking about but didn't buy, and remember, if you accept my opinion and lose money, or miss the profit express, it doesn't cost me anything. The ultimate responsibility is yours. Don't forget.

I'm staying in Treasury bills, or the money funds which invest strictly in Treasury bills, and we're putting some of Target's funds into the Capital Preservation Fund of California. The odds are that interest rates are going to be rising. That means the market value of interest bearing investments will tend to fall, and the longer the maturity, the wider the fluctuation. I'd rather be in short-term Treasury bills where there is no market fluctuation.

Again, let me repeat, the principal factor in investment is temperament—the ability to choose wisely—calmly letting your profits run, and staying out of the marketplace when things are not clear.

Perhaps the toughest investment decisions arise when you need investment income to live on. Many of my subscribers are widows, or businessmen who have sold businesses and retired and have no income other than that from their investments, such as annuities, or blue chips paying good dividends. But, today inflation threatens everything.

Back in November of 1976 I pointed out that when inflation is running at 6 or 7% you have to have at least a 13% return in order to break even, considering taxes and inflation. And with the present rate of inflation, you must have an even higher return just to break even.

Now, most people in the position we've just described, who have also become persuaded of my view of the future, are faced with some cruel decisions. How do you get income sufficient to meet your needs while, at the same time, protecting yourself against currency depreciation (inflation), and ultimately currency collapse?

There isn't any way to do it in perfect safety. You are faced with choosing the best of some bad alternatives but there is one solution which seems better than the others. You can buy precious metals and coins now, and bet that they will appreciate at such a rate that you can sell off some of your holdings at reasonable intervals, and assume that appreciation will be sufficient that the purchasing power of your capital will remain intact. You will be paying taxes at the lower capital gains rate or at least until Congress shoots down the preferred tax rate for capital gains.

(8/15/77) In an inflationary spiral, the person in the worst position is the long-term lender. He gets chewed up by being repaid in cheaper dollars than those which he loaned.

In the end, all securities issued by governments at all levels, as well as bank certificate and paper money will be instruments of guaranteed confiscation.

I favor the small guaranteed loss, as long as my holdings are totally liquid. I would not tie my money up in anything long-term that did not have an active "secondary market" where it could be sold. I would not hold a second mortgage. I wouldn't mind a first mortgage on a good piece of residential income property or a farm, especially if it's near a small town, as long as there is good equity protecting me. At least I would be able to repossess the property if anything went wrong, but this leads us to an interesting paradox. If things turn bad, the last thing you would want would be for your borrower to be able to get his hands on a lot of worthless money and pay you off, because he would have the land and you would have paper. If things do go bad, you, as the lender, would prefer that he default so that you could own something real and tangible instead.

It's a weird financial world, and inflation has made it so. It distorts every investment decision. The old rules no longer apply.

I want to help you to understand the alternatives. When the course is not clear, stand on the sidelines. You can't stand on the sidelines holding your cash in your hand, so you have to do something with it. Perhaps the best middle ground is a mix of high-yield government bonds and short-term Treasury bills. In effect, when you accept a small guaranteed loss, that's what you are doing.

(1/15/77) Now you have two more problems. One is the selection of the right investment from all those available to you, and the other is your timing in getting in and getting out, and again, we come right back to temperament. Do you have the guts to cut your losses and let your profits run?

Remember that any investments, whether they are real estate, securities, gold stocks or whatever, should be made only after you have taken a defensive survival position.

DON'T TAKE ANY PROFITS WITH YOUR SURVIVAL COINS! If you wish to speculate in gold or silver, that's fine with me, as long as you're not doing it with your survival assets. They are your life insurance policy. Selling them at this point would be the same as getting rid of your life insurance because you've been around for 50 years and you haven't died yet. You still need it.

FIXED-RETURN TYPE

(3/15/78) The two biggest traps in this inflationary spiral are (1) the need for income and (2) the search for tax shelter. More dumb investment decisions are made on the basis of taxes than for any other reason. Our whole tax structure has distorted the results of investment and has totally fouled up what might be normal business judgment. Also, remember when you buy bonds or put money in CDs you are a long-term lender, and the long-term lender gets ripped off by inflation.

Remember also, you will suffer capital losses when you try to sell your bonds if interest rates have risen, because the market value of those bonds will have fallen. And interest rates are, and will be, rising.

(10/15/78) Anyone who has invested in any kind of fixed-return investment in the last five years has probably lost money. Between inflation and taxes on the earned interest, you have lost money. The only justification for leaving money in banks or saving and loans would be that you have decided to accept a controlled, predictable loss, as opposed to the ups and downs of other investments—and you feel you won't outlive your money.

At today's rate of inflation, anyone who invests in CDs, bonds, cash value insurance, or mortgages is now losing money in terms of purchasing power, and it will get worse. Anyone who is spending his interest is consuming his capital, because it is necessary to reinvest every penny of interest to maintain even an approximation of staying even.

Inflationary money is fraudulent, and anything that guarantees a fixed return in today's dollars is also fraudulent unless the assured, guaranteed safe, pre-tax rate of return exceeds the rate of inflation by at least six percentage points, and then it's only a break-even proposition—if you don't spend the income.

I haven't even touched on the possibilities of a general inflationary

377

collapse requiring the government to freeze assets, which is highly possible. In that case, not only would you be losing purchasing power at a heck of a rate, but you might not be able to lay your hands on your money to switch to other investments during a full-blown monetary crisis.

I say keep your money under your personal control. Don't give it to other people to invest who don't understand the environment as we see it. If you must keep it liquid in dollars, invest it in T-bills, or a money market fund. Better still, put it into the counter-cyclical kind of investments we have been consistently recommending in this letter.

(11/1/76) Inflation and taxes have distorted the normal market-place. There is no way that you're going to get sufficient returns from any fixed-return investment which will beat inflation and taxes, unless you are willing to take considerable risks. It might be best for you to settle for a recognized small loss. If you want liquidity and security, that is what you're going to have to do. If you were to buy U.S. Treasury bills and Treasury notes, you are assured of a loss of today's real inflation rates, but it will be small and predictable. You will retain your liquidity until obvious profit opportunities arise. I am recommending that you do just that with some of your funds.

If you spread your money around among various recommendations, you will probably turn out fine. Treasury bills will give you liquidity and security for now (they will be the last thing to go broke), despite the aforementioned guaranteed small loss. Gold and silver coins will give you a hedge against runaway inflation or a currency crisis. Then you can decide which other investment will best suit your temperament and your pocketbook.

GOLD AND GOLD STOCKS

(7/1/77) Personally, I wouldn't have a penny invested in South Africa. Economically, they're depressed. The Johannesburg exchange is a disaster. Politically, they are an international Charlie Brown, with few friends. I believe that, sooner or later, their economy is doomed. There is also the possibility of severe political turmoil and race war. White against black. Zulu against other blacks. Black marxist states against white capitalist. And, strangely enough, the U.S. and Russia against white South Africa.

Even if normal commerce continues, investors will be nervous, and I can't see any big buying surge of anything South African, except their commodities: gold, silver, diamonds and other minerals. So buy precious metals, but avoid South African paper. The investment climate is lousy.

(8/15/77)   For those of you with some extra speculative money and are looking for a high rate of return, you might look at some of the South African gold shares, because some of them are paying dividends in excess of 20 percent, but where there's that high a return available there is almost always a reason for it. The market risk is considerable. South African gold shares will make money if the gold price turns up before South Africa's troubles get worse.

If South Africa's racial and business troubles increase substantially before gold turns up, the bad news could further depress that market, even in the face of bullish prices of gold, so be super careful.

(11/1/77)   The South Africans have had a good rise. I was on the sidelines, and so were my subscribers when they all moved, but that's OK. As I told you a long time ago, we are going to stay away from severe risk situations and we may miss some profit, and we did that time, but I don't regret it for a moment.

Incidentally, something to watch for in the movement of gold and South African shares is the relationship between the price of gold and the movement of the stocks. As long as they are moving together, South Africa's troubles have not become critical. If gold moves upward and the South African shares do not respond and they begin to diverge, it is time to take your money and run and either buy the metal directly or get into any of several North American gold stock issues. (see: Gold, Gold Auctions)

THE PITFALLS FOR LONG-TERM CREDITORS

By Gary North, Ph.D.

(5/15/77)   The total funded debt of the (German) Reich immediately before the (First World) War was about five billion marks, or, say, approximately 1,250 million dollars. This amount of indebtedness would be paid in full the latter part of 1923 by the number of paper marks that one could buy wih one-eighth of one cent United States currency. The entire mortgage indebtedness of the German people, which was estimated to amount to approximately 40 billion marks in 1913, could have been paid off in November 1923, with one American cent. (reference: Prof. E. W. Kemmerer, *MONEY* [Macmillan, 1937], pp. 299-300)

It is extremely difficult for everyone to remember exactly what was written in this or any other economic newsletter. It is even more difficult for people who went through the deflationary depression of the 1930s to comprehend the implications of inflation. Inevitably, like the generals of a defeated army, those who were scarred by the Great Depression try to protect themselves against the crisis that they remember.

They fight and re-fight the battles of yesterday never fully understanding that today's world is very different.

(France is a perfect example of Gary's point. After World War I, the French decided to never again lose to the Germans, so they built the Maginot Line, fortifications with concrete bunkers several stories deep and the world's most powerful artillery pointed towards Germany. When the paratroopers dropped behind the lines, the guns were all pointed in the wrong direction.

When the Japanese invaded Singapore, they didn't come from the sea as expected, they came down the Malay Peninsula, and again, the guns were all pointed in the wrong direction. Those who are expecting deflation, first, have their guns pointed in the wrong direction, and, second, by the time the inflationary spiral is over, they will be out of ammunition and won't be prepared to take advantage of the deflation.

Those who have experienced the European inflations over the last half century are less likely to mistake the signs of the times and are more prepared to fight the battles of our inflationary era, because they know what they or their parents went through. They know what inflation can do to the middle class.

I am on the telephone daily counselling people concerning their finances. Over and over, day after day, I hear the same questions concerning certain kinds of long-term credit investments coming from the over 50 age group. I do my best to explain to them that all their fears about the past are poor guides to solve the crises of the future. They have difficulty comprehending. They respond to a world over four decades old.

They ask me, for instance, to comment on the advisability of buying an annuity. Why, I ask them, do they want an annuity? The answer is always the same: to prepare for retirement. But what good will the money be then, I ask. The answer is also familiar: it's a first-class company that is selling this annuity. But that's not what I asked. I asked about the money, and they answered concerning the reliability of the company. Why? Because they remember the 1930's. Anyone who had an annuity then lived well, if the company didn't go bankrupt. They have missed the point. I'm not worried about the quality of the company; I'm worried about the quality of the monetary unit.

The company is probably sound; it's the money that is dying.

Another question I always hear concerns the sale of real estate. "Should I take 29% down and the balance over five (ten, twenty) years?" Answer: no, take cash. The response is inevitable: "But I'll have to pay capital gains taxes on the whole amount." My answer is: you'll have to pay the inflation tax later, and it will be higher than the capital gains rate. "But it's paying me 10%!!!" Paying you in what? "Dollars." Oh. I think the money will depreciate more than 10%, and the government taxes you on the 10% you earn. You lose. "But," comes the supposedly conclusive argument, "if the borrower goes broke and can't pay, I get the property back." They have not understood the crisis of our age.

The borrower won't go broke; the money will go broke.

(You might want to refer to the Real Estate section, PASS ON THE OLD MAID, for some alternative suggestions. HJR)

Let me quote from another, earlier book by Prof. Kemmerer, *KEMMERER ON MONEY*. (We professorial types keep rewriting the same book over and over; Kemmerer didn't even change the title much.) Whatever you do, never forget his description of Germany in 1923:

> In the latter days of the inflation, when it was feared that there might be a stabilization of the mark at a value higher than the prevailing one, creditors were reported to have been seen "running away from debtors, and debtors pursuing them in triumph and paying them without mercy."

People ask me about tax-free municipal bonds. There are no tax-free municipal bonds. There are only INCOME TAX-FREE municipal bonds. But the income tax is not the biggest problem today. The problem is the inflation tax. Any fixed-return investment denominated in U.S. dollars is going to lose if the rate of price inflation accelerates. The money's purchasing power drops, and the buyer of the investment is struck with a fixed quantity of dollars coming in. He loses. It doesn't matter how solvent the municipality is; the problem is the solvency of the monetary unit.

No doubt some of you are thinking to yourselves, "Why is he spending so much time on this point? It's so obvious." Well, it isn't obvious to anyone who has a pension plan, or an annuity, or a bond portfolio, or an investment in fixed-return mortgages. It isn't obvious to dozens and dozens of those who have called in and asked whether or not to buy or sell off such investments. In short, it isn't obvious to an entire generation of trusting people who went through the Great Depression and who are planning their economic futures in terms of that catastrophe—a very different kind of catastrophe from the one which is facing us.

Let me conclude with a quotation from Kemmerer once again, this time from the 1937 book. *MONEY*:

> Farmers and urban home owners paid off their mortgages at the cost of a few days' labor or a few bushels of grain. But what the debtor gained, the creditor lost, and the creditors were often the most worthy classes in the community, as, for example, the small investors who had put their life savings in government bonds or in the bonds of the large corporations, the middle class clerk or artisan with a savings bank account, the owner of a life insurance policy upon which premiums had been paid for many years, or the widow or orphan livng upon the income from trust funds invested in bonds or mortgages. The savings of these people were practically wiped out, as well as those of the wealthier classes.

Lest you be tempted to indebt yourself up to your ears in order to pay off these debts with depreciated paper money, never forget that modern governments never allow price inflation to go on that long. They impose price and wage controls. They ration goods and services. They allocate scarce economic resources. The public at large suffers. Those who prosper are those who happen to sell goods and services that aren't under the controls (used goods, luxury goods, repair services) and those who deal in black markets. But if you pay off the bank with cheap money, the IRS and price controllers may look into the source of the money. Where did you get it? Did you get it legally? So don't expect to win out just because you indebt yourself today. The debt pyramid may be difficult to get off from safely under price controls.

But one thing is certain: the long-term creditor is sure to lose.

So be prepared: if you ask us about your annuity, your 10 percent mortgages, your bonds, your preferred stocks, your cash-value life insurance policy, or any other long-term (one year or more) credit position that is not tied to some commodity, you will get the same old answer: they're as sound as the dollar. (see: Inflation)

PORTFOLIO OF INVESTMENTS

(3/15/78) Here is a sample portfolio for $10,000, $50,000 or $100,000.

Sample Portfolios (Family of Three)

	$10,000	$50,000	$100,000
Food Storage	2,400	2,500	2,500
Silver Coins (pre-1965 U.S.)	5,600	11,200	11,400
Cash (Demand deposits or concealed)	2,000	4,300	4,300
Gold Coins (survival)	-0-	15,000	15,000
Diamonds, Gold, More Silver, Gold Shares, etc.	-0-	17,000	(*) 66,800
	$10,000	$50,000	$100,000

(*) Could also include T-bills, real estate equities, antiques, stamps, rare coins.

These figures are obviously flexible, depending on current prices. As you can see, the more money you have, the more flexible you are, but the basic advice is the same for everyone. Your choice of optional investments (*) depends on your temperament and inclinations. Real estate requires aggressive negotiation, and management and some knowledge. Gold and diamonds are passive. It's a matter of temperament.

(Note: At 3/15/78, when this article was written, $5,600 would buy about 1½ bags of silver. Today, 1/80, however, that same 1½ bags would cost over $25,000!)

(10/1/77) Now a word about investments during both inflation and deflation. Well, we are going to have both, and precious metals are a good hedge in both instances. Inflation will first destroy the paper currency, and gold and silver will maintain their purchasing power relative to goods and services, and don't forget about diamonds. Diamonds, properly purchased, are an excellent hedge both ways.

My fondest wish is that some day we will all go back and read this article and say, "What a fool Howard Ruff was. None of his dire prophecies came to pass." But I'm sorry, folks, that's just the way I see it, and I don't like it any better than you do, so get your house in order. After all, you are paying for my advice. Why not take it?

DIVERSIFICATION

(1/1/79) Diversify! Diversify! Diversify! If there's any single message that I tried to convey to our friends who attended our Caribbean Cruise Seminar, it would be summed up in that one word—diversify! By now, you all know my basic fundamental advice. It's the same for everyone.

As the Cruise progressed, and I sat down with individuals to look over their investment portfolios, a startling pattern emerged.

Everyone seemed to have his "pet" investments. I talked to one man who had over half a million dollars in gold bullion and he was terribly worried about the November decline in gold prices. I suggested that he should divide his portfolio between gold, silver and diamonds if he felt vulnerable. He didn't want to be an active investor, so real estate was not appropriate for him. His response was, "I just don't like diamonds or silver."

Another gentleman "liked" silver but didn't like gold. Another very nice couple from Florida loved small town real estate but "didn't like" gold or silver.

The "all-your-eggs-in-one-basket" syndrome is a dangerous attitude. Each of these investments has strengths and weaknesses which can complement each other—if you diversify.

Gold is the world's "real" money, and also the world's scared money; however, it is also a political football. We've just had a graphic illustration of how Uncle Sam will bomb away at it if it serves his purposes. Anyone who has all of his money in gold is going to have some gut-wrenching, scary times. Over the long haul it will turn out great, but it will be a rocky sleigh-ride in between.

The person who has silver will see it move somewhat in tandem with gold, but actually, for reasons we'll discuss in another issue, its price is probably more closely related to soybeans. Besides, it's divisible into much smaller units and is real spending money in the event of a total paper currency collapse, and we recently came awful close to just such a collapse. If Carter had not acted as he did, the Arabs would have started withdrawing their money from the New York banks and we could have had a chain-reaction run on all the banks, and a total collapse of the monetary system of the Western world.

During all this scary decline in gold and silver, complete with margin calls and busted speculative bank-rolls, diamonds just sat there and didn't do anything very exciting except gently appreciate against the expected rate of inflation.

The gentleman who didn't "like" diamonds, may like the excitement of the gold market, but just bear in mind that, like a roller coaster ride, the sudden changes of direction are what give you the thrills and the ulcers. If you balance your investment funds between gold, silver, diamonds and real estate, you don't have all of your eggs in one basket, and a sharp decline in one will not ruin you.

A lot of lousy investment decisions are made because people develop pet investments—things they "like" or "dislike." I don't want any emotions to enter into my investment decisions. Not even an emotion as relatively mild as "liking." I don't like or dislike any investment. I just diversify. If I have my discretionary investment funds rather evenly divided between junk silver, numismatics, gold coins, a small percentage in Swiss francs or Swiss franc travelers checks, some real estate holdings in well-located small towns and some lovely diamonds for stability, then I don't feel there is much that can hurt me as long as we remain in an inflationary envivrionment.

I don't profess infallibility and I don't really know exactly what the future holds. All I am willing to bet on is that it holds surprises. Your investment position should be sufficiently diversified that, on balance, you will make out all right. Don't fall in love with any investments. You must be objective and cold-blooded about what you do with your investment money. Once you are prepared, hedged, and diversified, then live life positively and to the fullest. That's the way I handle my life and I find great happiness and personal satisfaction.

A LETTER TO INVESTMENT ADVISORS

(4/1/79) If you are advising people what they should be doing with their money, the odds are that most of the things you are suggesting for them are going to destroy them financially over the next few years. Now, if the shoe doesn't fit, don't wear it. At least give me a fair hearing before you jump all over me. The consequences of being wrong in the current inflationary environment are awesome, both in terms of preserving the wealth of your clients and the welfare of the country.

Whether you are involved in estate planning, the sale of cash value insurance, brokerage, trust management, or whatever, you have a fiduciary responsibility. You must be sure that what you do for your clients is right for the present and future financial environment. If you persist in selling them cash value insurance, or advising them to put money in certificates of deposit, bonds or the stock market, and leave their portfolios unhedged by precious metals, diamonds or real estate holdings, you will some day have to account to a wrathful client for the total loss of his purchasing power.

The only valid measurement of wealth is what it can be exchanged for in terms of goods and services: purchasing power! Inflation is now destroying purchasing power at a rate which is unprecedented within our lifetimes.

During January and February, the Consumer Price Index rose at an annual rate of about 15%, and it seems to be accelerating. This means that for the first time in the last several years, prices are beginning to out-race income. Until recently, the statistics indicate that most people's purchasing power, as measured in terms of their personal income, has stayed even with rising prices. However, the value of the stored money that they have sent ahead to take care of them in their old age has shrunk, but the average American is not aware of this because he hasn't had the shock of trying to spend that money yet. It's only when he attempts to live on the income from that stored money that he will find, with a rude shock, that his purchasing power has been confiscated by government through the inflation tax. But now, more and more people will be forced to go into debt to maintain their standard of living, which means that more and more of their daily paycheck will be eaten up in loan payments. Whatever is left will be rapidly shrunk by rising prices until their debt has overwhelmed them. The additional debt necessary to maintain standards of living, etc., is a vicious cycle, like a snake eating its tail. Each new loan increases the money supply and is inflationary. When people awaken to this incredible fact of life, they will flee traditional investments with their savings for precious metals, diamonds, and real estate, in a frantic effort to keep up.

Take, for example, that certificate of deposit. If your client has a 9% CD and the inflation rate is 15%, and he reinvests his interest, he has a 6% loss of purchasing power. If you factor in the tax on the earned interest, it is probably closer to 9 or 10%. It only takes a few years at that rate to get wiped out. And that rate will increase! We will look back on 10% inflation with nostalgia.

To make it worse, the current price inflation rate may be understated by as many as three percentage points. Any time you put a client into a fixed-return investment—meaning that they will be paid back the same number of dollars they loaned—if the interest return is not at least three points higher than the anticipated inflation rate, THEIR WEALTH IS BEING SYSTEMATICALLY DESTROYED.

If you are still unpersuaded about inflation, take a look at these numbers! Food prices are up 4.3% during the first two months of 1979, which is an annual rate of close to 30%. Prices are up 16.6% higher than they were in February of last year. The U.S. Bureau of Labor Statistics blamed the food increases on adverse weather conditions which affected the fruit and vegetable supplies. It added that further price increases, particularly from beef products, appear likely. (That's all kind of dumb, because the root cause of inflation is government, not weather.) The cost of owning a home has increased 20.8% during the year due to higher mortgage interest rates and material costs. The overall Consumer Price Index is up 12.7% since the same period last year, and it's worse in the big cities. If you factored out small town America, where the inflation rate is lower, you would find that the big cities where most people live are "enjoying" an inflation rate of close to 20%. Now you tell me how, in good conscience, you can commit somebody's money out into the future to be returned in fixed dollars, even at compound interest, at anything less than the rate of inflation? If you can sleep well after that, you just don't understand the problem. The search for income must be subordinated to the quest for capital growth to keep up. If you can get both, so much the better.

Up until now, we crackpots in the hard money crowd have been pretty much alone in this position. One of the targets of my wrath has been city or state pension funds, which I contend will do the workers little or no good when they retire, just based on inflation and the impact of inflation on the kinds of investments that these pension funds are making. Now it seems that the state of Alaska is seeking to invest its pension funds in gold and foreign securities. PETER BUSHE, the state's Deputy Commissioner of Revenue, says, "It's the only way left we know of to protect beneficiaries of our public pension plans against continuing inflation." There is now legislation before the House Finance Committee which will permit the state's public employees' retirement fund and teachers' retirement fund, with a total of $520 million, to invest in gold bullion or certificates of deposit denominated in foreign currencies and real estate.

At the present time, their funds are invested in mortgages, bonds, money market funds, securities and common stocks, receiving an average return of about 8 percent. "These traditional outlets simply can't maintain the purchasing power of the pensions' dollars," says MICHAEL J. RILEY, State Investment Officer.

This is the first public pension fund to move into the hard money camp. However, the funds are going to run into some trouble with the Municipal Financial Officers Association because they are questioning how far funds can move in this direction and still remain "prudent." Under the "prudent man rule," you just can't depart from the common herd, but the common herd consists of lemmings.

The bottom line is: inflation has destroyed traditional, conservative investments! Any fixed dollar investment will be wiped out by inflation.

Let's look at each of the investment markets and see what their future is in an inflationary environment.

1. BONDS. (see also: Bonds) Bonds clobber you two ways in rising inflation. First, long-term interest rates will rise along with the rate of inflation. That means declining bond prices, so you have capital losses. Second, the interest return is nowhere near enough to compensate for loss of purchasing power, even if there were no dollar decline in the face value of the bonds. Anyone who buys bonds in a period of rising interest rates and rising inflation rates, is crazy, stupid, or both.

2. STOCK MARKET. (see also: Stocks/Stock Market) The stock market is destroyed by inflation several ways. Don't you think there's some reason why the stock market hasn't gone anywhere since 1966? That's when inflation started taking off. That's when the money creation process began getting out of hand, forcing Nixon to close the gold window in 1971 because we were losing our gold hoard to foreign interests holding our dollars. And that's when the stock market peaked and started going nowhere at a rapid rate. If you adjust the Dow Jones Industrial average for inflation and state it in 1966 dollars it's about 370.

What does inflation do to the stock market? Well, first it overstates the value of earnings and dividends. If you adjust corporate earnings for inflation, they haven't gone anywhere. Second, it means the depreciation allowances for replacement of obsolete corporate plants and equipment are grossly understated and the cost of expansion is soaring. That means earnings are grossly overstated in terms of real numbers. The stock market, being smarter than all of us, understands this and is going nowhere.

If you have been reading *THE RUFF TIMES*, this is not news to you, but until accounting rules are changed and inflation reverses, the stock market is going nowhere for a long time. Even if it goes sideways, stocks will lose value at the rate of 15% to 20% a year at the present inflation rate. If you persist in attempting to beat the game with your clients' money you are betting them into the longest of long shots.

3. CERTIFICATES OF DEPOSIT. (see also: Money Market Funds) I've already touched on that. A CD is a long-term loan. A long-term loan rips off the lender, as the borrower pays off in cheap dollars. When the inflation rate is only 7 or 8%, it is like being nibbled to death by ducks. When it is 15 or 16%, as it is now, it is like being eaten by alligators. There is no way that interest income will replace the lost purchasing power of inflation.

4. KEOGH AND IRA PLANS. (see also: Retirement Plans) They are a little better, but not much. Some of the inflationary bite is offset by the tax savings. The higher the tax bracket you are in, the more valid it is to have a Keogh or IRA. But then, if the Keogh or IRA is invested in precisely the same kind of investments that are going to be destroyed by inflation, sooner or later those funds will be chewed up. It takes a little longer because the tax saving offsets it. If you have a 30% tax saving and you are talking about an inflationary loss of 15% a year, then it takes a couple of years longer before the losses begin. But the very nature of a Keogh or IRA means that you are betting on a long-term future. If you are doing it in fixed dollars, receiving a fixed rate of return, eventually you will be destroyed financially.

I could sum it all up by saying, "The money is going broke." I don't know whether the insurance company, the company whose stock you bought, the city, state or government who issued the bonds, is going broke. All I know is the money is going broke and they will pay you off in cheap dollars.

If I keep singing this theme over and over again, it's because I meet you folks all the time, and too many of you are doing the same things with people's money that you have always done, probably from sheer inertia. I see insurance agents putting clients into cash value insurance, which makes no sense at all when the inflation rate is anticipated to be over 10%. I see bonds being added to the portfolios of widows and orphans by bank trust officers and financial and estate planners.

If I were a financial planner and advisor right now, I would be examining my motivation in the selection of investments for my clients. Unfortunately, most of the income of the typical estate planner comes from commissions on the investments. I believe this creates an impossible conflict of interest, because in this financial

389

environment, the best commission rates also come from the investments which have the poorest long-term value, such as cash value insurance and annuity programs.

The only basis on which you dare continue to make these kinds of recommendations is if you are prepared to disagree with me about the future of inflation, and defend your stance. Then, in all conscience, you can proceed as you have done in the past. I submit as evidence, however, that the terrifyingly high inflation rates that we are experiencing now, are precisely what I forecast in the past. I am not looking at the distant future. I am looking at the numbers NOW. You don't have to wait for the future to see inflation destroying your money. It's doing it now. Don't expect government or the tax revolt to bail you out. Inflation is out of control. What this world needs now are men and women of principle who advise their clients properly for an inflationary environment, without regard to the financial welfare of the advisor. The client must come first. There are many good, honest advisors who have acted contrary to their own financial self-interest, if the client's welfare required it. It takes a lot of guts to say "I was wrong." If you simply don't agree with me, that's an honest difference of opinion. Just be sure that your motives are right, and please, please, please give serious consideration to the arguments in my book and *THE RUFF TIMES*. And if you can't believe what I have to say about the future, at least pay close attention to the present. It may have some constructive lessons for you.

Inflation is an evil so monstrous as to almost defy description. It's immoral and dishonest. I'm having to teach my children to be speculators rather than prudent savers, and I find this immensely offensive. If your advice does not take into account this monster, and if you do not understand how it gets out of control, you are merely contributing to the destruction of the nation's wealth.

Unfortunately, the advisors who most need the foregoing advice are not reading *THE RUFF TIMES*. Those of you who are probably don't need the advice, but that's the way it always seems to be.

Sincerely,

Howard J. Ruff

P.S. If you care about what you should be recommending, please read the "Survival Preparations" section of this book. You will find my basic recommendations there.

FROM A TO Z

JOIN THE BAND WAGON

(6/1/79) Well, I'll be darned! I just found something that reads like *THE RUFF TIMES,* or *HOW TO PROSPER DURING THE COMING BAD YEARS*, and it's in *U.S. NEWS AND WORLD REPORT*.

> Even with higher yields, saving a little for a rainy day won't be easy.
>
> Take the worker who planned ahead, scrimped and saved, and cautiously stashed away his dollars for retirement in an investment paying 5½%.
>
> Consider $75 banked in December, 1968, and left untouched for 10 years. By last December it was worth $129.51, a yield of $54.51 total.
>
> But during those 10 years, prices rose by 91%. So—The prudent saver actually lost $7 in purchasing power.
>
> What about the American who buys a series E $100 bond now for $75 and holds it for 10 years? If the inflation rate stays at the 1978 level of about 9%—he will take a real loss in 1989 of a whopping $18 per bond.
>
> Small change? Note that savers now hold 72 billion dollars in E bonds. Thin silver lining: Treasury has authority to increase the 6% paid on E bonds to 7%. If prices keep flying, they'll have to do just that. (April 16, 1979)

Actually, *U.S. NEWS AND WORLD REPORT* has been one of the more realistic publications in assessing the problems the nation faces. It's on my "must" reading list and should be on yours. In the meantime, congratulations, fellows, at *USN&WR*. You are right on target.

HARRY BROWNE NCMR REPORT

(6/15/78) I just returned from the annual off-shore investment conference, sponsored by the National Committee for Monetary Reform.

Perhaps the most interesting talk of the entire conference was from HARRY BROWNE. Harry is a towering giant of a man, physically and intellectually, and has, as DICK RUSSELL commented later, "a vast fund of common sense." That doesn't mean that I agree with everything he said, but it was a logical, well-thought-out presentation. Harry felt that the "buy and hold" era for stocks ended in 1966. From 1970 through 1974, we came through the "hard money" buy-and-hold

391

era where you could simply buy gold or silver and hang on and make a lot of money. It was characterized by high inflation rates and the beginning of financial chaos. He also concluded that gold is not an inflation hedge and never has been. That rather startling statement makes sense only when you look at his rather narrow definition of "inflation hedge." According to Harry, a true inflation hedge will correlate automatically to the rate of inflation. In the last few years gold has been both a big loser and a big winner at various times. The Swiss franc is a true inflation hedge because the franc tends to rise against the dollar in relation to our rate of inflation and gives you an inflation break-even proposition. He feels that gold's 1974 explosive rise was because it had been price-controlled for a long time with a lot of pent up demand. When Americans were able to buy it and it was released to "float" freely in the marketplace, it exploded and so did silver. He said that gold and the Swiss franc have caught up with the suppressed price control levels. When it does go up in the future, it will be for different reasons than in the past.

Also, he said that price inflation and the stock market have nothing to do with each other. Many people feel that stocks will fall as the rate of price inflation increases and that inflation is bad for the stock market. Harry felt that they are separate phenomena, both reacting to monetary inflation. Harry's basic strategy involved picking up the basic "tidal" movements and switching to catch those broad movements. Right now, the Fed is in a restrictive mode but inflation will continue to rise. He said that sometime early next year the bear market will bottom out around 480 on the Dow Jones.

He discussed the relationship between the stock market and gold. They move in opposite directions. When you are in the stock market, you should not be in gold, and vice versa. Gold tends to rise in times of difficulty because it has a fundamental value which is recognized by most of the world. Most of the people of the world live unstable lives and they look for dependable, transportable and hideable getaway money, bribe money, and chaos money. When things get uncertain, they tend to buy gold, and this obviously bids up the price. Money should be portable, durable and recognizable by everyone and gold meets these requirements for most of the world. According to Harry, gold performs two roles: (1) it's a chaos hedge, (2) it's a vehicle to make profits if you buy low and sell high.

Harry felt that gold is in a "super bull market" which is characterized by many smaller bull markets and retreats, with each retreat bottoming out at a higher point than the previous bottom and each upward move peaking at a higher point than the previous top.

He feels this current mini-bull market will come to an end but chaos is a long-term condition. He also expressed the possibility that silver coins may become money again when this cycle results in a breakdown of the monetary system.

He said, somewhat with tongue-in-cheek, that if you were to base your conclusions about investing on the actions of investors, you would conclude that the objective of all investing is to break even. For example, a lot of people bought silver around $5.50 during the bull market in '72-'74, and there's an awful lot of $5.50 silver waiting for the price to recover. Each time silver bounces up against that price, some more people will try to break even and unload, and eventually there won't be any more $5.50 silver around. There's no further resistance this side of $6.50. If he's right, silver is an excellent buy on any correction down around $5.25, either for the short-term trader or the long-term buyer. He feels, however, that we have a greater chance of deflation than we've had in the past and that would be bad for silver. He also feels that silver moves independently of gold.

He says to have nothing to do with real estate, bank CDs or Euro-currencies because they are all vulnerable. That puts him at direct loggerheads with Harry Schultz. It also puts him in disagreement with me. Although he's generally right about real estate, small town real estate is the one exception.

A Long-Term Strategy
After all that great background, he gave us his long-term strategy.
1. Buy gold. It's your chaos hedge.
2. Hold some Swiss francs, that's your inflation hedge.
3. You can go into the stock market and buy warrants, which are long-term options. Warrants cost roughly 15% of the price of a stock. Your loss is limited to your investment. When the market recovers, your profits would be considerable. This is a hedge against a miscalculation in your gold holdings.
4. You should hold some dollars in the form of T-bills for liquid funds.
5. A Swiss bank account to protect your money from confiscation. (I'm not sure I agree with that, because it may become difficult to move money across international boundaries as international monetary chaos increases, possibly before this year is over. HJR)

A Short-Term Strategy
He has a short-term strategy where you move from gold into stocks and bonds when the market bottoms out. Both he and DICK

RUSSELL feel that twenty-year government bonds will be the next big play at the beginning of the stock market uptrend. After recession or depression bottoms out, interest rates will again peak; you then move into long-term Treasuries on margin. When interest rates fall, bond prices rise. You can buy bonds with 10% margin, which is about $150. The interest on your margin account will be offset by the yield on the bonds, but as interest rates fall and bond prices rise, you could have capital gains of as much as $400 or $500 on your bonds. When interest rates are falling, gold prices also fall. So you have two choices. You can stay with the long-term trend over the years, and hang onto your gold, knowing it will eventually come back, or you can try to profit from the short-term trends. But the strategy is sound—if the system doesn't come completely unglued—but you can decide that as you go along.

MORGAN MAXFIELD said in Hawaii that gold not only moves contrary to the stock market, but also moves with interest rates. When you have a rising prime rate, gold is in a bull market. When you have a falling prime rate, gold is in a bear market.

Harry was asked from the audience whether or not he likes Swiss franc annuities where you are paid off in a gold-backed currency. His answer was that he didn't want to be tied to 20 year contracts in anything, but he felt that all paper currencies could be swept aside in a real international holocaust and that you need control of your investments so you can make adjustments based on trends. All in all, a most useful and helpful presentation.

LEVERAGE

(Special Report #4, 4/1/78)

Q. Can you explain "leverage?"

A. Sure. It's easy. Leverage means utilizing the principle of the lever in making money. Archimedes, the Greek, said, "Give me a lever and a place to stand and I can move the world." Use a little bit of your money and lot of someone else's and the rate of return on your investment is greater. For example, if you bought a piece of property for $100,000 cash and sold it for $110,000, you would have a 10% profit on your investment. If you bought it with $10,000 down and a $90,000 loan, and sold it for $110,000, your $10,000 profit is 100% return on your $10,000 invested, and you could have used your $100,000 to buy ten such properties and you would have made 10 times as much. I've ignored interest and taxes to keep the example simple, but the principle is still sound.

Leverage increases your risk as well as profit, when you use it with volatile investments such as stocks, commodities, etc., because they can fluctuate downward rapidly and wipe out your investment, if you go in with high leverage and a small margin. However, leverage can be safely used in a stable rising or slowly fluctuating market, and that, over the past several years, has been real estate. You must still use leverage with great care in the coming real estate market, and the principal risk is in whether or not you have selected a rising or falling market, again, location, location, etc. (see: Real Estate and Survival Preparations)

IRAN

SHAH OF IRAN

(2/1/77) The SHAH OF IRAN represents a capacity for mischief that had better be noted by the world. He has the fourth largest military establishment in the world. He is engaged in a major power struggle with Saudi Arabia for control of OPEC. His megalomania has created a precariously destabilizing set of circumstances.

Iran is, of course, one of the world's greatest oil producers. The Shah apparently has dreams of reestablishing the Persian Empire of Alexander the Great. Most of the billions which he has received from the sale of his "black gold" has gone into grandiose desert economic development, and military hardware. Most of it is offensive in nature. The Shah is not really threatened by anyone. He can only be a threat to others. Despite the billions in hard money that has flowed into his coffers, he is actually facing a deficit in his balance of payments and is hard-up for cash.

Here are the circumstances. Saudi Arabia is labor poor. The desert tribesmen scorn labor. Most of the workers that have flowed into the country to work in the oil fields are Iranian. They represent a potential fifth column, and Saudi Arabia is totally dependent on their labor.

The Shah has concentrated upon the development of his offensive capability. For example, he has purchased from England large numbers of troop-carrying hover-craft, which are extremely useful in traversing shallow water or swamps. Iran is separated from Syria and the Arabian Peninsula by the swamps of the Euphrates Delta. With this peculiar kind of military capability, Iran could sweep into Syria and down the west coast of the Persian Gulf and occupy 80-90% of that whole area's oil-producing capability in as little as 48 hours. There would be nothing anyone could do to stop him. The U.S. Fleet in the area is too weak. The Russians would cheer him on because he would be able to deny to the West their needed oil supplies, and this fits in with the Soviet mischief-making proclivities. This move would enable the Shah to control world oil prices at will, so that he could continue to implement his dreams. It would also save his country from financial disaster and instability which could result in his being dethroned.

This recent action by the Saudi Arabians to pull the Shah's teeth by asserting their economic power, because they own the largest pools of oil, could actually result in destabilizing the situation and trigger the Shah into military action. It may be his only recourse. There is no question that the Saudis have the economic and "oil-in-the-ground" power to impose their will upon pricing. The Saudis didn't do it to be nice to the Western nations. I believe that they are rapacious, pragmatic, and perfectly prepared to run the risk of renewed recession or depression in the Western economy, simply because they know they can come out of it sitting on top of the world's real wealth—oil in the ground. I believe that this is a power play to reduce the power of the Shah. It is a dangerous game.

Now, what are the world-wide implications of an Iranian invasion?

1. It would mean an immediate increase in oil prices—possibly as much as 100%, and would be the trigger of a plunge into world-wide depression overnight.

2. It would mean the end of the ability of many poor nations to pay the interest on their loans from American banks, which could topple the American multinational banks and take the entire banking system with them with a lightning-like domino effect.

3. It could result in American military intervention in the Near East and, in fact, probably would. This could trigger an Egyptian invasion of Israel and bring the Shah into direct conflict with the Arab nations. Bear in mind that the Shah is an Aryan and has no racial affinity to the Arab nations. Their ties are religious but the Moslem religion is as fragmented as Christianity. And he is an unstable, ruthless megalomaniac and cannot be depended upon to act rationally under stress if his country becomes economically unglued.

4. It could trigger a nuclear exchange between Israel and the Arab nations. I firmly believe that they are in possession of nuclear weapons, and to insure their survival, would not be afraid to use them.

What does this mean to you as an American? It means that one of Ruff's leading indicators telling you to bail out of the banks and paper money and into hard money assets will be military action or the threat of such action by the Shah of Iran. Watch for increased military shipments to Iran. Watch for press reports of Iran's balance of payments deficit increasing over the next few months.

Keep your eye on the Near East. It has never been far off center stage, and I believe it will soon be moving back into the spotlight.

AYATOLLAH KHOMEINI

(2/15/79)   Iranian Time Bomb

The events of the last few months in Iran have highlighted several major problems that will affect your life.

The AYATOLLAH KHOMEINI is one of the most dangerous people to come on the world scene since the GRAND MUFTI of JERUSALEM who precipitated the 1st Arab-Israeli war. The man even looks like the wrath of God, with an implacable juggernaut aura! He is the only Muslim leader today who could call a JIHAD, or holy war. It is believed that those who die fighting in a jihad go to paradise, and all their previous sins are forgiven. He now seems to be in control, but what if he's not satisfied with the purity of the Muslim religion in neighboring countries? He could call a jihad, which could spread down the Persian Gulf to Saudi Arabia, Kuwait and all of the other little oil-producing sheikdoms, to say nothing of Syria, Iraq, Lebanon and Egypt. And Israel! Remember her? And he has inherited the Shah's awesome offensive weaponry.

We don't know yet how much oil Khomeini will sell us, if any, or when, even if he wants to. And what about Russia? The end of civil war is good news, but what comes after? Most likely, U.S. government fuel conservation actions will be taken. You just might find yourself waiting in gas lines or unable to travel on weekends because of weekend service station closings. (The Department of Energy's first choice.) It is certain that you will see dramatically higher gas prices. Kuwait is now receiving $20 a barrel for light crude oil and, according to them, if the Iranian production is disrupted for another six weeks, the price of oil could triple. Gold has avoided a long overdue technical correction because of the fears of the gold buyers of the world that the Middle East energy situation is going to boil over and the Arab sheiks are leading the gold pack. It actually made new highs. It's a nervous market that could go drastically either way short-term, although the long-term trend is still up.

How can we protect ourselves from the Khomeinis of the world?

As you know, I believe there is no genuine energy crisis that is not politically caused. All of our energy policies have increased, not decreased, our dependency upon foreign oil. The big oil companies have their major investments either in Alaska or overseas. Any real effort to solve our energy problems that threaten that investment would meet with determined resistance. For example, we have 600 years of natural gas lying under the Louisiana and Texas coasts. Under the present price guidelines, no one can afford to go get it, but we are willing to allow the giant energy companies to import liquified natural gas (LNG) from Algeria and Indonesia at prices considerably higher than that which would be necessary to make recovery of Louisiana natural gas economically feasible. On a positive note, Mr. Carter is negotiating with Mexico to tap her natural gas reserves, but that's only patching up the huge blooper he made not too long ago. California wanted to sign a contract with Mexico to import natural gas at $2.80 per 1000 cubic feet, but that exceeded Mr. Carter's guidelines in his "moral equivalent of war," so he shot that down, and we are now trying to mend the fences with an offended Mexico.

What is the solution? Totally deregulate natural gas and oil —immediately! The Carter energy program provided for a phased-out deregulation of natural gas over several years, but *THE WALL STREET JOURNAL* has pointed out that rather than stimulating production, it will probably have the exact opposite effect, and that the intent of Congress in the energy legislation is probably reversed by an administrative action by THE FEDERAL ENERGY REGU-LATION COMMISSION. They held by a vote of 3-2 that gas producers cannot employ escalator clauses in their contracts to raise gas prices to the new legal ceilings. In other words, if you are producing gas and selling it to a local gas company, you cannot insert a provision into new contracts that the price will rise to the new ceilings as the ceiling is gradually lifted unless the local gas company "wants to," and, of course, they won't. So gas deregulation will not result in the higher prices necessary to stimulate production.

There is also a backlog of 20,000 requests for action from parties affected by regulation, and the new regulations will add thousands of new cases to that backlog. Some of the younger participants will have grey hair before some cases are settled.

Other features of the energy plan will motivate industry to switch from gas to oil, which, in the light of the Iranian situation, is an act of monumental stupidity. (see: Deregulation of Gas)

IRS

(4/15/77) I don't know whether to laugh or cry!

Perhaps you noticed in your local paper an interesting story about the IRS and a bank robber. It seems that the bank robber, with some help, had stolen approximately $20,000. He ended up in jail, and while awaiting trial, police found approximately $6,000 in his apartment. They were able to trace $100 of it directly to the bank robbery. The IRS stepped into the picture and seized over $2,500 of it to cover the bank robber's income tax on his $10,000 share of the robbery. The IRS has refused to release the funds to the bank.

Now this raises all kinds of interesting legal issues. If the bank robber was not allowed to keep the money, did he truly have a taxable profit?

Now it seems to me that the bank ought to have some rights in this matter. I am no lover of banks, but after all, fair is fair.

Now you might put this down as simply one of those peculiar things that happens every once in a while. I believe that this is a typical governmental bureaucratic action, blindly following regulations that are drawn by mere mortals who have no idea of how they might be applied at some future date. Remember, no one is capable of drafting a regulation that will not need modification at some future time and the IRS certainly is no different from anyone else. What I'm concerned about is that the IRS so often acts with no concern whatsoever for the rights of innocent parties. When they seize money from someone's checking account to cover an alleged tax deficiency, do they consider the rights of an innocent party who may have deposited a check in his bank, drawn on that account, which had not cleared yet? Do they care at all about equity or fairness?

Of course, the answer is no. It is exactly as I have said before. As the burden of government spending becomes greater and greater and the success of the tax rebellion begins to hurt, the IRS will become more and more repressive.

The tax rebellion is now only a drop in the bucket; however, if the government persists in its arbitrary and unfair actions, there is no question in my mind that the tax rebellion will gather steam, and it could result in a breakdown of the so-called "voluntary compliance" for which American taxpayers have been justly famous in the past. This nation's government cannot exist without the goodwill of its population and the evidence is that the goodwill is rapidly being dissipated. (see: Bureaucrats; Government, Big; Regulatory Agencies)

J

JANEWAY, ELIOT

(3/15/78)

Q. Howard, what do you think of Eliot Janeway as an economist and advisor?

A. I always read him. Sometimes he's dull, he's often very wrong, and just about as frequently has something worthwhile to say. I had to laugh when, in one of his recent columns, he was asked why he still advised his readers to put money in the bank instead of investing in Krugerrands or gold bullion, in light of the dollar's troubles and the ineptness of the government that he had been talking about. He responded by saying:

> The dollar is the only money the world has for doing its business. Gold is not usable money. It represents speculation, not investment. Prudent investors never fall for high pressure retailing campaigns like the mass merchandizing of the Kruger-rand.
> Washington's first try, early in January, of buying dollars instead of discouraging their sale, broke the gold market. (It's $10 higher now than when he wrote that—HJR) This proves that the price of gold is just a speculation against the exchange value of the dollar. If you decide that I'm wrong, don't say I didn't warn you when headlines announcing a return of strength of the dollar break the gold market. It will happen before 1980. (This is an interesting statement with gold now nearing $500 an ounce, 12/79—HJR)

Janeway's nuts. Gold is the world's scared money. It's not just a hedge against the dollar. It's a hedge against international troubles.

Money is anything that people are willing to accept in exchange for goods and services. I agree that right now the dollar is money and gold isn't. But it is a hedge against the falling purchasing power of the dollar, not only in the international markets but as a result of domestic inflation. Right now, it is only a commodity like any other.

Later on, it will again serve as backing for money when monetary systems fail and the world is forced to turn back to gold, but not before the dollar has collapsed.

Take Janeway with a dose of salts. I have to laugh every time I hear his commercials for savings and loans. He and all of the other traditional economists will be swept away in the troubles that will envelope all financial institutions. You just go right ahead and buy your gold coins. And even at $190, it's still in a good buying range.

JUDICIARY SYSTEM

OUT OF CONTROL

(Special Report #2, 1/76) THE CRIMINAL JUSTICE SYSTEM IS OUT OF CONTROL. And so is crime.

As of this date in the city of New York, the backlog of criminal cases is over 700,000. If the police made no new arrests at all—if the whole police department went on vacation—it would take 2½ years for the courts to dispose of that backlog.

If a man commits a felony, his chances of not even being arrested are better than four to one. If he is arrested, his chances of getting indicted are only one in five. If he is indicted, the chances of the charge being reduced before trial are ten to one. That makes it very hard to get into jail.

In New York, the system is so bad, so overloaded, that plea bargaining is the only thing that has saved the system from total collapse. Under plea bargaining, the guilty go free immediately and the innocent stay in jail. That's right. If a person pleads innocent, he will then be sent back to jail until the trial can take place, which could be as much as eighteen months. That's the way it works. Plead guilty, you go free, plead innocent, you go back to jail.

The whole system is designed to obtain guilty pleas by reducing the penalty to the point where the felon will plead guilty. As a result, rapists, murderers, muggers, heroin dealers, and arsonists all find themselves free on reduced charges.

If no defendants agreed to plead guilty, the criminal justice system would be destroyed within a month. Every day in New York, some 400 felons from City Jail plead guilty in court and are released or transferred to upstate prisons for short "wristslap" sentences.

As recession and unemployment create desperation, crimes against property (burglary, arson, car theft, etc.) will increase. As New York City's budget is cut, there will be less and less police to keep what degree of order there is. And New York is not the only city faced with this problem.

(7/1/76) As I've stated before, one of the greatest threats to freedom is the rise of judicial power—courts literally out of control.

In Gilbert and Sullivan's "Trial by Jury" the judge sings,

"And though my law be fudge, I will never, never budge. And I'll live and die a judge, and a good judge too."

There has been an immense increase in the use of the court order to bring about social change. We've already recounted two examples.

In Boston, Judge Garrity has taken total control of the school system. And not just by ordering busing. He has stopped the closing of schools in the face of declining enrollment and virtual municipal bankruptcy. He has ordered new construction and renovation, and assigned and transferred teachers, and then said in effect, "What it costs is not my problem. Raise the money or else."

Here's a forecast for you.

You will see judicial power rampant—out of control—when New York's finances finally collapse, and the city will be supported by the taxpayers—from Keokuk to Phoenix and New Orleans—and it will be ruled by a panel of Federal judges. The time is near when the elected officials will be stripped of all power over taxation, borrowing, and disbursements.

TYRANNY FROM THE BENCH

(10/1/78) The Supreme Court, voting 5-3, recently said that judges cannot be sued unless they act in "a clear absence of all jurisdiction." This is the conclusion of a suit over a 1971 court order which authorized the sterilization of an unsuspecting 15 year-old girl. She had been told she was going to have an appendectomy, but it turned out to be a tubal ligation (sterilization), which she found out four years later, after she was married.

It was the opinion of three of the justices that her constitutional rights had been violated. However, the justices upheld that no judge can be sued for making mistakes or is even guilty of malicious action. He can be sued only if he acts "in a clear absence of all jurisdiction," an immunity doctrine first fashioned in an 1871 Supreme Court decision.

But JUSTICE POTTER STEWART in his dissent said, "I think that what Judge Stump did . . . was beyond the pale of anything that could sensibly be called a judicial act."

Many flagrantly unconstitutional decisions are oozing from our courts. The Internal Revenue Service operates under the legal theory that you are guilty of tax evasion unless you prove yourself innocent, a clear violation of Constitutional guarantees. Also, IRS procedures clearly violate the Constitutional guarantees against "unreasonable search and seizure," self-incrimination, and double jeopardy. The courts have consistently upheld them in this regard.

Under our Constitutional separation of Judicial, Legislative and Executive functions, the other two departments should be a rein on the courts, but they are not. They either sit on their hands or merely affirm by "benign neglect" the power of the judges. (see: Government, IRS)

(4/15/79) Contemplating the possible consequences of my defiance of MR. HARTLINE, of THE FEDERAL HOME LOAN BANK BOARD (see: Banks, Robert Hartline letter), I did get a little shiver down my spine while reading an article which appeared in the SAN FRANCISCO CHRONICLE, February 10. I was reminded of the coercive power of the bench. It seems that the three commissioners of Carroll County, Ohio, did not grant the demands of JUDGE PATRICIA ANDERSON for a 23% increase in 1979 appropriations for her court, over the 1978 budget. So she sentenced them to 10 days in jail for contempt of court, plus a $500 fine from each commissioner, and then left for a weekend judicial conference in Washington. She said she was willing to forgive the remaining sentences and fines when she returns next week if the commissioners agree to her order.

The county prosecutor said, "I checked to see if they had changed their minds and they said 'no.' " Apparently, the Ohio Supreme Court in a Marion County case has upheld similar jailings but it stipulated that, "the rights of those affected must not be violated." I am sorry, but that escapes me. How can you not violate their rights and put them in jail? But I guess I just don't understand the law. The State Senator who represents that county said he was drafting a bill that addresses the problem, but don't count on him for a lot of help. He said, "There's not a whole lot we can do right now for this sentence. I'm not a lawyer but it looks like the law is on her side. In my opinion, she didn't use common sense."

It's just another piece of the pattern of increasing power of all levels of government, totally contrary to the concept of our founding fathers that government should be limited.

I hope this remains an isolated instance. If it isn't, it scares the heck out of me, and I sure hope I don't have Judge Patricia Anderson, or somebody like her, sitting in on my trial, should it ever come to that.

L

LESSER DEVELOPED COUNTRIES

(Special Report #2, 1/76) THE THIRD WORLD IS OUT OF CONTROL. Several months ago, I heard a speech by an ambassador from India to one of the European nations speaking before the Commonwealth Club in San Francisco. In a conversation after the speech, with several people gathered around, one member of the club asked, "If India has such a great need for economic help, why did you spend several billion dollars to build atomic weapons?" The ambassador, choosing his words very carefully, responded, "We will at some future time, be required to demand assistance in food and money from the wealthy nations of the world. When that time comes, we wish to be credible."

The Third World has discovered its power. In past decades, through our economic and military power, we were able to manipulate the natural resources of the lesser developed countries to our advantage. They were able to benefit from American investment, but there was no question as to who was in control. We were! Now, the smaller nations are flexing their muscles. Many of them are combining to form cartels to boost prices and make political demands in return for the export of vital commodities to this country. The Arab countries are only one example. Similar cartels are being developed in aluminum and copper. The Third World is demanding nothing less than a redistribution of the world's wealth: Robin Hood on a cosmic scale.

Now some of the poorer nations have atomic weapons. Sooner or later, nuclear weapons will be used. Can you imagine "The Bomb" in the hands of President Amin of Uganda?

LETTERS TO THE EDITOR

(8/15/76)   Love Letters
Dear Sirs,

Your comments on birth control are stupid and dangerous. Please cancel my subscription.

—John H.

* * * * *

Gentlemen:

I have never seen such drivel. If I see another copy of your rag in the mailbox, I will report you for mail fraud. I bet you won't have the guts to print this.

—Wilson M.

Wilson, stop beating around the bush. What are you trying to say?

—H.J.R.

* * * * *

Dear Mr. Ruff:

Your last issue was pure trash.

But, please don't cancel my subscription. I can hardly wait to see what's the next damn fool thing you're going to say.

—Mrs. Leona M.

* * * * *

There now, readers. Wasn't that fun? Fortunately for my peace of mind, about ninety-eight percent of our letter writers love us.

M

MARKETS

(12/1/78) Markets, and What They Can Tell Us
By R. E. McMaster

In the last century, wagon trains crossed the great Mississippi and headed west with regularity. Out front, breaking trail, finding the river crossings and mountain passages, were the wagon trains' scouts. The scouts provided the pioneers with advance information on dangers such as Indian attacks, prairie fires, and flash floods. They also provided the wagon train with favorable information, such as the location of deer or buffalo herds from which meat could be obtained. The scouts were the avant-garde. They had first contact with "experiences" that would affect the wagon train.

Each of us, in our individual occupations, makes up a portion of the U.S. economy's wagon train. Our scouts, our avant-garde, which process information and feed it back to us as forecasts, are the markets.

Throughout the history of the markets, many reputable and successful analysts have concluded that the markets are "discounting mechanisms" that foresee the future. Stated differently, markets move in anticipation of a news event. Once the news is in the market, or once you and I see the news item on the TV or read it in the newspaper, it is of little value to the market investor. The market has already discounted the event. "Buy on rumor, sell on news," is a good rule of thumb.

Markets are usually reliable indicators of coming change. Inflation and government manipulation of the economy have dramatically increased the volatility of our financial world and undermined its stability. The fact that there is a four-year economic/political cycle means that, by its very nature, there is continual change. Therefore, we are forced—all of us—into the role of the speculator. We must change our investment and business strategies so that we are in harmony with the alterations in the economic cycle, or suffer financially. The markets can tell us how to adjust.

Markets are not perfect predictors of change. The wagon train scouts didn't always pick the best place to ford a river. But, over the long journey west, they were reliable guides, and so are the markets.

Just what indicators should you watch to aid you in your day-to-day personal and financial planning? Since you probably don't have the time or inclination to be a market analyst, I will zero-in on those relatively simple indicators which can provide you with meaningful information on which to act.

Markets are made by people. Agreement between a buyer and a seller at some price is partially the result of the anticipation of future market movement by each party. The interaction of all the buyers and all the sellers creates a sort-of "mass mind" in the markets. Masses, whether they be a football crowd, a political rally, or traders in a market, can be predicted with a rather high degree of accuracy(probability). The herd instinct grips the masses. Therefore, predicting the psychology of the crowd is the most important consideration in the market place.

There is a mass psychological cyclical movement lasting approximately 50 years. As JAMES A. FUNK wrote in 1932 in *THE CYCLES OF PROSPERITY AND DEPRESSION*, the "Cyclic/Order" for a society is: "Depression produces thrift. Thrift produces confidence. Confidence produces investment. Investment produces activity. Activity produces prosperity. Prosperity produces easy credit. Easy credit produces over-production. Over-production produces fictitious sales and fictitious collateral. These produce an economic structure of fictitious paper value. When the structure is so recognized, it is abandoned, which is another way of expressing panic. Panic produces depression." The more things change, the more they are the same. It should be obvious that we are in the latter stages of that 50-year economic cycle.

One accurate gauge of the psychology of particular markets is "bullish consensus" figures, commonly called "contrary opinion" percentages. When better than 80% of the crowd in a market believe prices are going up, we will become suspicious and expect a market top to be close at hand. When 20% or less of the crowd believe prices are going up, we will be looking for a market bottom. The theory of contrary opinion is one of our most important tools. We also use cycles, technical analyses, and fundamentals in evaluating markets.

I focus most closely on the commodity markets. Why? The commodity markets are the nearest to reality. They are the "first fruits" from the good earth. They are the leading "scouts" of our economic wagon train. As the initial ingredient, or starting point, in our economic production process, commodity price movements often give us the best advance warning of changing trends. For example, the plywood and lumber markets give us clues to future activity in construction and real estate. They also hint at the direction of long-term interest rates. As plywood and lumber prices fall, interest rates usually rise. The long-term interest rate markets (T-Bonds and Ginnie Maes) tell us where we are in the economic cycle. As the long-term rates work higher, we know that the economic cycle is approaching its end. When the long-term rates become too high, businesses will refuse to borrow for capital expansion (new plants and equipment), real estate developers will retreat to the sidelines, and potential home buyers will decide not to purchase a new home.

The rise in short-term interest rates helps us gauge the increasing rate of inflation, as well as the government's decision to fight inflation. The decision by the government to fight inflation is marked by an increase in the discount rate, and is reflected in the T-bill futures market. These increases usually result in less borrowing. When this occurs, a recession should be anticipated.

The copper market is an important indicator of future construction and manufacturing activity. Cotton gives us an input to our understanding of the next direction of consumer spending and retail sales. Silver and gold reflect the inflationary pressure on the economy as well as approaching chaos, such as civil riots and wars. Sugar, potatoes, pork bellies, cattle, hogs, eggs, coffee, cocoa, soybeans, oats, corn and wheat prices are important barometers of future prices we will pay in the grocery store, as well as the rate of inflation.

The Commodity Research Bureau's Oil Seeds, Metals, Livestock and Meats, Industrials and Grains indices point to the prevailing trends of each of these groups.

The Dow Jones Industrials, Transportations, and Utilities are important overall economic forecasters, and, together with the commodity and bond markets, make up the overall market picture which anticipates our future.

In these increasingly unstable times, the markets are more emotional and therefore much more volatile. Therefore some parameters will be given so you can watch (with the help of *THE WALL STREET JOURNAL*) the market action in order to see how the trends are progressing or changing.

(R. E. McMaster is Editor of *THE REAPER*, a weekly trading advisory service specializing in trading the commodity markets and interpreting what the markets are telling us about the economy. P.O. Box 39026, Phoenix, AZ 85069.)

(1/1/79)   Markets, And What They Can Tell Us
By R. E. McMaster, Jr.

Our present economic recovery is now the second longest post-war economic expansion in history (three years, nine months old). Are economic expansions like markets? Can they go up too far, too fast, for too long? If they do so, without correcting, does it mean the ultimate correction will be more severe? Competent technical analysts will tell you so. A market that goes up for too long without a significant correction is approaching a final top, or will experience a very severe correction once the adjustment comes. Why? For each action, there is an equal and opposite reaction. The euphoria of extended over-bullishness gives way to fear as the bears take hold. This is the danger in our present overripe economic expansion—a sharp, severe break.

The Interest Rate Markets

The week of December 11th (1978), the long term Treasury security markets (Ginnie Mae and T-bonds) and the short term T-bill markets both shattered their support and broke to new lows. As markets tend to anticipate the future, and falling bond and T-bill prices mean rising interest rates, and vice versa, I have concluded that we will soon see higher long and short-term interest rates. This confirms the projection of the greatly respected HENRY KAUFMAN of SALOMON BROTHERS, who is looking for a 12% prime rate minimum. Interest rates usually do not peak until after a recession has begun.

Originally, there was some technical basis for hope of a near term peak in interest rates. When the Treasury bond market reversed and broke to new contract lows, the strength of the down trend was reaffirmed.

The rise in short-term interest rates above the long-term rates is also a major red flag, forecasting the imminent end of the business cycle and high inflation rates, as the business expansion rushes to its peak.

The Stock Market

Since the stock market is a reasonable indicator of future business activity, we need to watch it closely.

The "timing indicators" (cycles) correctly warned us of a stock market low (Dow Jones Industrials) in November. The cyclical low was confirmed by those "fundamentalists" who view the book value, price/earning ratios, and yields of stocks to be in bargain territory. *RICHARD RUSSELL'S DOW THEORY LETTER* notes that the

Dow Industrials are "actually selling below book value." This is rare, and "the Dow is now selling at approximately nine times earnings. In only 12 years since 1929 has the Dow Price/Earnings ratio dropped below 10, the area where it is now." Russell further states, "The yield on the Dow is now 5.9%, not far from the historically attractive 6% yield level. In the past, 6% on the Dow has always been considered the lower end of the 'bargain in values' zone, an area which was seen during 1932, 1942, 1949, and 1953, all major lows."

(I'm not so sure that today's 6% yield is such a "bargain" rate, after you adjust for an inflation rate at least twice as high as it was during those previous lows. And don't forget higher tax rates. By the time you crank in those two factors, true yields in real purchasing power are a lot less than six percent. If that is correct, the recent market lows may not be the real bottom, and my forecast of "truly terrifying lows" is still ahead of us. HJR)

Should stock prices break sharply and broadly below 780, followed by further lows, then we should suspect that the American economy is headed for serious trouble. A gentleman with whom I have done a great deal of technical research, TOM DEMARK of NATIONAL INVESTMENT SERVICES, felt that while the Dow could rally to 840, it was probably headed for 720-740. It would not be surprising for there to be another sell-off following the current recovery from the October panic decline. This kind of market action carries dire forebodings for the economy in general.

The Commodity Markets

The is an emerging overall unity to present commodity price action, which does not indicate more inflation, at least not near term. Soybeans have been dropping. Wheat is down. Cattle, pork bellies, and hogs are working lower. Only the metals are still in up-trends, but they are over-bought. As a result, the overall commodity indices (Dow Jones Futures and Spot Indexes and the Commodity Research Bureau's Futures Price Index) reveal "choppy" declines. If the Commodity Research Bureau's FUTURE PRICE INDEX again rises to challenge or exceed the 238 level later in 1979, then we will know we face increased inflationary pressures. This is not the case presently, but it needs to be watched closely.

Individual Commodities

The Swiss franc, German deutschemark, and British pound are moving as a unit against the dollar. Their recent, sharp five week decline following an extensive six month bull rise is typical of the end of a bull market, suggesting that the dollar has bottomed for now. Should this not be the case, then we will clearly have dangerous monetary problems. Let's state this differently: Should the March futures contracts in the Swiss franc and the German deutschemark rally to new highs, we should expect probable panic, possibly hyper-inflation, maybe wage and price controls, and general economic chaos. But for now, technical indicators project that the dollar has bottomed.

Don't be alarmed by steep rallies in these international currencies against the dollar. Such is a normal part of the distribution process. Markets don't go straight up or straight down. They oscillate up and down before they start to trend down. And, the steeper the decline (as we saw in the Swiss franc), usually the steeper the corrective rally. Fundamentally, the recent steep rallies we have seen in these international currencies, from historical support and oversold conditions, were fueled by the OPEC price rise and trouble in Iran.

Gold

The above comments concerning the international currencies apply to some extent to gold. Gold has been following the lead of the Swiss franc, so I monitor them together. The public is still very strongly committed to the bull side, and the public is usually wrong. A cyclical and technical peak is due in this market the last week of December or the first week in January, 1979. Then, the market should retest the 200 lows. If I'm right about the dollar, gold will break below 200, perhaps as low as 150. Interestingly enough, Tom DeMark is looking for the high 220s (London price), to be followed by a decline to 155. (Tom and I reached our conclusions independently.)

Silver is following gold, but is the "weak sister." At this time, it is anticipated that if gold breaks sharply, silver could "fall out of bed."

The failure of copper to break down (in any meaningful sense) has been encouraging for the U.S. economy near term. Copper's rally, however, in keeping with its seasonal tendency, has now approached the historic 71-72 resistance level. A sharp decline for the copper market would confirm economic trouble in manufacturing, fabricating, and home building. Housing starts are maintaining the two million unit annual rate. Shipments of electrical products and appliances are still running strong. Capital goods spending and nonresidential building's vigorous activity have been supportive of the copper market too.

Food prices will continue to increase in 1979. Commodities such as cattle, hogs, pork bellies, soybean oil, soybeans, potatoes, sugar, etc., are not cheap, by any means. But the processing costs (the middleman) continue to drive prices out of sight. And, the workers in the food processing industries have labor contracts up for renegotiation in 1979. Who believes the unions will follow Carter's voluntary wage guidelines?

Bearish action in the cotton market could be confirming a weakening of consumer spending and recession in 1979. Such would not be surprising, particularly since the U.S. consumer has increased his level of debt by 50% since 1974.

(2/1/79)   Markets And What They Can Tell Us
By R. E. McMaster, Jr.

Markets, as reflections of life, display the accelerating pace of life. Many traders are falling by the wayside and losing money. They can't stand the pace. Worldwide inflation is a big part of the problem, and it is further complicated by global political and military upheavals. Lately, bombs have been exploding all around us: Cleveland's bankruptcy, the fall of the Shah of Iran, the recognition of Red China, the fall of Cambodia. As the world becomes increasingly unstable, we need to dig in and seriously prepare for the coming bad years.

A month ago, I wrote, "Our present economic recovery is now the second longest post-war economic expansion in history (three years, nine months old). . . . This is the danger in our present overripe economic expansion—a sharp, severe break." It is interesting to note that the January 8, 1979 *WALL STREET JOURNAL* almost echoed *THE RUFF TIMES* "The current upturn, nearing birthday number four, is an extreme old-timer. . .business cycle experience strongly suggests that this expansion, already remarkably long-lived, is likely to end sometime soon." Question: Is the *WALL STREET JOUR-NAL* reading *THE RUFF TIMES*?

Red flags are flying! (1) We presently have an interest rate inversion. Short-term interest rates have higher yields than long-term interest rates. In the six times that this has occurred in this century, all but one time was followed by a panic, crash, and resulting economic contraction (recession or depression). (2) When the discount rate was raised one full point last November, 1978, another flag went up. When this occurred in the past, it led to the Depressions of 1921, 1929, and the bank runs and financial crisis of 1931-33. (3) Beef prices are soaring. Beef is a basic consumer item in our economy. High beef prices have historically signalled the onset of an economic downturn. Perhaps the psychologized effect of high beef prices and the resulting consumer withdrawal from that market is a forecaster of retrenchment in other areas as well. (4) Capital spending has increased. This activity classically occurs near the end of the business cycle. (5) Small, unsophisticated businesses are eager to expand. This was a red flag prior to the last recession.

So, why hasn't the economy turned down? One key to the matter is the monetary base, which has continued to grow. Increasing loan demand has resulted in higher interest rates. But as interest rates rise, instead of choking off the recovery, the Federal Reserve has increased the monetary base and, therefore, accommodated increased loan demand. Unless the Federal Reserve moves decisively to reduce the monetary base, we could experience a stair step effect: higher monetary base, higher interest rates, a still higher monetary base, and then even higher interest rates. This could result in runaway inflation, which is why we have had recurring dollar panics during the past year. (Eurodollar holders, who are said to hold a dollar amount equal to all the demand deposits in domestic banks, are not willing to watch their purchasing power rapidly diminish.)

What can stop this sequence of events? (1) A firm stand by the Administration to stop the creation of money and credit, and balance the budget. (2) Widespread fear or a panic of some type. The first is not likely because the politicians are all too aware that during the next economic downturn, falling tax collections could result in a $100 billion deficit. That deficit would make today's inflation look like a tea party.

The second is the most likely. Any surprise/fear can result in panic. And when the economic foundation is unstable, as it is now, and when people are tired, as they are now, a panic is possible.

Human action runs in cycles. We start with a depression. People become thrifty as a result of the depression. This thrift produces confidence. Confidence results in investment. Investment produces activity. Activity results in prosperity. Prosperity yields to easy-credit. Easy-credit results in excesses. These excesses lead to a panic, which then results in a depression.

The Interest Rate Markets

As predicted last time, we have seen higher interest rates (T-bills). The Federal Reserve has raised its target rate on Federal funds from 10 to 10½ percent. However, for the past five weeks, the short-term interest rate futures market (T-bills), and the long-term interest rate futures market (Ginnie Maes) have been in tight consolidations, called "trading ranges." Confirming "bullish momentum," these markets have rallied and have decisively broken out of their trading ranges on the upside. We should expect a near-term softening of interest rates. If they reverse down, and breakout through the lower boundary of the trading range, then a continuation of the trend to higher interest rates is forecast. An old, conservative market principle is to assume the continuation of a major trend until there is a clear reversal. Therefore, at the present time, we must assume that we have not seen the peak in interest rates even though, near term, they should decline.

The Stock Market

The Dow Jones Industrials' rally to the 840 level came exactly as forecast. As long as this market rises, we should not be overly concerned about dire economic problems presently in the news. In fact, the longer the stock market goes up, the greater can be our assumption that it has discounted (anticipated) the worst of our immediate economic troubles. Should the market break sharply and close below the all important 780 level, then we should become concerned. Many investors and financial institutions view a Dow Jones Industrial close below 780 as having dire forebodings for the economy.

The Commodity Markets
Gold and the International Currencies

Increased monetary inflation is now occurring in the Swiss franc, German deutschemark, and Japanese yen. Investors who traditionally sought protection in these currencies, against a decline in the value of the dollar, have had to alter their investment posture. During the week of January 15th, a major shift occurred. Pressure on the dollar did not result in dramatically higher franc, deutschemark, and yen prices. It resulted in an explosive price rise in gold and silver, preceded by copper. Could this be a vote of "no confidence" for any currency by sophisticated investors? In any case, this shift in relative strength in favor of the metals, against the major international currencies, marked a significant deviation from recent market action. The irony of it all is that gold and the dollar could both appreciate against the major international currencies.

The International Currencies

During the month of January, the major international currencies suffered a net loss against the dollar. They did rally enough, however, in sympathy with the rise in the price of gold. The near-term direction of the international currencies is down. It is clouded by central bank intervention, and the longer-term indicators are slightly bearish.

The Metals

The surprising break of the tie between gold and the Swiss franc casts a whole different light on the precious metals. Copper led the charge, followed closely by silver and then gold. Presently, however, they have rallied to levels where significant resistance is expected. All the "true believers" are long on these metals, which is at least a sign that some caution is advisable. Furthermore, one of the most unique aspects of the recent price rise has been that the precious metals have rallied with the news. Markets usually anticipate (discount) the news. While there is no question that survival gold is a must during these treacherous times, several generally incompatible markets are moving to the same direction. Gold and the bond market are rising.

The political risk remains to these metal markets. If the dollar stays firm against the international currencies, will the Carter Administration allow gold and silver to rise? Maybe. All in all, even with cycles favoring higher prices in the metals into February, one should recognize the risk and approach these markets cautiously. Technically, prospects for the metal markets are deteriorating near-term.

Individual Commodities

The recent cold weather served as a catalyst to higher meat prices. Higher futures market prices in cattle and hogs project still higher meat prices at the supermarket. Should the metal complex continue to rally enthusiastically, this could carry over into the soybean complex, corn, and oats, which have shown some improvement. Higher prices in basic commodities plus increased processing costs, could dampen discretionary consumer spending. Expect to spend a bigger chunk of your paycheck on food.

A word of caution. These comments are not intended as trading recommendations. The markets are very nervous and unstable. Harsh and unpredictable weather, explosive world-wide events, concern over interest rates and inflation in this late stage of the business cycle, and an increasingly volatile response to each and every pronouncement from Washington, D.C. have led to violent market turns.

(3/15/79) What The Markets Tell Us About The Future
By R. E. McMaster, Jr.

The stock market (Dow Jones Industrial Average) is still dangerously near the psychological critical 800 level and the technically critical 785 and 780 levels. A wide-range, heavy volume, low close below these important lows will put us on economic "red alert." Such a drop could possibly signal a more severe recession than 1974, with increasing corporate and personal bankruptcies. At a minimum, the violation of these important support levels will lead to retrenchment by professional investors. If the stock market is an anticipator of future news, a break below these lows must be viewed as a harbinger of really bleak headlines.

But there is hope. Adjusted for the Consumer Price Index, the critical stock market low, formed in November 1978, is nearly as low as the adjusted 1974 low. Some analysts point to this fact as a good reason to buy stocks. Cycle analysts are forecasting a higher stock market. Week after week, the fundamentalists on WALL STREET WEEK talk about how cheap stocks are in terms of yields, price earnings/ratios, etc. What's the point?

This unresolved conflict shows we are at a critical economic juncture. The stock market will probably indicate our next major economic direction. It is our most important indicator. If the market breaks to new lows in the face of (1) bullish cycles, (2) historically cheap stocks based on fundamentals, and (3) bargain basement prices adjusted for the Consumer Price Index, then we are headed for severe economic trouble.

Since last November, the bullish "star" in the commodity market has been the copper market. During the first week of March, 94% of all the copper traders felt prices were going higher. This usually signals a major top, according to the contrary opinion theory. Rising copper prices are a very positive sign for the economy from the viewpoint of some analysts. Copper is used for tubing in home building and other construction, as well as in manufacturing. Consumption has been rising. Copper stocks, meanwhile, have been dwindling.

These positive economic "demand" fundamentals are further supported by supply problems in the U.S., Zaire, Zambia, and Chile, which should continue. If copper prices fall in the face of these supply problems, this could mean a contracting economy.

An interesting perspective on the copper market came from MARTY ZWEIG, of *THE ZWEIG FORECAST* (747 Third Avenue, New York, NY 10017). "Copper tends to top very late in both the business and the stock market cycles. Currently, copper is in a super boom, especially in the commodity markets. Given that the Dow Industrials topped out nearly 2½ years ago, and the ZUPI peaked close to six months back, the resumption of speculation in copper is an insidious sign. Any phenomenon so reminiscent of '29, '70 and '74 is scary. Perhaps one ought to 'copper' the market."

A seasonal peak in lumber and plywood is due before May. If lumber, plywood, and interest rates drop severely at the same time, instead of the usual seasonal peak, the real estate boom is probably over.

Along a related line, DAVID RHOADS, of *THE RHOADS CONCLUSION* (P.O. Box 22675, San Diego, CA 92122), observed that personal bankruptcy in Southern California is becoming as common as divorce. Mortgage delinquency rates have not yet reflected this, but they will. As goes California, so goes the country.

If interest rates go higher now in the face of a contracting monetary environment, an overheated and overextended economic recovery, and illiquidity among banks, businesses, and consumers, then the probability increases that the hoped for "soft landing" will result in a "crash." While fundamentalists (like Howard Ruff) certainly have a valid argument for higher interest rates, the charts do not support their case at this time. This is not unusual in the first quarter of each year. Probabilities favor higher interest rates in the 2nd quarter. The T-bill market (short-term interest rates) and the Ginnie Mae and T-bond market (long-term interest rates) are in a neutral trading range. The 90-Day Commercial Paper market has been forecasting lower rates for several months now. (My fake-you-out scenario? HJR)

We may be forced to keep the rates on U.S. government issues (T-bills and T-bonds) artificially high in order to attract foreign investors and prevent another run on the dollar. This will aggravate any economic downturn. (Lower interest rates will be unavailable to credit-worthy and needy borrowers.) Historically, the stock market has not formed a bottom and rallied until after interest rates have experienced a healthy decline. (This was the case in 1970 and 1974.) This bodes ill for the stock market, and therefore, for the economy.

Commodities soar very late in the business cycle, during an inflationary boom. We have seen this from August 1978 through February 1979. Overall, the Commodity market should peak between now and the end of May.

Gold, the primary and most sensitive indicator of inflation, has been unable to advance recently in the face of soaring wholesale and consumer prices, in addition to the threat of war. Silver, which is an industrial commodity as well as a precious metal, has acted similarly. The dollar remains strong against the Japanese yen. It has also been doing better against the deutschemark and Swiss franc. All this suggests a near term softening of inflation, and some relief for the tattered dollar. (The fake-you-out phase again? HJR)

The futures market in cattle has entered a blowoff stage. This is historically a prelude to recession. While consumer prices will be considerably higher in the next year, a peak in cattle prices is thought by some analysts to call the top of the commodity markets.

If the meat market turns down in the face of bullish supply

fundamentals (cattle), this can only be forecasting declining buying power on the part of the consumer. (Consumer spending has made up between 2/3 and 3/4 of this business cycle.)

The four month decline in the cotton market may be a warning of a decrease in discretionary spending on the part of the consumer. The cotton market anticipates, to some degree, the level of retail sales. Certainly, the consumer assumption of record debt, coupled with his higher taxes and energy costs, means that he will be unable to spend to the degree that he has during the 48 months of this economic recovery.

Sugar prices, which were thought by some analysts to be in a bull market due to increasing world demand and inflationary expectations, have broken down. Should the July contract (New York) close below 8.4, then it will probably be forecasting declining economic activity and an easing of inflation.

Supply fundamentals, coupled with adverse weather, have been bullish for the grains. Soybeans, corn, wheat and oats have recently reflected declining demand near-term, which should not last for long. Over the next decade, adverse weather will thrust us into the era of "protein gold." (*THE REAPER* focuses on this subject.)

At this late hour in the business cycle, a stock market collapse will most probably signal recession. An accompanying commodity collapse would signal severe economic problems and probably a deflation and liquidity crisis.

MONEY MARKET FUNDS

(10/15/76)   We're interviewing JAMES BENHAM, President and founder of CAPITAL PRESERVATION FUND, Palo Alto, California. I became aware of Mr. Benham when, on the same day I had read an article in a national magazine about the successful performance of his fund, a subscription to *THE RUFF TIMES* came across my desk from Capital Preservation Fund. After getting acquainted with Jim, I concluded that he shared many of the same convictions that we hold here at *THE RUFF TIMES*.

HJR: First, Capital Preservation Fund is a money fund. What is a money fund?

JIM: A money fund invests exclusively in the money market. The money market is that market, primarily in New York City, where debt instruments with maturities of one year or less are transacted by telephone. Money market debt instruments include U.S. Treasury bills, bank certificates of deposit (CDs), bankers' acceptances, and commercial paper issued by corporations.

Most people and institutions lack access to the money market because of the large minimum denominations required. As an example, a "round lot" transaction in Treasury bills is never less than $1 million and is often $5 million.

Today, people with $10,000 can buy Treasury bills but they can't really participate in the money market. They don't have the clout or market contacts necessary to obtain the best prices.

HJR: Would you class yourself as a mutual fund?

JIM: Yes, we are an SEC "registered investment company" which is, by definition, a mutual fund. We mutually pool investors, money to gain effective access to U.S. Treasury bills which dominate the money market.

HJR: Then, people invest in your fund and their money is then invested in the money market, right?

JIM: Yes. Today there are 41 money funds with $3-1/3 billion from investors numbering close to 200,000. We were the second to open nationally and are the largest in the West.

HJR: Do you restrict yourself to U.S. Treasury debt?

JIM: That's correct—short-term "full faith and credit" debt of the U.S. government. We also take physical delivery of our investments.

HJR: I would like to add, for the benefit of our readers, that yours is a "no-load" fund, which means that there are no sales commissions to pay to security salesmen, either when investing or withdrawing money.

JIM: In fact, that's the only way anyone can invest with us.

HJR: Many of our subscribers have accepted our basic premise that, at this time, they ought to have a high degree of liquidity, that they should get out of investments which can't be quickly converted to currency. Do you agree?

JIM: I agree. The attractive thing about being liquid is that one maintains all investment options. The fund deals in the most liquid market of all. Round lots ($1 million or more) of Treasuries are completely liquid.

HJR: It seems to me that when you are going for liquidity and safety, you sacrifice some profit.

JIM: Yes, that's a fundamental fact of life in every market. Tying up money for a long period of time always rewards you more. For instance, a $1 million overnight investment in U.S. government securities yields five percent today, while long-term U.S. government securities are yielding close to eight percent.

HJR: How do you make an overnight investment?

JIM: Well, if you have $500,000 or more, you execute a one-day "repurchase agreement." An overnight "repo" investment is the ultimate in liquidity. We always have at least a small portion of the Fund's portfolio in an overnight repurchase agreement.

We believe that in this country, the paper investment with the greatest safety and least risk is U.S. government debt. U.S. government debt has no credit risk. There is a risk, however, the market risk. The Treasury sold 10-year Notes last August, paying eight percent. As lucrative as these notes seem today, I would not be surprised if, before maturity, eight percent will not look so good. England is paying around 11 percent right now on Treasury bills, and long-term British debts yield in the high tens. Not too long ago, eight percent was considered a high return in London.

HJR: Do you think we are catching the "English Disease?"

JIM: Yes. U.S. markets tend to follow many of the trends established in Great Britain. England's problems have emerged-throughout the world.

HJR: Then don't you think that at some future time, the U.S. Government might repudiate its debt?

JIM: I'm not predicting such an eventuality, but yes, I accept it as a possibility. For the time being, I believe in our paper money.

HJR: I agree that at the present time, U.S. government securities are safe to hold, but it is my opinion that at some future time the only safe haven will be precious metals, and people will have to move out of all paper, simply because government debt will become too huge to even service, let alone refinance as it comes due.

JIM: In my opinion, that may never happen. But it's all right for us to differ on that.

(11/15/76)   Jim Benham Interview, cont.

HJR: Mondale recently said that one of the first actions of the Carter Administration would be to loosen the money supply and reduce interest rates to stimulate the economy. How does that affect the investor holding any type of interest-bearing instrument?

JIM: It depends. If Carter is elected, we will probably see easy money shortly after his inauguration. Initially we will see more pump-priming, more Washington spending. I don't think that this is necessarily going to bring about lasting lowered short-term rates, because the debt markets are sophisticated. Whenever more dollars chase the same amount of goods and services, we eventually experience higher inflation rates. The market knows this. We might see huge increases in M-1 and M-2, the money supply numbers. Howard, that's the time I would be shortening the maturity structure of the Fund's portfolio, because interest rates wouldn't stay down for long. My feeling is that if, in fact, the government does turn out a stream of money, get ready for a higher rate of inflation somewhere within a few months.

HJR: You say you've read every issue of *THE RUFF TIMES*. I'd like to get some reactions from you as to what areas strike you as being useful, and some of the areas you might disagree with. It's great that sophisticated people such as yourself are taking note of what we're saying.

JIM: You have motivated me and stimulated my thinking and I've personally taken some steps that have been recommended in your writings, Howard.

I've expanded my holding of precious metals—coins—as you suggested. I have investigated various sources of food in case I decide it's time to stockpile. I now have what I think is a complete vitamin program and a storage supply of such vitamins. I am in complete agreement with you about not relying on the assumptions of the past. I don't believe the assumptions that were the basis for investment decisions in the past will necessarily be useful in the future. Markets are still undergoing dramatic changes.

HJR: If you were to go back five years and ask any conventional investment advisor, "What are the safest possible investments for a widow with insurance money?" He would say, "Municipal bonds, blue chip stocks paying good dividends, and mutual funds." And now, the world has turned upside down. The municipal bond market is trembling at every new hint of the New York City disease, and changes in the bankruptcy laws enable cities to go bankrupt and repudiate their debt. The stock market and stock-investing mutual funds have taken a pasting, despite the flirtation with a 1000 Dow level.

So all of our assumptions have been turned upside down, yet

advisors are still giving traditional investment advice, even though anyone who would step back and look at today's real world would see that those assumptions have been drastically altered.

(12/1/76)   Jim Benham Interview, cont.

HJR: It's my opinion that we are entering an era where the investor should be cautiously conserving his assets, and that this is no time to be sticking out necks and taking risks.

JIM: I agree with your position. I think that many people who used to play the investment game recognize new dangers in our system today, the uncertainties that surround us, and the lack of control in certain areas of our lives. Human behavior is a very strange thing to predict. That's why I want liquidity.

HJR: Let's say that someone came to you and said, "Mr. Benham, I have $10,000 in liquid assets. I haven't made any survival preparations. How should I divide up that money and what portion of it should I put in Capital Preservation Fund?" What recommendations would you make?

JIM: Well again, it depends. With $10,000 in liquid form and without an investment program, this tells me automatically that the money is in a bank or a savings and loans. That should be changed. I would not rely on the insurance provided by the FDIC or the FSLIC. I don't believe it would be adequate during times of extreme stress and crisis. The government deposit insurance program was not designed for that purpose at all. It was designed for normal times. (see: Banking Industry & Banks) And in my opinion, these are not normal times. So, my first recommendation would be to improve the safety behind that liquidity.

Secondly, I believe that some of that money should be spent on food. What is more liquid than something you can eat? It is up to the individual to decide how much.

HJR: Let's assume that it's a family of four, and they decide upon a year's supply of food and spend maybe $700 for each family member. They've spent just under $3,000. We have $7,000 left. Where do we go from there?

JIM They should obtain some silver or small denomination gold coins. Small denomination coins have excellent liquidity and will increase in value if paper money loses its acceptability. It's a form of insurance, you know. I've met people who were insured for millions of dollars and thought they were fully insured. They said to their investment counselors, "I want to have every base covered." Yet they haven't covered the one we're talking about today.

HJR: Well, they assume they will always be able to exchange their wealth for food and other basic needs.

JIM: Anyway, of the remaining $7,000, I would say $2,000 to $3,000 should go into coins. No bullion, just coins and/or currency as you recommend, to meet day-to-day needs or to barter for milk, bread and other essentials.

I can envision the possibility of closed banks and a period of time when people might have to go out looking for a gallon of gasoline or new chain for their bicycle. One might become relatively wealthy overnight with just a small portion of his money in coins.

The remaining $4,000 to $5,000 could be used to buy Treasury notes. I'd be careful about buying long maturities though, because you may have to hold them to maturity or risk selling them at a loss if you need cash when interest rates are at higher levels.

I like short maturities with the "full faith and credit" backing of the U.S. Treasury. They have a liquid market, although they are considerably less liquid when in small denominations. Liquidating a Treasury instrument through a broker or a bank can be a very costly operation. For these reasons, to maintain the utmost liquidity, some choose to use Capital Preservation Fund. The Fund lets them cash in at anytime. One could conceivably invest in the Fund for just one day and earn one day's income. For some, the Fund is, in effect, a demand deposit account that pays interest.

HJR: How can your Fund's investors cash out?

JIM: There are a number of ways. We provide our investors with free withdrawal checks. They decide when to write those checks and to whom. They can make checks payable to themselves or any third party immediately. The minimum Fund check is $500, because we can't absorb the expense of small denomination checks.

HJR: Someone can actually write a check on your Fund and take it down to the bank and cash it?

JIM: Yes. That's real liquidity. We also have a provision that has been in our prospectus since the day we opened that states that we plan to use U.S. postal money orders if necessary. This, of course, implies that it might be necessary should the banks ever close.

HJR: So, you were concerned about the possible illiquidity of banks four years ago.

JIM: Before that. These concerns are an outgrowth of my experience as a bank examiner for the Federal Reserve Bank of San Francisco. I learned a great deal about the banking system then, and continued to learn and gather information through-out my years with Merrill Lynch. I concluded that the banking system was in serious trouble.

HJR: Are there any tax advantages offered by your Fund?

JIM: Yes, the Fund offers tax-free retirement plans: The IRA and the Keogh program. We plan to offer an annuity type of investment in the Fund soon. Also, there are certain tax advantages available to those who own Treasuries outright. All interest from U.S. Treasury debt which is held outright by individuals is exempt from state and local income taxes. Only Federal taxes apply. Our Fund, as it is today, does not pass on this tax exemption. We tried, but the Internal Revenue says that even though we own 100 percent Treasury debt, the return to our investors is not "interest" for tax purposes. The Fund pays dividends, according to the IRS. (see: Retirement Plans & Taxes)

HJR: Do you care to comment on the money supply?

JIM: Yes, I do. The nation's money supply is described in various ways, the most common measure is called M-1. M-1, as de—fined, consists of the total amount of money in bank checking accounts (demand deposits), plus all the outstanding currency and coin. The composition of M-1 is changing. When M-1 grows through the currency and coin avenue, it makes me think the populace is hoarding coins and/or currency. I have yet to hear of others looking at this part of M-1 with any concern. But I'm concerned. I think it's another barometer that measures people's confidence in our economy.

HJR: I feel that when we try to measure the real growth in money supply using M-1, we've really ignored one of the major factors in expansion of the money supply, which is the increase in outstanding government debt instruments, which for many people, are used like money. For example, if I were to invest in Capital Preservation Fund, or short-term U.S. Treasury securities, I would consider that a cash equivalent.

JIM: That's true. When you invest, you draw a check against your bank account. M-1 goes down, yet the money goes into something just as liquid, and it's not counted in M-1.

Additionally, when corporations raise new money by selling stocks or bonds, they don't put that money in the bank like they did in the 1950s, in "demand deposit" form. Yet, all of the little checks from the people who bought those new issues reduce M-1. Today, corporations invest the money overnight in the form of "repurchase agreements," and repurchase agreements are not part of M-1. Or perhaps the corporation buys 90-day Treasury bills, or some commercial paper. They're not in M-1 either. I've always questioned the reliability of M-1 as a forecasting tool. It leaves out too much.

HJR: You're talking about a possible hidden expansion of the money supply, which could reflect itself in an explosive inflationary cycle.

JIM: And don't just look at the domestic money supply. Look at the world money supply. It's growing twice as fast.

HJR: If a European banker has a dollar on deposit, he generally can loan $15 to $20, and so the money supply increases as our money flows abroad.

JIM: As the amount of money throughout the world increases, it obviously has an inflationary impact on the prices of commodities and services everywhere, including the United States. Foreign bankers create money that is not subject to control by the Federal Reserve or the U.S. Treasury or anybody.

No government regulates the billions in the Eurodollar market. There are no reserve requirements for those banks.

HJR: Incidentally, I was interested in our balance of payments for the month of August. We've just had the largest monthly deficit in our balance of payments in something like four years.

JIM: The chickens come home to roost, don't they?

HJR: One way or the other, we're gonna pay the piper, and yet we hear such confident statements about how carefully they're controlling the money supply.

JIM: The government says it has the handle and knows which way and how far to turn that handle. I doubt that.

HJR: Jim, you made a comment at one of our seminars that the Federal Reserve might someday have to bail out the whole world. Do you remember that statement?

JIM: I do. My logic is this: Bank of America and Citibank, the two largest banks in the world, have most of their assets invested abroad. In other words, most of their loans were made abroad. Most of their income is derived from abroad. To be that exposed to the affairs of the other nations, particularly the more than 100 underdeveloped nations, is to be subject to great uncertainty. To have so many pieces of paper that may or may not be paid at maturity, is risky. If the paper turns bad, and our Federal Reserve has to bail out a large bank because of defaulting international paper, our central bank, in effect, becomes the lender-of-last-resort for the entire world. That's dangerous, Howard.

HJR: That's a very dramatic point.

JIM: The outgrowth of that could eventually be a nationalized U.S. banking system. That would be the day when the Fed could say "we have all your good assets over here. We've loaned you money against them. We control and own you. Now we are the 'owner of last resort.' "

HJR: And all this time, I thought those were just nice people who help us out and don't have any strings attached to their assistance. All right, do you have any other things you'd like to cover?

JIM: One final thing—it has to do with my concept of capitalism. People trained in economics say free markets operate best, and many feel the U.S. doesn't have free markets. I think we've always had free markets. We have free markets right now and we'll have free markets tomorrow. Why? Because we have done what we have by choice. We were free to do otherwise. Monopolies don't look like free markets. Yet it is our free choice that lets monopolies exist. We made things the way they are.

So, let's not be angry at anyone about what's out there, because we created it, and allow it to be. Besides, Howard, we can change it.

HJR: It's like Pogo says, "We have seen the enemy and he is us."

JIM: Yes. So let's take the responsibility and fix it. I'm concerned about my children's children. And so are you. And my grandchildren's world will work if I keep my personal scene in order. I'm talking about honesty, integrity, and ethics. This keeps our family in order too. When my family is in order, I read, think and effectively plan for the future without my thoughts wandering to something I haven't done. That's when I'm comfortable inside. I think our system works, and if we start with our personal and family lives, we can tune it up.

HJR: Jim, thank you. We're going to direct our subscribers who want further information about the Fund, or anything else that

you've discussed, to write directly to: CAPITAL PRESER-
VATION FUND, 755 Page Mill Road, Palo Alto, California
94304, PHONE: (From California) 800-982-5873, (all other
states) 800-227-8996. We appreciate the service you're
rendering for our subscribers.

JIM: I've enjoyed talking with you, Howard, and I hope to be
joining you at future seminars.

(11/15/77) A Money Fund has several advantages:

1. It is the equivalent of cash in the bank. You can deposit as little
as $1000 and receive the current yield on Treasury bills if the fund is
well managed. You pay no commission to get in or out, and the fund
supports itself by taking one-half of 1 percent of the assets of the fund
each year in management fees. If they are well managed, their yield
will be better than if you bought the bills yourself, as good
management can ride the yield curve and improve their return.

2. You can get out instantly. Most of the funds will wire your
money with a telephone call, and they all issue you blank checks
which you can write against your money at any time, although they
do limit you to checks to over $500.

Many large corporations and banks deploy their idle money in the
money funds because it combines liquidity with a reasonable interest
return.

Is the Treasury bill market safe? During periods of monetary
trouble, investors traditionally turn to short-term government securities as a safe haven. The day will come when even Treasury bills
won't be any good, but they will be the last of the securities markets to
collapse, and it is precisely during the time of panic that scared money
flees into these securities. You can then bail out and become fully
deployed in gold, as that's where all of your funds should end up
eventually, except those in rural real estate, silver coins and diamonds
for the long haul.

T-bill money should be limited to that which you need for liquidity.
This is not your long-range investment program. If you need a return
on your money to live on, put it into gold coins and sell off a little bit
at frequent intervals. You'll get a better rate of return that way, as all
the signs for gold are bullish.

Choose a fund that invests strictly in Treasury bills. Some invest in
bankers acceptances and commercial paper, also. I think the economy
still has several months to go, judging by all of the traditional
measurements, but investment markets signal these troubles months
in advance, and they affect your cash. Most of the statistics will

continue to look pretty good for several months. When the histories are written, the great story of this decade will be the reality of dealing with the massive amounts of wealth that we have transferred to the Arabs. Mark that down, and look at it a few years from now.

We may get through this crisis and buy ourselves another year or two of prosperity, but I doubt it. My suggestions are designed to make your money safe without burning all your bridges behind you. Move fast, and then you can sit calmly and see how things develop.

(1/15/78)   More Questions

Q. Why did you suggest that we use the Capital Preservation Fund now when their return is lower than other money funds?

A. Because they invest only in Treasury bills, not high-yielding bank paper or commercial paper, and their yields are rising. Also, they are the safest.

Q. Wouldn't a large investor be better off buying Treasury bills individually so that he can get the exemption from state income taxes?

A. Yes, but you need to buy in "round lots" of $1,000,000 or more. It takes at least $10,000 to buy Treasury bills. Money Funds buy in "round lots," and the combination of their lower purchase price and their ability to "ride the yield curve" will probably make up for any tax advantage that you might have received by owning the bills directly.

Q. How do I buy Treasury bills as an individual?

A. You go to your local Federal Reserve Bank or sometimes your commercial banker.

Q. Why are T-bills safer than passbook savings?

A. Because, if the banks get in trouble, money will be fleeing into T-bills and that will be the last liquid market. Eventually, even T-bills will be in trouble, but you will have time to make your final move into gold.

Q. I'd like to use a T-bill fund closer to me on the East Coast.

A. It's irrelevant. In fact, one way to increase your yield on your T-bills is to work through one of Capital Preservation Fund's banks on the opposite end of the country from you. For example, Capital Preservation is in Palo Alto, practically in our backyard. We are going to use a Florida bank for our transactions with the fund because the float gives us the use of the money and increases the effective yield. A money fund is a great place for businesses, banks and individuals to park working capital when it is not being employed.

MORTGAGE, HOME

(9/15/76) "Neither a borrower, nor a lender be."—William Shakespeare

Should you pay off your mortgage now, if you can?

There are three basic possible answers, and several variations.

1. Yes. Pay off your mortgage. Then you are protected from losing your home if your income is cut off. It's yours, you will sleep better.

2. No. Dont pay off your mortgage. As runaway inflation is coming, you will pay off your loan in dollars worth a lot less than those you borrowed. Also it's easier to sell your home if you have a big loan, and the interest is tax deductible.

3. Increase your loan, for the reasons in #2 above, and use the money to buy food, and gold and silver coins.

To make a proper choice, you have to understand some basics.

When inflation is rampant, it is best to be a debtor if you can borrow at interest rates lower than the rate of inflation, because you pay off in cheap dollars.

If deflation is the order of the day, it's best to be a creditor, even if the interest you earn is low, because you will be owed dollars that are increasing in value and purchasing power, if your debtors don't go broke.

If you live in or near the danger areas listed in Chapter 6 of *HOW TO PROSPER DURING THE COMING BAD YEARS* and have several months' cash reserve, keep a maximum mortgage on your home or any other urban property, and then sell out in a planned, orderly way.

The experience of the 30s shows us that property foreclosures occur early in a depression. As banks fail, or find themselves with foreclosed, empty homes, and unworked farms, all subject to neglect and vandalism, they begin making deals, and restructuring debts. Your problem is to get through the first few months. (see: Survival Preparations)

MYERS, VERN

(4/1/78)   I always read with great interest the work of C. V. MYERS, who publishes *MYERS' FINANCE AND ENERGY REPORT*. He is one of the grand old men of the newsletter advisory business, having paid his dues through fights with regulatory agencies and having been a lonely voice crying in the wilderness that we are headed for a massive deflation, rather than the inflation that I expect.

Vern Myers and I disagree on the scenario, but I immensely respect his opinions and his ability to gather hard data. It's just that we are looking at the same data and drawing different conclusions. On some things we agree. We both believe that gold is the best hedge to protect the value of your assets in either instance.

He also advocates the purchase of silver. He assumes that even though prices of these commodities might fall, the value of money will fall far more rapidly, so they will increase in value relative to money, and that's the principal standard by which we must measure these things. I don't care if gold falls 50% if other prices fall 75%. But, if he's right, you should own paper money which is oppisite to the advice of what I have given you.

I will soon ask Vern Myers to present his case for deflation in *THE RUFF TIMES*. I owe it to you to give you a choice of alternatives. Some of the monetary steps you would take if you are expecting deflation are different from what they would be if you are expecting inflation.

I think he's wrong, but you will soon get a chance to make up your own mind.

Here's why I think he's wrong. All societies that inflate their currency, as we have done, eventually end up with hyper-inflation. The bubble always bursts in a massive deflation, but not before a runaway hyper-inflation. You must remember that governments that inflate find they must continue to inflate or die. They have no other choice.

MCMASTER, R.E.

(9/15/77)   I've been watching with great interest the career of R.E. McMaster and his fascinating commodity publication, *THE REAPER*.

R.E. is a graduate Cum Laude of the University of Houston, in Management and Economics, and a member of four national honor societies. He did Master's work in Business Science at Northern Colorado University. He was an associate with the international real estate development firm, Trammell Crow Company, and he was formerly one of five nationally approved trading advisors at Hornblower-Weeks. He is now the editor of the liveliest, most interesting newsletter in the commodity field, *THE REAPER*.

R.E. doesn't just write a technical treatise on commodities, but he presents a picture of all of the factors in society that affect markets.

(11/1/77) R.E. McMaster phoned me today telling me that the way the commodity and currency markets are responding from a technical point of view, they are discounting something terrible. He confirmed to me that the monetary system is coming unglued. He feels that wheat is in a substantial uptrend and he expects it to go over $3.00 a bushel in the next few months. He also passed on the following tidbits:

1. The credit unions are overextended, their loans being roughly 104% of their deposits and they are borrowing to meet loan demand. Get out!

2. Savings and loans are going to be in difficulty in a major downturn if it becomes necessary for them to foreclose on many properties—and it will. Get out!

3. He also is just as worried as I am about the Arab money that is sloshing about the world like water in a sinking ship, now leaving the American dollar and going into the British pound, gold, and Japanese securities. He commented very astutely that the timing for the dollar to be in trouble couldn't be worse as the OPEC nations are meeting in November to evaluate the world economic situation and again in December to determine what their pricing policy will be.

(5/1/78) Perhaps the most shocking talk of the whole Hawaiian Conference (1st Annual Economic and Investment) came from R.E. McMASTER, the brilliant young investment technician and commodities advisor, on the subject of his recent book, *CYCLES OF WAR*. His book is brilliant, and his speech was also brilliant. He demonstrated, through a review of cycles of history, including climate, investments, economic cycles, even sunspot and planetary cycles, that we are coming to an amazing conjunction of downturns in all of these cycles somewhere between 1978 and '82, and historically the end result of such downturns is always war, in some form or another. It will be associated with economic toubles, civil disorders, and famines.

His book cites quote after quote from impressive sources and if you ever needed an impetus to prepare for hard times, this is it. I cannot recommend the book highly enough. In all the history of *THE RUFF TIMES*, we've recommended only five books, and this will be Number 6.

R.E. has made all previous "futures studies" obsolete. He also says that cycles can expand, contract, or even disappear, because most of them are directly influenced by man. If this book is read it could be one of the most influential books of our time. It's my hope that enough people read and believe it so we can collectively take action to prevent or minimize what he sees coming.

(3/1/79) R. E. MCMASTER gave us something totally different in his principal address at the 2nd Annual *RUFF TIMES* National Convention. He did not at that time discuss the commodities market, but saved that for his workshops. He assessed the world and his position in it in a most moving way. It will be hard to convey to you the emotional nature of what he had to say, but I'll try.

When he published his book, *CYCLES OF WAR*, he thought there was only a 60% probability of war in the next six years. Now he has escalated his estimate to 80%. He said, "All compass points, north, south, east and west are either smoldering or rising in violent conflict. But there is one area of my book I would change. I would document the evidence that supports the conclusion that we are headed for some combination of the great depression, the U.S. Civil War and World War II all wrapped together in the same unpleasant package. Further, I would document the overwhelming evidence that suggests that we are at the major turning point in Western Civilization—the end of the 510 year cycle."

He then gave us a moving account of how he concluded that it is not enough in this life to do just the selfish things. He told us how he decided to "come out of the closet" in the Flathead Valley of Montana where he lives. Speaking to every knife and fork club and church in his area about the future and the same kind of thing that are in *THE RUFF TIMES* philosophy, he began to make a major impact on his community. As a result, others in his community are getting prepared for difficult times. He said, "Too many Americans stand up for their rights but forget their duties. Each of you individually can make a major impact in your own community. You can be the instrument of change. People in this country are ready for meaningful change. All you have to do is cast your bread upon the waters." He even suggested that if one has a lot of money to invest, he might try buying the local newspaper and changing its editorial policy. He said, "You are one individual who can make a difference." He took a stand in his community. He shed some light, and he says others can do the same thing. "Meaningful change begins by the sharing of information, the shedding of light," he encouraged.

In his workshop, he indicated that the business cycle averages 33 months long, and the cycle we are currently in is approaching 48 months in April, and is long overdue for correction. A series of 50-year cycles seem to be pretty consistent in human affairs. It takes about that long for the mass of human mechanism to create the excesses and return to ground zero. The excesses tend to be self-correcting over the 50-year cycle. Weather also seems to run in a 50-year cycle. It's been approximately 50 years since the dust bowl weather of the '30s. The '80s may have the worst weather in history. Some harsh, variable weather patterns are seen for the future. Several down cycles are coming together and it is a reason for concern. When asked his opinion on agricultural products in view of worldwide inflation, he said that the primary preference now is towards "protein gold" (soybeans, corn, wheat), and these primary commodities will increase in value in the next decade, which has obvious implications for the commodity speculator and for the farmer, as well as the prospective farm purchaser. In response to a question as to whether the small American farmer can survive while receiving 1972-73 prices for production and paying 1979 costs, he said, "He might survive if his debt load is not too high or if he is not hassled too much by government control." However, he did not see much improvement in that situation in the future. On balance, if you are properly capitalized, however, you should be able to do well in the farming business with the explosion of the commodity prices expected in the future.

N

NATIONAL FOOD RESERVE

(12/75) We face famine from two directions: fiscally induced famine, and supply-demand famine. Both are inevitable.

The fiscally-induced famine will come from the inevitable economic convulsion from an overextended, weakened, artificially propped-up printing-press money system, which has been tried by every civilization since the press was invented, and which has always corrected itself by inflation, then explosive deflation.

It always results in depression, business failures, banking collapse, and a breakdown in delivery of goods and services.

When that will hit us, I don't know, but I think it's soon.

The classic supply-demand famine is the inexorable crossing of the food production line and the "population growth or food-demand" lines.

We now produce surpluses in America. We sell a lot, we give some away. It has prevented worldwide catastrophe. There were twenty two net food exporting nations four ago. Now there are three. The U.S., Canada, and Australia. Due to temperature changes in the far north and far south temperate zones, and new patterns of drought, Canada and Australia will soon contribute little.

We have made public international commitments to feed people and will continue to do so—first for "foreign policy considerations," then to try to save our allies and friends, then, out of fear, with our survival at stake as a nation.

Ordinarily, we could feel safe from India's or Pakistan's famine, but we have made their problems our problems. We have promised.

I think we need a NATIONAL FOOD RESERVE.

We can achieve it in the following way. All of these steps must be taken simultaneously.

1. Full-out production.
2. Free the farmer from all controls or subsidies. Let the free market rule.

3. Keep the government out of food storage. Past programs were a disaster. The cost of purchasing, storing or administering such programs are financed by the printing press and will skyrocket inflation.

4. Now, the guts of my proposal! Encourage the purchase of surplus grain by individual consumers, in time of plenty, for home storage. Make it a patriotic duty. GRANT HIM TAX CREDITS, DOLLAR FOR DOLLAR, FOR WHAT HE BUYS, UP TO A TWO-YEAR SUPPLY (400 POUNDS PER PERSON).

This will build up a home reserve of millions of tons in America that consumers will dip into in times of shortage or civil unrest, or just when prices rise too high.

This gives the farmer the marketplace he needs in America, so he won't press politically for "Russian Grain Deals."

It provides price stability at natural price levels.

It could mean millions of people who won't panic in times of trouble because they can still eat. They won't be on the streets protesting. They will be home enjoying their food.

It will be cheaper than subsidizing huge loans to foreign buyers and reestablish stability with our food supplies, because our reserves in our own homes will have reduced the domestic demands on current and future production.

(12/15/76) Why do we need such a reserve?

The NATIONAL OCEANIC AND ATMOSPHERIC ADMINISTRATION CENTER FOR CLIMATIC AND ENVIRONMENTAL ASSESSMENTS says the world's food producing system is much more sensitive to the weather variable than it was even five years ago. Why? Because the Green Revolution uses new strains of grain that require massive use of fertilizer and pesticides, a long growing season, and plenty of water at the right time. Fertilizer has quadrupled in price. The countries that need the most can't afford it.

The man who was responsible for this "revolution" is Dr. Norman Borlaug, 61, who was funded by the Rockefeller Foundation to develop these grains. Borlaug has recenty said:

> People are asking us why we can't develop plants that don't need so much fertilizer and water. I'm irritated by this looking for an easy way out.
>
> We never said the Green Revolution was a panacea that was

going to cure all the ills of the world, but we said that there was this chance we could, at least for the time being, produce sufficient food for all the people.

The Green Revolution is only a temporary expedient. It has bought us some time, but now there is not enough fertilizer being produced in the world today to meet the growing demand. This means a possible world disaster of epic proportions, and could create a chaotic dangerous situation which is a threat to world peace and commerce.

One bad weather year in the U.S.A. is all that stands between the world and this epic disaster.

I have proposed that Congress pass tax legislation granting dollar-for-dollar tax credits for Americans who purchase food for emergency storage from supplies that are judged to be in surplus. For example, if you were to purchase $200 worth of wheat in a year when we have surplus wheat (over and above our domestic demands), you would receive a $200 credit against taxes. I maintain that this is an important concept for Congress to consider.

(9/15/77) With the mountain of surplus wheat piled up in our warehouses and elevators, and Carter's proposal to take 20% of the acreage out of production next year, I am reminded of Joseph in Egypt, where the nation was blessed with seven good years, with a God-ordained responsibility to store food for the lean years. My first reaction was to have the government store this grain. When I recovered my sanity, my second reaction was that I don't want them to get their hands on my food. These are the same people that gave us the Post Office Department, Vietnam, and OSHA, and I don't want them to lay their spastic hands on my food supply.

We need the NATIONAL FOOD RESERVE I have written about before.

In previous writings I pointed out that we could find ourselves in an interesting dilemma. We could be forced to export food at a time when it was badly needed here, simply because we need the foreign reserves. We are running huge balance-of-payments deficits in 1977, almost five times that of any previous year. If, as a result, the dollar continues to sink, we will find it difficult to buy the oil we need, and it could destabilize the world's financial and monetary system. The Arabs might bail out of a sinking dollar, sell their U.S. Treasury securities, and withdraw their bank deposits. And who could blame them? This is no laughing matter. Central bankers and world financial officials are terribly worried about it. What if we were forced to continue to export in order to support the dollar after a bad crop in the United States and the Soviet Union, and we had this proposed reserve in the homes of America? As the price of wheat rises, at some point Americans would start dipping into their reserves to save money, and grain prices would stabilize. We would be able to export the necessary grain, keep the dollar from sinking into the ocean, and not suffer hardship.

It would benefit the farmer because it would stabilize his market-place. It would benefit the consumer, ultimately, because it would keep prices from rising too sharply. If we have the expected inflationary depression, it would also mean, perhaps, hundreds of thousands of people who will not be part of the panic that can occur when the economy gets really sick, as it did in the '30s and after the Civil War. Tax credits will be cheaper for our government than for them to allow the dollar to sink.

(10/15/77) Let's hear it for the American farmer. He is probably the last of the rugged, individualistic entrepreneurs. He takes tre-mendous risks. Sometimes he has a tendency to want to milk the government cow to take care of his troubles, and sometimes when he has a bad year, he forgets the good years and wants to be bailed out. But the farmer is facing genuine hardships due to this price-depressing abundance unless we provide him a legitimate marketplace. We cannot permit the farm economy to collapse. Right now, the price of wheat is well below the cost of production. The government storage programs and soil banks of the past were expensive scandals, and Mr. Carter is proposing that we fall into the same traps.

I believe that my proposal for a NATIONAL FOOD RESERVE would stabilize the farm economy, would harness the free enterprise system, and make it far easier for those of us who are survival oriented to buy these surplus foods. Fortunately, wheat is an ideal storage food, one of the central components of my recommended storage program. It stores almost indefinitely with relatively casual packaging. It is one of the most nutritious foods known to man (although some people are allergic to it). It can be eaten raw, if sprouted. It can be cracked with inexpensive hand grinders and made into a delicious whole-wheat cereal. Even whole kernel wheat can be made into a delicious hot cereal.

I think the most beautiful part of this proposal is the "tax credit" aspect. For most of you, it will end up costing you nothing. Too often when we see the problems and ills of government, we tend to throw up our hands and say that there's nothing that can be done. I do this sometimes, but deep in my heart I know it's wrong, even if there isn't much hope. We have to create conditions that will enable us to get through the troubles in better shape. I have given up on trying to prevent the troubles. We are going to have a major depression. The odds favor drought and unstable food production over the next five years. The dollar is going to sink into the Pacific, regardless of what we try to do. War in the Middle East, in my opinion, is almost inevitable. We are going to have a runaway inflation. But, doggone it, if we can implement some of the things I've proposed, we improve the odds for the survival of our essential institutions, and that's worth something because I do care about the political and social environment in which I live. (see: Food Shortages, Food Storage, and Survival Preparations)

NEW YORK CITY

GENERAL PROBLEMS

(Special Report #1, 10/15/75) The consequences of the financial failure of New York are so immense, so unsuspected, and so misunderstood.

To state briefly my thesis: THE FINANCIAL FAILURE OF THE CITY OF NEW YORK COULD DESTROY THE BANKING SYSTEM, CAUSE RIOTS IN THE CITIES, AND PERMANENTLY CRIPPLE OR INTERFERE WITH THE INDUSTRIES INVOLVED IN THE DISTRIBUTION OF FOOD AND OTHER VITAL COMMODITIES TO THE CITY. IT CAN TRIGGER, VIRTUALLY OVERNIGHT, THE GREAT DEPRESSION THAT I AND MANY OTHERS HAVE SUSPECTED IS IN OUR FUTURE.

New York is suffering from the same sickness that destroyed ancient Rome. I am not referring to its moral decay, but to its fiscal irresponsibility. (see: Economy, U.S.)

John Williams won the National Book Award for his historical novel *AUGUSTUS*. Williams noted that Rome, from 200 BC until about 200 AD, developed a policy that anyone coming in from the countryside would be fed by the government. As a result, the hungry streamed into the city. Soon the center of Rome became clogged with the hungry looking to be fed.

The next step for the government to consider was housing, according to Augustus. As the people of Rome left the city to set up

441

residences on the other side of the river—the first suburb—Augustus decreed that the poor would be swept up and placed in the first high-rises on record. The housing projects were six stories high. Many died in the fires that often occurred.

New York has followed precisely the same practice and the poor of the nation have responded by streaming into New York. New York not only accepted them but created an environment which attracted more of them as a moth is attracted to a flame.

New York described itself as "the city with a heart." Municipal officials decided that the poor should have sufficient welfare to live in "dignity." They decided that everyone in New York was entitled to a good education and should not have to pay for it, whether they were able to or not. Consequently, one of the largest universities in the country was established with free tuition and the highest paid professors in America. City politicians also decided that everyone should have health care at below-cost prices, so they established 19 hospitals and subsidized large deficits. They decided that the city employees should be the best paid in the country and should also have the most generous pensions so they could retire in "dignity," so they yielded ignominiously to union blackmail. Finally, they decided to help poor people hold down costs by slapping rent controls on property within the city.

All of these policies flowed from a kind heart, mixed with a little political savvy of New York politicians, who realized the first maxim of politics is "spend, spend, spend—elect, elect, elect!"

All these kind acts created gigantic deficits in the New York budgets. New York decided to solve its fiscal "shorts" by two devices.

1. They increased property taxes to such levels that the property owner, squeezed by rent controls on the top, and increasing costs and taxes on the bottom, simply abandoned buildings and refused to pay taxes. This decreased New York's income at a time when its outgo was increasing tremendously.

2. They resorted to the simple device of borrowing to cover their shortages and then borrowing more money to pay off the short-term loans they had previously made in order to cover the previous shortages, all the while accumulating an immense obligation with ruinous interest payments.

In the meantime, landlords began to simply abandon their properties because it was cheaper than paying the taxes.

As New York routinely went to the banks to fund some more current deficits and to "roll over" some of its short-term obligations, the banks began asking embarrassing questions. The banks, recognizing their responsibility and the developing quagmire of city debt, which perhaps would not be paid, began to request that the City of New York (1) give them better financial data as to their deficits and (2) begin to make some economy moves that would reduce their deficits.

To make a long story short, this soon resulted in the disclosure of New York's terrible financial problems, and the refusal of the banks to fund New York City any more.

New York is a classic example of the arrogance of man in assuming that he can do all things that he feels are worth doing without counting the cost or ultimately paying the price.

The problem has now reached such dimensions that the default of New York City on its bonds and obligations, and its financial collapse appears inevitable.

1. The city exhausted all of its credit resources, and as a last resort, went to the state for help. The State of New York agreed to provide and guarantee approximately $2 billion in notes, which would be sufficient to meet New York's needs through September, October and the first half of November, 1975. Shortly after they did this, the agencies which rate the credit status of cities informed the State of New York that their credit would be impaired and that they would be unable to raise additional money markets if they poured any more of their resources or their credit into the City of New York.

2. The city will have to raise incredible sums of money in the face of a total collapse of a demand for New York bonds, the skepticism of every banker in America, and the inability of the city to reduce its monthly obligations due to contractual commitments with labor unions, welfare recipients and city employees. They will be unable to pay their maturing debt as it comes due. They will be unable to pay their welfare recipients, policemen, firemen, and other city employees. They will be unable to pay the suppliers who contract with the city for goods and services.

Its effect upon the nation's economy is far-reaching. The first major effect would be the collapse of the municipal bond market. The tax-exempt municipal bond has been the favorite money raising tool of cities because they can raise money with a low interest rate. It has been the favorite target of the most conservative investor, because he gets a tax-free return and is willing to accept a low interest rate in return for that, plus the low risk. However, investors are now concluding that municipal bonds are high-risk investments and are refusing to buy them even though interest yields have climbed to an incredible high.

BUSINESS WEEK on September 1 reported that Felix Rohatyn, Chairman of the Finance Committee of the Municipal Assistance Corporation said:

> A default by the city would be catastrophic. It would force the state to default as well shortly thereafter and ruin the credit of other cities such as Detroit and Newark which are having their own financial problems. At the least, default would raise the cost of borrowing for every municipality and state agency in the country.

In the same article, *BUSINESS WEEK* stated:

> It is also difficult to predict with any accuracy how a New York City default would affect other municipalities. New York Senator Jacob K. Javits feared that a city default "would completely destroy the municipal market" and lead to "crushing borrowing costs." Some cities have already reduced the size of new offerings. Financial officers in such cities as Detroit and Philadelphia wonder where they would get the money they need if the New York default closed the municipal market to them.

Such a bond market collapse would, quite simply, lead to chaos in the cities. It doesn't take a genius to figure that out. San Francisco learned what happened when policemen did not report for work during their recent police strike of only a few days. The crime rate increased by ten times for that few days, as no one feared being apprehended. In a prolonged situation of this kind, it would be far worse.

Don't think for a minute that the cities can get by if they are unable to borrow. Mayor Alioto of San Franciso was reported on July 6, 1975, as saying, "New York could be a harbinger of things to come. The seeds of New York are in every American city."

Other cities find themselves precisely in the same condition. Evans and Novack, the widely syndicated columnists, reported in the *DALLAS TIMES-HERALD* of Friday August 22, 1975:

> Sober financiers see not only a strong possibility of default but also a frightened fallout: civil disorder in the cities, default spreading to the New York state government and finally even international difficulties.

Virtually every city in America faces this kind of problem. It is simply standard operating procedure to borrow money, short-term or long-term, to meet current cash needs. So many contractual obligations to take care of people have been built into law that there is no way of meeting these obligations without borrowing, and no way of reducing them without new legislation which no politician would have the courage to introduce.

The default of New York City on its obligations also could sweep the banking system with it. I do not stand alone in this opinion. The possibility has been considered seriously by such prestigious publications as *BUSINESS WEEK, FORBES, BARRONS, U.S. NEWS AND WORLD REPORT*. Statements of such possibilities come from the officials in the know in the City and State of New York, as well as high-ranking officials in the Federal Deposit Insurance Corporation, The Office of the Comptroller of the Currency, and the Federal Reserve.

The big question is: Could the banks survive if the City of New York defaulted on its notes? Let's look at their general vulnerability.

At the present time, the six largest New York City banks have total shareholders equity and loan/loss reserves of $8.1 billion. If you were to add together the face value of all the New York City bonds, all of the "Big MAC" bonds (the agency set up to try to save New York) and their Real Estate Investment Trust (REIT) holdings, half of which are presently in default, the total pitfall adds up to $5.3 billion.

That's 62% of the total shareholders' equity and loan/loss reserves of New York's six largest banks. That means if the City of New York defaults and takes with it the Big MAC bonds, and if the REITs continue to suffer from the present housing decline, the banks could virtually lose half their capital overnight. This is sufficient to topple New York's biggest banks.

The government has pressured banks into making shaky loans to such companies as Penn Central. Some of the corporate loans are so bad that the banks have been actually forced to throw good money after bad. For example, the W.T. Grant Company, one of the biggest and best known retail chains, is reporting enormous operating losses. It was widely reported September 30 that they actually now have a negative net worth. They have been unable to meet their maturing loans. With such problems, no banker in his right mind would loan them any money. However, W.T. Grant was pulled back from the brink of bankruptcy at the last moment by $600,000,000 provided by a banking syndicate headed by the Morgan Guaranty Trust Company. *FORBES* Magazine commented:

> Some companies are insolvent by ordinary standards. Certainly
> W. T. Grant is one. Last year's loss has wiped out half its equity
> capital—and future write-offs will certainly erase the rest. Many of
> the remaining assets are down for the count and the company has

liabilities of hundreds of millions of dollars that do not even appear on the balance sheet. Morgan Guaranty, Chase Manhattan and First National Bank of New York may each lose a whopping $97.5 million at one whack, if the W. T. Grant edifice comes tumbling down. (Just before press time, W. T. Grant filed bankruptcy —HJR)

Why would the banks make such loans? Because they literally cannot afford a major failure, and in attempting to prevent it, are merely digging a bigger and shakier hole for themselves.

The banks now face a greater danger. Up until now, when banks wished to raise money by floating bond or stock issues of their own, the Securities Exchange Commission had very liberal disclosure requirements. They were not forced to reveal to potential investors, depositors, or the general public the details of their financial heat like other corporations. Now, however, the SEC is going to require this information to be disclosed and banks which have to go into the money market to raise money will have to disclose this data. What would the effect be? *U.S. NEWS AND WORLD REPORT* had this to say:

> For depositors at some banks, however, the details about large and swelling piles of delinquent loans could come as a severe shock. Nothing like this (disclosure) has ever been attempted before, and neither the promoters nor the opponents of the "open book" rule for banking are sure what will happen. Fears that such news could spark disastrous runs on some banks have generated vigorous opposition to the SEC plans among the bank regulatory agencies —THE FEDERAL RESERVE BOARD, COMPTROLLER OF THE CURRENCY and THE FEDERAL DEPOSIT INSURANCE CORPORATION. The practice of these agencies for decades has been to work quietly with "problem" banks and sometimes to pour in millions of dollars in loan funds—to keep the institutions from failing.

> There are problem banks and according to public reports, the number of banks in this category during the past year is greater than any time in the recent past.

The *SAN FRANCISCO CHRONICAL* in its Business Section on Saturday May 3, 1975, went into this rather frightening subject in an article called, "THE BEST KEPT SECRET . . . LIST OF 'PROBLEM' BANKS."

> New York: One of the best kept secret lists in Washington these days is in the hands of a few people at 1550 17th Street N.W., the home of the FEDERAL DEPOSIT INSURANCE CORPORA-

TION. It is the FDIC's list of problem banks, one whose present or future solvency is in question.

Bankers and bank regulators get nervous when asked about the FDIC's problem list and if it were ever made public, panic at 1550 17th Street probably would be monumental.

'If the list were published, you would probably see a list of banks fail,' said one Long Island official. 'I think that that would be the end of any trust in one another when they honor checks drawn on other banks, and allow depositors to draw on those checks before they have cleared the issuing banks. A sudden and abrupt failure of a major bank could produce chaos at the clearing houses and have a devastating effect on all banks.'

But the real uncertainty occurs when depositors become aware of these things and begin to react. The classic public fear reaction is to withdraw money from the banks. Is this possible today? The only thing that prevents people from doing it is their belief that the banks cannot fail.

On April 21, *BUSINESS WEEK* devoted a substantial part of its issue to "THE GREAT BANKING RETREAT." Let's take a look at a few concepts:

> The banking system's problems are serious, with an overhang of very shaky loans the most visible one.
>
> ...There is a clear acceptance by bankers that they have reached too far, taken too many risks and must retrench before more big institutions get into trouble.
>
> 'Last summer scared the pants off some of those bankers,' says John C. Poppen of Booz, Allen, and Hamilton, the management consultants.
>
> The risk got so great that the banks in 1974 had to charge off an unprecedented $1.8 billion to cover loan losses and there still are billions of dollars in loans in considerable trouble—ten to twelve billion dollars in loans to real estate investment trusts alone.
>
> By mid 1974 the system was stretched dangerously thin: too much questionable lending, too much borrowed money, too little capital to support swollen assets, and monetary growth that has slowed to dead zero.

The basic and fundamental weaknesses are bad enough to hold a risk of dumping the entire banking system if the current recession were only to continue at its present levels, or if the expected recovery were not to occur. However, as bad as the general problems are, they represent nowhere near the threat to this critically weakened system that the bankruptcy of New York represents. And remember, when

New York goes broke, it adds the problems that I'm going to describe to the already dangerous situation that we have discussed previously.

The size of the New York problem, and the potential danger to the banking system has, for the first time, hit the press. I've been talking about this danger since November of 1974.

A rather strange ambivalent statement was made in *BUSINESS WEEK* on June 2, 1975:

> The spectre of the City defaulting looms large with the banks, but banking analysts say they could survive. If the City were to default on both interest and principal, the results for us would be 'severe' says a bank analyst at a large institutional brokerage firm. 'There is no way of gauging the dollars and cents effect,' he says. 'Even the banks don't know for sure—but it wouldn't break them.'

Brave words, but as the problem developed, various financial publications and analysts became not quite so sure about whether the banks could survive the problems. On August 4, *NEWSWEEK* had this to say:

> America gave New York City a resounding vote of no confidence last week and they sank measurably closer to a financial collapse that could, in turn, damage the country far more than it realized.
>
> 'What we are seeing today is a major confrontation which will determine whether or not the nation's cities are going to survive,' says Miami Mayor, Maurice Ferre. 'It's not just New York; that is only the tip of the whole urban iceberg.'

In an article in *BUSINESS WEEK* on August 25, entitled, "IF NEW YORK GOES BUST":

> The on-again-off-again fiscal perils of New York have made default an increasingly grim probability . . .
> . . . there was surprising disagreement on just how serious a default might actually be for the city and for the rest of the nation . . . and there was concern that outright default, a failure to redeem some of the billions of dollars in outstanding city obligations, might paralyze the municipal bond market completely, undercut the country's basic credit system, and even prompt a depression-style run on the banks, a number of which have invested in New York bonds.

What does all this mean to you? It simply means that if the municipal bond market collapses and cities are unable to maintain order, and the safety of the banking system is jeopardized, and depositors' fears cause depression-style runs on the banks, then your comfortable life, as you know it, could possibly end for a period of time. It means that your currency could become valueless overnight!

Look at it this way. 90 percent of the nation's money supply is neither printed paper money nor coins. It is simply bookkeeping entries on the computers of banks. If you put money in the bank today, the bank would loan much of it to someone else. Some of this money would be kept in the checking accounts and it would be reloaned over and over again. The money supply grows on that basis. The failure of the banks would wipe out all of that non-existent money.

A legitimate question would be: Could the Federal government prevent such a collapse? The answer to that question simply is "no." The collapse can be postponed, but in so doing, problems that would simply make the crash worse would be created.

For example, the Federal government could step in and guarantee the bonds of the City of New York. Immediately, people would be willing to accept them because of the backing of the Federal government and New York would be able to raise money and continue its profligate ways.

This would be a signal to every politician in every town across the country that it's alright to appropriate and spend more than the city or state receives in income because Big Sugar Daddy in Washington will be willing to bail you out.

On July 4, 1975, *FORBES* Magazine considered this possibility.

> UNCLE SAM CAN BAIL OUT NEW YORK, BUT WHO WILL BAIL OUT UNCLE SAM?
>
> For a decade or so, the local governments have been able to borrow against their credit using all kinds of strategems to explain why it was okay to go into debt to meet current expenses. Credit ratings go down, however, as borrowing goes up. For a while New York City could bludgeon its banks into buying its securities, but banks have obligations to their depositors. They can't go on lending increasing sums to any borrowers, even city goverments, who are habitually spending more than they have been taking in.

You can blame New York City for abjectly surrendering to its subwaymen, garbagemen, policemen and school teachers, but you can't get away from these uncomfortable facts about the Federal government.

Federal deficits have become at least as chronic as New York City's—15 in the last 16 years.

The Federal debt has reached such proportions that interest alone on it now amounts to $32.8 billion a year, involving a transfer of something like 10% of Federal tax receipts to Federal bond holders. (Editor's note: Please keep in mind the date this article was written. The Federal debt is much larger now.)

As the Sugar Daddy of last resort of sinking local governments, the Federal government may one day soon have to rescue the Mayor Beames or face chaos in the cities.

I have estimated that if the Federal government, by bailing out New York, gives the cities, in effect, a Federal spending license, the government deficit for this year alone could jump to an additional 30 billion dollars, and over 50 billion dollars for 1976.

Also, Oregon state officials recently pointed out that if the Federal government steps in and guarantees New York paper, then that would suddenly become the only paper an investor would want. Who then would buy Oregon's bonds and notes—or Los Angeles' or Detroit's?

Government would be forced to guarantee everyone's paper. This would probably break an already critically weakened financial system, and be the beginning of the end of city and state independence and our Federal system.

What is the government's plan to attempt to save the banks in case of default?

The Federal Reserve Board has announced that it will "open the discount window," the place where banks go when they need short-term money. They have also issued no accounting rules which would allow the banks to write off their loans over a six month period.

But the most amazing statement of all came from a director of the Federal Reserve, who said, "We will simply allow the banks to continue to include in their capital those defaulted loans and notes as though they were not in default." This simply won't work, because once it becomes generally known, depositors will grab their money and run.

This rather lengthy treatise has one objective only: To convince you that we are sailing through the most dangerous financial seas that the nation has seen since the 1930s. In fact, it looks worse. The greatest danger that we face is the incredible trust people have in government! When the government says that it can't happen here, that the banks can't fail, that a depression cannot occur, people simply believe it. Throughout history, nations who have inflated the currency and have overreached themelves in an attempt to provide more goods and services than they can afford, have failed, just as did Rome, Greece, and the British Empire.

I feel the responsibility as a father to see that whatever happens, we will not be caught without the basic commodities for a healthy survival. I include food, clothing, fuel, medicine, tools, etc.

You may be able to read all of the foregoing material and conclude that what I am predicting won't happen, but I don't see how you can possibly look at it and say it is impossible. With the possibility even within the 10% range, I think you would be foolish not to prepare for these eventualities.

One last piece of advice: Don't try to guess how much time you have. Act now, prudently, carefully and systematically.

(11/75)   New York has escaped default by the skin of its teeth, at least twice.

President Ford has vowed to veto any bill to prevent default.

Rockefeller has switched from opposition to Federal bailout, to all out support, and bailed out of the Ford Administration.

1.   The Federal Reserve has lowered bank reserve requirements on time deposits from 3 to 1%, and flooded the money market with $3 billion in new money to try to prepare for the shock, driving down interest rates and rekindling inflation (the wholesale price index rose at an annual rate of 23% in October).

2.   New York City and State politicians and bank officials have launched a massive public relations effort to scare the public into supporting a Federal bailout, much like a neurotic wife who bullies her family into getting her way, by making regular suicide threats.

Should we bail out New York with Federal guarantees, or let it default?

I'll answer that for you. It doesn't matter! The result will be the same. Depression! The only difference is the timetable!

Think of the nation's economy as a hurdler. The first hurdle is New York. And as the runner gets more and more tired, the hurdles get higher and higher. Sooner or later he trips over one. Unfortunately, New York's default is just the first hurdle, and not the highest one.

(Special Report #2, 1/76)   "All I know is just what I read in the papers. You know, of course, that never a day passes in New York without some innocent bystander being shot. You just stand around in this town long enough and be innocent, and someone is going to shoot you. One day there were four innocent people shot here. That is the best shooting ever done in this town. Hard to find four innocent people in New York."—Will Rogers

(11/75) Now I think Rockefeller is involved in criminal violation of Federal conflict of interest statutes because of his family's bank and his position as President of the Senate considering a bailout of the banks. But back to our scenario!

Immediately upon default, banks freeze New York checking accounts, and the lawsuits and welfare riots begin.

Now the government, or a Federal judge, has to decide what are "vital" services? Policemen and firemen, of course! But what about school teachers? Probation officers? Welfare clerks?

Walter Wriston, Chairman of First National City Bank of New York (Citibank) says

> If sanitation workers in Bedford-Stuyvesant aren't paid, will they drive their trucks right into the Citibank Branch in that neighborhood? And if the police aren't paid, will they stop them?

And funds could be frozen indefinitely and in an incredible landslide of litigation, probably beyond the ingenuity of a human judge to untangle for weeks or months.

Other cities that have bond issues ready will withdraw them. Municipal workers will be laid off, perhaps in violation of collective bargaining requirements.

More litigation, unemployment rises, corporations cancel expansion plans, and lay off workers. The struggling young financial recovery is aborted. This triggers personal bank loan defaults and personal and corporate bankruptcies, which are already at historic highs and climbing.

There are bills before Congress to guarantee New York bonds and restore New York's ability to borrow up to $7 billion.

These bills require New York to make Draconian cuts in payrolls and services, and city pension benefits, and drastically increase property and sales taxes. If Congress saves New York, it would be another scenario.

I don't think it's possible! It would lead to paralyzing labor and citizen protests. Pensions are protected by the State Constitution. Labor Unions never give up hard negotiated benefits. Volatile minority groups will protest welfare cuts, closing of day care centers, food stamp reductions, city hospital shutdowns, reduced police service, and the imposition of tuition for the city's 220,000 college students, now getting a free education.

If they do get past all those hurdles, we will have created a national problem.

New York bonds will be the only Federally guaranteed state or municipal bonds. Who will buy Atlanta's—or Oregon's? The government will have to guarantee those also. That means paying off bondholders when cities and states can't.

If they don't, cities and states, one by one, will fall into bankruptcy.

Then a Federal budget, already out of control, will run wild, as local debt is added to the incredible, unpredictable Federal deficit.

In sum, the effects of a default would probably be:

1. Collapse of the bond market.
2. A 150 point loss in the Dow Jones, followed by erratic ups and downs, then a fairly rapid slide.
3. Social chaos in New York, then other cities, as they are unable to borrow to meet their needs.
4. At the least, a loss of his party's nomination by President Ford, and a probable Rockefeller nomination.
5. Bank failures and a runaway inflation due to money supply increases to save banks.
6. Federal money ($3—$5 billion) poured belatedly into New York.
7. Default by New York State, Illinois, Massachusetts, Philadelphia, Oakland, Buffalo and others, in three to six months.
8. Worldwide depression and disruption of commodity distribution, with monetary collapse.
9. A fiscally induced famine.

On the other hand, the effects of a bailout would be:

1. Federal takeover of cities through Federal guarantees of all cities' debt.
2. A jump of 100 points in the Dow Jones, with possible further gains, until the plan falls apart, then a prolonged, gradual, but accelerating decline.
3. Breakdown of the bail-out plan due to resistance of pressure groups (labor, minorities, students, etc.) with civil disorder.
4. New York bonds immediately jump back to near par.
5. A possible temporary feverish boom in the economy, as everyone breathes a sigh of relief for 12 to 24 months.
6. A Federal deficit of $90—$110 billion next year.
7. Accelerating inflation, followed by recession, depression, explosive deflation and monetary collapse.
8. International cheering as New York is "saved," turning to dismay and depression worldwide as our runaway inflation is exported and the dollar weakens, then collapses.
9. Accelerating bankruptcies, civil disorder, and a breakdown of services and distribution of goods.

Questions

Q. Why did Ford oppose a bailout?

A: He's worried about the nomination. He thought he had a popular issue and a way to out-Reagan Reagan.

Q. Will he give in?

A. Probably, after New York has appeared to be sufficiently penitent, possibly before you get this letter.

Q. How did they persuade the Teacher's Union to loan New York $150 million to save them from default at the last minute in October?

A. They convinced Albert Shanker (the Union President) that pension funds already loaned to the city would be lost, if the city defaulted. He had no choice but to throw good money after bad to keep the city alive until help arrived from Washington.

Q. Where will the government get its money to bail them out?

A. The government has two sources of funds:

1. Take it away from you in taxes!
2. Print it.

They'll choose the latter! Slow suicide!

Stay liquid until you see which way New York is going to go.

(12/75)   A great controversy has been raging over whether or not a family or a doctor has the right to terminate heroic measures used to keep a patient alive beyond the time he would have normally died. The issue is not really the patient. The question is really the anguish of the concerned family.

Will they be forced to continue to pour their emotional and financial resources into a bottomless pit, destroying their health and bankrupting them, while destroying or mortgaging their future?

New York is just such a terminal patient.

The Ford-Carey-Beame plan to "save" New York is just such a "heroic measure" which maintains a semblance of life, misallocates resources, builds false hopes, and changes nothing. And it could bankrupt us! And the patient will die anyway!

It won't work. It's neither a default nor a bail out. The issue is not resolved, but merely postponed.

Even if all the pieces hold together, it is still billions short of solving the problem. The pension funds are underfunded now, and will require additional billions. The city's deficits are grossly understated. It's like handing a man in a fifteen foot pit a five foot rope.

But look at the pitfalls to be avoided to make the plan work.

1. The new taxes are regressive. They will result in reduced revenues. 10 percent sales tax? The commuters and tourists will shop at home, and plan to do so. New inheritance taxes? Nobody will want to die in New York. Get out while you're still healthy! These measures will merely accelerate the decline of the city, create more unemployment, and boost welfare expenditures, giving inflation a shot in the arm in the process.

2. Neither the city nor the state will be able to balance their budgets. Cities and housing authorities are going bust and will need help. The state just bailed out Yonkers, for example. And they haven't allowed for general inflation in projecting their future expenses.

3. The "moratorium" is illegal and is now being challenged in the courts. Those notes are contracts between the city and the lenders. The Constitution of The United States provides that: "No state shall ... pass any bill of attainder, ex post facto law impairing the obligation of contracts...."

That's just what the state has done, passed an ex post facto (after the fact) law repudiating those contracts. The city has been sued by the Flushing Bank on behalf of its customers holding this debt. If they win, the deal collapses.

Only through formal bankruptcy can debts be forcibly restructured, and that by a Federal judge. This is why Ford insisted on a change in the bankruptcy laws to make it easier for the city to file bankruptcy. This is why he said the government reserved the right to withdraw its loan offer if the state and city could not do their part. He knows the pitfalls.

4. The union leaders have to sell the rank and file on the changes in the pension ageements, and keep them from protesting further firings and layoffs.

The garbage collectors are on strike already.

5. Balancing the city budget is easy to agree to, but impossible to accomplish.

Will employees and welfare recipients sit quietly and watch their checks be eaten up by double digit inflation for three years, without protest?

Will students (with their marvelous record of rational cooperation) enthusiastically accept the imposition of tuition on the city's free university system? Remember, there are 220,000 of them.

Will the ghetto dwellers applaud the closing of the half-empty, city-subsidized hospital and free clinic in their neighborhood?

So we're back to square one. Bankruptcy, or a TRUE Federal

bailout! And let's be realistic. Bankruptcy means $8 billion to $13 billion in federal funds to prevent the total collapse and destruction of the city. Twenty-eight states have laws preventing the sale of securities of defaulting municipalities for ten years after default. That, plus investor distrust of bonds, plus the collapse of business and property tax revenues means New York will not be able to raise money. So, Uncle Sugar is stuck!

Federal bailout means just about the same thing. It's just more expensive. At least the bankruptcy court can restructure debts, or even write some off!

It is inflation and uncontrolled spending and "money creation" that has created a New York City. As Mayor Beame so aptly said, in reference to the Federal government: "They were the pushers, and we were the junkies."

(1/15/76) First National City and Chase Manhattan had the greatest exposure to New York's financial problems, although you can expect soon to see other New York banks added to the same list as their exposure was almost as great. There has been great debate and a series of conferences between the Accounting Board, the Securities Exchange Commission, and the various bank regulatory agencies, over what to do about all of those bad New York notes and bonds that are carried in the bank portfolios, over 5 billion from an accounting point of view. If they are no longer paying interest or have not been redeemed at maturity, they are technically in default. The question: should the banks be required to write them off now, write them off later, or write them off at all? The decision was made, as I forecast earlier, to simply carry them on the books at face value and not require assets of dubious value as though they were very valuable and continue to function as though they had a secure capital base.

Back in December I pointed out that nothing was really solved, it was only papered over. I am very concerned about this adverse publicity, and this leak of what is generally considered to be secret data, causing possible runs on these banks. I believe that CDs will not be renewed and that many large depositors will withdraw. Already, major withdrawals have been made by corporations who are moving out of New York.

In November, 1975, I said, "And also watch Chase Manhattan Bank. It will be seriouly affected by New York's problems, and because of its vast international influence and holdings, and its entanglements with foreign banks and foreign governments, it could represent serious problems for this country if it got into trouble. And I think it will."

This financial house of cards we are building can stand only as long as no adverse winds blow, and we are going to face some adverse winds. New York is still that wind. We are now only in the eye of the storm.

First, after watching the nation's biggest city imposing a moratorium on its debts, investors are showing reluctance to invest in the bonds of every other city. This is not fair, because some cities have managed their finances well.

Second, the new municipal bankruptcy law, which allows cities to go bankrupt without the consent of 51% of their creditors and to more easily default on their obligations, has changed all the rules of the game for the investors and the cities, just as I prognosticated in December. Nearly all cities have to borrow. If they can't borrow, they would have to do the same thing you or I would have to do if our credit was cut off, simply spend less money. This is virtually impossible to do in a time when more and more demands are being made for social services, police and fire services, etc.

Third, cities are also being forced to make far greater disclosure of their financial status. This has the paradoxical result of some cities conscientiously and responsibly disclosing their problems, and appearing to be worse risks than others who are not so conscientious and are much slower in disclosing problems. This distorts the whole investment judgment process.

In mid-December, the first round in a lawsuit between the Flushing Bank on the one hand, and the Municipal Assistance Corporation and the State of New York on the other hand, was won by the state and Big MAC. Flushing Bank had challenged the provision in the new state laws which required holders of New York paper to either exchange their notes as they came due, for lower-interest long-term Big MAC bonds, or accept a lower interest rate and retain their notes for three years without chance of redemption before that. As we have said in prior issues, this is in violation of both the State and Federal Constitutions, because it involved repudiation of a contract without recourse to formal bankruptcy. The state court upheld the legislature. However, state courts almost always do. The real battles will be fought before the State Supreme Court and then before the United States Supreme Court.

Protests are already underway with students at City University of New York, protesting economy moves there. So far, the city has not really attacked the problem. No hospitals are closed. No tuition has been imposed. No services have been substantially cut. So the moments of truth are still ahead of us.

The Federal government has so far loaned New York approximately $700 million of the $2.3 billion that they are authorized by Congress to loan. However, you can be assured that the Federal government will acknowledge shortly that far more money is needed than they have committed. The President will either go back to Congress for additional authorization for funds or will move to cut off any additional loans and will simply put a lien against Federal revenue-sharing funds and other monies which are owing to the city under various Federal programs in order to recover their loans. This will drive New York into bankruptcy.

As I forecast earlier, the new laws regarding inheritance taxes are driving large numbers of New Yorkers out of the city. New York is a nice place to visit, but I wouldn't want to die there!

Here's a collection of interesting quotes regarding New York City which have appeared nationally over the last few weeks.

NEWSWEEK (December 29, 1975): "CUNY students have vowed to protest the budget modifications at City Hall and in Albany. Some warned of possible 'unpleasant repercussions' at the Democratic National Convention when it meets in New York next summer."

FORBES (January 1, 1976): "There were perfectly good reasons for investors to shun some banks; they face horrendous loan write-offs. . . . Which are sound? Which face bathing in red ink? Unfortunately, only the insiders know. Banks do not have to reveal much information about the quality of their loan portfolios."

BUSINESS WEEK (December 29, 1975): "New York City may vanish from the headlines, but its place amost surely will be taken by the financial problems of New York State and a dozen other cities and states."

WALL STREET JOURNAL (October 15, 1975): (In reference to pension funding) "Is this only a New York City problem? Hardly. Many of the 2400 state and local pension funds are deteriorating, moving to a point where outrage will exceed receipts later in the decade."

THEODORE WHITE: "New York City has now reached a point where it is entirely incapable of self-government. We are a city burdened by an enormous underclass—a dependent, hapless, and increasingly predatory underclass.

In order to pacify and control this underclass, we pay not only huge sums in welfare, but extraordinary benefits to a body of 260,000 civil servants. These city employees . . . charge extortionately for their services. There are over a million people on welfare in this city. Our

260,000 city employees have wives or husbands and children. Most of them vote and they are all united in one great purpose: 'More.' No one can be elected in this city who promises 'less.' Only now there is no more.

You have to realize that the issue is not just a bankruptcy of one city, it is the bankruptcy of the goals and thinking of the 1960s, the decade of unreckoning good will."

BRENTON W. HARRIES, President of Standard and Poors Corporation: (In reference to the bond market) "Overall there has been an extreme loss of confidence. Most of the changes arising from the events of 1975 will be permanent.

(In reference to underfunding of city and state pension funds) In Los Angeles, we think $1 billion. In New York at least $3 billion. In Massachusetts, which has no funding at all—pension benefits are paid from current budgets—the figures may be as high as $8 billion."

What does all this mean? It means we've got to keep our eye on New York City. I still say it has the potential to completely abort the fledgling economic recovery and to drive this country into a deep depression. Don't be lulled into a false sense of security simply because politicians have turned their attentions elsewhere and it's not making headlines.

BOOK REVIEW: *THE FINAL FIRE*

(2/1/76)   Ordinarily, I would not bother to review a novel, but for this one I'll make an exception. Written by New York City fireman, Dennis Smith, it is a riveting account of what could happen in New York if the firemen went on strike.

I now understand the mentality of the labor leaders and the internal pressures of union politics that forces them to take militant positions on wages, hours, and benefits.

I can see the helplessness of city officials in trying to cope with public emergencies created by the unions.

Whenever I visit New York and feel the forces of those winds that roar and swirl down those concrete and steel canyons, I'll think of the terrible final fire that roars out of control, devouring whole blocks, leaping narrow concrete canyons, while striking firemen yell "scab" at those who, out of conviction, fight and sometimes die.

I've always contended that our cities were fragile entities, depen-dent on intricate inter-relationships of politicians, workers, and money, and much like the human body, could suffer permanent damage if a critical part ceased to function for only a little while. *THE FINAL FIRE* will convince you, and give you a bang-up, scary evening in the process.

Incidentally, there is a little of the mandatory "realism" in sex and language in his book. Not as much as most novels—in fact, most would consider it pretty tame stuff, but I thought you'd want to know about it, just in case it bothers you as it does me. (see: Banks; Cities; Bonds; Economy, U.S.; & FDIC)

NORTH, DR. GARY

(3/1/79) Based on the attendee evaluation questionnaire, DR. GARY NORTH was one of the most popular speakers at our recent 2nd Annual *RUFF TIMES* National Convention. He discussed price controls from his unique perspective, pointing out that inflation is a tax, "which is engineered from the Federal Reserve System, resulting in increased monetary demand for products, which then results in businesses reacting with a hike in prices." He quoted COLIN CLARK, who said, "Over the past 150 years, whenever a government had taxation in excess of 25% of the national income (it's 42% now), that government, without exception, turned to the inflation tax for the ultimate solution." He discussed the four tax escalation steps with the appropriate taxpayer responses to those steps. Step (1) is direct taxation. Taxpayer response to that would be direct evasion or avoidance. Step (2) is indirect taxation, meaning inflation, and the taxpayer response to that would be inflation-hedging. When you try to beat the inflation tax, you are a tax evader. Step (3) would be price controls, with the taxpayer response to that being the formation and patronization of black markets. Step (4) would be rationing, because of the resulting shortages, and the response would be barter and feudalization of the economy. Gary says the 5th step would be one of two final alternatives. Step (5-A) would be currency reform, with gold backing for the money. At that stage there would be hope of freedom, because we would be returning to Step 1. But the more likely scenario at that stage would be (5-B), a controlled economy through socialism or fascism, which, with few exceptions, most countries have chosen. He hoped it would be 5-A, not 5-B in our country.

He then laid out what we can do now while we can still legally hedge against this inflation monster. The principles are well covered in the chapters on price contols in my book, which were written with

Gary's help. Basically, it involves the stockpiling of non-luxury items, which are relatively small in profit margin and high in volume, as those are the ones most likely to disappear first from the marketplace.

Gary's workshops were mostly questions and answers. Here are some of the more interesting ones:

Q. What do you think about investments in blue chip stocks, like IBM?

A. The equity market for IBM, no matter how good IBM is, is dependent upon the confidence of the public in the stock market. You're not buying IBM. You're buying someone's willingness, at a later date, to buy IBM from you. IBM stock, like any other investment, is a discounted market value of an expected future return as denominated in the currency of the realm. When you buy IBM, you are buying the market which makes IBM possible, and I don't trust the market.

Q. What is the best long-term investment strategy after you have your survival gold and silver?

A. I recommend half T-bills and half numismatic coins for a "put-it-away-and-forget-it" investment. Numismatic coins have appreciated generally at 18% per annum compounded since 1967. *I believe in liquidity*. I want to be able to discard my mistakes rapidly.

Q. Why are most retirement programs no good?

A. They leave records. The tax escalation system (inflation) is the confiscation of all private wealth in the name of a central government. It leaves records! Those are the three worst words any investment can have.

NUCLEAR PLANTS

(4/15/79) The most tasteless joke of the year award goes to comedians BOB and RAY. On a television special, right in the middle of the nuclear crisis, when no one knew whether Pennsylvania might blow up, they announced they were holding a contest to select a new state capital for Pennsylvania.

I haven't investigated yet, but I'll bet there's some cheap real estate available in Harrisburg. The THREE MILE ISLAND nuclear situation may have been the most potentially dangerous man-created event in all of human history.

The day after the crisis, I was concerned enough to instruct our staff to phone each of our Discussion Group leaders with the following message and ask them to call their group members.

> THE NUCLEAR ACCIDENT NEAR HARRISBURG CAR-
> RIES A DISTINCT POSSIBILITY OF A MELT DOWN. IF IT
> HAPPENS, HUGE AMOUNTS OF DEADLY RADIOACTIVE
> FALLOUT WILL BE VENTED INTO THE UPPER PREVAIL-
> ING WINDS, WHICH IN THE HARRISBURG AREA, ARE
> FROM THE WEST AT UP TO 75 KNOTS.
>
> THE ODDS ARE THAT MELT DOWN WILL NOT OCCUR,
> BUT THE DANGER DOES EXIST. MY RECOMMENDATION
> WOULD BE TO IMMEDIATELY EVACUATE EVERYTHING
> EAST OF HARRISBURG FROM NEW YORK SOUTH TO
> BALTIMORE AS A PRECAUTIONARY MEASURE UNTIL
> THE EMERGENCY IS OVER. IF I'M WRONG, YOU CAN
> ALWAYS GO HOME AGAIN. HEAD NORTH OF NEW YORK
> CITY OR SOUTH OF BALTIMORE TO BE OUT OF THE
> FALLOUT AREA.
>
> PLEASE REFER TO THE *RUFF TIMES*, MARCH 15, 1977
> ISSUE, FOR OTHER STEPS TO PROTECT YOURSELF FROM
> FALLOUT.
>
> DON'T KILL YOURSELF BY RECKLESS PANIC DRIVING,
> AND IF A MELT DOWN OCCURS WHILE TRAVELING,
> KEEP YOUR CAR WINDOWS CLOSED AND THE AIR CON-
> DITIONING OFF.

Even though neither the NRC nor the power plant officials were talking about the possibility of "melt down" at that time, our information was that it was possible, and, after checking the winds, I knew that Philadelphia and New York were both downwind.

A melt down is a horrifying event. If you can't cool off or control the nuclear reaction, the atomic fuel eventually melts and fuses, heating still further, and in a matter of hours would burn its way clear through yards of concrete and steel and through the bottom of the plant. It would then burn its way into the earth, eventually hitting the ground water, which it would vaporize, sending an explosive geyser of radioactive water and dust into the air, combined with particles from the nuclear fuel itself. This could continue for days or perhaps even weeks. In the worst possible case (which can only be theorized, of course), there could be many deaths from radiation exposure in a period of a few weeks. How far downwind that would reach is anybody's guess. Many people would be exposed to radioactive iodine, which would mean anything from thousands to possibly millions of cases of thyroid cancer over the next few years. Strontium

90 also would be released, possibly causing bone cancer. I felt that there was no harm whatsoever in deciding to visit Aunt Matilda in Ohio for a few days until it became clear what was really happening. We were receiving confusing and contradictory comments from the NRC and the power company and, as transcripts of the NRC deliberations have recently revealed, it is evident that no one had the slightest idea as to what the situation really was. If I lived in that area, I wouldn't have stood around to find out.

Now what is the political, economic, and ideological fallout from the Three Mile Island near-disaster?

Those who are in favor of the expansion of nuclear energy will be pointing to this as an example of the safety of nuclear power. A potentially terrible accident was contained and there was no loss of life—obviously a point in their favor.

On the other side of the coin, the danger was real and the consequences of a melt down are greater than the consequences of a coal mine accident or an oil rig fire, which would only affect the lives of the workers in the area. A nuclear accident can affect thousands or even millions of people downwind.

The government has created an environment which gives us the worst of both possible worlds. First, we have developed a significant dependence on nuclear energy. The shutdown of existing nuclear power plants would have a devastating impact on the economy and could drive oil prices out of sight, as oil-fired plants would have to take up the nuclear slack.

At the same time, government, on all levels, has imposed regulatory construction delays which have increased the cost of nuclear plants to the point where they may not be economical, while at the same time, allowing nuclear plants with unsafe design structures to be put into service, often in unsafe places. This means unconscionable delays, coupled with unsafe reactors. The Three Mile Island plant is almost an exact duplicate of a plant at Rancho Seco in California, which recently had a near-miss accident almost identical to Harrisburg. This information was available to the Three Mile Island people and the NRC, yet the plant was allowed to continue to function with a basic design flaw which had been concealed from the public. The Three Mile Island accident was avoidable.

The regulators delay, but they do not protect. It is a typical example of government inaction. (see: Regulatory Agencies)

In all fairness, it seems that the NRC people on the spot at Harrisburg did give us more accurate information than the power company, so let's give credit where credit is due. Once the crisis

463

began, they seem to have performed well.

This accident means that we are headed for more energy problems. It only complicates and magnifies the problems we live with each day. (see: Energy, Nuclear)

NUCLEAR PROTECTION

NUCLEAR ATTACK?

(12/15/76) I just received the November 16, 1976 issue of *MCKEEVER'S MISL* and was immediately captured by the lead article called, "YOU CAN SURVIVE A NUCLEAR ATTACK." It is the most interesting, best-reasoned description of the effects of nuclear war that I've ever seen. It also describes some very simple and inexpensive measures that can be taken to increase your chances of survival, without being branded as some kind of a nut. These principles would also be valuable in the case of a nuclear power plant accident, or a terrorist bomb in one of our major cities. It is complete with fascinating pictures of fallout patterns in the U.S., one hour and twenty-four hours after a nuclear explosion, so you can get an idea of how well you are located.

All in all, it's a fabulous article and I suggest that you write for a copy immediately. Send your inquiry to *MCKEEVER'S MISL*, P.O. Box 41301, Medford, Oregon 97501.

INTERVIEW WITH MARLIN EBERT

(3/1/77) MR. MARLIN J. EBERT is President of RADIATION PROTECTION CORPORATION of Livermore, California.

He began his career in the nuclear industry in 1961, while attending Graduate School at Pennsylvania State University as a National Defense Education Act fellow. He spent 2 ½ years doing basic research, received his Master of Science in Molecular Biophysics and then spent five years as a regular officer in the United States Army, resigning in 1968 with the rank of Captain. He did two combat tours in Vietnam as an Army aviator. He is a full member of the Society of Nuclear Medicine, and a part-time faculty member of Chabot College.

HJR: Marlin, you are the manufacturer of one of the most fascinating products I've seen in a long time: an inexpensive

personal anticontamination kit and protection suit, which would protect against the effects of nuclear fall-out in the event of nuclear accident or nuclear war. Why do you feel there is a marketplace in the U.S. for these items?

MJE: If you take a look at the world situation and our military posture, you see that the U.S. is completely dependent on the nuclear strike deterrent for its military superiority. Conventional weaponry is in very short supply in our arsenal, and, in many cases, it is not even the best of equipment. This knowledge has been widely circulated. Our posture relies on the nuclear threat.

Then we have seen constant growth in the proliferation of nuclear materials. Communist China recently set off a couple of test bombs. Minor amounts of fallout were deposited in North Carolina, New York and Pennsylvania. Nothing you would care to have in your milk—and you will if you live in Pennsylvania— but it probably won't kill so many people that you might notice. If you multiply that sort of thing by a factor of 10 or 20, now you've got something you really should worry about!

Look at the proliferation of the weapons that we know about. There are many other countries who have not exploded a bomb, but extrapolate their technological capabilities and you can see that they have nuclear capability. Such countries would include South Africa, Israel, and probably Argentina.

We know how India got theirs. They bought a test reactor from ATOMIC ENERGY OF CANADA, LTD, seven or eight years ago, and they produced Uranium 238, wrapped it around the reactor, and transmuted it.

HJR: Do you think the Shah of Iran has the bomb?

MJE: He has the money to buy one, he is buying all sorts of fancy weapons. Therefore, I would conclude that he does have a bomb.

HJR: The development of a radiation fallout suit seems to presuppose that nuclear war is not the end of all life on earth, and that there is a way to protect yourself against it. Is this true?

MJE: Yes it is. Howard, I've taken state-of-the-art nuclear anticontamination capability, exactly like that used in the reactor business, where I've spent most of my business life. I've been in the very guts of a reactor, and taken apart nuts, bolts and screws in high radiation areas in the world's largest commercial test reactor. You can protect yourself. There aren't enough bombs to char the earth with the direct effects of the blast. What is really going to cause long-term suffering and death at some later time, is fallout. Fallout is pretty well gone, due to decay, in 2½ or 3 weeks. That which is left will be trapped by the soil, and some will get into the food chain, and that will not be good. Strontium 90 is one of the nastiest ones. It won't hurt you to hold it in your hands, as it emits radiation which is not highly penetrating. It gets you when you breathe it or eat it. It clings to the soil and most of it will not get into the food chain at all. What you have to contend with, if there is a nuclear attack anywhere around the world, is large clouds of fallout.

HJR: Are you saying that if you can avoid the direct effects of blast and heat, and you protect yourself against fallout, that you would have a chance of surviving?

MJE: Definitely. In the late '50s and early '60s many people built bomb shelters, not fallout selters. If they had tried to use those shelters, they probably would have contaminated them. The interior would have been as dangerous as the outside.

HJR: Unless they got in there before the blast.

MJE: If they got in there before the blast, and they had the appropriate air filtration equipment, and they stayed in, uncontaminated for $2^1/_2$ to 3 weeks, without coming out for food or water, they would be O.K. When you do come out, you are going to have to protect and decontaminate yourself. My kit is absolutely superb for that, and will give people a great deal of protection from the remaining contamination after the hard gamma radiation has decayed away.

HJR: What are the Soviets doing for their population?

MJE: Professor Leon Goure, an internationally recognized expert on the Soviet Union, and a Russian immigrant, is the Director of Soviet Studies at the CENTER FOR ADVANCED INTER-NATIONAL STUDIES, University of Miami, Coral Gables, Florida. He has reported his examinations of this problem in articles in the *CHRISTIAN SCIENCE MONITOR* and other publications. Professor Goure states that the Soviet Union has been spending billions of dollars since 1974 to protect her industry and her people by providing them with equipment such as that which I am offering, although Professor Goure says that mine is far superior to anything the individual Soviet citizen has, and he has written me a letter to this effect.

He further states that better than 90% of the Soviet people would survive a nuclear war. Further, the Soviet industry would be able to be back on the line in full scale production in two or three years. Conversely, in our own country, more than 50% of the people would die as a result of a nuclear holocaust and our industry would be down and out for 10 to 15 years. These figures are backed up by the prestigious report issued by the Boeing Aircraft Company in mid-November, 1976.

HJR: Isn't it true that when the Soviets provide nuclear war protection for their population, they are really making an offensive gesture? I don't think this country is capable of a sneak nuclear attack, especially because we have not done anything to protect ourselves. It seems to me that they are preparing against retaliation from us after an attack by them, and they would be able to warn their population to head for the shelters in time, even if they waited until they pushed the button. We don't have fallout shelters in the United States. All you can do is insulate yourself from the worst effects of what's going to happen. What do you think is the likelihood of nuclear war?

MJE: I think the likelihood is becoming greater and greater, and I feel almost certain we will see a nuclear exchange somewhere on the globe. World Communism will have no qualms about using the bomb, because, after all, their whole philosophy is "the end justifies the means," and the end is World Communism.

HJR: But isn't it true that the Chinese are not a nuclear threat to us? Only the Soviets have the delivery capability.

MJE: No, I don't think so. The delivery capability may be on the back of a person. There are units small enough to be carried. You can shoot them out of a 155 millimeter howitzer. And let's just take Allen Drury's scenario in his book *PROMISE OF JOY*, where the Chinese and the Russians start throwing bombs at each other. Those clouds of fallout are going to be all over this country, just as the little clouds were over Pennsylvania and North Carolina. And people are going to have to get out of the zone and get clean and stay clean, and that is what my unit will do for them.

HJR: People are concerned about the possibility of a nuclear reactor accident. Do you think this is much of a possibility?

MJE: Murphy's law says, "If something can go wrong, it probably will, sometime" and even though nuclear reactors have as many as a dozen redundancies, or backup systems, we have come awfully close with a couple of reactors. I don't think the chances are as great as the chances of my having an automobile accident as I drive home tonight. I wear a seat belt, but I don't stop driving a car. I do believe that this very same type of anticontamination capability should be available in the communities downwind from a reactor. Then, if there ever were a release, the people would have sufficient protection to safely evacuate the area and not breathe or eat fallout, such as Iodine 131, which is just terrible.

HJR: I read a rather interesting report recently from some Soviet emigres who talked about an area where a nuclear accident occurred some years ago in the Soviet Union. Years later they had to drive through fast with their car windows closed. The story was that this has been a dumping ground for nuclear wastes, and they had dumped so much that it created a critical mass, and there was a spontaneous explosion. Is that possible?

MJE: At a processing plant some years ago, a pipe broke. The material which was fissionable went into a sump, and it settled to the bottom. There was sufficient mass there that you would have had a "chugging reactor" and it would have settled to the bottom and then "gone critical." One of the engineers in charge evacuated the building and went in. The story I got from the people who were there is that he took a long pole and stirred this sump, keeping it from falling to the bottom, until they could get the appropriate pumping equipment in there to pump it out. Now, take that same scenario, and suppose the guy doesn't stir the sump. Now you have yourself a "chugging reactor" which wouldn't explode, but would spread one dickens of a lot of fissionable material around.

(3/15/77)

HJR: You have already mentioned one step: make sure you have enough necessities that you wouldn't have to venture out for two or three weeks. That's basic. What else could we do to protect ourselves?

MJE: If the fallout is heavy where you live, you are going to need some sort of shielding to protect you from the penetrating gamma radiation in the early days of the fallout. If you have a basement, you are really in good shape because you can use heavy materials, the denser the better, to make adequate shielding protection. You must be shielded by distance or mass. If you have a barn with a basement, you can stack up feed sacks about four or five feet thick. That would be a super shelter, and you could stay in there for a few weeks, especially if you have food or water. If you have my kit, you can make a foray out from time to time.

HJR: Does the shelter have to be airtight?

MJE: It would help if it were airtight, however, let's take the case of the barn. Fallout is large dust particles, so it would settle on the roof. Unless there were a lot of wind carrying it through the chinks and the cracks, you would probably be in good shape. The distance between you and the roof is a shielding factor.

HJR: How long will that kind of fallout remain dangerous?

MJE: You have 1/10 as much radiation after seven hours, and 1/100 as much radiation 49 hours after the first hour. That's a handy rule of thumb. By the way, I discuss that in my book that comes with the kit.

HJR: Now, let's assume that we have protected ourselves against the worst hard radiation, and now we decide we want to flee the neighborhood. Is that what your kit is designed to do?

MJE: Yes, it is, it definitely is.

HJR: Could we hop in our car and safely drive out of this hot fallout area?

MJE: Yes.

HJR: Recently, in *MCKEEVER'S MISL*, which is a fine "hard-money" newsletter, there was an article, with a map showing major fallout zones, based on prevailing wind patterns down-wind from potential nuclear targets. If you knew what the patterns would be, you would know which road to take and where to go.

Let's assume that one has such a map and wants to get out. What does your kit consist of and what will it do for him?

MJE: There are two kits—a heavy duty professional model, which has some renewable component, and is the type of thing you would wear in a hot zone in a nuclear reactor or a radiation laboratory. It meets all government specifications for this use.

HJR: Could you describe it so that someone will know what it looks and feels like?

MJE: Each kit contains a mask-type respirator which one puts over his chin, mouth and nose. These respirators are designed to inhibit the inhalation of toxic particles all the way down to 4/10 of a micron. They take out 99.999% of all particulates. The smallest bacteria is an E. Coli, and it is one micron in size, so the respirator will keep our particles smaller than the smallest bacteria. In addition to that, there is a body covering made specially to my design to give the individual user the optimum protection without having to go through a lot of special preparation. It has a hood which is integral to the unit. It provides you with just about the best dust covering you can possibly get. It is made of a DuPont space age fabric also used in the nuclear industry. There are shoe covers and gloves. The heavy duty kit has heavier ones and the lighter duty kit has lighter ones. But they all provide you with significant anti-contamination. There is also an instruction book. It's very carefully written. I've used many information sources and provided references. I wrote the book from my background in the business. Most of the references were prepared at great taxpayer expense by the Federal government.

I have provided decontamination agents. They are two specially made alcohol detergent sponges loaded with an alcohol detergent solution that can be used to cleanse exposed or contaminated areas of the body, even if you don't have water. Also, there are two surgical scrub brushes—the kind that a surgeon uses prior to an operation—which are sterile and individually wrapped. They can be used with a four-ounce bottle of specially formulated detergent, which does a very good job of removing metallic contaminants and typically metallic radioactive materials from fission of uranium. And there's enough in there to wash one's whole body about seven times. Also included are four large disposable, absorbent, surgical towels with nylon reinforcing, which can be used to wipe yourself off, either after using the alcohol sponges, or after a complete body washing.

HJR: But how much would a person increase his odds of surviving with such a suit while crossing a medium contaminated area?

MJE: That's a rough one to answer, but no one in his right mind would consider going into a minimally hot area in a reactor without this kind of equipment, because if you get it on your skin for any length of time, or if you breathe in just minor quantities of radioactive material, you're burnt for life. It's a very fearsome thing. Without such equipment, you increase your chances of fallout contamination by hundreds of times.

HJR: If everybody had one, how many more lives would be saved?

MJE: If you are right there where the bomb goes off, my suit won't help you. However, if everyone had one, and knew how to use it, and knew some other principles of protection, along with the food and water and other essentials, we would certainly decrease the fallout mortality rate by 90%.

HJR: Marlin, it sounds like this outfit of yours has to be incredibly expensive. How much does it cost?

MJE: Well, the medium-duty kit, which is quite adequate for the homeowner, the person who is not going to need long-term respiratory protection, sells for $22.50 and the heavy-duty, industrial, standard, professional unit with a reusable respirator sells for $39.50 (1977 prices).

HJR: That's incredible. I thought you would need something similar to a moon walker's space suit.

Marlin, I've learned from this interview that there is no need to believe that nuclear war is the end of all life on earth. You could protect yourself and your family for a small sum of money. There are a lot of people out there who are worried about this, and it may never come to pass, but how much more peace of mind would I have if I had protection. Maybe it's a good insomnia cure, if nothing else.

It has been my opinion that we may be faced with such great Soviet superiority, that one day the Soviets may just simply unveil to us everything they have, show how they could destroy us in a moment and say, "Now that you know this—now that this is understood clearly—let's negotiate."

We are becoming weaker and they are becoming stronger, and if we are not weaker than them by now, which is a matter of some debate, we will soon be, someday.

Marlin, is there any last thing you would like to add to all this?

MJE: One important thing about the kit is the shelf life. It is virtually indefinite. There's nothing to deteriorate.

HJR: How long does it take to put one on?

MJE: Less than a minute. I could put one on in the same time it takes you to put on a pair of Doctor Dentons—you know, the pajamas with the feet.

HJR: I've enjoyed this interview. It may be one of the most important we have ever had. Isn't it strange how many things come back to RUFF'S BASIC RECOMMENDATIONS? Store food. Prepare to be independent of society around you. Act to insulate yourself against forces that you cannot control or reverse. This is certainly one of them. It fits into our philosophy. I will tell you this—I will have a complete set of these outfits for my family, and I'm not going to worry about whether my neighbors think I am crazy or paranoid—I just won't tell them.

Many thanks for this interview, Marlin. (Note: For a transcript of a more recent interview with Mr. Ebert, please write to RUFF HOU$E Television, P.O. Box 2000, San Ramon, CA 94583.)

NUTRITION

The entire field of nutrition is examined in Chapter 16 of my book, *HOW TO PROSPER DURING THE COMING BAD YEARS*, but I want to give you the basics here in capsule format. For a more extensive exposure to this vital aspect of survival, please refer to my book.

(3/1/76) We've had a shocking experience that has reaffirmed some basic principles I have believed and written about.

Our five-year old son, Timmy, somehow managed to climb up and swing from the shower curtain rod over the bathtub, and fell across the edge of the tub on his stomach. Two days later he began to show the classic symptoms of a damaged spleen and we hustled him off to the hospital.

I am deeply appreciative of the loving care of the nurses. I'm grateful for the surgeon, who, when called in for a pre-operative consultation, said, "I'm not convinced. Let's watch and wait." And it did turn out that surgery wasn't necessary. I appreciate the diagnostic skills and gentle manner of the two pediatricians who examined him.

But, I'm appalled at the medical ignorance of the nutritional principles that can strengthen the body's defenses against injury and promote healing, and astounded at the total lack of awareness of the effects of stress on the body's nutritional status, caused by injury and X-rays and radioactive isotopes. But, most of all, I'm devastated at the hospital junk food diet.

We have to prepare for a time when medical services may not be readily available to us, when our only health protection may be the food and food supplements we eat, and we have to start before the problem hits us.

Let's go back to Timmy's experience for a few examples.

For two and a half days he was totally on I.V. feeding, consisting of glucose (a simple sugar), a saline solution, and potassium. His spleen was bleeding internally and his red cell count and hemoglobin were dropping.

Why was there no iron? When you are bleeding, you have heavy iron loss (red bood cells) with a corresponding loss of oxygen-carrying ability, which impairs healing.

Why no vitamin K, which helps normal clotting? Why no vitamin C, which is essential to the production of collagen, the healing connective tissue.

Timmy had three sets of x-rays and three series of radioactive isotopes to facilitate pictures of the vital organs. Why don't radiologists recognize the indisputable scientific evidence of the destruction of enzymes, vitamin C, the B complex, and amino acids, by radiation, and routinely require heavy supplementation of these nutrients.

When he was finally given food to eat, why was he given popsicles (loaded with sugar and red dye #2, just banned by the FDA), ice cream, potato chips, candy and gum, to burden his body with additional stresses? When we protested about his diet, the doctor told us we could worry about that "nutrition stuff" when he got home. We actually had to smuggle vitamins to him. I'm grateful that his nutritional status was good enough to see him through.

Skyrocketing malpractice insurance rates are driving doctors out of practice, causing them to withhold their services in protest and driving medical costs through the ceiling. It could jeopardize your ability to receive health care even if we didn't have a total economic collapse.

We may be facing a time when you dare not get sick, but if you do, remember vitamins and minerals can be used therapeutically in lieu of drugs and medicine in the prevention and treatment of disease and injury. If we should find ourselves with medical sevices unavailable, you may have to fight it out yourself without medical help. So, you'd better know how!

1. Start cleaning up your diet. It's probably loaded with "empty calories." This simply means food containing sugar, starches, fats or some protein, but with the vitamins, minerals, enzymes, etc., refined out. Stop eating for recreation and start eating for health. Be sure your diet consists of wholesome grains, vegetables, fruits, meats and dairy products.

Empty calories hurt you two ways. First, you will become deficient to the degree that you consume these foods. Second, sugar requires vitamins and minerals for its metabolism, so it robs your tissues of these nutrients. Sugar is actually a negative nutrient.

2. Routinely use good, natural food supplements, to build your nutritional status and protect you against infection and promote quick recovery from injury. You need a good multivitamin formula, vitamin C, calcium, and possibly vitamin E and vitamin A.

Over age 60, you might need a good hydrochloric acid supplement and some natural enzymes. If you have a cholesterol problem, you need lipotropic factors.

I believe the RDAs (recommended daily allowances) are usually too low, as they do not allow for increased needs under stress, and stress conditions are what we are preparing for, are we not?

Also, I know it is conventional theory that the water-soluble vitamins (B complex, and C) are not stored in the body, and amounts above the RDA merely are excreted in the urine. Admittedly, there is no one storage depot like, for example, vitamin A being stored in the liver. But there is evidence that quantities over and above the RDA do build up in body tissues until a degree of saturation is reached. This is non-toxic, and takes time to build up. Vitamin C, when saturation is achieved, can confer resistance to virus infection and accelerate healing of wounds and bone fractures. Some of the B vitamins increase resistance to the physical effects of emotional stress and can improve efficiency in mobilizing protein tissue for body repair.

In my opinion, preparation for possible hard times involves building up your body's health and resistance to disease. To assume that you can consume all of the junk food you want, paying no attention to diet, and then suddenly resist the demands of stress while switching over to your healthy food storage program is inconsistent and foolish.

I am a bit dubious of excessive claims made for supplements, however. I am not convinced that all diseases have a specific cure related to some particular vitamin or mineral. This great frontier is now being probed. Dr. Alexis Carroll, one of the great pioneers of medicine, said, "The nutritionist of today is the physician of tomorrow." Unfortunately, because of the anti-nutrition bias built into our scientific establishment, we're a long way from realizing this. I guess I will rest my case by asking: wouldn't you rather be sure?

I suppose it is theoretically possible, under today's conditions, to get all the nutrients you need from a normal diet, as is claimed by the Food and Drug Administration and the largest segments of the medical profession. However, before you decide against my suggestion to properly supplement your diet, consider these questions. Do you know how much nutrition you receive from the food you eat? Do you know that your diet is low in the junk foods that tend to dilute nutritional value? Do you know if the synthetic vitamins added to many of the foods you eat are in their most soluble and available form? Did you know that foods can vary widely in the nutrients they contain, depending upon the soil in which they are grown, and how long they were stored and how they were processed prior to eating?

Did you know that the Department of Agriculture has published an impressive study indicating that over 70% of the population of this country is deficient in one or more nutrients? Did you know that the FDA's anti-supplement position is a result of intense lobbying from the food processing companies, who object to people saying that their highly-processed, over-chemicalized, plastic foods are not providing sufficient nutrition? Finally, did you know that the National Research Council of the National Academy of Sciences, which sets the recommended daily allowances, consists of scientists who have been nominated by the food industry and that there is a built-in bias towards setting those RDAs very low (see: Food Storage; National Food Reserve; & Protein Supplements)

CALCIUM

(3/1/76)   The preferred supplemental form is a chewable tablet of calcium gluconate and calcium lactate combined with hydrochloric acid, vitamin D, and magnesium, as these other factors are necessary for complete utilization of calcium. If your diet is low in whole milk, cheese, cottage cheese or green leafy vegetables, you probably have a calcium deficiency. It is not just for replacement of bones and teeth, but it is also critical for the functioning of your nervous system. A deficiency can cause insomnia or sudden leg cramps at night. Your muscles don't relax readily without an adequate supply of calcium. Your heart cannot relax between beats without an adequate supply of calcium.

Some people with calcium deposits or arthritis have been mistakenly advised to avoid calcium. This condition is generally due to lack of proper distribution of calcium and can occur simultaneously with a calcium deficiency. Adding a hydrochloric acid tablet to the diet often solves the problem. Calcium's therapeutic role is in the healing of wounds and bones, insomnia, and as a natural tranquilizer. Calcium supplements should be low in phosphorus (at least 15 to 1) as your diet is generally rich in phosphorous.

HYDROCHLORIC ACID

(4/1/76)   Hydrochloric acid is manufactured in the walls of the stomach and is important for the breakdown of protein into amino acids, as well as the distribution of calcium and other minerals in the body. Unfortunately, as we become older, the body produces less and less hydrochloric acid and becomes less and less efficient in the use of minerals and protein.

When my mother was in the last three years of her life, whenever she visited our home and was taking her hydrochloric acid tablets, we would notice within a matter of days a tremendous improvement in her. We found she stopped losing weight (she was down to 78 pounds) and would have an increased appetite, and increased ability to digest high protein food, and the obvious loss of concentration and memory would begin to slightly reverse itself.

Hydrochloric acid supplements can be beneficial to arthritis sufferers, to those who have trouble sleeping at night after a meal of steak or fish or other high protein foods, and would be especially important if you are supplementing your diet with calcium, zinc, magnesium or any of the other essential minerals. A good supplement will be made from betaine hydrochloride, derived from beet roots. It will also be coated with a glaze coating to protect you from the bitter taste.

IRON

(4/1/76)   Dietary iron is yeast supplied from fresh green, leafy vegetables and liver. There's a shortage of these in most storage programs, but you get some from your stored wheat. Iron is critical to your body's ability to remanufacture red blood cells in case of bleeding due to injury, childbirth or menstruation. Iron supplements are generally given in the form of ferrous sulphate, however, it's my opinion that this form is highly insoluble and the body has difficulty utilizing it. Ferrous gluconate is the preferred form. It has been thought that iron and vitamin E are antagonistic, that is, that the two cancel each other out. That is true of ferrous sulphate. The ferrous gluconate form does not have this effect, however.

LIPOTROPES

(4/1/76)   The lipotropic factors are all of those factors found in foods which enable your body to break down fats. They emulsify fats just as a detergent does, i.e. break them down into tiny particles which remain in suspension in the blood until the body can break them down into free fatty acids and burn them for energy. It is believed by many health authorities that cholesterol and excess fat building up as plaque in the arteries are a major cause of heart disease, high blood pressure, senility, and stroke. The lipotropic factors keep these particles in suspension so that they will not "lay down" in the blood vessels and form these deposits. There is some evidence they can even dissolve existing deposits and reduce high cholestrol levels. Such substances as lecithin, lipase, B-12, choline, inositol, folic acid, etc., are lipotropes.

Pure lecithin can be beneficial, however, it does not store well. A good lipotropic adjunct can be several times as effective as lecithin alone. Your body makes its own lecithin from choline and inositol. It is possible to buy the lipotropic factors in supplement form in gelatin capsules with sufficient shelf life. I would not think of leaving a lipotropic factor supplement out of my food storage program. (see: Food Storage)

MILK

(9/15/76) In the past we've referred to the Pottenger Study on raw and cooked milk, using cats, as reported by Dr. William A. Albrecht, the world's most respected soil scientist. This fascinating experiment also will be of interest to farmers. It will teach you a lot about fertilizers. The cats were fed carefully controlled diets using various combinations of cooked and raw meat, pasteurized and raw milk, sweetened and condensed milk, evaporated milk, and one interesting diet used raw, metabolized vitamin D milk from cows fed dry feed, and green feed.

Here's what they found.

1. Cats fed raw meat and raw milk were healthy and reproduced naturally.

2. Cooking the meat or pasteurizing the milk resulted in physical degeneration that increased with each generation. Kittens of the third generation failed to survive six months.

3. The kittens fed only raw, metabolized vitamin D milk suffered rickets and early death in male kittens, vermin, and parasites. Skin diseases and allergies jumped from a normal five percent, to over 90 percent in the third generation. Severe osteoporosis was universal. This group suffered most from the degenerative diseases encountered in human medicine.

It is not known what precise food factors are destroyed by heat processing of milk (and we're talking about normal temperatures incurred in pasteurizing and drying), but it is suspected that there are alterations in globulins, albuminoids and minerals, together with partial destruction of enzymes, vitamins and amino acids.

Change occured not only in the immediate generation, "but as a germ plasm injury which manifests itself in subsequent generations of plants and animals."

Four generations of raw meat and milk were required to bring some of the cats back to normal.

Now, here' the weird part. The cat pens were allowed to lie fallow for five months. The weeds which grew in the excrement were hardy in direct proportion to the health and vigor of the animals that lived in the pens. Navy beans were then planted, and the same results were observed. In the two plots fertilized by cats on raw milk, the plants germinated early, and the beans formed earlier, grew faster, and were more abundant.

Ruff's Conclusions and Recommendations

1.   Don't rely too heavily on powdered milk in your food storage program. It belongs there, but you need other sources of uncooked, high-quality protein, such as a protein supplement, or freeze-dried meat, fish, or fowl.

2.   Feed your kids certified raw milk, if available. I've done it for years and it does make a difference.

3.   Avoid sweetened and condensed milk, and sugar-sweetened baby formulas. In the Pottenger study, the animals fed these products did the poorest, by far. (see: Protein Supplements & Organic Farming)

(4/1/76)   Milk, Powdered

There is a great deal of contradictory and controversial data on powdered milk. In my book, *FAMINE AND SURVIVAL IN AMERICA*, in the chapters on "The Deadly Errors," I concentrated rather heavily on the negative aspects. There are also positive aspects of powdered milk. My major concern was to demonstrate that it does have certain deficiencies and weaknesses, which become important only if you are intending to rely on it as your sole or primary source of protein.

Recently there has been considerable attention paid in the popular press to the X-O factor. This is xanthine-oxidase, a substance found in milk which develops during the pasteurization process. This substance clings to the walls of the blood vessels and provides the rough surface on which cholesterol and triglycerides can get a foothold. The solution is to bring the milk briefly to a boil. This breaks down the X-O factor. The X-O does not occur until the milk is pasteurized and that's why our family drinks raw milk from a certified dairy. It is my opinion that pasteurized milk, and by extension, pasteurized dried skim milk, because of X-O, may be a major factor in the epidemic of heart disease.

Another piece of data came to the surface as I was reading a book called *DIET DYNAMICS* by Dr. Bellow. Dr. Bellow refers to three studies.

Francis M. Pottenger, Jr., M.D., published a report on "The Effect of Heat- Processed Foods and Metabolized Vitamin D Milk on the Dental Facial Structures of Experimental Animals" in the *American Journal of Orthodontics and Oral Surgery* in August of 1946. In young cats fed dry milk as their primary source of protein, the experiment demonstrated that these animals were poor operative risks, that in some instances they were unable to reproduce. Their kittens presented deficiencies in development and in some instances the kittens were sterile. The most remarkable deficiencies were demonstrated when they were fed sweetened condensed milk. When raw milk, cod liver oil and some raw meat were fed to the animals, vast improvements in their health were achieved.

When roller dried skim milk powder was the chief source of protein for experimental rats in another study, the test animals died of liver necrosis within four weeks, even though their initial growth was satisfactory. The death rate in one experiment with roller dried skim milk products was 76%. With spray dried skim milk products, the low temperature process used in most dried milk, 40% of the animals died. Animals fed fluid skim milk survived the 120 day test period unharmed. Something apparently happened during the drying process.

In another experiment, when young albino rats were fed an otherwise normal and sufficient diet, in which the major part (52%) of the protein was derived from dried skim milk powder, it frequently happened that up to 100% of the animals died suddenly from an alimentary liver necrosis, even though, at first, they grew fast and attained a good weight. These rat experiments were done by Dr. H. Fink in Germany, and were reported in 1956 and 1959. They were abstracted by Dr. E. B. Pfeife for the article, "Milk, A Special Fluid," which appeared in the *NATURAL FOOD AND FARMING* magazine.

I do not hesitate to include skim milk in my storage program because it does contain many benefits, but I would never use it as my prime or sole source of protein. For that reason, I have consistently recommended the use of a good protein supplement. (see: protein Supplements)

VITAMIN A

(3/1/76) Vitamin A protects the mucous membranes of the body, such as lungs, mouth, bowel, etc. It is essential for good vision, protects against ulcers, and virus infections, as your body cannot manufacture antibodies without sufficient vitamin A. There is some evidence that it can provide protection against cancer. The maintenance dose is 10,000 to 20,000 IUs for adults, 5,000 to 10,000 for children under twelve, and 500 to 1,000 IUs for infants. Its therapeutic function is to help you overcome acute infections and allergies, to improve night vision and peripheral vision and, as I indicated before, to retard tumor growth. The therapeutic dose is 20,000 to 50,000 IUs per day. (CAUTION: 100,000 IUs per day for six months or more would be toxic. The synthetic form is more toxic than the natural.)

VITAMIN B COMPLEX

(3/1/76) The preferred supplemental form is a concentrate of yeast, as part of a multivitamin supplement. B complex provides elements for the chemical reactions by which your body converts carbohydrates into energy. It affects the health of your nervous system. Deficiencies of these vitamins can manifest themselves in mental and emotional symptoms similar to those of schizophrenia, depression, etc. The maintenance dose varies for each member of the B complex family. To make it simple, we feel that the amounts in the Neo-Life Formula IV come close to the ideal balance for maintenance. The B vitamins can be used for therapeutic purposes in the treatment of depression, nervousness, and other emotional conditions. Sometimes lack of energy and low resistance to infection can be related to the B complex. They are completely non-toxic, even in megadoses.

VITAMIN C

(12/75) Much concern has been expressed recently about the shelf life of vitamin C, largely through FDA dissemination in the press of a paper presented by I.O. Wilk at an undergraduate laboratory section of a recent American Chemical Society meeting.

It was alleged that vitamin C degrades rapidly under storage into harmful products. I have in my hands two documents: a technical bulletin from Roche Chemical Division of Hoffman-LaRoche, Inc., the largest manufacturer of vitamin C in the world, and a paper on vitamin C from the *Journal* of *Pharmaceutical Services*, Vol. 59, pp. 229–232 (1970).

I quote from the technical bulletin: "We have made extensive studies of a variety of formulations of ascorbic acid packaged tablets under a variety of conditions, including various temperatures and humidities, and found little or no loss of potency in periods up to five years."

The term "ascorbic acid" is used in the technical literature to mean "vitamin C," in whatever form, natural or synthetic.

In the paper from the *Pharmaceutical Journal*, water and temperature were controlling factors in shelf life. "Sodium ascorbate," a common synthetic form of the vitamin was most susceptible to loss of potency from moisture.

Oxygen seems to affect shelf life also. In the Wilk's study, scrapings from the surface of tablets were used.

Ruff's Conclusions

Vitamin C is essential in a food storage program. Most of the vitamin is lost from foods in processing for storage. Much is destroyed by additives used in dehydrated food, or heats used in canned foods, or during storage itself.

Vitamin C tablets should be stored to compensate for these losses, and to meet the body's increased demands for vitamin C under stress.

The natural forms should be used. "Sodium ascorbate" should be avoided.

If kept sealed, dry, cool, and dark, you can expect shelf life up to five years with no significant loss of potency, and up to six months after opening, if it is kept sealed between usages.

(3/1/76) The preferred form of vitamin C comes from citrus, rose hips, or acerola, because they also contain bioflavenoids or the "P-factors." There is much controversy as to the value of P-factors, but many authorities feel it would be very unwise to have anything less than the entire "C complex." I prefer the chewable all natural tablet form. Nearly all Vitamin C preparations are 60 to 80% synthetic ascorbic acid with small amounts of the natural sources added. It is possible to obtain it in the all-natural form, however, and we can assist you in finding it. The formal function of vitamin C is to enable your body to manufacture the unique protein tissue called collagen, which is literally the glue that holds you together. Scurvy is simply a breakdown of collagen. If you are deficient, wounds and fractures heal slowly, gums bleed easily, and you bruise excessively. Vitamin C is an effective antitoxin, it is combined with toxins and excreted in the urine, while being destroyed in the process. This is why massive amounts are recommended in the presence of infections. The maintenance dose is probably under 500 milligrams per day. The therapeutic dose at the onset of illness or injury, in my opinion, should be 500 to 1,000 milligrams per hour during the waking hours and 2,000 milligrams upon awakening in the morning. Vitamin C also combines with the B complex in assisting the nervous system to perform its many functions and has been used in conjunction with the B complex as part of the megavitamin therapy in treating schizophrenia and other forms of illness.

VITAMIN D

(3/1/76) Vitamin D is added in synthetic form to milk, and is probably adequately supplied in the diet. However, it is a fat-soluble vitamin, and skim or low fat milk are very low in this vitamin. When you are storing defatted dried milk, Vitamin D will have to be supplemented in approximately a one to ten ratio with Vitamin A. Its preferred supplemental form is fish liver oil. Its normal function is in the utilization and mobilization of minerals in the body, particularly calcium. A deficiency can result in poor bone growth and actual deformation of bones and teeth in children. The maintenance dose is 50-100 IUs per day and its therapeutic function is in the healing of broken bones. A therapeutic dose can, for a short period, be up to 5,000 IUs per day, but it is toxic if such dosage is continued for more than a few days, as it accumulates in the liver.

VITAMIN E

(3/1/76) The preferred supplemental source of Vitamin E is whole wheat oil or wheat germ oil. It is also found in other vegetable oils if it has not been processed out. It takes an incredible amount of wheat germ oil to produce a cup of vitamin E, which makes the natural form expensive in supplemental form. The only source of vitamin E in our recommended food storage program is wheat and, in my opinion, that does not provide adequate amounts. The best vitamin E supplement will be all-natural mixed tocopherols. Vitamin E is a complex of tocopherols. The alpha tocopherol is the most active. Synthetic vitamin E is all alpha tocopheryl. The other tocopherols, however, have important anti-oxidant functions to perform in the body. Vitamin E combines with unsaturated fats and prevents them from oxidizing, forming peroxides, or "free radicals" which attack the cells, and are believed by many authorities to actually shorten cell life and thus, life itself. If your diet is high in unsaturated fats (liquid oils), supplement with vitamin E. The maintenance dose is 200-400 IU per day. The therapeutic function of the vitamin is to improve the body's use of oxygen for athletic performance or high altitude performance, such as skiing, flying, etc. It has been used in the treatment of various forms of heart disease (but not rheumatic heart disease). It also has been demonstrated to protect against the effects of smog inhalation. The therapeutic dose is between 800-1,200 IUs per day.

(CAUTION: If you have a known history of high blood pressure, you should start with 1 unit a day for a week, add 100 units per day the next week, until you have built up to the recommended dosages. If you do not do this, it could cause temporary elevation of your blood pressure and pose some dangers to your health.)

VITAMIN K

(3/1/76)   This controls the clotting factor and should be included in any normal mutivitamin preparation. It protects against excessive bleeding from fractures, cuts, or even normal childbirth. It is especially important for young women during their child-bearing years.

O

OIL

OIL RECOVERY

(8/1/78)   It seems that GEORGE MERKL has founded an energy company and developed an inorganic "polymer" (a fancy name for a liquid chemical substance made out of silicone). When one barrel is injected into depleted "stripper" oil wells, they produce again. The principle is simple. The polymer separates the oil from the structure and actually "cracks" the oil to produce natural gas. The resulting increase in pressure starts wells free-flowing that haven't produced in years. In many instances it produces more oil than it did in its heyday. It also works to produce natural gas in shale formations.

I have personally interviewed Merkl, and he is for real. Here's why.

1.   He's not looking for any money. He is a wealthy man in his own right. He came here during the Hungarian Revolt and made his own fortune. He could have retired many years ago. He and some associates have put up all the money.

2.   Primarily, he isn't selling his product. He goes to independent operators who own these stripper wells, negotiates a joint venture and goes into business with them, sharing the profits. They are producing oil from stripper wells in Ohio, Kansas, and Texas, and are signing joint-venture agreements every day. He's willing to take the risks along with the producers.

There are a million and a half such stripper wells in the country less than 1,000 feet deep. The big oil companies are not interested because they own very few of these shallow wells. They have pooh-poohed this method, knowing that it would represent substantial competition. The Department of Energy rejected it without investigation or testing. In fact, when it was proposed that it could be used to clean the northern French beaches polluted by AMOCO's huge tanker wreck, AMOCO reported it was no more effective than other decontaminants. The

French government, however, found otherwise, and bought several million dollars worth of Merkl's product. It effectively separates the oil from the sand so that it can be safely removed and beaches decontaminated.

To give you an idea of the dimensions of his creation, these "dead" oil wells can flow between six and 35 barrels a day. With a million and a half of them, there is a potential flow of nine to 30 million barrels a day, which could make us energy-independent, from that source alone, for the next 30 to 60 years. These wells are not even included in our reserves.

OFFSHORE DRILLING

(2/15/79)   The other controversy, which is due to erupt, will be the battle over whether or not to allow additional offshore drilling for oil off the coast of central and northern California.

Somewhere between uncontrolled, careless drilling resulting in oil spills all over the place, and the environmentalists' opposition to and and all drilling, is some reasonable ground. Let me both ask and answer a few questions.

Q. Would drilling along the California coast create some oil spills?

A. Yes. Sooner or later some oil will be spilled.

Q. Will that not pollute the ocean, kill some sea life and leave some messy goo all over some of the most beautiful beaches on our coast?

A. Yes, but not as bad as is painted by the environmentalists. Accidents like the Santa Barbara oil spill are unpleasant and expensive to clean up, but seem to leave little in the way of permanent damage.

Q. Aren't these oil derricks unsightly, destroying coastal property values?

A. Some are and some aren't. There are colorful rigs in the Los Angeles-San Pedro-Long Beach area that are not at all unpleasant to look at.

Q. What about air pollution from unsightly shore facilities?

A. With modern new facilities it is certainly controllable. Every society has some unsightly industrial facilities. If we eliminated all that's unsightly in our basic industries, our society would grind to a halt.

Q. Wouldn't oil drilling destroy California's fishing industry?

A. Some of the best fishing in the world is around the oil rigs in Louisiana. Small fish congregate there and the big fish stick around to eat them.

OPEC

(6/15/77) I'm sure all of you have read of the sabotage of an important Saudi Arabian gas pipeline in which a pumping station and a substantial amount of pipe were destroyed. The "incident" was treated as relatively minor by the world press and the Saudi Arabians. I would like to suggest, however, that there may be more than meets the eye.

In my newsletter I have written about some of the problems between OPEC nations. I have discussed the internal problems of OPEC, particularly the rivalry between Saudi Arabia and the Shah of Iran. This has great potential for destabilizing the Mid-East, as the Saudi Arabian resistance to the 15% price increase wanted by Iran would create serious problems for Iran.

To review, the Saudi Arabians held the price increase to five percent and increased production. The result of this was that Near Eastern oil customers reduced purchases of the more expensive Iranian oil and bought more from the Saudi Arabians. The Shah of Iran is spending so much money on military development and grandiose civil projects to restore the glories of the Persian Empire that he has performed the absolutely incredible feat of running a balance of payments deficit, creating a need to borrow money from Western nations (see: Iran). The Shah might see fit to take some kind of action against the Saudi Arabians, and it this would have potential for war in the Mid-East.

Also, most of the laborers in the Saudi Arabian oil fields are Iranian.

This pipeline sabotage may be the opening shot in an internal war in OPEC, and the Saudi Arabians may have responded when just a few days after the incident, they sent out feelers indicating they might be willing to increase their price by another 5%, and thus, bring everything back into harmony within OPEC.

This, if true, may be only a tip of the iceberg in a monstrous world power play. It involves the European Central Banks, South Africa, the Arab oil producers, President Carter, and especially West Germany and Japan.

(10/1/77) WE MUST BUST THE OPEC CARTEL. If we don't, it's going to destabilize the world, if it hasn't already done so. Unless we deregulate the price of natural gas, we don't have a chance.

If we allow the price of natural gas to rise to $3.50 per thousand cubic feet, it will still be competitive with the current price of No. 2 fuel oil on a cost-per-BTU basis, and this will open up unimaginable amounts of known natural gas deposits that are now uneconomical. The direct energy competition would bust OPEC wide open.

Coal isn't the answer. We can't mine coal fast enough. It is too polluting to be acceptable, and the nation's railways are in terrible shape. It is estimated by Amtrak that it will cost between 20 and 30 billion dollars to repair the roadbeds to rapidly carry sufficient coal to come even close to Mr. Carter's requirement. It has been proposed that coal be pulverized and mixed with water and sent by pipeline, but the coal mining areas of the country are short of water. Atomic energy isn't the solution, as it would require 15,000 new nuclear plants to solve the problem which would take forever, and would create a waste disposal problem far beyond our present capability to handle.

There is plenty of natural gas, which is non-polluting and clean, and can be obtained at prices competitive with other sources of energy.

But Carter is determined to have his energy crisis and has threatened to veto any energy bill which deregulates natural gas.

(5/15/78)   As I forecast many months ago, some members of the OPEC cartel are jittery about the shrinkage of their dollar holdings. They are pressing to have oil repriced in gold or a "basket" of other currencies. Kuwait is now pressing aggressively for the price increase, as are the Arab oil emirates. The Saudi Arabians say they don't want to, but there is a chance they will cave in later because they are also concerned about the losses in their dollar holdings. The implications for the world monetary system and the banking system are immense because the Arabs are like a 600 lb. gorilla—they sit anywhere they want—and their economic clout with a vast amount of uncommitted dollar is almost beyond comprehension.

(6/1/79)   Oil For Food

I've heard a lot of talk about raising the prices of our grain to the OPEC nations in retaliation for their increases in oil prices. There's even been a big Country and Western hit song by Bobby "So Fine" Butler which was featured on Paul Harvey's broadcast.

The rationale is that, prior to the Arab oil boycott of 1973, the price of a bushel of wheat was about the same as the price of a barrel of oil. Therefore, we should arbitrarily raise the price of a bushel of wheat for export to OPEC to the price of a barrel of oil and demand a barter deal, because they need wheat as badly as we need oil.

Theoretically, this is a wonderful idea, but how does it hold up in the real world, the only world I'm interested in?

First, we need a lot more barrels of oil than they need bushels of wheat. Second, if we should take such a step, we must be positive of the total cooperation of Australia, Canada, Argentina and any other wheat exporting countries. Otherwise, OPEC would simply go around the boycott and buy wheat in the world markets at prices below our cartel price, although above what they pay today. Agreement would have to be absolute and ironclad.

OPEC's success as a cartel is due, in large measure, to their ideological bond. They are united in their hatred of Israel and they have stuck together in maintaining a floor on prices. For awhile it looked like they might come unglued before the Iranian problems, but they are now back in bed together. Could we be that unified in confronting them? Canada is close to energy self-sufficiency with her recent gas and oil discoveries. Why should she jeopardize her wheat markets for us?

We would have to be firm in our resolve that we weren't bluffing. Many of the Arab oil countries have stockpiled sufficient food to subsist for months without imports of grain. Could we go for months without their oil? If we bluffed and they called our bluff, given our vulnerability, we would have to crumble ignominiously. They hold all the cards, except, of course, the military card.

In the final analysis, if we were willing to form an airtight cartel, could be sure of our partners in that cartel, and were prepared to undergo the incredible dislocations in our economy that will occur when they test our will (like going for several months with huge cuts in oil imports), then I'm for it. But I am not until all those ducks are in a row. At the moment, I don't think the climate is right.

OPERATION CABLE SPLICER

(6/15/76)   In the midst of all of the optimism about our wonderful economic recovery a few years back, some realistic and worried California State officials were preparing for something less than the best.

OPERATION CABLE SPLICER was scheduled to begin operations in July, 1976, in California. It was a massive Pentagon plan to suppress potential revolt in the street. It was supposed to have been dropped in 1972. Under the title, "LAW ENFORCEMENT ASSIS-TANCE FORCE (LEAF)," a crack new National Guard unit was to be trained to handle civil emergency situations, including riots and demonstrations. Troops were being drawn from fourteen military police, air guard, security, and infantry units scattered around California. They were to be equipped with M-16 rifles, 12-gauge shotguns and military uniforms which had been "civilianized" so they would not be obvious. It was funded by the U.S. Law Enforcement Assistance Administration to the tune of roughly $1 million—$250,000 of which has already been invested in guns and ammunition.

The organizers succeeded in emphasizing LEAF's role as a harmless emergency group in civil disaster, rather than its function as a civilian police force in riots. The only major opposition to LEAF was California police groups who are concerned that it might be used to break police strikes.

The only public statement on the subject was raised by Major General Frank Schober, Commander of the California National Guard, who said,

> The last thing we look forward to is a situation where we may need to mobilize LEAF, but part of our sworn responsibility is to be ready to respond to appeals from local communities in times of major emergencies ... including riot situations.

The desire to protect the citizens generally doesn't arise until somebody perceive there's a problem. I've contended from the beginning that one problem we face is a possible breakdown in civil order resulting from economic problems. Be prepared to hear more in the public media about OPERATION CABLE SPLICER or LEAF. But remember, you heard it here first.

ORGANIC FARMING

(8/15/76)   I once claimed that it would be possible to reduce our dependence upon petroleum products such as gasoline, fertilizer, etc., while increasing food production, if we were to go to natural, organic methods of farming. I received some irate letters from subscribers who are farmers in the Midwest claiming it is not possible to continue to produce this nation's great cornucopia of foodstuffs with organic farming methods. This reaction stems from ignorance of what organic farming is all about.

We have traveled to the panhandle country of Texas—Deaf Smith County—to interview Frank Ford, the Chairman of Arrowhead Mills, one of the largest suppliers of natural, organically grown grains and seeds for the health food industry. Mr. Ford is also a leader in the movement to encourage the storage of food to protect us from possible economic or meteorologic calamities.

HJR: Mr. Ford, it's a pleasure to visit with you. I have two areas I'd like to discuss today. I'd like to discuss organic farming and food storage, but first, because the term "organic farming" is often misinterpreted, don't you think we ought to find another term to use?

FF: For those who understand the words "organically grown," the expression is very good. Perhaps we could call it "natural science farming," but regardless of the nomenclature, the facts are that here in Deaf Smith County we've seen this method of farming work very successfully over a period of ten years on thousands of acres under compost. We've given the soil an opportunity to not only renew itself, but to produce better crops on better soil each year. This is "eco-agriculture," or "natural science farming," or "organic farming." We're producing "organically grown" foods. All these terms are interchangeable. The nomenclature is not as important as the principles suggested in these questions: Do the methods of farming increase the ability of the soil to produce next year? Does it increase the soil's ability to renew itself? Does it improve the life of the soil? Herbicides, artificial and synthetic insecticides and fertilizers have a very negative effect on renewal.

When we use the beneficial insects and biological controls to a much greater degree than we have in the past, with good soil cultivation methods, rather than herbicides, to keep the weeds down, we're halfway home.

HJR: Some years ago, when Earl Butz first became Secretary of Agriculture, he was asked, "What about organic farming as a method of growing food on a large scale in this country?" His reply was, "organic farming is fine if we decide which half of the human race we would allow to starve." How would you respond to that?

FF: Well, I would hope that he's grown in his knowledge of world conditions since he's made that statement. He should know, for instance, that there's $8 billion worth of manures going to waste every year in this country. If these manures were composted, it would increase their value about tenfold. We have a tremendous multi-billion dollar potential input into soil fertility, which does not depend upon the good grace of the oil-producing countries.

HJR: It seems contradictory to me that one of our pollution problems is how to get rid of agricultural wastes.

FF: We've seen this resolved here in our own area. We're a high density feed-yard area and these feed yards had a runoff pollution problem so now we are saving the manure compost and putting it on the soil where it is not a polluting factor, but does affect the soil in such a positive way that we make better use of the rainfall and the irrigation water. There is less fuel required for tractors to pull plows through the soil, which is "tilthy" and loamy, and not hard as a brick. The beneficial insects are doing a much better job of controlling insect pests and pesticides, because the pesticides have caused the insects to mutate, to become more resistant over the years.

HJR: Assuming I knew nothing about it, give me a definition of "organic farming."

FF: Using fertilizers, beneficial insects and predatory insects to improve the soil's biological life.

There's much research being done now. Had that research been done years earlier instead of all of the chemical emphasis, we would already have all of these problems solved in this nation's agriculture.

Let me add that if any farmers in Iowa would talk to their very own Iowa Secretary of Agriculture, he would give them the names of the farms where they could go see what organically grown feed and food looks like, and how much more net profit the farmers are making. There are many, many successful natural science farms in Iowa. The Secretary is quite supportive of this method, and is most willing to answer questions about it.

HJR: Does the organic farmer's profit margin result from a higher price tag attached to the products that carry the label "organic?"

FF: No, most of these men feed their own livestock, or sell the wheat, corn and soybeans on the open market, but they have increased their efficiency of operation because of their reduced fuel requirements. I recently saw a series of slides, where grain raised with natural science farming, eco-farming—organically grown grain—was put in one jar, and "chemical-source" grain was put in another jar. Five or six years later, the latter had decomposed to a black mess of mold, whereas the food raised with ecologically sound methods was still good and clean.

HJR: Why?

FF: Because of the way it was grown. The good quality grain was mold resistant. It had balanced soil. It was raised with the knowledge that there are very many trace elements—at least 26—that are very important in the growing of grain, whereas, the chemical companies have mainly worked with NPK. NPK has been the watchword since World War I.

HJR: I have ridden with you today through some of the 7000 acres that you've farmed. For the benefit of our readers, let me describe what I saw. We drove down roads lined on one side with corn and feed crops grown on your land using organic method, and on the opposite side was an identical crop using chemical methods. You've had a prolonged drought down here, which was just broken four or five days ago with substantial rain. Even to my amateur eye, your crop was healthier looking, taller and darker green in color, as opposed to the pale green, and often yellowish color across the road. Your soil was still moist on the surface. The other, just a day or two after that rain, already appeared to be drying on top. You seemed to have much less weed problems. Is your method of farming any more labor intensive than your neighbors across the road?

FF: I would say it has much less labor requirement and less fuel requirement. Nature will work for you if you let it. For example, by plowing under green manure crops, the soil sponge (tilth) and the soil structure will be good.

HJR: Do you want to define "green manure crops"?

FF: Green manure crops are green crops, even weeds, that are plowed under so that the plant life is turned into life in that soil as it decomposes. The soil is going to utilize rainfall and irrigation water far more efficiently than soil which has been denatured by burning residue stubbles, or by applying anhydrous ammonia and other hot fertilizers, which have destroyed the carbon-nitrogen balance in the soil.

HJR: We have a lot of readers who are farmers in Iowa or Nebraska, what would be involved if one of those farmers decided to farm organically? Would it be expensive? Would it be difficult for him to change his methods?

FF: Well, of course, it's difficult after a person has "mined" the soil rather than farmed it to change the soil humus, but I think it's better to start now than a year from now. They ought to be in touch with farmers who have done this. If they would just get in contact with Iowa's Secretary of Agriculture, he will lead them to the farm of Ralph Engleton, and many other farmers in Iowa who are doing a tremendous job.

HJR: If the whole world were to suddenly get religion on the idea and switch to organic farming, what benefits would we see as a result?

FF: Well, I think the developing nations would be the greatest beneficiaries, because they're going to be the ones who will be hurt the most as energy supplies get short, unless they are raising all their own food. I think the poorer people of the world would be helped most.

What it really comes down to is the renewal of our soil, and using our worldwide resources correctly so that all will have enough.

HJR: I've contended in the past that we have made ourselves vulnerable to these weather and economic problems because we have become dependent upon strains of grain that were designed with modern chemical farming methods in mind. As the land is "mined" by intensive farming, we have to keep piling on more and more synthetic fertilizers. We have allowed ourselves to become more vulnerable to shortages of petroleum and natural gas from which fertilizers, pesticides and herbicides are made. This drives up prices, also. It has been my contention that, because of this vulnerability, we ought to be looking at methods which use less calories in the form of energy to produce calories in the form of food.

FF: Yes. We've boasted many times of the American farmer's efficiency. There are many wonderful things about American agriculture, including the amount of food that one man can produce with our technological capability; however, we must remember that we are unnecessarily dependent upon that OPEC oil, and it doesn't have to be this way. We can use the sun's energy better by having live soil that's open to the rays of the sun, utilizing the energy that naturally falls. We can utilize wind energy and other energies better. I think we also need to stop processing our food so much. That takes energy.

HJR: I wrote an article recently for another publication that rejected the article because they disagreed with my contention that the American farmer is not the most efficient farmer in the world. I think it was probably my fault because I didn't make my point clear enough. What I meant was, we're probably the most efficient in terms of the amount of food raised per person working on the farm. I don't think there's any question about that. But in terms of food raised per acre, we're not the most efficient. There are parts of the world where labor intensive methods closer to the organic approach are used which actually produce more food per acre. For example, Indonesia and Japan.

HJR: Do you claim that we could continue to produce as much food per acre and as much food per man-hour with a much lower expenditure of petroleum energy?

FF: I'd like to divide my answer into two kinds of farms.

Let's first take a large family farm, like mine. My sons and I do all our own tractor work. Now let's consider a 150-acre grain farm, with two people doing the work, which would be the norm in the dry land area of Deaf Smith County. An irrigated farm requires less fuel to pump, less water to do the job, if the soil is in good shape. Also, food that is grown on highly synthesized chemicals is far less resistant to spoilage. For instance, they have found in the vegetable area of Deaf Smith County that potatoes and other vegetable crops raised with natural eco-organic farming methods, will keep three, four, even ten times as long. So, to answer your question, yes I think we can produce more food with less energy by employing the organic farming methods we've discussed.

HJR: Thanks for your time. The interview has been most informative. (see: Farming; Food Storage; National Food Reserve)

ORGANIZED LABOR

(4/15/76) Earlier, regarding the Teamsters strike, I said, "Labor peace may be bought at the cost of another dramatic round of inflation." I believe that may have just happened.

Labor Secretary, W. J. Usery, representing the government as a mediator, when questioned as to whether or not the settlement was inflationary, said: "Given the circumstances, it was a good agreement." If you want that translated from the original Greek, it says: "Yes, it's inflationary, but they had a gun at our head."

The Teamsters got virtually everything they asked for. It amounts to a 9.1 percent increase this year. They will receive more than that, if our inflation rate exceeds seven percent, which it will, as they got an unlimited cost-of-living escalator clause.

Why did the industry cave in? For two reasons, in my opinion. First, even a moderate long strike would destroy the recovery. This one only lasted two days, but one General Motors plant had to close for lack of parts, idling 5000 workers. Another week and all General Motors, Chrysler, and American Motors plants would have shut down 100 percent. The wire services widely reported that food shortages would have been epidemic in a few weeks and that, of course, is social dynamite.

Second, it's an election year. The government would have been forced to issue a Taft-Hartley injunction, forcing drivers back to work for eighty days. President Ford can't afford to alienate labor anymore. They settled, with the trucking industry making almost all the concessions. These new benefits will be passed on to you in the form of higher freight rates, and increases in the cost of everything you buy that has to be trucked somewhere.

This strike was a near brush with disaster. I have contended that labor peace is essential to prevent a collapse of the economy. I hope we will realize that the door may have been opened for just a quick peek at hell. We had two bad choices: Renewed inflation or chaos. We got inflation. (see: Inflation/Deflation and Trucking Industry)

P

PANAMA CANAL

(5/1/78) The Senate Panama Canal battle is history, but the House has to approve the necessary expenditures and will battle over the Constitutional issue of whether the United States can give away territory without the consent of the House. Of course we can't, but Carter says the Zone was never really ours. The Supreme Court will probably just cop out and refuse to hear the issue.

Can you believe TORRIJOS the morning after? He said that if the treaty had not passed, he would have destroyed the Canal. We've just negotiated with a gun at our head, and we flinched. Torrijos also said that if we ever invoke the DeConcini Amendment by sending troops in to reopen the Canal, he would destroy it. He said that, "They (our troops) are six to eight hours away, and by then. . . . " That's precisely why we shouldn't give it away. We need our troops on the spot to protect it. With friends like that, who needs enemies? (see: Hatch, Senator Orrin)

POLITICIANS

(3/1/78) An interesting concept came out of our Anaheim Convention. One of the most appreciated services of *THE RUFF TIMES* is the recommendation of honest and dependable merchants. It became apparent after the appearance of Senator Helms and Senator Hatch that our subscribers would equally appreciate a recommendation of politicians worthy of their support. After the Hatch reception, a couple came up to me and said they had become so cynical about politicans in general that they had removed themselves from the entire political process and really appreciated meeting two good men. They suggested that, as a service, we should come up with a list of those who are worthy of support, by virtue of their integrity, effectiveness and principles. Now that's pretty tough, because there are some effective, honest men whose economic viewpoint makes them dangerous (Hubert Humphrey?) and, by the same token, there are some men whose economic politics are generally sound but I wouldn't trust them as far as I can throw them (Spiro Agnew).

Well, I've given a lot of thought to this suggestion and have decided to dip my editorial toe into the political waters. If you are interested, here's my rationale.

I don't believe that any combination of politicians is going to prevent major economic "readjustments." (How's that for a euphemism?) But there's no question that as the ship of state sails through stormy waters, an effective crew could keep it from capsizing. As a result, I am terribly interested in those who make our laws or who stand as effective opposition to laws which put more holes in an already leaky ship. I think it is a matter of great urgency that we have men in office who understand how we got into trouble and who can guide us when things get tough.

I have been busy researching some of these people and getting personally acquainted with them and I am going to try to develop a "good guy" list.

Let me make one point very clear. I do not believe that the political process will avoid a major depression. But, I do believe that it is only the political process that will determine whether or not the difficulties give way to the kind of unrest that would produce a Hitler, or a socialist, collectivist government. That process will begin and end on Capitol Hill. Hatch and Helms are the first two members of our good guy list. I dont think their voting records are perfect, as I tend to be a bit more libertarian than conservative, but I'm with them most of the time. There will be others, but we are still completing our research and interviews, and we will add to our list from time to time. It has never been more true that money wins political campaigns.

I also want to be very pragmatic about this and not have you pour your money into lost causes. I am only interested in supporting those who truly have a chance, and I will add names to this list from time to time once they have met all of our criteria.

POLITICS

RUFF'S VIEWS

(7/15/76) In this election year, I have received dozens of phone calls and letters asking me about my political views and forecasts. My articles on Federal regulation have always triggered a surge of passionate exhortations to support Ronald Reagan because "he will lead us out of this mess."

I think it's time to let you know where I stand, and maybe make some forecasts. First, I believe our political and economic system is out of control and beyond the ingenuity of human leadership. Second, no president will alter the basic trends in our style of government. He couldn't if he wanted to. Congress is where the action is.

Mr. Carter, Mr. Reagan, and Mr. Ford all have come out foursquare in favor of fiscal responsibility and less government. None of them will achieve it. Only a massive overhaul of Congress would achieve it. And that won't happen unless the voter decides to have the government spend less, and says "Let it begin with me." That's about as likely as Lester Maddox and Lena Horne dancing cheek to cheek.

Reagan is, of course, philosophically the most conservative of the remaining candidates, by a whisker, over Ford. But as Governor of California, he was not able to prevent massive increases in spending. He was only able to increase taxes to balance the budget. He had to break most of his campaign promises (no higher taxes, no with-holding, etc.) because of political realities. I think he was a fine Governor! But he can't be elected, although he can make it close. The only area where he can produce real change is in foreign policy. And that's why I'm pulling for him.

Generally speaking, when things go wrong, we load too much blame on our presidents. When things go right, they take too much credit. Both positions are distortion. Again, Congress is where he action is. (see: President of U.S.)

Carter—the Cheshire Cat

I find Jimmy Carter to be the most incredibly deceptive politician of our times. Some political observers have even called him a conservative. That's ridiculous. In every area where he has been cornered into taking a position, he is about as conservative as Hubert Humphrey or George McGovern. If he is elected, the fiscal brakes will be off. He, like Roosevelt and Nixon, would be elected on the basis of alleged conservative principles, and then would produce his equivalent of Roosevelt's "New Deal" or Nixon's "I am a Keynesian." At least Reagan would try to carry out his principle, and Ford would try to drag his feet a little.

Carter would whip Reagan by a bigger margin in the popular vote than he would Ford, but Reagan woud make the electoral vote closer, as Ford's strength is in the Northeast where Carter will carry most of the big states anyway.

In other words, where Ford is strong, Carter is even stronger. But Reagan has a chance to take some southern and western states from Carter to make it close.

Ford Or Reagan

Now, the tough one! Ford or Reagan? It's Ford, unless he makes a major goof. If he does, it will be in foreign policy, and it would have to be of the same dimensions as Kissinger's African policy announcement on the eve of the Texas primary. Possible, but not likely.

Interest rates will drop when the administration opens the money spigot, and stock prices will rise. So if Ford is nominated, buy top grade corporate bonds.

If Reagan is nominated, the lame duck Ford Administration will have lost much of its incentive to open the fiscal floodgates. Reagan's nomination would normally be interpreted by the stock market as bearish. However, if Carter holds his lead in the polls, that will be discounted.

If Carter is elected, the stock market will go nowhere for awhile until Carter produces his big-spending credentials. Again, interest rates will drop, bonds will rise, but inflationary expectations will eventually increase, and we will be into double-digit inflation by next spring.

Ruff's Recommendations

1. Ignore the presidential race.
2. Work politically on the Congressional and local level. It's our only chance!
3. If Ford is nominated, buy bonds, if you have discretionary funds.
4. If Carter is elected, buy bonds, again with discretionary money.
5. Be ready to dump them at the first sign of increasing inflation.

6. Prepare for two-digit inflation by next spring (1977).

(11/15/76) I believe that we are now being governed by economic ignoramuses with Marxist leanings. Mr. Lawrence Klein, who is Mr. Carter's principal economic advisor, has admitted before a Congressional committee that he had a brief flirtation with Communism in the 1940s and is a Marxist. He believes we need to immediately inject large amounts of Federal money into the economy, and if it should result in an increase in the inflation rate, we simply must use standby price controls. This is a prescription for Socialism and economic chaos.

MAN ON A WHITE HORSE

(5/1/79) One of the more frequent questions I'm asked (and this is true of the three-hour interview I had with *TIME* magazine) is: "If we should have the kind of runaway inflation and fiscal problems you are talking about, what is the possibility that we might have a 'Man On a White Horse,' a 'Strong Man,' possibly a dictator, arise out of the kind of fiscal chaos that could result from that scenario?"

My answer was wrenched out of context by *TIME* magazine, but it's a good question.

There is a chance that this nation could be taken over emotionally or politically by some charismatic, authoritarian personality who does not believe in our basic institutions. The odds are that it won't happen but it's possible, just the same.

I'm not sure I see such a person on the horizon but one indicator of the nation's vulnerability to this syndrome might be the political career of General Alexander Haig. Thus far he has not been considered among the serious contenders for the presidency, but he soon may be coming up fast on the outside. He was our Commander of NATO and was Richard Nixon's White House Chief of Staff during the dark days of the Watergate trauma. I'm not saying that General Haig is a fascist. I don't know enough about him yet, although I am disturbed by some of the things I've heard in the Watergate tapes that indicate he may not share your or my views of government. By the same token, both George Bush and Orrin Hatch told me they think Haig is a fine man, so I'll withhold judgment. But what I'm interested in is whether or not the nation shows signs of turning towards an authoritarian military answer to its problems, and Haig's candidacy might be one way of taking the social temperature, so to speak. I know he's serious about wanting the Republican nomination. Haig is embarking on an aggressive, carefully planned public speaking campaign to bring himself back into the public eye.

One of today's most dangerous realities is the total vacuum of leadership, which has resulted in a massive national distrust of institutions. All the polls show that the presidency, the Congress, the courts, the teaching profession, the ministry, and almost any other institution you want to name, are held in very low regard, and it's getting worse. It is only in such a vacuum of leadership that people cast around looking for strength, and will gladly follow someone who seems to know where he is going. This could be a dangerous time for our nation if a strong, manipulative personality with no scruples comes onto the scene.

If John Connally should become a serious contender for the Republican nomination, that might be another indication of the vacuum of leadership, because John Connally is a very potent personality. He has so many political liabilities that he could never be nominated or elected without that potent personality and platform charisma.

The best thing that could happen to this country would be the emergence of national leadership that would create a sound climate where prepare-for-hard-times books and newsletters were no longer necessary.

Someone once said, "You can judge a man by his enemies," and I'm rather proud of mine (and you probably ain't seen nothin' yet). There will continue to be a lot of out-of-context quotes, a few downright misrepresentations, and a substantial number of writers who honestly disagree with me. And, I'll reluctantly admit, there might even be some legitimate criticism, because my wife and kids might even be right in their assessment that I'm not perfect.

In the meantime, I say "three cheers for the capitalist system, and four cheers for profits: my profits, your profits, and anybody else's profits. When profits go away, we've all had it. And that's my Capitalist Manifesto."

In the meantime, keep an eye on General Haig. I'm going to learn everything I can about this man. I don't know whether I like him or dislike him, but I think he is significant. I'm reminded of the great humorist, Robert Benchley. He opened an account at a bank, then came back an hour later and withdrew all his money, closing the account. When asked for his reasons, he said, "I don't trust any bank that would have me for a customer." Anybody who wants the presidency has to be a little bit suspect. It is basically a futile job because you are circumscribed by what Congress will let you do, and everything you do angers at least some of the people in the country. It destroys men, their reputations, and their families. Whenever anybody asks me if I would ever, in some laughably remote future, want the job, I just say, "If nominated, I will not run, if elected, I will slit my wrists." And I mean it. I'll leave all that to someone who grooves on power, and also hope that he grooves on good, sound constitutional principles. Let's hope that such a man exists. (see: President of U.S.)

POPULATION CONTROL

A PHONY ISSUE

(5/15/76)   Whenever anybody looks at the picture on the back cover of my book and sees me, the father of eight children, they're often tempted to say, "Mr. Ruff, if you're so concerned about the world food problem, why do you have so many kids?" Implicit in that question is the assumption that the birth rate is at the root of the world's food problem and, somehow, if we could convince people they should have less babies, there would be no problem. After much study, I have come to the conclusion this is utter hogwash. I now understand the situation well enough to take a firm stand.

I really think birth control is a phony issue simply because our famines are political and economic in nature. A monetary crisis, a breakdown of the delivery of goods and services, municipal bankruptcy and urban chaos, or the socializing of farming are all far more urgent potential causes of famine than the birth rate.

Another phony issue, used by the "no-growth" advocates, is that we should limit births in America, because a baby born in America will consume fifteen times more energy, food, and natural resources, than a baby born in India or South America. Consequently, according to their reasoning, Americans are socially irresponsible if they have babies, and one American baby is depriving fifteen Asians or South Americans of their rightful percentage of the world's resources. The assumption is that this baby is a burden to the rest of the world and that our prosperity has been based only upon the exploitation and suppression of others.

Again, is is utter hogwash. Admittedly, America uses the world's oil supplies and natural resources at a rate considerably greater than that of the rest of the world, but don't forget, much of this is used in the production of food and commodities which, in turn, pour out in benefits to the rest of the world. Farming, as it is now practiced, is primarily the conversion of calories in the form of energy into calories in the form of food, which then is shipped around the world to feed the nations. If we were to look at the actual consumption of resources on a worldwide level, we would find that America is not only the world's largest consumer of resources (production), but its largest distributor. This being so, everything begins to average out rather nicely.

The real problem is that food distribution and production is vulnerable to the destruction of our economic monetary system, and it is our economic system I am worried about. I am afraid that if the no-growth advocates have their way, the world will be killing the goose that lays the golden egg.

I am distressed that India has taken steps to make it a felony to have more than two babies, and to punish by imprisonment this "offense against nature."

What I'm trying to say is that some people should have babies and some shouldn't, but no one has the right to control this vital decision in someone else's life.

SOVIETS' PROBLEM

(9/1/76)   Recently I read in *U.S. NEWS AND WORLD REPORT* an interesting analysis of the troubles of the Soviet Union. One of the major problems which they face is a plunging birth rate which is reducing the potential for growth of the work force and the economy. On the one hand, the Soviets are deciding that a lowered birthrate is a threat to the survival of their nation. On the other hand, many of those who are inclined towards socialism in this country, and who are advocating socialist controls of the nation as a solution to our problems, are advocating a sharp reduction in our birth rate. In other words, a reduction of birth rate is bad in socialist countries, but it is good in capitalist countries!

It is my opinion that if we ever reduce the birthrate below its present level in this country, it would be a disaster for the world. The United States feeds the world. It exports capital to the world.

In investment, there is an old adage that says, "Let your profits run and cut your losses." Perhaps the analogy to the word "profits" would be what's happening here in America. America's economy must continue to expand. It does not have a population problem. It consumes much of the world's resources in that they pour into this country. But those resources pour back out to the world in the form of food and capital, like a vast cornucopia to benefit everyone. If the United States economy gets the sniffles, the rest of the world gets pneumonia.

GROW OR DIE—A REVIEW

(11/15/77) James R. Weber, in his book *GROW OR DIE* just may have come up with an explanation of why our economy is sliding into such intractable ills. His beautifully documented thesis is that population growth in the developed countries, such as the United States, is absolutely essential to the financial health of the world, and the current decline in growth is a factor in our current weakness. Even those in favor of Zero Population Growth (ZPG) admit that the economy may slow down with a reduction in the birth rate, but they blithely toss off the suggestion that this can be dealt with "by appropriate monetary and public spending policies." The U.S. birth rate has been dropping steadily for years, and the immigration rate is way down despite the wetbacks crossing our southern border. He argues persuasively that economic well-being always has expanded during times of population growth, and contracted during times of population shrinkage.

The book presents a persuasive argument that the solutions of the world's problem will be accomplished by people, and population growth is essential for the necessary expansion of knowledge and technology to find the answers. GROW or DIE are our only two alternatives.

Weber also musters an impressive array of evidence from impeccable sources that our resource base is many centuries away from being depleted. Copper production, for example, is way below demand, but a growing percentage of our copper use comes from recycling existing copper. (That's why teenage arsonists burn down tenements in the Bronx to recover the copper tubing and wiring, because they have good market value.)

Weber's most telling argument is that our entire pension and social insurance system will collapse without a continued flow of workers coming into the labor force. When Social Security began, there were 90 workers for every person receiving benefits. Now there are three. In another fifteen years, it will be two. This has forced the government to recently impose a horrendous increase in Social Security taxes.

Approximately 40% of Americans now pay more in Social Security taxes than they do in income tax. If a $50 tax rebate were deemed sufficient to stimulate the economy, what do you think a tax increase of several hundred dollars per person would do to depress it? The recent actions of Congress in increasing the minimum wage rate and vastly increasing Social Security taxes, are perhaps the two most damaging blows it could throw at an economy, which is now delicately balanced and sliding into recession.

We have nothing but bad choices. If we let Social Security go broke, we face the specter of our parents starving if we can't take care of them. If they do increase taxes to keep the fund solvent, they place a burden on the economy it cannot endure. All you can do is batten down the hatches and get ready, as the Social Security system will bankrupt the country. *GROW OR DIE* is not easy going, but it thoroughly documents the intellectual bankruptcy of the Paul Erlichs of the world and demonstrates the weakness of their assumptions. The earth is millenia away from depleting its resources. It can accommodate many times its present population, and if the progressive, developed countries should reduce their population, while the poor of the world multiply, this is like buying a diversified investment portfolio, and cutting your winners as they show promise and throwing your money into losers. It is a purely economic issue, and our policy should not be aimed towards reducing our population growth in this country. If so, we will continue to reap the bitter harvest, and it may be too late already.

PORNOGRAPHY

(1/15/77) Of importance to me is how society can erode our efforts to pass our values on to the next generation. I have been concerned by the magazine rack at our local Seven-Eleven store, which is right next door to my office, and where my kids often go to pick up refreshments. It's a family store, run by a family, and structured for families. There, in the magazine rack, are *PLAYBOY, PENTHOUSE, HUSTLER, OUI,* and other examples of slick, well-structured, beautifully-prepared, hard-core porngraphy. I'm not too worried that my children will buy it or look at it. What I am worried about is that they will look at this nice, friendly, respectable store selling these products and unconsciously identify it with such unacceptable and unrespectable things.

I can remember when everyone in this country was "against sin and in favor of motherhood." Now, everyone seems to be opposed to motherhood and in favor of sin.

Now, you can tell me all you want that freedom requires us to allow these things. You can talk to me about freedom of the press and I would agree you have a point, even though I hate to. It is most difficult to pass laws against this sort of thing. I'm not sure it would be right to pass laws to prevent the Seven-Eleven from selling these things, but I do feel it is right to inform the owner that neither I nor my family will patronize his store for this reason, and to ask others to join in this. The answer is not new law, but public concern and outrage.

I have chosen this issue as an example of what I believe to be a corrosive, and perhaps, shattering trend in our society: the crumbling of values. In *Fiddler on the Roof*, Tevye tells us of the value of tradition in holding his society together, and we then watch the crumbling of the community and village when traditions, values, and standards begin to lose hold on the young.

Nowhere do I see a reversal of this trend. By refusing to patronize my local Seven-Eleven, I haven't really done much, but I have to try. (see: Crime; Family; Homosexuality; Sin-Tax; Values and Morals)

POVERTY

(10/1/77)   I'm so impressed with the story of the Selmon brothers, who were both football All-Americans at the University of Oklahoma, and first round draft choices in the National Football League a couple of years ago. They were poor as dirt. In fact, the floor in their home was dirt. But their mother, a strong woman of unbending character, demanded excellence. She insisted on good grades and taught them honesty, integrity and respect for their fellow man. Not only are they now great football players, but in every respect, they are fine men, because of a strong unyielding example set by a mother they loved and respected, and feared a little. They endured real poverty and racial discrimination, fought their way through life relatively unscarred by them, and became examples I would love to have my children emulate.

I am sick and tired of hearing how "poverty is at the root of all the world's problems." We've always had poverty. There will always be a large unproductive class! Humanity has always stratified itself by choice, as well as by circumstance. Slaves have risen to make great contributions to mankind. Some children of wealth and privilege have ended up as stumbling winos in drunk tanks.

This is an economic issue because there has been an incredible waste of taxpayer money in asaulting problems from the wrong perspective. The "War On Poverty" was doomed to fail, because of that natural stratification. I've been rich and I've been poor, and rich is better. A person's financial status bears little relationship to his character or his future, unless he becomes persuaded that poverty is a handicap and succumbs to it. Sociologists, politicians and agitators have been banging our ears with the concept that if you don't succeed in life, it's because you are poor and it's someone else's fault. A society that blames others for all its troubles is lost, because it will never attack the real problems. A society consisting of families who dump the responsibility for the creation of their children's character and sense of personal responsibility on the community, is lost. A society that justifies the abandonment of common virtues by the excuse of poverty, discrimination or whatever, is lost.

In all the great stories of the underprivileged rising from the depths, the most common theme is strong family moral leadership, and high expectations on the part of parent, which are enforced with loving strictness. Let's stop blaming others for our troubles. (see: Family; Values and Morals)

PRESIDENT OF U.S.

DOES IT MATTER WHO IS ELECTED?

(2/1/76) It doesn't matter who gets elected President. It could be a genius with all the right instincts, a highly moral and ethical man, but he would find it impossible to reverse the juggernaut we have put in motion. I believe that inflation is irreversible, that the adjustments will come in the form of a financial convulsion, and that we'll pay the price sooner or later. That doesn't mean I don't intend to vote for a man who shares my philosophy. But, realistically, I don't think it will make any difference.

FROM A TO Z

PAST PRESIDENTS

(7/1/78) I recently ran across a quote in the Salt Lake City *DESERET NEWS* that made me do a double-take.

When Franklin D. Roosevelt was President he gave this advice:

> If the nation is living within its income its credit is good. If in some crisis it lives beyond its income for a year or two it can usually borrow temporarily on reasonable terms. But if, like the spendthrift, it throws discretion to the winds, is willing to make no sacrifice at all in spending, extends its taxing up to the limit of people's power to pay, and continues to pile up deficits, it is on the road to bankruptcy.

(11/15/76) The Presidency tends to change people. Harry Truman grew into the job. Nixon was elected as a conservative and then, late in his first term, announced, "I am Keynesian." Roosevelt ran as a conservative, preaching fiscal responsibility. He only began making liberal noises after he was elected.

WHAT RUFF WOULD DO AS PRESIDENT

(10/15/78)

Q. Howard, what would you do if you were President of the United States?

A. Anyone has to be crazy to want that job. It has destroyed the last four men who held the job, either physically, as in the case of President Kennedy, or by reputation, as in the case of Johnson, Nixon, and Ford. Eventually, it will wipe out Jimmy Carter. It will destroy anyone. The job is impossible. You can't get elected president without telling people you have solutions to the world's problems, but there are no politically acceptable solutions to the world's problems.

The only time I would want to be elected president would be after the nation had been so punished by an inflationary spiral and the subsequent depression that the political promise of the past would be universally recognized as garbage. Only then would the nation be willing to accept the Draconian measures that would be necessary to restore things to normalcy. Only in that environment could a president truly do the things which would save the country. He can't prevent the punishing day of reckoning.

However, just for the sake of the exercise, I'll tell you what I would do if I were president.

509

1. I would immediately terminate the SALT talks and inform the Soviets we are making no concessions of any kind, and that we're going to build the strongest possible offensive and defensive military force. I would then instruct them to keep their cotton-pickin' hands off Africa and the Middle East, and to order the Cubans out or be willing to accept the consequences. Those consequences would be:

    a. The withdrawal of any loans or grain shipments to the Communist-bloc nations.

    b. The cancelling of all business and trade agreements with the Communist-bloc nations.

    c. Possible military retaliation, with a clearly defined "win" policy.

Detente and SALT are merely devices by which the Soviet Union strengthens its position vis-a-vis the United States, and that must end right now.

2. I would immediately throw my support behind the Rhodesian and South African governments, subject to their willingness to implement a genuine, careful phased-in democratization of their nations over a period of some ten to twenty years, through an education program preparatory to universal suffrage. After obtaining this agreement, I would give them all the economic, military, and moral support necessary to fight the Communist guerrillas, and would issue economic sanctions against nations that encouraged the terrorists.

3. I would go immediately to Congress with stiff budget cuts in every department of government, including the military. Military bands, etc., cost millions of dollars a year, and that's just one example of the waste of the military dollar. I would also instruct the Armed Forces to return to the same ratio of officers to enlisted men which won World War II. This would mean phasing out of approximately two-thirds of the Officer Corps.

I believe 30 percent could be cut out of the military budget. That money could be used to fund modern weapons systems, such as the B-1, the Cruise missile, and several other systems the Soviets have negotiated right out of our playing hand.

4. I would propose taking all of the judgmental and hearing functions out of the hands of all the regulatory agencies, so they could not sit as judge, jury and executioner over business and citizens. I would include the FDA, the SEC, OSHA, and all that "alphabet soup" that's strangling American industry.

5. I would immediately introduce legislation into Congress

that would restore gold-backing to the dollar by revaluing gold at a realistic price relative to the amount of currency in existence. This would stop inflation in its tracks. I would then announce that the dollar would be freely convertible into gold by both American citizens and foreign countries at that price.

6. I would immediately inform the nation that I was going to be a one-term president because the steps I was going to take would be very painful and politically unacceptable, but that I was prepared to accept the consequences. Then nothing I would do could be interpreted as "just politics."

7. I would rally public support for legislation that would prevent Congress fom insulating itself against the evil effects of its own actions, such as avoiding the unsound Social Security System with their own pension plan, and having their own salaries indexed against the rate of inflation caused by their irresponsible legislation.

That ought to give you the general drift. But it wouldn't work until the country had been so traumatized by economic troubles that it was willing to try almost anything. Then, and only then, would any sane man be interested in the job.

PRICE AND WAGE CONTROLS

PLANNING FOR PRICE CONTROLS

(3/15/77)   By Gary North, Ph.D.

A lot of forecasters have assumed that the coming price-inflation will be something like the awful German inflation of 1922-23. What lies ahead will be nothing like that. It will be like the German inflation of 1945-48. That inflation was much worse in its economic effects than the 1922-23 inflation.

Price inflation is coming, but will be disguised by PRICE CONTROLS—repressed inflation. This is the inflation usually associated with wartime economic controls.

The government creates monetary inflation through our nation's central bank, the Federal Reserve System. When this fiat money begins to raise prices, the politicians blame somebody else: big business, big labor, the weather, or any other easy target. But the cause of long-term price inflation is the creation of fiat money. When prices start rising above 10% per year, politicians are tempted to

511

impose price controls. This, they believe (along with most voters), will stop the inflation.

It will not stop inflation. It will stop the efficient operation of the free market economy. New York City and Washington, D.C. have rent controls. They also have very few apartments available to potential renters at the artificially low prices—politically imposed prices. What is true of apartments under rent control is equally true of all other goods and services under a system of general price and wage controls.

The government can wipe out sections of the U.S. economy simply by imposing price controls. The American economy is like a large auction. What would happen in an auction if the government declared a maximum price level for some product? What if it imposed a maximum price when half a dozen bidders were still competing? "That's all, folks," some bureaucrat would announce. "No more bids are allowed." How would the auctioneer determine the successful bidder? How would he see to it that the item would be claimed by one person, and only one person? How would the bureaucrat determine the "fair" price? What would happen to the auction? What would happen to all future auctions threatened with this sort of bureaucratic interference?

When I first wrote a series of articles on price controls and how to evade them, as well as prosper from them, few publications were willing to publish my findings. *THE RUFF TIMES* was not yet in existence. So I published them in my own newsletter, *REMNANT REVIEW*. My readers began to write me about their experiences under price controls in World War II and in foreign countries. It became clear to me that the techniques used by my readers in the recent past were the same techniques used by successful price control evaders over the last 4500 years.

The first and foremost technique is to begin stocking up on goods that invariably get scarce under a system of full-scale controls. They are those items that are mass produced, because mass produced items must be competitively priced. Manufacturers make profits by selling these goods to millions of middle-class buyers. Instead of thousands of Cadillacs, producers make more money selling millions of Fords or Chevrolets. Let's face it, there are more middle-class people than very wealthy people. The key fact is this one: these items have very narrow profit margins.

When the government slaps on price controls, it doesn't cease printing fiat money. No, it only stops the legal "auctions." It continues to create money, thereby debasing the currency. Shortages develop in those sectors of the economy that are the most vital to the largest number of citizens. In other words, the bureaucrats achieve just the opposite of their officially stated economic goals. They put on control in order to give the average citizen a break, and the result is the destruction an bankruptcy of those producers who try to supply the average citizen with price-competitive goods and services. The inevitable result is shortages.

Real costs keep going up. These costs cannot be passed on to consumers in the legal markets. So black markets develop. (I hate the term, "black markets." It's a term invented by government bureaucrats. I much prefer the phrase, "alternative zones of supply.") This means that people have to pay even higher prices in order to buy what they need (more risk to the sellers means higher prices for consumers). The auctions still go on, but they go on secretly.

Ironically, the so-called luxury goods—goods aimed at a narrow class of wealthy buyers—stay on the shelves far longer. They have much higher profit margins, though fewer sales. The suppliers have more flexibility. They can afford to stay in production longer. They can afford to buy raw materials in the semi-legal markets or even the illegal markets. The controls wind up subsidizing the wealthy at the expense of the poor.

I keep hearing a rumor about a secret currency that the government is about to impose on the nation. It's supposed to be a deflated currency that will be exchanged at 10 to one in a couple of years. Ten present dollars for one new dollar. This misses the point entirely. Yes, there is a new currency in the works, but it won't be recognized as a new currency. The currency of the 1980s, or in some cases the late 90s, will be the ration coupon. He who has only paper money will be able to buy goods and services only in the illegal markets. He will need ration coupons in order to complete legal economic transactions. This means that paper dollars or checks will be the *SECONDARY* currency of the realm. The real currency will be the ration coupon. (By "real," I mean the legal, necessary, and officially approved currency.)

If the controls are left on for more than 18 months, and if the government continues to expand the money supply, then there will be major disruptions throughout the economy. Controls make an economy very rigid. Supplies cannot be linked to demand. Production bottlenecks will appear in many industries. People will be thrown out of work because certain production tools or raw materials are not available at the maximum legal prices. Within 18 months after the imposition of full-scale price controls, we will be in the midst of the shortage economy.

What can the average citizen do about this state of affairs? On a national level, not much. On a personal level, quite a lot. They should start a mini-warehouse in their home to complement their food storage program. They can start stocking up on all mass produced, price-competitive goods. This means practically everthing sold in a supermarket, discount chain store, or other volume sales organization. Each family should draw up a comprehensive list of the goods that are purchased regularly. Chart a day's consumption or use of all durable and nondurable goods, morning to evening. Then expand the list to cover a week. Finally, look at a month's consumption to include those items that are used irregularly.

Families should begin with long-life tools or hard goods that require very little storage space. Hand tools are an extremely good investment for an era of price controls. There will be a need to extend the life of all equipment. Repairs will be crucial if people cannot purchase new equipment at the legal, below-market price. Any occupation connected with repairs, replacement parts, and used goods will be an ideal one for the coming period. "Junk" yards will be absolutely vital supply sources, since it is virtually impossible to control the profit spread between buyers and sellers of used goods.

How can anyone store all the goods his family might use over a period of five or ten years? Obviously, few have the necessary space or capital, so everyone has to make judgments about the future. Which items would be imperative for the survival of the family, both physically an psychologically? Those items are your first choice.

Price controls reduce the efficiency of the free market, leading to a narrowing of the market and, therefore, a reduction in the "division of labor." Everything will cost more to produce, since without "division of labor," we cannot enjoy the fruit of economic specialization. The jack-of-all-trades will be the king of the price control era. For example, the general practitioner will have a new competitive advantage, financially speaking, in comparison with medical specialists who are dependent upon the highly developed medical technology of the modern hospital. As markets narrow, in response to the disrupting effects of the price controls, the demand for less specialized laborers—competent in several fields—will increase.

We are frighteningly dependent upon the continued mass production of parts that are inexpensive today and may be virtually unavailable in the future. Consider the lowly spark-plug. If you can't buy them for that $7,000 car of yours, you've got a huge pile of junk, useful only for the parts you can strip out of it. Of course, what will happen is that spark-plugs will be selling (illegally) for a lot more than $1.25, if the lack of plugs is keeping cars in the garage. Yet the black market price will scare away many buyers for considerable time —time that may be crucial.

When I decided to publish my book, I worried that some readers might conclude that what I am advocating is immoral, illegal, or unpatriotic. Yet the basic steps that a family can take today are neither immoral nor illegal. "Hoarding" (the government's term for intelligent saving and planning) is not illegal today. It is not immoral, since the goods will be used to supply a family's need in a difficult future, thereby keeping its members productive and off the relief rolls. That's why it is so important to start a mini-warehousing program for the family immediately, before such steps are made illegal by the government authorities whose policies have created the program.

HERE COME PRICE CONTROLS

(4/1/78)   The New York Federal Reserve Bank has suggested that "an income policy" to restain wage and price increases might be necessary to deal with the nation's inflation problems.

According to *THE WALL STREET JOURNAL*, this suggestion, contained in the bank's annual report, surprised economists. In the past, the New York Federal Reserve Bank has opposed wage and price controls.

Although their opposition wasn't specific, you can take this as a harbinger of the future. It means the Fed sees additional inflation in the future and is prepared to deal only with the symptoms, not the basic cause. The Federal Reserve System will continue to create the new money demanded by the politicians, and the resulting rising rices will create public demands for price controls. Controls will create shortages, causing unnatural upward pressure on prices, as the money supply continues to grow.

Wage and price controls remind me of the dumb doctor who took a sick patient's temperature. It was 106 degrees, and the man's life was in danger. Truly inspired, the M.D. plunged the thermometer into cold water, driving the temperature back to normal.

THE KAHN JOB

(12/15/78)   Well, it seems that Alfred Kahn, the President's chief inflation advisor, has just announced one of the most dangerous

515

policies in the history of the republic. He said last week, in reference to the "voluntary" guidelines on wages and price, "It seems to me that you have to place a great deal of reliance on local community action, surveillance, protest, boycotts." While such an approach "does not represent a definite decision yet," Kahn said it is one of the measures the government is actually considering to put some clout in the largely voluntary wage and price guidelines.

He also said the administration is pondering whether to deny revenue-sharing fund to state and local governments where guidelines are exceeded, even though that would require a Congressional approval. He used the example of the approval by Illinois legislators of a personal 40 percent pay raise.

These positions by government are a greater threat to the republic than mandatory wage and price controls, which are bad enough. At least mandatory controls would be imposed by the vote of our elected representatives, and even though they would do great violence to the economic system, at least it would be done in accord with the constitutional system of a democratic republic. The present "voluntary" program is a form of vigilante-ism. When governments attempt to impose their will upon the citizens bond the statutory rights granted them by those citizens, government becomes an outlaw, acting far outside the orderly procedures that have stood this nation in good stead for 200 years. It is the ultimate illegal assumption of authority.

For example, the Illinois legislators gave themselves a raise. That's wrong and, given the present tax revolt environment, it's certainly stupid. But when the Federal government says it will withhold revenue sharing from a state because of their action, that becomes an unwarranted intrusion into the affairs of a sovereign state by the Federal government. This has opened up a Pandora's box of expansion of govenment powers that is probably a far greater threat than the proliferation of unwise laws.

Look what happens when a businessman raises his prices. He attracts the attention and disapproval of the Administration, which then launches a campaign to encourage boycotts, demonstrations, etc. The potential for violence is great. You don't even get a fair trial. In the meantime, you might be fighting a boycott or demonstration. The damage is done, with no semblance of due process.

When the storm of protest went up that limiting price increases to 7-1/2% might be unjust to companies whose raw materials come from other countries, where those prices are uncontrolled, the Administration decided that maybe they would allow larger increases. They gave the companies the option of measuring the legitimate level of price increases by limiting increased profitability. To justify their increases, a private company would have to make public its most intimate, private financial data.

What about the hardware store selling 20,000 different items? What an administrative nightmare! The cost of administering such a nightmare just might absorb the total allowable increase. It's madness! It is ultimately inflationary, as it increases costs, railing the pressures to pass them on in further price increases.

The President's "voluntary" guidelines should be fought tooth and nail. If he wants wage and price controls, let him go to Congress and get the statutory authority. I will fight that, but I will not fight their right to go and ask for it, nor do I fight Congress's right to impose it, as stupid and wrong-headed as I think it is. The history of tyranny is the history of people passively letting governments reach beyond their statuory power. Vigilante-ism has no place in government.

The only ray of hope in this whole thing is that Kahn's primary function as Chairman of the CAB was to dismantle it. Deregulating the airlines was very constructive. If he would dismantle Carter's voluntary wage guidelines as effectively as he dismantled the CAB, maybe he is the right man for this particular job. That would be something. (see: Energy Shortages)

THIS TIME THEY'VE GONE TOO FAR

(3/1/79)   Maybe YOUR ox is about to be gored.

I found an article buried on the back page of the first section of the Saturday morning *SAN FRANCISCO CHRONICLE* (a position that assures it will be seen by hardly anyone). The Carter Administration has disclosed it will take its "anti-inflation battle" to the arena of small business, as they intend to expand the fight to the monitoring of price increases by many small or medium-sized businesses.

"It seems that a lot of the big companies are cooperating with the President's voluntary wage guidelines," said Barry Bosworth, Director of the Council on Wage and Price Stability. But he also told a Congressional panel, "It appears necessary to begin monitoring smaller firms (those with sales under $500 million a year), because of indications that many price increases are far exceeding the guidelines. Too many smaller firms think the guidelines do not apply to them."

Bosworth told reporters that the Council will call in meat processors and shoe manufacturers, for example to explain why some recent increases have exceeded the "voluntary" standards.

517

Why does anyone have to explain their lack of compliance to a "voluntary standard?" If I received such a request, I would refuse to comply in no uncertain terms. If they want wage and price guidelines, let them go to Congress and get them. We cannot, as a matter of principle, allow this arrogant usurpation of authority, backed by no statutory or constitutional power whatsoever. It is this creeping tyranny that leads to wholesale loss of freedom.

I've made clear in past issues that the attack on wages and prices is like an attack on fever in curing a major disease. You can relieve the symptoms for a little while, but the medicine can have severe side effects after continuous use.

When I see the government attacking the real source of inflation, the money creation process in the public and private sectors, then they will get my wholehearted cooperation. Until then, I have nothing but contempt for them. (see: Business, Freedom, and Regulatory Agencies)

PRIVACY

"...MIGHTIER THAN THE SWORD"

(6/1/77) I just received a marvelous letter from one of our old faithful charter members. He's come up with a marvelous idea for protecting one's privacy in money transfers. In order for it to work, you would need the cooperation of merchants or businessmen with whom you are doing business.

Many are concerned that if they buy gold, silver, food, or other investments, their cancelled check is microfilmed by the bank and is part of permanent bank records—and could be easily reconstructed. Unless I were singled out for special attention by the IRS, I wouldn't be terribly concerned about anyone trying to find out whether or not I bought gold or silver. Here is my friend's idea, which I think is a great one.

> Get light blue checks from the bank. When making out a check that you don't want anyone to know about, use a very light green felt tip pen. These pens are designed for proof readers. The ink will not photograph.
>
> Result: When the bank microfilms your check, all they have is a record of your name, account number and the amount (imprinted on the bottom of the check by machine). The film will not record the name of the person to whom the check is made out.

518

One disadvantage, of course: The payee may take a big rubber stamp and plaster Pay to the order of ... on the back, which will give the game away. It might be a good idea to endorse the check for the payee, and clip a note to the check saying, "Please do not rubber stamp this check ...," and explain why you're asking that. Most of the people whom one would want to pay in this way would probably understand why you're asking that this procedure be followed.

It is an amazingly simple idea and another blow for freedom. Maybe there is some way to beat the machine after all.

RED CHECKS

(7/15/78) Some time back, I recommended you conduct your banking business on dark red checks printed by Liberty Graphics of Charlotte, North Carolina. This promotes personal privacy, as it is impossible for banks to microfilm them for their permanent records. I had no idea how much that would bother Big Brother.

The following letter went out from the Department of the Treasury to the Board of Governors of the Federal Reserve and was passed on to all banks in the Fourth Federal Reserve District by the Federal Reserve Bank of Cleveland:

Dear Mr. Ryan:

A number of Federal agencies, as well as the American Bankers Association have directed our attention to a new practice in the printing of checks. As reported by *TIME* magazine in its September 26, 1977 issue, a firm in Charlotte, North Carolina, is selling check forms printed on red paper.

Apparently, when checks written on red paper are routinely microfilmed, the microfilm copy is illegible. Since 31 CFR 103 contains a general requirement that each drawee bank must maintain the original or copy of checks written for more than $100, it may be advisable to alert banks to their responsibility in this area. If a bank permits its depositors to use checks which cannot be effectively microfilmed and fails to make other provisions to meet the requirements of the regulations, it may well be in violation of the law.

Please keep us informed concerning any action you decide to take with respect to this matter; we would appreciate receiving copies of any general communications that you may issue on the subject.

/s/ Arthur Sinai—Deputy Assistant Secretary (Enforcement)

The Supreme Court has ruled that the records of your account with the bank are the property of the bank and can be subpoenaed by the IRS in a criminal action against you or, for that matter, even a simple tax dispute. The Constitution supposedly protects us against being forced to incriminate ourselves. I find these principles in conflict if a third party can be forced to disclose your private records.

There is an interesting conflict of rights.

1. The bank is required by Federal Reserve and Treasury regulations to microfilm all checks as a permanent record, to be used for whatever fishing expedition government might wish to go on.

2. The law does not require you to make your check legible for microfilming.

3. The regulators have been trying to get around this by telling the banks not to accept your check unless you help them by having a check that can be microfilmed.

4. The courts have held on many occasions that checks can be written on anything, just so they are legible enough to be negotiated. They shouldn't be able to get away with this intrusion of privacy.

Here's the big question: Do you have to cooperate with the bank requirement to be microfilmed?

Legally, no. But as a practical matter you may have to yield to get the bank to do business with you. So how do you beat the game if you still want to maintain your privacy? There are several techniques, some requiring a little ingenuity and inconvenience.

I'm not quite sure why I'm doing all this, except that I have a visceral concern for my Constitutional freedoms, and even though I have nothing to hide, I never know which one of the hundreds of thousands of regulations I might inadvertently violate some day, giving them the excuse for a fishing expedition into my private affairs. Would you like your neighbors to be able to snoop through your cancelled checks any time they want? I think that principle is justification enough.

Here are some suggestions:

1. For those transactions you wish to keep private, withdraw cash and purchase money orders. That has the disadvantage of complicating your accounting and your tax record keeping, but with a little extra work, it can be done.

2. You can order checks printed in light green and write with a light green or light blue pen. This can be seen well enough to be negotiated, but is almost impossible to microfilm. You can buy such pens from LIBERTY GRAPHICS, P.O. Box 3614, Charlotte, NC 28203. (Copy-Not non-reproducing pens made by Eberhard Faber,

$8.28 per dozen, plus $.50 for shipping, are also available at your local office supply store.)

The checks you might be concerned about are those where government power *is* encroaching on constitutional rights. If we had Federal gun control laws and the government were chasing down gun purchases, the first place they would want to look would be microfilm bank records. You might not want to make that easy for them.

Things have come to a sorry pass when someone like me, who has been brought up to believe that the Constitution of the United States is an inspired document, should get to the point where he still loves his country but fears his government. Remember, all Carter has to do to assume dictatorial powers is invoke Executive Order 11490. (*THE RUFF TIMES*, August 1, 1977)

If you don't think it can happen, I suggest you look at the recent newspaper stories of Carter's announcement that he will not honor "legislative vetos." Congress often writes into a bill a provision they can veto or cancel it at any given time. Carter says he simply will not honor such clauses, and there is such a "legislative veto" clause in Executive Order 11490. The man has a latent fascist mentality.

When I was interviewing Rene Baxter for my TV show, he made a very profound statement. He said that The Founding Fathers knew that government was a singularly dangerous power and had to be chained, and we chose to chain it through the Constitution.

The entire Bill of Rights is a series of links in the chain with which we decided to bind government. Our Founding Fathers worried about any possible repetition of the repressive government of King George. The right to protection from self-incrimination was written, not to protect criminals, but to protect law-abiding citizens against the abuse of government. I simply want to prepare my life so that if the time comes when I have to stand against that power in order to protect myself and the Constitution, I will be able to do so. My bank records are my own business.

The founder of my church once said that at some future time, "... the Constitution of the United States will hang by a thread," and many other far-sighted men of other religious persuasions have made similar statements.

Whether an individual's actions in resisting government constitute a moral defense of the Constitution, or simply a violation of the law, is a "judgment call." The tax revolt is an example of that principle. I consider the direct confrontation methods of tax revolt to be needlessly dangerous and unnecessary at this time. The "confrontation" tax rebels are trying to bring down the taxing system and are, in effect, throwing themselves in front of the government steamroller to do so. I think that's unwise and premature. The steamroller is going to run out of gas and self-destruct anyway. But I want to be able to use every defensive position against the aggressive encroachment of government in my life, if I should need to, and the right to privacy and the right to avoid self-incrimination are among the rights that should be protected.

Let's try to keep one jump ahead of those rascals in Washington. Crank up the green ink!

BUM CHECKS

(8/15/78)   We've had several letters from bankers indicating that their banks copy checks on both sides, so the endorsement-on-the-back plan may not work for you.

Some of our subscribers' banks closed their accounts because their checks were not in copyable form—i.e., they were using the red checks from Liberty Graphics.

I believe this is against the law, and a violation of the Constitutional rights of the depositors. I can think of no more startling example of how far we have gone in relinquishing individual rights. It isn't just laws we have to worry about, but practices that the government can impose on controlled industries, such as the banks, which can affect your life without any law being passed.

As a practical matter, if you can't get away with the endorsement-on-the-back method, you will have to go back to the green-pen-on-green-checks method, or forget the whole thing and deal in cash while I figure out some other way to keep ahead of those dudes. If you have any new ideas, send them on. It's our move.

ON THE FACE OF IT

(8/1/78)   Tax deductible check expenditures, which you will have to produce if you should face an IRS audit, should be written in the normal way with ordinary checks and ordinary pens. For checks that are used to purchase items you would just as soon not have anyone know about, make out the check for the correct amount, payable to "cash," and then endorse it to the payee on the back. When checks are microfilmed, only the face of the check is photographed. (There are some exceptions, check with your bank.) This has several interesting advantages:

1. You maintain your privacy.

2. It won't alert the bank, because there's nothing unusual about the check. They process checks made out to "cash" all the time. There will be nothing to alarm anyone.

There is, however, one potential problem. Dr. Gary North, in his book, *HOW TO PROFIT FROM THE COMING PRICE CONTROLS*, quotes a long-buried Emergency Banking Order, to be implemented "in case of an 'attack' on the U.S.," which would require all checks over $1,000 to be photocopied, front and back. It also freezes your funds.

I don't know what Carter would construe as an "attack." An oil boycott? A threat? Who knows? The obvious solution is to haul your money out of the bank at the first sign of trouble, and ask for an immediate final statement.

YOUR MOVE

(6/1/79)   Hiding From The Watchbirds

Those of you who have been with us for awhile may remember Liberty Graphics and their red checks which the bank couldn't microfilm. Some of you may have had a nasty experience with them. Some banks cancelled accounts of people who used such checks, as, I am sure you all know, the government requires banks to microfilm all checks. There is no law that requires you to give the bank checks that can be readily microfilmed, but the Federal bank regulatory agencies require the banks to microfilm them, so some banks have tried to force people to make it easy for the bank to comply. If anybody would like to join me in this fight, there's an interesting constitutional issue here that I'd like to raise in court.

I believe that the microfilming of my checks is an invasion of my privacy and should be done only with my consent, especially since the Supreme Court has ruled that the bank's records no longer belong to me, and are not protected by the Fifth Amendment (the right to refuse to incriminate myself). When presented with a check that cannot readily be copied, the reactions of the banks can range from "ho-hum" to, "You must be a crook—what are you trying to hide." In the meantime, those of you who want to stay one jump ahead of the government in this privacy battle might be interested in writing again to Liberty Graphics, because they have again jumped ahead of the Watchbirds. They now have inconspicuous blue checks, which will not attract as much attention as the red checks. You must use a Copy-Not pen in order to obtain copy resistance, however. I've checked it out and it works. You can't photocopy a check written on this blue paper with a blue Copy-Not pen, but it is perfectly readable and negotiable. If you want to know more about it, write to Liberty Graphics. They will send you all the information you need.

I don't know what counter-ploy the banking regulators will come up with on this one, but if that kind of privacy is your bag (and it is mine), you might want to give it a whirl.

The Constitution, including the Fifth Amendment, was not designed to protect criminals, but honest citizens who run afoul of government. Most businessmen probably break a law a day in this complex world, even without knowing it. If that happens to you, or if it is merely alleged, preserving your financial privacy in advance might be your only salvation.

MARK SKOUSEN CONVENTION REPORT

(3/15/79)   Mark Skousen spoke on the subject of personal privacy. He felt you should maintain a low profile and restrict the use of your bank account to your routine purchases. Your sensitive purchases, such as gold, silver, diamonds, firearms, food storage, etc., should be kept outside your bank account by using money orders, cash and cashier's checks, with cash probably being the best. He indicated you should avoid divulging your Social Security number, except in the few instances where it is required by law. A safe deposit box should be put in a company or trust name to avoid the sealing of the box on your death. He felt that up to 20 percent of your funds should be kept in Canada, the Bahamas, Switzerland, or Mexico. For maximum privacy you should turn to such non-reportable investments as gold or coins bought at a coin show. Privacy is not a two-way street and you should be cautious in dealing with someone else who is maintaining a low profile. They may not disclose what you need to know for your decision-making process.

Generally speaking, he feels we should exercise our ingenuity to maintain a low profile and disclose as little of our financial affairs as possible. Leave few tracks.

PROPERTY RIGHTS

(6/1/78)   Certain conservative publications have lit up our hotline by stating that our government has recently, by treaty, signed away the right of Americans to own private property, which means the destruction of the free enterprise system.

The rationale is that treaties, according to our Constitution, are the law of the land and supersede other law, including the Constitution itself. Consequently, any treaty we sign has implications for domestic law. The UNITED NATIONS COVENANT ON CIVIL AND POLITICAL RIGHTS is being signed by a large number of Senators, as well as President Carter. We fought for some years to have a paragraph included that guaranteed to all people of the world the right to own private property. Of course, the communist countries could not agree to that because it is a denial of their fundamental premise. Finally, to get an agreement, we withdrew that paragraph. This has been touted by certain publications as meaning we gave away the right of Americans to own property.

Now think about that for a minute. We did not give away the right of Americans to own property. We simply weaseled on guaranteeing that all people everywhere had that right. If we had inserted a clause that said, "The right to own private property is hereby cancelled," then we would have something to worry about. It's a shameful document, but let's not misrepresent it as being something it is not.

The absurd logic is that every right not specifically granted to us in a treaty is somehow excluded. Well, the treaty didn't guarantee us the right to move freely within our borders, to hold the job of our choice, to go to college or not, to have a savings account, or to take a shower every day. The fact that these rights were not included in the treaty doesn't mean we don't have them.

Before I am misunderstood, I'd like to reiterate, it is an atrocious document, and another example of the hypocrisy of the Carter Administration and its loudly proclaimed human rights campaign. The treaty never should have been signed, but not for the reasons I've been reading about.

PROPOSITION 13

JARVIS-GANN SHOWDOWN

(6/1/78) The Jarvis-Gann Initiative is a State Constitutional Amendment that slashes property taxes by 60% and, for better or for worse, could cause great changes in the economy of our largest, most important state.

Jarvis-Gann has problems. If property taxes are cut, government has but two choices: Cut services to the citizens or find other sources of revenue. I believe it is politically impossible for them to cut services. Even if it passes, the people will demand continued services. Politicians will temporarily solve the problem with money from the state budget surplus, and then they will impose new taxes on business and probably on home sales. The net result will be that we will have only rearranged the deck chairs on the Titanic.

(3/15/78) If you don't pay property taxes, you will pay more income tax, sales tax, or some new and horrendous business tax. One way or another, the government will get theirs. That's why I'm just a little bit cynical about efforts to cut government income without similar vigorous efforts to cut government expenditures.

If you cut government income you will have to surrender benefits, and this will mean unemployment and abrupt reductions in government services. Therein lies the vicious, addictive effect of government services. We have built ourselves a velvet prison, and when we have to face the hard, cruel world, too many of us will suddenly realize we really wanted the safety and security of that gilded cage.

Does this mean I am opposed to the Jarvis-Gann Initiative or the Liberty Amendment? No, not necessarily. In the end, it will all feel the same. I don't care whether we go over the cliff skidding with our foot on the brake, or soaring with our foot on the accelerator, the end result will be the same. But if we can have a cut in government revenues, matched with a hard-nosed, realistic phase-out of government spending over a few years, the world will be infinitely better off. But that is an unrealistic utopian dream.

(6/1/78)   Opponents of Jarvis-Gann, who are generally government employees swilling at the public trough, have announced it will take policemen off the streets, shut libraries, close playgrounds, etc. Now that's bull!! No political entity will allow those kinds of cuts in services. There will be no reduction in spending as long as the state budget surplus (approximately $7 billion dollars by the end of 1978) lasts, and that surplus will give them plenty of time to pass new taxes. So don't get your hopes up that this will cut state and local spending. Then why should you vote for it? Because this may be the last chance to mobilize public opinion to send the message that says we've got to stop somewhere. Jarvis-Gann alone won't stop it, but it could start an irresistible movement toward the limitation of government's ability to extract our hard earned money from us. Maybe it will fuel a political juggernaut to impose something that will truly work.

The National Tax Limitation Movement is growing nationwide. If Jarvis-Gann passes they can expect floods of money from enthusiastic taxpayers all over the country. But I have one strong reservation. It attacks government at the wrong level. The best, most responsive level of government is generally city or county, and as you progress up through the state to the Federal government, it becomes decreasingly effective. But I'm still going to vote for it, because if we don't get a "yes" vote, the flood gates will be open, and the moving hand will have written and moved on. And the word it will have written is "doom."

JARVIS-GANN REALITY

(6/15/78)   The California JARVIS-GANN PROPERTY TAX INITIATIVE is sending shock waves all over the country. It's being heralded as the beginning of a massive tax revolt that will lead to the limitation of government spending. It has been damned as an irresponsible action, mostly by people who drink at the public watering trough. We are reading sad stories of government employees being fired, and cities imagine themselves being stripped of police and fire protection.

Now that it's a reality, I have had a chance to think through all this hysteria and make some observations.

I have learned a few things from this whole Jarvis-Gann episode:

1.   There is a tremendous desire to limit taxation because it hurts.

2.   There is not an equally potent grass roots movement to limit government spending and services.

3. Unless the tax revolt is coupled with an equally enthusiastic drive to reduce government services, it will be irresponsible and violently inflationary.

4. One negative effect is that it takes responsibility, money and power from the local level, transfers it to the State, and dumps the problem in the lap of Uncle Sam. The end result could be larger and more inflationary Federal deficits.

5. Property taxes are deductible on your Federal return and this loss of tax deduction will increase the Federal income tax liability of Californians by about $2 billion, taking back roughly 30% of what we just gained in property tax relief.

6. A letter to the *SAN FRANCISCO EXAMINER* stated one important issue very clearly. It said, "People find they are being asked to pay for the government they have demanded from their local representatives and now find they cannot afford it and don't want to pay for it." If we stop here, it may be one of the most irresponsible actions to come from a large segment of the American public. If we make some hard decisions about what we really must spend, lower our expectations, and make a concentrated, deliberate, ruthless attack on the bureaucracy, so the bureaucrats will be cut, not policemen and firemen, then this will be a great day in American history.

When the State surpluses run out and the Federal government steps into the breach, it will have to do so with printing press money—and this will be the budget buster of all budget busters. The State budget surplus of several billion dollars will buy time, but sooner or later it's all going to be dumped back on Uncle Sugar.

CHEWING THE FAT

(7/1/78) One argument in favor of Jarvis-Gann was that any bureaucracy is loaded with "fat"—useless bureaucrats and programs that could be cut without hurting anything essential. That's true in spades. The assumption was that if you cut off the income, then the government would be forced to cut out the fat. That's not necessarily so.

Let's assume California's budget is 40% fat and 60% lean meat and bone, with the lean portion consisting of the policemen, firemen, teachers of fundamental subjects in the schools, and other "essentials." The fat consists of the desk-sitting bureaucrats and the give-away programs to the unproductive segments of society. Let's also assume we cut the budget by 40%. They will leave the meat and bone and cut out the fat, right? Wrong! Why? Because the people who are in charge of doing the cutting are part of the fat and they are not about to eliminate their own jobs. And the taxpayers won't stand still for cuts in the lean. The result? A stand-off, as long as there are other money lodes to be mined.

In a state such as California, public employees make up a significant percentage of the voters. The predictable result (I know it's predictable because I predicted it) has occurred. In San Francisco the initial announcements about Draconian cutbacks were truly impressive. But the City restored nearly all of the cuts and may fire only 200 out of 18,000 city employees. The post-Jarvis-Gann budget is 94 percent of the pre-Jarvis-Gann budget. How did they perform this marvelous feat? It's simple. They increased several city taxes, and the State Legislature voted, as I said they would, to utilize $5 billion worth of State surplus funds to bail out the cities.

This raises some interesting questions.

1. Will the net effect of Jarvis-Gann be an overall reduction in taxes? No. It will, as I said before, shift taxes from the property tax to sales and business taxes, all passed on to the consumer.

2. What right on earth does the State have to tax us $5 billion beyond what it needs to conduct its business? Why wasn't this surplus money given back to the taxpayers in the first place? Just a thought.

Unless an independent Citizens' Commission with real power to make cutbacks is appointed, I can guarantee there will be little or no cutback in state, city or county expenditures. The cutbacks that will be made will be those designed to scare you the most, and leave the bureaucrats untouched.

We are now reading pitiful stories in the newspaper about the hardships of a few fired public employees. Why didn't somebody care about the hardships of those who lost their homes because they couldn't pay the property taxes? Life is always tough for someone. We've just decided to shift the burden from one group to another. There will now be an orgy of small symbolic economy moves, and possibly a big Federal tax cut, sharply increasing the Federal deficit.

These tax cuts will eventually stimulate the economy, which will make up for some of the lost tax revenue. That takes time, however, and unfortunately, the cut will probably happen at the time when inflation is leaping forward. The reinforcing effects on inflation could take us over the edge of the cliff before the beneficial effects of the tax cut could work themselves through the economy.

We now need to follow up with aggressive cuts on the state and Federal levels without regard to Civil Service or tenure in office—only public need is to be considered.

The Scriptures say, "If thine eye offend thee, pluck it out." And nothing less than the survival of the Republic is at stake. Continued inflation from government spending and huge deficits will destroy our monetary system and endanger our way of life, perhaps permanently. The politicians have gotten a message, but it came through a bit garbled. The message they got was that we only wanted to cut taxes, not spending, and the evidence of that is staring us right in the face in California. Little or nothing has changed, except we are now consuming our accumulated surplus tax revenues. Let's resend the message.

(11/15/78) Proposition 13 and the alleged "conservative movement" are not real forces against inflation, and, in fact, are inflationary. Everybody of conservative leaning wants to believe that the conservatives' fiscal approach to government is really gaining force. I am unconvinced, and I become more unconvinced as time goes on. There is a great constituency for cutting taxes, but there is no major *Effective* constituency in favor of cutting spending in particular. The conservatives want to cut transfer payments, welfare, and government agency budgets, while increasing our defense budget for protection against the Soviet threat. The liberals want to cut the defense budget so we can demonstrate our desire for peace while increasing the spending programs for the "disadvantaged" members of our society. Both groups are powerful enough to block cuts in their pet projects and neither of them is powerful enough to impose cuts in the programs favored by the other end of the political spectrum. What this means is that Proposition 13-type tax limitation initiatives and legislation are highly inflationary. They will reduce government income just at the time when government spending will be accelerating due to the recession. The deficit will be funded by inflationary "funny money."

If you make your future plans based on the assumption that fiscal sanity is in the process of being restored, you are going to make horrible mistakes.

There will be no real change until the nation has been terrified and traumatized by a gut wrenching, bone crunching, mind blowing depression. It is just around the corner.

PROSTITUTION

(8/15/78) I invited Margo St. James on my show, RUFF HOU$E, for several reasons:

1. She has been a very popular and frequent talk show guest on many of the top-rated network talk shows—and she's had a field day. When anybody has tried to challenge her viewpoint, she just trampled them. She's tough, aggressive, fearless, and a very articulate spokesperson for a particularly dangerous and demented point of view. I wanted to confront her. Someone had to take a stand against that nonsense. Sometimes evil has to be dragged out in the light to be examined.

2. When I did the Phyllis Schlafly interview, in opposition to "Women's Lib" and ERA, I wanted to come up with someone with a contrary point of view, and Margo St. James certainly represented that. Nobody could ever say I set up a "patsy." She was tough.

3. If I have nothing but people with whom I agree on my show, we won't be on the air very long. I can't make every broadcast a "love feast," so I invite guests whom I can use as a spring-board to express my most important convictions on important matters. Prostitution and the so-called sexual revolution are matters of great economic and social significance. In fact, I have devoted a chapter to the subject in my new book—an economist's perspective on the sexual revolution: Sin-Tax.

4. I believe prostitution is an evil that society can only tolerate as long as it is encapsulated by negative public opinion.

Society is rapidly reaching the point where it is accepting dangerous principles which are socially and personally destructive—and they won't go away by hiding from them.

PROTEIN SUPPLEMENTS

FUNCTION

(3/1/76) PROTEIN SUPPLEMENTS. (See *HOW TO PROSPER DURING THE COMING BAD YEARS*, pages 185-189). Protein's function is to provide replacement tissue for normal wear and tear, wounds, bone fractures, and the hormones and enzymes which are the key to every body function. Protein can also be used as a reserve energy source in the absence of carbohydrates or fats. The normal maintenance dose would be 22-30 grams a day. A therapeutic dose in illness or injury would be 45-60 grams a day.

JUNK PROTEIN

(1/15/78) The FDA recently released results of tests on the three best known brands of liquid protein used in the "Protein Fast" diet. They were shown to be of very poor quality. I'm sure you've seen in the news that several people were alleged to have died as a result of using liquid proteins, and that the FDA is considering banning them from the shelves. This is another case of government agency stupidity, where truth is mixed with terrible error.

The scientific testing probably is valid. I agree that the liquid proteins are of extremely poor quality. In rat studies, when they were used as the only protein source in an otherwise balanced diet, the rats stopped growing. I'd like to refer you to *HOW TO PROSPER DURING THE COMING BAD YEARS* (page 187). I discussed the concept of P.E.R. (Protein Efficiency Ratio) and listed standards by which you can judge the quality of a protein supplement. The liquid proteins in question are made from animal hides and have the same basic makeup as gelatin. Gelatin is a poor source of protein because it lacks some of the essential amino acids your body needs to utilize it. Don't confuse these liquid proteins with the protein powders I recommend as part of your storage program.

Where, then, did the FDA go wrong?

In the first place, when a minute percentage of persons die from using the liquid protein diet, it isn't because the protein is poisonous. They were fasting, and the protein was their only food, once a day. The low P.E.R. was inadequate to meet their bodies' protein, vitamin and (especially) mineral requirements, and they all (28 of them) died of heart troubles related to mineral imbalances. In order to safely use a protein fast, a protein supplement with a high P.E.R. is needed. In addition, supplement your diet with the right minerals, particularly potassium, magnesium and calcium. They are involved in the complex processes by which the muscles—including the heart—expand and contract. The protein didn't hurt anyone. It was the fasting regimen combined with the poor quality protein.

So what has the FDA done to protect us from this threat? They want to turn the protein supplement into a prescription drug and make it unavailable. They might as well ban gelatin. It's the same thing, only cheaper. That's the wrong solution for the wrong reasons. The FDA could require labeling stating that vitamin and mineral supplementation is needed with this regimen. There's enough conclusive research in this field to support that recommendation. But the FDA won't do that because of their "tablets of stone" bureaucratic position that all food supplementation is unnecessary. As a result, we'll never get an intelligent solution.

I also believe that the FDA is misusing their data to drive all food supplements from the marketplace, including protein supplements.

Don't allow this twisted reasoning to dissuade you from including protein powders in your food storage program, but remember, quality makes all the difference in the world. I've done my homework on that and my advice is still sound.

This is an example of my basic contention that government regulatory agencies generally do more harm than good, and the FDA is a prime example. Their conclusions are dictated by factors other than the public benefit. Bureaucrats are human beings with human weaknesses, and they simply cannot make a decision that would cast doubt upon their previously announced, publicly committed, preconceived conclusions.

It all boils down to this:

1. All the liquid proteins I have looked at are junk, but they haven't killed anyone.

2. An all-protein supplement diet is reasonably safe, *IF* properly supplemented with the right vitamins and minerals, if there are no discernible health problems going into it, and if your condition is monitored by a physician. The protein must be of high quality, and casein must be the first ingredient.

3. Protein supplements are vital to your food storage program, but that is an entirely different matter.

4. To ban protein supplements, even poor quality ones, is not the answer to the problem. It is merely a continuation of the war against supplements.

5. If you want to go on a safe diet, use the program I developed several years ago that was the forerunner of the liquid protein diet. It is safe and, with thousands of users, it has never resulted in any serious health problems of which I am aware. (see: Bureaucrats & Regulatory Agencies)

R

RACIAL PROBLEMS

(4/15/76) It seems that all the well-intentioned efforts to improve the lot of blacks in America may only end up in racial conflict.

I consider myself to be a non-biased American, but if I am, why do I feel so nervous when I'm driving through black East Oakland. Why does my heart beat faster when I am approaching two or three black teenagers on the sidewalk when I go downtown?

Why? Because I'm afraid they hate me because I'm white, I've been made to feel guilty for the racial sins of past generations, I feel race war may be coming. It could be started by blacks or whites, with plenty of reasons and justifications on either side.

On the black side of the ledger, unemployment is twice the national average. It is over 35 percent among teenagers. Alcoholism and drug addiction are of epidemic proportions. Several states have exhausted their unemployment benefits, and food stamps have just been cut by Congress. Our newspapers recently showed a picture of a Boston black man being beaten by a teenage thug with an American flag.

On the white side of the ledger, frustration and anger are rising over busing and recent Supreme Court rulings that attempt to compensate blacks for the sins of past generations.

Whites resent their children being carted for hours to a school across town, when they might live right next to a fine school. Busing limits after-school activities—music, sports, special tutoring, library, etc.—because the buses leave too early. So affluent white families move to the suburbs, leaving the poor blacks. Tax income drops and unemployment rises, increasing welfare, police, and fire protection costs. And white resentment also rises.

Recently the Supreme Court ruled by a five to three vote that black workers should be given special seniority if they were delayed in getting their jobs because of racial bias. If I were an all-powerful evil genius, trying to drive a wedge between black and white, I would have ruled exactly the same way! It seems wrong to award restitution to a victim of injustice by punishing an innocent bystander.

These factors, plus "hate rhetoric" from racists of both colors, could trigger some frustrated red neck or some cool bad dude from the ghetto to retaliate. The riots of the sixties were often triggered by minor incidents.

There are many events that could trigger another explosion, including: New York City bankruptcy, the South African issue, a postal workers strike, further cuts in welfare benefits and food stamps, militant black fire bombings, random violence and additional highly publicized white violence over busing.

In the meantime, I still feel guilty and fearful because someone hates me due to the color of my skin.

(10/15/76)   White suburban America fears the urban black. Many visualize hordes of black militants, armed to the teeth, pouring out of the cities to ravage, loot, and rape a helpless white countryside. There are enough real things to worry about without conjuring up unlikely events to scare you.

Here is what the real world probably will be like:

1.   Sooner or later the cities will go bankrupt, and there will be welfare and food riots, and general "trashing."

2.   Most of the resulting violence will be contained inside the city limits, due to the "dilution" factor as mobs spread out. The further they get from the ghetto, the less of a threat they become. However, neighborhoods adjacent to the ghettos may be in real danger, especially after fires drive the blacks out of the tenements. But the thing to remember is that safety increases geometrically as distance from the inner city increases.

Full-scale rioting, looting and burning, in the context of a full-blown depression and monetary crisis, with cities gone broke, will be a tragedy for America's black people, as the numbers and the guns are against them.

The white liberal politician, who created this dependent underclass by making promises that society inevitably could not keep, is the criminal who will be responsible for this terrible massacre.

As these problems develop, millions of urban whites will head for the small cities and towns, driven by fears both real and imagined. This will create an explosive, though short-lived, boom in places like Bakersfield, Salt Lake City, Boise, Davenport, and Albuquerque. The newcomers will buy land, farm equipment, food, and furnishings, all with rapidly depreciating currency. The boom will bust when these towns realize the social and economic stresses that this flood of newcomers has imposed on their communities.

Violence and looting in the ghettos will die down after 10 days to three weeks, when there will be no more food stores to loot and liquor runs out. Hunger and hangovers create lethargy, not violence.

(9/15/78) I've been watching pieces of another puzzle click into place, indicating the potential for serious racial troubles during the next several months. They ought to be watched very closely.

Let's take them one at a time:

1. THE BAKKE DECISION. Blacks and other minorities have had an unbroken string of legislative and judicial actions over several years, requiring society to make adjustments in their favor. "Reverse discrimination" has become a public policy whose goal is to correct the discrimination of the past. Now that this trend has been interrupted by this decision, developments should be closely watched.

2. SOUTHERN AFRICA. Our policies in South Africa may be leading us to military involvement in the middle of a black vs. black, or black vs. white confrontation.

3. TAX REBELLION. The property tax revolt sweeping the country could result in a cut in many of the benefits minorities take for granted. When this happens, the festering resentment could boil over.

All this reinforces my views that the big cities are to be avoided as places for investment and living. Nobody knows where the "flash point" is, and we may stay below the violence threshold. But I think you could safely argue that the events of the recent past have increased the danger.

I'm not opposed to the Bakke decision (part of it, anyway), the property tax revolt, or helping African whites against communist-backed outside revolutionaries. I'm just trying to be realistic as to the effect. When you withdraw expected benefits and promises, people get mad, and I think we ought to be ready.

REAGAN, RONALD

(5/1/78)

Reagan at Hawaiian Economic & Investment Conference

Ronald Reagan is obviously running again, and here are some quotes that summed up the key points he made in Hawaii. "Government costs the family more than food, clothing and shelter combined . . . seventy million taxpayers are supporting 81 million people who pay no taxes."

In discussing the economists who have been so wrong, he said, "It's not that the scholars are stupid. It's just that they know so many things that aren't true." He said, "If you had a billion dollars and sent your wife to the store to spend a $1,000 a day, she wouldn't be home for 3000 years." The anti-business climate in America is damaging to capital formation. Referring to alleged "obscene" business profits, he pointed out that pension funds own one-half of all the equities in this country, and everyone has a huge stake in business profits.

"If you earn $23,000, you are in the top 10 percent of the earners, but you pay 50% of the taxes. Government, in 1950, cost $1600 per family, and now it costs $9000 per family. Government debt is increasing four times faster than goods and services," and as a perfect example of the growth of government, he pointed out that the Department of Energy, which is supposed to save us from obscene profits of the oil companies, is costing us all about 10 cents for every gallon of gas.

REAL ESTATE

INTRODUCTION

(Special Report #5, 4/1/78) This section is not really about real estate. It's about people and money. Every real estate problem is a "person problem." For the majority of you, your principal asset will be some form of real estate: your home, a second mortgage or trust deed you are holding on a piece of property that you sold, or the real estate loans that are made by the bank, savings and loan, or insurance company with which you have your money.

An astonishingly large number of middle class Americans have built equity in their own home, or in rental property, a lot in the desert or the mountains, a vacation home, or an interest in a small piece of commercial or industrial property. The American dream is to own some of the land. And then, of course, we have the farmers who are trying to decide whether they should expand their holdings and pick up the farm next to them when it comes up for sale. Whether you like it or not, virtually everyone's life is touched by this subject.

This section will not cover all aspects of how to make money in real estate. There are too many good books already written on that subject. The best, by far, is Dr. Albert J. Lowry's *HOW YOU CAN BECOME FINANCIALLY INDEPENDENT BY INVESTING IN REAL ESTATE* (Simon & Schuster).

Fundamentals

Let me summarize the fundamentals against which we should measure our real estate decisions.

1.   We are heading for a major economic downturn. Inflationary and deflationary forces will be battling for supremacy, but, because government must inflate or die, general inflation will win.

2.   Big cities will go broke as the welfare and unemployment burden swells. Crime and frustration in the cities will create a climate of fear. Racial and social frictions, both real and imagined, will accelerate the trickle of middle class and prosperous whites from the cities. It will become a steady flow.

3.   The beneficiary of this exodus of people and money will be the small towns of America, as far from the large urban centers as is necessary to feel safe.

4.   That means a price trend reversal in the expensive suburban real estate markets on a random, unpredictable basis, and a general boom in small town real estate.

5.   In an inflationary spiral the long-term lender gets hurt, and the long-term borrower reaps windfall profits. The implications for real estate deals will be discussed later.

6.   To prepare for the depression environment in which we will find ourselves, it would be best to either pay off your home (if possible) if it's in a good location, or have it mortgaged to the hilt—nothing in between. If it's in a bad location, you either sell it or refinance it to the hilt—nothing in between. If you refinance, the money should be used for more real estate, coins or diamonds.

7.   As property taxes accelerate and the general wage levels increase, this will tend to drive up rents, and political pressures will create a demand for rent controls.

8.   Residential income property in the proper areas is an excellent hedge against inflation and depression.

It's not my intention to take a rank novice and make him a sophisticated expert in real estate by reading this section. Short of an extensive course, there's no way I could do that, but I can help you to understand some principles so that you won't make the kind of costly mistakes that will destroy your whole investment program.

My last piece of advice is: get an education! Read everything you can on the subject. Thoroughly digest the real estate sections of your Sunday paper. Buy every book you can find, including Nickerson's *HOW I TURNED A THOUSAND INTO A MILLION IN REAL ESTATE IN MY SPARE TIME*. In this business, knowledge is power and the person who understands certain key principles has great mental leverage in dealing with others. The average guy buys premium property at premium prices, with no room for improvement. He still does fairly well, but nowhere near as well as the guy who knows that most property is mismanaged and the world is bristling with bargains if you know how to find the "uncut gem."

Remember, you are ultimately responsible for your own success or failure. But don't go into it deaf, dumb and blind just because of some vague feeling that real estate is a "good deal."

BROKER'S FUNCTION

(Special Report #5, 4/1/78) When I buy or sell a property, should I use a broker? Yes, most of the time. A good broker is immensely helpful in arranging financing, negotiating as a third party, and helping with all the details in setting up an escrow and getting it completed. If you do an exchange as recommended in this report, the exchange counselor will perform all those functions. The only circumstance under which you might not want to use a broker is when you are the seller, *if* you are experienced in all aspects of real estate and know how to open an escrow and handle the entire transaction yourself. Even then you will probably need an attorney. Also, you would need to be positive that you can find your own prospects. If you wish to handle the deal yourself, then you should read one of the better books on the subject, *FOR SALE, BY OWNER* by Gerald M. Steiner.

Never negotiate to buy a listed property without using a broker on your end. The commission will be paid out of the sales price anyway. Usually the listing broker divides it with the selling broker.

Before you select a broker, ask for references from satisfied customers for the same kind of property you are buying.

You may have to guide the broker in all your transactions, because he probably does not understand the principles in this Special Report, and probably knows little about creative finance, but you still need him because he understands the mechanics of closing a deal that you probably could not handle.

FROM A TO Z

AS A PROFESSION

(Special Report #5, 4/1/78)

Q. What is the future for the real estate salesman?

A. If you are in the big cities, you may starve. If you are in a small town serving the people who will move in, you could have some glory years.

CITIES VS. TOWNS

(Special Report #5, 4/1/78)

Q. How can I tell whether or not the area in which I live is a good one?

A. Here are some questions to ask.

1. Has your neighborhood been in a long, explosive inflationary spiral, lasting several years? By explosive, I mean 15% a year or more.

2. Do you live within a few miles of a depressed racial or economic ghetto?

3. Do you live in an area that could suddenly become terribly depressed due to the closing of one major plant or industry?

4. Has there been a substantial increase in the listings of homes for sale in your area compared to last year at this time? (Check with any local broker for these figures.)

5. Have the homes listed for sale tended to remain on the market for longer and longer periods of time during the last year?

6. Has crime, particularly burglary, had a sharp increase in your area recently?

7. Have there been articles in local newspapers in the last several months about the fiscal instability of your community?

If more than three of these questions are answered "yes" I think that's a good place to get out of. How far? I don't know exactly' how far, because every town is different, but you should get beyond the ring of expensive suburbs and there probably ought to be some open country or farm land between you and the city. About 25 miles out, I'd breathe a small sigh of relief, and 75 miles away, I'd really feel pretty good.

Q. Wouldn't it be better to stay in close because of possible fuel shortages, so you could get to your job?

A. That makes some sense, but you will have to juggle your priorities:

your personal safety and the value of your real estate holdings, against the possibility of being isolated from your job. If you must work in the big city, and energy worries you, I suggest you sell your home and rent.

I'M NOT SUGGESTING THAT YOU MUST MOVE FROM THE CITY. I AM SUGGESTING THAT YOU SHOULD NOT HAVE YOUR MONEY TIED UP IN REAL ESTATE EQUITIES IN THE CITY. Most persons have their largest single asset in the form of equity in their home, and that should be removed.

I also believe that big city real estate prices are going to crash. Keep these two principles in mind: protection of your money and protection of your person are two different matters. Your personal safety merely requires that you be mobile. If you own a home, you can get out of the city just as well as if you rent one, but I'd just as soon not leave my money behind. If you sell your urban or suburban home, you can afford to buy something in a small town and rent it out until you need it. My immediate concern is financial protection.

Q. But I love my house and I've lived in it for twenty-five years and I don't want to leave it. What should I do?

A. You refinance and use the money to buy another place as described above. If you ever had to leave for fear of your personal safety in the city, the financial impact of abandoning your property would be far less. I believe that as big cities deteriorate, insurance will be difficult to get, that arson and fire are going to be real problems, especially if a city has gone broke and policemen are striking for higher pay—ditto firemen.

I would also maintain a relatively low profile. I believe there is going to be an anti-rich backlash. I don't think you should buy an ostentatious home in the most expensive suburb of a big city.

Q What are the criteria for judging a small town?

A. That's pretty easy. Keep it under 100,000 population. It should not be dependent upon one industry or plant for its prosperity. It should be surrounded by a diversified agricultural economy so that if we had a full scale depression with a breakdown of the monetary system, the town could be reasonably self-sufficient for food. By diversified agriculture, I mean livestock, chickens, grains, vegetables, etc. I'd also be concerned about the water supply. The area I've chosen has a huge underground reservoir which held up well even during the two and one-half years of Caifornia drought.

Don't buy a farm unless you are experienced at farming. Many intend to become self-sufficient farmers and just don't know how. Most of you would be better off living in a small town with most of the services you are accustomed to. My feeling is that big cities are dangerous, but living alone in the countryside could be equally dangerous. The best compromise is small town life. Right now, if you act quickly, your investment in a small town property could be the best financial move you've ever made.

Obviously, you all differ in your ability to take this advice. Some of you are making too much money with your big city job to leave, but if you have businesses that tie you to undesirable areas, I still would consider selling and renting, or refinancing. If you have a business in a large city, now might be an excellent time to take a profit by selling it. A doctor, dentist, or an attorney with a lucrative practice, might stay put and go the refinancing or rental route.

If you refinance, read the small print and be sure that your liability, if you had to walk away from the property, or if you lost it because of financial reverses, is limited to the property itself. That way the lender couldn't come after you for a deficiency judgment.

Q. Will the time come when we will want to go back and buy property in the cities?

A. Not for years in the central cities, but I would love to go back into the lovely suburban community I moved from, after everything settles down, and pick up some beautiful properties there at the depressed prices I think we will see later on. Remember, in 1929, those who prepared themselves for the crash were in an excellent position to buy a lot of things very cheaply in 1934, including stocks, farm land, income properties, businesses, etc. It is a valid philosophy to keep your money liquid—in diamonds, gold and silver—and wait to buy real estate later on. There is, however, great profit potential now in real estate.

Q. What makes you think the prices will break in the cities? Real estate prices have done nothing but go up over the last several years.

A Real estate prices don't always go up. Look what happened to Florida in 1974 when land and condominium prices broke badly. They are still recovering. All speculative bubbles burst, without exception, and the faster it blows up, the bigger the bust.

The Los Angeles and San Francisco areas are typical of what will happen in many parts of the country. Everything happens first in New York or California. During the building boom of the last couple of years, as many as 35% of the new homes were bought by speculators, leaving a dangerous overhang of properties threatening the market place. As of this date, only a small percentage of these have been dumped and no panic has developed. However, the other phenomenon that makes this over-hang so dangerous is that many people have borrowed to the hilt against their equities, in effect, leveraging their paper profits *AND SPENT THE MONEY*. It is dangerous to borrow against paper profits, unless you are investing the funds.

The market is vulnerable, and the ability of the average person to buy a home is being destroyed by inflated home prices, inflated replacement and construction costs, and inflated property taxes. Add to that the above-described fear of big city problems, and you could have a lot of homes on the market. In the county I just moved from, there are three times as many homes on the market as there were a year ago.

Q. Do you still see the collapse of big city real estate prices?

A. Yes. It's already starting in some places. There's evidence of a substantial slowdown. The principal evidence is that many buildings are being listed longer before they are sold and we are starting to see some discounts from listed prices. This is not true all over the country, but there is evidence of it in various states, including Texas, Montana, and parts of California. The bloom is off the real estate spiral, generally speaking, although there will be exceptions to this in some parts of the country.

(6/15/78) The large cities in the "sun belt" seem to be suffering from the same urban decay as the older cities in the Northeast. It's just in an earlier stage.

In 1974, the Commission On The Future Of The South called for avoidance of "Northern mistakes in a Southern setting." A recent study suggests that the problems of the older Northeastern and Midwestern cities are now the problems of even such revved-up growth spots as Houston.

The report, entitled "Growth And The Cities Of The South: A Study Of Diversity," was released this year by a Dallas consulting firm. Here's what they found.

Twelve Southern cities, including Atlanta, Dallas, and Nashville, are experiencing population decline in their central areas, even as their suburbs continue to grow. Jobs and tax dollars are fleeing the core of these cities.

Atlanta, Louisville, Miami, and New Orleans are suffering from a combination of increasing poverty populations, aging housing, overall population decline and economic schisms with their suburban satellites. Serious problems in the inner cities have been masked by aggressive annexation of suburbs, which has kept the levels of unemployment and poverty much lower than they really are. For example, Houston's overall unemployment rate is very low, but the number of unemployed in some of its inner-city neighborhoods is out of sight.

Mr. Kaplan, the principal author of the study says, "There's more substandard housing in Houston than in Detroit."

Another study by Walter X. Burns and Charles D. Kirkpatrick, of the Marketing Forecasting Division of Lynch, Jones and Ryan, has come to the conclusion that the mania in house prices is nearing its peak and the outlook is for "a Humpty Dumpty crash in the immediate future."

As reported in the *DALLAS MORNING NEWS*, the article went on to say,

> But the rapid rise in housing prices cannot really be attributed to population growth, scarcity of land, inflation, or greatly increased family income.
> Rather, we think we have an old fashioned mania on our hands. To date, all the criteria have been met except for the eventual collapse.
> When?
> It looks like the house price mania will break in the very near future. How bad might it be?
> The percentage declines after manias are usually enormous. We believe the decline might match the 80% drop in stock prices which followed the crash of 1929.

I still believe that well chosen small town real estate will be generally unaffected by this collapse, as long as the criteria explained in my Special Report are carefully met.

I don't believe there's a big city in America that is a good place to buy or build in the next two to five years; at least, none of those over a half a million or so in population, and very few over 200,000. For safety and opportunity, head for small town America.

FINANCING/LOANS

(Special Report #5, 4/1/78)

Q. When I find that new home, how should I pay for it? Should I put a big mortgage on it or a small mortgage?

A. The basic ground rule is as follows: Use as little cash as possible or pay all cash for it. (see: Mortgage, Home, for more detail)

Q. What about the sale of my property in the big city? What if I can't get an all cash buyer, and they ask me to take back a "purchase money" second mortgage?

A. The purchase money second is a simple device for helping to close the gap between the amount of cash the buyer has and the amount of money he might be able to borrow.

There are several ways to deal with that problem. First, that note is negotiable. Most people think the only way you can turn a second mortgage into money is to sell it at a 20 percent discount to a mortgage broker, but there are better things you can do. Think of the second as an asset that can be used to buy another piece of property. I recently purchased a property with a combination of (1) the assumption of their existing loan, (2) some cash, (3) a note and Deed of Trust against my present home, which I was going to sell. Here's how it works: Building A is available for $150,000. I want to buy it with as little cash as possible because I don't have enough money to pay for it in full, so I assume his $80,000 first mortgage, (take over the payments and have it transferred to me). I give him $30,000 cash, leaving a $40,000 gap. I still own building B, which has not yet been sold. I give the seller a second mortgage on Building B in the amount of $40,000. It's O.K. with me to have a mortgage on the home I'm going to sell because that, in effect, means I have my money now, rather than later, and I don't have to make my new purchase contingent on the sale of my old building.

If you are selling your property in the big city and you have to take back a purchase money second in order to sell it, think of it as the "Old Maid" that you have to pass on to the next guy. And when you look for a new home or for an investment property —such as a small apartment house—use it to help pay for your new property. The guy you are buying from would probably be willing to give you a purchase money second on the property he is selling you. Why wouldn't he be willing to accept a second on an equally good property somewhere else, in lieu of some cash?

Think about it. It takes a litle creativity to sell this idea, but it can be done. Be careful, however, because there are some possible adverse tax consequences.

If you have taken back a note as part of an installment sale to avoid taxes and use that note to purchase other property, there is a possibility the installment sale could be set aside and the tax on the profits of the sale could be immediately due and payable. This is not true if you take a note on the sale of your principal residence and use it to buy another principal residence. Under Section 1034 of the Tax Code, you can invest profits on the sale of your home in another property of equal or greater value, without any capital gains tax liability. But if you are trading for other kinds of property, be sure to check on the tax implications with your accountant or attorney. You may have to make a nasty decision between accepting the tax lumps, or holding a note in inflating dollars on a property in an endangered or depreciating area. That's not an easy decision, at least the above described technique gives you some alternatives.

My advice might require you to sell a parcel of highly appreciated real property, and you'd be faced with the dilemma of reporting a sizable capital gain, if the sale was for cash. Tax avoidance calls for an installment sale to defer the tax bite. But then you are stuck again with a long-term promissory note secured by the parcel.

An alternate solution is a sale requiring security for the installment note other than the real property sold. In this example, you sell to a buyer under a contract which requires an alternative security—gold, silver, diamonds or some other commodity securing an installment note. This proposed solution, however, has the taint of "constructive receipt," which the IRS often raises in such situations, and, in fact, the IRS has been highly successful in disallowing installment sales and causing the taxpayer to report the entire gain in the year of the sale. The IRS reasons that he has constructively received payment with the use of alternative security. This would be especially true if the taxpayer were to attempt to provide a gold inflation clause in the installment note and have the substitute security be gold bullion.

Accordingly, the ideal solution is to have the taxpayers form an irrevocable trust with an independent trustee, and trust beneficiaries other than the taxpayers (the beneficiaries might be children, grandchildren or other close relatives). Then sell the subject property to the trustee under an installment contract. The promissory note would be structured to qualify as an installment sale with a gold clause or other commodity inflationary index to hedge against dollar devaluation. The security for the initial installment sale will be the property sold.

Following the receipt by the trustee of the title to the real property, the trustee would then negotiate a cash sale to a new buyer for a value equal to or higher than the purchase price, with the tax result of very little, if any, gain to be reported.

The trustee would then invest the cash in gold, or any other inflation hedge commodity, as a hedge against his obligation to pay gold value dollars on the promissory note to the original taxpayer. The security for the note between the original taxpayer and the trustee will be the coins, bullion, or other assets held by the trustee.

The interest rate on the original sale by taxpayer to trustee should be six percent or more. As the coins appreciate, the trustee sells off enough to pay the interest on the note.

This, of course, presents an oversimplification of a very complex legal transaction. Actual documents, together with a legal summation of cases of other precedent setting programs, should be prepared by competent counsel.

The Old Maid

The desired net result when you sell your big city property is to not be stuck with paper. Your choices are: Go for a cash sale, use the foregoing trust technique, or accept the paper and pass it on in your next real estate transaction. Remember, the people you deal with do not necessarily share our philosophy. You also will be astounded at how often they will be willing to accept a second mortgage with interest payments only.

Now, to straighten out all these facts, let's list the fundamentals, one at a time:

1. When you are a seller, either do not accept long-term paper as part of the deal, or get rid of the "Old Maid" by using it in your next real estate transaction. You could also sell to a trust on an installment contract, with your children as beneficiaries and have the trustee resell for cash and buy gold coins with the proceeds. This would be security for the note, to hedge against dollar devaluation.

2. When you are a buyer, use as much "paper" as possible, or pay cash in full. Nothing in between. Remember, the long-term lender gets ripped-off!

Borrowing

Q. I already live in a nice town that meets your criteria, but I don't have enough money to buy gold or silver or diamonds, or even my food supply. What should I do about it? Would it be wise to borrow against my home?

A. Borrowing against your home would probably be the lesser of the two evils, although you don't have any real good choices. If you borrow, make sure you can meet the mortgage payments from dependable income. Also, be sure to borrow enough to be able to set aside some liquid reserves so you could make some payments if your income was cut off. If you put some of the money into gold or silver coins, then you have an off-setting asset that could be used to make the payments. If I am right about the future, they will appreciate enough that they will more than make up for the extra interest. It's also possible that they could explode through the ceiling and enable you to pay off your whole house at some future time.

But if you are going to borrow, don't make the mistake of not borrowing enough, but don't spend the mortgage proceeds for a trip to Europe. It's only wise to mortgage if those funds are prudently invested so that they are available as a cash reserve to meet payments.

Q. What do you think of fixed rate mortgages as opposed to the new variable rate mortgages?

A. Each has its advantages and disadvantages. Obviously, in a period of rising interest rates, you would want a fixed rate; however, rates must move sharply before the lender is able to increase the interest rate on a variable rate loan. When rates fall, he is forced to reduce his rates rather quickly. Generally, a "variable" is assumable, and you can sell your property more easily. Also, if your interest rate has jumped, you can pay off the loan within 90 days without a prepayment penalty, if you sell to a cash buyer. Also, most variable rate mortgages have a ceiling beyond which rates cannot be raised, regardless of how high interest rates go. On balance, I think I'd probably rather have a fixed rate mortgage on the home I know I am going to keep, and would probably lean toward the variable on property I knew I was going to fix up and unload.

At any given time, some institutions are loaded with loan money and you can often negotiate better terms. Don't think that when you walk into the savings and loan that the terms they present to you are the ones you must take. It does pay to shop.

Q. Why is it that the man at the bank who approves the loans isn't the same one who wrote the ads? I've found it awfully hard to get loans to buy investment property and my credit is pretty good.

A. That's one place where Lowry's book and his weekend course can be so helpful. He shows you how to go to a lender with a loan presentation that will have him conclude you are a good businessman who knows exactly what you're doing, and the bank will have a fine customer. Prepare your presentation so the loan officer knows exactly where the money will come from to fix up the property, precisely what the market value of the property will be worth, based on comparable sales in the area, and what the income will be from the completed improved property. Loan officers will often approve or disapprove loans based on the degree of professionalism they can read into the loan presentation.

Also, there are several creative ways to get as much as 100 percent financing. Again—Lowry's book. And if you intend to go into this business, Lowry's chapters on creative finance are worth many, many times the price of the book.

Q. How much cash reserve should I keep on hand?

A. I obviously can't give you a dollar amount, but you should have at least six months worth of mortgage payments in demand deposits, Treasury bills, Capital Preservation Fund, or in gold and silver coins. This safety margin would keep your investment alive in times of difficulty. Even if you get paid in worthless money for your rentals, your mortgage contract is also written in worthless money, and you simply pass the "Old Maid" on to them. The objective is to keep the property until such time as proper values are reestablished. It's a method of preserving your wealth and getting you from here to there across the gulf of depression.

INCOME PROPERTY (Investment)

(Special Report #4, 10/76) Residential

Q. How do you feel about real estate investment generally?

A. In the big cities, I am totally negative. In the suburbs, small towns, or in rural areas, I think it's very sound, as long as you stay with agricultural or residential property. And I would not put all my eggs in one basket. Rather than one large apartment building, I think I'd rather own several small ones, located in different areas.

Residential income property (rental homes or apartments) has been the best and the safest for the non-professional real estate investor. A properly structured residential income property deal will produce a substantial tax-free net income for you, and will show substantial appreciation in value when you sell it, if you know how to structure it.

Income property should be highly leveraged—by that I mean you should have the largest loan possible on the property and the smallest amount of your money invested. That way, the primary risk is taken by the lender. The interest reduces your profit somewhat, but the interest is tax-deductible and you can own more buildings. Remember, when people's funds are limited, they still have to pay for a place to live and for food, and those two items represent the two safest areas of investment.

(11/1/76)   Stay away from residential property in the big cities. Rural areas or small towns, or even medium-sized cities have greater potential for profit, without the social risks. The income will be tax-free and should keep you ahead of inflation. As the market value of a piece of income property rises in relation to its income, you can usually raise rents to keep up with costs, and the market value of the property tends to increase ahead of the overall inflation rate.

(5/1/77)   Regarding income property, here are some fundamentals. First, you should understand the difference between "SPECULATION" and "INVESTMENT". Speculation produces no income. The only profit to be realized is through resale. You are betting on trends, and can only profit if you guess right. And it costs pocket money to maintain.

Investments are predictable and do not depend upon future trends. They produce regular income sufficient to meet all the expenses, and produce spendable money in the investor's pocket. The property and its income can be improved by your own action. The future is in your control and can be determined by your actions. I am recommending investment only. This is no time to be speculating. Stay with fundamentals—the basic need of human beings to have a roof over their head.

Here is the step by step process to follow:

(1)   Buy older properties which are basically sound but have deficiencies which have reduced their value. Neglect will have made the property difficult to sell and will have driven down the price. It will also have made it impossible for the landlord to maintain fair rents, so there is ample room to improve the income after the property is improved.

(2)   Get the biggest loan possible. Dr. Lowry's course will teach you some ways to get more than 100% financing. He'll teach you how to go into a savings and loan or bank with a proposition they can't refuse. Obtaining financing is not an art, it is a skill that can be acquired. Use the maximum possible financing, because the interest is tax deductible, and you can buy more properties. The more properties, the more tax benefits, and the more net income.

The maximum loan reduces your risk. If you were a banker looking at two defaulting $50,000 properties and one had a $20,000 loan and the other had a $40,000 loan, which one would you be most likely to repossess? Just be sure that your loan is written in such a way as to protect you. The lender should have no recourse to your other assets, only the property. Your mortgage should provide for exculpatory provisions, which are possible under certain conditions.

(3)   Improve your property and make it a more attractive place to live.

(4)   You then improve the net income by raising rents, and reducing expenses. THE VALUE OF A PIECE OF INCOME PROPERTY DEPENDS UPON ITS NET INCOME. EVERY DOLLAR OF NET INCOME CAN COME BACK TO YOU TEN TIMES OVER IN INCREASED MARKET VALUE.

(5)   Sell, trade or refinance. You should be able to get a new loan based on the new value of the improved building. If you sell, you'll be liable for capital gains tax, and will have had to hold it for at least nine months (as of December 1979, one year) under the current tax law. You can, however, trade your equity for other properties, and you will probably need to use a real estate exchange counselor. If you handle it properly, there will be no tax on the transaction, and you can trade up into a larger property, or two like properties. The objective is not to sock away a profit, but to increase your holdings.

(6)   Keep on pyramiding until the market collapses, and hang on through the depression! Sock away some cash, so you can hang on if times get tough and your tenants can't make their payments. But remember, if times get that bad, the banks are going to be overwhelmed with repossessions. And whenever a bank writes off a loan, it has to show it as a loss. So they cannot write off too many, or they would become insolvent and would have to shut down.

If you follow all the steps above, you can rapidly pyramid your money showing a 15% to 30% tax-free spendable income from rentals, over and above expenses, and from 100% to 300% capital gain return on your invested money. The power of this method is utterly incredible, and it has worked for hundreds of thousands of successful real estate investors across the country. When all is said and done the big depression is over, the people who manage to hang onto residential properties will come out very well indeed. There is no way, short of writing a book, that I could tell you everything you need to know. You ought to spend the time and money to find out how to go about it.

I cannot overemphasize te importance of knowledge, and if this idea excites you, and if you feel you have the temperament, the drive, and the time to make it work, then by all means register for Dr.

Lowry's Real Estate Investment Seminar. (For registration information, call Toll Free 800-648-5955.)

(Special Report #5, 4/1/78) Stick with residential income property, preferably four-plexes on down to single family dwellings. One of the last ditch efforts to stop inflation will be wage, price and rent controls. Under previous rent control legislation in various parts of the country, four units or less were generally exempt. I prefer residential to industrial and commercial property because of the relative ease in finding tenants. Housing units are relatively standard, but business or industrial requirements can be unique, and a piece of property that is ideal for one company may be totally unsuitable for another. And when they become vacant, they tend to stay empty longer, waiting for the client who needs that kind of facility. Houses and apartments have numerous potential renters. I realize that during a depression, renters also could be in financial trouble and find it difficult to pay their rent, but safety lies in the fact that everybody has to eat and have a place to live. Those are the first things they will pay for.

(5/1/77) Like Will Rogers once said, "Real estate is a good investment because they ain't making any more." We're talking about fundamentals again, and in this uncertain future we face, the only thing we can be sure of is that fundamental human needs will still have to be met, and you should place yourself in a position to meet them.

(Special Report #5, 4/1/78)
Q. How can I determine what I should pay for a piece of income property?
A. I won't go into that in detail, as it is covered so beautifully in Al Lowry's book, but you do not buy a property until you know exactly what it's worth now, based on its net income, comparable sales, etc., and what it will be worth when you fix it up and increase the net income. After you determine what you want to pay, each step of the negotiating process is aimed at arriving at your pre-determined price.

   I have sometimes deliberately paid "too much" for a piece of property, but because I was able to buy it on such great terms, the return on my investment was acceptable. The old adage "My terms, his money; his terms, my money" is one of the most important lessons you can learn in real estate.

Q. How can you think about buying real estate with today's high interest rates?

A. The nature of the residential income property business is that the costs are passed on to your tenants. The market is competitive, but you can price the rent to cover your expenses if you have chosen your areas properly. Also, if you improve the property and make it a more pleasant place to live, your tenants probably will not move when you raise the rent. The interest is tax-deductible, which provides you some tax shelter.

Q. What if I build this investment pyramid by fixing up properties, trading them and selling them and acquiring more and all of a sudden I get stuck when the big crunch comes?

A. Well, I have a couple of alternate suggestions:

1. As we get close and when the signal goes out in *THE RUFF TIMES,* sell off enough properties to realize sufficient profit to pay off the rest and have them free and clear, or trade all your equities for one large, fully owned building. I think we still have at least a couple of years to go in the small town market. That's enough time to make some money.

2. Keep your buildings, and maintain some cash reserves, so you can make the payments for awhile if your tenants can't. If you spread your risk among several properties in three or four communities, the likelihood that you will need to do so diminishes. Then you think of your property as a time machine to get your assets from this side of the gulf to the other. I am convinced that if you can hang on for a few months, the financial institutions will have to start making deals to prevent their own collapse and you should make it through. Values for essential human needs tend to be quickly reestablished after economic collapses, and housing is certainly an essential.

(11/1/76)   Farm Land

Q. What about farm land as an investment?

A: In my opinion, a small rural plot of agricultural land with a home on it has marvelous potential for both short-term appreciation (six months to two years) and for long-term holding strength to get your assets through the coming depression.

(Special Report #4, 10/76) Keep in mind, however, that real estate is not as liquid as other investments. Therefore, make sure the money you would need to survive during the worst period is not invested in such illiquid things.

(Special Report #5, 4/1/78) If you want a farm, be sure it is either small enough so you could live on it and farm it for self-sufficiency, or big enough that the proceeds could support a resident manager. Nothing in between makes economic sense.

Don't buy farm land unless you know farming, have enough land to farm efficiently, and are prepared to be a good manager and good businessman. The farmers who are making it today are good businessmen, not just good farmers.

(Special Report #5, 4/1/78) Raw Land

Q. What do you think of land as an investment?

A. What kind of land are you talking about? Do you mean a lot in a mountain, desert or swamp subdivision? Do you mean farm land, or large tracts of land to be subdivided? My basic principle of real estate is to buy properties that can be improved in such a way to increase their intrinsic value. Land that can be subdivided falls in that category; however, I prefer not to speculate in land because (1) it takes more time and marketing attention than I am prepared to spend, (2) it does not earn income, so the ongoing expenses, including debt service, come out of your pocket. This tends to increase your investment and eventually lower your rate of return. (3) It usually takes a lot longer than you anticipated to get a parcel subdivided and properly zoned. Much of the profit can be drained off in expenses.

If you stick with improvable residential income properties, you get tax shelter, income from rental, and capital appreciation. The resulting profit is generally greater. And if you stick to small towns, you will have your mistakes covered by continued inflation, which is much less likely in the big cities.

Q. What about buying raw land and speculating on price inflation?

A. Speculation generally does not produce income and you are betting solely on the rise in price—either through a general inflation, the building of a new freeway or industrial plant, or some external event that you have forecast—to give you a profit upon resale. If you have forecast properly, your speculation will pay off. If not, then you could lose your shirt.

That's why I like the LOWRY-NICKERSON concept of real estate investment, which involves finding undervalued properties with deficiencies that turn off prospective buyers. If you are able to detect the swan under that ugly duckling, you buy it at a distressed price, improve it, receive income from it in the

555

meantime and market it at a profit. That way you are not betting on the general inflation rate. You are betting on improving its intrinsic worth—more specifically, its income-earning potential —through your own predictable action.

If you follow Lowry's plan, you will never buy a real estate investment until you know exactly what it will cost you to put it into shape, exactly what the income will be, and exactly what the expected profit from resale will be. There's no guesswork, and you are not betting on inflation to bail you out.

(Special Report #5, 4/1/78) Commerical
Q. How about hotels, motels and transient trailer parks and campgrounds?
A. Well, they are obviously a form of real estate, but they are really businesses, requiring advertising and a constant search for new customers. They also are a heck of a lot more work, and the rate of failure in these businesses is far higher than the rate of failure among those who simply buy residential income property, rather than depending on transient customers. Money can be made in those businesses but it's a lot harder and the returns are not as sure, and depression means less business and recreational travel. Stick with buildings where people make their home.
Q. What kind of use brings the greatest return from the land?
A. Cemeteries. The return is many times greater than any other form of real estate investment, and you will never lack for customers, but be prepared to market aggressively. It also takes substantial capital.

(11/1/76) Real Estate investment is a step you take *after* your survival position is assured and you have your own residence paid for, or the money set aside for six months of mortgage payments.

PERSONAL PROPERTY

(11/1/76) The best real estate investment you will probably ever make is your own home. It has proven to be a better investment than anything we've discussed thus far. The increase in residential real estate values over the past 12 years has kept you ahead of inflation.

(5/1/77) Most of us are real estate investors in that we own our own homes. Many own investment property, or would like to, but don't know how to go about it. I get zillions of real estate questions on the hotline, and they usually go something like this: "Should I pay off the mortgage on my home if I can?" "Should I buy a motel, or an office building, or a warehouse?" "Will real estate do well during the coming depression?"

My experience comes from my own investment program and my wonderful experience in helping to put together a real estate course some years ago, designed by Dr. Albert J. Lowry, in conjunction with William Nickerson, the author of the best-selling book in the history of the real estate business, *HOW I TURNED $1,000 INTO $1,000,000 IN REAL ESTATE IN MY SPARE TIME.* Dr. Lowry has developed the finest educational program of its kind. Tens of thousands of people have taken his weekend seminars, and you need some understanding of the principles he teaches, before investing.

Real estate fits beautifully into *THE RUFF TIMES* philosophy. During the hard times ahead, the things that will retain value will be fundamental to human needs, such as residential property and farm land. In a depression, these investments will be illiquid, so don't invest your day-to-day survival money. That belongs in silver and gold coins, and in food storage. But if you have funds left over, you should consider properly selected real estate.

How big a loan should you have on your home? As a general principle, I think your home should be debt free if possible, provided you, and the home, meet certain conditions. If you don't meet those conditions, you should have the largest loan possible.

If you live in a big city—an area that would be endangered by civil disorders, fire or riots—you should refinance it to the hilt right now, and put it on the market. The big loan will make it easier to sell. It also protects you if things should bust loose before you can sell it, because you can deploy the money in safe assets (gold, silver, diamonds, food, other properties). After you sell your home, you can rent and remain in the city, keeping your present employment, or you may wish to buy another home far enough out to be safe, or even change jobs. That's up to you. Either course of action is all right as long as you have prepared a place in a safer area that you can move to when things get tough in the big cities. Remember, when society begins to crack, the first cracks will appear in the cities, and they will be the least safe.

How far out should you move? I would consider a suburb over 25 to 35 miles out, beyond the band of large expensive homes.

If your home is in a safe area and if you can afford to, dump your speculative investments and pay off your mortgage. That way, no one

557

can take it away from you. Do this only if you have your year's supply of food, your bag of silver coins for each member of the family, and sufficient cash to meet six months' financial obligations, including taxes on your property.

If we have a general economic collapse, and everybody is having trouble meeting their mortgage payments, the lending institutions are in trouble also, and one of the worst things that can happen to a bank or savings and loan is to have an awful lot of loans go sour and have to be written off. This can force them into insolvency.

(9/1/77) In recent months, I've been writing more and more about the plight of our cities, and about your personal real estate. I recently suggested that now is the time to sell your property in the big cities. That advice is still good, and in spades.

After watching the real estate listings book, in both northern and southern California, I've concluded it's time for me to bail out. I've just purchased a home in a small town in the Central Valley of California. We have our own well with an excellent underground water supply. Our location provides the quiet privacy I need for reading and writing, and gives us the kind of outdoor life we enjoy. I will produce fresh catfish and bass from the stream that runs through our backyard, and a cash crop from the orchard in front of the house.

But the principal reason I bought it is that it would have cost me at least $80,000 to $100,000 more to purchase an equivalent property near our old home.

The real estate boom in California is setting records equaled, perhaps, only by the Miami Beach land boom of the 1920s. We have gone through a true buying panic. Homes in some parts of California have increased in value at the rate of 20 percent to 30 percent a year. Some new subdivisions have sold out within two hours of the time they opened, with people sleeping out all night in lines just to get a chance at a lottery. You could buy anything in the San Francisco Bay Area or the Los Angeles-Orange County Area and sell it at a substantial profit in months, or even weeks. I believe the real estate boom in these areas is in its last 15 percent of life, and when it turns down, the speculators will panic and begin unloading their properties, and the marketplace will be swamped with homes for sale.

Those people who believe real estate can only go up are fools. Any inflationary boom that is fueled by speculative buying can be shot down by panic selling. The time to be selling is when everybody is buying, and the time to be buying is when everybody is selling. Smart investors throughout history have understood this principle and it is almost unerringly true. I believe that almost any small town in America under 250,000 population, without a large welfare dependent population, is going to boom. If it is surrounded by diversified agriculture and not dependent on one big industry or plant, it's even better. Many smaller communities are adopting aggressive "no growth" policies, which means they cannot easily increase the supply of existing housing. This increases the value of available property. Almost any land near the small towns will appreciate. A home in a small town will inflate in value.

I'm not saying this is all going to happen tomorrow. It's very difficult to time these peaks, so the only thing you can do is be early. If you try to wait until it's started to turn down, you will be too late. You will become part of the panic selling. It takes time to sell a home. You have to start now and systematically prepare it for sale and offer it, giving yourself sufficient time to get the job done.

When you go home hunting, bear in mind that whether or not you pay too much for a home is still a matter of good selection, negotiation, and some active comparison shopping. You could probably pay too much and still do all right under the forecast future conditions, but there's no sense in doing that.

My "bailing out" advice applies not only to the heart of the cities, but to the expensive ring of suburbs surrounding them. Anytime you can get 50 to 75 miles away from metropolitan areas you will find that home values are at least 20% to 30% less, and in some instances, as much as 50% less for equivalent housing and a finer way of life.

(7/1/78) I've just run across a fascinating little newsletter. It's called *SMALL TOWN U.S.A.* Each issue is dedicated to a complete analysis of American small towns. If you are looking for a small town, as we have recommended, this just might be a heck of a good way to begin hunting. It does a beautiful job of describing towns. It discusses geography, climate, history, housing and utilities, taxes, medical facilities, employment, communications, transportation, schools, churches, shopping, restaurants and services, organizations and clubs, visitor accommodations, and even includes some sample real estate listings from the local newspaper. It's well written and costs only $24.00 a year. They will send you a sample copy for $1.00. They publish ten times a year (not in July or August).

Send your requests for copies to WOODS CREEK PRESS, P.O. Box 339, Ridgecrest, CA 93555, and address it to LEONARD DEGEUS, Publisher.

(8/1/78) I just saw in *THE NATION'S BUSINESS* that the median price for a new single family home is approaching $50,000, and since lenders will not usually make a mortgage loan that is more than twice the amount of the borrower's annual income, the buyer must be in the $20,000 bracket to take out a $40,000 mortgage, so homes are being priced out of everybody's reach. Right? Wrong. Some first time home buyers are hurt by this, but many homeowners are converting their inflated equities in older homes into large down payments in higher priced homes, and there is tremendous upward mobility in house ownership. Also, a lot of young couples have two incomes and are able to buy the new homes, although we will soon run out of new two-income families during the next recession.

In the year or so we have left, the best strategy for accumulating some counter-cyclical investments is to sell your home, invest some of the proceeds in a bigger home, and pocket the cash difference. Most of you would be much more liquid financially if you moved just once. I've done it four times in the last 18 months, and have ended up with a substantial investment kitty and a much nicer home where I intend to stay.

The size and quality of the home you can afford to buy is not necessarily determined by the price of the house but by the size of the mortgage and your available cash.

Most people who have owned a home for the last ten years have an equity that exceeds 50% of the market value. That's inefficient use of capital. You should either have your home paid for, for total security, or be substantially leveraged with a large loan and the borrowed money safely at work in some kind of other inflation hedge. A word of caution: DON'T, I repeat, DON'T, borrow against your home and SPEND the money. It must be invested in something relatively liquid. You need off-setting investments showing capital growth, or the whole process is dangerous. I chose gold coins because they are divisible into monthly mortgage payments and you can sell off a coin here or there.

TAX-FREE EXCHANGE

(Special Report #, 4/1/78)

Q. I now own an apartment house in a big city. Because I have depreciated it so far, I will take a tax beating when I sell it. Should I just take my tax lumps and sell out?

A. There is more than one way to skin a cat. I would suggest a tax free exchange. Perhaps the best kept open secret in the real estate world is the nationwide network of real estate exchange counselors who help people exchange properties. I recently spoke at a meeting in Phoenix where there were 40 or 50 counselors gathered from all over the country to exchange properties. If you want to exchange your big city real estate for small town real estate, somewhere there is somebody in a small town who has placed on the market the distressed property you are looking for (Mr. Smith). He may not want your property, and needs cash, but there might be a third party (Mr. Jones) who does want your beautiful, improved property. Mr. Jones would be willing to buy it at a premium price through the route of an exchange with Mr. Smith. Jones buys Smith's building, and then exchanges buildings with you. Now Smith has cash, Jones has your building, which he wants, and you have Smith's building and a tax free exchange under Sec. 1031 of the tax code. I've described a simple exchange. It usually gets more complicated than that. If you would like help with this, we can refer you to the Exchange Counselor Network and they will refer you to the local person with whom you should list your property.

Don't conclude that your property cannot be exchanged. These people are incredibly creative and a lot of things can be thrown in to make deals, including miscellaneous lots, the notes and deeds of trust we talked about earlier. And they can solve such problems as unequal equities, tax implications, etc. Sometimes even the sales commissions are taken back in paper or properties. A lot of these counselors get involved in these transactions to build their own estates.

Another way to deal with the tax problem is not to sell at all, but to refinance it and use that tax-free money to buy other properties, then later on you can trade your relatively small equity for something else when the right deal comes along. The property with a big loan on it will be easier to unload anyway.

TAX SHELTERS

(Special Report #5, 4/1/78)

Q. You haven't said anything about tax shelters. Can you still get some protection from taxes by owning buildings?

A. Yes. Real estate is one of the few remaining areas where you can. Most tax shelter loopholes have been plugged by recent tax reform; however, a properly structured real estate deal will produce paper losses through depreciation which are in excess of the income received from the property. You can use that excess to offset your ordinary income and reduce your total tax bill, while enjoying additional spendable income.

In summary, if you do this right, you will find an undervalued property, buy it cheaply with a lot of paper, fix it up physically and financially, and enjoy the income and appreciation while you are preparing to trade your newly created equity for another property.

WHY THE REAL ESTATE BUBBLE WILL BURST

(3/15/79)   If I had a dollar for each person who has asked me why I believe big city real estate prices are going to break, I could take my whole family out to the best restaurant in town. As I've looked back over what I have written on the subject, I don't think I've adequately explained my reasons, so here goes.

If you have read *HOW TO PROSPER DURING THE COMING BAD YEARS*, you know that I feel the big cities are going to have financial difficulties, which will accelerate the middle class exodus from the cities to small town America. (It's already 1 percent a year.)

This phenomenon, however, might not be enough to break the market all by itself. I am concerned that the motive power that pushed up the market over the last three years can suddenly disappear during the coming hard times, letting the air out of the real estate balloon.

The biggest single factor in this market has been the abrupt, explosive increase in the number of two-income families who are able to afford a more expensive home. Not very long ago, the U.S. government began requiring lending institutions to take into account the income of both the husband and the wife when determining credit worthiness. All of a sudden there were literally millions of families who could afford to buy a more expensive home. Even though prices were rising, they were able to keep their borrowing power equal to or ahead of the increased mortgage requirements. This law created a sudden lump of new purchasers which took several years to go through the real estate market, like a pig through a python. Also, due to women's liberation, a falling birth rate, and a lot of other factors, more and more married women entered the job market and added to this already existing pool of potential two-income borrowers.

Now, I'm convinced the python has almost digested the pig, and the coming recession will reduce the flow of two income families and reverse the trend. Not only will there not be large numbers of new buyers, but many of those people who used both incomes to qualify for a loan may find that the wife's income is unstable and that she was "the last hired and the first fired."

In addition to this, an increasingly common phenomenon has seen young couples borrowing the money from family for the down payment. This means that there is a heck of a lot more real estate debt than the official figures will show, because there are no records. It's just between kids and family.

Also, in many parts of the country, the number of unsold real estate listings is expanding and it's taking longer and longer to sell a home. The wild runaway price rise is slowing down. This is not uniform throughout the country, as there are obviously some exceptions, but there seems to be a pattern developing. The wild demand for homes could, in a matter of six months, turn into an immense surplus. The market, despite its past strength, is fragile. Demand could dry up almost overnight.

The small towns of America, in my opinion, will be somewhat insulated from this phenomenon because small town home buying is generally not as vulnerable to the two-income family syndrome, and people will be leaving the big cities and heading for those towns looking for a safer, more predictable way of life. Another major factor is the continued disintegration of big city schools, and the perception that small town life somehow recaptures the old fashioned values of America. If my travels have told me anything, it is that people of this country are terribly distressed by rapid changes in society, and the nostalgic pull of the small town will increase. That means that big city real estate will be in trouble and small town real estate should hold its own, and probably even boom. You must make a philosophical judgment as to whether your home is an investment or just a home. Either borrow to the hilt and reinvest the money, or fully pay for it (if you can afford it) and have a secure place to live. Nothing in between makes any sense.

A REAL REAL ESTATE CRISIS

(2/1/79)   By Gary North, Ph.D.

Judging from the huge number of telephone calls to *THE RUFF TIMES* hotline, real estate is the hottest topic on your minds. This is understandable, as we've said some alarming things about real estate. Spectacular profits have been made by real estate investors over the last three years, and real estate fever has spread throughout the nation. But the old warning should be taken seriously: when everyone and is cousin are getting on board the bandwagon, you are probably getting near the final phase of the speculative fever. When you run out of newcomers to bid up the price of the properties, the game of musical chairs ends. Then everyone is scrambling to unload.

We are now experiencing very high interest rates, with higher rates probable soon. While it is extremely difficult to predict interest rate movements, mortgage rates are likely to rise above ll percent in many areas before they turn down, and, given the predictable monetary inflation that Carter will have to promote to bail out his 1979 recession, they are unlikely to come down significantly. There could be some drop-off (perhaps temporary) from the peak by next summer, however, but don't expect eight percent mortgage money in the next few years.

Short-term rates are also headed upward and may not peak until March or April. When short-term rates exceed long-term rates, we can expect recession to follow. This is the case today. Short-term rates will probably ease next summer, but only as the economy shrivels in the recession.

The high long-term rates, when coupled with recession, a credit crunch, and rising unemployment, will produce sagging new house prices in most urban areas, and liquidity problems for home sellers. We may not see a sharp contraction in listed prices for most homes, but home sellers will probably have to wait many months to get a buyer who is willing to pay the asked price and who is also able to qualify for the high down payment, high interest rate loans. A lot of price cutting will be going on over the next 18 months in the housing markets. The sharp negotiator who has sufficient cash to pay 20 percent or 25 percent down may find some good buying opportunities.

There are possible exceptions to the rule. Prime waterfront property in popular areas in Florida and southern California may not be affected too much, since these are rich men's markets. The scarcity of properties and the fat wallets of potential buyers may keep these prices up. In certain cities, we have found in the past recessions of this decade that housing prices have continued upward despite tight money and rising interest rates. These cities include Phoenix, Tucson, Houston, Dallas, Wichita, and a few other unique areas. Reno, Salt Lake City, Denver, Seattle, and southern New Hampshire may also escape the effects of the crunch, along with Portland, Eugene, Medford, and other Oregon cities. ("The smaller the town, the better the odds." HJR) If enough new buyers migrate into an area, bringing with them substantial cash from equities from homes sold elsewhere, then the tight money problems may not be sufficient to reduce general demand in that area. But these are unique areas. Regions not experiencing strong net inflows of new residents will unquestionably find the local housing markets, especially new homes, softening noticeably.

This is not as bad for those who use the Lowry-Nickerson techniques for buying properties. If you spot an undervalued property with a problem you can cure, or sellers with a problem only a fast sale can cure, then you may be able to get in cheaply in expectation of mass inflation in the 1980s. The spring of 1979 could be an excellent buying opportunity. But I would caution builders to hold off, get liquid, and sit the next year out. The liquidity crunch is here. Discretion is the better part of valor today.

Most disconcerting is the great number of phone calls we receive from people who simply haven't understood Howard Ruff's insistence that small town real estate is imperative—not simply a good idea, but imperative. When we counsel people in big cities to sell their homes, they constantly ask, "But, why?" They have simply ignored Mr. Ruff's published warnings about food shortages, riots, disruptions of municipal services, and the middle class flight out of the cities that economic turmoil could cause. They seem to be suppressing the knowledge of what they are reading because they don't like what they are reading. How could any *RUFF TIMES* subscriber ask why he should sell his home in the city after reading *THE RUFF TIMES* or Howard's new book? It is understandable that people might not like the advice, or think that they can't afford to move, but why do they ask the hotline counselors why they must move?

If we had evidence that an atomic attack on our cities was imminent, and told our subscribers to get out, they all would leave if they really believed us. The talk about living near the grandkids or the high pay of their urban jobs would disappear. They would clear out. Yet when we tell our subscribers of the high risks associated with urban living, they keep talking about the grandkids and the high urban pay. What they are saying is this: we have considered the likelihood of Mr. Ruff's scenario, and while we are willing to buy some gold and food storage, since that only takes money to do, we do not think things are really so awful that we will forfeit the fringe benefits of urban living. We will stay in Orange County, Los Angeles County, the Bay Area, New York City, and so forth, because the risks of disaster are lower than the risks of lower pay or fewer fringe benefits in small towns.

You should make your own decisions and bear the resulting costs. But to wonder why we recommend getting out of the great urban centers is to ignore the nature of our predictions.

It may be possible that "big money," meaning large quantities of depreciating paper money, might be made in the suburbs of big American cities over the next few years—after 1979, in other words. ("I doubt it." HJR) But are you really after large quantities of taxable paper money? Isn't the whole idea to transfer your capital assets into less dangerous, less conspicuous, more stable regions of the country? Isn't the whole idea to get your assets out of the city? Sure, you may make a lot of paper money by using Lowry-Nickerson techniques on the fringes of the large population centers, and it may work until the panic flight away from the cities begins. But never forget: this kind of real estate speculation is just that, speculation. The long-term goal should be to trade out of the cities into small towns close to food-producing areas. Even better would be a few acres, a wood-burning heating and cooking stove, your own well, a 4,500 watt gasoline generator (to get that well water pump pumping in a power failure), 500 gallons of gasoline or diesel in the ground, and the back acres planted with crops. You might want the kind of self-sufficient home described in Joel Skousen's important books on survival housing. For those of you who are really serious about getting out of the cities and getting set up in a safe area, you ought to buy all three volumes of Skousen's books. Skousen also sells plans for homes in various price ranges ($70,000 and up).

If you're looking for an urban or suburban home, stay on the sidelines over the next year unless you get a very special bargain because of some unique problem faced by a particular seller. Keep shopping. Keep an eye out for problems. Buy the book by Al Lowry, *HOW TO BECOME FINANCIALLY INDEPENDENT BY INVESTING IN REAL ESTATE.*

If you are thinking of selling your house, get it on the market right now. If you think it's so desirable that you don't need the broker's services, buy a copy of Gerald Steiner's book, *HOME FOR SALE BY OWNER.* But speed is imperative. If you want to sell your home during the next 18 months, then get your house on the market soon.

It is not certain there will be a total collapse of the housing markets. The U.S. government is so deeply committed to bailing out the housing markets and buying the votes of potential homeowners, not to mention saving the savings and loan associations from bankruptcy, that it might try to prevent a collapse—as denominated in fiat dollars—of the housing markets. If they can, that is. But a serious crunch, forcing substantial discounts, is quite likely, unless the government steps in sometime in 1980 with lots of Federal money for low and middle income home buyers. This means opportunities for buyers over the next year and a half.

Don't panic. On the other hand, move rationally and systematically to get your main assets outside the major urban and suburban areas. Get into safer, smaller, semi-agricultural towns. If you think you will miss cultural activities, locate a small town with a college of under 5,000 students. Get a standard college handbook (like the one published by *BARRON'S*), grab a map, and start looking for colleges in the state where you intend to start looking for property. The college gives you cultural and sports events, a more cosmopolitan atmosphere, and some local protection against depression, especially if it's a state school, since the students will always be spending money locally. It will ease the "cold turkey" effects of a sharp urban-to-rural transition.

Why do people call the hotline and ask if we regard places like Orange, California as "small town real estate"? We do not. If you're in the following telephone area codes, you're not very safe: 213, 415, 914, 212, 312, 215, and the urban portions of 714. We recommend that you start looking for a safer area to own property.

For survival on little money, consider buying a few acres in a county that allows mobile homes anywhere in the county. Then get about an eight-year-old 12 by 60 foot mobile home ($3,000-$5,000), sink a well, put in a septic tank, put in gasoline storage facilities, and buy a generator (the Onan is very good: 1400 73rd Ave., N.E., Minneapolis, MN). This is the least expensive way to buy survival recreation property. Any county that has restrictions on mobile homes has failed my "bureaucratic litmus test." Forget it; there is too much government and too many urban voters in that county.

Your home is the largest single investment item in your portfolio, unless you are very poor (no home) or very rich. You would be wise to invest $24 in a year's subscription to the *HOMEOWNER'S MONEY LETTER*. This newsletter provides important information that can help you to improve the value of your property. Write: Homeowner's Money Letter, Route 3, Box 127, Shelbyville, IN 46176.

RECESSION

(8/1/78)   We are seeing the same signs we saw early in 1974: rising interest rates, a falling bond market, an international monetary crisis, a collapsing dollar and a stock market that can't make up its mind which way to go, despite the fact that it is at historic lows (if you adjust stock prices for the purchasing power of the dollar). Consumer confidence is at an all-time low, and gold, that most infallible barometer of world troubles, is exploding. It burst through its all-time high, and brushed aside the $200 barrier as though it wasn't there.

Yes, we are in a recession. It will probably take several months before it is reflected in labor statistics and business numbers, but the recession has already begun.

I have developed a theory of interest rates that is a bit unorthodox, but I'll pass it on to you for what it's worth.

It is thought by most experts that interest rates are determined strictly by demand for money and Federal Reserve policy in relation to the money supply. That is true to a degree, but now there is another powerful force that, over the long run, will overwhelm the other factors. That is the rate of inflation.

Throughout history, lenders have always demanded interest rates high enough to compensate for the rate of inflation, plus three percentage points of real profit. As the rate of inflation increases, the percentage they need for profit also increases, as their interest is chewed away by inflation. As inflation rises, over the long haul, the basic interest rate becomes less susceptible to market and government forces on the downside, although they will determine the short-term fluctuations. Over the next little while, we might see a slight reduction of pressures on the money markets, which could result in an easing of interest rates, but not much, and not for long.

I don't think I've ever made a forecast about which I'm 100 percent sure, but once the probabilities have been determined, you have to act firmly. I also have prepared strategies to switch to if these forecasts don't turn out to be true. If the inflation rate should turn down and interest rates really begin backing off, I have an investment strategy that will be just as profitable as the gold/silver/diamonds approach. I think the odds are against it, but I'm ready for it if it comes.

I'm always a little dubious of those who feel they can forecast well in advance how far some investment will go in price and the exact date when the trend will reverse itself. I feel much more comfortable with Dick Russell's approach (mostly because it's always been mine), that it's a lot easier to identify a bottom or a top when you reach it, than to tell you when, or how far up or down it will be.

In the meantime, the trends are still intact, nothing has changed and the recession has begun. Will it turn into a full scale depression this time? I believe so, but we will have to watch very closely, just in case we manage to spend our way out of it one more time.

(11/15/78) The recession is developing on schedule. You will see the prime interest rate in excess of 15 percenty—in the next year! Ditto, inflation! And that will only be the admitted inflation rate. Albert E. Sindlinger, who has been polling consumer attitudes for the past 23 years, believes the current inflation is really running at a 14½ percent annual rate, rather than the admitted 9.6 percent rate.

You will see a sharp drop in consumer spending. Sindlinger feels that the following reasons guarantee the drop.

1. Nearly a quarter of U.S. households no longer have any savings. Five years ago the figure was less than nine percent.

2. Four out of every ten American households are now living off their savings— more than double the rate of five years ago.

3. Through much of the '60s and the early '70s, about 90 percent of the monthly pension benefits to pension fund holders and Social Security recipients went into savings. Now 80 percent of the benefits are going, instead, into checking accounts to meet bills. People have been living off their savings, and now they are living off credit, so the consumer is not going to be able to carry the ball for the economy in 1979.

As Sindlinger says, the economic prosperity of the last year has been fueled by inflation-hedge buying—people buying now to avoid higher prices later. But now they are consuming much of their savings, they have utilized much of their borrowing capacity, and I don't believe consumer buying will sustain a continued rise in economic activity. That, coupled with the government's sharp contraction in monetary expansion and the increase in interest rates mandated by the Carter Administration, guarantees us a continued accelerating, dramatic slide into recession. At the same time, the continuing demands on government, reinforced by the tax revolt, and the recession-caused deficits of the next year also guarantee us a classic monetary expansionary inflation. Put that in your pipe and smoke it!

(11/1/78) There's an old proverb that says if you want to boil a live frog you don't throw him in hot water. He'll jump out. You put him in cold water and gradually raise the heat until, before he knows he's in trouble, he is cooked.

You frogs are on the verge of being parboiled.

I've commented in the past that nations in decline rarely know it. When our economy is sliding into recession, we usually don't know it until after we're deep into it. We spent the first six months of the last recession arguing whether or not we were going to have one. Only with the perspective of history can we look back and see what really happened.

Washout Wednesday

The signs of early recession are all around us now. The dollar continued to crumble abroad until Uncle Stupid suddenly turned up the heat. On Washout Wednesday, November 1, 1978, we woke up to find the Carter Administration, in coordination with the Federal Reserve, moved brutally in support of the crumbling dollar with the most massive intervention in history—$32 billion worth of currency swaps with Germany, Japan, etc., with the borrowed foreign money being used to buy up dollars. The Fed raised the discount rate one whole point, and the Treasury doubled the amount of gold to be sold in December to 1½ million ounces—all overnight and without warning.

The immediate reaction? A roaring rally in the stock market, with the biggest one day advance in history, gold and silver markets panicking, foreign currencies down limits, and bonds rallying furiously.

What does it really mean?

1. We were probably forced to take these steps by the Germans and Japanese (our traditional friends). They unloaded their dollars, we unloaded more of our gold, and we now owe them a bundle in their strong currencies.

2. We've shot our wad! If this doesn't permanently turn the dollar around, we have nothing left. It probably will have only a temporary effect.

3. We have opted for a recession with the one point jump in short-term rates, pushing short-term rates above long. We might have a pause in the inflation climb, but the political screams from the left will again force us to inflate.

4. When the panic in gold and silver is over, they will resume their climb.

5. We will see an even greater explosion in the prime rate. Two or three more percentage points in the next six months would not surprise me at all.

Drat it, I'm scared, and you sit there and take it like that proverbial frog because all of this doesn't seem to be having much of an impact on your life. You still take home a regular pay check. Prices are rising slowly enough at the supermarket that you adjust to them, usually by simply accumulating a little more debt. Unemployment hasn't started rising yet, nor have sales fallen off sharply. Those are the LAST confirming events. Any fool can recognize a recession when that happens. On the surface, nothing much seems to have changed, but the underlying structural changes are deep, permanent and ominous.

Some people think I get some kind of kick out of being a "prophet of doom." Well, I don't. It runs contrary to every instinct I have. By nature, I'm an optimist. I like to laugh. I want a happy future for my children. But I have to sit here week after week pumping out this gloomy prose simply because everything I'm studying confirms to me that I'm dead right, and I'd rather be right than ignorantly happy. You're not paying me to be gloomy or optimistic. You're paying me to be right. (see: Economy of U.S., Possibility of Collapse)

RECOMMENDATIONS

FREEZER SENTRY

(2/15/78)   I have found a dandy gadget to recommend. It's called FREEZER SENTRY. It's a little hard to describe, but it is a card with a visual temperature alarm that you put in your freezer and check from time to time to see whether thawing has occurred. With the kind of intermittent power shortages I expect in the future, it would be awfully nice to put this in your freezer when you go away on vacation. You check it when you get back and if it has turned red, you will know the power has been off and that thawing has occurred, even if everything has refrozen. If you are interested, it can be bought from INSTITUTIONAL PRODUCTS CORPORATION OF AMERICA, 8100 Capwell Drive, Oakland, CA 94621 (415-569-3600).

MO-PEDS

(7/1/77)   I have just been turned on by one of the greatest survival items I've ever seen. I just bought a Mo-Ped.

If I'm right about the development of an energy crisis due to government meddling, rationing, or whatever, it could be a lifesaving, business saving investment.

A Mo-Ped is basically a motorized bicycle, although some of them are almost motor scooters. The principle is that you have a light-weight vehicle that can be pedaled like an ordinary bike, and a motor can be used as a boost to get you up a hill or if you just get tired. I've bought a Solex, which is made in France and is probably the most popular brand on the Continent. It gets 150-200 miles to the gallon and provides me with much needed exercise, and on top of that, it's a heck of a lot of fun.

Here's how it works. It has a tiny 8/10 horsepower motor mounted on the front fender. When you wish to use the motor, you merely push forward a lever that engages the motor with the outer surface of the tire. This starts the motor and then the motor drives the tire by direct contact friction. There is no ignition, merely a magneto. It has a centrifugal clutch so that when you stop, it will idle. It doesn't have an awful lot of zip, but it will do about 18 miles per hour on the straightaway. Going up hills, you have to use the motor and pedal, too. If you want to just pedal, it works fine, just like a nice free-wheeling bike—without ten speeds, of course.

You can't ride double and it's really designed for relatively flat country. It is tremendously economical. It uses a 50 to 1 mix of gas and oil, like a lawnmower or an outboard motor, and runs very quietly. With its big one-third gallon gas tank, I can go about 50 miles between refuelings. The mechanism is so simple that anybody can fix it, especially if you stock a few spare parts.

Mo-Peds are really catching on. They are generally treated by state and local licensing agencies as a bicycle, not as a motorcycle. Their speeds are low enough so that they are no more dangerous than the average bike. They can go anywhere a bike can, but are not licensed for freeway use because of their obvious lack of power and speed. They seem to be great for old and young alike. Anybody who can ride a bicycle slowly on level ground can ride this vehicle.

There are several different kinds of Mo-Peds. Some of them can only use the pedals for getting started. They are, in effect, pedal starting motor bikes. The Solex is the only brand I know of that is a genuine free-wheeling bike. They are still pretty expensive. I paid $320 for mine, but if you are concerned about having basic transportation in a fuel crisis, I can't think of anything better to have around. I wouldn't hesitate to start out on a trip of 50 to 75 miles. I may not get there fast, but I'll have a heck of a lot of fun doing it.

FROM A TO Z

OUR VENDORS

(2/1/78) Why do I recommend commercial products and services?

When *THE RUFF TIMES* was first conceived, it was basically a consumer's guide to dependable services. When I recommended the purchase of food, gold and silver coins, I also recognized I might be leading you into a trap, because both of those industries have high mortality rates and a lot of people had been badly hurt. The food storage business, in particular, was in great disarray. A lot of customers had bought expensive food storage units from dealers and distributors who went broke before they could be delivered. In some instances, the dealers were O.K. but their supplier went under. This started us on our policy of actively seeking out and recommending good vendors. Because this business was obviously potentially profitable for us and for the vendor, there was the danger of the charge of conflict of interest, and I would have no credibility when I made a recommendation. So we made the policy decision that neither I nor my family could ever benefit financially from any vendor with whom we did business, and after two or three months of publication that decision was implemented.

We entered into an agreement with these vendors that they would give free counseling in the areas in which they were expert, to any of our subscribers, whether they did business with them or not. They understand that is the price they pay for having our recommendation.

We also decided to settle on only one or two firms in each of these areas and not come up with a long "laundry list" of recommended firms all over the country, because the products we recommend can be handled nicely by mail order. I much prefer to have one dependable firm that will reveal to me their most intimate financial data, will subscribe completely to *THE RUFF TIMES* philosophy, will deal with our people at fair prices, and resolve any genuinely debatable dispute in favor of our subscriber. I am prepared to endorse them. Fortunately, because of the care in selecting the firms, these disputes are infrequent, and there are no unresolved problems of which we are aware.

Some of the people we recommend are able to sell you products at prices much lower than you can get elsewhere. In other instances, their prices are competitive with others, and there is occasionally a very small price premium over and above that which you might obtain from other merchants. But we continue to recommend them, simply because their financial stability, dependable service, and willingness to give good advice more than compensates for that small difference in price.

Because we refer so much business to these firms, it has given us some real influence, in that they will do most anything to please us in order to maintain our endorsement. After all, we are referring 80,000 clients and as a result of that recommendation, they have become among the largest firms in their fields. This clout is used to your benefit.

We consider them an extension of our staff, and thus have been able to pull together a wide range of highly expert people to help you.

WOOD STOVES

(8/15/77) I've never recommended panic measures you would regret if my forecasts turned out to be wrong. But I cannot, under any circumstances, see anything wrong with having a well-designed, properly installed, woodburning stove in the house. What's wrong with using an abundant self-renewing resource like wood?

Ruff's Recommendations

1. Buy a woodstove. I own a GIBRALTAR, but there are lots of good ones. The modern stove is a far cry from the old pot-belly. On the new stoves, you can control the oxen flow. Mine has a glass panel on the door where you can see the cheery flames, and a fat cooking surface on top. One load of wood lasts up to 12 hours, and there is almost complete combustion, leaving few ashes.

2. Store wood, preferably hardwood, and don't wait until winter.

3. Buy extra blankets, warm pajamas and socks, and plenty of winter clothes.

4. Even if you live in a temperate or warm climate, you still have to cook, or heat water. And remember, the weird weather patterns that brought a freeze to Florida and record snows to the Eastern half of the U.S. are likely to continue, according to the meteorologists who have been the most accurate so far. At the least, have a grill and a good supply of charcoal for cooking.

5. Install your stove according to directions. Comply with local building cod. Improperly installed, it can be dangerous, even fatal.

I've asked Reliance Products to prepare a catalogue of acceptable woodstoves, with some super discounts. You will be receiving it in the mail soon.

(10/15/77) I've just had an advance look at an amazing document. Reliance Products has produced the catalogue on woodburning that we promised you in our August 15 issue, and it is a lot more than a catalogue. It offers a lot of products for sale, most of which have been carefully researched by me or my staff, which can aid you in heating your home or cooking in power shortage conditions. It doesn't just contain sales material. It also tells you how to convert your fireplace for heating and cooking, and how to reduce the loss of heat. It is full of useful information and is a logical extension of our woodburning article.

REFERENCE MATERIALS

This section, added primarily for the benefit of non-subscribers, should put you in closer touch with more of *THE RUFF TIMES* philosophy. All the books can be found in your public library, and most (except those noted with an asterisk) can be purchased through Target Publishers by writing to Target Publishers, P.O. Box 2000, San Ramon, CA 94583. (Prices listed may not reflect current inflationary increases.)

The newsletters listed also form a useful part of *THE RUFF TIMES* philosophy. You may write to the addresses indicated for subscription information.

BOOKS

How You Can Become Financially Independent by Inve ting in Real Estate, Albert J. Lowry, Simon & Schuster, $10.00.

Cycles of War, R. E. McMaster, War Cycles Institute, $10.00.

War on Gold, Antony Sutton, '76 Press, $9.95.

The Insider's Banking & Credit Almanac, Mark Skousen, Kephart Communications, $14.95.

Mark Skousen's Complete Guide to Financial Privacy, Mark Skousen, Kephart Communications, $14.95.

Grow or Die, James A. Weber, Arlington House, $11.95.

How You Can Profit From The Coming Price Controls, Dr. Gary North, American Bureau of Economic Research, $10.00.

How To Manage Real Estate Successfully In Your Spare Time, Albert Lowry, Capital Printing, $19.95.

How I Turned $1,000 Into Three Million In Real Estate, William Nickerson, Simon & Schuster, $11.95.

Home For Sale By Owner, Gerald M. Steiner (paperback), Hawthorn Books, $7.95.

Common Sense Economics, John Pugsley, Common Sense Press, $12.50.

The Biggest Con, Irwin Schiff, Freedom Books, $5.95.

The Great Inflation, William Guttman & Virginia Meegan, Saxon, $14.00.

Harry Browne's Complete Guide To Swiss Banks, Harry Browne, McGraw Hill, $12.95.

The ABC's of Home Food Dehydration, Barbara Densley, Horizon Publishing, $3.95.

Just In Case—A Manual of Home Preparedness, Barbara H. Salsbury, Bookcraft, $5.50.

Field Guide to Edible Wild Plants, Bradford Angier, Stackpole Books, $6.95.

Making The Best Of Basics, James Talmage Stevens, Peton Corporation, $5.95.

The Paper Aristocracy, Howard S. Katz, Books in Focus, $4.95.

War Mongers, Howard S. Katz, Books in Focus, $12.50.

Let's Try Barter, Charles Morrow Wilson, Devin-Adair Co., $4.95.

The International Man, Douglas R. Casey, Kephart Communications, $14.95.

The Survival Home Manual, J. Skousen, Survival Homes, $25.00.

Stocking Up, Editors—Organic Gardening and Farming, Rodale Press, $13.95.

Your New Swiss Bank Book, Robert Kinsman, Dow Jones-Irwin, $14.95.

Kinsman's Guide To Tax Havens, Robert Kinsman, Dow Jones-Irwin, $17.50

The Hard Money Book, Steven K. Beckner, The Capitalist Reporter Press, $10.00.

How To Make Profits In Commodities, W. D. Gann, $25.00.

New Profits From The Monetary Crisis, Harry Browne, $12.95.

How To Prosper During The Coming Bad Years, Howard J. Ruff (hardbound), Times Books, $8.95.

How To Prosper During The Coming Bad Years, Howard J. Ruff (paperback), Warner Books, $2.75.

FROM A TO Z

Finding And Buying Your Place In The Country, Les Scher, MacMillan Publishing, $6.95

Mother Earth News Handbook of Homemade Power, Mother Earth News, $2.50.

Sunbelt Retirement, Peter A. Dickenson, E. P. Dutton, $8.95.

The Age Of Inflation, Hans F. Sennholz, Western Islands, $8.95.

Energy: The Created Crisis, Antony C. Sutton, Books in Focus, $10.95.

The Complete Real Estate Advisor, David J. DeBenedictus, Simon and Schuster, $9.95.

How To Avoid Probate, Norman Dacy, Crown Publishing, $12.95.

* *On The Brink*, Benjamin and Herb Stein, Simon and Schuster, $8.95.

Final Fire, Dennis Smith, New American Library,

The Invisible Crash, James Dines, Ballantines Books, $10.00.

Skill For Survival, Esther Dickey, Horizon Publishing, $6.95.

Herbal Handbook For Farm & Stable, Juliette Levy, Rodale Press, $7.95 (hardbound), $3.95 (paperback).

* *Money*, E.W. Kemmerer, MacMillan (out of print)

A Time For Truth, William E. Simon, McGraw-Hill $12.50, Berkeley ($2.50 paperback).

NEWSLETTERS AND ADVISORY SERVICES

(10/15/76) (revised 4/79) There are several newsletters I never miss. I read most from cover to cover, and would like to recommend them to you. Each one focuses on some aspect of our economic world and all play an important role in *THE RUFF TIMES* philosophy. I've often picked up an idea or concept I otherwise would have missed. You may not be able to afford them all, but you should subscribe to those which fit your peronal interest and budget.

You must understand that, while I enjoy them all, none is as good as *THE RUFF TIMES* (totally unbiased opinion). I do disagree with some of their conclusions from time to time, but all the editors are in general agreement with me, and I always get something of value from them.

Finally, for a synopsis of most newsletters listed, please refer to Chapter 20 in HOW TO PROSPER DURING THE COMING BAD YEARS. I have devoted a few pages to them.

Here they are:

RICHARD RUSSELL'S
DOW THEORY LETTERS
P.O. Box 1759
La Jolla, CA 92038

THE REAPER
P.O. Box 39026
Pheonix, AZ 85069

VIEW FROM THE PIT
1595 Little John Ct.
Highland Park, IL 60035

GOLD NEWSLETTER
8422 Oak
New Orleans, LA 70118

MCKEEVER'S MISL
P.O: Box 4130
Medford, OR 97501

TAX ANGLES
P.O. Box 2311
Landover Hills, MD 20784

MYERS' FINANCE AND
ENERGY
642 Peyton Building
Spokane, WA 99201

WORLD MARKET
PERSPECTIVE
P.O. Box 91491
West Vancouver, BC
Canada V7V 3P2

THE RHOADS CONCLUSION
P.O. Box 22675
San Diego, CA 92122

GARY NORTH'S
REMNANT REVIEW
P.O. Box 35547
Phoenix, AZ 85069

DAILY NEWS DIGEST
P.O. Box 39027
Phoenix, AZ 85069

PERSONAL FINANCE
LETTER
P.O. Box 2599
Landover Hills, MD 20784

HARRY BROWNE SPECIAL
REPORTS
207 Jefferson Square
Austin, TX 78731

PRECIOUSTONES
NEWSLETTER
P.O. Box 4649
Thousand Oaks, CA 91359

THE RETIREMENT LETTER
8401 Connecticut Ave.
Washington, DC 20015

WORLD MONEY ANALYST
1300 Connecticut, NW #307
Washington, DC 20036

THE INTERNATIONAL
HARRY SCHULTZ LETTER
P.O. Box 2523
Lausanne 1002
Switzerland

THE SPOTLIGHT
300 Independence Ave., S.E.
Washington, D.C. 2003

SMALL TOWN, USA
P.O. Box 339
Ridgecrest, CA 93555

*ORGANIC GARDENING &
FARMING*
33 East Minor Street
Emmaus, PA 18049

THE ZWEIG FORECAST
747 Third Avenue
New York, NY 10017

*ROBERT KINSMAN'S LOW
RISK ADVISORY LETTER*
P.O. Box 881
San Rafael, CA 94901

THE DINES LETTER
P.O. Box 22
Tiburon, CA 94920

*THE WELLINGTON
FINANCIAL LETTER*
P.O. Box 1287
Honolulu, HI 96807

ACRES, USA
10227 E. 61st Street
Raytown, MO 64133

MOTHER EARTH NEWS
P.O. Box 70
Hendersonville, NC 28739

*LET'S TALK...SILVER
AND GOLD*
Sibbet Publications, 61 W. Lake
Ave.
Pasadena, CA 91101

*INTERNATIONAL
MONEYLINE*
25 Broad Street
New York, NY 10004

DEAKNEWS
1800 K St., N.W.
Washington, D.C. 20006

*PERSONAL SURVIVAL
LETTER*
P.O. Box 598
Rogue River, OR 97537

*THE COMSTOCK TRADING
POST*
P.O. Box 8020
Walnut Creek, CA 94596

REGULATORY AGENCIES

GENERAL PROBLEMS

(9/1/77) "Bureaucracy is a giant mechanism operated by pygmies."
—Honore de Balzac

I just ran across a marvelous discussion of the financial effects of government regulation, and the cost to you, by J. R. Johnson, President of Royal Industries. It should give you pause.

> It took 142 years—1789 to 1931—for our Federal government to spend $100 billion. 31 years later, in 1962, our government managed to spend $100 billion in one year. It took only nine more years to get to the $200 billion per year level, and three years later, in 1975, we went over the $300 billion mark. Now it's getting easy! This year the Federal government will spend over $400 billion. That's a billion plus per day.
>
> What is a billion? It's a lot. One billion seconds ago the first atomic bomb had not been exploded. One billion minutes ago Christ was still on earth. One billion years ago men were still living in caves, yet one billion dollars ago, in terms of our Federal government spending, was yesterday.
>
> The labor force employed in private industry grew about 36 percent in the years from 1955 through 1973. In that same period, the government labor force—Federal, state, and local—grew about 90 percent, or a rate two and one-half times that of the private sector.
>
> In 1953 the average family in the U.S. had an income of $5000 and paid 12 percent of that in Federal, state and local taxes. In 1974, the family income had increased handsomely to $13,000, however, 23 percent of that income went for taxes.
>
> We can give thanks to those who wrote our Constitution. They provided for our government of checks and balances. The more checks the govenment writes, the worse the balance becomes.

This mounting pile of government spending results in inflation. Nikolai Lenin said, "Through inflation government can quietly and unobservedly confiscate the property and prosperity of its citizens." And that is precisely what is happening.

Mr. Johnson goes on to say, "Government regulation, by its very

580

nature, causes all kinds of reports to be submitted to the regulators. Recently someone counted 15,000 types of Federal forms. Businesses file more than 114,000,000 forms every year. Twenty-five years ago the Hoover Commission reported that a million reports a year were filed reporting there was nothing to report. A major oil company stated last summer that 636 miles of computer tape are required simply to store the information required by the Federal Energy Administration alone. General Motors recently stated that in 1974 they spent 1.3 billion dollars on compliance with government rgula-tions. The Federal Office of Management and Budget was asked recently to calculate what consumers pay for the regulations imposed by the government. They replied that while impossible to calculate precisely, the annual cost "might" be as high as $2000 per family, or a total cost of $130 billion per year—an amount roughly equal to all personal income taxes. They are about right."

(7/1/76) We've written before about government bureaucrats (see: Bureaucrats) and their abuse of power, but I have some new perspectives on them I'd like to pass on.

It's the fault of Congress. Every congressman or senator wants to have his name on a piece of important legislation. And the real plum is to create a new agency. It's the best way to become immortal because your creation will never die.

Congress repeats the same mistakes over and over again.

1. An evil is perceived. Then it is decided the evil can be corrected with new legislation. Then an agency is set up to oversee the correct application of the "remedy."

2. The agency is given a broad mandate with power to issue regulations with the force of law and with appropriate penalties.

3. The agency is given power to ferret out violations of its regulations, bring charges, prosecute the violators, and sit as judge and jury, determining guilt or innocence. It then pronounces appro-priate sentence. Strangely enough, the agency rarely loses a case!

4. Agency personnel are made immune to personal liability, and you receive no damages, legal fees or expenses, even if you win.

(9/1/76) This year Congress will introduce about 25,000 pieces of proposed legislation. Out of these 25,000, perhaps 400 will eventually be enacted into law. In short, with 535 people on both sides of Capital Hill working full-time, less than one bill per congressional office gets signed into law.

This results in approximately 200 pages of the Congressional Record daily, at about $286 per page. (Thank goodness it wasn't two bills per office!) And very little of the voluminous Congressional Record involves actual laws that affect your life.

However, every day a book equally as large as the *Congressional Record* arrives at each Congressman and Senator's office—*THE FEDERAL REGISTER*. Unlike the *Congressional Record,* the *Register* means business. All of the fine print is law. Every day of the work week, 52 weeks a year, the *Register* is published—about 60,000 pages a year. It is the law of the land. Very few of these laws are challenged by Congress. Most of them are immediately applied. Congress only gets 1.6 percent of its proposed legislation into law. ALL of the regulations issued in the *Register* become law, complete with civil and criminal penalties. This also includes Executive Orders. We now have a body of law that has reached the point where it cannot be understood or obeyed. It is too complex. It is too huge. It is possible for you, if you are a small businessman or professional man, to inadvertently violate the law 20 times a day and never know it. But you could be held liable for fines or imprisonment, or be required to publish corrective advertising telling the world you've lied, or any number of penalties for laws innocently violated.

We found out during prohibition that when laws are not respected, law and order breaks down. Our nation is built on a basic voluntary respect for its institutions and for law based on reason, which we firmly believe has been enacted by our elected representatives who are responsible to us, and who must curry our favor for reelection by pleasing us.

Perhaps you're not aware that government pay scales and GS ratings are based, to some extent, on the number of employees supervised by the individual being rated. Consequently, there is a built-in financial incentive accomplished by a multiplicity of regulations that need to be supervised, and require more enforcement, legal, and clerical staff.

Here's how this idiotic system hurts us.

1. It increases the costs of government so that the tax burden confiscates the money that might have been spent in the economy to stimulate business activity.

2. It increases the budget deficit to the point where money has to be created by government to pay its bills.

3. We lose our freedom bit by bit. I read a book recently by Rene Baxter. He used the analogy of Gulliver. As you recall, Gulliver was shipwrecked and washed ashore unconscious. When he woke up he

was tied down, not by a large thick rope or chains, but by thousands of threads, none of which individually had the power to bind him, but collectively were able to restrict his freedom, and he found himself in bondage to a race of tiny pygmies.

I believe we are rapidly reaching the point where we will be in bondage to the pygmies who run our bureaucracy. If we cannot choose which school our children attend, if we cannot decide to have a Fathers and Sons Banquet, if we cannot control those who are supposed to be serving us, then we have lost something far more precious than money. We've lost freedom.

There is no question about it. Regulatory agencies are "out of control" and can literally destroy the basis of freedom which built this country. We are the most powerful, productive, and influential nation on earth because of our freedom. When we lose that freedom, we will find ourselves beset with the same kind of troubles that plague Communist countries, and which are solved only by repression of the population.

But, remember, when you have all-powerful, all-seeing, all-knowing bureaucracies controlling every aspect of your life, you have lost your freedom. Controls can only proliferate. Unfortunately, rather than recognizing the root of the problem and freeing us of our shackles, most of those people who make our public policy have decided the best thing for us is "a little hair of the dog that bit us." More controls! More regulations! More misguided attempts to legislate out of our lives every problem that a bureaucrat can dream up to expand his influence within the bureaucracy! (see: Bureaucrats)

RUFF'S FIRST PRINCIPLE OF GOVERNMENT

(Special Report #2, 10/76) Perhaps the nation's greatest misdirected resource is Ralph Nader. Here is a man who performs a tremendous service in pointing out those things which are wrong with society, and then completely negates the value of that service by proposing the strengthening of government regulations, the passing of new laws, and the establishment of new government agencies to deal with these evils.

Ruff's First Principle of Government is: "When government solves a problem it invariably creates TWO problems of equal or greater dimensions." And the corollary to that law is: The true function of government is to make small problems WORSE."

Government regulatory agencies are truly out of control. They are trampling upon the rights of individual citizens and corporations. They are driving small businesses to the wall with the proliferation of rules which are impossible to follow, expensive to administer, and so easy to violate unknowingly. They trample on freedom of speech. They have the power to put you out of business temporarily before your guilt has been determined. The sheer amount of paperwork required by the FTC, IRS, OSHA, FDA, CAB, EPA and all the rest of the alphabet soup makes it virtually impossible to function unless you are large enough to have an army of accountants and lawyers.

They create one of the great hidden costs of government: the cost of dealing with Federal and local agencies, initially borne by business and industry, and eventually passed on to you, the consumer, in the form of higher prices.

THE WATCHBIRD AND RUFF'S REMEDIES

(10/15/77)   I'd like to devote some space to some remedies that might make it easier for us, as a nation, to get through the difficult years ahead. There are several constructive changes that might insure the survival of the Republic. If you agree, make a photocopy of this article and send it on to your congressman, senator, governor or state legislator. Ask for an answer and an opinion. The following story seems fitting.

The Legend Of The Watchbird—1999 A.D.
By Ray Bradbury

Man has finally achieved perfect freedom from violence. He has invented the WATCHBIRD—a system of intelligent, flying robots that blanket the Earth, programmed to detect violence before it occurs, and strike down the violent one before he can do harm. And they can transmit their experiences to each other, learn, and make increasingly sophisticated judgments.

Their first action prevented a New York mugging. Their second prevented the first shot of an African border war, to the cheers of a grateful world. The third struck down a hangman and prevented the death of a rapist. Then the Watchbird network decided animals should not be killed, and destroyed a slaughterhouse worker to save a hog. Soon the victims included a surgeon about to make an incision, a child pulling the wings off a fly, a nine-year-old schoolyard bully, a mother spanking a two-year-old, a farmer reaping his wheat (plants are living things). Within two days, every predatory animal—every lion, ferret, snake and spider—was dead, as the Watchbird expanded its definition of violence and performed his new self-appointed tasks.

When man recognized what he had made, he tried to deactivate his creation. The Watchbird concluded that he was also a living thing, and struck down his creator, and soon the Watchbird presided over a silent, but perfectly orderly world.

The greatest single threat to freedom and the free enterprise, capitalist system is the tremendous increase of governmental regulations, often freed from Constitutional restrictions. To review the principles:

1. For every law passed by elected bodies in the United States, there are now 11 regulations passed by unelected bureaucrats, which are binding upon you and often have the force of law, with criminal penalties, including jail and fines.

If they are defeated in the courts, they often repeat the process in another jurisdiction until you are bankrupt. We generally knuckle under. We'll knuckle under to the IRS if the money involved is smaller than the legal fees it would take to fight it. So government often wins by default, simply because they can throw their battalions of attorneys at you. Constitutional guarantees don't apply. The Supreme Court has ruled 8-0 that you are not entitled to jury trials in administrative proceedings.

Let's say the FDA claims that your health food store is in violation of the labeling laws, because on one shelf you sell a book advocating vitamin C for the common cold, while the vitamins are on the other side of the store. This constitutes "misbranding" of the product by "claiming a cure" for it, which, by their rules, makes a drug. They can then arrest you and your clerk, and confiscate the vitamins and burn the books under current regulations. And you are bankrupted even if you should win the legal battle. Most health food store owners don't have the resources to fight, so freedom of speech and freedom of the press are stifled.

If the IRS comes after you, as they did Harry Margolis, you lose, even if you win. Harry Margolis is a San Francisco tax attorney who utilized what he felt were legitimate loopholes in the IRS code. He set up off-shore tax havens in the Cayman Islands for his clients. The IRS knew he would, but this was done simply as a lesson to any enterprising attorney or accountant who attempts to take advantage of gray areas in the IRS code. The IRS didn't care if they lost. Harry Margolis has been dealt a severe financial blow, and I'm sure the lesson is not lost, as every tax consultant in America was watching.

So here is my proposal, Ruff's Remedies, if you please.

1. We need simple legislation stating that, if a Federal agency brings an action and the citizen or corporation prevails in the courts, the agency will pay all legal fees and out-of-pocket expenses of the defendant, and must advance the money for the defense, if the defendant is unable to pay for his defense. This will reduce Federal bullying, and enable people to fight when government comes down on them unfairly.

2. The trial procedures should be separated from the agencies. Under the present system, the agency decides whether to bring action, acts as a grand jury, then prosecutes and tries the merits of their own case, before its own administrative judges. The hearing examiners (judges) are subordinates to the heads of the agencies who are bringing the action. The potential for mischief, and the built-in bias shoud be obvious to anyone. We must set up a separate examiner agency. This would not add to the number of present government employees, but would merely separate this already existing function. We need to clearly establish by statute that all Constitutional guarantees, including freedom of the press, of speech and of jury trial, are applicable, just as though it were an action brought by a law enforcement agency.

These procedures would eliminate much of the abuse. It falls way short of solving the whole problem, as most government regulation is harmful. But at least it would be a step in the right direction toward helping the "little guy" under assault by government.

These steps will not save the Republic from the troubles we face, but will give us a heck of a lot better chance of getting through it with our institutions intact.

FDA

(7/1/76)   The Food and Drug Administration is charged with the protection of the nation's health. The nation's health has not noticeably improved because of them, has it?

They reacted to the Thalidomide tragedy by making it so difficult, time consuming, and expensive to clear a new drug application that many effective, life saving drugs, in use for years in other civilized countries, are illegal here. They require extensive animal testing, before the drug can be used on human volunteers. Fleming, the discoverer of Penicillin, said that his drug could not have been developed today. It causes such severe side effects in rats and dogs that it could not have gotten through the FDA to the human volunteer stage.

Many drug discoveries are dropped because the bureaucratic costs of a new drug application are so high that it becomes uneconomical to continue to develop and market a drug that might save only 5,000 or 10,000 lives. The market is too small to support the artificial costs of government regulation.

Because of the FDA, you probably pay 50% more for drugs and vitamins and are denied the use of effective remedies. Your freedom of choice is impaired, and if you seek illegal drugs in other countries where they are legal, and bring them home, you can be jailed for smuggling.

I've watched the vitamin and health food industries locked in a death struggle with the FDA, with the industry screaming about the preservation of everyone's freedom to be able to take the vitamin of their choice. Then I see the same people screaming for the FDA to regulate or ban food additives. On the one hand they claim freedom is at stake, on the other, they want stricter regulation of the bad guy.

This is a microcosm of society. "Give me freedom, but there ought to be a law to put that bad guy in his place." We can't have it both ways. As Pogo says, "We have seen the enemy and he is us."

(4/15/77)   Rat Poison

The best way to kill rats is to give them cancer, using huge injections of SACCHARIN directly into their bladders. From this it is reasoned that saccharin causes cancer in humans. Saccharin may not seem an appropriate subject for *THE RUFF TIMES,* but stay with me, I have a very important point to make and some recommendations, and it involves your freedom.

Under the DELANEY AMENDMENT, passed by Congress, any substance found to cause cancer in laboratory animals must be banned by the FDA. It seems that giving rats the daily equivalent of 800 cans of soda pop worth of saccharin gave them tumors. Obviously, no human being is going to consume that much saccharin, so the decision to ban saccharin is silly. Right? Wrong! And right, too.

Animal experiments, using massive doses of chemicals compress into a relatively small number of experimental animals the equivalent experience of very large numbers of human beings. The risk, based on the rat studies, is quite high for the population of the United States. If you drank ten cans of diet soda each day, the odds of developing cancer would be four cases per 1,000 persons. One can a day during a lifetime would result in four cases per 10,000 persons—a very low probability. But this adds up to 120,000 cancer cases a year. That's two and one-half times as many cancer cases as we have highway fatalities.

Not everyone in America uses saccharin, so there wouldn't be 120,000 cases of cancer, but the incidence of cancer would be a major health risk.

Now we come to the question I'm trying to get at. Assuming it does represent a health threat to Americans, should saccharin be banned?

The answer is no.

I have no objection to the FDA being required to label each saccharin product in big letters, to the effect that it has produced cancer in experimental animals. I even think people ought not to use saccharin. I'm opposed to the consumption of additives in our food and certainly in such unnecessary things as soda pop. Not that any one of them might kill you, but we are ingesting from three to seven pounds per American per year, and no one knows what the effect of the combination of these chemicals will be. We don't know whether it's going to sterilize the third generation or cause every sixth American to turn green. Nobody has the slightest idea. All of the animal experiments are based on the administration of one isolated chemical. What is the combined effect of thousands? What is the cumulative effect? What is the effect on future generations? No one knows. I prefer to eat a diet as low in colorings, preservatives, flavor enhancers, etc., as possible. This is especially true of my food storage program. But we still shouldn't ban saccharin by law. Let me choose for myself! Disclosure is O.K.

And now the crowning blow. The Supreme Court just ruled 8 to 0 that the Seventh Amendment, guaranteeing jury trials, does not apply when you are under attack by a government regulatory agency. They just held, in a case with OSHA (Occupational Safety and Health Administration), that the defendant was not entitled to a jury trial and that the Seventh Amendment right was not absolute. This is utterly incredible. Our forefathers recognized that we had a right to a trial by a jury of our peers. Remember, if you are a businessman attacked by OSHA or the FTC, or a seller of vitamins under assault by the FDA, or any other target of bureaucratic meddling, the penalties can be as severe as a criminal offense. And you will be tried by the agency that is accusing you. That is bad enough, but now you cannot have a jury trial if the agency doesn't want you to. This is one of the most serious Constitutional threats since the founding of this Republic. It is not possible to overstate the seriousness of this matter.

President Ford started a commission on Federal paperwork, enthusiastically seconded by President Carter. This was an attempt to reduce the paperwork load on businessmen. Trying to reduce paperwork without reducing the regulatory activities of government is the equivalent of launching a massive attack on fever while at the same time encouraging the spread of disease. This regulatory monster will inundate us. It can be the difference between survival and failure of a small business during its formative years. The small businessman cannot remain price competitive, simply because the costs of regulation are so great. Government regulation may be the death of the American entrepreneur.

Then there is science and government. When regulations are passed in areas that are essentially scientific, government begins setting standards by which fraud is judged. For example, the whole vitamin and protein supplement controversy is based on the opinion of mainstream nutritionists. They say supplements are useless. However, a very talented and respected minority vigorously disagrees, and says they are essential to the health of the country and that everyone should be using them. This includes such men as Dr. Roger Williams, a Nobel Prize winner at the University of Texas, Dr. Linus Pauling, and many others of equal credentials. The FDA holds hearings and sets up regulations governing potencies and allowable doses. The majority opinion is frozen into law, and it becomes "consumer fraud" to advocate unpopular views or the minority position. It becomes illegal to compete in the free marketplace with products and ideas which do not adhere to a government approved conclusion. It can even become dangerous to continue research to demonstrate otherwise, as you come up against the great power of the government propaganda mills. Bureaucrats never back down. They never make a mistake, and as a result, scientific progress screeches to a halt, frozen into concrete, based on the current consensus.

To see how dangerous this is, just look at the long list of advancements in science and medicine which resulted in the ridicule and heartbreak of the great pioneers. The electro-cardiograph, the electro-encephalograph, Dr. Lister and his germ theory of disease, the poly-unsaturated fat approach to the reduction of the risk of heart disease, not to mention Galileo.

Today, Lister would not only have to fight the AMA, but they would have behind them the regulatory power of government, which would jail and fine him for promoting his unpopular views.

(4/15/77) Now, I do not question that the government has done some good. By isolating the facts, you could array an impressive mountain of evidence in favor of government benefits. That's precisely why it exists. It does provide benefits. All I'm trying to say is that the benefits are far outweighed by the long-term damage. It is an uneconomical tradeoff.

One of these days we will wake up and find that every aspect of our life is so controlled that freedom is gone and the economy has been paralyzed and stagnated. It is a great force out of control, which assures that a great American productive machine will sooner or later creak and groan to a halt.

My only consolation is that when the major collapse comes, and government repudiates its debt, it will be so impaired in its functioning that all of this immense regulatory apparatus will wither away, and American business will rise unshackled from the ashes like the Phoenix of old, and perhaps we will not repeat these same mistakes for a hundred years or so. Just be grateful we aren't getting all the government we're paying for.

(1/1/78) Government regulations kill people. I've previously pointed out how FDA drug regulations have postponed or completely blocked the development of drugs that would save lives. Now, in the recent grain elevator explosions, you have a perfect example of mindless government at work. These chain explosions completely destroyed four huge grain elevator storage complexes. Grain dust is up to fifteen times more explosive than coal dust, and an explosion is easily set off when the humidity drops below 35 percent or 40 percent. The obvious answer is to vent the accumulated dust out of the silos. However, EPA rules prevent this, as it would pollute the atmosphere. Well, O.K. Let's use humidifiers to raise the humidity level above the flash point. Oops! This is forbidden by the FDA, which says that the increased moisture would "adulterate" the grain. So the dust accumulates, and as a result, more than 50 people have died and millions of bushels of grain are gone, all because of stupid, mindless government.

FTC

(Special Report #2, 10/76) In McCammon, Idaho, a local plumbing inspector invited himself to John Schoonover's house to "check his plumbing." He had a vent from the bathroom toilet through the wall to the roof, which was fractionally smaller than 3 inches in diameter, but perfectly functional. According to the National Plumbing Code, this is a misdemeanor, punishable by a $10 fine. Schoonover offered to pay the fine, but was refused and cited with a felony complaint that could send him to prison for five years. To replace the present vent pipe with another slightly larger one, walls from the lower level bathroom to the roof needed to be torn out. So Schoonover went to court. He is now contemplating a court order to modify the plumbing in his house, or else. The prosecuting attorney advised Schoonover that if he pursued the case further, other technical violations will be found. Three times, this bureaucrat of the bathroom has walked into the Schoonover house uninvited—once when no one was home. He is legally immune to prosecution for trespassing.

Recently, the Federal Trade Commission has moved to expand its powers. Under legislation passed by Congress last year, the Commission now has authority to go immediately to court against persons suspected of evil doing.

The Federal Trade Commission now wishes to take legal action in the following areas: advertising that misrepresents potential earnings for business opportunities; deceptive demonstrations; testimonials or endorsements on behalf of products or services (Joe Namath can't sell pantyhose).

I would be all for the FTC's objectives, but power in the hands of these bureaucrats is being constantly abused, and the business cost of defending against frivolous actions by government is always passed on to you, the consumer.

According to *NEWSWEEK* magazine, this great web of protective legislation, may cost the average American family over $2,000 a year. If it continues at its present growth rate of eight percent a year for the next two decades, the cost of regulatory government will be 58% of the gross national product, and most Americans would find themselves working more than half their time just to pay for their own chains. We have put the razor to our own wrists.

(4/15/77) Some years ago the FTC was doing a routine "surveillance" of advertising, and ran across my weight control program ad. One of their newest field repesentatives came to see me, and I gave him all of my materials to examine. He informed me that my advertising was "fraudulent." It seems that when I said the program was guaranteed, I did not state the full text of the guarantee in the ad. When I stated that we had highly trained counselors, we didn't list them by name and state their qualifications in detail. I was using a certain brand of vitamins in our program and he wanted me to put in the ad that all people on the program would be required to use that particular brand of vitamins, and so on, ad infinitum, ad nauseam. They were all granted a money-back guarantee if, after reading all of the materials, they decided they didn't want to go on the program. And we had records proving that I had scrupulously honored that guarantee. If I had done as he wanted, it would have doubled the size of my ad, the cost of which would have been passed on to the customer.

They prepared a "consent decree" for me to sign. A consent decree is an interesting document in which you say you haven't done anything wrong, and you promise not to do it anymore. It is published in the newspaper and all of the government allegations are included in the press release, along with your statement that, without admitting guilt, you agree not to do it anymore. I knew I had done nothing fraudulent. I finally told them I refused to sign. He said, "Well then, we will have to take legal action." I said, "Fine. Go ahead. I will fight you." He then said, "You don't have the financial resources to fight us. You will be bankrupt before you get past the first appeal process." I said to him, "I've already been bankrupt once. That doesn't scare me at all and I'll fight you from every radio and T.V. show and newspaper interview that I can get, and I'll name you personally."

He went away and I didn't hear a thing for six months. Finally, I received a letter signed by the High Commissioner in Washington, D.C. saying, in effect, that they had decided not to take any action against me at this time. But that didn't mean that I hadn't done anything wrong, or that they might not change their minds later, so "watch your step, buddy." They had no case and they knew it. All they wanted was a trophy scalp to dangle from their belt.

Many of our subscribers are small businessmen strangled by government regulation. As this monster grows, the American dream of starting on a shoestring and becoming wealthy will be lost. Whether the Socialists like it or not, that is the basic strength of America. The government will have cut off our roots.

(12/15/78) Would You Buy A Used Car From This Government?
FORBES recently carried a fascinating article on the FTC's proposed used car window sticker. Somebody in Carter's inflation-fighting program ought to take a look at this one because it's going to add billions of dollars to the cost of used cars in America. And guess

who buys those used cars? The poor, the blacks, and others who have too much month at the end of their money, that's who.

When you buy a used car you are buying someone else's problems, but the government has decided to protect us all. They are proposing the accompanying sticker. Look it over carefully. This means that the used car dealer will be responsible for anything that goes wrong with the car during a warranty period, after you buy the car. The vice president of the National Automobile Dealers Association says it will cost $200 or more to inspect a car well enough to fill out the sticker. The government says it's only $15, but you can't even get a mechanic to raise the hood for that. And that's just the pure inspection cost, not including the cost of repairs.

If the dealer marks something "not OK," you pay the cost of fixing it. If they mark something "OK," the dealer is required to pay the cost if it breaks down. And it doesn't matter whether you buy the car with a warranty or "as is." I don't think that's fair. This means that when a dealer sells a car, he has no idea what his liability might be for eventual problems that were not apparent on inspection. If he has any sense at all, he will jack up the price $100 to $200 to protect himself. There ain't no free lunch. They are not imposing this same requirement on individuals who sell a used car, because according to the FTC, "individuals are more honest than used car dealers."

This is another example in a miles-long list of dumb-headed efforts on the part of government to protect us from everything under the sun without weighing the cost. The cost of creating a perfectly risk-free world is beyond the ability of any society to pay. It doesn't seem to be beyond the ability of any government to fantasize. This proposal should be laughed into oblivion. I know I might offend some people who are interested in "consumer protection," but I am also interested in the consumer's pocketbook. It's just one more assumption of authority way beyond the statutory intent of the legislation that set up the Federal Trade Commission in the first place.

(2/1/79) The Federal Trade Commission has me between an ethical rock and an emotional hard place! I've been watching with great interest the fuss between them and the cold cereal industry over the FTC's desire to regulate advertising on children's television shows. Here is a classic, clear-cut example of the debate between government paternalism and free market forces.

On the one hand, I have a visceral, emotional reaction in favor of anybody who will help me to keep my children from being seduced into begging for fattening, tooth-rotting cereals. Apparently some of my kids have inherited my predisposition to sugar addiction, and in the case of one child, a persistent weight problem. To that child, sugar-loaded cereals are like alcohol to an alcoholic, or dope to a junkie.

My kids are like your kids on Saturday morning. They like to get up and watch their cartoon heroes, and because Saturday morning is the one time I can sometimes sleep in, when I do go downstairs they have been watching those deceptive commercials for an hour or two.

I'd really appreciate some help. Many of those cereals contain up to 40 percent sugar, and all of their advertising is directed at children. It's deceitful and immensely seductive.

On the other hand, the FTC is one of the more dangerous of the "Watchbirds," and now they are posing as my friend, protecting my children from the "Cookie Monster." The FTC has found the perfect issue. On their side will be every parent who worries as I do about my kids, but who does not understand the corrupt, sugar-coated nature of government regulation. Arrayed against them will be an unlovely self-interest group of cereal and toy manufacturers, network advertising executives, ad agencies, and a few lonely free market voices. Those easy-to-hate corporate so-and-so's in the cereal industry, who don't care what they do to my kids' teeth, will be hiding behind the legitimate freedom issue. They are precisely the kind of predatory wolves I would just as soon not have on my side.

How do you resolve the dilemma? Well, I've got to come down on the side of freedom. It's my responsibility to regulate my kids' diet and their TV viewing habits, not the FTC's. It's my responsibility to instill in them sound principles of good nutrition and healthy eating so they will, of their own volition, decide to stay away from those things. It is my responsibility to get up early and sit with them when they watch those commercials, and tell them all of the sneaky, deceitful things that are built into those potent messages. It is my responsibility to encourage my wife to plan good healthful breakfasts that are so attractive they won't want that junk. And, unfortunately in this case, it's also my responsibility to defend the free marketplace of even unattractive ideas. I would support a district attorney who would go after those people in the courts for fraud, but not on the basis of our need to be protected from a potentially harmful product.

I detest tobacco and alcohol, but I defend the right of these people to expose their products to the marketplace of ideas. To complicate the issues still further, I concede that our children should be protected against certain things. I am in favor of a free press, but I'd like local laws with stiff penalties for allowing pornography and mind altering chemicals, including alcohol, to get into the hands of children. My only real defense against pornography is parental training, and the creation in my home of such healthy attitudes toward sex that my kids don't have to go after illicit thrills in a quest for sexual knowledge. In other words, it is my responsibility and that of my wife to protect and educate my children against assaults on their minds and bodies. We live in a free marketplace of ideas and we must keep it that way. We should not abdicate our responsibilities to some government agency.

And heck, some people have decided that some things said on my TV show are dangerous, and I don't want to arm government with a sword to use on my enemies, because they might use it against me.

Every loss of freedom is preceded by a popular demand that the government "do something." I want to clip the wings of the FTC, not give them more statutory authority. I don't want them to win this fight. I'll take care of my kids. Let's all take care of the FTC. Remember The Watchbird!

EPA

(7/1/76)   The Environmental Protection Agency will protect the air and water by raising the cost of your new house or apartment. Construction can be delayed for one to two years for new developments, while an "Environmental Impact Report" is approved. In the meantime, inflation increases the cost of construction 25 percent a year, taxes on the land pile up to be passed on to you, the buyer, and the house or apartment might end up being priced out of your reach by the time construction is complete, and your freedom of choice is limited.

Regulators initiate actions against corporations and individuals to meet quotas, to grind an ideological axe, or through sheer stupidity. And they never have to pay for their mistakes.

PIONEERS SAVED

(9/15/76)   From this fictitious report, which appeared in my newsletter a last years several sincere inquiries were generated. It's really just for laughs—really!

(September 23, 1859)
    North Platte, Nebraska (UPI) The Federal Trade Commission and Department of Transportation, together with the Department

of Commerce, have just recalled all stagecoaches of the Wells Fargo Company and the Bison model of the soft-top vehicles manufactured by the Connestoga Wagon Company of Independence, Missouri.

The noted consumer advocate, JIM BRIDGER, pointed out that high-speed motion pictures taken of an Oregon-bound wagon train being chased by Indians, showed that the wheels tend to turn backwards, creating a safety hazard.

It is anticipated that westward migration will be delayed up to two years, and some families will be forced to bivouac along the Oregon Trail.

Washington has assured the travelers that food relief shipments, food stamps, and Federal troops will be provided. They were also assured that they would be on their way within two years.

(see: Bureaucrats; Government, Big; and Government Debt)

THE LITTLE RED HEN

(9/1/76) Once upon a time, there was a little red hen who scratched about the barnyard until she uncovered some grains of wheat. She called her neighbors and said, "If we plant this wheat, we shall have bread to eat. Who will help me plant it?"

"Not I," said the cow. "Not I," said the duck. "Not I," said the pig. "Not I," said the goose. "Then I will," she said. And she did.

The wheat grew tall and ripened into golden grain. "Who will help me reap my wheat?" asked the little red hen.

"Not I," said the duck. "Out of my classification," said the pig. "I'd lose my seniority," said the cow. "I'd lose my unemployment compensation," said the goose. "Then I will," she said. And she did.

At last it came time to bake the bread. "Who will help me bake the bread?" asked the little red hen.

"That would be overtime for me," said the cow. "I'd lose my welfare benefits," said the duck. "I'm a dropout and never learned how," said the pig. "If I'm to be the only helper, that's discrimination," said the goose. "Then I will," said the little red hen.

She baked five loaves and held them up for her neighbors to see. They all wanted some, and, in fact, demanded a share, but the little red hen said, "No, I can eat the five loaves myself."

"Excess profits!" cried the cow. "Capitalist leech!" screamed the duck. "I demand equal rights!" yelled the goose. And the pig just grunted and they painted "UNFAIR" picket signs and marched round and round the little red hen, shouting obscenities.

When the government agent came, he said to the little red hen, "You must not be greedy."

"But I earned the bread," said the little red hen.

"Exactly," said the agent. "That is the wonderful free enterprise system. Anyone in the barnyard can earn as much as he wants, but under the modern government regulations, the productive workers must divide their product with the idle."

And they lived happily ever after, including the little red hen who smiled and clucked, "I am grateful. I am grateful."

But her neighbors wondered why she never baked bread anymore.

THE CLAUS CLAUSE

(1/15/77) If you noticed a different pattern in Santa Claus' visits to your children last year, you can blame it on government. This is an exclusive for *THE RUFF TIMES*. It has come to our attention that during the months of August and September there were six weeks of secret hearings in Washington, D.C. The star of the show was S. Claus from Northern Alaska and he was in Washington at the demand of the Federal Trade Commission. It soon will be announced that Santa entered into a consent decree with the FTC. Without admitting guilt, he agreed that beginning in 1976 there would be no discrimination between "naughty" and "nice" in his gift-giving to children.

This infamous decision has taken away one of the last weapons at the disposal of parent in maintaining authority over their children.

This is but another example of government intrusion into our private lives.

RUGGED INDIVIDUALISTS

(3/15/78) A young man attended public school, rode the free school bus, and participated in the subsidized lunch program. He entered the Army, and upon discharge retained his National Service Insurance. He then attended the state university on the GI Bill.

Upon graduation, he married a public health nurse and bought a farm with an FHA loan, and then obtained an RFC an to go into business. A baby was born in the county hospital.

Later he put part of his land in the soil bank, and the payments helped pay for his farm and ranch. His father and mother lived on the ranch on their Social Security; REA lines supplied electricity. The government helped clear his land. The county agent showed him how to terrace it, then the government built him a fishpond and stocked it with fish.

Books from the public library were delivered to his door. He banked his money and a government agency insured it. His children attended public schools, rode free school buses, played in the public parks, and swam in the public pools.

He was a leader in obtaining the new Federal building, and went to Washington with a group to ask the government to build a great dam. He petitioned the government to give the local air base to the county.

Then one day, after hearing that Carter's $500 billion budget for 1978 added up to $2,000 for every man, woman, and child, he wrote his Congressman:

> I wish to protest these excessive governmental expenditures and attendant high taxes. I believe in rugged individualism. I think people should stand on their own two feet without expecting handouts. I am opposed to all socialistic trends and I demand a return to the principles of our Constitution and of state rights.
> ... Author Unknown. (Edited slightly)

The same guy is probably voting for the Jarvis-Gann Property Tax Initiative in California and the Liberty Amendment to eliminate deficit spending.

The above story illustrates why I believe a tragedy will play itself out and the process is irreversible. Everyone thinks they benefit from the status quo. There is a chance, however, that such movements as the Liberty Amendment or the Jarvis-Gann Property Tax Initiative will bring the system tumbling down a lot faster.

SPEED LIMIT

(2/15/79)   While walking down Michigan Avenue in Chicago, I was stopped by a television reporter doing a "Man on the Street" interview. It was pretty funny, I had just done three TV shows. He asked my opinion of the bill introduced by Senator Hayakawa to set aside the 55 mile an hour speed limit. My answer was, "55 miles an hour has saved a lot of lives. Why don't we make it 15 miles an hour and save the rest of them." My brilliant, sardonic wit was somehow lost on him.

FROM A TO Z

If gasoline prices rise, people will find they can't afford to drive as much, so a lot of discretionary driving will disappear. In the meantime, the Wyoming legislature has voted to rescind the 55 mile an hour limit, and they will lose some $75 million in Federal highway funds. The threat of withdrawing those funds is the Federal club that bullies the states into enforcing this limit. The question of lives saved is really a relative one, as you obviously could eliminate all traffic death by banning the automobile. Who knows what the optimum safe speed limit is? I do know that I spend many more hours on the road than I ordinarily would because of that speed limit, and I get sleepier than I would have without it, and a sleepy driver is a menace.

RENT/RENTING

(9/15/76) Should you buy a home or pay rent? It depends on where you live. In the large cities, I think I'd rent. In the outer suburbs, or on a farm, or in a small town, I'd buy. But if I rented in a big city, I'd sure be planning where to go when the city becomes untenable. (see: Real Estate, Personal Property)

RETIREMENT PLANS

KEOGH PLANS

(7/1/78) I don't generally like IRA and Keogh plans. They are based on the assumption that if you can set aside tax deferred money for retirement into an investment fund and have it earn for you, when you do take it out years from now, you will supposedly be in a lower tax bracket. With an IRA (for wage earners not covered under a company retirement plan) you can set aside up to 15 percent of your income up to a maximum $1,500 of your wages, tax deferred each year. The Keogh (for self-employed) is 15 percent of net business income to a $7,500 maximum, as of this writing.

If they are such a good deal, why don't I like them?

1. I don't think it's a safe assumption that you will be in a lower tax bracket later on. Inflation is accelerating us all into higher tax brackets. The odds are you will be in an equal or higher bracket and the tax savings will be nonexistent.

2. Rising inflation will chew up capital faster than you earn interest.

3. They are inflexible. It is difficult, costly, or impossible to switch them from one kind of investment to another, and in this changing environment you need to be able to switch between hard money and paper without severe tax penalties.

4. I am most concerned with the programs offered by insurance companies and savings and loans which are totally inflexible and oriented in the direction of paper investments.

There are some Keogh plans allowing purchase of gold and diamonds, which makes them more acceptable. That's the only way I would do it. As I see it, with inflation at its current levels and climbing, they are simply guaranteed instruments of confiscation over the long haul.

(1/1/79)   Gold Keogh

I've just received a note from Ronald O. Holland, Assistant Vice President and Trust Officer of the First-Citizens Bank & Trust Company, P.O. Box 3028, Greenville, SC 29602. The text is as follows:

> Dear Mr. Ruff:
> The Trust Department of First-Citizens Bank and Trust Company sponsors a Self-Employed Retirement Plan (Keogh) in which an owner-employee may direct investment in Krugerrands, coins, gold, etc.
> If you have questions or desire additional information, please call me at 803-271-8844.

Sounds interesting. You should check it out. I'll be interested in hearing what kind of service you receive.

RETREATS

AN INTERVIEW WITH SURVIVAL WRITER DON STEPHENS

(11/75)

HJR: Don, I appreciate your taking time for this interview for the first regular issue of *THE RUFF TIMES*. First, I'd like to tell our readers you are probably the best-known writer on the subject of survival. You've spent many years writing for prominent newsletters, including *INFLATION SURVIVAL LETTER* and *MCKEEVER'S MISL.* You've studied dehydrated and freeze-dried food storage companies. You are a consultant on retreats and, like me, a controversial character.

Why do you feel that the group retreat concept is necessary? I'm not converted to it, but I'm sympathetic to those who are, as I understand their concern. I want our readers to have an opportunity to make up their own minds on this issue. What is a retreat?

DS: Retreating means having an alternate lifestyle to turn to if you feel that the way that you are living now may no longer be feasible in a big city due to a shortage of food or collapse of the monetary system, or, possibly, nuclear war!

HJR: Then would you say that the people you deal with believe there is a high likelihood that society is heading for some very abrupt changes and they want to prepare for it?

DS: They are at least concerned about the possibility.

HJR: Is there more than one basic approach to retreating?

DS: Yes. Many. The simplest approach would be for a person who lives in a less populated area to simply establish a retreat within his home. He puts aside food and other essential supplies he feels he might not be able to obtain later. He puts aside silver coins for exchanges which could not be made with worthless paper money. If his conscience tells him it's the right thing to do, he can put aside arms to protect against those who will not be as well prepared.

The second alternative would be location. People who feel that they live in hazardous areas might decide to own a home in a small town away from populated areas where they feel that the people would be more self-sufficient and more cooperative under crisis conditions.

Some might want to continue their lifestyle, with an option of having a motor home, possibly with a trailer behind it stocked with supplies, fuel, etc., to get away from the populated area and ahead for a rural or a wilderness area where he can start a new life with what he is carrying with him. This would be a "land mobile approach."

The next alternative would be an individual retreat in the woods somewhere, or at an isolated spring in the middle of the desert somewhere away from people. They would build a home, or a mobile home, or a modular house. There should be space for gardening, an orchard, perhaps a pond where they could raise fish, and some wild planting and salt licks for the attraction of game, so they could live off the land.

The last step would be to join a group retreat where they would have predetermined neighbors with a variety of professional skills—doctors, lawyers, dentists, farmers, foresters and hunters. In essence, they would be transplanting a community to a remote area. Each family would have its own food supply and the potential of exchanging skills to the extent that it was mutually profitable.

I learned a long time ago from Harry Browne the importance of knowing the difference between the things you control and can predict, and those which you do not control and cannot predict. So, I can't say for sure what I'm preparing for but I can say what I'm concerned about, and I think this generally reflects the concerns of my clients.

Their primary concern is that this country, over a period of the last 50 to 100 years, has based its whole approach toward living on interdependence rather than independence. A person in one part of the country is dependent upon fuel from other parts of the country or other parts of the world for his automobile and to heat his home. He is dependent upon food grown a thousand miles away, or possibly in another country half a world away to stock his table. For defense and protection from law breakers, he's dependent upon a professional law enforcement staff financed by taxation, which may or may not remain effective. In every instance these things are lubricated by money. He obtains the things that he needs through exchanging money, and, of course, the money supply is losing its value rapidly.

I expect inflation to increase, with temporary interims, until money loses all value. Once it gets there, there is instability in distribution. So, we move from interdependence, to a vulnerability of our money supply, to a shortage of food resulting from breakdown and this is where civilization really comes unglued. As long as a man has a full stomach and his children are well fed, tomorrow may look bleak, but it has promise. When his children are starving and he can't get more food for them, and his money is worthless, he may turn to violence. This could result in the breakdown of our normal systems.

For example, we depend on the fire department. In Los

Angeles, one of the larger storage food distributors has told me that among their major clients are policemen and firemen. Many of them have retreats as well. When a fireman has a food supply at home, he might be hesitant about leaving his family while he goes out to fight a fire in another part of town. The same thing with the policemen. We may have a situation in which the police are not reporting to duty because they are at home protecting their own families, or they have left for their retreats. Once fires get started, they could spread, so large portions of cities might well go up in fire storms.

On the other end of the spectrum, in remote areas or the farming communities or wooded areas where the population density is low, the effects of the whole thing might be very minor.

HJR: What percentage of probability would you, in your opinion, assign to the worst type of collapse that you have been talking about?

DS: I would guess that it depends upon time. I would say that the sooner collapse occurs, the less drastic it would be. If we get the full collapse with total loss of faith in the money system, where paper money is not accepted at all, and with it the government fails to function, we are talking about maybe ten percent of the people in the cities getting out, so maybe five percent who remain in the cities survive.

A friend of mine who is in computer work has done some profile projections, models, whatever you want to call them, feeding in as many factors as he can, relating to fuel availability, depletion of agricultural potential, weather patterns, and has come up with the fact that by 1985, 1986, at the latest, these things are all going to come to a crashing intersection, if it hasn't hit before then.

HJR: As a certified member of the "Prophets of Doom and Gloom," I suddenly find myself in the unaccustomed position of being on the sunny side of one of the calamity issues, as compared to you, Don.

My study of financial panics and famine indicates that, generally, periods of chaos and difficulty are relatively short lived, that order is generally restored quickly, even if it is through totalitarian means. I've been postulating that you'll have a relatively short period of violence and distribution breakdown, that there will be two or three very difficult years and probably a period of rather stagnant recovery, and the world will be permanently changed in many ways. I have not, in my wildest vision of calamity, foreseen 85 percent to 95 percent of the population losing their lives, as you have forecast several times in the past. To assume that 90 percent of the people in the populated area will lose their lives assumes that no food will be distributed. It assumes that the other 10 percent will probably kill for it. That doesn't seem reasonable.

DS: My feeling is that a small percentage of those who die will actually die at the hand of another human being. I think that there will be many people who will die of nothing more than the shock of the situation, as much as several months after the initial crisis. Another large percentage of people will suffer from disease or drought.

Our cities, Los Angeles is a classic example, are almost totally dependent upon water pumped by power from far distances. It must be distributed and purified to make it safe, so I would guess that we probably are talking about all of the "horsemen of the Apocalypse." I would guess that hunger will take a number of people, fire will take a sizeable number of the people, particularly in older wood construction areas of the city.

HJR: I think we will agree to disagree on that. It is my opinion that mankind has more resilience. In my studies of famine and financial panics, I've seen a mortality rate of eight percent to 10 percent, with possibly the exception of the days of the black plague where 40 percent of the population was lost. It has been my opinion, and I think it still is, that depression and financial collapse can create difficult, dangerous times, with sickness, illness, famine and epidemics; but even in the great San Francisco earthquake, where something like 55 percent of the buildings were either damaged or destroyed, the mortality rate was less than two percent of the people. So let's agree to disagree on that! I think we can both agree that the people should prepare for hard times.

(12/75)   Don Stephens Interview, cont.

HJR: The "group retreat" concept has received some recent publicity, most of it unfavorable, particularly relative to one retreat in Northern California where the media chose to tee-off on it as an example of exploitation of fear by money-hungry promoters who reap unconscionable profits. Let me hear you respond to that.

DS: I think there are a number of reasons why it isn't unfair exploitation. In fact, I would compare that with one that is very clearly exploitation. One of the largest financial interests in this country is the life insurance industry. I'm not talking about term insurance where a person agrees to bet a certain amount against the company that he will die and the company would have to pay. I'm talking about "cash value" insurance as one of the most unconscionable exploitations around. (see: Insurance) If you bought a "whole life" policy in 1965 and cashed it in today, you would have lost 50% or more of your buying power.

   The retreat concept, with assets appreciating in value in the group retreat, is a response to people's genuine concerns. It provides them with these three things: 1) Peace of mind, 2) Recreational potential between now and such time as they should need it for emergencies, and 3) Real life insurance —living insurance when and if they need it.

   I haven't seen anyone making any huge profits in group retreats and if I had, I would certainly expose them to my clients. But knowing as intimately as I do a number of projects, I too am concerned about these firms being able to make a reasonable profit.

HJR: Let's dig a little deeper into that particular question. If a promoter of a group retreat buys some mountain land cheaply and charges ten or fifteen thousand dollars for a small lot to put a trailer or store some food, that's an extremely high mark up. He has to have some high expenses somewhere. What are they?

DS: With the exception of one in the Caribbean, I don't know of a group retreat that is charging $15,000 for a membership.

   First of all, the group retreat developer has to spend a good deal of time and, in many cases, consultation fees with myself and other people to establish criteria for what kind of facilities that would be necessary in order to have a valid group retreat. Second, he has to spend a great deal of time looking for the right piece of land, because once those criteria are established, it may take six months to a year and an examination of hundreds or more pieces of property to find the one that, with a free conscience, he can offer as a group retreat.

   Most sellers look for at least 29% down on a large parcel of land. This capital comes from the developer's pocket. You can't sell what you haven't got. Now he has to develop the property in order to make it saleable. It must provide visual shelter and seclusion and water. It must have disposal capabilities. It must be defendable, and have access capabilities. It must have access developed to each location where people can set up their trailers or mobile homes or whatever.

HJR: How large a piece of land goes with a membership?

DS: I generally recommend from two to five acres per family. Compare this with an eighth or a sixteenth of an acre lot in a trailer court for the same money. This means longer distances to run water lines and waste disposal lines. The waste disposal system must be self-sufficient, rather than hook up to the city sewer system. It means an independent water supply and purification system. You need power generating equipment, electric lines to the various lots, which again are scattered more widely and require much more line per house than a conventional development.

HJR: Some group retreats have had a lot of publicity and newspapers have published where they can be found and how to get there. This could draw unwanted attention to you. Promoters of group retreats do have to let the world know they are there or they don't sell their memberships. And what about the individual retreat in the mountains, isolated from help. I've always considered this dangerous. Perhaps you would be better lost in the anonymity of the masses, if you could quietly stockpile the basic supplies. How do you compare the relative safety factors?

DS: A group retreat in the wrong location with sufficient publicity and an inadequate capability to protect itself could be a very deadly place to be. On the other hand, I think that either a group or an individual retreat can be a relatively safe solution if it's planned and set up right. The idea of blending in with one's neighbors is fine as long as one's neighbors' houses are not burning and one's neighbors are not lying dead on the floor. In small towns away from urban areas, to be part of a local community offers an alternative, and for some people the best alternative. This is something that I often recommend to elderly people who don't feel that they could manage to put in their fair share of labor at a group retreat. On the other hand, I think it's very possible, if a person chooses to go remote enough, to have an individual retreat which is completely safe.

I have a client who has a retreat in a National Forest in one of our less populated states which has been in existence for five years now, and has not been discovered by hunters, forest rangers, or anyone else. He has electric power, running water, sewage disposal, the whole thing. Our own retreat also is in a very remote location, and we don't expect any great mass of people because it is in such an unpopulated area.

HJR: If enough people conclude that retreating is for them, your ability to remain secluded or isolated is diminished by the number of people looking for isolation.

DS: This is true, except that the kind of people who are looking for isolation are people who also make the best kind of neighbors.

HJR: Well struck! Don, how do people obtain more of your expertise?

DS: I charge $100 an hour for personal consultation. However, I figure the best way to reach the greatest number of people at the lowest cost per capita is by printed material, and this is why I write newsletter articles and booklets that sell for a few dollars. For the self-starter, this should be enough to get him on the way. I have written in excess of thirty columns for *INFLATION SURVIVAL LETTER.* I have written a number of columns for *MCKEEVER'S MISL* and will continue to do articles for both publications, as well as others. That's the most economical way for a person to acquire my assistance. To do that kind of writing, it's necessary to limit my personal consultation. I found that I was sitting for three and four hours with lonely people who really felt that for just $25 or $35 an hour, it was worth their money to have somebody to talk to, and so I increased my fee to $100 an hour.

HJR: There's one concept you have sold me on and that's the concept of a mobile retreat. In our family council, we decided our next vehicle would be a motor home and that it wouldn't hurt to have a very small inexpensive piece of land off the beaten track where nobody would think to look. It doesn't have to have any facilities other than water and possibly an underground fiberglass food storage tank. The family concluded it was a good idea because we could also use the recreational vehicle for recreation and transportation.

Don, do you want to make further comment on the social consequences of mass famines and financial panics?

DS: The sorts of crises we are facing are unknown. There is a cliche that history repeats itself, but it doesn't. It plays on the same themes, but very loud or very soft. To find any parallel with America in past history you must find a nation of over

200,000,000 people that was dependent upon the massive nationwide and international transportation of essential goods, based on a rapidly depleting supply of petro-chemicals. We are unique.

People have tried to compare a future depression with the 1930s, when over half of the population of this country lived on farms and had the potential to grow their own food. Today, over 85 percent of our population lives in cities. Farmers used to raise a flock of chickens and have a garden. Their wives made their own bread and canned fruits and vegetables. They probably had a milk cow or two and raised a couple of hogs or steers for meat.

Today a farmer has a cash crop. He goes to Safeway and buys his meat, milk, and eggs just like everybody else. Our condition is not parallel with 1930, nor with the situation during the German inflation, nor the situation during the French hyperinflation, nor the one in China. In Germany, as you said, there was a small mortality rate and a short period before order was restored, but Germany was a very small country. It was surrounded by neighbors with stronger currencies, and as soon as the German Mark went to a point of little or no value, foreign currency started flowing in and was exchanged for goods, and in essence replaced the German currency until it could reestablish itself. In China, during their hyperinflation, every coinage in the world was floating around and the U.S. dollar was king.

The U.S. is not in that kind of position now. We don't have available to us any strong, tangible coinage from an adjacent country. Canada's economy is as vulnerable as our own, or more so. We certainly can't depend on Mexico, nor any other country in the world, to bail us out. So we can't depend on currencies from other countries to reestablish orderly commerce.

The other situation that is unique today is the fact that we are so dependent upon fuel. Our agricultural potential is based on huge petroleum-fueled combines which harvest thousands of acres at the hands of a few men. In the 1930s we had much smaller dependence upon petro-chemicals for the production of our food.

HJR: Are you saying that perhaps we would be unable to harvest our crops even if they were able to be planted?

DS: Very definitely. We might have the bumper crop of the world, but because of the fuel situation, and the lack of economic stability, we may not have the ability or the incentive or the crop to be harvested. Further, we might not have the fuel for trains or for trucks to carry it to the cities.

HJR: Your message is very bleak and alarming, but I've always felt that one should alert people to all possible dangers, expose them to all of the possible alternatives, and then let them choose what they should do. This is the only sound and reasonable approach.

One last question. How would you answer someone who says, "Well, gee, if it's going to be that bad, and I don't have the money to establish a retreat, and can barely buy the food I have now, why bother to do anything. I might as well just take my lumps."

DS: I think that is something they will have to decide upon individually.

HJR: From merely a deep depression with a lot of people out of work, to the kind of financial and social Armageddon you are talking about, there is a wide range of possibilities in between. To assume that because you can't prepare for the ultimate calamity, you should not prepare at all, would be foolish, in my opinion.

DS: Right. I think a person has to decide how much preparation he would need in order to feel at peace with himself so he could go on enjoying life from day to day. To help people with this decision, I wrote *Retreating on a Shoestring*. It shows people how, with a few dollars, over a period of months, they can prepare themselves to have a chance to survive, or to get out of the city if necessary. It gives them a list of readily available supplies that they could stockpile. They can buy them a few at a time. Each step will be a step toward peace of mind. But my primary interest is to solve the concern that they will have when they realize the problems. I feel it is my job to help people to become aware of the concerns that I feel are real, and to show them how to have peace of mind through proper preparations.

HJR: Don, you don't seem to have your ego wrapped up in being right. I think that you and I pretty much share the same philosophy. We would be happy to lead the cheering if it turned out we were both wrong. Don, thank you for taking the time, we appreciate it.

IS A MOUNTAIN RETREAT ADVISABLE?

(Special Report #5, 4/1/78)

Q. What do you think of having a retreat in the mountains, either as an individual or part of a group, in case things get a lot worse than you think they are going to get, which incidentally, I think is going to be the case?

A. Well, I'll have to disagree with you on what the worst case will be, because I don't believe the nation will collapse into total anarchy, at least not this time around. I'm expecting a depression, not a new "Dark Age." Other than difficulties in buying the things you want, life in the small towns should go on pretty much as before. The big cities are where the trouble will be concentrated, with a possibility of sporadic problems elsewhere. Being off by yourself in a retreat seems dangerous to me. If there is no national anarchy (and I don't think there will be), a retreat is unnecessary. If there is anarchy, roving bands would look for isolated homes. If people leave the cities looking for trouble or food or money, I don't think I'd want to be all by myself. Above all, I don't want to be put into a position where I would have to shoot somebody, although I have recently bought some hunting rifles so that I can become self-sufficient off the land, if necessary. The thought of using a gun on a human being is totally abhorrent to me. The big cities will be dangerous. Being alone could be dangerous. The small town represents more safety and security because you can have a common bond with others who wish to protect their interest and safety.

A group retreat can be a reasonable alternative as long as the developer is selling lots at a fair price and it also can be used as a vacation home with recreational potential. If it makes you feel good to live in a group retreat, there are several good ones around and we can refer you to some through Member Services, but it doesn't particularly turn me on. I think the retreat concept is an excessive reaction and unnecessary.

(Special Report #4, 10/76) If you are still thinking of a group retreat, don't buy before visiting it. There are many well-intentioned promoters who don't know what they're doing. Look to see whether or not there is adequate water, provisions for electrical power generation, mutual security, accessibility, etc.

RUFF HOU$E TV SHOW

(12/15/78)

Q. I notice that on your TV show, RUFF HOU$E, you often interrupt your guests. Why do you do that? I'd like to hear more of what they have to say.

A. I have a total of sixteen minutes to interview a guest. They are all instructed prior to the taping that we need to have a lively exchange with relatively short answers, otherwise it's just not good television. And, whether we like it or not, we must attract and hold an audience. When I break in on a guest, it's usually because he's giving me a lengthy monologue or has made a cryptic statement that needs clarification, so I try to serve as a monitor.

These guest appearances aren't supposed to be "interviews." They are conversations, as that's the style of our show, and I reserve the right to express my opinion.

Now, after all that disclaimer, I've looked back at a few shows and decided you are partly right and that I've occasionally hogged the camera, so I'll be a little more careful.

RUFF TIMES, THE

SO, WHY ANOTHER NEWSLETTER?

(11/75) *What's So Different About THE RUFF TIMES?*

1. Our function is to digest data from all sources and identify the stress points and weak spots in our society so that you will be looking in the right direction and won't be caught by surprise. The New York crisis is an example of that. I called the shot on November 11, 1974.

2. We have a broad perspective. I'm qualified to interpret weather data and its effect on crops and food. I've been a stockbroker and investment counselor, and a nutrition reporter and writer, so I feel qualified to advise you on preparations and constructively criticize the burgeoning survival industry. We will discuss all areas relating to economic forecasting and survival.

3. We will be comprehensive, simple, and thoroughly documented. I will read the complex technical literature for you, strip it of

the intellectual posturing, translate it into information that affects you, and show you how to apply it. You won't need to be a "gold bug" or have an understanding of economics to understand this letter. I may go down deep, but I won't come up dry.

4. We won't be afraid to make commercial recommendations. It doesn't do you any good to hear what you need, and not know where to get it.

5. We will expose you to views we don't agree with. We will let you know when we agree or disagree, but you can make your choice.

6. We'll make general investment recommendations. I am not an expert on gold, silver or foreign currency, but I have such experts to refer you to if you call on our 800 number. I will identify trends, forecast events and probabilities, and make general recommendations, then refer you to experts.

7. We will give very specific advice on food, books, and survival items. I will name good guys and bad guys in the survival industry. And last....

Any advice we give will have to pass two tests:

* Will it give you real protection against future problems?

* Does it give you a flexible position? Would it be a good move, even if we didn't have a total collapse?

PRINCIPAL SERVICE

(Special Report #4, 10/76)

Q. What do you think is the principal service that you will perform in *THE RUFF TIMES*?

A. I believe that after you have taken all of the advice we have offered you in my books, *FAMINE AND SURVIVAL IN AMERICA* and *HOW TO PROSPER DURING THE COMING BAD YEARS*, our principal service to you will be to let you know when circumstances change, so you can change your strategy.

We will not always be recommending that you have your money in Treasury bills.

We will not always be recommending that you keep your precious metals in a safe deposit box in the bank.

From time to time there will be serious matters of legislation pending in Congress, or regulations from regulatory agencies, which you need to be aware of so you can make your protests known.

From time to time we will have insider information relative to gold in the international marketplace.

We will also give some basic instruction on some very important economic issue, so you can help to educate your friends and neighbors on the survival concept.

Life is dynamic. The economic scene, the investment markets and our social environment are subject to dramatic change. It's my function to stay ahead of this change and to let you know about it in sufficient time to act.

Perhaps the most valuable service we offer is the privilege of calling on our hotline for advice to assist you in individual investment and lifestyle decisions.

RUFF'S REVIEW

(12/1/76) During the Thanksgiving holiday I had a rare opportunity to sit back and contemplate the work of the last year. I read all of the back issues of *THE RUFF TIMES* to see whether or not I had made any contribution to the sum total of human perception.

I have but one regret.

Sometimes *THE RUFF TIMES* seems too strident in presenting the nation's problems and trying to persuade people of the coming calamities to get them to prepare.

If you relied on *THE RUFF TIMES* for your only view of the world, it would be a frightening and perhaps depressing perspective. However, I assume you can achieve balance by looking about you and seeing the good and wonderful things in the world. There are so few around who are willing to wade past all of the conventional wisdom and keep an eye on the fundamental economic rot.

When nations die and economies fall apart, it always comes as a surprise! Historically, nations on their way down never look like it to those who live during such times. It's only after it happens that the signs seem clear to those who are raking through the historical ashes.

It's also a bit of a paradox that the guy who was farthest out in front with his forecasts is the guy who has to hang on the longest through the ridicule.

And the saddest part of all is that when vindication comes, it comes in the form of the calamity which was forecast, which brings misery to everyone, including the forecaster. There's no pleasure in being right in these matters.

The only satisfaction is in knowing that a lot of people are better prepared and sleeping better as a result of *THE RUFF TIMES*.

ITS CONTENTS

(1/15/76)   Every time I devote a page or so to a moral or ethical issue, I get a few complaints from subscribers, suggesting I ought to stick with hard data, facts, and tangible advice. That's a mistaken view. Hard data and facts have often been a secondary influence in the world, compared to the great intangible, emotional and spiritual forces that have caused wars, founded religions, motivated exploration and discovery, and built or ruined nations and civilizations.

So, Dear Reader, some pages of *THE RUFF TIMES* will and must always be devoted to principles I feel are relevant to spiritual and intellectual survival (see: Survival Preparation, Emotional). You don't have to agree with me, but if you stop reading everything you don't agree with, you'll never learn a new thing, and perhaps that is a good definition of spiritual and intellectual death.

RUKEYSER, LOUIS

(5/1/77)   The Master of Ceremonies for the Hawaiian Economic and Investment Confernce was Lou Rukeyser, host of public television's "WALL STREET WEEK." Lou has about 8,000,000 regular viewers and is one of the most perceptive and witty people I've ever heard. The first question he asked was, "Why is the stock market jumping around so much?" The answer: "Its because we are jittery about Jimmy.'' Carter's actions have produced a schizophrenic marketplace. He said, "He has misled us, and that's not all bad. If we had to take seriously everything that comes out of his mouth, the country would be in deep trouble."

He brought the house down with the statement, "Carter against inflation is like the anopheles mosquito against malaria." He has contradictory policies in almost every area. For example, he says government should be smaller, but he has proposed programs that make it larger. He says unemployment should come down, but he has approved policies which will drive it up. He said we must fight inflation, but there have been at least thirty inflationary proposals in the year he has been in office. He has at least three different policies on capital investment. Lou believes he will eventually try wage and price controls, which have failed clear back to the Emperor Diocletian in 300 A.D.

He had some fascinating views on Arthur Burns, which coincide with my own. Arthur Burns has the image of being the crusty inflation-fighter, but Lou says, "There is the public Arthur Burns and there is the real Arthur Burns," and there is very little similarity between the two. He has presided over the largest inflationary expansion of money in the history of mankind.

Lou believes that 1978 will be a blurred carbon copy of 1977, with no major economic difficulties. He stood alone in that respect.

One comment about the power of the Treasury printing press was, "If Abe Beame had had a printing press, he'd still be mayor of New York City."

RUSSELL, RICHARD

(1/15/77) RICHARD RUSSELL, in his *DOW THEORY LETTER* (December 1, 1977), made a most interesting observation relative to we "prophets of doom." He wrote:

> Most recently I've been interested (I should say fascinated) by the vehement and continuing bearishness of the number of these reports (newsletters like *THE RUFF TIMES*). The facts they present are well-known and for the most part, irrefutable, but the scenarios that these services offer are positively hair-raising.
>
> It seems to me that the market is telling us another story, one that seems to have escaped all the super-bears. The market is saying, Look, you guys may be right and the worst depression collapse since the dawn of history may lie somewhere ahead, but we are now in a primary bull market, and it isn't finished yet—it hasn't done its stuff yet. The party's going to get a lot hotter up ahead than you ever thought possible, so either sit on the sidelines, join the party or hold your peace. Perhaps the whole thing can be wrapped up by quoting a few paragraphs from William H. Hamilton, that great Dow Theorist and old-time editor of *THE WALL STREET JOURNAL*. Hamilton said, "The graveyards of Wall Street are filled with men who have been right too soon."

I think Russell is dead right. The further ahead you see the problem, by the time the events actually occur, you will have probably been discredited.

Dick may very well be right about a bull market. His track record is outstanding and his letter is one of the most thoughtful of any in this particular genre.

(11/1/77)   Well, it's finally happened. Dick Russell, has declared a bear market.

Over the last several months, he has contended that we have been in a correction prior to the third speculative phase of a bull market, and he had all of his subscribers put their money in bonds and T-bills or cash while waiting for the correction to run its course. He expected an oversold market and a third speculative surge in which money could be made. Last week, however, he saw a major bearish confirmation by the Transportation Index and has concluded that this is not just a correction, but the primary phase of a bear maket.

Dick Russell is a man of great integrity, tremendous ability and immense writing skill. His newsletter is one of the first I will read. He has been consistently right over the years. If you want to know anything about timing your movements in the stock market, I can't think of a better newsletter.

The most recent bull market differed substantially from others in the past, in that it was only 22 months long and did not have that third speculative phase. If we are in the grip of the bear, then the market is telling us there is something terrible in our future. I think Russell's right. Get out of the market! Now! Everything but gold shares! Also, get out of bonds and into Treasury bills or money funds for liquidity. And do it now! Interest rates are going up, which means bond prices are going down.

(6/15/78)   At the Bahamas Monetary Conference, Dick Russell gave a very informative, illustrated lecture using charts, as he does so beautifully, to clarify his points. He pointed out that we are at a speculative peak in the stock market, as indicated by the tremendous rise in what he calls the "cats and dogs index." It took 12 million shares of trading for each point in the Dow Jones during this recent rise, and he finds that distinctly unimpressive.

He said that in terms of the consistency of the move, the 17 month slide of the stock market was the worst in history. It slid from over 1000 D.J. to below 750 without so much as a five percent correction, and that was totally unprecedented. The recent explosion in stock prices was an accumulation of several corrections that you would ordinarily expect in such a slide. He felt that there is a "roof" over the averages at 870 where massive amounts of stock are available that would be unloaded at that point. Recent market action bore him out.

He said that commodities are giving us a "flash inflation signal" and that there will be an explosion in Treasury interest rates, which are currently 20% below the 1974 yields. What that means, of course, is that the market value of your bonds will continue to fall. If you have done what we told you, you were out of them a long time ago. The time to get back in will be when interest rates peak, and Dick thinks that a 12% to 14% prime rate is not unlikely. He showed us charts on silver and gold, which were both bullish. In reference to the recent surge in the stock market, he observed that never has a bull market in stocks begun in a time of rising interest rates. Right now he is 80% in Treasury bills, 20% in gold, and zero percent in the stock market. The municipal bond funds merited some comment. (These are mutual funds invested strictly in municipals.) Their recent declines have wiped out two years of income. So many subscribers say "But I need bonds for the income." The municipal bond market is illiquid and is headed nowhere but down. He also said that there are no certainties when it comes to investments. We can only deal with probabilities.

(3/1/79) Richard Russell, the editor of *THE DOW THEORY LETTER*, was one of our featured speakers at our recent convention. He expressed great concern that more and more debt is producing less and less stimulus to the economy and we are seeing one of the most dramatic financial struggles of all time—the struggle between inflation on the one side and debt on the other. The power of the compounding of debt is the most potent financial force alive. He believes that the debt monster could come crashing down. The collapse of the debt structure would be deflationary and he is now "less and less interested in inflation." He pointed out that six times since 1928, short-term interest rates have risen above long-term rates and every time this has happened, it has resulted in a recession. Due to this phenomenon, he believes we will experience a recession, probably towards the end of this year, but no later than 1980.

Mortgage debt is increasing at over $100 billion per year, the highest rate in U.S. history. He said, "The country is absolutely exploding with mortgage debt." He also believes we are near the top on gold on an intermediate basis, even though silver is blowing its top. "Commodities are the last great areas subject to inflationary explosion."

"The stock market is acting very, very tired. I would be a seller here," Dick points out. As to the future, he said, "If I had to guess, by July or the 3rd quarter of this year, there will be an extraordinarily bearish and unforeseen event come up which will knock the stock market to its knees. My general advice is to move to a liquid position.

Buy gold and T-bills. I'm bullish on T-bills because they are outside the U.S. banking system. The exact proportions of how much of your investment should be divided between gold and T-Bills I leave to the individual." Dick concluded by saying that the Constitution guarantees us freedom of religion and freedom of speech, but he wants "freedom from robbery by the U.S. government. We are going into the most volatile markets we have ever seen, wherein costly mistakes can be made, so my advice is to move to liquidity. Get liquid with gold and T-bills."

As you know from past letters, I respect Dick immensely, but, even though I fear debt as much as he does, I do not see an imminent collapse of the debt structure. I think government can keep feeding it, and the increase of debt will continue to be inflationary. I see more inflation, not less, but I don't worry about Dick's position, as his advice is the same as mine—gold, silver, T-bills, commodities. Not a heck of a lot of difference.

S

SAFETY

(9/1/77)   Every once in awhile, I look back through all requests for information and review all the correspondence to see if there's any pattern developing.

One persistent pattern is a sense of concern about the hostility of others if one has silver coins and an emergency food supply in a time of social chaos. Personal security, as a point of discussion, will get you about as many opinions as there are people, so let me throw my oar in the water.

Personal safety, in my opinion, is not going to be secured by having guns and shooting people. I'm planning my life in such a way as to reduce or eliminate that necessity. The safest thing you can do is live in a small town with a tradition of law and order. Other than the difficulty of obtaining imported commodities, I am convinced that life in the small towns will go on pretty much as before, and that the brief period of chaos in this country will be concentrated almost entirely in the cities.

I don't think you have to head for the hills to some remote retreat. (See: Retreats) In fact, that might be dangerous. I'm not opposed to it. I just feel that you should consider the following points.

We are gregarious animals, and need some degree of socialization. I also believe we need the varied services, goods and skills that only a community of reasonable size can provide. Very few of us are rich enough to buy land in a remote area, build an adequate retreat and stock it. I just don't accept the scenario that civilization is going to come to an end and that we are going to have years of anarchy. We possibly will have weeks of anarchy, and it will be centered in the big cities. Your odds for personal safety, and the safety of your home, improve greatly as you move farther from the city, but I think you are safer in a small town than you would be out on a farm. Stop and think it through. Remoteness has disadvantages.

But whether you live in a small town, or a metropolitan suburb, this does not eliminate the question of personal security.

Your personal security depends upon the security of those around you. If your neighbor has a food storage plan and some silver coins, he is not a threat to you. He will be secure and not part of a general panic that might occur if we have a monetary crisis, a nationwide trucking strike, a Mideast war, or an energy crisis. You want people around whom you can call on for help—people you will not have to fear.

The most common question is, "How can I persuade my friends, relatives and neighbor to get ready for hard times? They think I'm a crackpot." My advice is this: Arrange your life so your world is not dangerous for you. If you live in a place that is potentially dangerous, structure your life so you can relocate. Be an influence on those around you, but if you can't persuade them, then let us try.

(Special Report #4, 10/76)

Q. What can we do to improve the safety and security of our home?

A. I would begin by bringing in a locksmith and making sure that every door in your house can be locked and that your windows can't be forced. Also, I would suggest a couple of good, noisy dogs. I don't think you need a dog that will bite anybody, but you do need one that sounds like he might.

Prepare your home so you could operate if there were interruptions in electric power or gasoline supplies.

A good wood stove could be invaluable. (See: Energy, Alternate Sources) There are many stoves now being made that are vastly superior to the old Franklin Stove. These stoves can throw out a steady heat for many hours and also can be used for cooking. The proper installation of such a stove can be lifesaving in our very cold climate.

I would also suggest that you provide for candles, flashlights and plenty of batteries. You might want to keep the batteries in the freezer, as their shelf-life is prolonged if they are cold or even frozen.

Try to develop an association with neighbors who are like-minded, who have also set aside emergency supplies of food and who share your concern so you can call for help if you should need it, and you'll be available to assist others.

Even if we do not have a complete economic collapse, crime rates do rise during a depression, so it would be best to be prepared, even if you live in the suburbs or a small town.

Q. If we should have a major monetary crisis, is there any part of the country that will be safer than another?

A. Yes. I would avoid the large cities (anything over 100,000 in population), particulary those with large welfare populations, and I am not simply referring to blacks. In the United States today, 55 percent of welfare recipients are white. I'm talking about an economic class, not a racial group. I would be concerned if I were living within five miles of such an area. The suburbs, anywhere from 30 to 35 miles out, are probably all right. Best of all would be a small town away from the larger metropolitan areas. They will be less susceptible to panic buying of food and other commodities, urban disorders, and welfare riots from government collapse.

I feel best about the Intermountain West (Idaho, Montana, Utah, Colorado, parts of Arizona and New Mexico), the Pacific Northwest (outside of the Seattle Metropolitan area), parts of North and South Carolina, Georgia, Arkansas, Texas, Oklahoma, Missouri, Indiana, and Ohio, Minnesota, North Dakota (outside the larger urban areas). These areas are generally agricultural in nature, and would be more likely to be self-sufficient.

My primary concern is that you reduce your dependence upon transportation for the survival of your area. Those areas which are totally dependent upon food and commodities to be transported on a regular basis will suffer the most. I wouldn't want to live in Honolulu, Las Vegas, New York City, Philadelphia, Detroit, the Los Angeles basin, San Francisco, St. Louis, Chicago, or any other large metropolitan area.

(6/15/77)

Q. All right. Let's say I took your advice and I stored up food and bought coins, and was ready to ride out the problems, but my neighbors didn't. Wouldn't they take away from me what I had stored?

A. The question assumes there will be a complete breakdown of law and order for a prolonged period of time. What you are postulating is perhaps the end of the world as we know it. I don't know how to prepare for the end of the world. No one else does either. But if I don't store food, I'll starve to death by default. If I do store food, there's a chance I'll be able to keep it and take care of my family.

Q. Well, Mr. Ruff, it must be very frightening to live with such fears.

A. No problem at all. My philosophy is that if you can see and understand a problem and prepare for it, then you sleep well at night. People have written to me by the thousands to thank me for the peace of mind they have, now that they have made some careful preparations.

Q. What if you turned out to be wrong? You could be the laughingstock of the U.S.

A. I know that. That's the chance I'm taking. However, I've carefully structured my advice so that if it turns out to be wrong, you won't be hurt. I'd like someone to explain to me how getting out of debt can possibly be harmful. I'd like to know how storing food could be damaging to your life. I'd like to know how putting a little "insurance money" into gold and silver coins as a hedge against a loss of value of other investments is a bad idea.

SAFE-DEPOSIT BOXES

(12/1/77)

Q. Is a safe-deposit box really safe?

A. It had better be. That's where I've got all my coins. Here are some facts.

1. The contents are your property, not that of the bank. That is not true of the money you deposit. That can and will be lost if enough banks are in trouble to overwhelm the FDIC, but safe deposit box contents are your property.

2. The IRS does have the power to open a safe-deposit box, but must go to a Federal judge and show cause that a crime has been committed and get a court order. If you are having a squabble with the IRS, I suggest you empty your safe-deposit box, but if your tax affairs are generally in order, the odds of it being opened are zilch.

The principal risk is fire or theft. You can generally get a cheap rider to your homeowners' policy insuring the contents of your safe-deposit box.

If the banks should go broke, you may have trouble getting to your box, because the doors will be shut. But after the dust settles and the panic is over, you will have access to your box. Maintain a separate inventory of everything for insurance purposes. Don't put your will in there because in many states it is illegal to remove anything until appropriate authorization, in case of death of one of the co-owners. Your will should be on file with your attorney, or in a safe place at home.

The time will come that you ought to haul your stuff out of the safe-deposit box to avoid the inconvenience of not being able to get into it during a period of panic, but that time has not come yet.

It might be a good idea to have more than one safe-deposit box in more than one bank, and if you keep cash in the box, spread it around among the boxes.

SCHULTZ, HARRY

(2/15/78) Harry Schultz has agreed to address our *RUFF TIMES* Convention by telephone from his home in London on February 21. Harry is the world's highest priced investment consultant and has a marvelous percentage of market calls over the last several years. He is not perfect, but his record is among the best in our industry. He was one of the original "gold bugs" and probably knows as much about that metal as anyone alive. It's a pleasure and an honor to have him participate in our program.

(6/15/78)   The famed Harry Schultz has left us with an interesting approach to investing. He said that we must all become traders and speculators in order to survive. He referred to the famous book on the stock market by Loeb, *THE BATTLE FOR INVESTMENT SUR-VIVAL*, which he retitled *THIS WEEK'S BATTLE FOR INVEST-MENT SURVIVAL*. We are moving into an age where three weeks is long-term. The day when you could buy something and set it aside is over. You need 12% a year just to stay even, and you are not going to get that without assuming fairly high risks. Inflation rewards the trader. You can trade anything as long as you are willing to go short or long. You can trade in bonds, stocks, foreign currencies and precious metals futures. But you must stay right on top of it, check the markets two or three times a day, educate yourself, and make your own charts. If you want to trade in currencies, there are several ways to do it. You can buy shares of stock in foreign companies on foreign exchanges. You can exchange dollars for foreign currencies and make time deposits in Swiss banks. You can buy currency futures, which you should chart personally or use a good advisor. You must be willing to cut your losses or hedge in the opposite direction. If you are "long" on a currency and you think that it's going to go down temporarily, rather than selling, take a corresponding "short" position so the profits and losses will offset, until a trend is clear in the right direction. He says you should base all of your decisions on the day's closing prices.

I found the talk very interesting but it seems to me that his advice can be used by a very small fraction of the people, because it requires a risk-taking temperament, lots of time, tremendous knowledge and a willingness to be on top of it every moment. You just can't ever turn your back on the marketplace.

Money has two characteristics: (1) It pays no interest, and (2) it's an asset for which there is no corresponding liability. Gold is money and Harry feels that gold should be an essential part of your portfolio in either an inflationary or deflationary scenario. He likes coins.

He also says that when you do invest you should not use "stop orders." You should keep stops in your head and know precisely where you want to stop yourself out. If you have issued a stop order to a broker and you are not watching, you might be stopped out when you might not have wanted to.

SCRIPTURAL PROPHECY

(12/15/78)

Q. Mr. Ruff, your advice is foolish. The next depression is the "beginning of the end troubles" prior to Christ's coming and the righteous will be taken from the earth before the troubles, so they need no stored food or coins.

A. I am a Bible believer too, but history is littered with the reputations of those who profess to know exactly when certain Bible prophecies were going to be fulfilled. I don't know whether the next economic downturn is the last one prior to the coming of Christ, nor does anybody else. Similar prophecies were made prior to 1932, during World War II and before the last recession. There's a legitimate theological debate as to whether or not the believers will be taken from the earth before or after a period of tribulation. My job is to act as if it were all up to me, and pray as if it were all up to God, and trust Him. Then if this is merely a passing phase in our history, as I think it is, my family's well-being is secure. If I read the Scriptures correctly, they tell me that charity begins at home and Paul has informed us that if we do not take care of those of our own household we are "worse than an infidel."

When Christ comes, my money won't be important anymore, but between now and then, it is important. I'm not going to bet my future on an interpretation of the Scriptures that says I don't need to store food or take care of my money, when betting on the safe side won't hurt me spiritually at all. Please stop sending me letters on this subject. Food storage, precious metals and defensive investments are not religious matters, and I refuse to make a judgment that affects your life and safety based on a sectarian interpretation of scripture. This letter is for Christian, Jew and nonbeliever alike, and I value you equally as subscribers and friends, even if we should disagree on theology.

SENNHOLZ, DR. HANS

(5/1/78) Dr. Hans Sennholz was fascinating at the First Annual Economic and Investment Conference in Hawaii. He was so concerned about the generally pessimistic tone of the conference that, although he intended to deliver a similar address, he felt compelled to show the other side of the coin. He pointed out, as I did, that this is an unparalleled age of opportunity. But we must take advantage of the coming major changes. The greatest opportunities come when there are basic institutional changes. Instability leads to opportunity. The entrepreneur or speculator does not want stability because it's difficult for him to do well during periods of stability. We should study the fundamental radical changes that come from Washington. One rather pithy comment on current social trends was, "Social justice is what I receive, socialism is what others get." He pointed out that he had decided never to accept any benefit of any kind from government, taking the same stand that I have.

When asked whether he thought we were headed for inflation or deflation, he said deflation would come only after inflation and price controls. Under price controls, profits would flow to those who invest or deal in uncontrolled commodities, as under controls money flows into such uncontrolled marketplaces as single family dwellings, spare parts, and most basic farm commodities.

When asked during the panel discussion what he would recommend for a retired couple with $100,000, he said that they should take at least half of it and bet on youth by funding some young entrepreneur with an idea that was right for our times. When we succeed we owe something to the next generation and to the country, and not all of our investments should be selfish. We should look for reasonable profits while helping new ventures to get off the ground.

Dr. Sennholz is one of the most exciting, interesting and creative people I've ever met.

HOWARD RUFF

(3/15/79)

The Second Annual *RUFF TIMES* National Convention

Dr. Hans Sennholz identified three types of income. First, LABOR INCOME—the proceeds from the labor of your hands or your mind—your paycheck. As a percentage of all income, this has been declining at about one percent or two percent a year. The second type of income is what he called TIME INCOME, income earned in interest. He felt that we would have much higher interest rates in the future, but not enough to keep pace with inflation. The third type of income is ENTREPRENEURIAL (investing, forming new businesses, etc.), which results from the proper anticipation of change—population change, interest rate change, social change, all types of change. He felt we were going to go through a period of great change and said, "If you can't make it now, you couldn't have made it 100 years ago, because the world now has many more changes, and the entrepreneur seeks change." He also said very provocatively, "Society gets poorer through over-consumption, thus reducing our standard of living." He sees more inflation in the future, not a classic deflationary depression. He disagrees with the deflationists.

He said, "I can see price controls but not wage controls." He indicated he did not see the disintegration of the money supply (deflation) through debt liquidation and bankruptcies in the next few years, as do some others. He also felt that other currencies are not much better than the dollar, and will all be damaged by inflation. "The game that must be played today is the inflation game," said Dr. Sennholz, and I agree.

He also buys real estate. He likes farms and income-producing property. He said, 70% of all great personal fortunes are made in real estate. Don't knock real estate. I believe that percentage will rise in the future. The best way to insure a good location in real estate is to buy your neighbor's home, then buy another neighbor's home, then buy the entire neighborhood." The tax shelter benefits of real estate are substantial. The average American pays 43% of his income in taxes. He said that there are two basic laws of survival in today's environment: (1) Stay out of money, or in other words, invest all of your savings in non-monetary forms. (2) Invest in inflation hedges that give tax benefits. Real estate accomplishes both. He said, "I'm convinced that real estate prices over the next three to four years will double again, recession or no." He expressed the same concerns I have in the past about urban real estate, although he was not as bearish as I am on suburban properties.

SILVER

(9/1/76) I have just found an unusual way to accumulate some silver. I've just read a booklet by Werner Pauson telling you how to recover silver from waste photographic and X-ray developing chemicals, and how to get your raw materials free. It sounds kookie when I describe it, but the booklet makes sense. You could acquire from $320 to $4600 worth of silver in a year with his well-thought-out scheme. Write to: W. M. Pauson, P.O. Box 425, Willow Grove, Pennsylvania 19090.

(4/1/78) I'm also getting more and more bullish on silver. I have always advised silver coins as your basic hedge against currency collapse, because it's spendable money in small denomination. I'm now getting excited about it. It has burst through the $5.00 level in one big move to almost $5.50, and backed off to around $5.30. It may back off a little more, but I believe it's building a base for a long upward move. In my opinion, it's now on a par with gold as an aggressive vehicle for long-term capital appreciation. (see: Gold)

SIN-TAX

(11/1/77) Recently, I stood in the Greek and Roman Antiquities Rooms of the the famous Louvre in Paris. My family and I gazed with awe and wonder upon the Venus de Milo, the great Winged Victory, the statues of Apollo and of Roman Emperors and Greek gods from ages long past. A question passed through my mind: How could this civilization, great enough to have created these works of great beauty and technical skill, have slid into such a decline that they could not or would not protect their great art treasures?

As we examined buildings from civilizations that were centuries old, and particularly as we looked at the great architectural and artistic wonders of Renaissance Italy and the Greek and Roman Antiquities in the Louvre, I gained a little better perpective on the accomplishment of man. Almost every civilization believes it is the highest flower of man, but civilizations do rise and fall, and

627

subsequent generations build upon the rubble. But why do they fall?

Their days of decline are marked by shifting values in nearly every area of human behavior: reverence for life, sexual behavior, business ethics, and most other values we consider essential to a stable society.

Nearly all were guilty of inflating their currencies, and it was fiscal problems that helped bring them to their knees and made them vulnerable to a variety of other malignant influences. And Rome was no exception.

(9/1/78)   The Roman Empire faced bankruptcy 2000 years ago as more and more power was concentrated in the central government and government spending grew.

Cicero spoke out against the trend. The great Roman senator said, "The budget should be balanced, the treasury should be refilled, the public debt should be reduced, the arrogance of officialdom should be tempered and controlled, assistance to foreign lands should be curtailed lest Rome becomes bankrupt. The mob should be forced to work and not depend on government for subsistence."

Romans ignored Cicero, Rome fell.

Cicero, where are you now that we need you?

I do have one ray of hope. The '70s are in many ways a replay of the '20s, including the sexual revolution, the youth revolt, women's lib, inflation and a lot of other similar social developments. But the sexual excesses of the '20s were swallowed up in the economic holocaust of the '30s. People simply had neither the time, the money, nor the mood to indulge in hedonistic pleasures. The pendulum swung back and we went through a period of Puritanism in movies, on the stage and in public life. That consensus did not begin to break down again until the '60s.

I'm not sure whether nations fall because of sexual revolutions, or whether a sexual revolution is a symptom of deeper ills, but there's no question they do go together. Sexual excess seems to be a reinforcing factor in the rate of decline.

Let there be no mistake. The sexual revolution costs you money. Every time a family breaks up due to sexual rivalries, unfaithfulness, or "doing-your-own-thing," the odds are that you will have to pay some of the social cost through the taxing system or the Federal money creation process.

(Special Report #2, 1/76)   Can you remember the days when the politician felt that his safest stance was to be against sin and in favor of motherhood? Now, of course, it's fashionable to be in favor of many sins and be opposed to "excessive" motherhood. It's not so much that there is pornography, or prostitution, or lax moral standards. Those things have always existed, but now those things are being thrust upon us in the most public way possible. It's even piped into your home through your television set.

When I was young, an enterprising teenager who wanted to do something he shouldn't do could find a way to do it. But he knew he was doing wrong. And it was not approved by society. Today, that same teenager can find people whose names are respected and admired coming out in favor of many of the things that used to be considered wrong. The schools, and even the churches, which were once bastions of moral strength, are now, in many instances, officially taking positions that are contrary to standards which the spiritual thinking people of this country are still convinced are sins.

It is my opinion that only the direct intervention of a Divine Providence can save this nation from terrible trouble. As I drive through the nation's cities on business and look about me, I can only conclude there is little evidence that this nation as a whole warrants such Divine intervention.

(7/1/77)   Much of what organized religion calls "sin" is a set of essential behavioral standards, the violation of which will destabilize society. Violation of these standards leads to fiscal instability, confiscatory taxation, and inflationary ruin.

Economists should study human moral and ethical behavior, along with traditional economics, when they try to understand the present and forecast the future.

Thoughout history, advanced civilizations have had very restrictive, somewhat puritanical sexual codes during their ascendancy and peak.

Codes of sexual behavior were sometimes "honored in the breach," but even when they were being violated, it was understood that a standard was being violated. Civilizations in decline eventually tend to reach the point where the violation become the accepted norm.

In Biblical times, there was a complex set of rules and regulations regarding sexual behavior. Incest, adultery, fornication, homosexuality, bestiality, and sodomy were all forbidden, and the penalties were severe.

It is my opinion that these were rational attempts to control behavior for the salvation of a society. Please hear me out.

The family has been the "nurturing unit" of society. The family is the means by which society protects its children against physical harm and against the errors of judgment that are natural to the inexperienced young. The family is the means by which the values of one generation are passed on to the next. It determines whether succeeding generations will be neurotic, criminal, unstable and a threat to society, or whether it will be strong, progressive, moral, and emotionally and spiritually stable. In fact, when we train our children, we are, in effect, training our grandchildren. I'm convinced that the sexual codes of society serve to proscribe and condemn anything that endangers the integrity of this family unit.

Take a close look at these rules. The rules prohibiting incest, for example, are aimed not only at preventing genetic problems from multiplying, but they also prevent divisive sexual rivalries in the family unit. Adultery brings jealousy and sexual rivalry which can poison or break up the family unit and create unstable atmospheres for the rearing of the young. When society relaxes its attitudes against premarital sex, you begin having, as we do today, unmarried family units formed without long-term legal or emotional commitment. There were one and one-half million unmarried family units, mostly teenagers, begun in 1976. Most of these will break up, leaving fatherless children, for the most part, and no statistical tracks.

I know what it is like to grow up without a father. My dad died when I was six months old and I never knew him. When society condones casual sexual relationships that create children without a father role model, with little girls being starved for male affection, and little boys not experiencing father-son "male bonding," the end result is always promiscuity, illegitimacy, and its accompanying burden upon society. Society ends up paying the bill for crime, drug addiction, Aid to Dependent Children, welfare and all of the other problems that tend to come from children raised in broken homes.

Now, there are exceptions to this. I think I turned out O.K., growing up without a father. I'm talking about society collectively.

I am convinced that loosening sexual morality always ends up hitting society in its pocketbook. The incredible growing welfare load and property taxes, in my opinion, can be traced directly to unstable home environments, and a relaxation of traditional sexual morals is the major contributing factor. And don't forget to count juvenile crime, alcoholism, abortions, drug addiction, and disrupted schools that can no longer teach but can only "police." And they do that badly, too.

I'm not trying to preach religion, It's just that I believe sexual morality has survival value.

(9/1/78) Any economic system functions within the context of its social structures, and the family is the basic structural unit of our society. Out of it will come our presidents, athletes, philosophers, saints, whores, drug addicts, murderers, and medical researchers. In short, the structure of the American family will determine the wisdom, judgment and emotional stability of the next generation. It will not be many years before the new history books will tell us whether or not we had the restraint and judgment necessary for the conduct of a free enterprise based democratic society. If the "nuclear family" continues to decline in influence and strength, we won't. It's just that simple.

There has been a recent flurry of articles about the American family and the sexual revolution. They have great relevance for anyone who's trying to predict the future so he can make his life decisions. If the family is healthy, the nation is healthy. If not, the nation is sick. Professor Urie Bronfenbrenner, of the Psychology Department of Cornell University, recently observed that the American family is falling apart. Violence and vandalism are rampant in our schools and more people are living alone. These disturbing trends must be reversed if we are to survive as a nation.

> Changes of this magnitude have never occurred before except in times of great national upheaval like wars, depressions and floods.
> The family will either become more important again or we will go down the drain like Greece and Rome did. As soon as the family fell apart in Greece and Rome, so did the whole society.

If you are having trouble making the link between this and financial advice in a newsletter, let me point out to you that I believe the family break-up and the sexual revolution are becoming increasingly dominant factors in the largest single expense most of us have—the taxes we pay.

For example, 50.3 percent of the newborn black babies in this country were illegitimate. Among whites, the illegitimacy rate has nearly doubled, from four percent of all births in 1965 to 7.7 percent in 1976. According to Peter Schuck, a Deputy Assistant Secretary of HEW, "There is definitely a high correlation between out of wedlock births, welfare costs and many of our most pressing social problems."

$11.7 billion is spent yearly in Federal, state and local Aid to Families with Dependent Children, the welfare program for poor families with no father at home. The Urban Institute in Washington, D.C. said that women who began their drift toward dependency as teen-age mothers cost taxpayers about six billion dollars a year in welfare payments.

Only 50% of the unwed mothers manage to get even a temporary job during the first four years of motherhood, and nine out of ten land on public assistance rolls, which is five times the rate of married mothers.

Psychologist Bronfenbrenner says, "These people are going to put a growing burden on our society, not only to sustain them but to repair the social and economic damage they do."

Let' get back to some numbers. The Carter Administration has offered a new bill on adolescent pregnancy prevention and care, which would finance more counseling, contraceptives, classes and day care for pregnant and unwed teenagers. It will cost about $60 million a year. That would bring to $344 million the total that HEW is asking Congress to spend on teenage pregnancy, an increase of $148 million over the current level.

Murray Straus of the University of New Hampshire directed what seems to be the only national study of violence in American families. The study found an astonishing range and severity of violence toward children by their parents. 1.2 million children of ages 3-17, at some time in their lives, had been attacked by a parent with a lethal weapon. More than 1.8 million wives are beaten by their husbands at least twice annually. 2.3 million children have used a knife or a gun on a brother or sister.

The sexual revolution and the breakdown of the family are dreadfully dangerous trends. Don't think this is something that is limited only to the poor ghettos or the wife-swapping super-rich. An associate judge of the New Mexico Court of Appeals ruled a few months ago that a 23-year-old school teacher, by engaging in sexual intercourse with a 15-year-old boy, contributed to his worldly education—not to his delinquency. It was determined that the act was "consensual." (That's a strange legal term to describe a "sensual" act.)

Because the child consented and the school teacher consented, it was legal, and the judge said, "To me a legal act does not tend to cause or encourage juvenile delinquency. A consensual act of sexual intercourse engaged in by a young man is nothing more than sex education, essential and necessary in his growth and maturity and subsequent domestic family life."

Judge Lewis R. Sutin, then reversed the conviction of Ernestine Favela, charged with contributing to the delinquency of a minor.

Let's read a little more of this "enlightened" proceeding. Sutin said:

> The legislature abolished fornication as a crime. In doing so, it
> cast aside the ancient religious doctrine that forbids such practices.

It recognized, as a matter of public policy, that this conduct did not violate the mores of the 20th century. Today, sexual intercourse is recognized as normal conduct in the development of a human being. As a result, this subject is taught to children in the public schools.

Once upon a time, the burden of teaching this important subject rested upon parents, but generally it was forbidden as a subject for discussion in family life. It was too difficult for parents to explain.

The fact that a normal young man experiences one act of sexual intercourse does not tend to cause or encourage a perversion of the sexual instinct.

In the same edition of my local newspaper where that story appeared, there was an article about Roman Polanski, whom you will remember as the famous film director who was convicted of having sex with a 13 year-old girl. I wasn't so concerned over the fact that he was guilty of such a crime, although it is terrible. The consequences to society at large would not be too great if we duly punished our sexual criminals and their criminal acts were condemned by most everyone. What disturbed me about this story is that when he skipped the country, most of his most famous Hollywood friends were getting together a big party to celebrate his expected light sentence for that heinous crime. How far have we come from the days when Ingrid Bergman almost had to go into exile when she had a baby out of wedlock?

Now back to economics. I am prepared to forecast that if society proves unable to recover from the future economic ills, it will be because the inner structure has deteriorated to the point where family units will not be able to stabilize society. Inflation will have insured that there will be no wealth left for this generation to pass on to the next one, and we will go the way of Rome.

(11/1/77) I am more and more convinced we are a civilization in decline, and that this nation is leading the rest of the world into a financial abyss with great social and economic consequences. A nation without stable spiritual moorings and well-rooted values cannot be protected from the consequences of the economic dislocations I see on the horizon. However, if we are determined, we can get through the chaos in reasonable shape.

(9/1/78) In the meantime, I would suggest that you do anything and everything within your power to strengthen your family unit. Make a closer connection with the church that will help to reinforce your views of traditional morality. Draw your family together with you once a week for specific training to pass your values on to your children. Without continuity of useful values from one generation to the next, any society is doomed. You might well adopt the Mormon practice of "Family Home Evening" every Monday night. Without that mechanism, I don't think I would have a real chance in today's world of giving my children a basis to get them through the difficult and destabilized world in their future—with their principles and values intact.

(5/15/79)

> The success of a market system in the Western world was attributable in no small measure to the existence of strong non-market institutions such as the family and religion. The fruits of the market system—science, technology, urbanization, affluence—are undermining these institutions which were the foundations of the social order.
>
> Professor Victor Fuchs of Stanford University

I recently ran across an article in the *OAKLAND TRIBUNE* (Wednesday, April 25) which adds a little ammunition to my arguments that the sexual revolution is imposing a heavy cost on America.

> UPI-Washington: Unmarried teenagers unable to discuss sex with their parents and ignorant about contraception are producing thousands of babies and boosting welfare costs as a result, Congress said yesterday.

The article went on to say that more than $4.5 billion has been disbursed annually to women who were teenagers when they first gave birth. Now there's a number you can get your teeth into—$4.5 billion!

Guess what Congress said would be the solution? A-ha!! Government money! $400 million a year spent on contraceptive research. And guess who is leading the government fight for Right? Representative Paul McCloskey of California, that's who, one of the biggest spenders in Congress. He said that government should devote more attention to the problems of young women and give us more research on the birth control pill. Government should also give more money to family planning services to reach low-income women and adolescents.

And how about special programs to be devised for teenage men and boys. He said, "It is senseless not to expand the family planning service that saves individuals from personal trauma and saves society enormous economic burdens."

I don't want to get embroiled in a debate with McCloskey on this issue, but I will reiterate my frequently expressed position that the sexual revolution has an adverse economic impact on this country —and especially on the taxpayer. And that burden will grow if McCloskey has is way. The cost of illegitimacy and an unstable generation of children, born to and raised by other children, has awesome implications for the future of this country. And I'm not terribly happy about that $4.5 billion tax bill that I help pay for, either.

SOCIAL SECURITY SYSTEM

(Special Report #2, 1/76)   The Social Security system is out of control. Of all the possible disasters I have discussed in the past, the one I believe to be absolutely inevitable is the collapse of the Social Security system.

The unfunded deficit of the Social Security system (future liabilities for which there are no payment provisions) is estimated by the system's own trustees at $2-1/2 trillion, or, if you prefer, $2-1/2 thousand billion. This is equal to all assets owned by American citizens: all stocks, bonds, government securities, cash, bank deposits, savings and pension funds. The assets of the Social Security system are only 60 billion. Realistically, there is no chance whatsoever that this enormous deficit will or could be made up out of either future withholdings or general tax revenues. Social Security taxes deducted from employee checks will either have to increase up to 50 percent of the payroll, or the government will have to make up the deficit from the general fund.

What they will do is merely print enough extra money, with correspondingly low purchasing power, to meet this staggering obligation and other expenses as they arise. Currency will be as common as toilet paper. I have had my paycheck docked for almost thirty years, allegedly to provide for my old age, and I will wind up in thirty more with nothing more than a fistful of scrip for my pains.

Perhaps the greatest problem created by this out of control monster is the hidden problem of the discouragement to savers. It is the savings of Americans that has provided the great pools of investment capital for the expansion and modernization of industry, which create the jobs on which we all depend. Vast sums of money are being drained into the Social Security trust funds—hundreds of billions of dollars—and are no longer available for productive work in our society. The Social Security trust funds are only allowed to invest in Federal bonds, notes, and Treasury bills. This captive source of government borrowing will never be turned loose for productive investment in corporate bonds or stocks. We face a great capital investment crisis. After taxes, corporate earnings are insufficient to meet the demands for expansion and replacement of obsolete and worn-out plants and equipment. These corporations must go the nation's savers for investment funds. Those potential funds are now, to a great extent, tied up in the Social Security system.

This great Social Security monster will eventually destroy the system! When? By 1985, perhaps, and possibly sooner!

Social Security is perhaps the greatest single contributor to inflation of any program ever launched by governmnt. The increases in Social Security withholding tax that we are seeing this year will merely be passed on by business in the form of higher prices. It is irreversible because so many people depend on their Social Security payments that the screams of protest would be heard from here to Mars if any proposal was made that would even begin to cut back on benefits. The tragedy is that when it goes broke, those whom it was designed to help will be the first victims of this monstrous Ponzi scheme.

(3/15/76) Articles telling us the Social Security system is in no danger go something like this: The Social Security system now provides income to so many people with so much political power that there is no way Social Security benefits could ever be cut. The Federal government will simply dip into the general fund and make up deficits in the system out of tax revenues. Consequently, no one need be concerned for the safety of the system.

There are some major problems with this explanation.

The system's proponents have missed the point completely. It's not so much that the Social Security system is in danger of going broke. *The danger is that the Social Security system will break America.*

The growth of the Social Security system is so "ordained" because of the automatic increases built into the law. This hurts the nation in two ways.

1. It will take a bigger and bigger bite out of everyone's paycheck

and will hit hardest on the poor—who can least afford it—and the middle class, the nation's "savers."

2. The system cannot possibly fund itself adequately because of the increasing number of people who will be covered by the system. People are now being covered who never paid into the system. Over $2.5 trillion will be required to meet these unfunded obligations.

Any pension fund is required to set aside an amount equal to that which is expected to be drawn upon by anyone covered by that pension. If the amount in the fund is not sufficient, then the deficit is referred to as the "unfunded obligation." Such a deficit is considered fraudulent dereliction of duty on the part of any professional fund manager, corporation, or municipality. The City of Oakland recently reported that in order to catch up with its unfunded obligations, it is going to have to extract from the general funds of the city, each year for several years, an amount equal to 120% of the city's payroll. This could bankrupt the city. New York City's pension funds not only have a huge unfunded obligation, but what funds there are have been loaned to the city or the state to try to save the city—a dubious investment at best. (see: Cities)

The Social Security fund is incurring obligations several times faster than it is accumulating funds, primarily because the fund is required to support more and more pensioners by fewer and fewer workers.

Perhaps the greatest damage done by the Social Security system is that it is mandatory and virtually forces people to retire at age 65, unless they are in business for themselves and can set their own rules.

This is a tragic waste for America. When people have accumulated the greatest wisdom, judgment and maturity, government decrees them unproductive and a drain upon the rest of society. The Social Security concept is another example of government attempting to do that which appears to be good and compassionate, but over-reaching itself to the detriment of society in general.

Sooner or later we will be faced with the unpleasant choice of either repudiating the system with its unfunded obligations, or allowing it to continue until it has bankrupted the country.

Consider also the manner in which the funds are administered. This may come as a surprise to you, but the Federal government is very inefficient! The percentage of money paid into the system that actually ends up in funding or benefits is only 60%. A 40% bite goes to support the bureaucracy. My concern is that this great truth is not recognized: The Social Security System truly will bankrupt America.

(6/1/76) The worst thing about the whole problem is that the promises made by the proponents of the system and by the Federal government have seduced millions into depending totally upon this as their principal source of sustenance when they retire. It has discouraged savings because people felt that it was not as necessary to save, because "Social Security will take care of us." The system has, in effect, made Social Security "junkies" out of our population. No one even seriously questions that Social Security will be there in their retirement plan. But there is no question in my mind that the time will come when the benefits will not be there, simply because the Social Security system will have been the most likely cause of a general collapse of the economic system. Those who will be hurt most will be those who were promised the most.

The system is immoral, dishonest, unethical, and most of all, addictive in the worst sense of the word. But the greater cruelty is yet to come, when the system is recognized for what it is, and collapses of its own weight.

(6/1/76)   Ruff's Recommendations
1. If you are now receiving Social Security payments, you must somehow cut and scrape to set aside a little each month. You may live until the system fails, taxpayers could revolt and cut your benefits, or inflation could rapidly outpace increased benefits.

2. If you are approaching Social Security retirement age, don't plan to depend on it completely. Work a few more years and sock away a cushion.

3. If you are in your forties or fifties, make your retirement plans as though Social Security didn't exist.

4. If you are still comparatively young, and if your parents are alive and approaching retirement age, plan to care for them. They deserve it.

5. Remember, inflation eats up pensions. One way to beat inflation is to stockpile commodities—clothes, food, medications, etc.—at current prices.

(5/15/77) Mr. Carter has announced that in order to prevent the Social Security fund from being depleted, we've got to raise Social Security taxes and make some payments out of the general fund. That's a joke. For years, all FICA taxes have been mingled with other taxes in the general fund. Whenever the Social Security Administration needs to dip into the alleged trust fund, which it does all the time, the government has to create money to redeem the bonds. The so-called depletion of the Social Security trust fund is a farce. There isn't any fund to deplete.

It's a typical governmental accounting, slight-of-hand absurdity that has been institutionalized to the point where this criminally deceptive process has achieved respectability.

Mr. Carter proposes to increase the employer contribution to Social Security by collecting on the employees' entire salary, while the so-called "employee's contribution" stops when the salary passes $16,500. The assumption is that employers are rich and can afford it, and we don't want to hurt the poor employee—not the "little guy." In support of this concept, Mr. Mondale has told us that it won't hurt the economy because company profits are so good, and corporations so rich, that it won't hurt anyone.

Ordinarily I try to maintain a cool, detached, cerebral attitude in such matters, but every once in awhile, something makes me so mad I feel like striking out in every direction. This stupid, hypocritical, woolly-headed, dishonest approach to funding our social welfare program is about the last straw for me. It's coming pretty darn close to thrusting me into the arms of the tax rebellion.

The Social Security system can destroy America. I don't mean that old people will destroy America. I mean that the Social Security system has made promises it can't keep. I just don't think it's too much to ask for them to be honest about it. It's apparently more palatable to divide it up into categories such as FICA, Withholding Tax, etc., but it's all the same thing.

If the Social Security system is to be funded on a pay-as-you-go basis, it will sooner or later tax American business out of business, as it is simply another corporate tax. Corporations pay no taxes, as we know them. They don't pay FICA, Corporate income tax, or any other kind of tax. The public pays taxes. Corporations merely collect taxes. People think that the employer has to absorb the increase, but it is passed on to you and me in the form of higher prices. It's passed on to the employee in the form of lower wages. Any businessman is a fool if he doesn't recoup his costs in his price and wage structure.

If you're asking who got raped, make sure you understand that corporations are not the victims—consumers and employees are! And government is the pervert that did it. Let's also remember that there are no funds to pay Social Security benefits. The government is in deficit to the tune of $60 billion. This will be paid with newly created, inflationary funny-money. Now, I can understand trying to meet the contractual obligation to our elderly people. It's too late to hassle about that. But if you really want to create hardship for our senior citizens, just put American corporations out of business.

Don't pretend that someone else is paying the bill. You are! You always have and you always will!

(2/15/78)   Social Security Soft-Soap

With appropriate hoopla, President Carter has announced that the Social Security tax increases have "assured the solvency of the Social Security trust fund for at least the next 50 years."

That's such a flagrant lie that I wonder how he had the guts to utter it. There's not an economist in the country that doesn't know the sheer, bald-faced audacity of that remark. That projection is based on the assumption that inflation will average under four percent, and so will unemployment. The rate of population growth will have to double. Any prolonged recession, depression, or period of double digit inflation will destroy these assumptions. Other fallacious assumptions are that no new classes of people will be covered under the Social Security system, National Health Insurance won't be lumped under that plan, and that benefits will not be increased.

(4/15/78)   Social Sacrifice

I had an interesting comment from a member of our staff, which makes an interesting addition to my discussion of Social Security. I said recently, "How many of you rugged individualists are accepting your Social Security check whether you need it or not? Even while you recognize the fund is in danger, are you still counting on it in your estate planning? Have you already figured out how you are going to spend it for your retirement? If so, don't point your finger at the farmer."

The comment was that most people feel they have been forced to pay into the Social Security fund and that it is their money and they are entitled to it, and I should not make people feel guilty for merely taking what is rightfully theirs. Several letters have expressed the same opinion.

Now, I will have to admit that this argument would have a certain amount of merit, if that money you paid in had really been set aside for you.

After all I've written, some of you still don't grasp that the Social Security system is not a funded pension plan. It's a tax, pure and simple. It is no different from the money that is taken out of your pocket for property taxes or income taxes and given to those the government has decided to help. The government is even beginning to admit this, calling Social Security "the pact between the generations." You are betting your children will honor that pact even when their tax burden doubles or triples. I may be cynical, but that's a lousy bet.

It is indisputable that if every person accepts his Social Security, the fund will go broke. It would be a great act of patriotism if those who did not need it would not accept it. It's our only slim chance of saving the system from bankruptcy, and if even it is futile, I wouldn't sleep well unless I tried.

Let me say that I am not totally opposed to a government retirement and pension program for those who do not have funds or family to take care of them—but only for them. I know that makes me a dinosaur in this socialistic age. Let's just hope that, unlike the dinosaurs, I don't drown in the tar pits to be looked upon as a curiosity by some future generation.

The FOUNDATION FOR ECONOMIC EDUCATION (FEE) had an interesting discussion of the same subject in their March letter.

> How does one make it clear that accepting coercively confis-cated "benefits" is just as sinful as the confiscation itself? It would seem self-evident that if no one would accept Social Security payments there would be no government plundering to finance the program, and the same is true of thousands of other ignoble schemes. "He sins as much who holds the sack as he who fills it."

That puts it a little more strongly than I would have, but that's another reason I've decided not to accept my Social Security, if there is such a thing when I retire. I'm going to try to make myself personally financially independent so that I'm not tempted. I consider it a moral issue.

It is not right to judge those who have no other means of support than Social Security, especially when the government has made it impossible for them to accumulate savings by ripping off a portion of their paycheck every week throughout their earning life. I only object to those who take it and don't need it.

Here's another Social Security fact of life.

There has been a drastic drop in the birth rate to its current level of 1.8 babies per woman, not even enough to replace us all (a birth rate of 2.1 is considered the rate necessary to maintain a stable population, or "zero growth").

When Social Security began, there were three retirees per 100 workers. There are now 31 retirees for each 100 workers. Unless the U.S. birth rate rises substantially, in 2030 there will be 52 for each 100.

You do not have to be a mathematician to see that Social Security taxes will have to rise steeply. And that does not even assume substantial increases in benefits, which you can bet your life will occur; the retired vote is the biggest single voting bloc in America.

In addition, income taxes will have to increase to keep up with spiraling benefits paid to retired government workers and retired military personnel. Property taxes and state income taxes also will rise sharply to cover retirement benefits for the increasing number of retirees from state and local governments. After all those taxes, what's left to spend or invest, or save?

The great irony is that a cure for cancer, for example, would place a gigantic unanticipated burden on our already shaken system of pensions and cause the day of reckoning to arrive that much sooner.

Here is the question. Will the workers of the future carry their burden without complaining, or will they turn against the elderly? If they do become restive and try to force cutbacks in Social Security benefits and government pensions, their mission will be a difficult one. Although worker/voters will still outnumber retiree/voters, the median age will be 50, and workers over 50 can be expected to side with the retirees, giving them a clear edge at the polls.

I believe that the only thing that can save the Social Security system is if those who can afford to do without their pensions voluntarily decide not to accept them.

This position is Utopian, and I admit may not work in the real world. The government may insist on sending it to you. If it were me, and I didn't need it desperately, I would give it to my church, support a child, or provide a scholarship. I'm open to suggestions. Let me hear from you.

(9/1/78)   Social Security Inflation

I just received an incredible document in the mail from one of our faithful subcribers in the Midwest who works for the Social Security Administration. A memo was circulated for all the local staff and he sent me a copy. It is "Public Information Program Circular" (or PIPC) No. 424, dated March 6, 1978, and entitled, "BENEFIT PROJECTIONS UNDER THE 1977 AMENDMENTS."

The table projects the amount of retirement benefits that will be necessary to maintain purchasing power over the years, and it's the darndest admission of inflationary expectations I have ever seen.

For example, the maximum benefit received by a Social Security recipient in 1978 is $5,727. By 1980 it's $6,855; 1990, $11,980; the year

2000, $22,725. If you live to the year 2010, it will take $42,451 to keep you even. It also assumes that the maximum earnings on which your Social Security deductions will be based, in order to be able to pay such marvelous benefits, will have risen in the same period from $17,700 in 1978 to $25,900 in 1980. In 1990, it will be $52,800; in the year 2000, $93,600; and in the year 2010, $163,800.

By the year 2045, it assumes that you will be paying payroll deductions on $1,157,700 in order to receive a possible maximum benefit of $306,736 a year.

The economic system can't stand that. The actuarial liabilities of the Social Security system are over $4.5 trillion and rising. That's more than the value of everything that everyone in America owns.

The press has been telling us that the recent increase in payroll taxes that our legislators decreed last year has "restored the financial soundness of the cash benefit program." According to *THE WALL STREET JOURNAL,* Monday, July 10, 1978,

> No actuary would agree with this as the trustees implicitly concede elsewhere in their annual report that the increase merely postponed the inevitable crisis. If the system is to avert ultimate catastrophe, more people in Washington are going to have to submit to actuarial discipline.

The article goes on to say in reference to new revenue:

> While $227 billion may sound large, it begins to look more and more like a Band-Aid when compared to the still looming multi-trillion dollar unfunded future liabilities of the system.
>
> Congress has taken the ridiculous attitude that it could promise lavish benefits and let future Congresses find the money. It has broadened benefits to dependents and survivors to the point where today only about half the beneficiaries are actually retired workers. Disability retirement was liberalized and it's been growing rapidly. Benefits were double-indexed to both wage and price inflation in 1972 and began soaring upward when inflation took off a short while later. The declining birth rate, meaning fewer workers to support future retirees.
>
> The trustees of the Social Security system see payroll taxes soaring to 17% to 20% of wages sometime early next century.

They are ravingly optimistic. Sometime in the next ten years the Social Security system will be the great public issue of the day. Inflation will wipe out the purchasing power of all those who trusted government and politicians. (see: Inflation and Government debt)

SOUTH AFRICA AND RHODESIA

(3/15/76)   Southern Africa is the next great explosive area, and Russian and Cuban meddling in this area could be the cause of great social disorder and civil fallout in the United States. We have great vital interests in South Africa. It is the source of much of the world's gold and diamonds. It commands the crucial sea lanes between the Indian Ocean and the South Atlantic, the route followed by most of the world's giant tankers as they transport oil from the Near East to Europe and the United States.

The South African government has been quietly making efforts to bring the black people of their country into a position of responsibility within the government, having seen the handwriting on the wall.

It is my opinion that the Soviets, through their client states and guerrilla movements, will apply increasing pressure, both politically and militarily, upon Rhodesia and adjacent South Africa, in that order.

In this country, we will have to decide whether or not we will lend support and aid to those two nations. If we decide to support these regimes, we will see a rise in international and internal tensions. The Third World will condemn us for our "racist" attitudes, and minority groups in this country, led by radicals, will condemn us for supporting "repressive, racist regimes." The next great domestic issue, the "Vietnam" of the last half of the seventies, could well be our relationship with Rhodesia and South Africa.

(4/15/78)   The U.S. government has consistently positioned itself on the side of black Marxist revolutionaries. It has ignored the human rights injustices and made pious pronouncements about the defects of South Africa and Rhodesia, while standing in the way of every reasonable solution to the problems of those troubled countries.

When the United Nations was founded, the only conditions for membership were to pay your dues and take no aggressive military action toward other sovereign states. Now the rules have changed. Now your internal policies have to be satisfactory to the majority of that debating society on the East River. The majority of the world's nations are Communist, Socialist, or Marxist dominated, and we have been afraid to buck the majority opinion of that organization on African matters.

Our Rhodesian policy is absolutely incredible. Responsible leaders, including blacks, accepted by a majority of the blacks in Rhodesia, have come to a sane, reasonable accommodation with the Ian Smith regime—a peaceful transition to black majority rule over a reasonable period of time. But because the agreement does not include the black guerrilla revolutionaries based in surrounding Marxist police states, we are doing our best to pretend that no solution has developed. By the very nature of our position, we have pretty well guaranteed that the reasonable solutions arrived at will not work. We have virtually assured a rising tide of blood in that troubled country. It won't be black blood or white blood, it will be red blood. It's all the same in the eyes of God.

The reaction of the Rhodesian blacks to the internal agreement indicated that it enjoys the overwhelming support of the people. There is no evidence of similar support for those terrorist fanatics who are only interested in acquiring power. If we don't reverse our position, a white racist regime will be replaced, after a long, confused, many-sided war. The hatred of the black racist regime will be directed not merely toward the white man. It will be directed toward all those who opposed them politically, including tribes not of their own persuasion.

We are so self-righteous about South Africa. What earthly right do we have to interfere with the internal affairs of that country, no matter how distasteful we think they might be? We have rejected the right of the rest of the world to make moral pronouncements about our racial problems, our injustice in the courts, our poverty pockets in the cities. What gives us the right to sit in judgment of others?

Our African policy is immoral, illegal, unjust, inflammatory, tragic and, above all, hypocritical. While condemning Rhodesia and South Africa, we are cozying up to Cuba, providing aid to Vietnam, saying nothing about the incredible atrocities in Cambodia, negotiating treaties with the Soviet Union, and expanding our contacts with Communist China. Those countries are among the most vicious, repressive, blood-drenched societies on earth. Why are we nice to them and nasty to Rhodesia and South Africa? That's simple. Power politics determines that we should swallow our principles and be nice to them. South Africa and Rhodesia can't fight back. But I would like to suggest another very important difference, and it revolves around the world's favorite subject: money.

One of our actions against Rhodesia was to boycott her high quality chrome, upon which we depend for our defense posture. It's a critical element in the building of missiles. There are only two sources of this high quality chrome—Rhodesia and the Soviet Union. So we punished Rhodesia for her sins by boycotting her chrome. Where do we now have to go for our chrome? Why, the Soviet Union, of course. Where did they get it? They bought it from Rhodesia, marked it up nicely and transmitted it to us. The winners? The Soviet Union. At the same time that Mr. Kissinger, in the last days of the Ford Administration, was pressing for Congress to honor this chrome boycott, a consortium of European and New York banks put together a fund of several hundred million dollars to loan to the Soviet Union for the development of its chrome deposits. One of those banks was Chase Manhattan. After Mr. Kissinger had assured it would be a good investment for Russia and the banks by giving them a monopoly of this crucial commodity, he then retired comfortably to a $75,000 position as a consultant with the same Chase Manhattan bank. And guess who guaranteed the New York bank loans? The United States government, of course. Who sponsored Mr. Carter on the international scene when he was a lame duck governor and peanut farmer? David Rockefeller, Chairman of Chase Manhattan Bank, who invited Jimmy to join his Trilateral Commission, which experience Jimmy publicly credited for his foreign policy expertise.

Did you know that six months before Mr. Kissinger's secret visit to China, which preceded the dramatic Nixon visit, David Rockefeller spent a month in that country on a secret visit? There's no secret about it. He's admitted it publicly. Did you know that New York banks are vastly increasing their banking presence in Hong Kong and developing expanding relations with the Chinese? Did you know that free world banks are involved in between $50 and $60 billion worth of loans to the Soviet Union for various forms of commercial development, and they have their eye on Cuba? Did you know that the only real security they have is the value of Soviet Union gold and diamond deposits? Do you realize that the communist drive on South Africa could very well be aimed at putting South African gold mines out of production, vastly increasing the value of the Soviet gold reserves? When you add this to the fact that the Soviets are talking about gold backing for the ruble, a pattern begins to develop. Mr. Carter seems to, in all instances and in all cases, be acting in the best interests of the American international banking establishment. Examine it yourself. The countries we are being nice to have extensive current or contemplated relationships with the New York banks. And that goes double for Panama. The countries he's being nasty to do not have extensive relations with those banks, or are worth sacrificing as markets in return for greater gains elsewhere. (see: Trilateral Commission)

SOVIETS

ECONOMIC PROBLEMS

(11/75)   Russia has lost one-third of her grain crop this year. Communist leadership does not survive crop failures. Look for a Kremlin shake-up, then the standard Leninist tactic of diverting the people's attention from their hunger and privation by stirring up adventures abroad. Watch for a troop buildup on the China border. The danger of war somewhere—South America, Africa, China, Korea, the Near East—increases exponentially in inverse ratio to Soviet internal problems.

It just doesn't add up. We will ship Russia all the grain she needs, and humbly bow to her verbal abuse, while the Russian citizenry knows nothing of our help, but hears us blamed for her troubles.

(9/1/76)   One of the reasons for the recent collapse of the gold market is that the Russians have been forced to sell a lot of gold to raise foreign exchange because they have recently been denied credit by Western banks. I know of two such loan requests totalling over $1.5 billion. They are suffering from severe economic problems that we don't hear much about. These problems don't affect us at the moment, however, sooner or later, their internal tensions have great potential for mischief. As I said before, one of the ways in which dictators of Communist regimes secure the loyalties of their people around them is to create an external threat, such as dabbing in international affairs and fishing in someone else's troubled waters.

(11/1/78)
Q. If the United States economy gets in trouble and we have financial and social disorder in this country, won't the Soviet Union take advantage of it? Isn't war really our greatest danger?
A. Every cloud has its silver lining. I believe the Soviet economy is so fragile, so delicately balanced, and so dependent upon loans and food imports from the United States and other western countries, that the financial difficulties of this country could result in a collapse of the Soviet system.

The CIA recently reported the Soviet economy is in trouble and may be headed for larger problems. And the State Department has concluded that this might explain signs of renewed Soviet interest in detente and disarmament.

If we should have real monetary chaos and a collapse of the western monetary system, the Soviets might be preoccupied at home and on the Chinese front and will not be interested in launching a preemptivewar against us, although we could see trouble in Europe.

So, I guess the news is not all bad.

NUCLEAR THREAT TO U.S.

(3/1/77)   In my opinion, Mr. Carter stated an absolutely disastrous policy when he said that we want to "completely and totally eliminate nuclear weapons from the earth." The Soviet conventional military power—in troops, tanks, aircraft, naval vessels, and nearly everything else you can mention—is so vastly superior to NATO and the U.S. military forces that the only thing preventing that power from being used is the threat of nuclear retaliation. Russia has been moving since 1972 to prepare underground shelters for all of its people, so that in the case of nuclear exchange, it would be safe (see: Nuclear Protection). The Russians also realize there would be tremendous damage to their country, and at this point in history, they consider the damage they would sustain as being unacceptable, although that judgment could change.

If we were ever successful in gaining an honest nuclear disarmament, it would merely mean the beginning of Soviet domination of the globe, because there would be no deterrent to their overwhelming conventional military forces. Why are we so concerned about disarming ourselves when we know we will never strike first? Why do we wish to totally alter the world's balance of power by eliminating our Sunday punch and our threat of retaliation?

If Mr. Carter's objective is achieved, it will be a disaster for the entire world, and one of these days the Soviets would simply say to us, "Here is where we are deployed. Here is what we intend to do, and you do not have sufficient force to stop us—now let's negotiate." Don't think those immoral monsters in the Kremlin wouldn't do it if they thought they had a chance.

Let's not only keep our nuclear deterrent, let's expand it and make the cost of aggression so great that it will never occur. There is some merit in "the balance of terror" concept.

(5/15/77)   I don't believe the Soviets are building their military machine to never use it.

On February 11, the *BOSTON GLOBE* ran a story on a lecture by BREZHNEV for the benefit of other Communist leaders. He told them that they were accomplishing far more through detente than they would have through confrontation. He also said that within three years they would be able to work their will anywhere in the world.

Militarily, they can demand economic benefits from us at our expense, and the time will come when they will use that power.

CIVIL DEFENSE PLAN

(6/1/78) *PARADE* Magazine recently featured a devastating article on the Russian civil defense program. It seems that the Russians have stockpiled enough food underground to feed their entire population for a year. Eighty percent of their population also would be safe from nuclear attack. Countries don't make such preparations unless they expect war. And there is no question the Soviets are preparing for it. The other possibility is they simply wish to present themselves to the world as being so invulnerable to attack that they can demand what they want and get it.

I haven't devoted much space to this subject, but it may be more important than anything I've discussed. The Soviets are moving with increasing aggressiveness in Africa, and I don't think they would do that unless they felt very secure in their own homeland.

The next time someone derides you for storing food and criticizes you for your "bomb shelter mentality," I suggest you point out to them that the Russians think that's a pretty smart thing to do. (see: Food Storage)

STOCKS AND STOCK MARKET

STOCK MARKET

(2/1/76) I spent five years as a stockbroker. I'd like you to understand a few things about that marketplace.

Small investors lose money by the billions because of "the fear of the loss of profit." Another name for it is greed. It is axiomatic that the public, the "little guys," jump in near the top of each rise and get out near the bottom. They don't want to be left out. The big investors are in and out long before you are. In every transaction there is a winner and a loser, and the loser is usually you, the public.

Stockbrokers and "customers' men" are caught in essentially an immoral position. They are paid on commission. Big volume, big paycheck! What does a man do when his guts tell him that everything is on the way down, and yet he makes his living selling stock? If he doesn't sell stock, he doesn't eat. If he does sell stock, his customers will lose money. If he has the ethics of a saint, he starves. So when he's working with a bull market, he gets hot and calls all his accounts and gets them on the bandwagon, and often continues to do so even when the smart institutional managers are out of the market.

It's a vicious conflict of interest and that's why I got out of that business a number of years ago.

I say: "get out and stay out." Watch the market reports and amuse yourself with your hypothetical profits after it's all over, if you wish.

(7/15/76) Everyone's thrilled when the Dow-Jones nears 1,000. Big deal! In terms of purchasing power, it would have to go to 1,750 just to equal 1966 market levels. You're watching the deterioration of America's faith in American economic strength. The stock market is a barometer. The Dow Jones between 1,000 and 1,200 is a sign of weakness, not strength.

(2/1/76) Uncle Sugar! Billions in printing press money! That's why the prime rate is dropping. The stock market equates low interest rates with a rising market. Rising stock prices strengthen the value of bank investment portfolios. Unfortunately, increasing the money supply triggers inflation about six months down the road. Inflation depresses the stock market. That's the main reason why this market really won't last, although it could have a pretty good run.

The Mad Bull
How strange is the madness of crowds!

As this is written, the stock market is pausing slightly on its mad rush toward a 1,000 DOW, which is distinctly possible. I believe it is building for a fall, and we will see the bears on a rampage sometime this year.

Here's why.

Optimism is in style, and every small piece of tentative or possible good news is stated in the most favorable light and touted as evidence

of coming prosperity. Contrary information is merely shrugged off by this market as unimportant.

Be cautious of statistics as they can lie!

Look at the tremendous boost the market received from new car sales figures for the first ten months of January. This is an excellent example of a statistic! General Motors was up 49% in sales over the same period the previous year! Up goes the DOW 15 or so points in record volume. Let's see how deceptive this can be.

This is a comparison with the worst car sales period since World War II! A 49% increase over that period in 1975 is still a disaster. In 1975 car sales were down 70% from the same 1974 period, which itself was a disaster, falling right in the middle of the Arab oil boycott!

It's still a disaster this year. GM officials had hoped for a 55% increase. Also, these are mostly small car sales. These small cars use less fuel, aluminum, plastic, rubber, shipping capacity, etc., and sell for half the price of a big car. This means continuing declines in dollar sales volume. Now, American Motors, Chrysler and Ford are shutting down some of their production lines. Some "recovery!"

Even improved consumer buying, which is up sharply, is, in my opinion, the pent-up need to make long-postponed purchases or replacements. Like the government's famous tax rebate, it will go through our economy in one lump, much like a pig through a python.

I believe that inflation has done its thing. Officially, its down to seven percent but it has already destroyed 25% to 30% of the value of all savings and income over the last two to three years, and people's discretionary spending assets have been eaten away.

If you think inflation is really only seven percent, ask the Pentagon, a school system, or a contractor how much they have to allow for inflationary increases in construction costs on long-range projects. Twenty to forty percent is more like it. Inflation is like a termite. You don't always know it's there, but it's steadily destroying you.

(1/15/77)   Super Bears

If you have the temperament for the stock market, then you can follow the advice of a good investment advisor and market theorist, such as Dick Russell, and perhaps make some money. My years as a stockbroker, however, convinced me that most people lose money even in bull markets, simply because they do not have the temperament to handle the marketplace properly. Why?

1. The are afraid to buy when prices are low and everyone is discouraged. Their temperament and fears will not allow them to do it.

651

2.   When they have made a bad choice, they are afraid to "take a loss," and they end up letting their losses run on, and then they sell at the first sign of a profit. Stock market profits come to those who have the temperament to deal with that marketplace. If you feel that you have the guts to handle it, the stock market has some possibilities.

(2/1/78)   I feel so bad every time someone calls me or walks into my office and says, "I knew I should have liquidated my stock market holdings when you told me to, but I just couldn't bring myself to do it. Grandpa left me that stock. Now everything is down. Should I hold on and wait for it to come back, or sell now?"

How in the heck am I supposed to answer that question? I think we are in the middle of a continuing downtrend, and I have no way of knowing whether there will be a major correction. I still think you ought to bail out. The losses you may have now are nothing compared to what you are going to see if I'm right. We are in the middle of a bear market.

(5/1/78)   The Bull Trap

A stock market buying panic recently rallied the Dow Jones 43 points in three trading days with record volume. This is a trap to catch the unwary bull who has been itching to get some action. The bear market has not seen the bottom. It was "over-bought" before the rally, and it is now grossly "over-bought." Bear markets end with a broadly-based selling panic at the bottom, and we haven't seen that yet.

FORECASTS

(11/15/77)   Market Signals

I watch the performance of the stock market, commodity markets, and the international monetary markets, not because I want to speculate, but because in the past they have been such accurate indicators of either trouble or prosperity, and right now they are telling us there's trouble afoot. The stock market has just signaled a major bear market and commodities are telling us there is terrible trouble in our future. The explosion to the upside of gold and silver is signaling depression and monetary troubles. I expect all commodities in general to turn upward, signaling inflation, sometime in the next few months, with perhaps wheat leading the charge.

Gold is probably the best indicator of monetary troubles, as it is traditionally the world's scared money. As of now, it's mostly European and Arab fear, otherwise we would see silver rising faster. Americans buy gold and silver when they're worried, whereas Europeans' prime interest is gold. Gold has exploded to the upside, and is probably in a runaway market. (see: Gold, Silver)

(12/15/77)

Q. You said you think the stock market is going down and that we ought to be out of everything. We've had 1000 shares of A.T.& T. for years and we depend on the income for retirement. Do you really mean I should sell my good performing stocks? Can't I keep my utility stocks? Or my blue chip energy and oil stocks?

A. This is not a stock market advisory letter, and I'm not going to advise you on individual stocks. There are others more qualified than I. However, I think I know as much about the general marketplace as anybody, and I do feel qualified to comment on general conditions. I think the stock market is going down. The so-called blue chips have been big losers during the current general decline, along with everything else. Just because it's called a blue chip doesn't mean it's immune to fluctuation. There was a time when the blue chips fluctuated so narrowly that they were considered to be "widows and orphans" stocks, and you could count on your dividend. Inflation and government policy have destroyed that safe haven and you now get sharp fluctuations, even though the dividends may have remained stable. I believe we are entering into a period of rising interest rates and falling stock market prices. You can choose to ride it out and hope that the next economic downturn is only a recession like the last one and that there will be a quick recovery, but I'd like to reemphasize something. In a spiraling inflationary depression, or a runaway inflationary spiral, the people who trust conservative blue chip, interest-bearing, or dividend-paying instruments, are the ones who will be hurt the most. That's precisely the time you'll want out of your stocks and into gold and diamonds, or you'll take a terrible beating. But remember, if you take my advice and I'm wrong, it doesn't cost me anything.

I can't prove there's going to be a collapse tomorrow but the trend has been signaled, and either an upturn in inflation, an upturn in interest rates, or a downturn in the market can hurt you.

Incidentally, the oil company stocks are the biggest puzzlement of all. With the demand for energy, and the government-mandated profits they will receive under almost any energy plan passed by Congress, you would think that they would be big winners for the future, but there are powerful forces working to force them to divest themselves of alternate energy sources and to break them up. I don't like to invest in anything that is so heavily regulated by government. As regulation increases, so too does the risk of the investment vehicle.

(12/15/77) Now, within that general climate of conditions, you are going to have to make your own decision or find a market advisor to help you. The only stocks that I am quite sure will do well are those which are related to the price of gold for the long pull. South African gold shares are risky, stick with the North American goods.

SURVIVAL PREPARATIONS

EMOTIONAL/SPIRITUAL

(1/1/78) Many of you have expressed confidence that I will be able to guide you through the difficult times ahead. Now that's scary, because I'm fallible. If that sounds like an uncharacteristic bit of humility, let me assure you it's very real. We newsletter writers are all egotists, or we wouldn't even believe that what we have to say is worth reading. However, we can get in trouble when we begin to believe that we're omniscient. My most accurate judgments seem to come after quiet periods when I realize how small I am in God's great plan, and when I acknowledge my Maker as the source of whatever talent, intelligence or insight I might have. It is then that I receive, bubbling up from the deepest wellsprings of my subconscious library and data storehouse, the insights that have stood me in good stead over the years.

(5/15/78) Here is perhaps the most important advice of all. We are facing a time of great stress. Personal peace of mind and spiritual serenity will, perhaps, be more important to you than all the money in the world. Develop a systematic weekly time to pass your values on to your children. If we were to get through this trouble with all of our money and lose our values, it would be hardly worth surviving. Those who get through sucessfully will shape the new world. I hope they are concerned with basic religious, moral, ethical and governmental values, as they will mold our "brave new world."

(12/1/78) After some serious soul-searching, I've decided to share a very personal matter because it might give you a little insight into why I feel the way I do about certain things, and it might help you in your planning.

My father was Chief Financial Officer of one of the nation's largest supermarket chains in the late 1920s. He was a mathematical genius. He could run his finger down a column of figures of up to seven digits and give you an instant total. He could do a store inventory in his head and accurately transcribe it on the train on the way to the next city. He was also a stock market speculator. When the market crashed in 1929, he took a fearsome beating. He unsuccessfully tried to recoup his losses through gambling, and lost even more. He became terribly depressed, which led him into a lot of other personal problems. He had no religious convictions or sound philosophical basis for his life. Also he was not what you would call a "family man" and, as a result, when his troubles piled up on him, they overwhelmed him, so in mid-1931, when I was only six months old, he killed himself. I have no sense of personal grief because I never knew him, nor do I have bad feelings, but I've learned a lot from the life and death of a man who loved money more than spiritual values.

Emotional and spiritual preparation for difficult times is infinitely more important than financial preparation, and that does not mean that I don't believe in financial preparation. After all, I devote 95 percent of each issue of *THE RUFF TIMES* to that subject. It's just that I believe that when the stresses hit our society, even if you have managed to preserve your money and eat when others around you are hungry, you could be deeply distressed and very unhappy if you have not made the emotional and spiritual preparations necessary to sail through these times with judgment, health and emotional stability intact. I'd rather be broke and happy than rich and distressed. Of course, all other things being equal, rich is better, meaning I'd rather be rich and happy. Here are some suggestions for "tidying up" your life to prepare for difficult times.

Ruff's Recommendations

1. Do some major soul-searching and come to some conclusions about where you stand in relation to the universe. I'm biased theologically, just as many of you are, and I think the world would be better off if it adopted my religion. But I wouldn't presume to impose it on you. Spiritual serenity is critical to survival. If you do not have

that inner serenity when things get tough, you will be the victim of your emotions and fears—and you will do and say stupid and dangerous things. You need spiritual stability to sail through these stormy seas with a cool mind and a clear head. Sit down by yourself and decide who you are and what you stand for. A lack of spiritual moorings killed my father.

2. Organize your family. Experience has told corporate managers that employees won't implement a plan unless they are involved in the planning, because it isn't "theirs." Families are very much the same. I don't think parents can unilaterally make major decisions and have them accepted by other family members.

My family uses the format of a Family Group Planning Session and weekly Family Home Evenings.

The Family Group Planning technique was taught to me by TERRY JEFFERS, my partner, who used it at IBM to train clients to arrive at orderly corporate decisions. This same planning technique is adaptable for the family. It generally involves one or two whole days away from the pressures of the world, where you sit down with your family and work out (1) your goals, (2) your objectives, (3) the problems standing in the way of meeting the objectives, (4) the solutions to the problems, and (5) a "to do" list, including specific assignments with completion dates for members of the famiy. Using this system, my family has devised the family rules and standards to which my teenagers have agreed, and we have developed our survival plan which suits our needs and with which we all feel comfortable.

Terry has published a small "how-to" booklet which is available from Target ($2 plus 50¢ postage and handling) for those of you who are interested in learning how to conduct such a planning session.

The second phase of our program consists of the Mormon weekly Family Home Evening, which could be easily adopted by other religions without sacrificing any theological purity. Our family meets every Monday night to discuss family problems and to have a lesson on some matter of ethics, morals, or religion. It is an organized, systematic way of passing our values on to our children, the most important thing we will do in this life. We can also check up on our family group plan progress, adjust the timetables, or add additional elements to the plan.

If you are interested in how the Mormons organize it, we can get you some free Family Home Evening Manuals if you will write us for one.

Unless you are spiritually and emotionally ready, all the money in the world might only bring you misery. Some people might get through in good financial shape, only to be overwhelmed by the social misery around them. We must develop that hard, inner core of strength that's rooted in an understanding of our relationship to God, the cosmos, and those we love. With that behind us, we can get through most anything.

PERSONAL/PHYSICAL

Since November of 1975 I have been advising my readers to store food, get liquid, provide security for their homes, stay out of big-city real estate and, in short, to take a defensive stance and face the fact that inflation and government policy have turned this world upside down.

Now I'd like to offer my basic recommendations in order of priority. First, the personal or physical aspect; then I'll make some financial recommendations.

1. (5/15/77) BE PREPARED TO SECURE PERSONAL SAFETY FOR YOURSELF AND YOUR FAMILY. As we move into a major recession, several things are possible.

If the cities go broke, as I believe they will, we could experience civil disorders. Unemployment will rise, and the people who receive unemployment and welfare checks will either not receive them, or the Government will fund the cities at the cost of tremendous inflation, and rising prices will cause an angry reaction on the part of the action-prone segment of our population. If this happens, you will need to protect yourself from crime and from the breakdown of the delivery of goods and services.

Much of what you eat is transported thousands of miles. No community is self-sufficient. Farmers raise cash crops which are processed, canned, frozen or whatever, and shipped all over the world. This complex distribution process is vulnerable to disruption. We are totally dependent upon truck transportation, and this could be disrupted by civil disorders in our major transportation hubs (see: Trucking Industry). A breakdown of civil order in major cities would result in almost immediate shortages. These shortages would be aggravated by panic buying, as people realize that transportation is the key to eating.

If we have runaway inflation, or troubles in our banking system, then your check might not be accepted at the local supermarkets. But even if there are no banking problems, and you have access to your funds, dislocations in the marketplace could cause you personal

657

suffering. I don't care how much money you may have. If there's nothing available to buy, you can't buy it. Therefore . . .

2. (5/15/78) OBTAIN AN EMERGENCY FOOD SUPPLY. I suggest a one-year supply. *HOW TO PROSPER DURING THE COMING BAD YEARS* gives you all the specification necessary to select a good food storage program. If you wish to go to the time and trouble, you can visit your local food storage dealer and buy from his shelves. By using my book as a guideline, you can put together a pretty good program. I've already done that for you, however. It's easier to buy from our recommended supplier (see appendix in book).

(7/1/78) You need to seriously ponder this question, which I've asked many times before: "Do you honestly believe that during financial chaos you can take your gold and silver coins down to the supermarket and find it full of food?" If you believe there will be chaos, you have to believe the marketplace will be disrupted. There is no way that you can have both fiscal chaos and normal markets.

(5/15/78) When people who don't have a food storage program write for advice on financial matters, I wonder who's wasting whose time. If you won't accept my most basic advice, how will you accept my advice on more complex issues? If worse came to worst, you'd end up eating the food, and dehydrated and freeze-dried foods can be downright luxurious. It will be the surest investment any of you will make. In an inflationary spiral, food prices will rise. Your return from your investment comes from not having to buy later when prices are at their highest. I can't think of a better investment or choice of barter items than Emergency Food Storage.

3. TAKE AN INVENTORY of all consumable items—those things that would make life difficult or uncomfortable if you didn't have them—and stock up. (I suggest such things as clothing, medicine, toilet paper, tools, light bulbs, candles, ammunition, etc.) Prepare for the shortages that price controls will bring.

4. Have an alternate SOURCE OF HEAT for comfort and cooking. A wood stove is a good start (see: Energy, Alternate Sources). If possible, have a generator and an underground supply of diesel fuel or gasoline, with appropriate additives.

5. RELOCATE, if you live in an endangered city, or at least

become mobile enough so that you could quickly relocate without losing a large real estate equity to market reverses, civil disorders or insurance cancellations.

(2/1/78) If you can't get yourself out, at least get your money out by selling your property and renting a home or an apartment. Many cities are broke. Those that aren't yet, because they have good credit and can still borrow, soon will be, as the cities are our weak link, and will be the breaking point in the next recession. This is where the troubles will first become apparent: the first domino. Please, get your money out of the big cities!

(4/15/77) If you can't sell your big city property, get as large a mortgage on it as possible and invest the money in counter-cyclical items.

This pretty well sums up the basic survival advice.

FINANCIAL

1. (5/1/78) **HAVE ENOUGH GREENBACKS ON HAND** to make at least six months of payments on installment contract debt, such as home mortgages. This can be in cash, T-bills or in a money fund! Get rid of all financially unproductive consumer debt.

2. (2/1/78) **GET YOUR PERSONAL FINANCIAL LIFE IN ORDER** by getting out of "consumer debt." Take a second job, or cut back on your expenditures, but get yourself out of debt so that you could survive in reasonable shape if you lost your job or your business went broke. That's precisely the kind of thing that will happen in our scenario. Become as independent as possible.

3. (5/15/78) **BUY ONE BAG ($1,000 FACE VALUE) OF AMERICAN "JUNK SILVER" COINS** for each member of the family minted prior to 1965. These bags contain dimes, quarters and halves. In the event of distrust of paper money, history tells us they can be spent.

(4/1/79) They have risen in value because of inflation and the depreciation of paper money. As long as that trend is intact, silver will rise. I expect an explosion of silver prices. $20 silver within the next 18 months would not surprise me at all.

(5/15/78) An equivalent dollar amount in bullion gold coins also makes sense. (Krugerrands, Austrian Coronas, etc.) These coins all tend to appreciate in value in either inflationary or deflationary times. They are the world's "troubled money," and when trouble looms, demand bids up the price.

4. (5/15/78) MAINTAIN LIQUIDITY. If you need liquid operating funds, you can invest them in a money fund such as CAPITAL PRESERVATION FUND. You can buy the shares with no commission and earn interest. You can write checks on your account. You can get your money back by bank wire the same day you ask for it. Eventually, even this won't be safe, but for now, it is the best place to keep liquid funds. Those are the basics.

(5/15/78)   Opportunity Money

Now we come to the exciting part of the whole plan. Periods of great change and difficulty have great opportunities (as Rhett Butler said in GONE WITH THE WIND, " . . . there is just as much money to be made out of the wreckage of a civilization as from the upbuilding of one." You have several alternatives.

1. PURCHASE MORE GOLD OR SILVER BULLION COINS.

Whether we are forecasting inflation or deflation, gold will do well, because it is a chaos hedge, any kind of chaos: inflation or deflation.

2. INVEST IN NUMISMATIC (RARE) COINS.

3. BUY DIAMONDS. (4/1/79) Diamonds between 1 and 2 carats, bought at true wholesale prices (check Reliance Products).

4. INVEST IN SMALL TOWN, INCOME-PRODUCING REAL ESTATE. (4/1/79) By small town, I do not mean bedroom communities, which are merely satellites of large metropolitan areas. I am referring to small towns where the traffic flows into that town in the morning, not out of it towards some big city. A diversified agricultural economy, a good community feeling, and a sense of small town pride are all important in your selection. It could be anywhere in the country.

Buy income-producing real estate, rather than speculating in raw land. If you figure out the rate of return after holding a piece of land and pumping your pocket money into it in installment payments, taxes, and other expenses, you will realize you can have better rates of return on investment if the property produces sufficient income to service the debt. In fact, I think it's the only valid income-producing investment for our inflationary times, because it's the only way I know, other than running a business, to get investment income without loaning money at a fixed return. If you think you are too far along in years to do something like that, remember, you *can* teach old dogs new tricks, so hustle your bones and get cracking with a real estate program. Buy some apartment buildings in a small town somewhere, and inflation will cover most of your mistakes. Your only other income choices will result in the destruction of purchasing power through inflation.

5. BUY COLLECTIBLE ITEMS, such as baseball cards, comic books, antiques, old cars, fine art, rare coins. You must become a hobbyist and enjoy collecting things, and make a real study of it. Don't do it unless you are either prepared to enjoy it enough to spend a lot of time at it, or unless you have an advisor whom you can trust completely to make your buying decisions for you. Otherwise, leave it alone. Don't just go out and buy some stamps or comic books because someone says it's a good deal. You can get hurt paying too much for inferior merchandise unless you know what you are doing.

(5/15/78) When people are looking for an inflation hedge, they tend to bid collectibles out of sight. Just when the market is at its wildest, you should sell and convert to gold.

6. There are some other interesting SPECULATIVE OPPORTUNITIES at times like this, including gold shares, gold and silver futures contracts, and small town real estate. As the quality of life in the cities deteriorates, which it will, affluent people will be moving from large cities to small towns. This will bid up property price. While the rest of the nation is going to Hell in a hand-basket, the small towns could prosper (with the exception of distribution of vital commodities).

(7/1/78) Unless you have both time and a speculator's temperament, you shouldn't even get involved in aggressive capital accumulation. It is in this area that Harry Schultz's advice to be a trader would be valid. If you are prepared to assume substantial risks in search of great profits, only then should you trade foreign currencies, precious metals on margin, commodity futures and stocks. If you do this, you should prepare for trading losses along with your profits. You should limit yourself to no more than 20% of your total liquid assets in this area. The judgment and nerve required to make money in this area are immense, and 90% of the people who try it end up losers.

The LOWRY approach to pyramiding real estate assets is for the person who wants to aggressively accumulate assets in a short time. It really works, and will continue for a year or more in the small town, residential income property market. But eventually, even there you will want to get off the debt pyramid and trade all your properties for one fully owned building, and hang on for the long haul.

(5/15/79) Incidentally, my son Larry has recently obtained his real estate license and is helping me acquire properties in the Provo area. If you are interested in having him look around for you, drop me a note and I'll pass it on to him. He knows what to look for.

(7/1/78) The preservation of your capital should be your primary investment objective, not the elusive search for wealth. Make your money in your profession or business and be as aggressive as you want there, but then hang on to what you make through defensive and counter-cyclical investments. They will get you through the financial quicksand on which we stand today.

(8/1/77)   More Financial Recommendations

1. If your money's in the bank, don't have it tied up in CDs. Be sure you could withdraw on a moment's notice, and I'll tell you when. You might get two or three false alarms, but I'd rather have you take it out once or twice and put it back in, than not be able to get it when you need it. I'd rather err on the side of safety.

2. Get an underground fuel storage tank, if possible. One marvelous suggestion from one of our Discussion Groups was for a group of you to go together and rent or lease an abandoned or out-of-business gas station. Use that as your private gasoline supply in case of rationing, allocation or shortages.

3. Get yourself a compact car that gets good mileage. Also, take a look at the article on Mopeds published in our July 1, 1977 issue.

4. Send to the U.S. Government Printing Office, Washington, D.C. and ask for a copy of Executive Order No. 11921. This contains revisions of Executive Order No. 11490, which appeared in the Federal Register, Volume 41, No. 116, Tuesday, June 15, 1976. Read it carefully so you understand the total context.

5. Conduct your financial transactions with as much privacy as possible. Realize that banking records could be seized at some future time. Deal in cash when you can, and try to accumulate some funds for which there are no records. Then put this money into gold and silver coins. This emergency could be declared immediately, and becomes effective on the day of the Order.

I seriously doubt any organization as ineffective as government would be able to immediately implement all the provisions of this Order. However, if it is implemented, you can bet your life that the

President will have alerted those agencies that deal with the critical areas; they will be ready to move quickly, so get ready for trouble.

(5/15/79)   You might want to speculate on falling long-term rates by taking a position in bonds, LONG-TERM TREASURY BONDS. You can nail down some high interest yields (which admittedly won't be sufficient to cope with inflation but will come close), and the difference will be made up by the capital gains possibilities. With current high rates, some of the older bonds can be bought at good discounts, and when we get the downward correction in long-term rates, the price of those bonds will rise. When the rates turn back up, in 6–15 months, we will be out of bonds and into a 100% hard-money position again. You might put anywhere from 20% to 50% of your money in these bonds. Right now you can get higher yields in Treasury bills, but you have no capital gains opportunities, as you do with bonds. If you buy a bond and interest rates fall, the market price rises. In other words, bonds are not like CDs or annuities. They do fluctuate with the market, and I think it's time to place a small hedging bet on a scenario of falling long-term rates for the next little while.

However, the major change in strategy I am suggesting is to take advantage of the high yields in bonds for awhile. This means income, and could hedge you against a classic recession. Don't go 100% into anything. Spread your risk. Buy some gold, some silver, some diamonds, some real estate, and some bonds for income. If it looks like the decline in long-term rates may be steep, we'll suggest that you expand that portfolio. Buy long-term Treasuries. Stay away from Series E "Savings Bonds." They soon will be a bigger rip-off than they ever were. They were a lousy deal at 6% for five years, and starting January 1, 1980, the five years will become eleven years. That is precisely what you should not do.

Gold

If you think the chances are four-to-one I'm right, then you might want to put $1 out of every $5 into gold. If you think it's fifty-fifty I'm right, then put half of your money into gold. In other words, you set your own odds and invest accordingly. I do not think it's wise to bet 100% on my scenario, or anyone else's, for that matter.

SELF-SUFFICIENCY

(2/15/77)   Ruff's Recommendations

1.   If you haven't completed your food storage plan, try to do so now—at least your vegetables and grains, as prices will probably never be as cheap as they are now.

2.   If you have agricultural land with good ground water, hang on to it. It will be valuable, as we are going to lose the productivity of some of our choicest land.

3.   Pray for rain and a softening of the elements. As much as man knows about the management of his financial affairs, he does not know how to insulate himself from the ill effects of weather. You should plan your life, as your ancestors did, to be self-sufficient —regardless of what happens.

4.   Contact a local firm that installs solar heating units, and install them in your home and in your swimming pool. They may not do the whole job, but they will certainly reduce the fuel demand, and you might be able to get by without undue discomfort in a rationing situation.

5.   If you can, drill a well. We can refer you to a company that sells home drilling equipment reasonably. Be independent of delivered water, at least to some degee.

6.   Make sure you have a home water storage supply in the form of a waterbed and containers filled with water. At least you would be able to cook and drink if you live in any of the areas that are prone to water pollution and drought.

7.   If you live downstream from areas where there has been heavy precipitation and cold weather, prepare for flooding. Above all, let's acquire a new sense of humility for our dependence upon the whims and vagaries of nature. We are not invulnerable.

(5/15/77) Self-sufficiency is critical. Be sure you could stay in your home without leaving it for awhile, if necessary. Secure your home with at least minimal protection against crime: dead-bolts, burglar alarms, and a very noisy dog. These should discourage the amateur, and there will always be lots of amateurs. Crime will rise as economic troubles worsen. You must relocate if you live in a vulnerable area (see: Real Estate). Remember, personal security comes ahead of financial security, so do the prudent things necessary to secure it. To do otherwise is gambling with the safety and lives of those you love.

(Special Report #5, 4/1/78)

Q. What degree of self-sufficiency should I try for?

A. By all means you should have food storage and/or a garden. If you can also have some chickens, rabbits or geese, that's even better. If you live in town, the neighbors might not want crowing roosters, but rabbits are pretty quiet. You should have a well and an auxiliary generator so you can always pump water. Have a good, modern wood stove and a nearby source of firewood. I would like to have an underground gas storage tank and, of course, a safe place for my emergency supply of food. I would want a safe concealed under carpeting and sunk into a concrete slab floor, if possible. I would like a bicycle, a moped, or a Honda Civic or its equivalent, so that I could always get someplace in a fuel shortage. There should be good hunting and fishing nearby so I could supplement my diet. But I also want to be able to live comfortably in the world as it is now, so I'd like to be relatively near stores, schools, job opportunities and all the other things that I consider important in my life. So what's the best compromise? A small town, but I think you've heard that before.

DO THY PATIENT NO HARM (HIPPOCRATIC OATH)

(5/15/78)   All this advice is designed to not hurt you if I should turn out to be wrong. I don't believe in burning bridges behind you. Think of it as an insurance program. When you buy automobile insurance, you aren't disappointed if you don't have an accident. We would rather not pay for insurance, but no prudent driver would be without it. Along this perilous road, let's be properly insured. If the worst happens, we are prepared, if it doesn't, our chances of loss will be small.

How do you decide how much gold or silver you should have? If you think there's a 20 percent chance I'm right, put 20 percent of your assets into gold or silver. If you think it's 50-50, then half of it should be in these counter-cyclical investments. If you are absolutely convinced, then throw everything you have into these basic suggestions, bearing in mind that you will need to retain some liquidity.

Now, become politically active on the local and Congressional levels, as we need good men in office to keep the ship of state afloat as we sail through stormy seas.

WHAT IF ...

(4/15/79) It might be a useful exercise to pass on to you a question that I receive so often in the mail and on radio and television shows. It usually starts out, "If everyone took your advice . . . ." and then follows with a list of all the bad things that could go wrong, such as banks failing because of everybody withdrawing their money, food shortages from everybody stockpiling food, etc. The analogy is used of "yelling 'Fire' in a crowded theatre."

Well, I think there's nothing wrong with shouting "Fire" in a crowded theatre, if you are sure that all but two or three people are deaf, which is precisely what I am doing now. If I thought everyone would try to take my financial advice, I'd stop giving it publicly, because it would no longer be valid. The kind of instructions I'm giving can only be followed by a minority, otherwise the markets turn upside down, prices of the inflation-hedge investments go up , and my advice just won't work anymore. Whether or not what I say could be harmful if everyone took my advice, is an interesting theoretical exercise and lots of fun to debate, but in the real world, only an infinitesimally small fragment of the population is going to take my advice. But let's look at whether or not my advice is good or bad for the nation.

If we find ourselves with runaway inflationary distortions, and significant numbers of people lose their incomes, look what would happen to *THE RUFF TIMES* subscribers who had stockpiled food, bought gold and silver, reduced their consumer debt and pulled their money out of lending situations.

1. They wouldn't need welfare, so they would not be a burden upon the public purse.

2. They could eat the food they had stored, and would not be competing for scarce goods with others.

3. They would probably have a wood stove and would not suffer from heating and cooking fuel shortages, because wood is still a widely available and relatively inexpensive source of energy.

4. They would have some liquid reserves, probably in the form of gold coins, whose prices would be going through the ceiling if we have those kinds of troubles. They would be able to service their debts and wouldn't run the risk of losing their properties.

5. They would have investments that are growing, not shrinking, because of inflation.

6.   They would not be part of any banking panic when it occurs. They would be mostly out of the banking system, well in advance of any such troubles, so they would not be contributing to a domino collapse when the dominos start falling.

7.   They wouldn't be hurt by loan defaults, because they would not be lenders.

8.   They wouldn't lose their big city home equity when the real estate market breaks, because they would have sold their big city real estate.

In sum, my advice is stabilizing, not destabilizing. It is anti-panic, not panic-inducing. The nation is nervous and apprehensive, but fear of the unknown is a lot worse than knowledge of a finite known factor that can be hedged against. I will continue to say all the things I'm saying, as long as I know I am talking to a minority in the country who can, in the real world, act upon my recommendations. If I reach the point where the majority will be acting, I'll probably shut up. But don't hold your breath. Guys like me never acquire a majority following.

THREE STEP PROGRAM

(2/1/79)

Q. I just cannot plan my life based on the assumption of a collapse of the American economy. I've got to live in the here and now. Can you help me? I'm confused.

A. When people are confused I can't always blame them. Maybe the communicator is at fault, and in this case, that's me. So I guess the buck stops here.

I am not asking you to make all of your investments based on the prospect of total calamity. My advice really falls into three basic categories.

1.   THE SURVIVAL PROGRAM. This is based on the assumption that there is a possibility of a major economic calamity in our future. That means food storage and the accumulation of other storable, consumable items, from spark plugs and toilet paper to canned goods and flashlight batteries. This survival plan assumes the worst, but it also has positive benefits —even if the worst never happens.

For example, if you want to get a 30% to 40% tax-free return on your money, I suggest you stock up whenever there is a major sale of any items you consume or use on a regular basis. To give you a better handle on this principle, it's the same as if you had bought an investment that went up in value 40%, sold it, and went out and bought something that had risen 40% in price. You realize your profit not by selling but by consuming, thus avoiding a taxable transaction from which Uncle Sam would get his piece.

Will Rogers said: "Invest in inflation, it's the only thing that's going up." So the trick is to own things that are going to rise in price. Just be sure that they won't rot on the shelf, and your imagination need have no bounds. So, even my survival advice is not based totally on the assumption that only a future calamity will make it worthwhile.

2.   THE BREAK-EVEN OR BETTER STRATEGY. This is not based on the prospect of future calamity. This facet of our investment plan is pragmatic and deploys our funds without regard to ideology, dogma, or other preconceptions, but based on the world as it is. There is no investment for all seasons, but there is a season for all investments. And this is the season for precious metals. As long as the interest rate is rising, the inflation rate is rising and there is increasing instability in the world, you can count on these metals being in a generally rising trend.

In this stage of our break-even-or-better strategy we will use diamonds, more gold coins, additional silver holdings, antiques (in fact, collectibles of all kinds) and small town real estate.

3.   THE LEVERAGED, GET-RICH STRATEGY. This is a totally different strategy taking considerable risks to not just beat the rate of inflation, but to beat it many times over. It involves the futures markets, perhaps gold mining stocks on margin, highly leveraged investments in farm land, raw land speculation, plus other non-income producing, volatile assets. This area is not for the faint-hearted, and frankly, most of us have faint hearts. It's only for those with guts and the ability to sleep through almost anything.

Strangely enough, gold could fit into all three categories. (see: Gold, Three Investment Strategies)

We must be concerned with the "here-and-now" with the bulk of our money. The survival position must be executed before you consider any of the other things that we have talked about. Once you are secure, you can have the emotional security and stability necessary to make good judgments about the rest of your investment portfolio.

SURVIVAL FOR THE NON-RICH

(6/1/79) Here's a letter I received from one of our subscribers who has saved a lot of money while implementing my suggestions. Most of you could apply some of these principles.

For those with adequate funds to whom time is money, the commercially prepared, dehydrated, freeze-dried food storage route might be more appropriate. For those of you for whom money is in shorter supply than time, this is a great way to go, or at least part way.

Dear Mr. Ruff:

I am a new member. I joined about two months ago. Since that time I have done the following:

1. Purchased two—55 gal. drums that food was stored in. One I filled with wheat and corn, the other with soy beans, cooking oil, dried yeast and a little rye (10#).

2. I have learned to make bread, soy milk, soy butter, sprout grain and make a good coffee substitute from the rye. (I purchased a flour mill at a garage sale for $5.00, a new one costs $25.00.)

3. I ran ads in my local Penny Saver and purchased silver coins, gold rings and sterling silver at wholesale or below (by paying the owners' prices if they were within reason, or bartering, if not).

4. I purchased several good books on survival, read them and packed them with my bulk food.

5. I purchased at garage sales and in response to my Penny Saver ad— two .22 caliber rifles in very good condition; and 2,000 rounds of .22 cal. ammo at K-Mart's spring sale (about 40 percent off list price).

Things to do yet are: complete a first aid kit, purchase a wood stove and pipe, purchase gas-powered electric generator, store some gas and oil, get a water purifier. I have two gallons of chlorox on hand to purify water and to use as a disinfectant.

A Civil Defense Radiation fallout book I had from the time I was in service helped calm my friends and neighbors.

For trading material, I have stored two—#1 cans of tobacco and a large amount of cigarette papers given to me free for buying the tobacco, two cartons of cigarettes (Germany was on a cigarette economy for five years after WWII), 12 pints of vodka (also can be used as medicinal).

Since we have been buying our toilet tissue and facial tissue by the case, we were prepared for the impending national truck strike and the near disaster at Three Mile Island (I am only 150 miles away).

Sample of Prices I paid:

two 55 gal. food storage drums, $8 each	$16.00 + tax
one flour mill	5.00
Grains—soy beans, wheat, corn, rye	34.00
Yeast and cooking oil	6.00
	$61.00

It doesn't have to be expensive to get started. From Penny Saver ads—(three weeks for $2.00) I have purchased $100.00 face value U.S. coins and $25.00 Canadian silver dollars, also 23 10K gold rings, 14 14K gold rings, three 18K gold rings, to be used in a barter economy, two nice antique rings I gave my wife, two diamond rings (small diamonds) with gold settings and several pounds of sterling silver, which I have traded for a Krugerrand.

Once you get off your duff and start doing for yourself and your family, it is surprising how much you can do to improve your lot, even on a limited income.

Thanks for giving me the incentive to get going—I enjoyed your book.

D. H.

I really appreciate this shared information, and the super "can-do" attitude. If you have success stories along the same lines, I hope you will let us know. We will try to pass them on whenever we have space.

SUMMARY

(2/15/76) Admittedly, all of these things are a bit scary. It's not my fault. I merely reported it. But we can't let fear distort our lives.

Herbert J. Grant, a great religious leader, was pruning his fruit trees one day when he was visited by a friend who asked what he would do if he knew the Second Coming of Christ was tomorrow. He said:

"I would finish pruning my fruit trees."

His message was twofold.

If you aren't ready the day before an event, one day of panicky action won't make any difference. If you are prepared you have peace of mind and go on with your daily pursuits and sleep well at night. Preparation is the key to peace. Physical preparation (food, clothing, etc.), financial preparation (preservation of capital, gold, silver, etc.), personal preparation (corrective surgery and dental work, diet improvement, exercise to build general health, etc.), and spiritual preparation (family strengthening, religious training, meditation, etc.). If you've done these things, then sleep well. Comfort yourself with the knowledge that even with the troubles we face, the U.S.A. will be the best place in the world to be in case of a world-wide financial convulsion. Feel secure in the knowledge that if you have done all you can, the odds are highly in your favor. Work like it's all up to you and pray like it's all up to God. Therein lies peace and safety.

SWISS BANK ACCOUNTS

(1/15/78)

Q. Should I have my money in a Swiss bank?

A. I'd rather have my money where I am. You would have done very well if your money had been in the Swiss franc recently. But that's hindsight, and currency speculation is dangerous. In an unsettled world economic climate, it might be difficult to repatriate your money. So much money has flowed into Switzerland that it is creating problems for the Swiss. Currencies get in trouble not just when they are going down, but also when they rise too rapidly. It creates internal and international commerce problems. Right now, the Swiss really don't want your money. In the recent past they have imposed a negative tax on money flowing into their country, and the laws regarding Swiss bank secrecy have been weakened considerably by treaties between the United States and Switzerland. Also, during World War II, we impounded Swiss money in this country and used it to blackmail them into refusing to do business with the Germans. Because they were surrounded by Axis occupied countries, they almost starved to death. I don't think they've forgotten that. There are plenty of ways to hedge your money right here in the U.S.A. Dick Russell raised an interesting point in one of his recent letters. The reason why the Swiss currency is so trusted is because it is substantially gold-backed. Right now, gold is under-valued in relation to the currency. These kinds of spreads don't often occur, and they tend to adjust themselves either by a fall of the currency or a rise in the price of gold. If they maintain their historic ration, the metal is now a better buy than the currency.

On my recent visit to Switzerland I decided that it's the only other country where I might like to live. It's beautiful, clean and self-reliant. The Swiss can put 400,000 citizen soldiers in the field in 24 hours. In 72 hours, they could have one million men under arms. Every male is trained in mountain guerilla warfare and is required to own and know how to use a gun. No one would attempt to invade them, but they could become isolated in a chaotic Europe, and the next economic downturn is going to result in unpredictably chaotic conditions. Switzerland would probably remain a relatively safe island, but even given that, I prefer to have my money where I am. If I had all my money in Switzerland, I might want to have a home there, and at the first sign of trouble I might fly to Switzerland to be near my money, but that's definitely second choice. The United States will be the best place to be during the world troubles and will be the first to recover.

(Special Report #4, 10/76) Investors in Mexican banks were thrilled to death by their 14 percent interest rate, until the peso was devalued, despite all the protestations of the Mexican Government and the investment counselors who were recommending such investments. When a monetary crisis occurs, the transfer of money across international borders becomes more and more difficult. That's why I prefer to have my money in this country.

T

TAXES

CAPITAL GAINS TAX

(7/15/78)   "I Will Never Lie To You"—Again

In a recent press conference, President Carter turned his demagogic rhetoric on the STEIGER AMENDMENT to his tax bill, which proposes to lower the capital gains tax from a maximum of 48% to a maximum of 25%. The figures which the President used to buttress his opposition were dishonest, and he knows it. They were designed to stir up class hatred in a manner reminiscent of Huey Long at his worst.

He said that 80% of the tax benefits from that cut would go to taxpayers who make more than "$100,000 a year," and he came up with the ingenious, emotionally loaded statement that it provided, "huge tax windfalls for millionaires and two-bits for the average American."

Let's expose the calculated dishonesty of that statement.

Do you know what he means by "those who make over $100,000 a year?" He is using a figure which the Treasury defines as "expanded income," which was, as *THE WALL STREET JOURNAL* says,

> ... a description developed by tax reformers some time ago for political purposes. Expanded income means ordinary income, plus the full amount of any capital gains. Thus, it would be possible for a family with an ordinary income of $25,000 and a capital gain of, say, $75,000 on the sale of a long-term residence, to be part of that illustrious group making $100,000.

Many a blue-collar middle-class American has a home that he bought a long time ago for $30,000, which is worth $100,000 to $125,000 in inflated funny money. If he should be forced, by property taxes, to sell that home, or if he just wanted to retire from mowing lawns by moving to an apartment, he could be stuck with a capital gain of $70,000 to $100,000, which when added to his $20,000 to $25,000 salary, could put him right up in that rarified class of those who "make more than $100,000 a year."

Carter's estimate of $2 billion in tax revenues lost, is based on the ridiculous assumption that a tax can be reduced without having a beneficial surge in economic activity and additional taxable profits, to at least compensate for the lost tax revenue. If there is any tax cut that would produce that benefit, it is the capital gains tax.

A lot of real estate and stock market investors go through incredible, uneconomic, distorted gyrations in the management of their investments to avoid the capital gains tax. If the capital gains tax were cut, the gyrations would be a lot less worth the trouble, and a lot of people would simply decide to pay the capital gains tax and forget about it, which would probably result in an increase in tax revenues. Also, the potential rewards of investment would be greater and more people would be willing to risk some money in funding the new businesses that have always been the life-blood of the American miracle.

THE WALL STREET JOURNAL used several examples to illustrate how this tax cut might yield major benefits to ordinary non-rich Americans. Here's one.

> A New York cabbie paid $24,000 for his licensing medallion five years ago and he now sells it for $58,000. His total long-term capital gain is $34,000. His earned income was $13,200, excluding the capital gain. He has a wife and two children. Under the present law, his Federal income tax liability would be $8,850. With the Steiger amendment, it would be $7,800, a saving of $1,050.

And then the JOURNAL concludes:

> It will be noted that none of the above are millionaires. They are ordinary individuals forced by circumstances to take a capital gain in grossly inflated dollars, and who, under present law, would pay a heavy tax on inflation. Obviously, the Congress understands all this better than the President. Backers of the Steiger Amendment might be forgiven if they categorized the statements at the Monday press conference as two-bit politics.

And, incidentally, the "two-bits" figure was computed by adding up all capital gains tax savings under the Steiger Amendment (exclusive of the "millionaires"), and averaging it over all the rest of the taxpayers. The actual tax saving for "non-millionaires" who take a capital gain is over $500. Jimmy's statistical technique is like determining the number of cans of dog food eaten by American animals, and averaging in the parakeets and hamsters.

Shame on you, Jimmy. You are either cynical, dishonest and reckless, or you are stupid, and I don't know which is the most dangerous to the Republic. Frankly, it doesn't matter. All I know is that I hope the Steiger Amendment comes to you with so many votes that it's veto-proof, because it is one of the most constructive steps that could be taken to strengthen the American economy and make it safer for those who wish to venture their capital. It is a function of a President not to incite class envy but to strengthen the unity of a nation through moral leadership. The least we should expect from you is to understand how the system works. Or maybe you do, Jimmy, and that's mind-boggling! (see: Real Estate)

THE INFLATION TAX

(10/1/78)   The argument in Washington seems to be over whether or not we should be paying 50 percent or 25 percent capital gains tax. Let me tell you about the real capital gains tax. In many instances, it is well in excess of 100 percent. The average person who thinks he has a capital gain has made nothing whatsoever. His Potomac partner ripped-off the whole thing.

In order to understand this concept, you have to remember that inflation is also a tax. Let's look at some numbers.

Let's say you bought some land two years ago for $100,000 and you sold it two years later for $125,000. The capital gains tax on the $25,000 "profit" (the difference between the $100,000 purchase price and the $125,000 sale price) could be approximately $6,000, depending on your tax bracket.

However, the true profit on that transaction was not $25,000. Two years of land price-inflation around 10 percent accounted for $20,000 of the profit, and in the real estate market, as measured by your ability to go back into the marketplace and buy a comparable property, $20,000 of the nominal gain was inflation, and consequently, was no gain at all. Only $5,000 of the total gain represented true profit. Your capital gains tax of $6,000 means that the true tax rate on your $5,000 true profit was 120 percent.

We not only need a meat-axe slash in the capital gains tax, we need to index capital gains for inflation. You determine the rate of inflation, figure out the inflationary gain in value and pay a capital gains tax on only the remaining true profit. In the example above, the tax should be paid only on $5,000.

The Income Tax can be even worse. Let's say you are receiving a yield of eight percent on a bond, and let's be charitable in assuming that the inflation rate is only seven percent. That means that after adjusting for the drop in purchasing power of your money, your true profit was only one percent. You had a seven percent inflationary loss and an eight percent dividend return, netting out a one percent gain. However, your tax will be based on the entire eight percent, meaning, of course, that if you are in the 25% bracket, you would pay out in taxes approximately one quarter of your total additional interest income, or two percent. Now you don't have to be a genius to see that if you have a one percent net profit and are paying two percent in taxes, the true tax rate for you is 200%, and that ain't no way to get rich.

Indexing is a genie that is hard to put back in the bottle once you get it out, but I would not mind seeing indexing of the capital gains tax and the tax on income from investments so that nobody is taxed on illusory inflation profits. But don't hold your breath. Government's very survival depends on that income.

(11/1/76)   Inflation and taxes are the villains that have stripped away the profit potential of almost every investment opportunity. Whatever is left is under direct governmental attack.

Here's how.

For an investment to be profitable, you must have a return of at least three percent AFTER INFLATION AND TAXES. If the inflation rate is 10%, and you are in the 33% tax bracket, your gross return after expenses would have to be 19.4%!!

19.5%	Gross Return
−6.5%	income tax (1/3)
13.0%	After tax profit
−10.0%	inflation (One year loss of purchasing power)
3.0%	Real Profit

Inflation increases the yield you must receive, while at the same time creating uncertain business conditions.

I believe that the true rate of increase in the cost of living ranges anywhere from two to five percentage points higher than those figures given out by the government, the so-called consumer price index.

Many major cost factors are not even considered in the CPI. It doesn't include automobile insurance, union dues, interest, Social

Security taxes, state taxes, Federal income tax, and property taxes. Insufficient weight has been given in the CPI to services, such as repairmen, attorneys, and medical insurance.

You can bet that if Uncle Sam says that the inflation rate is 6.5%, it really is 8% to 11%. If he says it's 11% in California, it's 13% to 16%.

(1/1/78) Unfortunately, the proposed IRS solutions are not solutions at all, but are a little more of "the hair of the dog that bit us" which has a temporary "feel-good" effect, but merely deepens our addiction. Let's look, for example, at the upcoming Carter tax cut which is supposed to stimulate the economy.

There will be no tax cut at all, but there will be the appearance of one.

MILTON FRIEDMAN has produced some mighty clear thinking on this subject. There are three basic principles.

1. The amount of money taken from your paycheck by the IRS is not the true indicator of the tax level. TAXES ARE WHAT IS SPENT BY GOVERNMENT, NOT WHAT THE IRS COLLECTS. For example, if government spends $400 billion and collects $325 billion through the IRS, where does the other $75 billion come from? It comes from the inflation tax, which gets us all. Carter offers us a $25 billion "tax cut," which means that the budget deficit will be increased by that amount, so the government has merely hiked the "inflation tax" to make up the difference. The INFLATION TAX simply is the AMOUNT BY WHICH YOUR PURCHASING POWER HAS DIMINISHED AS GOVERNMENT HAS CRE-ATED MORE DOLLARS TO SPEND. Their gain is your loss. The true tax level is the sum of the inflation tax and the IRS collections, and that adds up to the total amount of government spending. You can rearrange a pile of manure, and it's still a pile of manure. As the inflation tax increases the general price levels, government will have to spend a lot more money just to do the same things, because the cost of services and goods purchased by government is increased, right along with yours.

2. The inflation process triggers cost-of-living escalator clauses and, even though apparent take-home pay is increased, it throws us into higher tax brackets, which means we will pay a larger percentage of our earnings in taxes. The tax cut will be balanced out by the higher tax rates. This gives politicians the best of all possible worlds. They can appear to be voting for a tax cut, while spending (vote buying) is still escalating.

Friedman says that he would rather have a $200 billion Federal budget with a 100 billion deficit, than a balanced $400 billion budget with no deficit at all. Again, because taxation is the amount spent by government.

3. The $25 billion that Mr. Carter is so kindly giving back to us is approximately equal to the increased Social Security tax. Government takes $25 billion more in Social Security taxes, gives you back $25 billion in tax cuts, and says we've solved our problems and it hasn't cost us anything. A miracle!

But let's not blame government. If you weren't demanding these expenditures, they wouldn't be made. Remember Pogo's statement, "We have seen the enemy, and he is us." If that's what you want, government will find some way for you to pay for it, and they'll getcha, one way or another. Because of our increasing demands to swill at the public trough, our taxation and reward system is biased in favor of consumption rather than production. The producers who succeed are ripped-off to provide more funds for those who consume, so that they can continue to consume, and vote right. The majority now appears to benefit temporarily from this process.

Now, let me move to the financial bottom line of all this. When the economy turns downhill, probably before June of 1978 (unless we get lucky and manage to postpone it for a few years), all of society's problems will be exposed and demands for Federal aid will explode, and the Federal deficit will soar. I would not be surprised to see a Federal budget of $800 billion within two years with monstrous deficits and runaway inflation. It is politically irreversible. Not enough people really want to change it.

What will be the total impact upon Federal government?

1. The cities will need $100 to $200 billion a year in Federal support.

2. The banking system will need at least $150 billion to bail them out of its coming troubles (as the FDIC and the Federal Reserve are now the lenders of last resort to the entire world) caused by massive international loan defaults as the world-wide depression deepens.

3. If the farmers get their way, it will cost the government another $15 billion.

4. Direct foreign aid, or better stated, blackmail, by the commodity-rich, money-poor countries could take another $80 to $200 billion of our substance over the next two or three years.

The Federal government can only get money from two places—your paycheck, and by creating inflationary funny-money and there is no way that this can produce anything other than an inflationary explosion and a dramatically altered financial system. (see: Proposition 13)

TAX DEDUCTIONS

(3/15/78)   Let's Jail Rape Victims

Did you know that everything you make belongs to the government and anything that they don't take away from you in taxes is a gift? I just learned that myself. Where did I learn it? Why, from Teddy Kennedy, the renowned economist and stunt man. Teddy said recently that the "three martini lunch" tax deduction, which President Carter wants to cut in half, still amounts to "food stamps for the rich."

As a part of his tax package, Carter has proposed limiting the deduction of business meals to one half of the cost. "The only thing wrong with President Carter's proposal is it doesn't go far enough," Kennedy said. "Even a deduction for half the cost of an expense account meal is too much. The tax deduction for business meals is nothing more than a lavish and unnecessary Federal subsidy for highly paid executives—food stamps for the rich," Kennedy said.

"The business lobbyists working overtime to defeat President Carter's proposals would get short shrift from Congress if they came hat in hand to Capitol Hill seeking $1 billion a year in direct subsidies for their noontime gastronomical indulgences," Kennedy said. "And Congress should give equally short shrift to their current effort to preserve the present subsidy through the back door of the tax laws."

Subsidy? The vicious view that any money not taxed away from us is a "tax subsidy" is the most dangerous economic-political doctrine of our times. The U.S. Treasury has an even cuter label for the money that escapes the tax man. They call it a "tax expenditure."

The "three martini lunch" is just symbolic of a much larger problem. As the Chairman of the Board of a corporation, I don't allow my staff or employees to put a lunch on the expense account unless I feel it serves a legitimate business purpose. With most companies, it's the salesman on commission, struggling to make a buck by entertaining a client at lunch, who is reimbursed by his company. The business luncheon is a respected American business tool and every company I know watches that expenditure very carefully to make sure that it isn't abused, but that's almost beside the point. The point is that government feels it is entitled to everything you own, and, thus, we should be grateful for everything we keep, and should hate those who deduct business expenses with which we don't agree.

Teddy Kennedy, probably flogged on by guilt over his unearned money inherited from his buccaneer father, is one of the most dangerous anti-business, anti-capitalism, anti-Free Enterprise forces in America. When you compound that with his moral bankruptcy and his total ignorance of anything economic, and gloss that over with his Kennedy charisma, you have a dangerous, dangerous man. Taxes are, at best, a necessary evil and, at worst, a rape, and Teddy Kennedy is telling us that, just because most people are getting raped, we should stir up public opinion against anyone who has escaped the rapist until they are violated too.

The pernicious doctrine of "tax subsidy" plays on the envy and the basest emotions of the have-nots and can cripple the ability of the producers to continue to produce. You show me a businessman who abuses the expense account lunch for business purposes and I'll show you a fool who won't be in business very long.

This same anti-business thinking is reflected in Jimmy Carter's request to Congress to limit fringe benefits for people who own more than 10 percent of a corporation. He wants only 25 percent of the benefits for all employees to be for the owner. Any excess would be taxed to the owners. Thus, a one-owner firm can spend $400 for the owner's medical insurance if it spends $1200 for the employees, or it can buy the owner $16,666 of life insurance if it buys employees $50,000 worth. As a result, many small firms will just say, "To hell with it" and the owner will raise his salary, pay for his own coverage, and buy his employees nothing.

This proposed rule discriminates against owners of small, closely held firms with few employees. A Treasury official has conceded that it will hurt some small businesses but says, "Something should be done about owners who get free medical and life coverage from their firms and give their employees little or nothing." What's that again #??!!&*?

Whose business is it what the owner of a company decides to do with his money? What right do employees have to share in the corporate pie to any greater extent than the free marketplace for labor can bargain for wages and benefits? I yield to no one in my generosity to my employees, as any of them will tell you, but I do that because it makes me feel good and because it's good business.

This proposed rule is obscene, insane, and immoral, but worse than that, it's stupid, because there won't be any golden eggs unless the owner of the goose gets to use some of the proceeds of the egg sale to prime the goose. (see: Business)

(11/15/77) Now is the time of the year to consider taking some losses for tax purposes. I don't know how many times I've advised people to get out of certain kinds of money situations and they say to me, "But I can't sell now. I can't afford the loss."

That has to be the dumbest response I've ever heard. There's only one legitimate question, and that is, "Where should my money be now in order to safely grow?" The price you paid a year ago is quite irrelevant to that decision. If you invested $10,000 and its only worth $5,000, you don't have $10,000 any more. You have $5,000 worth of investment and you should be realistic and face up to it and put it where, under current conditions, it will grow best. If you have made a bad choice, you might as well recognize it.

If you sell something at a loss at this time of the year, you can balance those capital losses against any capital gains. So consider some "tax loss selling," then look around and see where your money ought to be.

As long as you have a loss, you might as well take advantage of it and turn that lemon into, at least, weak lemonade—a tax benefit.

TAX LOOPHOLES

(7/1/76)   Representation Without Taxation

No, I haven't got it backwards. I didn't say "Taxation Without Representation." A revolution was fought over that concept, and in a world turned upside down a revolution is now being waged over the reverse concept.

Congress is fighting its annual mock battle over tax reform, accompanied by lurid press releases about millionaires or corporations who don't pay their "fair share" of taxes.

Every tax revision in the last 20 years, however, has resulted in a larger, not smaller, percentage of American income being exempt from taxation. Without our noticing it, an incredible shift has occurred where the majority of voters benefit from loopholes and a huge, politically decisive group of voters pays no taxes at all, while electing officials who will spend the money taxed from others on their non-taxpaying constituents.

Not only do the non-taxpayers outnumber the large taxpayers, but they are determining that the money will be spent for their own benefit.

The net effect is that the political process has produced a tax-revenue system with a built-in bias in favor of consumption.

Let's do a political head count.

There were altogether 16.7 million individual tax returns in 1972 which reported no taxable income. That represents 21.5 percent of all 77.6 million returns. 92 percent of those "no-tax" returns were in the under-$5,000 adjusted gross income (AGI) bracket. 7.6 were in the $5,000-10,000 AGI bracket. 0.4 percent were over $10,000 AGI.

The low income "non-taxpayer" outnumbered the high income "non-taxpayer" 15-1/3 to one.

Add to this another 15 to 20 million voters not required to file returns at all for various reasons, usually because of low income, and you have a huge voting bloc.

Now, on whom are most of our non-defense federal and state tax-dollars being spent? That's right! On the low income non-taxpayer.

On what group is it proposed that the tax burden should increase? That's right! The "Rich" or "Big Business," in short, the producers.

In the light of these basics, lets look behind the screaming about tax "loopholes" and see where the real loopholes are. We'll be working with 1972 figures.

The amounts we are talking about are huge. All personal income totaled $945 billion, of which only $445 billion showed up as taxable on Federal Income Tax return. In other words, over $500 billion—or 53 percent of all personal income—went tax free in 1972, up by 48 percent from 1969. This is explained by the fact that several "tax reform" measures went into effect between 1969 and 1972, especially the Tax Reform Act of 1969 (more affectionately known as the Lawyers and Accountants Relief and Full Employment Act). At least $70 billion crept through loopholes solely as a result of that act.

Let's look at the loopholes and see who is truly benefiting, in descending order of tax revenue lost.

1. $155 billion in personal exemptions at $750 a head.

2. $97 billion in itemized deductions, representing 55 percent of reported income (on returns itemizing deductions) in the under $5,000 AGI bracket, 20 percent in the $14,000 to $25,000 bracket, and 22 percent in the $100,000 and up bracket. A huge bias toward the lower incomes.

3. $93 billion in tax-free income from Social Security, unemployment compensation, public assistance, veterans' benefits, employer contributions to pension and welfare funds, and other transfer payments, all extracted from producers. Obviously, these benefit lower and lower-middle income persons.

4. $70 billion in standard deductions, mostly from lower income earners. Under the liberalized provisions of the 1969 Act, standard

deductions went up 218% between 1969 and 1972, from $22 billion to $70 billion, while income rose only 26% and itemized deductions, 21%.

5. $10 billion in homeowners' deductions for interest and property taxes.

6. $7 billion to $10 billion in long-term capital gains tax exemption (usually taxed at 50% of the rate for ordinary income).

7. $4 billion in tax-free income from municipal bonds (of which $3 billion is refunded to states, cities, schools, etc., in the form of lower interest rates).

8. A few billion in miscellaneous deductions and exemptions.

The income exempt from taxation is heavily biased toward the lower end of the income spectrum. And they vote.

What can we conclude?

1. More than half the voters benefit from huge "loopholes."

2. As a result, no meaningful tax reform will take place until someone figures out how to persuade the majority to forego the benefits.

3. That would be political suicide for any elected official, so don't hold your breath.

4. The people who elect the guys that make the tax rules also elect the guys who tell us where our taxes will be spent, and they sure as heck won't give it back to the rich. They'll spend it on the voters.

I said in my book, "He who robs Peter to pay Paul will always have the vote of Paul."

The division of the American people into two groups—those who support the government and those who are supported by it—has created an irreversible "Representation Without Taxation." It will put down the Free Enterprise system.

If you were a politician, faced with an ever-growing mass of people who clamor for greater benefits from the government, to whose support they do not have to contribute, whom would you favor, the 51% who report an income under $8,000, or the eight percent with an income over $50,000?

The growing irresponsibility of "Representation Without Taxation" poses a grave threat to the preservation of the government of the United States.

What practical value is there in knowing all this?

First, we all need to understand the nature of what threatens us. If you are in the higher brackets, you need to understand the nature of the rape, and squarely face the fact that you will be the first to go. You must protect yourself.

Second, if you are in the lower brackets, you must realize that by supporting this transfer of wealth from the high producers to the low producers, you are administering slow death to the goose who lays the Golden Eggs. The result will be first the death by taxation and inflation of the middle class workers, investors, savers and producers; second, the nightmarish realization that the goose has died, by the low income, low production, dependent class, with their subsequent suffering, revolt and anarchy; and third, the escalation of economic and political power of the Super-Rich who will use their real wealth to accumulate more, just as they did during the 1930s.

What can you do about it?

Ruff's Recommendations

1. Throw out the spenders in the next election. It probably won't change anything, but we have to try.
2. Recognize that if we succeed in reversing the trend, it will result in depression, and a violent reaction from the non-producers, which will produce a very sick society for awhile.
3. Be prepared to say, "Let it begin with me" if you truly want to reverse the trend.
4. Prepare for the depression that will result either from a successful reversal, or from the playing out of the drama, by doing what the Super-Rich are doing (or as much as you can on your own small scale).
*Become self-sufficient in food.
*Buy agricultural land—preferably small plots.
*Become energy-independent if you can.
*Invest in precious metals to preserve real buying power.

In summary: I want you to recognize that the political and taxation process now is in the hands of those who don't have to pay the bills. We are seeing nothing less than the redistribution of wealth by ballot. When the producers have been stripped of incentive and assets, only totalitarian control can keep things working, unless there is a kind of upheaval that tears everything down, and allows us to start over.

(4/1/78) Government poses as the protector of the masses in tax policy, alleging that it is going to plug the loopholes for those rich and dirty guys because it wants to lighten the tax burden on the little fellow.

Well, let's see just how they help the poor struggling middle class, drowning in a sea of expenses, not the least of which is his taxes.

A member of the Senate staff, PAUL CRAIG ROBERTS, says it is dishonest to talk about ending deductions that let the rich avoid taxes. Actually, the present deductions benefit middle-income earners more than the rich, according to IRS data. Roberts is a professor at GEORGE MASON UNIVERSITY. He says, "Government is fashioning its tax net to catch those it pretends to protect."

If you want to plug a tax loophole, plug the one that benefits Uncle Sugar.

The biggest loophole of all is the way inflation increases the tax "take" for government. A 10% inflation rate produces a 16½% revenue gain for the government because taxpayers are pushed into higher brackets. Roberts says, "The central issue of tax reform is to close this inflation loophole."

Roberts further asserts, "IN RELATIVE TERMS, OUR POSITION TODAY IS WORSE THAN THAT OF A MEDIEVAL SERF WHO OWED THE STATE ONE THIRD OF HIS WORKING TIME."

WHY? BECAUSE GOVERNMENT NOW HAS A CLAIM TO 42% OF THE NATIONAL INCOME IN 1976.

Aren't we glad we live in more enlightened times?

TAX REVOLTS

(6/1/76) I've watched with great interest the development of the "Tax Revolt" around the country. Many of our subscribers have called to ask my opinion of the movement, led by Rene Baxter and others, to challenge the validity of the American tax collecting system.

The essence of the tax revolt concept is that much of the money taken from us by government is illegally extorted and the tax system is unconstitutional, immoral and unethical. The tax revolt rests on the assumption that you can avoid the payment of taxes with the use of novel legal and Constitutional strategies. The tax rebels are plowing new legal ground. They use such devices as forming their own church and becoming ministers of the church or declaring our currency not to be legal tender, as the Constitution specifies gold and silver coins as legal tender.

I am in complete sympathy with the tax revolters. I agree with them that our present taxing system is unconstitutional and illegal. I also agree with them that our currency is not technically legal tender. I agree that many of the arguments which they are using in court and many of the steps which they are taking are legal and should hold up in court.

From a selfish point of view, I'd like to cheer the tax revolters on. I'd like them to win. I'd like them to create sufficient trouble for the system, that it has to be revised. But I cannot, in all conscience, advise any of my subscribers to become part of the tax revolt, unless they are prepared to be martyrs. Sooner or later, enough revenue is going to be lost that the Federal government is going to move massively against the tax revolt. Until now, the IRS has handled this in a rather gingerly fashion whenever they have challenged it. Sooner or later, however, it will become evident that this is not working, that they are losing ground, and they will move massively in several ways that are available to them, even though their actions may be illegal and unconstitutional and may ultimately lose on appeal in higher courts.

Here are my reasons.

The Internal Revenue Service has incredible power. It can seize your property without notice and without legal determination as to what your liability may be. It simply moves to protect its interest and tie up the funds, and then waits to see what the actual liability might be.

A friend of mine had a recent experience where he had a piece of land which he had received as a gift from a grandfather. He sold the property and, expecting to receive the proceeds of the sale, made some business decisions based upon the availability of the money. The Internal Revenue Service, however, stepped in and seized the property and blocked the sale, while it conducted a lengthy and time-consuming fishing expedition against the estate, to see whether or not the grandfather was liable for any back taxes (over sixty years back). In the meantime, it was found that the IRS agent who issued the attachment had been bribed by a third party who wanted to block the sale for reasons of his own. The IRS did not admit fault for almost two years. The proceedings dragged on with the IRS getting postponement after postponement, almost bringing about the bankruptcy of several parties and causing great economic loss to all the parties concerned. Eventually the IRS was forced to capitulate, and not only had to release the property, but also had to pay damages and legal fees. in the meantime, my friend had been forced to sell his business. This didn't seem to be a matter of much consequence or concern to the IRS, though. It simply continued its blundering, unethical, improper actions until it was forced by circumstances to back off.

Now remember, right and justice were on the side of my friend. Eventually he won, but there were immense hardships along the way.

The IRS has the right under the law to seize your property and hold it for years until a leisurely determination is made. Its position is, "It will all come out in the wash, so you are not damaged." It does not consider the consequences of having your funds tied up.

I also had an experience with the IRS. One day I found that they had seized $12,000 from my checking account. Most of that money was there to pay against checks that had already been written. I didn't know that I owed the IRS anything. I had had no prior contact with an agent. As it finally turned out, I owed them $35 from a past return. The agent had just arbitrarily selected $12,000 as the figure to assess, "To get your attention," as he said. He would have gotten my attention just as well with a phone call or a letter. The agent's reason for not notifying me was, "If we had notified you by telephone or letter, you might have removed the funds, and we would not have been able to secure our interest."

That action on the part of the IRS was within the power granted to them by numerous court decisions. They can go into your bank and obtain bank records without your knowledge or consent. They can seize your funds and hold them. In my case, over 45 checks written on my business account bounced all over the United States.

As government spending explodes and taxes increase, taxpayer resistance grows, and stronger totalitarian methods become essential in order to collect the taxes due. Congress has hesitated to strip the IRS of its dictatorial powers because it is caught in the dilemma of individual freedoms versus the necessity of government to collect the increasingly objectionable tax burden. Heavy taxation to raise money for social spending will always result in loss of freedom because of increasingly repressive methods necessitated by increasing taxpayer resistance.

Right is on the side of the tax protestors, the Constitution is on the side of the tax protestor, even the law may be on the side of the tax protestor, but in the meantime, the IRS with its summary powers can destroy you. I cannot urge caution too strongly. Only join the revolt if you are prepared to be a dead hero.

And if you do, God bless you. My prayers and best wishes go with you.

(7/15/76) A taxpayer revolt is brewing. Los Angeles is up in arms over immense property tax increases (up to 88%). Payroll taxes and FICA are near the limits of tolerance. And an ever-insatiable spending monster will demand more, not less. Remember, our freedom can be taxed away. (see: Government Debt, Proposition 13, & Taxes)

(4/1/78)

Q. I attended a meeting held by some noted tax rebels and they recommended that to avoid taxes when selling a piece of property, I should demand payment in silver coins. I didn't understand exactly what they meant. Can you explain it to me?

A. Right now, a bag of American silver coins with a face value of $1000 is worth almost $4000 (please note date of article). Theoretically, if I sold a home, or anything else for that matter, worth $40,000, then I should demand $10,000 face value worth of junk silver coins. As money is defined in the Constitution as gold and silver coins, I would only have received $10,000. Consequently, I would not have had a taxable profit on that home because I only paid $25,000 for the home and I have sold it for $10,000 of legal tender, so I have turned a potential $15,000 capital gain into a $15,000 capital loss.

The theory is great, and I happen to think it's Constitutionally sound; however, the IRS has already issued a ruling saying that they would value the sale of the property at the fair market value of the coins. Deak and Company reported an interview with Forest D. Montgomery, an attorney in the Office of the Mint. He said that if there was an exchange or barter of property for property (house for coins) and properties of equal market value were exchanged, there would be no capital gains tax on the difference between the silver dollar's face value and the property's market value. There still will be a capital gains tax if the property is sold above the price paid for it by the seller. If you sold something for $10,000, and accepted coins in payment at market value, and later sold them for more than $10,000, you would be liable for capital gains tax on the difference.

If that sounds confusing it's because it is. Government positions on this are inconsistent. (For more on silver coins see: Survival Preparations and Silver)

(3/15/77) When you file your 1040 this year, DON'T USE THE FRIENDLY HELPFUL ADDRESS STICKER PROVIDED BY THE IRS. It has a code number that helps the IRS computer select returns to be audited. The law doesn't require you to use it, so write in your name. Also, if you have large charitable donations, send copies of the receipts with your return. This could also stave off an audit.

688

(1/1/78)   There's going to be a special place in hell for those who have led people into the tax revolt without warning them that they are joining an army that's going to get shot at with heavy artillery.

Perhaps it is time for all brave patriots to, metaphorically at least, take up their arms. Some of those who are recruiting you are not telling you about the danger. If you understand those dangers and believe in the cause, then by all means, be my guest and join the tax revolt; start your own church; file your Fifth Amendment tax return; or whatever, but don't do it with your eyes closed. This is not just a way to avoid taxes. It is a militant confrontation with an awakening government giant to bring down our oppressive taxing system. I have chosen not to join this revolt, as an IRS confrontation can destroy any small business, and *THE RUFF TIMES* must survive and continue to do whatever good it can accomplish.

Let me give you an idea of the kind of pressure beginning to be brought to bear by the IRS. I am in receipt of a letter from A. W. McCANLESS, IRS District Director in Dallas, Texas, sent to employers in that area. Many are using a Form W-4E, Exemption From Withholding, to avoid payroll taxes. McCanless's letter says, "As you know, entering in an excessive number of exemptions on a Form W-4, or improperly using the Form W-4E to avoid withholding of income taxes, can lead to tax difficulties for the individual and possible criminal prosecution."

The letter now goes on, rather subtly, to scare the employer by pointing out what they call, "the employer's responsibilities," under Treasury Regulation 31.3402(n)1, which states, "If the employer has reason to believe that the withholding exemption certificate contains any incorrect statement, the District Director should be so advised." The employer is then advised that if they think the W-4 forms are inappropriately filed, they are to contact the IRS directly. Now, look at the next paragraph.

> During future examinations and other contacts with taxpayers, we will be inquiring into use of these forms. However, our efforts may come too late to aid individual taxpayers who have been misled by leaders of the so-called "tax protest movement" into believing that income taxes are unconstitutional and that the Internal Revenue Service will not act to correct these activities.

This is just a gentle early step in the IRS assault on the tax revolt movement. I recently had a call from two subscribers who had joined the tax revolt, set up their own church, used all the methods advised by Drexler, Baxter, and others, and then found out that all of the things they were told the IRS could not or would not do, were being done to them. It's going to cost them at least $30,000 in legal fees to stay out of jail, as the Revenuers, in this case, were not satisfied with back-taxes and penalties. There is the threat of criminal action.

Our system has not yet reached the point where we must break the law in order to alter it, even if we think the law is unconstitutional. I yield to no one in pointing out the dictatorial powers that are being gathered by the IRS but, as of this moment, we still have recourse to our national legislature and the courts.

My principal point is: do not be led into taking these actions under the assumption that there is no risk. It is not safe and the danger is growing. I object to those who might sweet talk you into a suicidal charge by telling you the enemy is asleep or that its guns don't work.

(2/1/78) There are some people like my friend, IRWIN SCHIFF, author of *THE BIGGEST CON*, who is a militant tax protestor. He has fought the IRS to a standstill on several occasions. He has the temperament to fight, in fact, a genuine zest for the battle. Those people who are prepared to accept the fact that this is a confrontation with government, not merely a method of saving taxes, can, and should, follow their conscience in this matter.

My position on the tax rebellion could be summed up as follows:

1. Government is becoming repressive and the Internal Revenue Service bureaucracy is increasingly resorting to unconstitutional acts or illegal methods to collect taxes.

2. There is a time when such methods become so repressive that revolt is justified.

3. It is a matter of individual judgment as to when that time is reached.

Our founding fathers considered themselves Englishmen with a grievance against their King for many years, until finally they reached the point at which their problems boiled over and they realized that all avenues of redress had been exhausted.

I think that we should attempt to "work within the system" (remember that phrase?) to arrest the trends and bring about change and I am not prepared, at this moment, to officially declare the battle lost.

(11/1/77) Remember, being a tax protestor could be dangerous! The family trusts are also a matter of great concern to the revenuers and are beginning to make them mad. I know of at least five IRS

District Directors who automatically disallow family trust returns. As I reported in the last issue, the government is bringing criminal charges against people who merely utilize loopholes, let alone join the revolt, and several of the promoters of the family trusts have come under criminal indictment. (see: Estate Planning)

The IRS has the power and the will to move massively against you in disregard of statutes and court rulings. One of my subscribers recently sent me a copy of an article which appeared in the *ARKANSAS GAZETTE* on October 25, 1977, headlined, "IRS DECIDES TO IGNORE '76 RULING." It was syndicated from the *WASHINGTON POST* and said, in effect, that the IRS decided to ignore a 1976 Federal Appeals Court ruling and will continue dunning hundreds of retired military veterans for some of their disability benefits. The IRS Chief Counsel, Dean Whitaker, said, in an interdepartmental letter last year that, "The opinion of the court is erroneous and should not be followed." And, he told IRS agents to ignore the ruling. The IRS has not even appealed the ruling to the Supreme Court. This incredible arrogance should be sufficient warning of the totalitarian mentality of the Feds.

Over the next few years, the Federal government is going to become increasingly desperate to find the funds to conduct its business. We are headed for a depression which is going to cut tax revenues and increase welfare and social spending requirements as determined by our unelected bureaucratic rulers.

So, if you want to become a "Freedom Fighter" and tangle with the government, make sure you have your eyes open. Tax protest is not a royal road to tax savings. Just make sure that temperamentally and financially you are prepared for the battle before you join up for a hitch in the tax war. (see: Proposition 13)

(2/15/78)   One reason why I don't side with the tax protestors is that they are attempting to precipitate the collapse of the system by refusing to pay taxes. That is a dangerously unnecessary confrontation, because the system is going to self-destruct anyway, as RENE BAXTER, one of the tax rebel leaders, said when I interviewed him for my forthcoming television show.

WELFARE TAX—
THE CASE OF THE BORROWED HAM

(3/15/78)   A welfare recipient "borrowed" a country ham from a farmer without telling him.

He went downtown and sold it to a grocer for $27. Of this sum, he

691

used $20 to buy $80 worth of food stamps.

He then bought $51 worth of groceries, and also bought the ham back for $29 (which he put back in the farmer's smokehouse before it was missed).

The grocer made a $2 profit, the welfare entrepreneur got $7 in cash and $51 worth of groceries, and the farmer got his ham back.

It's kind of funny until you figure out who paid for it.

TERRORISM

(11/1/77)   Another important impression from my European trip is the great concern over terrorism. The death of leaders of the Baader-Meinhoff gang in prison and the recent hijackings and bombings have most Europeans on edge. I don't know if it received great publicity here, but there was extensive left-wing rioting in Rome and Milan, with several people being killed or injured, most of them being police or young leftist students. Repressive measures are now being taken. Our van was stopped in Belgium just because we had French license plates and a lot of young people in the car. Police and security officials are paranoid about terrorism.

There are probably no more than 10,000 terrorists in the whole world, but open democracies are so vulnerable to their actions.

THANKSGIVING

(12/1/76)   I would like to devote a few lines on Thanksgiving Day to give thanks for some choice blessings.

First, I'm grateful for a loyal, lovely wife and strong, fine children. I'm grateful for spiritual knowledge and the blessings of a loving Heavenly Father.

I'm so thankful for America and its freedoms, opportunities, and unimaginable abundance.

I'm proud of 200 years of honorable history, where we have been a beacon to a world which so often can only dimly sense the great principles of freedom and individual opportunity.

I'm grateful for time—time to get my house in order for the coming depression—time to persuade others to restructure their lives, as I will feel more secure if others also are prepared.

But my gratitude is mixed with sorrow. I feel schizophrenic when I love my country, but fear my government!

How tragic to look about at the millions of people who are making long-range plans on the assumption that our cities will not collapse; that our government will never repudiate its debt; that the Arabs will never cut off our oil again; that inflation will be stopped; that Social Security and pensions will be paid as agreed and that government will somehow stop its landslide toward regulation of business and personal life, somewhere short of the loss of essential freedoms.

TRUCKING INDUSTRY

(4/1/76)   There is probably no industry in America that can affect the rate of inflation more than trucking, with the possible exception of oil. Virtually everything that we consume has to be shipped from one point to another. It wasn't many years ago when the railroads were the most important factors in transportation. Now trucks have assumed this role. The trucking industry is one of the so-called "middle men," along with the distributor, the processor, the packer, and the wholesaler.

Supermarkets have, at most, three or four days of food on hand. A truck strike means no more deliveries. The same is true for gasoline and other vital commodities. Trucking is the nation's life blood.

Here is what can happen and what to do about it!

If they strike, the government could obtain a court injuction under the Taft-Hartley Act sending the Teamsters back to work for an eighty-day "cooling-off period" while negotiations are attempted. If a contract is not agreed upon, then comes the strike.

Some influential locals are so militant in their demands, that even if an agreement is ratified by the union, strikes are still likely at some key transportation hubs and shipping points. Also, the key Chicago local negotiates separately. In 1967 and 1970, this local struck and forced the union to renegotiate terms already agreed upon with the industry.

Remember, many of our farm workers are now members of the Teamster's Union. Remember also, that the ripple effect of a truck strike could be sympathy strikes from other industries, as well as the usual honoring of picket lines by other segments of organized labor.

Ruff's Recommendations

1.   Take an inventory in your home of all the articles that need replenishing regularly.

2.   If you have been procrastinating the purchase of your emer-

gency food supples, buy immediately.

3. If your business or livelihood depends upon items which must be transported regularly from one part of the country to another, consider yourself vulnerable and become as financially liquid as possible, so you can ride out the storm for whatever period is necessary. (see: Food Production and Distribution)

FROM A TO Z

V

VALUES AND MORALS

INTEGRITY OF POLITICIANS

(8/1/76) On Tuesday, July 27, the *SAN FRANCISCO CHRON-ICLE* published an editorial called, "HOWE'S TROUBLES." Here are some excerpts.

> Now that Representative Allan Howe, Utah Democrat, has been found guilty of soliciting sex from two police decoy prostitutes, one result of the whole matter may be looked at dispassionately and in proper focus. Even in this emancipated era, that's probably too much to expect, the mixture of sex and politics, being the heavy concoction it is. . . .
>
> There are loud and righteous calls now in Congressman Howe's community for his resignation. Three aides have left his campaign staff and he is under heavy pressure to abandon his bid for reelection. This state of affairs contrasts with that of Suisun City Congressman, Robert Leggett, whose active sex life also hit the public prints recently, but a recent survey of Leggett's district showed his constituents making a live-and-let-live attitude. Such revelations are becoming commonplace and the voters' main concern is with whether he's doing a good job in "that wasteland between Vallejo and Sacramento."
>
> So, a little perspective is needed. Howe's act involved what is known as a victimless crime and had no overtones of a character disorder. On this basis, his private life should be allowed to remain his own. The Utah voters should forget the drama of the last few weeks and concentrate on whether he's the man they want to vote on the next arms budget or foreign aid bill.

After reading this editorial and many other similar ones taking somewhat the same position, I have come to the conclusion that most people have missed the point. I don't know how many times you've heard me say that, but so often it is the case.

I believe that the personal integrity of our legislators is a matter of some consequence.

Congressman Howe, early in life, had served a two-year mission for The Church of Jesus Christ of Latter Day Saints, and was excommunicated from the church for sexual misbehavior during that period. After an appropriate period of repentance, he was reinstated in the church, only to be caught up again in similar activities.

Whether it is wrong, based on rules guarding sexual behavior, for any person to have an extramarital affair, or a "one night stand," is really rather irrelevant. It is a question of integrity. Having served a similar mission, I know that when I accepted that responsibility for two years, at the age of nineteen, I promised with the most solemn of covenants, that I would not do such things. When Mr. Howe was married in the Church, he also made a solemn covenant, which he has probably reinforced many times if he was a regular attendee at his local temple, that he would be true and faithful to his wife. It is not a matter of sexual behavior, it is a matter of keeping one's promises and covenants.

I have always been of the opinion that I would never have close to me, in a business capacity, someone who would not keep his marriage vows, because it was a question of the man's integrity. Would he violate his most solemn covenant to the person who is closest to him, for pleasure? If so, he might violate his most solemn commitments to me, for pleasure, money, or any number of motivations. It is a simple matter of personal integrity and willingness to keep one's word. I don't think I want a Congressman who resorts to deception, secrecy, and all of the other things that are necessary for one to have an extramarital adventure. There is no way to do that without compromising one's integrity.

And incidentally, he did willingly break the law.

Perhaps we can boil it down to a simple question of whether or not a man will keep his word, even if he thinks he won't be caught.

In my opinion, that is precisely the issue we face over Congressman Howe and many other Congressmen and Senators in the light of the revelations coming out of Washington, D.C.

I have no desire to put someone down or destroy their career, but this man represents a lot of people. Is his vote for sale to a person with advantages to offer? Could he be seduced by some Senator's good-looking secretary, to influence him to vote contrary to his own convictions? These are the questions that Congressman Howe has raised and these are the questions that such editorials as the scurrilous one in the *CHRONICLE* have missed.

I know there are subscribers who will not agree with my views. I know that there are those who have treated their marriage vows lightly, have rationalized it in their own minds and feel that it has nothing to do with personal integrity. I am not sitting in judgment of you, because you are not my public servant. Nor am I considering taking you into business with me. We can be friends, regardless of your behavior, based on this simple fact: do I like you or not? But when it comes to giving one's confidence and trust to one who has publicly demonstrated his willingness to break his word, I draw the line at that.

BASIS OF SURVIVAL

(10/15/76)   The root of the coming depression is not really the technical factor of monetary manipulation. It begins with moral issues—is it morally wrong to spend money we don't have, to saddle the next generation with debt, to make political promises that can't be kept, to press for more control of individual lives in order to "protect" us? Intangible concepts caused the rise of Alexander, Hitler, Mao, Jesus and Muhammad. Principles, not money, drove Lawrence of Arabia, Columbus, Rembrandt, Thomas Jefferson, Admiral Rickover, and Winston Churchill.

And it is intangibles such as courage, resilience, cooperation, patience, and family ties, that will determine whether you survive the next depression, or whether it's worth surviving. I don't care how much gold, silver, food, guns, and real estate you have. It will all turn to bitterness if we don't get through this holocaust with principles intact, with families unified, with communities prepared to function cooperatively, and a determination to build an even better world. (see: Family; Sin-tax; Economy, Collapse of; and Survival Preparations, Emotional)

VALUES OF FOUNDING FATHERS

(1/1/78)   How many times have you asked: What are the root causes of this runaway growth of our demands upon government to give us what we want, or think we need? Well, I think we can dig even deeper than the "swilling-at-the-public-trough" concept. These things are symptoms of a deepening spiritual malaise which now afflicts our society. I'm not using the term spiritual in the religious sense exclusively, although that is included. I am referring to the intangible attitudes that have made this country the greatest social and political phenomenon in the history of the world. There were fundamental principles that made this nation work, on which the majority of the population were agreed, and when those principles are rejected by a majority of the people, the system will no longer work.

When BENJAMIN FRANKLIN emerged from the Convention Hall in Philadelphia he was asked what kind of government the delegates had created. His answer: "A republic, if you can keep it." JOHN ADAMS, our second President said, "Our Constitution was made only for a moral and religious people. It is wholly inadequate to the government of any other." He was really talking about shared values (which are also shared by many who are not "religious"). Edmund Burke elaborated on this principle still further: "Men of intemperate habits cannot be free. Their passions forge their fetters."

The framers of the Constitution, from their own experience, knew that government could become a means of legalizing plunder. Therefore, they specifically limited government's role to protective functions. Nowhere can you find in the Constitution the right granted to the Federal government to redistribute wealth through taxation and to coerce people into participation in social welfare schemes. Whenever we hand more power to the Federal government we violate the most important single principle that was held by our Founding Fathers. Thomas Jefferson warned of this danger: "What has destroyed liberty and the rights of man in every government which has ever existed under the sun? The generalizing and concentrating of all cares and powers into one body." (Thomas Jefferson, WORKS 6:543, H. A. Washington, Editor. Townsend Mac Couns., 1884, 9 volumes.)

Madison warned further (FEDERALIST PAPERS, No. 10), that if we permit the democratization of our republican system of government by eliminating the electoral college, we will have turned government over to the whims of the majority, leaving minority and individual rights unguarded and unprotected. We will then be vulnerable as a society to "spectacles of turbulence and contention."

This nation has worked because there was a consensus that we had a responsibility to the general good, that every man was responsible for his own personal welfare, that individuals were to be charitable to those who were unable to care for themselves, and that there was no compassion for those who did not work. We were willing to take up arms to defend our country. We believed that we could pull ourselves up by our own bootstraps and that life rewarded those who struggled. We looked up to those who achieved, and did not punish success by excessive taxation. We were willing to sacrifice security for the opportunities that complete freedom offered us—along with the risks. People avoided "the dole" because to be dependent was humiliating, and this attitude motivated achievement and was a strength to society in general.

We believed in secure, stable money, and several times we have learned, through hard experience, what happens when we violate this principle, as our currency system has collapsed more than once, but the effects were relatively muted because of the higher degree of decentralization and independence than exists today.

There was a consensus as to what was "right" and "wrong" in ethics and morals. Family was honored as the basic structural unit of society and the "three generation" family was the mainstay of our society.

I could go on and on about basic structural changes. It is the intangible "spiritual" consensus that determines the strength of a society. This nation can become ungovernable as more and more people reject this consensus. I agree with John Adams that our Constitution is "wholly inadequate to the government" of any people who do not, in general, accept these basic principles. True freedom requires restraint, but that doesn't go with "swilling at the public trough."

These are the great realities that mark our times, and 1978 is probably the year in which all of the great developing structural weaknesses will cause visible stress fractures in society. This year will probably be the beginning of a time of great change.

To base my life on the assumption that we will escape the next swing of the pendulum is just too dangerous. This nation faces civil chaos in our big cities and, at the very least, the intermittent breakdown of the delivery of goods and services that you depend upon for your well-being. And if you don't make plans to relocate or to prepare yourself with the basic necessities of life to get through that difficult period until the nation comes to its senses, you are a fool and there is nothing I can do for you. Now if that makes you mad, I weep for you, because that is precisely the way it is and nothing you or I can say will make it any different. (see: Family; Sin-tax; & Survival Preparation, Emotional)

VOICE STRESS ANALYZER

(8/1/78)   RICK BENNETT is the manufacturer of a VOICE STRESS ANALYZER, which is basically a device used by Law Enforcement Agencies to determine whether people are telling the truth. It works on the theory that people are under stress when they lie and, therefore, certain frequencies disappear from their voice. It has a series of red and green lights on a horizontal line. When a person is telling the truth, most of the green lights will light up. When the red lights are lit he is under stress which means he may be lying, but that is not conclusive. So it's a "truth detector." I had one at home to play with for a week, so I know it works.

Incidentally, Rick Bennett had some pretty interesting things to say about his voice stress analysis of Jimmy Carter and Richard Nixon. When Nixon was interviewed by Frost, he was telling the truth most of the time. When Carter was on television, he was in the red most of the time. That may simply indicate stress, or it may mean he's lying, but Mr. Bennett does not believe Carter is a truthful man.

What does all this mean to you? It means that there are some solutions to our energy problems if they are not squelched by government, or laughed into ridicule, or not properly funded.

W

WAR

(7/15/78) I'm concerned about the prospect of war. War in the Mid-East could affect us all. I'm disconcerted by the recent significant turn of events in Africa. We encouraged Soviet incursions into Africa through their surrogates, the Cubans, and now, all of a sudden, President Carter is complaining to Congress that he doesn't have the authority he needs in case he should wish to intervene militarily. He has weakened our position in Africa, and now he gets belligerent. He is inept, and capable of a serious miscalculation.

If you're a Conspiracy fan, consider the possibility that a nice, neat, limited war just might be what Jimmy thinks we need to stimulate our economy and pull us out of the next recession, just as World War II pulled us out of the depression of the '30s.

If you want to really keep up on this subject, I suggest you read R.E. McMASTER'S book, *CYCLES OF WAR*, which I have recommended before. (see: Arabs, Africa, Carter, Soviets)

WATER

PURIFICATION

(3/1/77) Some months ago I did an article in *THE RUFF TIMES* about the WATER WASHER portable water purifying unit and the SUPER STRAW. These units remove particulate matter and kill most bacteria that might threaten your life, if you should ever be forced to use water that you are not sure of. We really appreciated our little portable WATER WASHER the other day when the water in our neighborhood was shut off for a few hours.

We have stored water in our home as a matter of course, and probably have enough in half gallon plastic milk bottles to last our family two or three weeks, but when the water went out, we looked at those bottles and knew that the water in them probably wasn't pure, and certainly wouldn't taste very good. We simply poured it through our WATER WASHER and it came out sparkling clean, and we were sure of it, and it tasted great. It really made us feel good to know that we could endure such a minor emergency with no major problems.

We have been so pleased with our portable unit that we have installed an under-the-sink permanent purifier from the same company. Because of the drought in Northern California, the East Bay Municipal Utility District is going to bring us water from the Delta which is of very dubious quality. This will dilute our fine Sierra Nevada Mountain water and produce some bad taste, as well as an increased need for chlorination. When we installed our under-the-sink unit, we found that we again had "spring-tasting" water.

We also are going to drill a well in our property, but because of the many septic tanks in the area, we are concerned with its purity. We would prefer that our drinking water be super safe. This under-the-sink unit gives us a separate cold water tap right next to the regular faucet on our kitchen sink. It operates on the same principle as the portable water washer with a silver-impregnated activated charcoal filter, and the water it produces, is not only safe but delicious. When you prepare frozen juices or hot beverages, the difference in taste is truly remarkable, and there is none of that chlorine smell or aftertaste.

I consider this a survival item simply because I believe our water quality is undependable, and we may find water shortages forcing us to use semi-polluted water, inadequately prepared by overloaded municipal water purification systems, or contaminated by floods in the East or drought-spawned problems in the West and Midwest. When you match this up with your portable unit for survival, which is a gravity-fed unit that's not connected into your plumbing, I believe that you have protection against the most vital of human deficiencies —the lack of safe water. I would never be without them and recommend your adding them to your survival inventory.

(3/1/78) A year ago I recommended a small, hand-held portable water purifying unit selling for about $20.

I also recommended an under-the-sink unit so that the water you drink every day would be equally purified; however, that unit was $149.50.

Now, I'm thrilled to announce that AMERICAN WATER PU-RIFICATION has come up with a beautiful compromise. They have developed an inexpensive counter top purifier which sits next to the kitchen sink and hooks directly onto the faucet, and doesn't require any plumbing installation. With an adapter you can use your portable unit, which has a replaceable cartridge.

That means that you can have the benefit of the inexpensive, hand-held, portable purifying unit connected to your water system, without the disadvantages of high cost plus expensive plumbing installation.

Here's how it works. It snaps onto the end of your faucet and it conducts the water to the unit via flexible tubing through the unit, and back through a tandem tube to the faucet, where it then comes through like a normally operating kitchen sink faucet. The unit is chrome and black, and about the size of a tea kettle, and sells for $39.95. You can install it yourself in minutes and it has a bypass button to use when you don't want to use up your filtering capacity, such as when you are doing the dishes.

Since writing that last article I've had some excellent demonstrations of the value of a water purifier. Traveling as I do, I have to drink some pretty crummy-tasting water. I always carry my portable Water Washer, and it removes the chlorine and makes everybody's water taste like it just came from the Sierra Nevada Mountains. This helps, especially in Los Angeles, Philadelphia and New Orleans where the water tastes particularly objectionable to me. Also it was helpful on our family trip through southern France and Italy where so many people end up with the Italian version of Montezuma's Revenge (called Montezumastrami's big-a-retaliation). I can even travel safely in Mexico without fear of a trip-ruining seige of the Aztec two-step.

Contact AMERICAN WATER PURIFICATION, 1990 Olivera Road, Concord, CA 94520, and ask for the counter-top model.

As is always the case, I make no money from this recommendation and am only trying to help. I think it is a great product and worthy of your attention. Remember, if times get really tough, the water filtration plant may not be working properly, in which case your water purification unit might be life-saving.

SHORTAGE

(5/1/77) We are running out of water, and not just because of drought. Many industrial processes use vast amounts of water. I'm not sure how authoritative this is, but one expert says that the amount of water necessary to cool a nuclear plant would provide most of the domestic needs of a city of 500,000 population. When I was on a Los Angeles T.V. show with a California Farm Federation official, he said that if we had energy we could get water, because it takes power to pump water from deep wells, and if we have water we can have energy, because we can produce hydro-electric power or use it to cool nuclear plants. We must have both. Within 15 years we will be using up to 85 percent of the flow of our major rivers. This cannot be done without completely destroying the environment of our coastline and the estuaries, which are the cradle of seal life and the source of much of our food. We somehow have to develop means of conducting our lives with less water. Water shortages are not a short-term phenomenon. The simple matter is we are using more than we have, and you can't do that forever. (see: Farming)

STORAGE

(Special Report #4, 10/76)

Q. How can I store water, and how much should I have on hand?

A. You're going to need approximately 500 gallons per person per year. That doesn't mean you should attempt to store it all. You must operate on the assumption that there will be some water available, but its purity may be questionable. For this reason, I recommend that you have on hand at least a two-week's supply of cooking and drinking water for your family, and a method for purifying your supply. We simply put water in every kind of container that comes into our house, as soon as it is empty. We put it on a shelf in the basement. As I said in my book, we also recommend a waterbed as a storage unit. Your hot water heater is a source of water. You might want to make a deal with a neighbor who has a swimming pool. My main concern is that you have a home water-purifying unit (see previous section on purification).

WEATHER AND CLIMATE

(Special Report #2, 1/76) The weather is out of control. What a great blessing last year when the rains came just in time to save the great Midwestern corn crop! Despite the huge crops we had last year, world grain reserves are at an all-time low.

This year, it does not appear that we will be so lucky. Eighty percent of the nation's food supplies are grown in California and the great Midwest. These two areas are being seriously affected by the adverse weather that I forecast over eighteen months ago in *FAMINE AND SURVIVAL IN AMERICA*. California is suffering from the worst fall and winter drought in over fifty years. Rain is only a fraction of normal, threatening the success of summer agriculture. Flows from lowland dams are being cut back to try to preserve water. Since the grain crop has been planted in Northern California, the dry weather has seriously endangered germination of, for example, the new wheat crop. There is talk of having to replant. This will affect livestock feed as well, and irrigation water supplies for the coming growing season. Usually, by this time of the year, the hills of California are green and cattle are out to pasture. Now, ranchers are having to import grain to feed their cattle. This increases the drain on already-thin reserves. Since October 1, precipitation has only been 6% of normal in Los Angeles. It has been 40% in the San Joaquin Valley and 60% in the Sacramento Valley. There's only seven inches of snow on the ground on one of the major snow gauging stations at Norden, at the 5000 foot level in the Sacramento River watershed. The normal snow depth at this station is 40 inches on New Year's Day.

In the Midwest, the situation is about the same. A bumper winter wheat crop hinges upon good fall rain to give the wheat sufficient root to nourish it during the long, cold winter. Next, there is snow cover required to protect the grain from a hard freeze.

As a result of fall drought, on December 23 the government announced that despite a slight increase in winter wheat plantings, the 1976 crop will fall at least nine percent from 1975's record winter wheat harvest. In its first forecast, Agriculture Department officials said dry weather already has spoiled prospects for a harvest equal to last year's. They cited poor crop prospects in the Great Plains wheat growing states of Kansas, Nebraska, Oklahoma and Texas, as well as eastern Colorado. In areas where growers earn extra money by allowing cattle to graze on their wheat fields during the dormant winter months, only 6% of the fields were ready for pasturing by fall, compared to 23% last year.

Wheat sprouts a few main roots and stalks shortly after planting. Later, the wheat (called "tillers") puts forth a second, more profuse growth of stocks. The grain that grows on the tillered stalks produces big yields.

"Because of the slow start, some wheat probably didn't tiller properly before winter closed in," says TOM OSTRANDER, president of the KANSAS ASSOCIATION OF WHEAT GROWERS.

R. I. Cross, manager of Santa Fe Railway Company's agricultural development staff in Amarillo, Texas, said,

> Some Growers are comparing it to the drought of 1953-1955, which is second in severity only to the devastating dust bowl days of the 1930s. The stunted wheat is going to be more vulnerable to winter weather and wind damage next spring.

The Southwest is where the national crop is made or busted. Add this to Russia's terrible 1975 crop and an equally bad or worse start for the 1976 crop, and the fact that Argentine crop conditions appear to be deteriorating also, due to poor weather. But in any event, the weather is out of control.

In *FAMINE AND SURVIVAL IN AMERICA*, I forecast that we were moving into a major new weather cycle, which would be characterized by erratic, unpredictable weather and drought in the food producing areas of the country. This was not based upon astrology or reading the entrails of chickens, but based on an examination of the weather data by leading climatologists who have been studying broad climatic cycles.

TIME's science writer said on April 28, 1975:

> There are ominous signs that Earth's weather patterns have begun to change dramatically and that these changes may portend a drastic decline in food production—with serious political implications for just about every nation on Earth. The drop in food output could begin quite soon. . . .
>
> The evidence in support of these predictions has now begun to accumulate so massively that meteorologists are pressed to keep up with it. In England, farmers have seen their growing season decline by about two weeks since 1950. . . .
>
> If the climatic change is as profound as some of the pessimists fear, the resulting famines could be catastrophic. "A major climatic change would force economic and social adjustments on a worldwide scale," warned a recent report by the National Academy of Sciences, "because the global patterns of food production and population that is involved, are implicitly dependent upon the climate of the last century. . . ."

The evidence of such change is beginning to appear in California and the Midwest. California is going through its worst drought in 200 years.

In the Midwest, things are even worse. According to *THE WALL*

STREET JOURNAL, Wednesday, February 4, 1976, tons of Iowa Topsoil, in which planters had hoped to plant corn and soybeans next year, have drifted like dry black snow into roadside ditches and fence rows. The winter has been the mildest and driest in anywhere from 10 to 70 years. Iowans got a hint of what is feared may come when 50 mph winds whipped up dirt plowed last fall, causing dustclouds so severe that some Western Iowa motorists, in order to see, had to turn on their headlights at noon.

The same problem holds true in Texas. Bill Nelson, head of the TEXAS WHEAT GROWER'S ASSOCIATION, said, "We harvested 130 million bushels last year. We'll be doing well to get 60 million bushels this year. We had our first little dust storm around Amarillo last Saturday."

U.S. NEWS AND WORLD REPORT on February 16, 1976 exposed a great concern that the record-breaking harvest of 1975 will not be duplicated. The heart of America's winter wheat belt, according to this magazine, is in the grip of a severe winter drought, stretching from Texas to North Dakota. *U.S. NEWS AND WORLD REPORT* also acknowledges the drought edging into the western corn belt in Nebraska, Kansas and Iowa. The long-range forecast for February from the National Weather Services, called for more dry days ahead.

The Oklahoma Crop and Livestock Reporting Service says a drought in the northern and western parts of that state already has cut deeply into this year's harvest. As things now stand, the service estimates that the winter wheat crop will fall 30% short of last year's record harvest.

In Kansas, the outlook is even more bleak. Myron Krenzin, Admnistrator of the KANSAS WHEAT COMMISSION says, "Right now, there's only a 10% chance of a crop in Western Kansas."

Some of the nation's newspaper writers are just now beginning to wonder whether or not these problems are part of a new cycle of weather. I have made my forecast of the weather based on an understanding of these cycles.

Henry Schact, Farm Reporter for the *SAN FRANCISCO CHRONICLE*, says that the plains were once described as part of the Great American Desert, so it is not surprising that the wheat there should be threatened by this dry winter.

To make it even worse, December was much drier than usual in Europe. And the Soviet Union's wheat crop again was endangered by lack of snow cover.

And finally, the Agricultural Department announced February 10 that the nation's winter wheat crop is continuing to deteriorate because of drought in the Great Plains. In the top-producing state of Kansas, according to the USDA, growers say their 1976 harvest will be the smallest in eight years. The conditions cited have led to only one conclusion—the weather is indeed out of control.

(3/15/76) Drought continues in the Midwest and in California. Many farmers are giving up on their winter wheat crops and are plowing up the land to turn up large clods, which are less susceptible to wind erosion than fine topsoil. They would rather save their land from blowing away and lose their potential crop, than take a chance on losing both. There has been enough rain in parts of the Southwest recently to briefly put down the dust, but that's about all. Much of the winter wheat crop is already lost.

In the face of this problem, the United States government announced that the Soviets are preparing to come into this marketplace for another five to six million tons of grain. I can't believe it! The reserves simply aren't that great. I believe that we should fight this Soviet grain deal tooth and nail. And I say this knowing that I am going to offend some of my subscribers who are farmers or who are dependent upon the farming economy. But I do believe that we have to build stockpiles in America. These stockpiles should be in the homes of individual American citizens (see: National Food Reserve). We have to keep this food here. The time will come when we will need it!

(5/15/76) I finally found out just how inefficient our government is. In *FAMINE AND SURVIVAL IN AMERICA*, published in September 1974, I said that the world is facing climatic changes which will cause serious food shortages, and would affect us here in America. I quoted from the work of climatologists Reid Bryson, and Dr. O'Hare of Canada, and others, who contend that a minor shift of climatic conditions could reduce food production, causing chaos throughout the world. Now, almost two years later, we find that the Central Intelligence Agency, with all of its tremendous resources, has just discovered what was published two years earlier within the pages of my book. I don't think I beat them because I'm that smart. I think the government is just that dumb. (see: Regulatory Agencies and Bureaucracy) But for the records, let's hear what they have to say.

The report warns of a global political and economic upheaval almost "beyond comprehension" because of climatic changes that have already occurred.

It contends that the world has entered a period of adverse weather that is likely to last forty years, and possibly centuries.

It seems that the CIA has also discovered Dr. Bryson, because the report is based on a study by him, in which he states that long-term changes in the weather may cause a major drought in India every four years, which would result in the starvation of 150 million persons, a major famine in China every five years, and the loss of the Soviet wheat fields in Kazakhstan.

Dr. Bryson also said that he expects a return to something like the climate of the last century, which I also reported in my book.

He feels that the northern half of the United States will receive more rain, but it will be drier in the Gulf Coast, and the Southwest and Northern Rockies.

Interestingly enough, he says that the unbalances probably would not significantly affect U.S. food production. I disagree with him here, because we are talking about upsetting an already precarious business, the farming, where you're dependent on weather even during periods of relatively stable climate. Now we may face a permanent major shift of the world's patterns. It cannot help but upset the entire farm economy and the production of food. The report says:

> The change of climate is cooling some significant agricultural areas and causing drought in others. If, for example, there is a Northern Hemisphere temperature drop of 1 degree Centigrade, it will mean that India will have a major drought every four years and can only support 3/4ths of her present population.

The most devastating statement in the report is the following:

> The new climatic era brings a promise of famine and starvation in many areas of the world. .... The economic and political impact of major climatic shifts is almost beyond comprehension.

This brings to mind echoes of another CIA report made public last year, which said grave food shortages would prompt increasingly desperate attempts upon the part of the powerful, but hungry, nations to get grain any way they could.

Massive migrations, sometimes backed by force, would be a live issue, and political and economic stability would be widespread.

I've always acknowledged the great implications of the shift in weather patterns, but I do not believe now, after studying this problem for three years, that we will ever reach the point where U.S. food production would be reduced to the point where we would not grow enough to feed our own people. It simply isn't true.

It also means that the glue that holds civilization together—our food—would no longer be available to the rest of the world. Much of the rest of the world would be starving. I think it's dangerous to be comfortable and healthy when surrounded by the sick and hungry. There is a great American Empire out there, an economic empire, tied to us through American investment and multinational corporations. We differ from England.

(12/15/76)   The 1976-77 drought phenomenon in Northern California is typical of the strange and unpredictable weather patterns that the world has seen over the last three or four years, causing over $2 billion in weather losses to California ranchers and farmers alone in 1976.

During that same period, AUSTRALIA'S drought was so severe that most of its wheat crop was lost, and millions of acres that had been reclaimed from the desert, at great cost, were lost to that desert again.

The drought in the Midwest was so bad that the Mississippi River's flow was reduced to almost half, and late in the summer and early fall of '76 there was some question as to whether or not the barges that transport most of America's grain exports to New Orleans would be able to use the river.

And yet, during all that drought, we accomplished a miracle in producing very large wheat and corn crops by a fortunate confluence of three things:

1.   Many farmers switched to irrigation and pumped water from deep wells.

2.   The price of fertilizer dropped somewhat from the previous embargo high and there was more fertilzer applied to the land.

3.   The largest number of acres in history were planted so we ended up with good crops, despite the fact that yield-per-acre was down sharply.

How can we be confident of feeding a growing world population when world weather patterns have changed to the extent that England now gets North Africa's weather, North Africa gets Central Africa's weather and Central Africa appears to be turning into a desert?

How can a farmer in a free enterprise economy look for a reasonable profit when the weather has become totally unpredictable? In addition, the climate seems to be changing permanently.

If there is one thing that I have learned in my studies of economics, it is that everything affects everything else. Nothing occurs in a vacuum. Every event in the economic world makes waves, and these waves bounce back and forth with seemingly undiminished power until they have run their course. The outlook for world agriculture could only be described as unpredictable at this time. We are seeing drastic changes, not just weather, but climate! When you add to that the inefficiency imposed by the march of socialism on world agriculture, you have a combination of circumstances that have great explosive potential.

(2/15/77)   All around us we have tangible evidence that something has gone terribly wrong with the entire weather system of the Northern Hemisphere. It seems as though an outraged Providence has chosen to wreak vengeance upon mankind for his indiscretions. Or perhaps it is just nature returning to normal.

I'd like to discuss, not weather, but climate, which is a totally different matter.

The circum-polar vortex is a band of winds that circles the top of the earth traveling from west to east. They undulate up and down like a skirt in the wind, sometimes dipping low at one point or higher at another. They determine the temperature during the winter, and they also determine how far north moisture will be drawn from the south tropic waters to drop on the land in the form of rain or snow. The weather of the last forty years may have been an aberration, and the changes which we saw coming, starting in 1974, might be indications that the world's climate was returning to normal, and that we could expect longer, colder winters and drier weather in the Great Plains and in the Midwest. If the climatologists who espouse this view are correct, no longer could great abundance be depended upon from the American heartland, at least not enough to feed the entire world. We have made ourselves vulnerable by creating technology and strains of grain which would only be effective if the world continued to go as before, and we should not make our plans on those assumptions.

Every farmer knows that weather is chancy at best, and good years can be followed by bad years. But over the long haul he believes he can depend on the climate. He knows that over the years he can grow corn, because corn is well suited for his climatic pattern and the length of his growing season. Or he can grow winter wheat because the average rainfall is X inches, and winter temperatures fall into such-and-such a range, and his growing season is relatively predictable.

His data are based on the experience of the last forty years when the dependability of the American climate, plus the innovations and technology introduced into the American farm system have produced an abundance incredible to behold. We produce, according to some experts, over 70% of the total food exported in the entire world. We produce enough to feed ourselves, and still export over 50% of what we grow.

We have made some long-term agricultural changes which are based on the false assumption that conditions would remain the same.

Here are some of those assumptions:

1.   Climate is predictable and can be depended upon.

2.   Modern farming methods can produce great abundance through the application of modern technology (see: Farming).

3.   Energy, in the form of petroleum and natural gas, is abundantly available and inexpensive. Consequently, we can use them liberally in producing food from the ground.

4.   Because the climate can be depended upon, we have produced strains of grain and other crops which have sacrificed hardiness in the interests of yield.

All of these assumption are now in question, as the evidence is all around us.

Sunny California

Just a few days ago I was in Palm Springs, California, making some radio and television appearances. I picked up the *LOS ANGELES TIMES* and found to my shock that they had abruptly imposed water rationing back in my home community of Danville, California.

Water from the East Bay Municipal Utility District (East Bay MUD) had been disappearing from Pardee Reservoir which supplies our area. We are in the second year of a terrible drought. The snow level at one of the measuring stations in the Sierras, which is normally over four feet in depth, is less than eight inches. Pardee Reservoir has lost 91% of its water. Marin County, across the Bay from where I live, has been in a desperate condition, and has instituted water allocation, with heavy penalties.

Efforts were made to raise money to bring a pipeline down from the Russian River to the north, which would have solved part of their problem. But this was blocked by environmentalists who were fearful of destroying the Steelhead and Silver Salmon and Striped Bass runs in that river.

I was not emotionally ready for the severity of the restrictions that hit us in our area, although (thank goodness!) I was physically ready. We had just purchased an older home which we were remodeling. One of the reasons we bought it was that it had a swimming pool for an emergency water supply. The previous owner had emptied the pool.

We were about to fill it when we discovered that we were going to receive an allotment of only 280 gallons a day, effective immediately. Now for a family of ten, that's twenty eight gallons per day per person. When you realize that anywhere from 5 to 10 gallons are used every time you flush the toilet, and you have been trying to teach your youngsters to flush the toilet every time they use it, you can begin to realize the dimensions of the problem. When you have athletes in the family who wish to shower every time they have been out jogging or playing a special sport, again you realize how much water is needed. And then, add up how many washings have to be done. We have averaged over four a day. Also, when there are that many people in the family, it is pretty hard to do dishes by hand, so we run the dishwasher. And our pool was empty—20,000 gallons empty. Well, fortunately, we were told there would be no penalty during the first month while we were "getting used" to the idea, so we went ahead and filled our pool.

These are minor inconveniences compared to what the farmers in the Central Valley of California are suffering. This is the richest agricultural area in the entire world. It produces 25 percent of the nation's food, and over 40 percent of its vegetables. They depend almost totally on irrigation from the great Central Valley river systems, fed by gigantic reservoirs which trap the copious snow-pack runoff from the heights of the Sierra Nevada Mountains. Because there's no snow-pack there, for the second straight year, farmers were told that their agricultural water allocation for irrigation would be 75 percent below the guaranteed minimum. Farmers with orchards were told they would receive just enough water to keep their trees alive, but not enough for them to bear fruit. Rice production probably will be cut in half. California's grain crop probably will be a dead wash-out. (That's a horrible analogy.) Hundreds of thousands of acres of rich farmland in the great fertile delta formed by the confluence of the San Joaquin and Sacramento Rivers will probably revert back to salt marshland.

California (south of the Tehachapi Mountains) has received more rain than normal, and yet we are still piping water from the delta to fill the swimming pools of Los Angeles. Salt water intrusion has crept into the great Salinas Valley north of Monterey, which grows about 80 percent of the artichokes for the United States, and untold tons of other vegetables to feed much of the nation.

Now bear in mind that California is an agricultural economy, and even the prosperity of its great cities depends upon the stabilty of that one great industry which far transcends in dollars the value of any other industry in the states. If this drought does not end soon, I can visualize the GRAPES OF WRATH in reverse, as farm workers, and workers in industries that will suffer from the ripple effects of this calamity, lose their jobs and begin to look for salvation elsewhere.

This strange weather pattern has its counterpart in the Midwest, and it is related to the California drought.

Here's what has happened. Some place out in the Pacific was a patch of warm water extending over many miles, diverting the jet stream north, carrying warm tropic air to Alaska, creating a winter-long spring. It was warmer in Anchorage for three or four days than it was in Miami, Florida. One of the great Alaskan dog sled races has been called off for lack of snow.

The jet stream then sweeps down across Canada, cutting south across the Midwest and into the Southern states, bringing snow and freezing weather into Texas, Mississippi, Alabama and Florida, as it carried the cold air down from the northern climes. This peculiar pattern also created drought. In ways that I don't think anyone understands, the California weather and the Midwest weather are related. As long as the drought holds in California, the strange pattern will continue in the Midwest. It has meant cold dry weather in Minnesota, Wisconsin, the Dakotas and parts of Iowa, and this has created an incredible combination of circumstances that will be remembered for years as "the winter of '77."

First, winter came early and froze the ground hard. In some parts of the northern Midwest it is frozen as deep as six feet. In some areas in winter wheat country it is frozen 15 to 18 inches deep causing a heavy winter kill. No one knows how much, but it is severe.

After the big freeze came more bitterly cold weather, with the "wind-chill factor" in some states as low as 80 degrees below zero. On the other side of this great vertical jet stream line, as it swept south, came tremendous precipitation in the form of snow, hitting major parts of Ohio, New York, Pennsylvania, Virginia, West Virginia, and all of New England, and we've all read about the tremendous problem of cities like Buffalo.

Now here's the effect it will have. First, let's look at crops:

1. The winter wheat crop will be way below expectations. How much below, no one knows, but in my opinion, it could be devastating.

2. The ground is frozen so hard that even recent snow, when it does thaw, will run off without soaking in, and we went into this year with dangerously dry soil conditions. Also, my climatological advisors tell me that we will have a long winter with very severe cold spells,

followed by a sudden transition into summer with very little spring.

This sudden transition is generally associated with high winds. The combination of dry soil and high winds could mean that after all of the snow has run off, much of Minnesota, Wisconsin and the Dakotas could end up somewhere over England.

We could also lose millions of tons of topsoil as it is swept downstream in floods to further silt up the MISSISSIPPI, which, after flooding, will probably return to even lower levels than we experienced last year, and we will have further problems with barge traffic.

3. The major export of the United States is food. Arms run a very close second. Again, I will repeat it, it is American food and capital that is the glue that holds civilization together. If we can't export food in large quantities, our balance of payments falls further into deficit.

Now the United States could feed itself very well indeed even if it lost 50 percent of its crops, but in the realities of the international community, we know that we must maintain the strength and stability of those nations to which our banking systems have loaned money. We cannot allow these countries to default on their international loans. We cannot allow them to become destabilized and descend into chaos. The integrity of our banking system depends on it.

It is my opinion that the answer of this Administration will simply be price controls, which, of course, will lead to additional shortages. We might find allocation of food supplies and government interference in the free market economy. The rules are already in place in existing Executive Orders for the government, under conditions of national emergency, to control the distribution of food supplies in this country (see: Executive Order 11490).

The other effect of this cold winter has been the vast increase in consumption of natural gas, and the exposure of the shortage of this most valuable material. For years the government has held the price of this product down to about 56¢ for each one million BTU's. This is an incredibly low price for energy, and its sheer cheapness has created an artificial demand for the product, while at the same time reducing the incentive for exploration because the profits are low or non-existent. Many of them have capped their wells to wait for a better day. Certain politicians in Congress, of course, call this a conspiracy to force up prices, but it is simply the response of a businessman not wanting to lose money selling his product. This certainly hasn't done anything to increase the supply. As Milton Friedman said recently, "We economists may not know much, but we do know how to create a shortage. Simply reduce the cost of tomatoes to 2¢ a pound by law, and watch tomatoes disappear from the marketplace."

That is exactly what we have done with natural gas. However, in this crisis we have pumped unprecedented amounts into homes to counter the effect of this incredible cold weather and, in so doing, we now have created a shortage of the product. Natural gas is one of the major raw materials used in the manufacture of anhydrous ammonia, a major fertilizer product used by our farmers. There now will be a shortage of that fertilizer, and what remains will be terribly expensive. Farmers can no longer depend upon cheap fertilizer and cheap energy. The price of gasoline will rise at the gas pump, as some petroleum has been diverted to the manufacture of heating oils rather than gasoline. We will further increase our dependency on Middle East oil, with all of the vulnerability that that proposes for the American system.

Add it all up. What do we have? A rat's nest of circumstances similar to that which we faced in 1973 and 1974, that gave us a recession and 15 to 20% inflation, only this time we are going into it in a much weaker condition, and the possibility is not just for recession, but deep depression. Can you conceive of the impact of a major permanent shift of North American agricultural zones, due to changes in weather, coupled with the migration of population from the state of California, coupled with a terrible drought that cripples the economy of our largest state, coupled with destructive floods in the Ohio, Mississippi, Hudson and Delaware River basins? Can you understand that the effect of ballooning heating bills for the winter is the same as if the government had imposed a tax to retard the economy? It drains purchasing power out of the hands of the American consumer.

Jim Benham made an interesting point at our Seminar in Los Angeles when he indicated that interest rates tend to rise when certain things happen weather-wise. For example, if there is a shortage of soybeans, and the price of soybeans rises sharply, this means that the farmer can borrow far more money based on the value of his crop. As his borrowing power increases, interest rates rise, simply because demand for money creates an increase in the price of money, that is, interest rates.

The weather problems we are facing this winter are severe, have far-reaching consequences, and may be permanent. They may be a fact of life for the rest of our lifetimes, or they may last only three or four years.

Ruff's Recommendations

1. If you haven't completed your food storage plan, try to do so now.

2. If you have agricultural land with good ground water, hang onto it.

3. Pray for rain and a softening of the elements. As much as man knows about the management of his financial affairs, he does not know how to insulate himself from the effects of weather, but you should plan your life, as your ancestors did, to be self-sufficient regardless of what happens.

4. Contact some local firm that is installing solar heating units, and install them in your home and in your swimming pool.

5. Drill a well if you can. Be independent of delivered water, at least to some degree.

6. Make sure you have a home water storage supply so that you would at least be able to cook and drink if you live in any of the areas that are prone to these problems.

7. If you live down-stream from areas where there has been heavy precipitation and cold weather, prepare for flooding if we should have a sudden thaw.

8. Above all, let's acquire a new sense of humility for our dependence upon the whims and vagaries of nature. We are not invulnerable.

WOMEN

(9/15/76)   Men tend to perpetuate the myth that women are not capable of understanding or handling financial affairs. About 40% of the calls that we receive on our Hot-Line (and about half of our subscribers call us) are women. I find women equal to men in sophistication. I find them extremely motivated, and most perceptive in foreseeing the nation's problems. And, I find them agreeing with me, which, of course, makes anybody pretty smart.

I recently read a book by Irving Stone called *MEN TO MATCH MY MOUNTAINS*. It is the story of the settlement of California, Nevada, Colorado, Utah, and Oregon, and it is a marvelous piece of history, engrossingly written. I could not put it down. Many of these pioneer companies found themselves in great difficulty, in desert heat or mountain snow. And in so many instances, when the men had given up and were dying, it was some little slip of a woman who found the physical, emotional and moral resources to get some of them through.

An especially dramatic story involves a party that got lost in Death

717

Valley, and it was only the sheer force of will of a 95-pound sick woman, that got any of them through safely.

You men out there, if you're smart, will not underestimate the power of a woman. You should share with your wife all your financial affairs and you should both be equally well-informed on the matters we discuss in this newsletter.

Recently in New York City, I had a delightful evening with one of our subscribers, Belle Green. Belle is a senior citizen, living in a beautiful apartment on Park Avenue. She became a subscriber several months ago, and has been most helpful in sending us clippings from New York publications and keeping us posted on things we may not have seen. She manages her substantial estate knowledgeably, carefully, conservatively, and with great understanding of the issues involved. She won't be rushed into panicky decisions, and I find nowhere in her the mythical "feminine reaction" to financial problems. In fact, I believe that such a reaction could be exposed for the fiction it is, if we would only assume the same degree of intelligence for women that we do for men.

I believe that the women of the world may be our salvation.

What I'm getting to is the chance to tell you a bit about my wife. Kay is the mother of our eight children. She's maintained her physical beauty and her tremendous love for everyone. She is a person "without guile." I don't believe that she is capable of even the smallest deception. She loves everyone and everyone loves her. She has open-heartedly taken into our home, at various times, five or six foster-children, in addition to our seven living children. Many a morning at breakfast, we have had thirteen or fourteen people around our table. It's like managing a lumberjack camp. She's been with me through the sudden death of our child, through a total business failure in 1968, and through the stresses and ups and downs of building businesses. She remains serene, confident, and totally supportive. I believe that she is my moral and ethical superior and I trust her instincts, as she trusts my special skills. As she is strong where I am weak, we feel that we make a powerful partnership.

It is largely because of my wife's inspiration and her gentle persistent pressure that we have a complete food storage program. It is largely because of her that the book *FAMINE AND SURVIVAL IN AMERICA* was written, because she created the climate that caused me to be motivated to write such a book when the proper combination of circumstances arose. I love her deeply and trust her implicitly.

The safety, security, and value system of my family is the most important thing in the world to me. And without Kay's loving strength and wisdom, we could never have achieved the degree of success that we have had with our wonderful children. Without her attitudes, I would never have made the effort to touch the lives of other children who also needed a stable home.

Men, take a look around you and see if you appreciate what you have. And if you don't, swallow your chauvinistic pride and see what you're missing.

Z

Zzzz

Well, by now you should be convinced of a few things. First, my long-term scenario is one of hope and optimism, making me not quite the dark-cloud-over-your-head advisor the media has occasionally attempted to project. Second, on balance, I have been right more often than not, in spite of a few inevitable, embarrassing mistakes along the way. Third, there are definable strategies for dealing with seemingly undefinable problems. Further, using those strategies can turn "problems" into understandable, ordinary circumstances with which you can comfortably cope. In other words, you can escape the unpleasant prospect of suffering, which inevitably comes from inaction and apathy, with prudent planning and courageous action, forgetting what criticism you may receive, and you'll get it. It will come from those who don't understand that the rules have changed, that unconventional approaches to solving problems are your only chance for survival. Finally, you should be convinced that information on a wide variety of subjects, about which I have written over the years, is now at your finger tips for future reference, contemplation and use.

Knowing all this, I can't help but think you'll be able to close the covers of *FROM A TO Z*, turn out the light, and get a healthy, restful night's sleep. By the way, thanks for buying my encyclopedia. May you have success and pleasure in planning your financial, physical and spiritual future. And happy Zzzzing.

INDEX

A

B

H

J

M

O

T

SOME COMMENTS ON HOWARD RUFF

According to Ruff, if the reader follows his plan, in at least five years your money will buy what it can today and you will retain a decent lifestyle even if a depression occurs. After reconstruction of the current economic system, the reader will be in a unique position to prosper from the rise in the value of the dollar.

—Terry Anderson, *Denver Post*

. . .Mr. Ruff offers timely advice to his subscribers on how they can make a go of things in this era of economic disruption. Mr. Ruff and I agree that inflation is one of the worst evils ever foisted on the American people by Government. (Mr. Ruff) has put together a proposed way of utilizing gold clause contracts and I believe it deserves serious consideration.

—Senator Jesse Helms (R), N.C.

Ruff is an evangelist of economic disaster, predicting that the economy will soon rush out of control along the roller coaster to disaster, carrying with it all those who fail to prepare long in advance for the worst. And how better to prepare than to buy Ruff's book and subscribe to his newsletter!

—Frank Vogl, the Cleveland *Plain Dealer*

It's apparent that Mr. Ruff is more sophisticated than many people give him credit for. Besides gold and bonds, he has recommended investment-grade diamonds, rubies, sapphires, emeralds and small town real estate. Mr. Ruff doesn't knock those who want to put their money in Switzerland or other foreign money havens, but he declares: "If America goes to hell, you know the rest of the world will be disaster. I believe the smartest thing is to invest in the long-term future of America while preparing for short-term troubles. That's what the Arabs, Swiss, Japanese and West Germans are doing.

—Jim Powell, *The New York Times*

Howard Ruff is a charming "crackpot," a word he says is often applied to him. But he talks enough plain common sense to convince almost anyone that his "outrageous commentary," a phrase he has been known to apply to his opinions, is revealed wisdom and that the nightmares he sees ahead are real.

—Edwin Darby, *Chicago-Sun Times*

. . .Howard J. Ruff has written a most useful book called *How to Prosper in the Coming Bad Years.* It is a clear and readable analysis of the sickness of the dollar, and a detailed strategy for protecting yourself against it.

—John Exter, Former Vice President, Federal Reserve Bank

. . .Howard J. Ruff's comments on coin investments alone, are worth their weight in gold.

—Congressman Phil Crane

. . .If you ever wondered what has really happened to your money, read Howard Ruff's book. You will also know who is responsible for it.

—Senator Orrin Hatch

. . .There is one practical book that I recommend for people to read in order to prepare on a personal level for the coming difficult years, it is *How to Prosper During the Coming Bad Years*.

—R. E. McMaster, author of *Cycles of War*

. . .Although some of it is too pessimistic, it contains, in addition to a well-deserved warning about inflation, some sound financial advice to help an inflation weary investor end an eloquent plea for fiscal security.

—George Bush

I don't know whether its Howard's gifted writing or the simple logic of Howard's predictions, but I couldn't put the book down. I read it in a night, and ended wiping sweat off the palms of my hands. I was surprised at how many things I learned from Ruff'n Ready Howard.

—Richard Russell

Howard Ruff is a man who practices what he preaches. When he tells readers to stock up on gold and silver coins in preparation for an inevitable depression, you can be sure that Ruff has followed his own advice.

—*Atlanta Business Chronicle*

How to Prosper. . .is good reading. It's practical, productive and often brutally realistic. Ruff believes in America, but he calls a spade a spade. He doesn't have all the answers, but as the book prods, "Can you afford to be without this man's advice?"

—Tom Beaudin, *Valley Pioneer*

The Third Annual *Ruff Times* National Convention has come and gone, but the opportunity to benefit from that hard-hitting fact-filled seminar has not. If you would like, you can have the Convention right in your own home.

Republican Senator Orrin Hatch (free market Senator from Utah), William E. Simon (former Secretary of the Treasury), Howard Jarvis (Godfather of Proposition 13), Nicholas Deak (foreign exchange expert and banker), Richard Russell (astute stock market advisor), Dr. Hans Sennholz (real estate investor and economist) and many, many other knowledgeable and respected experts will give you the latest and most useful information on politics, food storage, diamonds, gold, silver, numismatics, tax planning, trusts, financial privacy, stamps, foreign banks, barter, precious and semi-precious gems, money funds, commodities, investment management, and survival homes.

It's all here in beautiful binders, and you have your choice of tapes or transcripts. Just send $125.00 (cassette tapes) or $225.00 (transcripts) to: **CONVENTION TAPES, POST OFFICE BOX 2000, SAN RAMON, CALIFORNIA 94583.**